Photo by Karsh, 1987

"Yes, you can save your hair without drugs, chemicals, and mail order miracle products! The Natural Method of Hair Care shows you how. You can also have a clear, glowing, youthful, and healthy complexion without spending huge sums on 'miracle cellular skin creams,' injections, chemicals, or facial salons. Mother Nature and I will show you how step-by-step with color photos, articles, and diagrams. My book will make you a 'cosmetic maven,' because this is the definitive book on natural cosmetics."

Aubrey Hampton

What the experts are saying about
Natural Organic Hair and Skin Care
by Aubrey Hampton

"Aubrey's book is excellent, thoroughly researched and persuasively written and deserves the attention of a wide public."

Lawrence Durrell, author
The Alexandria Quartet

"I read Aubrey's book with delight. It is both witty and abounding in good sense. The technical passages are first class and well researched. It deserves every success."

Ludo Chardenon
The Herbalist of Sommieres
in Southern France

What the experts are saying about
Natural Organic Hair and Skin Care
by Aubrey Hampton

"This is not just a book: it's an encyclopedia! I can think of no better reference work on the elements we can use today to care for our appearance. Aubrey guides us through the maze of exotic names and points out the healthy, natural products we can use without worry. This will be a valuable addition to my library."

Annemarie Colbin
Founder of The Natural Gourmet Cookery School in New York, NY
Author of *The Book of Whole Meals*
and
Food and Healing

"In the pursuit of health and beauty, what you put on your skin can be as important as what you put into your mouth. *Natural Organic Hair and Skin Care* explains the differences between natural life-giving cosmetics, which can actually add beauty, and the "war paint" cover-ups which contain chemicals that may be harmful. This informative book is also enriched by warm and colorful anecdotes from Aubrey's own experience."

Paul Obis
Editor and Publisher
Vegetarian Times

"In an age of petrochemical intrusion into every realm of life including cosmetics, *Natural Organic Hair and Skin Care* offers an alternative: natural cosmetics formulated from organic herbs, seeds, vegetable oils, and clay without synthetic additives. Aubrey presents a whole approach to natural beauty--cosmetics derived directly from nature without harming test animals or the environment."

Luc Bodin
Natural Aesthetician
The Quern
Athens, VT

What the experts are saying about
Natural Organic Hair and Skin Care
by Aubrey Hampton

"Personal and household products that do not contain animal ingredients and that are not the product of animal suffering are the wave of the future. Organica Press takes the lead in making this reality a sooner one with *Natural Organic Hair and Skin Care*. Aubrey proves that animal experimentation has absolutely no value in creating cosmetics and their safe use. Aubrey's book is a tour de force for animal rights."

Doug Moss
Publisher
The Animals' Agenda

"This is a book that comprises very important compendia of just about every worthwhile subject in the cosmetic field. With a fine sense of wry (not rye) humor, Aubrey has thoroughly elucidated the many diverse areas of skin and hair care for which every woman as well as every man has sought common sense explanation (and was afraid to ask). Now everyone can get the answers they need in a book that digests high-powered scientific jargon and reforms it into everyday understandable and usable language."

Dr. Maurice Siegel
Executive Vice-President
Research and Development
Fabergé, Inc.

"The enormous research that went into the writing of *Natural Organic Hair and Skin Care* warrants its reading. As a perfumer I know the demands Aubrey makes of the perfumer. The hundreds and hundreds of perfume formulas specifically developed for him and the very few found acceptable attest to the integrity of the man and his products."

Ferdinand Perrone
Founder
Perrone Perfumes and Flavors

What the experts are saying about
Natural Organic Hair and Skin Care
by Aubrey Hampton

"This is not just another book on cosmetics. This is dynamite! Yes, dynamite to those who have been yearning for a clear, honest explanation and treatment on skin care. Those who know Aubrey would not expect less."

Harry Markarian, President
World of Nutrition, Inc.
Newington, CT

"Aubrey's *Natural Organic Hair and Skin Care* is packed with necessary information for the professional and the consumer. It's presented in an understandable, sometimes humorous way. Excellent reading!"

Marianne Blakeslee
Natural Aesthetician
Belmont Skin Care Clinic
Belmont, CA

"*Natural Organic Hair and Skin Care*:
Many meaty messages mentioned in there!
More than the hennas and camomiles,
Aubrey flushes some frowns and spawns some smiles,
Critiquing the synthetic snare.

If our past would be prophetic,
Dead mice tell taller tales,
Increasing greedy sales,
Pushing simplistic synthetics.

It's never really cheaper!
Ask the LD-50 Reaper!
Petrochemical "solutions"
Only double the pollutions,
As the acid rain drains deeper.

"Economic" energetics
Inundate us with synthetics.
Dare we delegate our duty
To bolster natural beauty
With the natural cosmetics?"

Dr. James A. Duke
Botanist and author of
numerous books on herbs including
Medicinal Plants of China

NATURAL ORGANIC HAIR AND SKIN CARE

Including A To Z Guide To Natural And Synthetic Chemicals In Cosmetics

AUBREY HAMPTON

Organica Press
4419 N. Manhattan Ave., Tampa, FL 33614

PUBLISHED BY
Organica Press
4419 North Manhattan Avenue
Tampa, Florida 33614
First Edition, Third Printing

Hampton, Aubrey, 1934-
Natural Organic Hair and Skin Care: Including A to Z Guide
to Natural and Synthetic Chemicals In Cosmetics
Library of Congress Catalog Card Number 86-61883
ISBN 0-939157-00-4

Printed and bound in the United States of America

Distributed to the book trade in the United States and Canada
by Organica Press, Inc.

DISCLAIMER

No part of this book is for the purpose of the treatment of disease;
the author and publisher assume no liability for such use of this book.
Those who have a disease of the skin or other parts of the body should seek
competent medical advice. The use of any products or substances discussed
in this book rests on the judgment of the reader, and any products or
substances discussed herein are for educational purposes only and are not
intended as recommendations of the author or publisher.

*To the many men and women in
the natural foods industry
who accepted my idea of
natural and organic
cosmetic products
and the Natural Method
of Hair and Skin Care
and, of course, to the many
consumers who keep the idea
of natural and organic hair, skin,
and body care products alive.*

*To those who know that animal
testing is inhumane and
unscientific, and base their
lifestyle on this principal.*

ACKNOWLEDGMENTS

No book is written solely by the author whose name appears on the cover of that book; many people's contributions, in fact, go into its creation. I can't name all of them, but I will name a few of the ones directly concerned with the creation of this book.

Susan Hussey, the editor of this work, is more than just an editor. A good editor aids the author in the creation of the book from the first rough, through the galley proofs where each word is isolated and discussed, to the finished book hopefully to be bought and read. Ms. Hussey is much more than this. If I could say to any writer, "I have an editor for you who will not only labor over the work as if she is your alter ego, but also can set type like a printer's devil, though she's actually a godsend, would you beg, borrow, and steal to get her?" "Yes" would be the quick reply of any writer. Ms. Hussey re-writes; she corrects mistakes; she types; and yes, yes, she actually sets type and knows the difference between Mallard and Melliza, Bauhaus and Bodoni. She is, in the long and short of it, a working editor. She actually set the type you will be gazing at in this book. Many thanks to Susan.

Greg Tozian took time away from his own writing projects to read the entire manuscript and make suggestions. He was that much needed sounding board every writer must have. Many thanks to Greg.

In my youth I was very much like a young Ben Franklin: writing was not enough for me. I worked in the lab and invented special etches for the press, special plate cleaners, and fountain solutions for the press. I also had to put the black ink to the white paper. There is absolutely nothing more exciting than seeing the first printed sheet come off the press. I pity the poor writer who hasn't had that experience. My thanks to the young Ben Franklins at Organica Press: we need more like them: Roland Gerke, senior pressman, Curtis Barrow, Scott Shaw, and Barry Boyles.

You can't tell a book by its cover. This is quite true, but so many of us first notice the book because of its cover. Susan Meadows designed the cover of this book and did a series of cartoons in the book called Organitoons. A big thanks to Sue.

Debra Pantley created the layout and did the excellent illustrations in this book. They make the "how to" sections of this book so much easier to follow. A writer's thanks to an artist like Debra (who also looks after my herb garden because she likes herbs).

Josef Karsh created the photo of myself on the back cover. What writer wouldn't want a portrait by Karsh? He has created lasting portraits of writers such as Bernard Shaw, H. G. Wells, Auden, Hemingway, and so forth. Mr. Karsh didn't want to take just a picture of me. He wanted my Bichon Frise, Robespierre (who was born on Bastille Day), to be in the picture with me. Robes had other ideas. He didn't want to make the trip to New York which has far too many poodles to his taste. I told Mr. Karsh that this time around he would have to settle for just my face. "It's just as well," said Karsh, "because if Robes were in the picture nobody would be looking at you." This cracked me up, and it was then that he shot the picture you see on the back cover. Many thanks to the great photographer with the eye of an artist.

Table of Contents

Introduction i

PART ONE: The History and Science of Natural Hair and Skin Care, Or Mother Nature as Cosmetic Chemist

In Search of the Organic World 1

CHAPTER I
The Cosmic You, Or
*Why A Natural and Organic Cosmetic Puts You In
Harmony With Nature* 15

CHAPTER II
In the Beginning Cosmetics Were Natural, Or
When It Came To Preservatives Mummy Knew Best 19

CHAPTER III
The pH Stuff, Or
Are You In Balance? 37

CHAPTER IV
Does Your Skin Really Absorb and Use Nutrients? Or
"I've Got You Under My Skin, Collagen . . ." 41

CHAPTER V
Cleo and Clay, Cleo and Henna, Cleo and Aloe, Or
Groucho to Cleo: "Aloe, I Must Be Going." 47

CHAPTER VI
Aromatherapy, Thalassotherapy, and Phytotherapy, Or
*Roses are Red/Violets are Blue/You Can Put Them In A Vase
Or Rub Them On Your Face* 53

CHAPTER VII
Charting the Hair and Skin Care Herbs, Or
*What Do Arnica, Betulla, Ivy, Horse Chestnut, and
Bladderwrack Have In Common?* 79

CHAPTER VIII
Mucopolysaccharides, Glucosaminoglycanes, Hydroxyproline,
Eicosapentaenoic Acid, and Other Natural Tongue-Twisters, Or
*If Peter Picked A Peck of Potent Pipessewa and a Pint of
Pomegranates, Pelargoniums, and Polypods For His Pop's
Poke, How Many Potent Pipessewa, Periwinkles,
Pomegranates, Pelargoniums, and Polypods Did He Pick?* 131

CHAPTER IX
How To Make A Natural Cosmetic in Ten Easy Lessons, Or
Mother Nature May Have Some Surprises For You 147

CHAPTER X
Paint Your Face, Color Your Eyes, and Dye Your Hair, Or
Color Me Dead! 159

CHAPTER XI
The Advantages and Dangers of UV Rays, Or
Here Comes The Sun! 167

CHAPTER XII
The East Of It, The West of It, The Yin and Yang Of It, Or
Does the Acupuncture Face Lift Really Work? 171

CHAPTER XIII   Love Thy Neighbor, Or
Animal Testing May Be Hazardous To Your Health 211

CHAPTER XIV   Preservatives, Or
Nothing Lasts Forever 219

CHAPTER XV   Anatomy of a Natural Product, Or
Putting It All Together 239

PART TWO: A to Z Guide to Natural and Synthetic Chemicals in Cosmetics, Or Mother Nature's Cosmetic Dictionary

PART THREE: Natural Organic Hair and Natural Organic Skin Care, Or The Natural Method, Or Mother Nature As Cosmetologist

CHAPTER XVI   How To Save Your Hair 321

CHAPTER XVII   The Natural Method of Hair Care 335

CHAPTER XVIII   What Your Skin Needs is Based On How Your Skin
Works 345

CHAPTER XIX   The Substances Found In Nature That Promote A
Healthy, Youthful Skin 351

CHAPTER XX   The Natural Method of Skin Care 377

PART FOUR: Resources, Or Mother Nature's Buying Guide

Introduction 397

Reading Cosmetic Labels 405

Carcinogens and Suspected Carcinogens in Cosmetics 416

Cosmetic Manufacturers 417

Herbal Suppliers 427

Index to *Natural Organic Hair and Skin Care* 431

Illustrations, Color Plates, and Diagrams

Organitoon: The Litmus Paper Freaks 36

pH Chart 38

Amino Acids in Dermal Proteins (Chart) 44

Organitoon: "Coconuts are being labeled just like cosmetics!" 52

Prostaglandin Synthesis for Essential Fatty Acids 69

Organitoon: "It's the greatest herbal face cream, Bob! It has every herb
in Aubrey's herb chart . . . one drop of each!" 78

Herb Chart (149 herbs for cosmetic and other uses) 83-129

Organitoon: "This contains mucopolysaccharides, glucosaminoglycanes,
phytosterols. hyaluronic acid, hydroxyproline, octacosanol, primrose oil,
jojoba oil . . . what are those things?" 130

Organitoon: "Glue-on nails have become ridiculous . . . maybe eyelashes will catch up!" 158

Synthetic Color Additives to Cosmetics 165

Non-Certified Color Additives to Cosmetics 166

Loophole Color Additive List 166

Chart of Ultraviolet Rays (Wavelength of Various Light Sources) 169

Yin and Yang Chart 172

Four Methods of Stimulating Acupressure Points for Face Lift (Illustration) 177

Acupressure Points For Face Lift (Diagrams) 178-182

Acupressure Points on Other Parts of Body 183-185

Chinese Medicinal Herbs (Chart of 235 Herbs Used in Chinese Medicine) 186

Organitoon: "Animal testing doesn't work for animals or humans!" 210

Glossary of Preservatives 225-234

Organitoon: "How do you come up with all these great ideas for products?" 238

Skin Diagram with Collagen Fibers (Example of Non-Crosslinked
and Crosslinked Collagen) 277

Organitoon: "The new hucksters have M. D. Degrees and FDA approval!" 319

Diagrammatic Sketch of a Section of a Hair Fiber 324

Diagrammatic Sketch of the Hair Root to Paniculus 325

Pauling-Corey Structure for Alpha-Keratin 327

Illustrations, Color Plates, and Diagrams

Structure of Crystalline Regions of Keratin....................................328

Organitoon: "The secret ingredients from an old medicine man still must
meet FDA labeling laws."...343

Diagram of the Skin...344

Organitoon: "Baa baa, black sheep, have you any youth reviving secret
cellular extracts that can be used in a moisturizing cream so gullible
women will plunk down over a hundred bucks to rub on their mug and dream of youth?"....350

Rose Hip Seed Oil Technical Specifications...........................353

Topical Applications of Herbs (Chart of Over 100 Herbs for Skin Care).........361-366

Organitoon: "We make our masks with specially purified mud from the
Dead Sea, sand from Tahiti, a few glops of French green grit, and a
sprinkling of grains from high in the Himalayas. Then we wash it off and
if you still don't like your face, we let you pick a mask to take home!
Joan Collins is our all-time favorite!"...............................367

Color Plate No. 1: Dr. Fabiola Carvajal, *Rosa Mosqueta* Rose Hips, Photos
of Patient Treated with *Rosa Mosqueta*...........................369

Color Plate No. 2: Patients Treated with *Rosa Mosqueta* For Wrinkles...........370

Color Plate No. 3: Patient Treated with *Rosa Mosqueta* for Aging and Acne
Scars...371

Color Plate No. 4: Hair Repair with *Rosa Mosqueta*...................372

Color Plate Nos. 5-8: Natural Method of Skin Care Step-By-Step..............373-376

Diagrams of Natural Method Massage with Photos of Each Step..............382-387

Diagram of Hydro-Occlusive Mask Step-by-Step........................393

Diagram of Easy Version of Natural Method Facial......................394

Organitoon: "I've invented so many anti-aging formulas...I've made
millons and my boss has made billons...and yet every day I look in the
mirror and my face is looking older and my hair is falling out..."................396

Organitoon: "Look! There's the guy who wrote that book *Natural Organic
Hair and Skin Care*! Let's get him!".................................430

Introduction

When I was a boy my father would pack us into our old Ford every summer to go to our country place until the end of autumn. In the winter he was in the foundry business; in the summer, he was a farmer. We had a few acres of good black Indiana soil and about two hundred acres of woods. Dad sat behind the wheel nursing the old Ford up the Floyd Knobs; next to him was my mother, and in the back seat, surrounded by our summer supplies, were my brother and me. Queen, our dog, restlessly paced around in what space she had and hung her head out the window. She hated car rides. My rabbit Herbie was on the ledge just under the rear window. He sat there patiently and calmly, like a secure king content in his position. Herbie, unlike Queen, didn't care that much for the country. He was a city rabbit. Every so often Queen would squeeze onto the back seat with us to look out the rear window, but, like as not, Herbie would drop-kick Queen in the nose. Queen, at that moment more insulted than hurt, wanted to bite Herbie in the worst way, but she was not allowed to let the wolf side of her nature turn my regal rabbit into a royal feast, and Herbie knew this. Herbie was my prize rabbit, and he had won countless 4-H contests.

Herbie was far more domesticated than Queen who had never worn a collar, had never known the pull of a leash. Herbie liked to go for contented hops with his red collar and leash because he was a grandstander. He was pure white with dark blue eyes, and when he paraded in front of the judges, there was no contest. He always won some kind of prize. Besides the fact that he could do a few tricks (if he was in the mood), he had those blue eyes. Like an American beauty queen, he knew his looks gave him the edge, but he put all he had into hopping just so, turning just so, and flashing his blues at the judges (with a few extra wiggles of his nose and a slight up-and-down movement of his ears).

This celebrity status made Herbie highly egotistical. He had nothing to do with the other rabbits and had even sublimated his rabbit libido into show business. This was, of course, our own fault because we pampered him and paid more attention to him than people should pay to animals. People try to attribute human traits to their pets and some people even put rain shoes and hats on their dogs and cats. Dogs, cats, rabbits, monkeys, birds are all animals we tend to "cartoonize" as human, but they're not human. They have their own traits. They are aware of their own species and can't understand the foibles of humans. I think it would be safe to say that pets patronize us, or at least indulge us.

Our old Ford barely made it up Floyd Knobs, and when we got to the top, Dad would always glance out of the window at the huge drop and nod his head at a break in the fence at the sheerest point and the most deadly-looking curve.

"A whole carload of people went over there last year," he'd say. We climbed over the boxes and looked out the window at the scary drop and the downed fence. "All of 'em burned to death . . . nothing left of 'em." He said this every year, and I always thought that the Floyd Knobs took one entire family per year. I always tensed when we approached the top and waited to hear the obituary of the family that went through the fence, over the Knobs to their death.

When we arrived at the top and gradually began going down the other side of the Knobs, Queen would get car sick, and we had to let her out. One time when we let her out, for some reason she went off into the woods and didn't come back. We called her and looked for her in vain. My brother was very attached to Queen, and he wanted to stay parked on the shoulder of the road until she came back.

"We can wait a while," Dad said, "But we can't go on waiting. We got a lot to do."

We had to leave her. I saw my brother cry for the first time; the second time was when Queen got hit by a car. He never cared for any other dog. My brother moped around all summer that year we left her behind. Each year he'd say she was coming home. Then about three years later we were going up the Knobs and there beside the road was Queen. It was as if she knew we'd be going by. We opened the car door and she jumped in, whining, barking, wagging her tail, wiggling her whole body, and licking us all in the face. She even forgot how much she detested Herbie and gave him a lick right on his wiggling nose. Herbie, true to his nature, ignored her.

Our summer farm was at least twenty miles from everything. We had no electricity or running water. We used the well for washing and a limestone spring for drinking water. This spring was in a special place in the woods. I always brought back the spring water. I loved the woods, and that special spot in the woods by the spring was my favorite. The water gushed out of moss-covered green rocks and cascaded down about four feet into a sparkling stream. I'd go to the woods and be there for hours. Sometimes I went alone, and sometimes I took Queen and Herbie with me.

I have lived much of my life in the city. I think the music Gershwin composed to capture Manhattan is exciting, but I wonder what he would have written if he had come to the quiet of the woods. It's true that Copeland was able to capture the Midwest in his writing (composed in his apartment in Brooklyn), but the quiet and the sounds of the woods has never been captured, except perhaps by Debussy. Nothing compares with actually going into the woods, but what's amazing is that once you've experienced the woods you can have it with you no matter where you live. You can be in a Greenwich Village apartment (where I lived for quite a few years as a student) and have the windows open to the sounds of the traffic, the horns, the shouts, the din that can only be created in a city where asphalt and glass towers funnel the sounds into a cul-de-sac of noise that releases itself into every open door and window. All you have to do to escape the noise is to relax and think about the woods. The Big Apple melts away into the peace of the limestone water, the rustle of trees, the sounds of the woods that come easily once you've been there.

I have a feeling, though, that you've got to be a young boy or girl to experience the woods like that. Most people take the wood on their own terms: they go there taking pieces of civilization with them. They pitch tents; they line up their cans of synthesized foods; they light fires and create an intrusive civilization in the woods. Oh, there's nothing wrong with that (if they clean up after themselves), and you can expect it of a city person who never really wants to leave the city conveniences for what he or she sees as the "inconvenience" of the woods. When I talk about the woods, however, I mean actually going to the woods, being there as part of the woods, on nature's terms and not ours (which distort nature). I know I had a great advantage of getting to know the woods and being able to go home only a few miles away. I admit this is ideal, and it is also true that there were no campers in our woods, no camp fires, no rusty empty cans, cigarette packs, beer bottles, and the other rubbish left by man. My woods was not a hunting ground or a government park or a tourist spot where trailers would hook into electric plugs and water spigots. It was pure woods! It was nature as she really is. This was the magic of it, and it's what I loved. I could lay down and look straight up and see tree limbs and sky. I could slowly lift the flat leaves of a May apple plant and savor the cool tart juices of that unique fruit not obtainable in any market or at any fruit stand.

When you first enter the woods the animals go quiet because they don't trust man. In fact, at first the woods are stark and quiet: it takes time to be accepted there. Time has shown the animals and the plants that man is destructive and usually only leaves his house and comes to the woods to do damage: kill animals, cut down trees, burn and destroy.

I was never like that farmer's son who experiences the woods with his father and the hounds at the crack of dawn tramping about looking for game. My father, though he had hunted, didn't care for it, so he didn't bring me into this violation and rape of the woods. It's just as well that I never learned to hunt because I would not have taken to it and then the response would have been that I was "sissy"; that I wasn't manly. There's so much of that kind of derision inside people who kill things, whether they do it in nature in the name of sportsmanship and manhood or in the testing lab in the name of science and progress. The hunters and spoilers see a child's nature, which is not to kill things, as a lack of manhood and if the child becomes a man he must take up the hunt; the scientist, whom we can easily equate with the hunter, sees any scientist who does not see animal testing as another step forward in the discovery of scientific fact as a pseudo-scientist, or at best, untrained.

As a child I would spend hours in the woods and did so daily and in time the whole aura of the woods accepted me. The silence ended. The animals didn't hide or go quiet when I came there. I could taste the woods, feel it, hear it, sense it, and was part of it. You can't get that if you're bending nature to your own whim and enjoyment, and if you're killing nature, you'll never experience the woods.

My dad worked the land and my brother helped him. Sometimes I helped, but usually I got to help my mother make soap, shampoo, creams, and lotions out of herbs. My brother, who was clumsy and might knock over a batch of soap before it cooled or mix things incorrectly, opened for me the opportunity to assist my mother in making cosmetics. I would line up the wooden boxes, place the waxed paper inside, and pour in the soap mixture. We would lower a tray of these soap cakes into the cool well where they hardened quickly.

"Grandmaw's Lye Soap," as my mother called it, was a strong brownish-yellow cake of soap mostly for doing laundry, but it was also a "scrub bar" after a day in the fields. It was excellent for bites, cutes, and bruises. Wash the area with "Grandmaw's Lye Soap," and by the next day the area was like new. A wasp sting was easy to care for with this soap. Cut a sliver of it, wet it, and bind it against the sting for immediate relief. We also made a milder soap for the face and skin, and my mother liked lots of glycerine and rosewater for this soap.

Years later there was a top-selling record by a comedian named Stan Freberg. The song was called "Grandmaw's Lye Soap." It perfectly described this unique bar of soap. As one of the lyrics said, "It's good for everything."

If my mother could read this book, what would she think? I've got charts on herbs that describe chemical components; I discuss the coloring principal of henna; I use nature in a method of hair and skin care called **The Natural Method**, and I discuss modern cosmetic technology where cosmetics are colored to look like candy and have no part of nature in them. As much as I try to think of this book as "natural and organic" I know it would not appear that way to my mother. The very idea of making millions of dollars on a face cream that's pink and packaged in a frosted bottle with a gold cap would be foreign to her. Most of her concoctions were brown; her creamy products were not pink, yellow, blue, or even white. They were off-white and eventually turned brown or yellow. Some had pleasant odors, and others didn't. Lavender and rose water were her favorite essential oils, so many of her creations had that fragrance, although lemon-citrus was another of her favorites. Her liquid soaps smelled like peppermint candy, and once she got a bottle of eucalyptus from a druggist in Louisville. This was a find for her, and for a while everything smelled like eucalyptus.

My mother knew nothing about the Latin names of plants or the various chemical components of plants. She'd say, "This is slippery elm, and it's good to gargle with. This is rosemary, and you boil it with lemon peels and rinse it through your hair . . ." She made soap but never knew the word saponin, and if I told her that saponins were a group of amorphous glucosidal steroid compounds that could form natural emulsions and that foamed in water, she'd probably wash my mouth out with some of her soap (but she still wouldn't know what I was talking about).

Down the street in the small town where I lived during the winter was Mrs. Hamilton. She lived there with her brother who taught me to ride a bike. I knew nothing about the two except for much of the day they'd sit on their big porch and watch people go by. One day my father came home from the foundry limping. Some hot molten metal had fallen down into his boot, and he had a horrible burn on his foot. He sat down on our porch steps and took off his boot to let the huge festering burn cool in the air. Mrs. Hamilton came by leaning heavily on her cane.

"Do you want me to cure your foot?" she asked.

"Oh, it'll get better on its own. I've been burnt many times."

"No sense in suffering. I can cure it by noon tomorrow."

"May as well do what you can; you won't give me no peace until you do."

Mrs. Hamilton removed a tiny jar from her bag and took the lid off. She smeared a thick brownish-looking grease on the wound. It looked like brown axle grease. Then she waved her hand over the area and mumbled some words. White witchcraft!

My father's foot was not completely cured by noon the next day, but within two days it was almost completely healed.

"I could make a fortune selling that stuff to foundry workers," he said.

"Yes," I said, "But we don't know what words to say when you wave your hand over the burn. I don't think she'd tell you that."

"That doesn't matter. I'd make up some words to go with each jar."

"Like 'Abracadabra'?"

"That would do just fine, but you'd have to say it seven times."

"For good luck."

"Yes. Whisper it as you pass your hand over the burn."

"Would the salve still work even if 'abracadabra' is the wrong word?"

"It's worth a try. I'd call it Hugh's Magic Ointment."

While my mother didn't really sell her cosmetics (she gave them to people), my father was always inventing things, selling things, and talking about how much money could be made on this idea or that invention.

I got to know Mrs. Hamilton. Her house was lined with jar after jar of herbs. All were labeled with the Latin as well as the common names of the herbs. She'd sell them to anybody who wanted them. She'd mix up brews of herbs for various ills, but if you asked her about a love potion, she'd laugh.

"They either like you or they don't," she said. "Most people are lonely and if you're kind to them, they'll like you."

My mother would read the coffee grounds or tea leaves in a cup, but Mrs. Hamilton was like a carnival's gypsy. She read the tea leaf residue in my brother's cup. She told him if he wasn't careful he would have an accident soon. He broke his arm. That was not really fortune-telling, though, because my brother was always having accidents.

I learned about herbs in a more studious way from Mrs. Hamilton. She talked differently from us because she was from New England, and the fact that her dialect was not Midwestern made me respect more what she told me. I asked how she made the brown salve and what she spoke over my father's foot.

"You can make that salve any dozen ways out of any variety of healing herbs," she said. "In New Hampshire we make the salve out of molasses and flour. The molasses keeps the flour moist and prevents the burn from festering. A little peppermint oil, elder, St. John's wort, and fir balsam is added to the salve to speed up the healing."

"What about the words?"

"You can just whisper, 'get well fast.' That'll do fine," she said with a smile.

This was my beginning in cosmetics, and even after working in some of the largest cosmetic manufacturing establishments these early lessons were the best. The woods and these people who made simple natural products that had a purpose together made the finest school for me.

This book will not have my mother's cosmetic formulas in it nor the magic salves and secret incantations of Mrs. Hamilton. It will have ideas for having natural healthy hair and skin, natural substances, and their positive results for hair and skin care, and if you are like me and read all the labels on products, there is enough information to make you an aware consumer. I don't make cosmetics like my mother, Mrs. Hamilton, or the European and American folk medicine remedies. I have brought my own sense of herbals and natural substances into a more modern environment, and I can draw on a world of botanical knowledge which was not known to the folk medicine practitioners. What I have done, however, is kept the basic idea of natural and organic methods as more important than the synthesized and chemicalized. As a cosmetic chemist my soul is in the woods. Let me distort an old saying: you can take the boy out of the woods, but you can't take the woods out of the boy. In this book we will be going into the woods more often than we'll be going into the lab.

Aubrey Hampton
Tampa, Florida 1987

Part I

The History and Science of Natural Hair and Skin Care

or

Mother Nature As Cosmetic Chemist

In
Search
of the
Organic
World

When Aristotle was tutor to the youthful Alexander the Great, he advised the young king, who collected curious plant specimens, to conquer those territories that contained aloe vera in abundance because it was a strong curative. Early explorers of the Pacific Northwest found the native Indians using bark which we know as *cascara sagrada*, a strong emetic and highly rated as a tonic for the intestines. The Countess of Chinchon, wife of the Viceroy of Peru, supposedly fell ill in 1638 with a fever so virulent that the physicians gave up hope for her survival. When the governor of Loja sent the countess a package of bark to take as a tonic, she promptly recovered. The bark, which became known as the Countessa's Powder, is today refined into quinine, the classic treatment for malaria. The Swedish botanist, Karl von Linneé, named the fever-bark *cinchona*, in the countess' memory, but he misspelled her name. In any case, the story about the countess being miraculously saved by the bark isn't true, but it served to persuade people to use the bark to reduce their fevers (and also made the countess famous throughout the ages).

Robert Talbot, a young apothecary's apprentice and medical student, set himself up as a root doctor in London in 1670. He charged outrageous fees but, unlike the physicians of the time, did not bleed or purge his patients. He instead fed them herbal mixtures which he kept a secret and loudly asserted that the doctors did not understand nature and therefore could not understand sickness and the cures of sickness. His unorthodox methods enraged the Royal College of Physicians who set out to ruin him. Their plot failed when he was called in to cure King Charles II and succeeded in doing so. He was knighted in 1678 and became Sir Robert Talbot, Physician to the King. Soon after he was called to France to the royal bedside of the feverish son of Louis XIV, the king's only son. Upon his arrival, Sir Robert met a wall of French physicians in the royal chambers, ready to challenge the root doctor. "You can't cure the king's son because you're not a true physician," they told him. "You can't even define 'fever'."

"You define it but I cure it," was Sir Robert's reply, "which is something you can't do." Sir Robert did just that, and the king's son lived to be the next king of France. Louis XIV then offered Sir Robert Talbot 3,000 gold crowns for the secret herbal remedy, and he promised him that he would not reveal the secret of the formula while Sir Robert was still alive. Sir

Robert couldn't resist the offer, and when he died in 1681 at the age of 39, his formula was published: 6 drams of rose leaves, 2 oz. of lemon juice in a strong infusion of Peruvian bark. To protect his formula, Sir Robert mixed it into different wines to keep his patients off the track. The doctors considered him an ignorant quack, but he was far from ignorant. He cornered the market in fever bark and caused his fees to increase five-fold (while thousands died because only he knew the secret). But Sir Robert also knew that he was regarded as a quack, that he could never enter the sacred priesthood of physicians, and that he could never persuade them to use his herbal formula.

Some people think that the early times represent the truly natural and organic times, but as we've seen, the supposedly scientific community and the physicians of the day regarded "root doctors" or "herbalists" as quacks. Though Kipling wrote "Anything green that grew out of the mold/was an excellent herb to our fathers of old," our "fathers of old" were no more free to create their natural and organic herbal elixirs than we are today. The term "folk medicine" is not simply a designation of a type of natural treatment; it is also a derisive term at the root of it (excuse the pun). Simple folk create simple nostrums, but the true doctor or scientist rises above nature with his complex substances from the test-tube: the miracle drug!

Just as the medical profession rose with the synthetic era in the late 1900's, the cosmetic industry began to tap the synthetic chemical stocks for their products. In the early 1900's, eighty percent of all medicines and cosmetics were obtained from roots, barks, and leaves. Today, there is a mere drop of some herbal in the most herbal-sounding name. We have been left without the herb itself; only the name remains. As you will see, even the words natural and organic have been redefined by the synthetic advocates and the merchandisers to the complete confusion of the consumer. The search for a simple herbal product is like an attempt to find the silver fox: both are almost extinct. In fact, natural and organic products are, even if they are quite natural, attacked as dangerous or phony.

Look around yourself. You are surrounded by synthetic chemistry, and artificial objects and substances. When you eat foods, you are more often eating non-foods than you are real foods; that is, you are consuming various synthetic chemicals. When you fill your glass with tap water, you are drinking water that is often treated with synthetic chemicals. In some places, you are drinking water that may even contain toxic chemical waste. When you eat a vegetable, it was probably grown in land laced with various synthetic chemicals. When I was a boy, I would go with my mother to Kron's Ice Cream Shop. It was a hot Indian summer, and we'd carry enough cones for everybody to sit on the front porch and have an ice cream. The ice cream was all natural, made fresh daily, and it was superb. We sat on the porch and ate ice cream and talked. The ice cream and the family together on an Indian summer day made it special. Today ice cream is mass-produced and synthetic, even if hand-dipped. The ice cream factory puts a chemical called carboxymethylcellulose into the ice cream to expand the viscous liquid to make you think you're getting more. Mono and diglycerides, emulsifiers, and artificial fats are also added to make more cream out of the cream (real cream is expensive). There are so many artificial flavors that the ice cream factory must dream up artificial names with a natural sound (chocolate ripple is not chocolate though it may be rippled). There are about 2,112 flavoring agents and 1,610 of these are synthetic chemicals.

If you think you are safe at your local health food store, you'd better think again. The health food store manager would have to spend all his time simply reading labels and have a chemical dictionary next to him to begin to control the flow of synthetic chemicals that find their way into the health food products from supplements to cosmetics. A few stores even sell pills that are completely synthetic. BHT (butylated hydroxytoluene) has long been a synthetic antioxidant in the processed food industry. Perhaps you have read food labels to avoid it and went to health food stores to buy foods that didn't have it, but now you can buy BHT pills and take them to supposedly increase your lifespan (thanks to a recent popular book on life extension). Life extension, however, depends on a healthy metabolism free of stress which is the exact opposite of what BHT did in lab tests. Two researchers in Australia (W. D. Brown and A. R. Johnson) found that BHT combined with fats reduces growth, causes an increase in the liver weight and reduces the important detoxification role of this vital organ. When the liver goes, your life span quickly goes with it! Due to the dangers of BHT, the British only allow its use in lard, butter, margarine, and essential oils. The British Industrial Biological Research Association and the British Food Standards Committee have recommended that BHT be taken off the list of permitted antioxidants, and BHT was banned from use in foods in Romania due to tests in 1950 that revealed metabolic stress. But in America, you can take your synthetic juice straight up by pill!

We seem to live in a society that is supportive of the most synthetic chemicals without a knowledge of the problems a continually chemicalized world is bringing to us. We use millions of pounds and gallons of fossil fuels every day (coal, oil, gas) without being aware that they are not simple combustion products for the purpose of creating energy, but are also profoundly changing our air, food, water, cosmetics, and every inch of our existence. Our beds and bedding, clothing, rugs, rug pads, furniture, walls, and draperies contain these chemicals known as petrochemicals. Petrochemicals are used in artificial colors, plastic, polyester, foam rubber, cosmetics, perfumes, pesticides, alcohols, formaldehyde, cleaners, sprays, waxes, tars, printer's inks, paints, solvents, toothpastes, mouthwashes, hair sprays, shampoos, lotions, gums, glues, drugs, and preservatives (that go in any number of products including foods, drugs, and cosmetics). Theron Randolph, M.D., and Ralph M. Moss, Ph.D., pointed out as early as 1951 that petrochemicals, though seemingly harmless chemicals, were responsible for a wide variety of mental and physical problems even when they were present in tiny, supposedly non-toxic doses (T. G. Randolph, M.D., and R. W. Moss, Ph.D., *An Alternative Approach to Allergies*, New York: Bantam Books, 1951).

I am skeptical of industry's ability to determine that a particular chemical or combination of chemicals is good for me. I am more comfortable with Mother Nature's ability to create superior beneficial substances. This is obviously both an emotional and an analytical reaction. It is an emotional reaction in that I intuitively feel that natural substances are better for me than synthetic ones. This is not, however, 100% true. Nature creates poisons, like rattlesnake venom or poison ivy, and sometimes individuals react badly to other natural substances. Sometimes, too, substances are both beneficial and poisonous, as is the case with aconite (*aconitum napellus*) which has been used successfully to reduce pain and fever in a tiny amount (two drops of the fluid extract to a cup of warm water), but if taken in excessive amount could cause the heart to stop. This knowledge does not cause me to turn away from this natural substance to a synthetic drug; it alerts me to the potential hazard of this substance which has been known for hundreds of years. The fact that I am working within an ancient tradition means that the potential hazards of these substances are known, unlike the effects of synthetic chemicals on our bodies. Every day we are becoming more and more aware that the chemicalization of our earth is having a disastrous effect--a long range effect--on the ecological balance. My knowledge of this makes me emotionally attached to natural substances rather than synthetic substances, but the studies I have been involved in make me analytically in favor of natural substances and against more synthetic substances in general.

If you are like me, you are an avid label reader, and you want to know about everything. I have a theory that as you become synthetic from all the synthetic juices taken into your body and rubbed outside your body, your mind becomes synthetic as well. You see synthetics as no different than substances created by nature. You become desensitized to synthetics so that you are about as alive as synthetic chemicals. The saps (i.e., synthetic apologists, which is what I call people who try to compare Mother Nature's substances to the lab people's substances) always say the same thing: "All foods, vitamins, and nutrients, and all other substances of life are chemicals." It is true that they are labeled as chemicals and many have long complicated names, but all this hair-splitting means nothing to the body. All this debate means nothing to our air, land, and water. Mother Nature did not contaminate and synthesize our earth--it was, and still is, the synthetic apologists. They are part of the problem, because they are not part of the solution.

The concept of my book is that everyone needs to avoid synthetic chemicals in cosmetics (hair and skin care products) by recognizing them, knowing some of the possible problems their presence in a product can cause, and presenting actual natural and organic alternatives. The first step to gaining this awareness is to understand what the words natural and organic mean and how these meanings have been manipulated historically.

In 1807, the Swedish chemist Jons Jakob Berzelius created a division between things that are natural and things that are synthetic by dividing chemicals into two groups. Those from organisms, living or dead, he called organic; the rest he called inorganic (the Latin "in-" means not). Today chemists refer to any compound that contains carbon atoms as organic, and they use inorganic to refer to a compound that does not contain the carbon atoms. We know today, that even though the German chemist Friedrich Wohler upset the work of Berzelius by preparing an organic chemical without any tissue--living or dead--as a starting material (in 1828), the distinction between the two terms holds fast. Organic farming is a classic example of using only natural substances to grow crops. The word "organism" came before the word "organic" which the ancient Greeks used (*organon*) for any musical instrument. This Greek word was used to create the word "organ" for a specific keyboard instrument, but the most general use of the term outside the field of music is that of a specific structure in a living creature such as the heart, lungs, skin, and so forth--the organs. One of the reasons cosmetic manufacturers put preservatives into cosmetics is to destroy unwanted organisms known as microorganisms (from the Greek *mikros* meaning small).

The Dutchman, Anton van Leeuwenhoek, created lenses so powerful that he could see single cells (1675), and he looked into this world of single-celled animals with great fascination. Until this time, we did not know that there were living organisms that were unseen by the naked eye, or at least we could not prove that these organisms existed. Leeuwenhoek called them "protozoa" (from the Greek *protos*, first; and *zoon*, animal), because he said these had to be the first animals to exist on earth. He also created stronger lenses and discovered even smaller organisms which were neither animals nor plants. To name these tiny organisms a Latin word was chosen--*germen*--meaning a tiny bud, representing the very beginning of life. Germs! While the word frightens hypochondriacs to the point of apoplexy, we all start as ovum and sperm, which are germ cells, just as a plant seed that develops into a plant (a process called germination). When you eat a nutritional supplement called wheat germ, you are consuming a germ. The name most used today is bacteria from the Greek *bakterion* (which means tiny rod which is how the microorganisms appear through the lens of the microscope.)

The cultivation of microorganisms is called a culture. Yogurt is a bacterial culture eaten as a health and diet food; acidophilus is a culture which you take for the purpose of restoring bacteria to your system if it has been depleted by chemical preservatives or antibiotics. These (wheat germ, yogurt, acidophilus) are bacterial cultures found beneficial to humans. Antibiotics are chemical cultures produced by fungi and other microorganisms and used in diluted forms to destroy or inhibit bacteria. Obviously there are benefits to this culture, but there are also problems. Antibiotics and certain destructive cultures not only destroy the harmful bacteria but also destroy the favorable bacteria inside our body.

All the living creatures from tiny microorganisms to you are organic. You are organic. A sunflower is organic; a piece of wood is organic; a protozoa is organic; wheat germ is organic; a marsupial is organic; perhaps your garden is organic; proteins are organic; a neuron is organic; chlorophyll is organic; isoprene (which doesn't sound organic but is in fact one of the building blocks of Vitamin A); amino acids are organic; wood can be burned to potash which is organic; but plastic is not organic.

Still, since organic compounds can be combined with synthetic chemicals and still be considered organic (coming from living organisms), and since an organic compound can be considered any compound which contains a molecule containing carbon atoms (not to mention the fact that any chemical can be made organic without tissue living or dead), we can become very confused by the term organic. By expanding the word organic to include any chemical that has a carbon atom, we can even support the fact that the synthetic chemicals and pesticides an organic farmer would never use may be called organic. It is for this reason that I like to see the terms "natural" and "organic" together, but I still think we should honor the inventor of the word "organic," Dr. Berzelius, by accepting his definition--"material that has once been a part of living tissue whether alive or dead."

If the word organic is complicated, shouldn't the word natural be simple? Dictionaries and lexicons say the word natural means pertaining to nature; produced by nature; not artificial; in conformity with the laws of nature; connected with the existing physical system of things; pertaining to foods, vitamins, and body care products that contain nothing synthetic and are sold in health food stores. The last definition is interesting because it comes from a book of new definitions not found in conventional dictionaries. All these meanings of the word natural lead us to believe that anything called natural must be produced by nature or at least contain only natural and non-artificial substances. This is not always true. Just as the word organic is abused and misused so is the word natural.

> "Nowhere does the idea of [natural products] take a more gratuitous bruising than in the field of cosmetics. Ever since the 1960's, when hostility to technology began turning the so-called natural look into a hot advertising gambit, the cosmetics industry has been overworking its overripe imagination to convince customers that naturalness is to be had only through the use of ointments, lotions, tints, and other exotic stuffs. Gillette's new FOHO--For Oily Hair Only--system all but inelectably boasts 'natural ingredients.' Jojoba oil is plugged as 'nature's own deep moisturizing formula from the legendary desert plant.' The epitome of the natural cosmetic notion must be a product called Natural Image by Granny's Girl: 'all-natural, grown-up cosmetics especially for little girls! Blushers, lip glosses, and eyeshadows that give gentle hints of color, shine, and scent...' What is easily forgotten under the enchantment of such copy is the unadorned fact that cosmetics exist entirely as interventions against natural appearances" (Frank Trippett, "Little Crimes Against Nature," *Time*, October 11, 1982).

This is Frank Trippett's criticism of those who don't know the meaning of the word natural and more directly of those who use the word for financial gain when there is nothing natural about what they are producing. He points to the Chiffon margarine commercial with the line "It's not nice to fool Mother Nature." "It is even less nice," says Trippett, "to blame and credit her for things beyond her doing."

One supposedly natural cosmetic company which did not make completely natural cosmetics ran a series of ads educating the public that natural substances worked better with synthetic chemicals in them. Also national health magazines, distributed through health food stores and through subscriptions, define a whole variety of synthetic chemicals as natural or at least organic. The view is that as long as there's a drop or two of something natural in a product it is natural, no matter how synthetic the formula happens to be otherwise. This is obviously a good way for the magazine to protect the advertisers by shabby editorial policy. One article went to the trouble of discussing the thousands of years that leaves (which are natural) decay in the ground so that we can have oil and hence a "natural" preservative called methylparaben, a petrochemical and a known sensitizer. One cosmetic label has a long list of chemical names and after each one is the phrase "derived from coconut oil," which has become a misleading term that you should question when purchasing a cosmetic. What was the purpose in deriving this substance (instead of using the entire plant or animal source), or was anything done to this substance once it was derived? Some derivatives are removed from sources because certain qualities of the whole substance are undesirable. The coloring agent in henna, for instance, is a good example of this. Once this is removed, the henna can be used as a conditioning ingredient in hair care products, and it will not color your hair. Another reason to derive or remove a substance from its source is to concentrate and isolate its particular quality: for example, mucopolysaccharides, derived from the aloe plant, condition your hair. The term "derived from" is misleading, however; some manufacturers list a chemical such as cocoamide DEA and then insinuate that this is a natural and organic substance by adding the magic phrase "derived from coconut oil." The cocoamide DEA in your shampoo may or may not have been derived from coconut oil, but in order to become cocoamide DEA, synthetic chemicals were added to it, and it is therefore no longer natural and organic. A friend of mine who loves coconuts resents the cosmetic chemical manufacturers' abuse of the word coconut. "They say sodium lauryl sulfate is from coconut oil; they say triethanolamine is from coconut oil; TEA lauryl sulfate is from coconut oil, and there's one shampoo that has them all in it. Some of these chemicals are listed as cancer-causing agents. The coconut is getting a bad reputation from these synthetic chemicals. Pretty soon we will have to put a label on the coconut that says 'may be hazardous to your health.'"

Can you picture the mass-producing cosmetic manufacturer actually boiling the essence from herbs? I make an herbal base in the cosmetic lab by actually creating a huge drum of tea. I put a variety of herbs into boiling water and steep. This becomes a hair rinse and a base for other herbal hair and skin care products. If the modern cosmetic chemist can't find the ingredient in a chemical book and get it at a most economical rate, he would never bother with it. Boiling a vat of herbs is old-fashioned, and smacks of folk medicine, kitchen cosmetics, and witchcraft.

The hard fast truth is that very, very few foods, vitamins, or cosmetics are partly natural, and even fewer are completely natural. Even those cosmetics that are partly natural have little natural substance in their products due to the cost of natural raw materials and the difficulty in getting them. Those things devised by humankind and those that issue from Mother Nature often get blurred in the cause of merchandising. The commercial rush to exploit the popular sentiment and notion of what is natural is getting absurdly out of shape, and the preposterous habit of putting the word "natural" on synthetic stuff has created a distrust in those who are learning to know the difference as well as increasing the ignorance of those who do not know the difference. In view of all these apparent criticisms and inaccuracies, I felt that a comprehensive book--*Natural Organic Hair and Skin Care*--would fill the need of those who were interested in what is natural and organic and what is hype and how Mother Nature fits into today's world of mass-produced synthetic products. Though Trippett's essay was simplistic and lacked the understanding of how nature and humankind can work together harmoniously, it still pointed out that "natural vinyl" and "natural nylon" are human artifacts, that a raccoon's coat is natural but a raccoon coat is not, as well as the belief that a human head of hair is natural, but once products containing synthetic chemicals are put on it, its bond with nature is weakened because the hair is no longer working with nature but against it. It is most unnatural to rip off the raccoon's coat (which murders the poor animal) in order to sew the pelts together for your own back, but a fake fur or "natural vinyl" coat is actually working harmoniously with nature in this case. Though I personally prefer cotton and wool, which are natural fibers, I will encourage synthetic furs if it means that one less animal is destroyed. It is, as I've indicated, simplistic to view nature as separate from man and woman: we are all extensions of nature. Your hair, for example, is natural. If you dye it or perm it, it is still natural--damaged by synthetics, but still natural--but a shampoo made from natural extracts (without synthetics) complements your hair's naturalness. I have found that the hair, skin, and body react differently to completely natural hair and skin care products than they do to those with various amounts of synthetic chemicals added to them. Using natural ingredients results in safer products because we know what natural ingredients are and what they do, unlike synthetic substances.

A journalist--or any type of writer--runs a risk when he or she writes about something without intensive knowledge and close experience with the subject being written about. There is nothing wrong in bending over your typewriter in a room surrounded by books on a subject, and most subjects are written in that way; however, nothing beats the first-hand experience of a concept or a product. I am reminded here of an article by a beauty writer for a well-known health magazine who recommended a complexion spray that would magically attract moisture to the skin due to a chemical called NaPCA (2-pyrrolidone-5-carboxylic acid). A very popular book on life extension had just been published that discussed the benefits of this chemical. The beauty writer was caught up in the hype and wrote an article praising the product and even suggested spraying the stuff on house plants (to attract moisture to them). People followed the advice of this beauty writer, but instead of attracting moisture, the product dessicated the skin and killed the house plants. The unfortunate beauty writer had to print an apology and a warning. I had run many tests using this "wonder product" NaPCA and found that it did exactly what the magazine readers complained about. What had happened is that the beauty writer had gathered her facts by talking to those who sold the chemical and by reading the book praising the substance. She did not talk to anybody who had looked at it from a more objective viewpoint, and at the time she wrote the article, she had not tried the product on her own skin. NaPCA may be manufactured by our own bodies, but it is inaccurate to assume that if man synthesizes this chemical, it will do the same job as the substance we make naturally in our own bodies. After using the humectant in its pure form, the beauty writer broke out with a very strong irritation response (as had a number of readers who tested the product on themselves). She then wrote a retraction article stressing the importance of patch testing. One wonders that if patch testing is so important why the beauty writer didn't patch test herself before writing the first article praising the synthetic substance. What I wish to point out here is that writers--as well as consumers--have a responsibility to recommend nothing except what they have found to be true first-hand. I don't ask that you take my word that natural substances are better: I only ask that you learn to recognize the difference between natural and synthetic substances so that you can make an educated choice between them.

I have made it a positive requirement of this book that everything I discuss in detail be natural substances I have actually formulated with, tested in hair and skin care research clinics, field tested in the marketplace, researched through various monographs by others, and have found to be commonly used throughout antiquity. A whole mass of synthetic chemicals are too new to meet this requirement, and most of the petrochemicals being used today were not even discovered until after World War II.

Many cosmetic books and hair and skin care books will suggest products for you to use. These books are frequently written by M.D.'s (dermatologists) who feel, due to their practice, that they can pass on brand names without fear of admonishment. However, after reading every skin and hair care book written by dermatologists, the fact is borne out that they know nothing about hair and skin care though they may know about treating disease. As Mary Ann Crenshaw pointed out in her best seller, *The Natural Way to Super Beauty*, (New York: Dell

Publishing, 1974):

>"[Dermatologists are] great when it comes to skin diseases where we couldn't make it without [their] medical expertise. But after skin-problem years of unnecessary, and possibly dangerous X-ray treatments, and more years of being told such things as to wash my face with tar soap or live on antibiotics--well, quite frankly, I'd feel more comfortable if the dermatologists kept their hands off my face."

One supposedly "no-nonsense plan for keeping your skin and hair healthy and vibrant" written by a dermatologist suggests the following shampoos: T Gel Shampoo (Neutrogena), Polytar (Stiefel), Sebutone (Westwood), Zetar (Dermik), DHS Tar (Person & Covey), Dermalab X-5T Shampoo (Derma Laboratories), Xseb-T Shampoo (Baker/Cummins), and Vanseb-T (Herbert). All these shampoos are coal tar shampoos.

One book suggests seven name brand shampoos for oily hair, and if you bought every one of these shampoos (all at different prices) and read the label of ingredients, you would see most of the same ingredients in all of them. Few of the ingredients are natural, and some of the ingredients have already been listed as cancer-causing agents. In two "medically-written skin and hair care books," there is absolutely nothing about nature, and there are no natural products tested. This is obviously because the dermatologist has been "detailed" by synthetic chemical companies. He can only try out what he gets samples of, and he is often looked at by his fellow doctors as strange if he slides too far into the "natural and organic" ranks. It is somehow a kind of heresy if you are a physician and you look for products that contain natural substances. It is a link that never ends. Synthetic foods, synthetic clothing, synthetic drugs, synthetic cosmetics, synthetic thought, and everything preserved, sprayed, colored, and denaturalized. Doctors usually call their books "no-nonsense," but they are filled with nonsense, because they treat you with a "doctor knows best" attitude rather than as a thinking person. You are a thinking person, and the more you are allowed to give free rein to that thought process the more likely you are to decide for yourself what is nonsense and what is not nonsense. It is hardly nonsense to seek out more natural substances to bring into your life: natural foods, natural cosmetics, natural supplements, and a more natural existence. The new breed of physician is aware of the chemicalization of our society, and I know many of these doctors. It would be nonsense to suggest that all physicians are the same and come from the same mold, but we have to be aware that the training of the usual physician is done by the chemical industry. It is a rare physician who can take this training and use only that which is needed, but look for the most natural methods. To take one example, millions of people are prescribed antibiotics every year, yet antibiotics destroy important bacteria in the small intestine which aid in the digestive and elimination process, yet very few doctors will suggest that the patients take acidophilus to restore the bacteria. One story concerning the use of acidophilus comes from a woman who achieved remarkable results after suffering with acne for over 20 years. Her letter points out that as long as she took the acidophilus, the acne did not return. When the letter was shown by another woman to a dermatologist, he dismissed the remedy as an old-fashioned joke. This woman also took acidophilus with excellent results (Mark Bricklin, *Natural Healing*, Emmaus, PA: Rodale Press, 1976) (Also see **ACIDOPHILUS**, in this book).

Because I have a close association with several natural cosmetic manufacturers and have had an association with large cosmetic manufacturers, I will give no brand names because it would be construed as favoritism. However, I have, here and there, suggested a brand name where there is absolutely no other product with a certain natural ingredient which I feel is of value. This book has a step-by-step **Natural Method for Skin Care** and **Natural Method for Hair Care** (with photos), and I have not included the brand names of the products that are used in my Hair and Skin Care Research and Training Clinic nor the ones used in Natural Method Salons and Clinics known to me. Obviously the success of the **Natural Method** is based on the natural substances used as well as the method and the massage used. In order to make it possible to make the hair and skin care sections of this book of value, I have taken the time to discuss the ingredients most beneficial in these sections and throughout the book. They are natural ingredients and/or natural derivatives, but it is still the formulation that makes them valuable to the hair and skin. I am including, therefore, a resources section in this book which lists raw materials manufacturers, cosmetic manufacturers, and examples of labels from these manufacturers. Obviously, I can't list every cosmetic company that says it's natural or that is natural. I consider the resources section of this book important because the **Natural Method for Hair and Skin Care** is based on completely natural substances used in a particular way. The Resources Section can supply the "missing link" to make the **Natural Method** work more effectively.

This book will not prevent you from having an allergic reaction to a product whether natural or synthetic, but it will put at your fingertips the most allergic chemicals, which have almost always been found to be synthetic or one of the petrochemicals. You can also be allergic to a natural substance, and if you were allergic to lecithin, for example, my definition that it was safe would be of no use to you and would be erroneous as far as you were concerned. It is impossible to say whether or not you will be allergic to something, and whether or not you are really allergic to what you think you are allergic to in a product. Again, let me use the example of lecithin, which is a natural substance and a constituent of your skin. A cosmetic manufacturer was preparing a product in which one of the main ingredients was lecithin. When they performed patch tests with the lecithin, they found a high incidence of allergic reaction, but it was discovered that the allergic reaction was due to a bleaching agent in the lecithin which had not been adequately removed when the lecithin was processed (Kramer, Sylvia, "Hypo-allergenic Cosmetics," in *Cosmetic Science and Technology*, New York: Interscience Publications, 1957, pp. 878-889).

Some years ago, I created a roll-on deodorant containing high amounts of vitamin E. The product was based on the fact that vitamin E is an antioxidant and will, without changing the body and in a natural way, reduce the odor by preventing the oxidation that causes this odor. Right after my product was in the marketplace, Mennen also manufactured a vitamin E aerosol deodorant, and their ads followed the same reasoning. However, thousands of people were allergic to the vitamin E in the spray deodorant, and Mennen had to stop manufacturing the product. There were no allergic reactions at all to the vitamin E deodorant I made, and it still sells today twelve years later. Why were so many people allergic to the vitamin E in the spray deodorant? Obviously, there was a difference in the E I had used, and the E they had used in the aerosol spray. There was, of course, a difference in the formulations as well as in the delivery systems. Again, if I write in this book that vitamin E is non-toxic and safe, and you use, for example, an aerosol E deodorant and break out in a rash, then my definition that vitamin E is safe is silly to you. It's important to bear in mind that there is a term called synergism. In chemistry, this usually means that two or more chemicals are working together to produce a more effective result than any one of the single chemicals could produce alone. It is for this reason that a natural substance can be excellent and safe but when combined in a formula can have an adverse effect. I have had people tell me on more than one occasion that certain natural substances caused them to itch and break out in a rash due to allergic reactions. I gave them a natural product containing that substance, but they had no allergic reaction to the natural ingredient in the natural formula. I am not allergic to synthetic chemicals because I am unhealthy. I am allergic because I am healthy. The body is natural, and if your immune system is doing a good job, it will attempt to reject chemical allergens.

Some researchers in the field of allergies are of the opinion that about 20% of the population suffer from some form of allergic reaction, but there are not many figures as to how many are allergic to cosmetics. Due to the fact that cosmetic formulas are always changing, and new chemicals are being introduced almost daily, there is no way of knowing who is allergic to what or why. In recent years hair dyes have been found to be one of the principal allergens in the cosmetic business. In one study, the types of cosmetics highest in allergic reactions were the following: lipstick 48%, nail lacquer 15%, creams & lotions 19%, face & body powders 4%, soap & soap products 4%, miscellaneous 10%. But these figures are not helpful because there is no way of knowing which ingredient or ingredients (which may or may not be present in more than one category) is responsible for the reaction. Another problem is involved when an ingredient is believed to be pure but actually contains impurities. It has been said that the simpler formulas are the better formulas, but if there are impurities in one or more ingredients, then the theory of a simpler formula means nothing. There is no doubt, however, that cosmetics do cause allergic reactions, and that many of these reactions are caused by synthetic substances.

In the American Colonies of 1721, synthetic chemicals had not found their way into foods, drugs, and cosmetics. In Boston, as well as Europe, lard, mutton tallow, white and yellow wax, and essential oils (herbs) were the ingredients used in all pomades for the hair and ointments for the skin. While the appearance of these cosmetics was quite primitive, it is documented that they had excellent positive results in the hair and skin (Cosmetics were part of the herbal doctors' wares). Products were preserved with essential oils and alcohol. Nothing synthetic was used, not even chemicals to color them or thicken them or solubilize them (the term "Shake Well Before Using" was much in vogue).

Approximately two hundred years after the first colonists arrived in Jamestown, the country was wild, and few physicians would venture into this new uncivilized territory. Why should they go there? There were no hospitals or medical schools; few drugs could be imported to the area; the only old world recipes one could find had to be gotten from old newsprints and almanacs, and if a drug was not available to save your life, the only consolation was that others would die just as you did. High prices were a fact of life due to the absence of all but a mere suggestion of industrialization. Oatmeal, which we take for granted today at about a dollar a box, was sold by the ounce for use in cosmetics, as a poultice, and even as medicine. Cosmetics were made in the home from time-tested remedies with herbs, simple kitchen products, garden vegetables and fruits. All natural ingredients were used because they were the only ones available. Even the commercial soapworks made their cosmetics the same way. Kitchen fats were saponified with potash made from wood ashes and quicklime. It made a strong soap, but the purpose of the soap was to clean and even have medicinal properties.

In colonial America, the men and women who used herbs to treat the sick were called root doctors, and the root doctors had more luck with illness than the conventional college-trained M.D.'s who used blood-letting, blistering, mercury, antimony, vitriols, and other popular European medicaments and methods that were the modern medicine of the day. Epidemics often ravaged entire cities in early America, and in 1793, the yellow fever epidemic returned to Philadelphia for the second time killing 4,000 people in a three month period. The disease baffled the most skilled physicians, but one root doctor by the name of Samuel Thomson who lived in Alstead, New Hampshire, used ginger root for anyone exposed to the disease or who showed early symptoms. The patients held the ginger root in their mouths and chewed on it like tobacco, swallowing the juice a little at a time. Physicians of the day, however, prescribed bleeding twice a day for ten days which weakened the patients and succeeded in killing off over half of them, while the ginger root saved well over half infected patients. Dr. Thomson was so popular that he was sent for by people all over the Eastern part of America, but his farm suffered from this demand. He was paid little or nothing for his medical practice because he was not an educated doctor (nor was he even approved of by these doctors). Eventually, Dr. Thomson put his time entirely to healing the sick with roots and herbs. His medical bag contained an ounce of emetic herb, two ounces of cayenne, two pounds of powdered bayberry bark or root, one pound of poplar bark, one pound of ginger, and an internal and external elixer for pain (which he recorded in 1831). This was a mixture of one-fourth pound of myrrh, one-fourth pound of gum guaiacum, one-half ounce oil of wintergreen, one-half ounce of red pepper mixed in a gallon of alcohol. He gave this in ten drops to a glass of water, and also as a rub for any painful areas.

The extravagant medical claims made for herbal treatments and cosmetics by rustics, pioneer settlers, frontiersmen, and medicine show pitchmen were to instill faith in their concoctions. Today all this is a matter of stretching the truth a bit with advertising, but what is interesting to me in all this is that the finest products are still natural or based on natural ingredients. The great advancement of synthetic chemicals has contributed little to the actual care of the hair and skin; quite the contrary, the danger of synthetic chemicals is making us seek the concoctions of the past to improve our hair, skin, and general health.

Today, the consumer has not only come of age: the consumer has grown beyond the manufacturers and retailers who sell products. In earlier decades, the consumer was regarded with disdain and contempt by the manufacturers of products. The attitude has shifted from contempt to condescension to the consumer, but today the consumers have organized to the extent that they question and question and question. This is as it should be. I receive hundreds of letters every month from consumers who don't like the synthetic chemicals being used in cosmetics, for example, and I can confirm the fact that this distrust is not a passing phenomenon but a growing one. In the space of two or three years, I've seen large manufacturers buy small natural cosmetic and vitamin companies. Wilkson-Vicks (of Vicks' Vapo-Rub fame) bought Plus Natural Vitamins and Mill Creek Natural Cosmetics, and Gillette bought a natural cosmetic company called Apri Cosmetics. These large corporations which have nothing natural or organic in their product mix obviously wanted a small natural product company. I think the main reason for this is the mass movement towards natural and organic cosmetics, vitamins, and foods.

But natural and organic cosmetics can't be compared with synthetic ones, and this is apparent when large cosmetic manufacturers attempt to get into the natural cosmetics game. Some call their product lines natural when they are not, as is the case with Fabergé Organics and Clairol's Herbessence shampoos. Other companies, such as Natural Organics Plus, which introduced a mass-marketed (though synthetic) jojoba shampoo, later introduced a completely natural product only to find that the product and its natural ingredients were (and are) incompatible with mass manufacturing and distribution techniques. What is needed are cosmetic companies who are opposed to synthetic ingredients, dedicated to optimal synergetic formulations, and who are flexible enough to design their businesses to fit the needs of their products and their customers. What is needed are consumers who are educated to know the difference between natural and synthetic products--the benefits of the natural products and the hazards of the synthetic ones. Many people do want natural cosmetics (as well as natural foods and vitamins), but they must be prepared to accept the products "without frills" as natural products, that are plainly and simply natural. "Shake well before using" may have to be revived!

The purpose of this book is to offer alternative methods of caring for your hair and skin, and at the same time to get to know all the various chemicals, both natural and synthetic, used as ingredients in cosmetics: what they are, where they come from, and what they can do for your skin and hair. Choosing cosmetics doesn't have to be a guessing game; we want to show you how easy it can be once you know how to read cosmetic labels. Adequate nutrition, natural cosmetic products, and uncomplicated daily care of the hair and skin are also part of what we advocate and explain in this book. Our purpose is not to represent a particular line though much of the work and results of natural hair and skin care are due to specific products that are as natural as humanly possible. Our purpose is to teach a system or regimen of hair and skin care known as **The Natural Method** which I have been using and teaching for well over a decade and have, thereby, gained knowledge about natural substances and their use on the hair and skin. Natural and organic are both words that have been abused by advertising companies to sell products which usually are neither. Some years ago, the cosmetic industry discovered that the consumer wanted natural products, and they began their natural buzz word labels and advertising. One of the early products to deceptively use this label was Clairol's Herbessence Shampoo. Their ads of a beautiful woman playing in a clear bubbling stream of water was to be imitated by many other cosmetic manufacturers marketing mostly through health food stores (i.e., Mill Creek, Spring Brook, Country Road, etc.). Because of the similarity of other advertising campaigns to theirs, Mill Creek (which had been purchased by Wilkinson-Vicks) decided to sue and force the other "brooks" and "roads" and "streams" and "paths" to walk the straight and narrow by leaving their old-fashioned mill alone. They won some of the suits, against, for example, General Nutritional Centers' Pioneer Brand. This company used the same bottle, and some of the same generic product names (i.e., Keratin Shampoo), but instead of an old mill, they used a covered bridge (another sort of path combining a brook and a bridge as a pathway). The courts agreed with Mill Creek that the consumer would be confused. Consumers are still confused. What does all this mean to you as a consumer who may be simply looking for natural products? It means nothing, of course. The purpose of this book is to urge you to ignore packaging and ads and slogans for the most part, and to emphasize the part of the packaging that should interest you most: the ingredients label.

I find so much excitement in the world of herbs that I could spend every day working with cosmetic herbal ingredients alone, and if I spent the rest of my life working with herbal extracts in various formulations I would not get through all the known and unknown herbs. I could come up with literally thousands of cosmetic products for hair and skin care; I could create thousands of natural herbal medicines and foods; and there would be lots of room for discoveries and progress for future generations. Think about this: in only the past few years, we have discovered two herbal oils that are high in protein and essential fatty acids (EFAs). One of these herbal oils is jojoba oil, which is more of a liquid wax than an oil. The seeds contain an oil which is an excellent replacement for sperm oil and thereby protects the sperm whale from being murdered for its oil (used in cosmetics). Jojoba oil is even superior to sperm whale oil because it never becomes rancid and is milder on the skin. The meal left over after the oil has been extracted from the seed is an excellent livestock feed high in protein, and I've used it as a beauty mask (See **JOJOBA** in Chapter VI).

The other oil is evening primrose oil which is high in EFAs and contains a rare fatty acid known as gamma-linolenic acid (GLA) which is needed for the formation of prostaglandins in the body. These are hormone-like substances that balance or regulate cells. Chemically, GLA is very similar to alpha-linolenic acid, but the body knows the difference and uses GLA. (Dr. David Horrobin is one of the researchers involved in discovering the GLA content of Evening Primrose Oil.) Some of the claims made for the medical use of evening primrose oil are weight loss, arthritis, hyperactivity, alcoholism, premenstrual syndrome, schizophrenia, multiple sclerosis, cardiovascular disorders, the induction of natural labor, and hair and skin care (See **EVENING PRIMROSE OIL** in Chapter VI).

I have used both jojoba and evening primrose oils in developing products for the care of the hair and skin. I was among the first cosmetic compounders to use jojoba oil, the first to use jojoba meal, and the first to use evening primrose oil. I have found that both these oils are excellent for the hair and skin when used in shampoos, hair conditioners, and skin lotions or creams.

What this points out, especially to those who say that there is no progress to be made by utilizing nature and limiting synthetic chemicals, is that more discoveries are ahead. Far from being a limited field of research, natural substances are a wide open field of research. In the case of the two herbal oils singled out here it is easy to see that they both contributed something new and opened a whole new field of research for internal and external use.

I have a simple saying: "It's the juice in the bottle that counts," but when you buy a cosmetic, it isn't just the juice in the bottle that you pay for. You pay for a fancy package which winds up in the trash can; you pay for the TV ads, the magazine ads, the celebrity endorsements, and even for the word natural on the bottle. What you want to know most about they never seem to tell you about: the juice in the bottle. I hope this book gives you more knowledge about the juice in the bottle and also what it can or can't do for your hair, skin and body. I hope you not only make use of the "A to Z Guide to Natural and Synthetic Chemicals Used in Cosmetics," but that you also utilize the **Natural Method for Skin Care** and **Natural Method for Hair Care** to get the advantage of a long range plan to youthful healthy hair and skin.

As much as possible I have kept the perimeters of this book within the hair and skin care area, but I have at times edged over into the fields of nutrition, herbal medicine, and dermatology to add to your present knowledge or expand the world of nature to areas of health care where it is needed. You will find an herb chart in Chapter VII, for example, with many herbs that are said to benefit ailments and optimize health, as well as improve the condition of the hair and skin. I have worked with about all of them at one time or another and find the success of herbals in cosmetics to be far superior to all the synthetic chemicals and animal oils in most modern cosmetics (including supposedly antiaging animal extracts that many men and women buy today at outrageous prices).

There is another herb chart in Chapter XII which lists the herbs used in Chinese medicine. I have included this because I think you will find it interesting. Though most of these herbs have not been used in cosmetics or investigated fully for that purpose, I think there is probably quite a bit to learn here. The main attraction to this chapter will be the acupuncture face lift described and diagramed in detail. You need not "needle" your face, however, because the use of acupressure works just as well for this face lift. Combined with the facial massage diagrams and **Natural Method of Skin Care** (in Part III of this book), you can find no better natural and organic way of caring for your skin.

If you go in search for the organic work in the modern cosmetic company you won't find it because cosmetic chemists don't bother with natural extracts unless they suddenly become a "hot word" and can be merchandised to sell a product. So the "hot word" cosmetic isn't even created to make use of the "hot word" ingredient in the product, but to ride on the crest of a marketing trend. (After all, cosmetic chemists who have been working in large cosmetic companies don't believe that anything works.) For example, a product development manager, who was an excellent cosmetic chemist, told me about a new hair care product for men (a grooming agent) which kept the hair well-groomed without being sticky and gave the hair a thick, full look.

"Does it have panthenol?" I asked him. "That can make the hair thicker and fuller-looking." I should have known better than to ask if it had anything natural that did anything positive in it, but I slip up sometimes.

"Panthenol?" he said, puzzled. Then he laughed. "Ah, the magic feather!"

Now it was my turn to look puzzled. "The magic feather?" I repeated. "What is that?"

"Dumbo the elephant thought he needed the magic feather in order to fly," the product manager explained, "but he soon found out he could fly without it."

This book is loaded with natural (mostly herbal) cosmetic ingredients, or "magic feathers," as the product manager thinks of them, but in truth, they aren't "magic feathers" at all. Many of them have been around for thousands of years, but they usually haven't been used in modern cosmetic products because most manufacturers don't want to take the trouble to hunt them down and use them in the completely natural formula they require to work their best. Panthenol DOES WORK to make the hair thicker and fuller-looking, but don't tell this to a cosmetic chemist. Keep the magic feathers in this book to yourself; use them to make your own cosmetic, or look for a cosmetic with them in it. If there isn't enough in the product to do the job (check the ingredients list), get some of that ingredient, and add it to the product. Don't feel that a cosmetic product is sacrosanct in any way. There isn't a product made that can't be improved, and the mass-produced cosmetics need more improvement than any of them. In fact, it's the magic feather that's missing!

A healthy looking skin and a full head of hair is a sign of good health, because no matter how we feel we are still looked at by others. There is absolutely no magic cream you can buy through a pulp magazine box number or even invent yourself which will give you the health and beauty that a **Natural Method** can attain. If this is learned and utilized through this book, then the time you spend looking at these pages will be a valuable investment to you many years from today.

CHAPTER I

The Cosmic You

or

Why A Natural and Organic Cosmetic Puts You In Harmony With Nature

The word "cosmetic" is derived from the word "cosmos," which was introduced by Pythagoras in 550 B.C., when Greece was world foremost in mathematical ideas and development. The Greeks developed the first rigorously defined mathematical system--Euclidean geometry--which allowed them to measure the diameter of the earth and chart the stars (although inaccurately because they placed the earth in the center of the universe). The word "cosmos" was originally defined as the order of the universe, and this universal order could be expressed in every aspect of human existence. The highest form of this universal order was the music of the spheres, sublime harmony that expressed the perfect order of the stars. Pythagoras defined "cosmos" as the order of the universe, and if we consider this word in its most ancient and precise meaning it signifies ornamentation or adornment (of man or woman); in speech, it means its rhetorical power; in music, the perfection of harmony. Thus, the meaning of "cosmos" could extend from Bach's Brandenburg Concertos and Lincoln's Gettysburg Address to the Euclidean golden mean of geometry. Carl Sagan chose Vangelis' composition "Heaven and Hell" to represent musically the space-time continuum for his TV series "The Cosmos." William F. Buckley chose Bach's Brandenburg Concerto No. 2 as the opening theme for his "Firing Line" discussion show to express the point-counterpoint development of ideas.

We don't often think of cosmetics in such "heady" terms, but the intimate relationship of appearance to one's own visual harmony was obvious to the ancient Greeks and before them the ancient Egyptians. To be physically beautiful was to be in harmony with the universe, and one's own physical beauty represented in miniature the "cosmos." In the late 19th century, A. Von Humboldt's *Cosmos: A Sketch of a Physical Description of the Universe* pointed out the link between universal order and adornment. "We may hope to comprehend and describe the universal all in a manner worthy of the dignity of the word cosmos in its signification of universe, order of the world, and adornment of this universal order" (London: G. Bell & Sons, 1880).

Just as cosmos can be linked to a harmonious you (in Greek, the word is *kosmetikos*), the contrasting word--chaos--which is the formless matter that preceded the existence of the ordered universe, describes a disorganized, dishevelled, disharmonious you. And so it is, if you have skill in *kosmetically* perfecting yourself, you are in harmony with the universe; you are not chaotic, dishevelled, disorganized, or disharmonious. Listen to Vivaldi's "The Four Seasons" and see yourself in the same balanced, harmonious, and melodious perfection. How do we know when we are in harmony and at one with the universe? I believe, based on my study of harmony in nature, that most of today's cosmetics have become artificial and do not give us the ancient meaning of the word. The highly synthetic look that today's cosmetics bring to our lives represents the chaotic side and not the cosmic side of our beings.

In the alchemy of China (400 B.C.), two basic axioms of thought were presented in *Materia Prima* and *The Polarity of the Masculine and Feminine Principles*. The purpose of the alchemist was to study the course of the stars, the cycles of the seasons, and if possible, to look into the heart of matter as well as the matter of the heart. The grand purpose was to live one's life in harmony with the cosmos, to understand its laws and workings, not cerebrally or philosophically, but realistically in the studies of medicine, cosmetics, and religious studies.

In this cosmology, the formless matter (chaos) that precedes the existence of the ordered universe (cosmos) is the *materia prima*. The physician, alchemist, and cosmetics scientist, Paracelsus, who taught at the university in Basel from 1526-1528, described the *materia prima* as fire and water. He called it *increatum* (the uncreated) and asserted that because it was immaterial it couldn't be described. "It is the one unique mother of all mortal things," he said, "a mother to all the elements and in them likewise a grandmother to all stars, trees, and creatures."

> "After nature has planted the mineral root of a tree in the center of its matrix, whether to produce a metal, a stone, a gem, salt, alum, vitriol, a saline or sweet, cold or hot spring, a coral, or a marcasite, and after it has thrust forth the trunk to the earth, this trunk spreads abroad in different branches, the liquid of whose substance--both of branches and stalk--is formally neither a water, nor an oil, nor a lute, nor a mucilage; in fact, it can only be conceived as wood growing out of the earth, which is, nevertheless, not earth, though it sprung from the earth."

When Paracelsus said this he was describing the way Mother Nature manufactures one substance from another; in this case, a tree from a "grain" in the earth. Each creature, plant, or mineral that Nature creates is unique, yet each class of beings partakes of every other. A plant grows out of the earth to become a part of the cow that eats it. The cow gives milk that we drink. We are all Nature's creations, one and inseparable, yet each individual and unique. To me, this is the difference in the natural cosmetic made of natural substances, and the synthetic or artificial duplication of natural substances.

We can make a formica table that looks like wood, but it is not wood and when placed in a room does not have the same effect on us that wood would have. The real wood--the tree--as described by Paracelsus can neither be duplicated nor improved. The wood contains the essence of the earth from which it sprang and the mark of Mother Nature's hand. This mark can't be imitated or duplicated or synthesized. The essence that is nature is--as is nature herself--eternal. For example, I make a shampoo out of herbs and the bark of a tree called the quillaya tree (pronounced "ki-li-ya"; called "the soap tree" by the Indians). This element--the ground bark of that tree which grows high in the Andes--can't be synthesized or duplicated, and though I can buy a synthetic soap that is said to be exactly like the soap tree bark, it is not like it. The natural essence is not there; the primal evolution from earth, water, air and sunlight is not there. There is no substitute for the pungent ground bark.

Another example is jojoba oil, a liquid wax that is squeezed from the bean of *Simmondsia Chinensis* that grows in the deserts of Arizona, California, and Mexico. A unique oil that is superb for the hair and skin, jojoba oil is an expensive ingredient but can replace sperm whale oil which makes it ecologically desirable. One company (Wickhen) makes a synthetic jojoba oil for half the price of the real thing which they say is exactly like jojoba oil. One cosmetic chemist told me that I could replace jojoba oil with synthetic jojoba oil. "You can even mix them 90% synthetic to 10% natural jojoba oil. Nobody could tell the difference...nobody," he said. "Not even with an analysis."

I got some synthetic jojoba oil--not to formulate with but to see if I could tell the difference. I could tell. The synthetic jojoba oil was not as good as Mother Nature's real thing. In fact, I checked out almost every synthesized copy of natural extracts. Can you guess what I found out? There was invariably a difference between the synthetic and the natural extract, and the difference was that the body responded differently to the real substance than to the synthetic substance. Using the synthetic copy of a natural extract on the skin or hair in cosmetic formulas gave me an inferior product every time from every standpoint. Pure vegetable glycerine, for example, is thicker, richer, and a far better emollient than propylene glycol (the petrochemical replacement), but the synthetic chemical is usually substituted for the natural extract because the manufacturers believe the pseudo-scientific hype: you can't tell the difference. Looking at a chemical salesman's analysis sheet will not tell you the difference because the chemical companies only synthesize what they see; they approximate, with their synthetics, the measurable qualities of the natural extracts. What they can't predict or measure, however, is the body's response to natural substances that is the recognition of their common primal evolution. Like the tree, we too were born out of our Mother Nature's earth, and to that earth we will return. Natural substances reinforce the cosmos within you, but synthetic substances create a "chaotic you."

But what does all this have to do with you and your daily life? Exactly how do you change from a "chaotic" you to a "cosmic" you? One way you can change from "chaotic" to "cosmic" is how you look at make-up. Many women put on make-up every day to supposedly improve their looks or to cover up aging skin, and this is exactly how they are programmed to respond by the chemical industry and by society. The image to which women are pressured to conform is a painted and artificial one. Women in the work world are expected to have a well-defined "professional" look, and make-up is a part of that look. Women who are portrayed as desirable are always shown wearing make-up. Yet these responses are conditioned and can be replaced in both sexes by a natural image. When women have rubbed flesh-colored make-up on their skin, painted their mouths red with red circles on their cheeks and black around their eyes, they do not look natural. They look like a paint job, and, in most cases, not a very good paint job. There is another part to this picture, however, and it is only right that you should know about it. Manufacturers may sell make-up with the idea that it will make women look younger, to hold back the years so to speak, but make-up and the chemicals in them actually speed up the aging of the skin. This is a well-established fact. Women who use more and more make-up more and more often will need more and more as the years pass. It is, after all, a mask--a cover-up, and the more often women apply the chemicals, the more toll these chemicals will take on their skin and on their whole health.

There are women who say that they feel naked without their make-up. They have a naked face fear. If you happen to be one of these women, then I strongly suggest that you do something to improve your skin every day. In fact, if you care about your skin, you need to spend at least the same amount of time (or more) on skin care that you do on make-up application. When you throw your skin out of harmony day after day with synthetic make-up masks you can expect to look awful in a very few years. But you can put the **Natural Method** to work to "save face." The proper natural skin care day after day will mean that you do not need make-up as a cover-up because your skin will be healthy and beautiful. Your skin and hair will be in superb condition because you will be in harmony with nature.

Is there a place for make-up? Yes. Make-up means to color yourself for a certain fashion look. So if you want to use make-up for a special occasion, go ahead. You should learn to apply it, however, with a very light touch so that you look fresh, natural, and vibrant. Also, there are more natural make-ups you can use. They are made with more natural formulas, and the natural colors are softer and more earthy looking. But even when using natural colors you should use as little as possible--just a touch and no more. Even natural colors can look unnatural!

To help you see this picture, let me tell you about a young woman who came to our **Natural Method Hair and Skin Care Clinic.** She wanted a facial, a completely organic facial using only natural ingredients. She had make-up on when she arrived. Of course, the first step in the facial was to get rid of the make-up. Now it happened that this woman used the **Natural Method** at home so when we looked at her skin under the skin lamps we found that it was in excellent condition, and she was beautiful. There were few dead skin cells piled up on her skin, which can be easily detected with a Wood's Lamp, and we couldn't see why she would want make-up on her skin. We gave her a completely organic facial. When we were through we asked her if she wanted a touch of natural blush or highlight. She said that her skin felt so natural and relaxed that she didn't want anything on it. She was in harmony, and her skin felt it. And, she looked better without the make-up she came in with on her face (although it was expertly applied). There was, in fact, a whole change about her. Did she become "cosmic"? Yes, I think in a way she did. She looked and seemed in harmony, and we perceived her as natural and more beautiful than when she had the make-up on. Why did she wear it then? I think she wore it because she thought it was expected of her, and because she thought it made her look younger. Yet when she was relaxed and saw her skin after it was clean and natural, she reverted to her real feelings and went with a totally natural look.

If you put on the most natural products you can find and you spend the same amount of time caring for your skin that you spend making it up, you will discover that you look better and feel better. A make-up habit will not be of benefit to you in the long run. A blotchy skin can become a healthy skin, but only through daily natural care, not through the daily application of make-up.The make-up will cover up the problem but will not get rid of it.

In conclusion, the more natural the product is the more advantages it has for your skin, and by reducing or eliminating the use of synthetic chemicals, petrochemicals, and hydrocarbons on your skin (and in your hair), you will be in harmony with nature. The vibrant unmade-up and chemical-free complexion is the ideal complexion, and the way to attain this healthy look is to care for your hair and skin with the **Natural Method.** Remember, the high fashion industry applies make-up, powders, and eye shadows by the pound, but the life of a high fashion model is very short. Most models are through by the time they're thirty--and so is their skin and hair. Some models use the **Natural Method** and have for the past few years. Those who do have been able to comply with the high-fashion painted mannequin or "Kewpie Doll" look and still keep their skin fairly healthy. One model told me she advertises all kinds of make-ups and chemicalized products, but she has a simple natural method of skin care and avoids all make-up off the set. Actors and actresses also know the damage that make-up does to the skin and know they must counteract that damage with natural care.

The **Natural Method** and the natural substances discussed in this book are long range methods of skin and hair care. There are no quick-fix skin or hair care products; in fact, the quick-fix products are actually the "quick-kill." They quickly part you with your money and give you a worse hair and skin problem because they take away from the importance of the long-range and effective way to care for your hair and skin. Nothing replaces actually doing a few things for your skin and hair every day, and the more natural, the better.

CHAPTER II

In The Beginning Cosmetics were Natural. . .

Or

When It Came to Preservatives Mummy Knew Best

Ancient Egypt, the Ptolemaic Period, 30 B.C. Fustat-Kal walked leisurely along the rich mud flats of the Nile. This particular stroll was the Sun Walk, but more than a simple celebration of the Re the Sun God had brought Kal out this morning. He was scantily dressed in his white muslin schenti so that his body could take in the sun. The alchemist Renuatum had told Kal to walk here so that the sun could act on the red scales of his body. Kal would also eat a special weed that grew on the Nile and rub a lotion made from this weed and other herbs into his skin. In a few months, his skin would be clear. Not until 1974 would the Harvard Medical School and Massachusetts General Hospital create *methoxysalen*, a derivative of this Nile weed, which has a photoactive substance that, when correctly combined with UV light therapy, slows the wild proliferation of skin cells that characterizes the skin disease psoriasis. A doctor in Vienna had used the same ancient Egyptian method to clear up many of his patients' skin disorders, but he learned that *methoxysalen* was not the only link to ancient Egypt; the skin must also be treated to the same wavelengths of light found in the Nile Valley. Nothing else would work.

Renuatum was a prince and an alchemist with great knowledge of the power of plants and the combined chemical and electrical force of the Pyramids. He would later in history be identified as Zozimus. He had taken the name Renuatum because it unified the cosmological elements of Re, the sun god; Nu, the motionless primordial ocean; and Atum, the god of the primeval hill that grew out of the wastes of Nu. My name, he would often say, was the basis of all life: air, water, earth, and man. But it was his sister, Theosebia the Hermetic who would be a major force behind the advancement of cosmetics.

Theosebia, who had just turned twelve, had come with Fustat-Kal on his healing walk in the sun. She had painted her body with a pale yellow color that seemed to glow in the sun. Her fingertips glistened with the color of orange henna. Two colors of kohl, green and black, outlined her eyes. Her breasts were outlined in blue, and the design was contoured to her veins, as if to illustrate the flow of blood to her heart. She was wearing a long braided beard attached with a gold strap.

"Only the queen can wear a postiche like that," Kal reminded her, "But that doesn't seem to worry you. Sometimes you think that just because your brother is the most important alchemist at court and known as Cleopatra's instructor you can do anything you want."

"I am as good as my brother."

"Then perhaps you know the secret of the Sun Walk and why my skin is cured by the power of the sun?"

"Yes, I do know. I take nothing for granted. I tested the whole process on my own skin. I ate the magic weed and put the lotion on my body and took the Sun Walk. All I got was a very bad burn."

"Of course," laughed Kal, "That was Re's way of showing you not to put your nose in the affairs of the gods."

"No, I learned something. Your skin needs more sun and can take in more sun than mine. There is also some kind of substance in the weeds that makes the sun stronger, more powerful, so that it takes very little time for the skin to burn. Other lotions protect the skin so that the sun cannot burn it, but this lotion has the opposite effect."

"You are lucky that Renuatum is your brother and you can learn all these things, but I can see that you know something of the art of cosmetics. Everybody knows that you taught the queen the art of make-up."

"Kal, when you look at me, what do you see? You see what I want you to see about myself. The purpose of cosmetics is to create an illusion of our real selves, but make-up also represents the harmony of the cosmos. The heliopolitan and hermapolitan traditions of primeval units are well-planned creations by the thought creator god Ptah who created all the gods. Cosmetics aren't just adornment, Kal, but herbal medicines that can cure or kill. Our job is to know the proper mixtures and how to use them, even down to the phases of the moon and the brightness of the sun."

"May the gods protect you! You do talk like a Roman." Kal rubbed his eyes, which were beginning to burn as some of the lotion got into them.

"I am nothing like a Roman! The Romans are businessmen who talk, talk, talk about everything but know nothing. They think everything can be solved on the floor of the Senate. They stole our cosmetic secrets, but they misuse them because they split up the compounding of cosmetics from the selling of them. Then the physicians came here, wrote down our formulas, and created their own compounders. Now the alchemists and their compounders have their followers, and the physicians and their compounders have their followers, and all have their prices set by the Senate. Everything is organized along economic lines and governmental ideals. Somewhere along the line the gods have been forgotten and the power of nature compromised. The physicians look with disdain on the alchemists and regard them as charlatans, but both groups forget nature and the gods of nature because their only real interests are money, the class structure, and the government's slogan that 'when in Rome, do as the Romans do.' They forget that nature alone lasts forever and that Rome will die. The magic of Egypt does not work in Rome, and nature cannot be bartered like the slaves they sell."

We can see many similarities in our own society and the new Roman society that Theosebia describes. Egypt, however, had a different social structure from Rome, one that was quite mystical, and Egypt boasted a large number of female alchemists. The early Egyptians were also considerably advanced in their preparation of cosmetics in that they used methods of distillation, extraction, fixation, and maceration that were unknown to previous periods and were not re-discovered in some cases until centuries later.

The first cosmetic chemist was an alchemist, and thereafter cosmetics took on the mystical aura of the hermetic arts. The secrecy and symbolism of the hermetic allegories beginning with the famous myth of the phoenix, and continuing with strange formulas and esoteric theories (like the existence of the philosopher's stone that would transmute base elements into gold--a theory that is postulated into the radioactivity of contemporary science) are part of this mystique. While herbal remedies were founded in folk medicine and passed from generation to generation, herbal cosmetics usually involved the closely held secrets of alchemists, ointment artists, and *unguentarius* who often died with their secret formulas. Possibly some ancient cosmetic compounders who wrote books containing formulas left out key ingredients or procedures vital to the compounding of the mixtures. They did this to give themselves an aura of mystical ability or special expertise not attained by anyone else. They fantasized that someone would read the formula, attempt to make the product, and fail. The would-be compounder would then be amazed and awe-struck at the superior genius of the original formulators. Of course, this thought process only took place in the mind of the alchemists because the compounder would probably go on to something else or simply improve on the formula. For example, the peculiar substances listed in ancient Egyptian scrolls as cosmetic ingredients, such as "blood of ibis," "tail of scorpion," etc., which seem silly and disgusting, were actually symbolic terms for actual herbal extracts and oils. But only the creators of the formula knew what the symbol stood for so that anyone preparing a mixture using their notes would come up with a revolting mixture for that special facial cream (i.e., hair of bat and tail of rat mixed well in the milk of one goat. Yech!). Modern cosmetics manufacturers today follow the lead of the alchemists and protect their formulas as trade secrets. The best known cosmetics manufacturers frequently make claims to secret formulas and ancient miracle ingredients, and until the late 1970's, the ingredients in cosmetics were never required to appear on the label. And, to the consumer, most of the ingredients on today's cosmetic labels might as well be listed as "eye of newt and toe of frog" for all the real information they contain. Chemical technology has replaced alchemy in the cosmetics industry, but selling techniques haven't changed a bit--mystique and secrecy still surround the marketing departments of modern beauty elixirs.

In 150 A.D., Rome was already in political turmoil, but the phrase "All roads lead to Rome" was still in effect. Rome had established cosmetic manufacturers, distributors, and retailers, much as we have today. As Theosebia pointed out, the manufacturing and distributing of cosmetics had been separated. But, more importantly, the physicians and the commercial cosmetic manufacturers each made their own cosmetics and had their individual methods of distributing their wares--a trend that has continued through history to the present day. The commercial cosmetic developers were called *unguentarius* and the shops where their products were sold were called *sesplasaria*. The physicians of Rome ordered their own medical cosmetics from a *confectionarius*. Medical cosmetics were administered at a clinic called a *medicamentarius*. The physicians would warn their patients not to go to the *sesplasaria* because only qualified *confectionarius* knew the correct way to use the products. This division is similar to that between estheticians and dermatologists today.

Crito, the court physician of Emperor Trajam (98-117 A.D.), developed many formulas and treatments for the skin, including cleansers, emollients, bleaches, make-up, and remedies he touted as excellent for removing wrinkles, freckles, warts, scars, and unwanted hair. He also developed hair dressings, bleaches, dyes, scalp lotions, and touted *Crito's Magical Hair Growth Elixir*, which was also said to be good for removing lice, scaliness (dandruff, psoriasis, etc.), and for thickening the hair. Before Crito's cosmetic nostrums, Pliny the Elder (whose original name had been Gaius Plinius Secundus, but nobody could remember his name, or else he liked the "old sage" feeling the name Pliny the Elder gave him) had written a book called *Natural History*. It contained over five hundred chemical formulas, including a section on cosmetics.

After these physician-cosmetic chemists made their mark on Rome, a physician of Pergamum (Asia Minor) started a thriving cosmetics business. His name was Galen (130-200 A.D.), and after Hippocrates, he is considered the greatest physician in antiquity. He was not only a doctor and cosmetic chemist but also a writer. He wrote the first systematic, scientific textbook devoted exclusively to cosmetics. Galen's cosmetic company, let's call it "Galen's of Rome," manufactured a cream that was in demand all over Rome and its environs. It is believed that his unique formula was all his own, not borrowed from Crito or Pliny the Elder. Galen mixed beeswax with olive oil, herbal extracts, and water to create an emulsion. What he found was that when this cream was applied to the face, the skin was softened due to the oils in the emulsion and cooled due to the evaporation of the water. Galen's *ceratum refrigerans* (cooling ointment) became the prototype for all cold creams and cleansing creams today. Galen's formula was (we think) 56.0% olive oil, 24.5% beeswax, 14.5% water, and 5% rosewater or other herbal waters. His staff of slaves who labored all day making the cold cream had to create hundreds of small pots of the stuff because the formula was unstable. Cosmetic manufacturers who came after Galen discovered that by adding borax (a mineral) to the cold cream, a whiter-looking and more stable product was obtained. One of the early refinements of Galen's cream was 55.5% almond oil, 24.5% beeswax, 14.5% water, 5% rosewater, and 0.5% borax. Due to the almond oil, the skin was even softer and smoother than with the original Galen mixture. Of course, after we entered the latter half of the 20th century, the natural cold cream dreamed up by Galen became pretty much of a synthetic petrochemical mix that the old Roman would never recognize: petrolatum, Tween 40, mineral oil, glyceryl monostearate, triethanolamine, zinc stearate, and ozokerite! The new Galen cold creams, or cleansers, as they were finally called, had very little of Galen's natural art in them. What changes would the modern cosmetic chemical salesman make if he called on Galen in his cosmetic shop in Rome, 150 A.D.?

Chemical Salesman: Doctor Galen, I'm from the PETROHYDRO Chemical Corporation of Padua. My card, sir.
Galen: You want to buy some of my *ceratum refrigerans*? I do well in Padua!
C. Salesman: Listen, doc, your idea is great . . . there's no doubt about that . . . but I've improved on your cream. Look at this fantastic cream. See how white it is! See how soft it is!
Galen: Yes . . . yes. I can see that what you say is true. What is the alchemical idea behind this cream?
C. Salesman: No beeswax, for one thing! After all, doc, why wait on the bees when you can call PETROHYDRO any time of the day?
Galen: No beeswax? Hmm . . .
C. Salesman: And no olive oil either.
Galen: No olive oil?! The olive tree is the oldest and most dependable tree in the world!
C. Salesman: Let me set you straight, doc--olive oil costs much more than mineral oil!
Galen: Mineral oil! Oil from minerals? That's interesting.
C. Salesman: For half the price, sir!
Galen: No beeswax, no olive oil, but what about plain water? Do you have plain water in it? Water's cheap!
C. Salesman: Yes, well, it's mostly water, doc! It's over half water, compared to your formula which has only 14% water.
Galen: What replaces the beeswax?
C. Salesman: Ozokerite.
Galen: Ozo--? Ozo-what?
C. Salesman: Ozokerite.
Galen: What is this "Ozokite"?
C. Salesman: Ozokerite, doc. It's a bituminous hydrocarbon wax derived from petroleum.
Galen: Petroleum, eh? Bitu--Bitu--er, eh--Hydrocarbon?
C. Salesman: Doc, we're going to change your operation here. You can cut this staff down to half, and you can make up gigantic pots of cream because mineral oil will not spoil. Bugs

can't live in hydrocarbons, doc!

Galen: That's fantastic! But where does all this stuff come from?

C. Salesman: From our chemical plant in Padua, doc. I'll tell you something else, doc--I've got this idea for using petrol in your chariot--I saw it parked outside--and it'll put plenty of hot horsepower in that rig!

This scene would have brought the twentieth century age of petrochemicals barreling down on Rome, and the Romans would have soon discovered that all the roads that led to Rome had become as polluted as ours are today. Petrochemicals pollute, and even though "bugs can't live in hydrocarbons," most cosmetic manufacturers load their products with synthetic preservatives--such is their fear of the demon "bacteria." Galen, one would suppose, had his method of preserving his *ceratum refrigerans*, but he used herbs and minerals for that purpose. When King Tut's tomb was unearthed, cosmetics were found, perfectly preserved after thousands of years. The Egyptians also knew how to preserve the bodies of their kings and queens, but they did so with natural means because they had no alternative: they didn't have a huge industrial chemical complex cranking out hydrocarbons and petrochemicals as we do today. The Egyptians also did not rely on animal tests because they were more sensitive to the cosmic chain and the balance of nature: both concepts were vital to their way of life. While in the present time we cut hearts out of baboons, they regarded animals as a productive part of their culture. Destroying animal life uselessly--as in the animal experiments of today--was unthinkable. When a supposed authority, such as Heinz Eilerman, Director of the FDA's Division of Cosmetics Technology, says there are no effective natural preservatives available for use in cosmetics, he is not speaking knowledgeably about the history of preservatives. In fact, the FDA could easily be renamed the Federal Disappointment Agency because it does not protect the consumer, contrary to popular gullibility. It exists to provide favoritism to more chemicalization due to the cozy relationship that has developed between this agency and the food, drug, cosmetic, and industrial chemical complex. It also exists to perpetuate animal testing.

The leaders, mystics, and natural scientists of ancient times were greater thinkers than all the researchers who have created the chemicals that are supposed to improve our lives, our land, our water, and our air. One Cleopatra, one Plato, or one Aristotle is worth the whole lot because these individuals knew the reverence of nature: it was sacred to them.

> "Man can and should indeed use his ability to be creative. Within the sphere of technology, the relevant products have their justification. This is, after all, a new kingdom created by man, and here their anti-life qualities do not immediately become apparent. Synthetic products can therefore be outstandingly useful technical aids for man . . . We need to consider what is aimed at and what the long-term consequences are. Is the whole man, in all his aspects, being considered? Synthetic products can indeed be useful to man, but if he allows them to enter too much into his sphere of life, they will, in the long run, have a destructive effect" (Otto Wolff, M.D., "Natural vs. Synthetics," *Weleda News*, Weleda AG, Arlesheim, Switzerland, 1980).

After Rome fell to armies of assorted invaders from the North, the medical arts were gradually reduced to such a weakened state that there was no recovery for the next two centuries. A few Hellenistic practitioners survived to preserve some cosmetic and perfume knowledge. Oribasios of Pergamum, personal physician to Emperor Julian, left behind some of the scant information that was available.

The designation of the Middle Ages as the "thousand years without a bath" may have been illustrative of the lack of cosmetic growth, but it wasn't literally accurate since the Danes reintroduced bathing to England during this period. There is, however, no record of any make-up or hair dyes, although curling irons were used. Aromatic materials were used in various religious services, but the use of perfumes was limited to the most affluent. As the Middle Ages developed in the West and in Europe, the nucleus of scientific knowledge moved eastward where cosmetic technology flourished. Two important historical movements brought this about. First, the Benedictine monastery was established in 529 A.D. at Monte Cassino in Italy. This resulted in an extensive library of manuscripts on medicine, philosophy, and other subjects. Secondly, when the famous Academy of Athens was closed by Emperor Justinian, the unemployed professors found refuge in Persia, and in India at the great medical school of Jundishapur where they introduced the latest Greek thoughts on medicine, philosophy, and science. Information on local customs, medicine, pharmacy, botany, perfumes, and cosmetics filtered out from Jundishapur. This brought physicians and scientists direct information on the ancient system of Hindu medicine. A kind of mix resulted. A Hindu system known as Susruta (founded in the sixth century B.C.) combined with what remained of the Hellenic system, equally as ancient. The Susruta demonstrated advanced knowledge of cosmetics, and even were familiar with surgery of the nose (rhinoplasty). More recently, during the Gupta period in India (320-500 A.D.), cosmetic hygiene was far advanced. The compounding of creams, oils, pastes before the bath, make-up of every kind, and hair dyes have been chronicled. The amount of these products used by men was almost equal to that used by women.

Eventually cosmetics would be regarded separately from medicine, although there was nothing automatic or immediate about this separation. One of the first moves to separate cosmetics from medicine was probably made by Henri de Mondeville (1260-1325). He was a Norman who had studied medicine at Montpelier, Bologna, and Paris. In a textbook he wrote in the early 1300's, he distinguished between the pathological conditions of the skin that merited medical treatment and the application of cosmetics for embellishment. However, Henri was not a pure scientist because he had his ideas on the separation of cosmetics and medicine mixed up with God and righteousness. He believed that a skin treatment was for health and therefore godly, whereas the application of a cosmetic was a disguise, or some such deviltry. But like most physicians, who are tied to the treatment of the upper classes (who could afford his services), Henri de Mondeville was not above the ungodly practice of helping his affluent clientele with cosmetic difficulties. "The favor of women cannot be overestimated," he said in the manner of a true Frenchman, "Without it one comes to nothing; without it no one can obtain the good will of the men, and occasionally that is as useful as the love of the Pope or even God." Henri had treatments for skin diseases, burns, minor disorders, and many recipes for dyes, ointments, depilatories, pomades, soaps, make-ups, and so forth, but it was one of his pupils, Guy de Chauliac (1300-1368), who did more to widen the gap between cosmetics and medicine. Guy's textbook broadened the concept of cosmetics to include defects of the eyes, ears, nose, mouth, and teeth. He also caused physicians and surgeons to accept the delimitations. In other words, legitimate medicine was to be restricted to internal ills and to serious disorders of the skin. The physician was not to bother with cosmetics.

The first chemists--both cosmetic and general--were alchemists, but they and their profession were surrounded with secrecy and suspicion. In fact, Chaucer's "Canon Yeoman's Tale," published in 1400, relates several anecdotes of unscrupulous alchemists who fool people and steal their gold. Alchemists and their preoccupation with gold, the philosopher's stone, and the *elixir vitae*, were to be turned around in the sixteenth century. Philippe Aureolus Bombast (the word "bombastic" is based on the personality of this man), who was called Paracelsus (1493-1541), came out of Switzerland to shock alchemists out of their effort to make gold. He said that the alchemists must work to manufacture substances to cure disease. Paracelsus said they were wasting their time sitting around reading old books written by old alchemists. To illustrate his point, Paracelsus piled the books of Hippocrates, Galen, and Ibn Sina into a pile in the public square and burned them. He told the apothecaries that their formulas were polypharmacal messes that were of no value to anyone. He refused to lecture in Latin (to further insult them), using the German language instead. He said Latin was a silly and useless language just as was the search for gold in base metals. Though his personality and bombastic methods infuriated many, he did eventually succeed in initiating a new period known as iatrochemistry. As time passed, this replaced alchemy, and the views of Paracelsus caught on. He introduced a large number of drugs and caused a revision of the pharmacopoeias throughout Europe, which included many new herbal formulas as well as the old botanicals, thus facilitating the study of medicinal plants.

"Resolute imagination can accomplish all things," he said. "If you prevent infection, nature will heal the wound all by herself." In a way he was the "natural and organic" voice of his time, and, despite his bombastic blunders, the Paracelsus name and fame spread throughout the known world. His lecture hall was always filled with cheering student-disciples as he venomously attacked worthless pills, salves, infusions, balsams, drenches, fumigants, and electuaries.

Even though Paracelsus caused the final elimination of cosmetics from the general textbooks on medicines, physicians in France and Europe continued to actively pursue an interest in the practice of cosmetology. André Le Fournier, dean of the faculty of medicine at the University of Paris (1518), published a comprehensive text on beautification. Jean Liebaut (1535-1596) practiced medicine at Dijon and Paris, and wrote several books on cosmetics, toxicology, and gynecology. In Italy, many physicians and scientists continued to be concerned with cosmetics. Giovanni-Battista Porta (1540-1615) devoted a section to cosmetics in his medical book *Natural Magic*; Girolamo Ruscelli (mid-sixteenth century) wrote a comprehensive collection of "Secrets" on everything related to cosmetology, perfumery, hygiene, and contemporary dermatology. He wrote the book under a pseudonym (Alessio of Piedmont) to protect himself from the criticism of physicians who looked down on the art of cosmetics. Three generations of physicians in the Martinello family served to illustrate a changing attitude towards cosmetics. Giovanni Martinello (fifteenth century) included a section on beauty culture at the end of his medical textbook, a section that was greatly influenced by the cosmetic findings of the Arabs. The last of the Martinello family (who died in 1580) made a valiant stand for cosmetics in medicine, but was not supported by his professional colleagues. It was during this era that cosmetic products were finally dropped from what was then the accepted scope of medical practice.

The Renaissance was a period of great activity and progress in cosmetics due to the advancement of industry, the popularity of travel, and the more prominent role of women in cosmetic development. Often their voice was one of the establisher of vogues and trends, rather than as the inventor of products, although there is no doubt that they encouraged the compounders to bring new plants and herbs from faraway places for the purpose of creating cosmetics. Travelers such as Marco Polo (1254-1324), Giovanni del Plan (1182-1252), Giovanni di Montecorvino (1247-1328), and others from England, Spain, Belgium, and Scandinavia made Europe better acquainted with India and the Orient. Their discovery of cosmetics was highly encouraged by the royal women of the time who carried the information from country to country as they were married to foreign noblemen. For example, Catherine de Medici of Florence, skilled in cosmetics, married Francois I of France. Their son married Mary Queen of Scots, who, after the death of the French dauphin, returned to Scotland, carrying the cosmetic secrets of France and Italy to the British Isles and, indirectly, to her cousin, Queen Elizabeth I. Cosmetics remained, however, the domain of the ruling class because of the scarcity and price of the ingredients. For example, the price of soap was so exorbitant that Queen Elizabeth I could only afford three baths per month. Soap was created by an essential ingredient that could only be obtained through a tedious and expensive method of soaking wood or seaweed ashes in water, followed by boiling in vegetable fat. Soap remained a rare commodity until around 1791.

The first perfume shop in Paris was brought about as a result of an international marriage. The wealthy and powerful Medici family married their ward and niece Caterina to their eldest son Henri who lived in France. When Caterina went to France for the wedding (1553), her retinue included her favorite astrologer, Ruggiero, and her favorite perfumer, Renato Bianco (also known as Rene of Florence). Rene established a perfume shop near the Pont au Change in Paris, which became a rendezvous for the ladies of the court. It was an interesting shop that did a business in perfumes, powders, pomades, make-up, and even poisons (employed by ladies who wished to dispose of those they found superfluous or objectionable). Rene's shop was destroyed during the French revolution, but the location is still pointed out to interested visitors as being the first major French perfume shop.

The most important advancement in the perfumer's art--and in cosmetology--was in the knowledge of alcohol and the methods of distillation. In the beginning alcohol, or spirits, was obtained from fruits and later from grains. Brandy was used as a medicine only until the volume increased enough to use it as a beverage (in the fifteenth century). Tinctures can be traced to the Arabs who used them as medicines, but the first published recipe for a toilet water, based on the herb rosemary, was prepared by Queen Elizabeth of Hungary: it was called, logically enough, "Hungary Water." She maintained that the secret formula kept her skin youthful far into life. Another contributor to distillation and its use in cosmetics was from a man known best for the invention of perfumed gloves, Mutio Frangipani, the last of an aristocratic Roman family that had existed from the twelfth to the sixteenth centuries. He made an alcohol extract from a dry mixture of herbs and spices, known as "Frangipani Water," which became popular all over Europe. Finally all the knowledge of alcohol and distillation was presented in a book by Hieronymus Brunnschwick (1440-1512), which included every type of apparatus used for distillation and every type of "water" that anyone would wish to prepare for distillation.

From the seventeenth to the nineteenth centuries, two opposing trends became apparent. One was an attempt to re-associate cosmetic treatments with medicine, and the other emphasized cosmetics as mere external embelishment only to be associated with fashion and beauty, but by the ninteenth century cosmetic treatments were still considered accessories to fashion and beauty and not medicine. This line of demarcation became rather evident in England where the number of hairdressers went from two in 1740, to hundreds in 1795. By the end of the eighteenth century, most alchemists were willing to turn from their quest for the philosopher's stone and their efforts to convert base metals into gold, to turning cosmetics into financial gold through the sale of "beauty waters," love potions, amulets, and various hair and skin care products.

Another modern trend--celebrity advertising--perhaps had its beginning in 1780, when a Dr. Graham opened his "Temple of Health" in London, using for his presiding goddess a famous beauty of the time named Emma Lyon whose duty it was to convince the patrons of the Temple that her lovely face and trim figure were the direct result of Dr. Graham's mud bath, beauty salon treatments, massages, and cosmetic products. Courtesans as well as celebrities figured in the development of cosmetics. Louis XIII of France was having dinner with a courtesan and they began to argue. The king became so annoyed with his guest that he filled his mouth with red wine and spat it across the table at her. The wine sprayed all over the courtesan's face and bosom which gradually developed a flattering pink tint. Quite by accident, Louis XIII brought about the first commercial color used in cosmetics, but because the natural-looking pink tint had first appeared on a courtesan, it became the mark of one, and respectable women painted themselves in garish reds and whites to avoid being taken for prostitutes. Simple cleanliness, however, lagged behind social and fashion improvements in the middle class until the early nineteenth century; bathing, i.e., washing the entire body, was considered a quaint habit indulged in by Puritans and Quakers, even though soap was first manufactured in England as early as 1641. The favorite skin cleanser was an almond paste compounded with cacao butter and vanilla, imported from Spain. In later years, Spain came to be known for its *castile* soap made with olive oil, which differs in appearance and method of manufacture from most castile soaps today, which are hard-milled, "super-fatted" toilet soaps.

While the advertising slogan "blondes have more fun" is relatively recent, the desire to "go blonde" is as old as recorded history. Recipes for bleaching the hair were common in Rome during the two centuries that bridged the beginning of the Christian era because the Roman women admired the golden hair of the slaves brought from northern countries and sought to imitate it. Native minerals such as rock alum, quicklime, crude soda, and wood ash were combined with wine and water for a favorite blonde look of the time. The Venetian women were particularly known for their beautiful golden-red shade of hair which was immortalized by the artist Titian (1447-1576) in his paintings. This shade of hair was produced by sponging a solution of soda, rock alum, black sulfur, and honey through the hair and allowing it to dry in the sunlight. The same method was introduced into France late in the sixteenth century by Marguerite de Valois. For over two hundred years, it remained the standard method for producing blond and reddish shades of hair, although every book of "medical" secrets written during the Renaissance contained recipes for bleaching the hair. Various crude soaps, soda, alum, borax, niter, and other mixtures were combined with decoctions of various plants such as birch bark, broom, celandine, lupine, mullein, myrrh, saffron, and so on.

Darkening hair was also popular, and for this purpose metallic salts have been used for millenia. Men and women of ancient Rome darkened their hair by dipping a lead comb in vinegar and then passing it through the hair. However, metallic dyes are not compatible with hair that has a permanent wave, so their sale today is limited to the types used by men as color restorers, not dyes.

Henna is often associated with Queen Cleopatra, but the first recorded user of this herb as a hair dye was the Egyptian Queen Ses, mother of King Teta, of the Third Dynasty. The plant has always been called Egyptian henna, even though it is also found in Arabia, Tunisia, Persia, and India. Henna can be purchased in many colors and is included as a non-coloring conditioning ingredient in some hair care products (See **CHAPTER 3**).

Initally, hair waving was a skill practiced by artisans using cumbersome apparatus and secret formulas. The method of cold waving the hair, without applied heat, began in 1930 with a process that required six to eight hours for completion at room temperature. After 1940, cold wave lotions based on thioglycolates became almost universal.

Nail lacquers, in one form or another, can be traced back to ancient Egypt when the fingertips were dipped in orange henna. A true nail lacquer was first made commercially in the 1880's from nitrocellulose, a natural, fluffy, white, fibrous material manufactured by the nitration of cellulose from wood pulp. Cellulose is natural plant fiber, and the nitration process is also natural, consisting of repeated washings of the cellulose in large volumes of water until the acid has been removed and the water replaced with alcohol. But then various chemicals are added to the nitrocellulose, and it is at this point that the product becomes less natural.

Today the cosmetic industry is quite different from the eras we have been discussing so far in this chapter. There is, so to speak, a big difference between Cleo and Clairol. In the beginning cosmetic chemists relied completely on nature; they were closer to great chefs than to today's chemists. If we could prepare an outline, a kind of summary on the development of cosmetics, it would look something like this:

I. Religious Phase of Cosmetics

Early Egypt, Early Greece, Early India--Cosmetics are tied to medicine;

both are part of a highly secretive alchemical tradition. Man and nature, in this cosmological world view, are perceived as inseparable.

II. Medical Phase of Cosmetics (Early, Alchemy)

1. Ancient Period (Alchemists in Ancient Egypt, etc.)

2. Hellenistic Period (400-600, B.C.) The arts of medicine and cosmetology were advanced during this period. By 500 B.C. medical schools were established in Greece, and Hippocrates advocated the use of cosmetics in medicine, dermatology, diet, exercise, herbal baths, and massage for health and beauty.

3. The Renaissance (1400-1600 A.D.) Cosmetics began to be considered as decoration rather than medical treatments during this period; this was a gradual dissociation, though, and much of the extant cosmetic literature was written by physicians. Alchemists, led by Paraclesus, stop looking for gold in base metals and begin to research drugs and cosmetics.

III. Trade Phase of Cosmetics

1. Roman Empire (27 B.C. to 476 A.D.) The Romans took the Egyptian cosmetic secrets to Rome, but they became divided between the physicians and the alchemists.

2. 1700-1900. After the art of decoration and adornment became separated from medicine and considered part of fashion, the making of cosmetics fell into the hands of kitchen maids, barbers, and assorted charlatans. Shops of hairdressers, perfumers, and wig manufacturers prospered in Europe and England. Some doctors, however, wanted to retain cosmetics as part of their art since it was related to maintaining a good appearance.

IV. Nineteenth Century (Industrial Revolution and Cosmetics)

1. Medical connection to cosmetics disappears.

2. Consumer services prosper (beauty shops, etc.)

3. Chemical industry begins.

4. Educational movement in cosmetic industry takes place (i.e., beauty schools in England and America are founded, and cosmetic chemists evolve through training in cosmetic industry).

V. Twentieth Century Growth of Cosmetics

1. Federal Food, Drug, and Cosmetic Act (1938) passed in America to separate drugs from cosmetics and bring about delimitation and testing of food, drug, and cosmetic chemicals.

2. Beauty Without Cruelty, a non-profit animal protection organization, was founded in 1959 and began circulating names of cosmetic manufacturers who do not test on animals. The widespread animal torture in cosmetics thus became known to consumers on a wider basis, and the ethics and validity of tests like the LD50/LD60 and Draize Tests are questioned by consumer groups and scientists alike. *In-vitro* alternatives are now being developed.

3. FDA institutes labeling in the cosmetic industry (1977), and for the first time, consumers see what they are paying for in a cosmetic formula and the great array of dangerous chemicals being used in products.

4. Many large cosmetic manufacturers, such as Fabergé and Clairol, added products in the late 1970's that featured "natural and organic" advertising slogans: the new lines were quite successful although not natural. In health food stores, some truly natural cosmetics became available during the 1960's and 1970's, although, just as with the major cosmetic companies, many health food store brands contained synthetics and unsafe ingredients, and many consumers became skeptical of the "natural and organic" claim. There was also a revival among consumers and manufacturers alike of ancient cosmetic ideas: the use of herbs in cosmetics, aromatherapy, Chinese medicinal cosmetics, henna hair coloring, etc.

5. The Natural Source Vitamin E Association was founded in 1984 in an effort to provide consumers with accurate source information for natural vitamin E in vitamins and cosmetics. This is one of the first efforts to control the use of the word "natural" in products; "natural" has previously had no limitations as to its use.

6. Public Citizen's Health Research Group, begun by consumer activist Ralph Nader, filed a suit against the FDA in February 1985, charging that the federal agency had abused its power in failing to state whether or not ten widely used food and cosmetic dyes are safe, although this declaration was a requirement for marketing the food dyes as stated in a 1960 law. The FDA had, in 1984, already recommended a ban on six of the ten dyes. These six dyes are FD & C Red 3; and D & C Orange 17, Red 8, Red 9, Red 19, and Red 37; the other four are FD & C Yellow 5 and Yellow 6; and D & C Red 33 and Red 36.

We began our cosmetic history with a visit to the Ptolemaic Period of Egypt (30 B.C.) and took the sun-walk with Fustat-Kal along the mud flats of the Nile. Then we imagined a meeting between ancient cosmetic magnate Galen (of Rome) and a modern chemical salesman. It's only fitting that we end with a visit to the Big Apple and a contemporary cosmetic manufacturer.

Manhattan, the Nuclear Age, 1986. The Cleogale Company was located on the 32nd story of a modern glass and steel structure on the Avenue of the Americas. It was in the neighborhood of the Exxon building, ABC television building, NBC television building, and the world-renowned Rockefeller Center. This little strip that runs from 47th Street to 50th Street is the glossy peel of the Big Apple: probably the most costly piece of office real estate in New York. Cleogale paid the high rent of this area to justify the high position they thought they held in the cosmetic industry, but the location of their offices was their only prestigious characteristic. Take, for example, the treatment of their employees. Their neighbor Exxon could boast high salaries for their executives and big benefits for all their employees along with job security. Though it was unlikely that you'd find any women in the oil drilling fields, on the oil barges, or making deals with the sheiks in the desert, you would nevertheless find some women in executive positions in the fountain-decked Exxon building. This was also true of ABC and NBC. But Cleogale Cosmetics, which sold products to women, had one token woman executive named Betty. All the other women held secretarial positions, clerks, switchboard workers, and other functions. In all fairness, however, in this regard Cleogale was no different than most other cosmetic manufacturers (with the exception of those owned by women) and could outdo its TV neighbors as well in sacking marketing directors and product managers. In the cosmetic industry, marketing men were known to keep their personal effects (awards, diplomas, the wife-and-kid-picture, etc.) in their attachés for the first few weeks of work to avoid the embarrassment of packing them up when they were told to leave. One piece per week would be removed from the attachés and placed on the desk, the last item being the family photograph. By then they would begin to feel secure in their position, and this was, quite often, exactly when the office boy would be sent in to help them pack their things. At Cleogale it was said that one marketing man didn't make it through his first day. He arrived at 9:15 a.m. sharp and got his coffee from the coffee wagon, but by the time he got to his office, his brother-in-law had his job. His brother-in-law, however, had already received two weeks' notice. Both decided to leave the cosmetic business to go into a more secure career: selling printing in Miami.

Cleogale, like other top cosmetic manufacturers, only revered one executive position--the job of research director and cosmetic chemist. Nobody understood this man (and they were always men), but nobody felt threatened by him either. He was usually nicknamed "doc," because he sometimes had a Ph.D., although it was usually in some obscure field of science or in metallurgy. But with a Ph.D. or without, the cosmetic chemist was immune to the executive purges that so frequently ravaged marketing departments because cosmetic chemistry was magic and the cosmetic chemist was the high priest who made it all happen. How else could a mere mortal man throw together a brew of petrochems for fifty cents and sell it as a rejuvenating skin cream for fifty dollars? The marketing men and other executives were expendable camouflage experts, and their hype a sham that had to stay one step ahead of the consumer activists and the FDA, but the doc was vital. The doc could dress as he wished, come and go as he wished, be as absent-minded as he wished (the more the better), and make the most blatant mistakes without so much as a reprimand. Unlike the doc, if a marketing man made even the slightest insignificant error he would be out the door and forced to go to work (for next to nothing) at some direct sales cosmetic company in California or Florida: Siberia in the cosmetics game.

The lobby of Cleogale Cosmetics was more bedazzling than the lobby of Fabergé (decorated disco-style with flashing lights and black walls). Cleogale, not to be outdone by any other cosmetic company, had a merry-go-round revolving lobby with a rheostat that could be speeded up or slowed down. Chemical salesmen were known to walk towards the elevator and wind up in the men's room. The lobby gave them more nausea and worse headaches than the cosmetic filling plants where the ammonia and thioglycolate stench hung rotten in the air. Nobody explained why Cleogale had a revolving lobby, but it was rumored that the president, Irving Finegold, liked to bring his grandchildren into the office on Saturdays for a ride. A higher-placed source (Finegold's son-in-law Bobby) said that the merry-go-round was there to spin the deadwood executives out the door. (This was before Bobby got revolved out the door when Finegold discovered that his son-in-law was giving trailer loads of cosmetics to prostitutes for their favors. His infidelities were easy to understand though because his wife looked, talked, and was exactly like Finegold. But Bobby was no beauty either: he resembled a cross between a cabbage patch doll and Peter Lorre; hence the trailers).

Our visit to the Cleogale executive offices would not be complete without attending a product meeting. The meeting began promptly at 10:30 a.m. in the conference room. The first person to arrive was the office boy who placed yellow ledger pads and a sharp pencil at each chair (although he broke the pencil point at the new marketing director's chair). That evening the office boy will be given a free case of hairspray by Bobby, who aspired to be the marketing director one day. Bobby will become the marketing director; the office boy will put a broken pencil at his place, and the executive director will give the office boy a case of hairspray. As we know, Bobby will be revolved out the door. Bobby will take a trailer load of hairspray with him for his secret cosmetic distributorship in Hoboken. The office boy will break the pencil point on the executive director's pencil, and Finegold will give the office boy a half case of hairspray. The office boy will be fired for stealing hairspray. He will open his own stationary supply store in Newark which is well-stocked with the pencils, pads, erasers, etc., that he took with him. He will also sell hairspray. Cleogale's hairspray aerosol plant in New Jersey will catch fire and blow up a few months before the FDA outlaws aerosol hydrocarbons due to the danger to the ozone layer caused by aerosols. This little area of New Jersey will have almost no ozone layer, and people at the Jersey shore will get more severe sunburns that year. Cleogale will increase its sales of Super Sunmask SPF 15. People will also purchase more of their aerosol SunBurn PainAway. This spray will reduce the ozone layer. The aerosol cans at Bobby's Beauty Supply in Hoboken will catch fire, and the whole business will burn down. Bobby will buy a small cosmetic manufacturer in an obscure town in Florida. The office boy's stationary store will burn to ashes when his hairspray cans catch fire, and the insurance company must take his word for how much stock was there. The office boy will open a printing business in Miami.

All the executives including Betty (the token woman), James (the token *goyim*), and Doc arrived at the meeting. In the center of the table was a bottle of shampoo that everyone agreed would revolutionize the art of cleaning hair (if it can be called an art). Finegold arrived last and took his place at the head of the table. The notes prepared by the marketing director said that the new shampoo will be called Fine Gold Shampoo. (This shampoo will be about as successful as a cologne named after the president of Fabergé called "By George," but nowhere near as successful as a cologne named "Charlie" after the president of Revlon. The idea of a Gold Girl was about as appealing as a Charlie Girl and a George Girl, but nobody considerd this. According to their marketing experts, there was no underestimating the taste of the American public.)

"Fine Gold Shampoo is made with the golden oils of nature," intoned the marketing director, "and at the same time bears the name Finegold."

"A clever play on words," agreed the sales promotion manager, "but what are the golden oils?"

"Golden camomile oil, golden jojoba oil, golden wheat germ oil, and golden honey," gushed the marketing director. "These natural golden oils are the secret of Fine Gold Shampoo." He frowned when he noticed his pencil was broken, but he carefully edged it over to the token *goyim*'s pad.

"Yeah, but all these golden oils cost a lot of gold!" hollered Finegold. "Doc, how much is this formula gonna cost us? Doc!!" Finegold, like all the cosmetic industry, was against spending too much on the juice in the bottle. They firmly believed the consumer bought based on packaging, hype, and celebrity endorsement. The product inside the bottle was insignificant, and since nobody else made an exceptional formula, why should they? In fact, this was the **ONLY** way a cosmetic chemist could get fired: if he put more than a drop of something expensive in a product, he could count on a ride on the merry-go-round that would take him right back to his teaching assistantship in the community college metallurgy department teaching arc welding at night. When Finegold was a child, his mother sang a lullaby when she rocked him at night that went like this: "Buy low, sell high . . . Buy low, sell high . . . Buy low, sell high." The baby Finegold never forgot this: he used this lullaby as the slogan by which he ran his cosmetic empire.

"What?!!" The Doc woke up. He usually fell asleep during the product meetings. Quite often he slept so soundly that everyone left him slumped in his chair after the meeting was over.

"Doc! How much will it cost to make this shampoo?" Bobby asked the all-important question.

"How much do these golden natural oils cost?"

"What golden natural oils?"

"The stuff you put in the new Fine Gold Shampoo. Doc, is it expensive?"

"It's a shampoo," Doc yawned. "You make it with water and sodium lauryl sulfate . . . some betaine . . . or cocamides . . . it's just shampoo," mumbled the Doc. "You pour it on your hair, it makes suds, you rinse it off, it goes down the drain, and you buy another bottle. It's just shampoo."

"Yes, we know that, Doc, but what about the golden herbal oils in it? I. F. wants to know if they cost a lot," asked the advertising man who always called Finegold I. F. or "The Big Man."

"There's just a dash, They don't do anything anyway, so why put much in?" The Doc edged down in the chair and closed his eyes.

"Betty, did you try this Fine Gold Shampoo?" asked Finegold. His main reason for keeping Betty around was to ask her typical woman-type questions of this nature.

"Oh yes, Mr. Finegold. It really cleans the hair and leaves it soft and . . . and . . . golden-looking too," said Betty. Actually it made Betty's hair dull and dry, but this didn't matter to Betty because who would listen to what she had to say anyway? The Doc was god as far as Finegold was concerned, and Finegold was too cheap to make a good shampoo. Betty bought her hair and skin care products at a health food store, and she was secretly on a macrobiotic vegetarian diet. This was just a job to her. One day she wanted to open a health food store in Greenwich Village, but for now she had to play the role.

"I. F., we got that blonde TV star what's-her-name . . . the one who plays the detective's girl friend . . . she's going to plug the new stuff in our TV promotion . . . 'Fine Gold is for me' is all she's going to say, and all she's going to wear is a polar bear rug," pitched the advertising manager.

"Oh yeah, and how much is she gonna cost us?"

"She's a big star, I. F., but we got her for a hundred thou. It was quite a deal."

"God! For that much I should get to lay her!"

Everybody laughed. Betty gave out a tight smile and a faint titter (she recently joined NOW, and did volunteer work at a rape crisis center, but a job is a job). The Doc woke up again because of the laughter.

"You know what I always say," continued Finegold.

"What's that, I. F.?"

"That the only reason a woman uses cosmetics is to get . . ."

Laughter served to save everybody from the usual F word that Finegold used to refer to women and his secret disdain for their lack of taste in buying his products. The only women who got Finegold's interest were the ones who told him his products were synthetic junk and that he was a capitalist pig who was poisoning the earth with his support of the industrial chemical complex. These were usually younger women he met at the health food conventions he attended to get ideas for products. Last year he had even given a thousand dollar check to the Society for Alternatives to Animal Testing because the young woman asking for donations had a sixties' look that turned him on.

"Is the shampoo pH balanced?" asked the sales promotion manager. "I think it's a good time to revive the pH balanced slogan and do some ads with the blonde dipping litmus paper into the shampoo and saying, 'Fine Gold Shampoo is pH balanced so it has the same pH as your hair.' After all, Redken got a lot of mileage out of that old pH story."

"I'll throw in some citric acid and some triethanolamine," says Doc. "I can turn the stuff into battery acid if you want me to."

Finegold picked up the bottle of shampoo and opened it. He gazed down into the bottle. The shampoo was yellow. That pleased him. A shampoo should always be yellow or green--the clean colors--the money colors. "How much does it cost to make, Doc?"

"About fifty cents, but I can use synthetic jojoba oil, synthetic camomile, and get the cost down to maybe forty cents. I can add propylene glycol to make the shampoo seem soft and smooth on the hair . . . that stuff is cheap."

"If only you could make it for a quarter," whined Finegold.

"Nothing costs a quarter anymore. Bunch of damn millionaires in the chemical business today," grumbled Doc. "Even petrochemicals are expensive. Lots of people think inflation is over, but it never goes away. Tell you what, boss, I can bring it in for maybe thirty-five cents."

"This man is a genius," cried Finegold, coming to his feet. "He could be a great scientist, but he's here with us, boys, here with us. You could all learn from him. You guys spend all our money on ads and fancy gold caps and fancy boxes and give some blonde *shiksa* thousands, but the Doc comes through for us. This man's a *macher!*"

Everybody nodded approval. The Doc dozed off. Then the advertising manager began passing around story boards and art for the magazine ads which would introduce Fine Gold Shampoo . . . the shampoo with the golden oils from nature. "What is a *macher*?" asked James, the token *goyim*.

As this fictitious high-level board meeting illustrates, there has been a back to basics movement that has caught the imagination of the cosmetics industry. More and more cosmetic manufacturers of the 1980's are marketing brands of "natural cosmetics," but most of them are not doing it out of any real scientific curiosity; they are doing it because there is a market for it. Most of the so-called natural products are mass-produced and highly synthetic, but the very fact that hype and production are increasing exponentially in this area tells you that there are many people who want natural products for their hair and skin. I could list cosmetic company after company that are in the "natural cosmetic game." For example, at the end of fiscal 1983, manufacturers had introduced many cosmetics based on all kinds of slogans and hype. Hair care products linked with the name "Farrah Fawcett," a perfume called "Babe," and a skin care line called "Great Skin" were among the products introduced by Fabergé. What products made it big that year? Only two really caught the consumer's approval, and ultimately their buying power. The old breadwinner was Brut, but the new breadwinner was Fabergé Organics. Notice the name of the new breadwinner. Yes, people look for the *natural* and *organic* link, and in company after company this has been the big winner. Even though most of the natural cosmetics are mass-produced synthetics with "natural" on the label and a "natural" hype advertising campaign, people buy these products seeking their connection with nature. They trust nature.

Most marketers look down on the consumer and ask the cosmetic chemists to make the same old shampoo but to throw in some magical elixir from nature that they can plug in their ads and on the labels. And the cosmetic chemists see the chemical formulas and the price and say, "what's the difference?" One chemist I spoke with told me that I could replace my natural jojoba oil, that was selling for $250.00 per gallon at the time, with a synthetic chemical copy of jojoba oil for only a few dollars a gallon. Due to their cheapness and availability, the synthetics usually win out, but this attitude and this substitution in products that are claimed to be natural denigrates the consumer. I have found that a truly natural product is important to the people who care, not simply because they have nostalgic feelings towards a simpler era (as many cynical merchandisers believe, substituting hype for quality), but because they have found that the natural products really work for their hair and skin. They have found that various natural substances such as aloe vera gel, squeezed out of a leaf and onto a burn, really work. This is why a truly natural and organic product requires more than a hype label. It must have cosmetic chemists who know and love nature more fervently than synthetic chemists who love petrochemicals and man-made substances; in addition, it must have consumers who know the difference between natural hype and natural truth in the products they buy.

It has been suggested that the future of the field of cosmetics may include preparations that are essentially physiological, taken internally for cosmetic effect. The authors of *Life Extension* suggest taking *canthaxanthin* pills for a sunless suntan, but as we investigate further into absorption of topical substances through the skin, we are aware that many chemicals are finding their way into the body from the outside. We are already aware that by rubbing a cream on the face, or even washing your hands with soap, absorption can take place and cause unexpected reactions. Today we are aware of a topical birth control cream for men which is still in the research phase. Men would simply rub a cream on their chests, and absorption would alter the fertilizing process through hormonal contact. Kimberly-Clark has just come out with a tissue with ingredients that are designed to help you get over your cold from the outside in. Fabergé, a cosmetic company, has developed a chemical dye process that is put into the fabric of a bra and will change to a certain color in order to alert the woman wearing it to the early stages of breast cancer (although this product was not approved by the FDA). These sound like new products or new discoveries, but they are actually applications of very old principles. It is not important whether or how Renuatum of ancient Egypt had more knowledge about psoriasis than we do today, but rather that we use all knowledge available to us, ancient or modern, to fight health problems; we can augment our technological knowledge of disease by searching out the knowledge contained in nature.

I believe that the alchemists of ancient times did not know the secret of life, but that they were aware that they were part of nature and were able to use her secrets in a form of natural chemistry free from synthetic chemicals. Modern men and women, on the other hand, have detached themselves from nature. We sit in tall structures of cement, glass, plastic, and steel surrounded by polluted air; our base is a lump of asphalt. We are told "the future lies in synthetics" which are far superior to nature. Nature is too delicate, they tell us; nature can't be controlled, and the plants of nature die and wither with the whim of the weather. However, man is not a lethal force, and the Earth is not delicate; the vegetal growth of the land is the toughest membrane imaginable in the universe, almost impermeable to death. Plants grow season after season; minerals abound in the land and seas; and all contain yet-to-be-revealed therapeutic values for all species. Nature is not vulnerable: it is we who are transient and vulnerable, and our problems with nature occur when we try to force her to fit into the puny economic structures we have created.

Man imagines his existence is above the rest of life--he views himself as more powerful than nature. This is an illusion; worse, it is folly. The ancient alchemists knew that man is embedded in nature, not separate or above nature. It is this simple fact that makes natural substances more powerful than synthetic substances created by man. The realization of how interlocked we are with nature and the past will be one of the hardest problems for the advanced technological society to face or even understand. In fact, they will not be able to cope with nature because of their isolation from it. The old idea that the new technology will destroy nature will become outmoded; if anything, nature will turn and destroy the new technology-- and us along with it. We can only hope that neither takes place.

One of the modern tendencies that I have become aware of is the fear of microorganisms in foods and cosmetics, and our struggle to create more and more poisons to destroy them before they destroy us. This was not a problem of the ancient peoples, because obviously they could create preservatives by working with nature that were far in advance of those we could create with our own chemical and technical ability. Their superior ability is now an accepted fact by any knowledgeable researcher. But by creating more and more preservatives and poisons to protect us from the dangers of microorganisms, we have not created a safe haven from the dangerous microbes; instead we now have our own allergic reactions, chemical sicknesses caused by a variety of poisonous substances. In fact, more sickness results from chemical reactions than ever could from microbes. Perhaps the ancients knew that there is a cycle and protection within nature. Today, those involved in new discoveries are finding that the microorganisms, even viruses, begin to look more like mobile genes, rather than as single-minded agents of disease and death. Bacteria, for example, are beginning to be studied as social animals and as models for the study of interaction between forms of life at all levels.

Obviously we can't jump into H. G. Well's Time Machine and go back to the Ptolemaic period of ancient Egypt to take the Sun Walk with Fustat-Kal, or discuss the cosmos with Renuatum, or learn to create unique natural cosmetics with his sister Theosebia. We can, however, become aware of the natural substances, how they differ from the synthetic chemicals, and how to seek out the best natural products for our own use, creating our own hair and skin care products. In the beginning cosmetics were natural, but whether you seek out a more natural commercial product, or make your own, I hope this information will help you to tie the knot closer and tighter with Mother Nature.

organitoons

The Litmus Paper Freaks!

CHAPTER III

The pH Stuff
Or
Are You In Balance?

On any given day you can stand at a health food store cosmetic counter and watch the Litmus Paper Freaks dipping their vile chemical strips into shampoos, cleansers, creams, and lotions. Some are a little nicer about it and wait until they get home to dip the litmus paper into the product. If the paper turns vile purple they rush back to the store with the now violated product, wave the paper under the store manager's nose, and declaim, "Look at this! Look at this! This is not a pH balanced cosmetic!" Some of the Litmus Paper Freaks check the pH on everything: urine, saliva, sweat, and the evening meal. If the paper turns a vile purple on any of these things, they gasp and worry. To a Litmus Paper Freak there is nothing worse than being out of balance, and they don't care what is in a product as long as it has the balance they are searching for. The phrases "acid balanced" or "pH balanced" mean nothing, though, because they don't really tell you about the juice in the bottle; they're just "hot words" to confound consumers.

The term pH stands for potential hydrogen and refers to the degree of acidity or alkalinity of a substance. The neutral point is in the center at 7. Anything below 7 is acid, and anything above 7 is alkaline. Though the center measure of 7 is neutral, the neutral range is considered to extend from 6.5 to 7.5. The table on the following page shows the potential hydrogen of various substances. You will notice that the various elements in the chart have a wide pH reading. If you mix an alkaline with an acid, a natural pH adjustment occurs. If the acid was highly acidic and the alkaline weak, the resulting mix would be slightly acidic, but if the alkaline substance was more alkaline than the acid was acidic, then the mixture would be weakly alkaline. The pH of a substance can be measured, although not precisely, with an indicator paper called "litmus paper." When the strip of litmus paper is dipped into a substance that is acid, the paper will turn pink or orange. If the substance is alkaline, it will turn green or purple. This is science; this is how pH works, but the term "pH balanced" is not science--it is an advertising slogan and has nothing to do with science. The claim "pH balanced" means that the pH of the product has been adjusted so that it is at the pH of the hair and skin, usually around 5 or so. The purpose of this pH manipulation is to protect consumers from the irritation that supposedly results from using too-alkaline products. Alkaline shampoos and cleansers allegedly

pH Chart

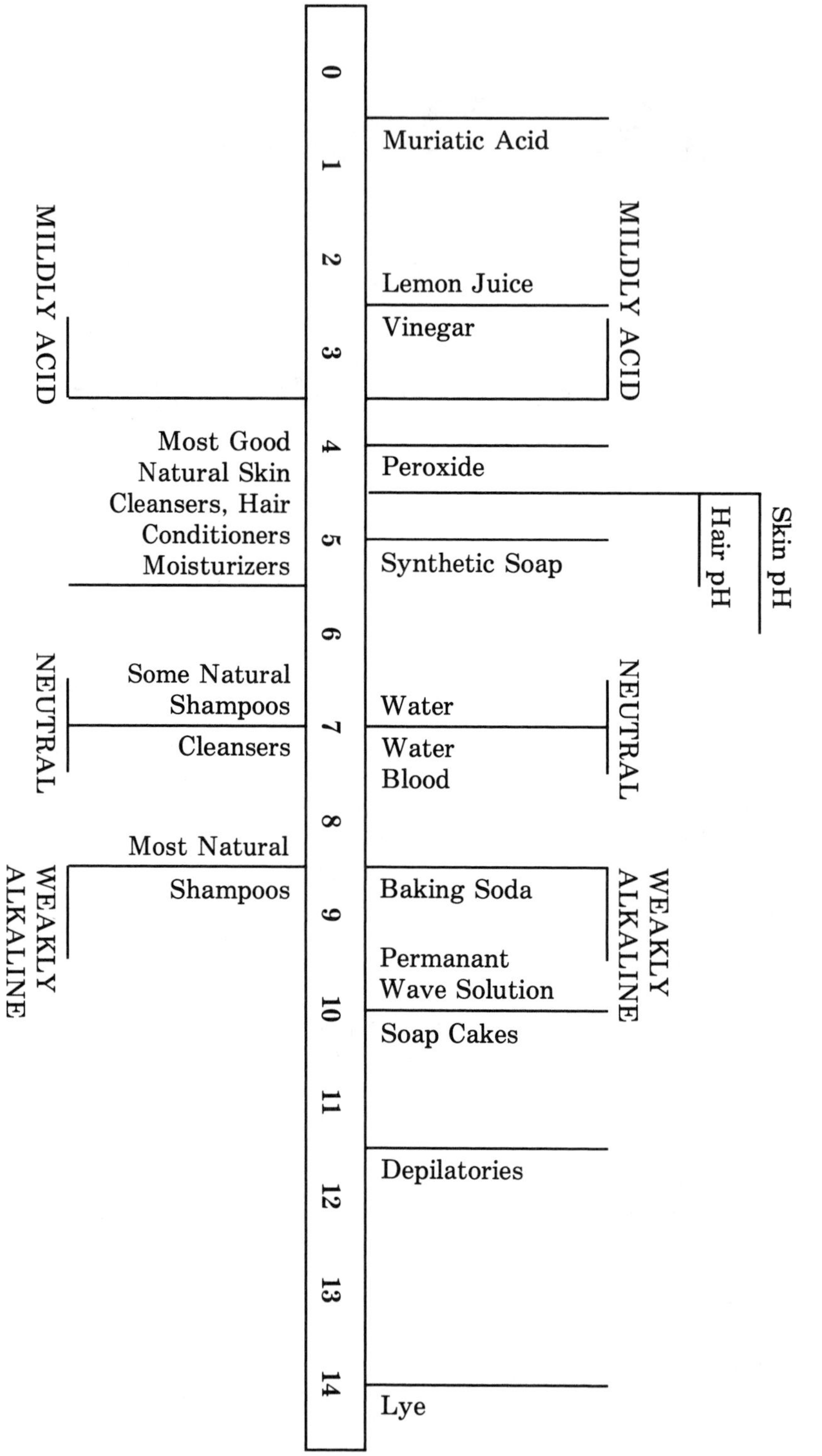
0
1
2
3
4
5
6
7
8
9
10
11
12
13
14
Muriatic Acid
Lemon Juice
Vinegar
Peroxide
Synthetic Soap
Water
Water
Blood
Baking Soda
Permanant
Wave Solution
Soap Cakes
Depilatories
Lye
MILDLY ACID
NEUTRAL
WEAKLY ALKALINE
Skin pH
Hair pH
MILDLY ACID
Most Good
Natural Skin
Cleansers, Hair
Conditioners
Moisturizers
Some Natural
Shampoos
Cleansers
NEUTRAL
Most Natural
Shampoos
WEAKLY ALKALINE

"destroy" the skin's "acid mantle," while "pH balanced" products protect the skin from the deadly bacteria that are ever-waiting to invade our bodies. For millenia mankind has been washing faces and shampooing hair, but only with the advent of "pH balanced" hair and skin care products can we finally do it right! What the Litmus Paper Freaks--and the advertising people who dreamed up "pH balanced"--don't realize, though, is that a product's pH has very little to do with how irritating it is to the skin. Recent studies have shown the the pH range of 5.5 to 10.5 has no influence on the irritation of the skin or hair. A "pH balanced" product does not protect the skin's "acid mantle," and, in fact, the substances used to adjust the pH can dry out the skin and hair. Even the claim "pH balanced" is suspect because pH varies over time and with changing temperatures. No manufacturer can guarantee that the pH of every bottle of shampoo or cleanser will be at exactly 4.5, or even 4.5 to 5.5, when consumers use them.

To understand why "pH balanced" products don't protect the skin's "acid mantle," you must understand what the "acid mantle" is: a layer of fatty acids from the sebum. These fatty acids are formed from triglycerides by the action of bacterial lipases. Triglycerides are fatty acid esters which are produced by the esterfication of three hydroxyl groups of fatty acids. The lipases are a class of enzymes that break down the fats. It is this continuing action that creates the protective "acid mantle" of the skin, which is called acid, but whose pH actually fluctuates constantly from 4.0 to 6.75, which is quite a range considering that 7.0 is neutral (the pH of most water). This has been found to be more variable in women's skin than in men's skin. The Litmus Paper Freaks have bought the rather shaky theory that skin acidity--or hair acidity--is of value in limiting the range of organisms that can successfully inhabit the surface of the skin or hair and in creating an environment that is unsuitable for pathogens, in particular fungi. While this sounds feasible, it really isn't since the growth tolerance limits of pH differ so widely for various microorganisms. The range of species that can contaminate a cosmetic product vary in pH from 3.0 to 11.0; this range covers virtually all hair and skin care products. For example, many fungi grow prolifically in an acid pH, but some can grow in a pH of 9 (especially in a facial cream or mask).

As many advertising slogans that induce fear in the consumer catch on, the products with the slogan "pH balanced" captured a big percentage of the market place by needlessly scaring the public, but the questions you should ask yourself are "balanced with what? And why?" For example, detergent bars that contain the chemicals known as alkyl sulfates are irritating to the skin whether they have a high pH or a neutral pH. If the soaps are made more acid, the sulfates still have an irritating effect on the skin (as will, for that matter, other synthetic chemicals). The alkalinity of the soap is not what is harmful to the skin; it is the alkyl sulfates (P. Frost and S. Horowitz, *Principles of Cosmetics for the Dermatologist*, C. V. Mosby Co., London, England, 1982). The skin has a superb buffering capacity and can adjust alkaline products that fall between 8.0 and 10.5 so that these substances will not harm the skin, but it cannot protect itself from alkyl sulfates and other synthetic chemicals. The point that both the Litmus Paper Freaks and the advertising men who thought up the "pH balanced" slogan forget is that the normal pH of the hair and skin is quickly restored after regular washing, so that any alleged value to the "pH balanced" protection lasts about as long as it takes the products to wash down the drain. A quick glance at our "pH Chart" gives another example. Which would you rather pour on your hair--lemon juice or hydrogen peroxide? Common sense tells you that a lemon juice rinse would leave your hair shiny and free from soap films, but the peroxide would change and possibly damage your hair. Yet, which substance has a pH that is closer to the 4.5 pH of your hair--the peroxide! Shampoos with a pH of 4.5 do not clean the hair well and are usually synthetic. Furthermore, the chemicals that are used to make the shampoos "pH balanced" are drying to the hair, cause itchy scalp, and have a bad long range effect on the hair and scalp. They may give the hair a shiny look, but a good natural conditioner or herbal rinse can do this job safely and without the harsh synthetic chemicals used in "pH balanced" shampoos. A simple lemon, vinegar, or rosemary and sage herbal rinse gives a natural glow to the hair, removes any soap films, and is far superior to a "pH balanced" shampoo or a harsh detergent shampoo.

While the pH rule is hardly a good method of self-sterilization or of product sterilization, some weak acids do have a preservative action, and this is why benzoic acid and the actual herb, benzoin gum, are used in this way. Sorbic acid and ascorbic acid (from citrus) also depend on an acid pH to preserve. I have also found that natural fatty acid cosmetics seem to be more protective to the skin and scalp than many other natural or synthetic substances.

In the long run, it is the quality of a cosmetic's ingredients and the quality of the formulation that give you an excellent product. For example, essential fatty acids are natural ingredients that are important to hair and skin care. They have a slightly acidic pH--naturally. When you buy cosmetics, don't look for the "pH balanced" hype--look for natural ingredients, and you'll find that the product--with its natural, unmanipulated pH--will work beautifully for your hair and skin.

CHAPTER IV

Does Your Skin Really Absorb and Use Nutrients?

Or

"I've Got You Under My Skin, Collagen . . ."

According to the Food and Drug Administration, cosmetics are "articles which are intended to be rubbed, poured, sprinkled or sprayed or introduced into, or otherwise applied to, the human body for cleaning, beautifying, promoting attractiveness or altering the appearance *without affecting the body's structure or function*" (our italics). If a product is discovered to alter the body's structure or function, then its classification is changed to that of a drug (and it is henceforth governed by an entirely different--and much more stringent--set of regulations). This is a definition whose major purpose is to limit advertising claims by manufacturers; a cosmetic manufacturer is not supposed to claim that his products "get under your skin"--whether they do or not. It's like Kellogg's use of the information that adding fiber to the diet can help prevent certain types of cancer--it has been proven to be true and it can't be said too often, but when it's printed on the side of their bran cereal boxes, an issue ensues.

Of course substances can be absorbed through the skin into the body; DMSO and hexachlorophene are both potent and fast-acting examples (one seemingly beneficial and one tragic). Much remains, however, to be discovered about this process, most importantly how it can be used therapeutically. The mechanism whereby certain substances penetrate the epidermal layer and dermal layers and are absorbed into the systemic circulation is called the pilo-sebaceous apparatus because it occurs through the hair follicles and the sebaceous glands. Many people think absorption takes place through the sweat glands, but studies have shown that they play a negligible role in percutaneous absorption (*peri-*, beyond; *cutis*, skin). The palms of infants, for example, which are devoid of hair follicles and sebaceous glands (but not of sweat glands), allow little penetration even with the application of fast absorption substances (F. Hermann, M. B. Sulzberger, and R. L. Baer, "The Penetration of Allergens into the Human Skin," *New York State Medical Journal*, 44:2452, 1944). The gradual absorption that characterizes the pilo-sebaceous apparatus allows certain substances to work more effectively when applied topically than with either a pill or a hypodermic needle, as with the corticosteroids. Someday, in fact, we may even take all drugs or nutritional supplements "by skin" rather than in a pill or needle, but regulation and dosage control will then undoubtedly be a problem. By government regulation, though, all this talk of percutaneous absorption and the pilo-sebaceous apparatus belongs to the medical profession and not to the cosmetic industry. The cosmetic manufacturer is supposed to represent the skin as a sort of old shoe that can be polished but not penetrated. Luckily, the skin doesn't recognize government regulation, though, because it can be nourished and treated from the outside in.

An absorption base is what allows active ingredients such as vitamins or collagen to penetrate the surface of the skin, but it is not just a carrying agent--it is also a humectant, an emulsifier, an emollient, a barrier agent, and a healing agent.

The word humectant is a good one to know and to understand because of what humectants can do for your skin. Humectants control the moisture exchange between the product and the air: they attract moisture. They also have the ability to release water gradually, which is important to your skin and the cream in which they are compounded. Glycerine and rose water is one ancient combination that consists of 50% humectant and 50% water. It has been said that humectants make water wetter, but I did not get my first lesson in humectants as a student in a chemistry lab but in my part-time job as a printer. The offset printing press works on the principle that oil and water do not mix. Therefore, the inky (oil) image on the plate will transfer to the image roller of the press and to the sheet of paper because water continually flows over the printing plate and keeps the plate wet and clean, yet will not mix with the oily image to be printed. Of course, the wetter the water is, the better the printing process works. I found that I could mix a little glycerine with the water in the printing press and get a cleaner and sharper image. By making the water wetter, I was actually controlling the exchange of water and air on the printing plate and getting a darker image with a cleaner background. Some of the humectants you will read on cosmetic labels are propylene glycol (a petrochemical), glycerol or glycerine (can be natural or synthetic), and sorbitol (natural). Though all three of these humectants are considered innocuous, there have been more reactions to the petrochemical than to the natural substances.

The emulsifier is what holds two ingredients together that normally would not mix. For example, in Galen's cold cream (original recipe) made of olive oil, beeswax, and water, the beeswax acts as the emulsifier that holds the olive oil and water in a homogenous mixture. An emulsifying action can be provided, though, by vigorous mixing, which is how you make another popular emulsion--mayonnaise.

An emollient lubricates and softens skin tissue. From a biochemical standpoint, an emollient action is a phenomenon related to the conservation of the water content of the skin. Water is the most effective emollient. Many people think that oil moisturizes the skin, but this is not true unless the oil manages to mix with, or hold more moisture on the skin. Studies have shown that chapped skin could be returned to normal when the dew point was above a critical level, and that a high incidence of skin chapping was directly related to a fall in the dew point. The dew point is the air temperature at which the gaseous moisture in the air begins to condense (I. E. Gaul and G. B. Underwood, "Relation of Dew Point and Barometric Pressure to Chapping of Normal Skin," *Journal of Invest. Dermatol.*, 19:9, 1952). An emollient then performs two important functions: it prevents dryness and protects the skin, thus acting as a barrier and healing agent. It also softens the skin. Some emollient oils that also absorb well into the skin are lanolin, cod liver oil, olive oil, coconut oil, avocado oil, castor oil, and various other vegetable oils.

An absorption base should, finally, allow the active ingredients to be absorbed into the skin. Among the most penetrating substances are essential oils which are a complex mixture of a wide variety of organic compounds (e.g., alcohols, ketones, phenols, acids, ethers, aldehydes, esters, oxides, sulfur compounds, etc.). If you are applying a collagen cream, an elastin cream, a mucopolysaccharide cream, a placenta cream, or a vitamin cream, the most vital function of the base or carrying agent is penetration. If it doesn't get into the skin and only lies on top of it, you are not getting the therapeutic value of the product. From lanolin to DMSO, nature provides the best absorption bases. In a moisturizing cream, however, maximum absorption into the skin (or scalp) is not always desirable because softening the skin and protecting it from loss of moisture--both of which take place on the skin's surface--are part of the expected results.

I have found that for both moisturizing and absorption purposes a base containing the essential fatty acids (vitamin F) softens and nourishes the skin, scalp, and hair. For example, a combination of essential fatty acids, an excellent lactic acid protein called lactalbumin, and herbal extracts (such as rosemary oil and sage oil) makes a superb hair conditioner that cleans the scalp and leaves the hair smooth, soft, and silky. The essential fatty acids, or EFAs, are polyunsaturated fatty acids with long carbon chains (linoleic, linolenic, or arachidonic acid). They cannot be synthesized by the body. There are two ways of obtaining the EFAs--one is through your diet, and the other is through application to your skin. Tests have shown that skin that is deficient in the EFAs exhibits enormous water loss, and scaliness and loss of hair are also apparent. Essential fatty acids have excellent moisture-retaining properties. They also produce occlusive films that attract moisture to your skin, with the added advantage that, because they are natural, your skin will recognize, at least biochemically, EFAs more readily than hydrocarbons, i.e., mineral oil, petrolatum, paraffin wax, ozokerite, etc.

Because mineral oil and its derivatives absorb very poorly, inhibit the skin's own moisture-producing capacity (thereby producing dry skin), and are phototoxic and allergenic, they are not at all recommended for any cosmetic product. More and more people are recognizing that although some form of mineral oil is in almost every cosmetic--including many so-called "health food store" brands--petrochemicals are BAD for your body, whether taken in as a food or rubbed on as a cosmetic.

An absorption base made with essential fatty acids is a highly penetrating and nourishing emollient on its own; however, many ingredients can be added to this base to increase the therapeutic value to each component of the skin.

Sebum - One of the reasons the essential fatty acids work in an emollient and absorption base is that they are similar to the skin's sebum, or lipids, which is a substance synthesized by the sebaceous gland in the epidermis. There are about one hundred sebaceous glands per one square inch of skin. The purpose of sebum is to lubricate the skin and help prevent the evaporation of moisture; it is also believed to help preserve the *stratum corneum*, the outer horny layer of the skin. Thus, sebum is a natural emollient and barrier agent. The raw materials necessary for the synthesis of these lipids are amino acids, long chain fatty acids (e.g., the EFA's), and carbohydrates.

Ribonucleic acid is a large molecule that carries cellular blueprints, or genes. It has received some publicity as a beneficial ingredient in hair and skin care products. The RNA included in cosmetics, however, has not been found to benefit the hair or skin. The claims of hair growth are not substantiated by current applications of RNA; however, we cannot rule out some positive effect RNA might have when combined with other substances. Be suspicious of label claims for RNA and DNA in most cosmetics, though, because the amount of these ingredients is likely to be minute, and any synthetic chemicals present in the formula would probably reduce any benefit they would have on the skin and hair.

Protein - One of the major products of the skin, protein is synthesized in the epidermis and hair follicles in much the same way as other tissues. Most of the twenty-two amino acids are found in the epidermis and the hair, with *histidine* being found in the highest concentration. The amino acids are assembled into chains by attachment to ribonucleic acid (RNA) and are then joined together into specialized particles in the cytoplasm of cells known as ribosomes. These are then released as protein molecules.

Collagen is a dermal protein. It is the fibrous material of the skin, in short, what holds you together. Collagen makes up about one-third of the total body protein, and 70% of your connective tissue. When your skin wrinkles and becomes dry, thin, and inelastic, your collagen has become cross-linked, which is an aging process of the skin's protein that is similar to the tanning of leather.

Young connective tissue contains mainly non-crosslinked, flexible collagen; in other words, its molecules are displaced in relation to one another. We call this "soluble collagen," which signifies connective tissue that has a good capacity for absorbing moisture and is therefore capable of swelling. When the sulfur-containing amino acids in protein oxidize and begin to react to form a disulfide bond, crosslinking occurs, and the result is known as "insoluble collagen," which is inelastic, cannot absorb moisture very well and is therefore incapable of swelling.

Aged connective tissue contains mainly crosslinked, inflexible collagen, whose molecules are no longer displaced in relation to one another. The skin has forfeited most of its elasticity, and this loss of elasticity manifests itself in increased formation of lines and wrinkles in the skin, particularly in those areas continually exposed to light, such as the face, neck, and the backs of the hands. When this crosslinking takes place, there are not only oxidative alterations in the collagen, but also in the elastin (another dermal protein found in the artery walls and the dermis), and in the reticulin (the third of the dermal protein complex). This oxidation also alters the lipids (unsaturated fatty acids) and the proteins. The crosslinking oxidative process also affects all the components within the connective tissues which includes amino acids, along with elastin, reticulin, the ground substances of mucopolysaccharides, mucoproteins, proteins, aqueous nutrients, and electrolytes. (*See chart below*).

Amino Acids in Dermal Proteins (By Percentage)

Amino Acid	Reticulin	Collagen	Elastin
Aspartic Acid	6.6	5.5	1.9
Threonine	3.8	1.9	1.4
Serine	3.5	3.5	1.4
Glutamic Acid	11.0	9.5	3.5
Proline	7.5	13.8	11.3
Glycine	15.7	22.5	22.3
Alanine	12.7	9.4	18.8
Cystine	0.2	0	0.2
Valine	7.1	2.2	13.9
Methionine	1.6	0.7	0.3
Isoleucine	3.1	1.4	3.0
Leucine	7.5	2.7	7.8
Tyrosine	0.9	0.2	1.1
Phenylalanine	2.5	1.9	4.5
Histidine	1.6	0.7	2.0
Lysine	4.0	3.9	1.4
Arginine	4.6	7.4	2.0
Hydroxyproline	6.1	12.0	3.2
Hydroxylysine	0	0.8	0
	100.0	100.0	100.0

The amino acid content of collagen, elastin, and reticulin gives these substances their unique benefits to the hair and skin. The amino acid hydroxyproline is characteristic to collagen, but is present in lesser amounts in reticulin and elastin. While collagen's amino acid content is the most complete, all three dermal proteins are excellent skin care topicals when therapeutic results are desired.

In recent years, extensive knowledge has been gained regarding the physiological behavior of collagen, its structural alteration, and its becoming insoluble on aging. The findings indicate that the loss of soluble collagen in the skin could be arrested or compensated by supplying the skin with soluble collagen externally. Histological and clinical experiments have shown that a natural soluble collagen cream stimulates the formation of new collagenic fibrils and consequently leads to the regeneration of the skin. A natural soluble collagen cream also increases the elasticity of the skin and elevates its moisture content, thus bringing about an overall revitalization of the skin. These results have been well documented by clinical tests and are objectively measurable. However, the way in which the cream is formulated determines whether or not the collagen will be absorbed.

One of the problems with introducing soluble collagen to the skin topically is that just as the soluble collagen within your skin can be altered through chemicalization, so can collagen as an active agent in a cream be altered if synthetic chemicals are added and alter the structure so as to render the collagen insoluble. We have found that natural soluble collagen is altered in the presence of various synthetic preservatives. Many manufacturers who package natural soluble collagen for sale as an active agent warn that a preservative may alter it. Soluble collagen is thermolabile and therefore cannot be added to cream emulsions above the temperature of 35° C. A collagen cream must have a pH between 3.7 and 6.5 because of the weakly acid character of soluble collagen. Soluble collagen should be incorporated predominantly into creams of the oil-in-water type because collagen is a water-soluble active agent and will be contained in the outer or "water" phase of oil-in-water preparations and will therefore be better absorbed by the skin. In a water-in-oil preparation the collagen would be enclosed in the inner or "water" phase, and not be well absorbed by the skin. (J. J. Eller and S. Wolff, "Permeability and Absorptivity of the Skin," *Arch. Dermatol. and Syphilol.*, 40:900, 1939, and R. G. Harry, "Skin Penetration," *Brit. Journal Dermatol.*, 53:65, 1941). Soluble collagen is also denatured by alcohol. I have found that more than 15% alcohol suspensions with soluble collagen have a rapid denaturization, and that the collagen precipitates out.

If you have tried a commercial collagen cream without much success you must be aware that most commercially prepared products contain either insoluble collagen or collagen that has been prepared incorrectly in either the compounding or manufacturing phase. For example, a cream containing methylparaben, propylparaben, formaldehyde, formalin, or other synthetic chemicals will alter the collagen. If the collagen creams you tried listed collagen as one of the main ingredients and yet were quite inexpensive, you should be suspicious that perhaps the collagen used was insoluble collagen (which is much cheaper as an ingredient than the soluble kind). Mineral oil, or one of its derivatives, in a collagen cream formula, will greatly inhibit its absorption. I have found that mineral oil often reduces the absorption and the therapeutic effects of not only collagen, but many other natural substances.

The American Board of Plastic Surgery feels that collagen creams are of no use except for moisture, but condones the use of Zyderm injections (collagen-in-a-needle), which are painful and extremely expensive. And, while the injections may temporarily "plump" up sunken areas in the skin that have been caused by scarring or wrinkling, the beneficial effects of these injections do not last. Topical application of collagen in an essential fatty acid base does penetrate into the skin but, unlike the injections, does the skin no violence.

With the current outcry against abortion, many cosmetic manufacturers--particularly those who use ingredients such as collagen or placenta--are besieged by letters and telephone calls from individuals who are deeply concerned that these substances are obtained from the fetuses of aborted babies. This is not true, and it is not true for a sound economic reason: it's cheaper to obtain collagen and placenta as by-products of the beef industry than it would be to obtain these ingredients from abortion clinics. There is plenty of bovine collagen available, and to obtain it from the beef industry is the easier and cheaper way. We can't say the majority of the cosmetic industry does anything for a moral reason, but we can state categorically that they do want to manufacture products in the easiest and cheapest way possible. But, good soluble bovine collagen is not cheap, and some manufacturers will substitute insoluble collagen which will result in a very inferior product. If you decide to buy a collagen cream, be sure the manufacturer specifies "soluble collagen," and read the label carefully. The collagen should be high on the list of ingredients, and the list should not include mineral oil or its derivatives, nor should it include synthetic preservatives such as methyl or propyl paraben. The best base--- one that will be moisturizing and yet provide collagen absorption--is one made with essential fatty acids. Treatment vials that contains pure collagen, elastin, etc., are, usually, not as positive in their results as one in an EFA cream base.

In conclusion dermal protein creams can be excellent skin care treatments, but the absorption base is vital, and the base is not what is advertised about most products. Don't get carried away by "hot words" on a cosmetic label; turn it around and read the ingredients list and see for yourself whether the product can deliver the benefits and the absorption it promises.

CHAPTER V

Cleo and Clay, Cleo and Henna, Cleo and Aloe

Or

Groucho to Cleo: "Aloe, I Must Be Going . . ."

In the tomb of Queen Heterpheres, mother of the Pharaoh Cheops (who built the Great Pyramid of Giza), a complete cosmetic kit was found by archeologists. This ancient kit contained vases and jars made of ivory and alabaster, wood and onyx, porphyr and gold containing *kohl* (a natural color), stibium pencils, lip pomade, aromatic unguents, rouge, perfume oils, combs, mirrors, tweezers, razors, manicure implements, and royal wigs. Other digs dating as far back as 1550 B.C. suggest that Queen Ses, mother of Pharaoh Teta, was one of the first to use henna as a rinse. In 1922 when the tomb of Tutankhamen was discovered by the British archeologist Howard Carter, the unguent containers still contained the young king's personal blend of coconut oil, balsam, valerian, broom, and animal fatty acids as a base. Obviously, after thousands of years, the boy king's cosmetics had withstood the ravages of time without the use of a single synthetic preservative (pyramid power perhaps?). However, of all the famous people of ancient Egypt, the one we most associate with beauty and cosmetic knowledge is Queen Cleopatra. Cleopatra could not be more remembered if she had signed a public relations contract handed down throughout history for the purpose of keeping her name and beauty alive. She has been publicized into a romantic legend, and her name has become a symbol for the best and most exotic cosmetics (some of which are manufactured in places like Brooklyn, New York, with synthetic chemicals of which Cleo had no knowledge at the time of 30 B.C.). Her name is used on products because it often attracts more consumers than a famous movie star's endorsement, which makes sense, if you think about it, because Cleo was more than just another pretty face. She was reputed to be thoroughly skilled, not only in the art of applying cosmetics, but in the art of compounding them as well. This makes her a very rare individual, even by contemporary cosmetic standards--a cosmetic chemist and cosmetologist rolled into one! Unfortunately, history has not preserved any record of Cleopatra's cosmetological expertise; all we have is the literature her legend has inspired throughout the centuries. If she had left a record of her cosmetic secrets, though, they probably would have included clay, henna, and aloe. All three have been used since, or even before Cleopatra's period, and all are used today. The benefits these substances can have for the hair and skin are truly worthy to have belonged to one of the first cosmetic wizards, Queen Cleopatra.

Cleo and Clay

There are many clay products in the beauty industry today. Health food stores usually have a few clay products, beauty salons and skin care clinics use clay as masks, and one beauty manufacturer has a whole line devoted to clay. Some European spas coat the entire body with "healing" clay, burying clients up to their necks. This treatment is also famous in Japanese health establishments.

Different regions produce different clays, but the clay most highly prized for cosmetic purposes is the white clay known as "kaolin" because it could only be obtained originally from Mt. Kaolin in China. This mountain supplied the royalty of Europe with the white powder for their pale faces and white wigs because the superb quality of kaolin could not be duplicated in Europe. The Chinese controlled the production of white clay until the expansion of the American frontier brought about the discovery of kaolin that could compare with China's. It is interesting that today we have products called "French clay," although the aristocrats of France had to beg their clay from China. In today's marketplace are also many colored clays, but they are usually artificially colored. Although kaolin is pure white, it takes color very well which has led to its use in powders, rouges, foundations, shadows, pastes, creams, and other products used to color and highlight the skin.

Some of the minerals found in clay are silica (57%), aluminum (19%), iron (7%), calcium (4%), magnesium (3%), sodium (2%), potassium (2%), and other trace minerals (6%). Kaolin is most often used for manufacturing a beauty mask. Another less expensive substance used is bentonite, which is not actually a clay, but a volcanic product composed of silica and aluminum (as is kaolin), but with a significant difference in its structure that makes it hard to mix in water. Thus, only a small amount of the bentonite powder remains suspended in water, as a kind of gel, whereas the true clay, kaolin, mixes easily with water to create a paste or clay pack.

A clay mask, or any beauty mask, should produce a noticeably tightening effect on the skin after application and drying. It should also possess sufficient absorbing power to achieve a cleansing effect, yet not irritate the complexion. The tightening and drawing effect of clay is produced when the water separates the clay particles, increasing the volume. Then, as the clay dries due to evaporation, the volume decreases, causing the tightening effect you feel on your skin.

To make a clay beauty mask, measure out two parts water for every part clay. If the mixture is too dry (after allowing the water to be absorbed by the clay), then carefully add water in small amounts. By mixing honey and other extracts with the clay, you can create a massage mask that can be very beneficial to the complexion. Clay will tend to dry your skin, so if you already have a dry complexion you may want to consider using an herbal mask rather than a clay one, or add some moisturizing ingredients (such as egg or avocado) to your clay mask.

Cleo and Henna

Of the many ingredients whose discovery and use are attributed to Cleopatra, henna is the one most commonly associated with her, yet the use of henna definitely predates Cleopatra by over a millenium. Though, as mentioned on the previous page, it is believed that Queen Ses first used henna, there is no way of knowing from the ancient writings exactly what kind of henna she may have used or what other substances she included in her henna compounds. Different varieties of henna make different colors, as was discovered by Dr. J. Mahmoudi, an Iranian botanist, who tested various samples of henna and found three classes. One is red henna (*Lawsonia inermis*, *Lawsonia alba*, and *Lawsonia spinoza*); another is neutral henna (*Lyzifus spina christi*); and the third is black henna (*Indigofera tinctora*). By blending the various hennas and treating red henna with iron oxide, browns and blacks can be made.

Though the Egyptians have been closely linked with henna, it is also found abundantly in Tunis, Arabia, Persia, and India as well as in other tropical countries. It has been used in all these countries, not only to dye the hair, but also the nails, palms, and soles of dancers, and the manes and tails of horses. Red shades of hair were out of favor for several centuries, and henna became difficult to obtain. In the late 1800's, the Spanish-born Italian singer Adelina Patti (1843-1919), came to sing in the United States and brought with her the idea of coloring the hair with henna. Her dark purplish-red or mahogany shade of hair caught on in the United States and remained popular for decades.

In 1916 Dr. Tommasi isolated the active coloring principal in henna (*lawsone*) and determined its chemical formula to be *2-dydroxy-1, 4-naphthoquinone*, which makes up about one per cent of the herb. A color rinse made of henna will bring out highlights on dark hair. Henna leaves are steeped in boiling water until all the dye is extracted, and the solution, when cool, is poured several times over freshly shampooed hair. For a more lasting shade of color, a henna paste of powdered henna leaves and boiling water is used. The cooled paste is applied to the hair and allowed to remain until the desired color is obtained.

Henna is a natural hair conditioning ingredient and has been recorded as such by many researchers (M. Weinstein and L. Smith, "Henna--The Natural Way to Condition Hair," *Soap/Cosmetics/Chemical Specialties*, 5 [1979], 40-42). In a conditioning rinse, henna has been quite successful for some types of hair. Although it is used on all hair types, it seems to work best for oily or dry hair that has a tendency to become oily (or oilier) as the day progresses. It also helps remove "scurf" or dandruff flakes from the hair. The coloring ingredient (*lawsone*) can be removed from the henna so that it will condition your hair without coloring it.

Because henna works best as a hair coloring in an acid medium, henna shampoos are not for coloring the hair, but they can be used for highlighting, cleansing, and conditioning the hair. In other words, don't expect a henna shampoo to color your hair red or orange. You can make a henna shampoo that will bring out warm highlights in dark hair by mixing 5% henna extract and 5% boric acid in a shampoo base. Make this up fresh as a kitchen cosmetic but be sure to wear rubber gloves as the henna may stain your fingers.

The main asset to henna is that it is practically the only widely-available semi-permanent hair coloring that is non-toxic. It does not generally irritate the skin or scalp. The main disadvantage is that henna does not always color predictably. If you want satisfactory results, you must read the directions on the henna package carefully and follow them exactly. Fair or gray-haired people particularly need to try out the henna color on a few strands of hair before applying the henna all over the head. People with temporary hair rinses should not use henna coloring as the two colors may mix in technicolor stripes. People with permanents or who plan to have them should also avoid henna, as the color may interfere with the waving process or may "take" differently on waved hair that is growing out. Furthermore, with continued use, the color accumulates on the outside of the hair shaft. Shampoos and rinses, however, with neutral henna do not color the hair, nor will they leave behind any accumulation of henna.

Cleo and Aloe

Like henna, aloe has an ancient and cosmospolitan history. The use of aloe originated in southern Africa, where the Africans hung aloe plants over their doors to ward off evil spirits. In addition, African hunters rubbed aloe over their bodies to reduce the human scent as they crept close to their prey. The women of Java claimed that aloe rubbed into the scalp stimulated hair growth. Aristotle of Stagira (384-322 B.C.), teacher of Alexander the Great, felt that aloe was so priceless that he persuaded his imperialistic pupil to conquer the island of Socotra

(East Africa) just to get the aloe crop to treat soldiers' wounds. In the New Testament, the apostle John mentions aloe among the plant extracts and spices used to anoint the body of Jesus after his death on the cross. Pedanios Dioscorides (first century A.D.), an army physician and scientist of Asia Minor, wrote a medical textbook that reported that the aloe plant could be used to alleviate pain, wounds, stomach disorders, constipation, headache, to grow back hair, to aid blistering, mouth and gum diseases, kidney ailments, skin care, sunburn, and blemishes. One of the oldest documents to record the use of aloe is the *Papyrus Ebers*, Egyptian papers written around 1500 B.C. Thus, although we have no proof that Cleopatra used aloe, the tradition that she credited the beauty of her skin to the aloe plant has historical support.

Aloe vera is a member of the lily family, cousin to onions, tulips, and asparagus, but it looks like a cactus. Aloe vera does flower, but it is better known for its leaves, which can grow to a length of two feet and are arranged in a rosette. The outside skin of the leaf is smooth, thick, and has a rubbery structure. Right below this outside layer are the cells which secrete the juice used to make *aloin*. The inner chamber contains clear gel, or pulp, which is semi-thick but thins shortly after exposure to air. The pulp is believed to contain "biogenic stimulators," first discovered by the Russian biologist and physician, Dr. Vladimir Filatov, that are used in cellular skin therapy. The active ingredients of this pulp are steroids, organic acids, enzymes, amino acids, glucomanna, and other polysaccharides. Chrysophanic acid has also been discovered in the aloe vera gel which is important as a healing agent to the skin.

Our interest is in the topical use of aloe vera, which involves the pulp of the plant and not the juice. The pulp or gel is 96% water, which moisturizes and 4% "biogenic stimulators" that heal and regenerate the skin. Plain fresh aloe vera gel is one of the best treatments a healthy face can get, but aloe vera helps skin problems of all descriptions.

Modern Egyptian doctors have found that aloe vera gel is a good treatment for acne, dandruff, and seborrhea, and there even have been some positive findings related to hair regrowth in seborrheic baldness. In the Soviet Union, at the Moscow Stomalogical Institute, where many studies on the uses of aloe vera take place, scientists have found that aloe vera extract in water regenerated nerve fibers. Even periodontal disease was treated with aloe vera by a Russian doctor who found that aloe vera influenced the activity of cell enzymes in the gums. Three to four injections reduced bleeding of the gums, and after six to eight injections, secretion from the gum pockets went away. Even the unpleasant taste and odor in the mouth went away as well as toothaches and gum pain (S. Levenson and K. Somova, "Periodontosis Treated With Aloe Vera Extract," *Medical Journal on Aloe Research*, published by Aloe Vera Research Institute of California.)

An interesting test on human skin with aloe vera was performed by I. E. Danhoff Ph.D., M.D., and B.H. McAnalley, Ph.D., at the Southwest Institute for Natural Resources in Grand Prairie, Texas. Using cell cultures from human tissue, the effects of aloe vera gel and aloe vera sap were observed. They found that the extracts of fresh leaves and commercially packaged aloe vera gel had lectin-like substances. Lectins are a group of proteins found primarily in plant seeds, that stimulate production of white blood cells that fight disease. Lectins also help bind together red blood cells. Aloe vera's similarity to lectins may be what causes its wound and burn healing ability. The Southwest Institute's research also supports the Russian findings concerning the benefits of aloe vera as gum healer.

One of the big problems in utilizing aloe vera is purity, which is essential if the important biochemical elements are to be effective. Many aloe vera cosmetics are so chemicalized that the cellular activity is simply not there. Pure aloe vera gel or extract in a natural formula is what you should watch out for in your aloe vera cosmetics. I have found it be be an excellent ingredient for use in topical hair and skin care products--shampoos, hair conditioners, hair rinses, face moisturizers, celltherapy creams, hand and body lotions, and of special importance in sun protection products. Aloe vera gel can definitely be considered a good cosmetic ingredient.

Whether or not Cleopatra used clay, henna, and aloe vera is unimportant really. It's fun to speculate how the legendary Egyptian queen may have used these natural cosmetic ingredients, but it's much more rewarding to see them at work on your own skin and hair!

organitoons

THE COCONUT REALLY CONTAINED ALL THOSE CHEMICALS COSMETIC LABELS CLAIM AS "DERIVED FROM COCONUTS" THE POOR COCONUT WOULD HAVE TO BE LABELED AS "MAY BE HAZARDOUS TO YOUR HEALTH!"

COCONUTS ARE BEING LABELED JUST LIKE COSMETICS!

NATURAL COCONUTS & COSMETICS

SPECIAL

S. Meadows

THIS COCONUT CONTAINS: Sodium Lauryl Sulfate, Cocamide DEA, Triethanolamine (TEA), TEA-Lauryth Sulfate, PEG 100 Stearate, Stearalkonium Chloride, Sodium C14-16 Olefin Sulfonate, Cocamidopropyl Betaine, Cetereth-20, Isopropyl Palmitate, Sodium Laureth Sulfate, Amphoteric-2, etc.

CHAPTER VI

Aromatherapy, Thalassotherapy, and Phytotherapy

Or

Roses are Red, Violets are Blue, You Can Put Them in a Vase, Or Rub Them On Your Face

What is the first thing we do when we pick up a cosmetic? Whether it's a shampoo, a face cream, or a cake of soap, we all put it to our noses and take a big whiff. As far as cosmetics are concerned, this is an automatic olfactory response. Only after we've smelled a product will we turn the bottle or package around and read about what's in it.

An interesting complication to this process is that today we have so-called "fragrance-free" products that are not supposed to have a fragrance, but guess what most people do who buy fragrance-free products? They open the bottle and smell the contents and then turn it around and read the label. We are all victims of habit, and one habit, as far as cosmetics are concerned, is to smell them even if they're not supposed to have a smell.

Fragrance-free products are sold with the advertising hype that if you buy them you will be safe from those awful fragrance chemicals that pollute other products. It is true that more people are allergic to fragrance ingredients than to any other type, but it is not true that a fragrance-free product does not have a fragrance material in it. Cosmetics will obviously retain the odor of their combination of ingredients, and even fragrance-free products can contain substances that could be considered fragrance ingredients, based on their composition and their purpose in the cosmetic. The purpose of a fragrance is not always to give a specific odor but to perhaps also mask some malodorous ingredients. Since the FDA labeling law does not require specific listing of fragrance in a product, this masking ingredient in the fragrance-free product is not listed on the label or is not recognized by the consumer as a fragrance. Those who read the ingredients list do not see the word fragrance anywhere on the label and are pleased that they're buying a pure, less allergenic product. When they smell the product, this intuition is reinforced because they smell a type of fragrance that smells like "no fragrance," i.e., a fresh or neutral odor, but this is as much a fragrance as any other.

However, a product could be considered fragrance-free naturally if it contains no ingredients that were added to make it smell a particular way for marketing reasons or to mask the odor of other ingredients. Whatever fragrance the cosmetic possesses will then be one of its characteristics. Let me give you an example: if you have a menthol cleansing cream, it will smell like menthol. It is fragrance-free because you did not add the menthol because of its fragrance.

Menthol is an essential oil that acts as a natural disinfectant. Other essential oils have their own particular fragrances and therapeutic values as well and are the sources of fragrance in the best perfumes. There is even a blend of essential oils offered as a "medicated fragrance" which is put into products to give them a medicated odor (a menthol-camphor type smell). This odor is meant to make you feel that this particular cream is going to help your complexion, and, in fact, the essential oils in the medicated fragrance are very beneficial for blemished or problem skin.

Some products have such an obnoxious odor that they are almost impossible to mask, and to try to do so makes them smell even worse. For example, cold wave solutions and thioglycolate depilatories are a class of chemicals that can never be given a pleasant odor, and cosmetic manufacturers always add a mask of some sort. Cold wave chemicals are so malodorous that they literally make your eyes water from the stench even if they have a perfume oil of the strongest type put in to mask the odor.

A cosmetic classically has a beautiful odor because it is created to make us more beautiful, or so the marketing logic seems to tell us, but I don't buy this excuse because it could be the reason that cosmetics are so frequently made more synthetic by the addition of a synthetic fragrance. Remember, the first thing you do is smell the product, so you have already sent a message to the cosmetic manufacturer that you will base your buy on how it smells. By the same analogy, you have been told that if it smells bad and tastes bad it is probably "good for you." The Norman Rockwell drawing of a kid being given a spoonful of castor oil and holding his nose with his eyes closed tells the whole story. It may look, smell, and even taste bad, but it will be good for you. This assumption can be just as erroneous as the other. These assumptions, however, are exactly why a medical skin cream smells medicated and a fragrance-free product smells as if it has no fragrance. Whether the product smells pure, antiseptic, or beautiful, its fragrance indicates why it's being purchased, but not necessarily whether it's natural or not. An avocado face cream can get its fragrance from a treeful of avocados or from a lab, but either way it will be green and smell like avocados because that is what the consumer expects.

In the cosmetic industry, fragrance is considered to belong to the merchandising area and not to the chemist. Although it is a part of the formula, fragrance is, like color, considered packaging, or at least a point-of-purchase consideration. Cosmetics are thus given the "board treatment" and passed under the sniffing noses of the ad men around the long table. I have found, however, that a natural cosmetic formulated without synthetic fragrances does not need the approval of the ad men sniffers. Only essential oils are used in natural cosmetics, which have a therapeutic as well as an esthetic value.

Aromatherapy, thalassotherapy, and phytotherapy are the therapeutic use of essential oils from land and sea herbs. These oils have powerful benefits that were well-known to ancient practitioners of these sciences but are practically unknown today. In this chapter I will discuss the various uses, traditional and modern, of essential oils in hair, skin, and body care products.

Essential Oils

The raw materials used in fragrances and as important active ingredients in cosmetics are essential oils. Essential oils may be either natural or synthetic, but even the natural oils are not known in their pure form in nature and must, in most cases, be isolated from natural products. From the plant kingdom we have essential oils (obtained by distillation or expression), flower oils, resins, gums, and exudations. From the animal kingdom we have musk oil and fish oils. From the chemical lab we have derivatives from plant materials and synthetic organic substances.

A cosmetic can contain just one or two of these raw materials, but more than likely it will contain dozens in a blend which is often called a compound or a perfume oil. This blend of many different ingredients can cause a problem if you have an allergic reaction to that blend because it can be difficult to isolate the one that is causing the problem, but most of the natural cosmetics I have seen contain only a few essential oils which are usually included for a therapeutic value rather than an odor to please the ad man's nose. A natural cosmetic chemist views essential oils not as perfume but as the oil obtained by the steam distillation of plants which can serve a purpose in a product other than a simple esthetic purpose (although this is also a consideration). The oils that come from flowers are known as "absolutes" and are used almost exclusively for the fragrance effect in a product. In Europe, however, where aromatherapy is valued by massage and facial professionals, the aromatic absolutes are recorded as having benefits for the skin, hair, and body, the best known of which are jasmine, rose, lavender, and camomile.

Little is known of the chemical make-up of essential oils because they are usually considered just "perfume oils," but we will single out and discuss a few that are used in the field of aromatherapy, thalassotherapy, and even in nutrition. It will be helpful to keep in mind that I will discuss essential oils from the natural cosmetic viewpoint and not as a perfumer.

The Olfactory Response

What if you picked up a bottle of vitamin pills and smelled them as you do a cosmetic? You probably wouldn't want to buy them. This is especially true of the B vitamins which have an unpleasant odor. I have compounded many natural cosmetics that did not smell like pretty perfumed products simply because I wanted certain natural elements that had an excellent effect on the hair and skin. What I learned in time was that by using essential oils I could blend or compound a natural cosmetic just as a perfumer uses essential oils to make a perfume, but I also discovered that many of the essential oils had a positive therapeutic effect when absorbed into the body as well as topically (and most essential oils have fantastic absorption abilities). Some of the products I compounded with essential oils are bath oils, massage oils and creams, but I also discovered the oils had their place in other hair and skin care products as well.

Olfaction is the perception of odors. It is a complex chemical sense which works with the substance being smelled (*odorvector*), the organ being stimulated (*odorceptor*), and the brain which receives and interprets the stimulation. The olfactory organ is located on the lateral nasal wall and covers an area of about five hundred square millimeters. Within this olfactory membrane are olfactory glands, olfactory cells, nasal mucus that contains olfactory fibers, and olfactory nerves. Not only do odorants affect the olfactory receptors in that we smell the substance in the air but also through the skin as well, and this entire process is related to taste.

Before we move on to discuss *aromatherapy*, I think it is a good idea to understand a little bit about the chemical process that causes you to be affected by an odor. It is an enzyme activity which conditions the biochemical reactions. In order to perceive a sweet odor as sweet, and a sour odor as sour, and a rose as a rose or a lemon as a lemon, two things are at work. First, the brain is involved in a complex memory association which is neither completely understood nor easily explained. The olfactory sense of newborn babies is so well-developed, for example, that they not only perceive odors but can distinguish them. In adulthood a slight odor can recall a chain of events dating back to early childhood, and the perception of the odor can even bring on a total recall of the previously experienced odor (Think of Proust and his enormous novel *Remembrance of Things Past*, partially based on the memory of the odor and taste of a tea-dipped cookie). Smell acuity varies little, and the variations that do exist are based on smell consciousness and association (a mental process). The "sensitive nose" is merely one that has been cultivated to perceive minor variations in odors. An example of this is most obviously the "nose" of a perfume company. For example, I have seen my friend, Fred Peronne of Peronne Perfumes and Flavors, Bunker Hill, West Virginia, put a bottle of perfume to his nose and reel off the many compounds it contained. Another example is a wine taster who can by smell and taste tell the harvest and the label of a particular wine. There are also coffee experts who can through smell alone perceive individual coffee blends that others could not perceive through taste. The second process involved in our sense of smell does not take place in the intellect, but in the biochemical activity that results from the chemistry of the odor we have perceived. The odor produces its effect by a chemical action involving biocatalysts or enzymes. The odorants are absorbed upon the enzymes at the olfactory cells' surface, which produces nerve impulses as a result of the chemical reactions catalyzed by these enyzmes.

Sometimes cosmetic chemists who compound with essential oils or add them to their product batch become unable to smell what they are mixing. This can cause, if they do not follow the formula exactly, an incorrect amount of essential oil in a product. The cosmetic chemist may say he has olfactory fatigue from smelling the same strong smell too long, but this is simply sensory adaptation. The adaptation of the sense of smell changes as soon as you smell an odor, and the longer you experience the odor the more difficulty there is in sensing it at all. Yet this phenomenon is neither sensory loss nor a fatigue of your olfactory response, but a normal part of the way you experience an odor, whether you are a cosmetic chemist or a person who wears perfume or aftershave. One incident that often occurs when you wear a scent is that somebody remarks how much he or she likes it, and at that moment you realize you can't smell it at all. Then, thinking it has worn off, you put on more, and perhaps more, and then somebody can pick up your scent across a crowded room! The reason for this is that when you use your favorite cologne, your experience with the odor raises your perception of it so that very little is needed for you to get a strong impression of the smell, but, at the same time, just as with the cosmetic chemist who can't smell what he is mixing, your awareness of the odor wears off quickly, and the result is that you become unable to judge how much scent you are wearing. The correct way to use a perfume or cologne is to put it on the first time for your own perception, and establish the amount you are always going to use based on this first perception.

As far as perfumes, colognes, and aftershaves are concerned, the amount of odor the person perceives is based on what is known as its *threshold*, and there are different sorts of thresholds that correspond to different levels of recognition. The *absolute threshold*, for example, is the amount of an odorous substance needed to produce a barely noticeable odor that can't be identified. The *recognition threshold* is the amount of odorous substance needed to produce a just noticeable increase or decrease in the intensity of the odor. Many factors, however, affect how an odor is perceived. The conditions under which the odor is introduced and the formula both play an important part in threshold and perception. If, for example, you put the odorous material in a hot steaming tub of water or a facial steamer, the recognition threshold is greatly increased. It is for this reason that in the art of aromatherapy only drops of the essential oils are used in a vaporizer, though much more can be poured into the hands and massaged on the body. In aromatherapy formulas, the essential oils are used in an odorless vegetable oil such as peanut, jojoba, sunflower oils, etc., or in a natural odorless cream.

Aromatherapy

Aromatherapy is a type of health and beauty care in which aromatic essential oils of all kinds are used as active ingredients in various beauty preparations and in various treatments. The essential oils can be used as basic ingredients in a massage cream or oil, and thereby used to give a body or facial massage, to vaporize the skin as a fine mist or steam, or even, poured into a tub of water, to prepare a whirlpool bath or hot tub. There are really two functions expected in aromatherapy: the function of the aromatic principals of the oil as absorbed into the body through the olfactory membrane and cells and the calming or stimulating effects of the aromatic oils. Here is an example of a combination of essential oils that will produce relaxation in an aromatherapy bath: combine two drops of lavender oil, two drops of orange blossom oil, and one drop of rose oil; pour it into a hot tub of water, sit back, and relax. If you want a cooling summer aromatherapy bath, combine four drops of lemon oil, two drops of peppermint oil, and the juice of one half lemon.

The first aromatherapists were early physicians who employed aromatic oils in their practice, for example, during the 12th dynasty in Egypt when the use of scented unguents was popular. The early Greeks and Romans used essential oils in their steaming baths and aromatherapy massages. Today, when you have a cold or a clogged nose, and you put a medicated inhaler to your nose and draw the vapors into the olfactory cells, you are utilizing a modern application of aromatherapy. Certain essential oils are contained in the inhaler that give relief to the swollen membranes. The same is true when you use a home vaporizer to help congestion and a sore throat. The old herbal remedy of a chest rub is a form of aromatherapy at work as is the mustard plaster popular in early America.

From biblical references we are aware that aromatherapy was prevalent in ancient times. In the *Aquarian Gospel* (74:3), the healing of the sick was brought about by Jesus not only with the "laying on of hands," but with healing pools (baths) and anointing with oil. Throughout the Bible there are passages on essential oils. "Then took Mary a pound of ointment of spikenard, very costly, and anointed the feet of Jesus, and wiped his feet with her hair: and the house was filled with the odor of the ointment" (John 12:3).

One of the earliest books on essential oils and herbal medicine was written in 2650 B.C., *The Yellow Emperor's Classic of Internal Medicine* (translated by Ilza Veith, 1949). The Chinese are credited with discovering the use of musk which they believed to have healing powers. Perhaps it was Huang Ti (the author of *The Yellow Emperor*) who discovered herbal and animal musk. If so, he began the success of all the musk oil colognes you see on cosmetic counters and hear advertised on TV. Huang Ti's book deals not only with Oriental herbal medicine but is the first complete text on the art of acupuncture (See **ACUPUNCTURE** in this book). Today China still has "barefoot doctors" who use herbs and acupuncture to treat the sick, and the modern version of this ancient form of herbal medicine is found in herb shops throughout China, and in Chinatown in New York and San Francisco where herbs are sold loose or in capsules or tablets, and in health food stores (see **NATURAL TONGUE-TWISTERS** in this book).

Rene-Maurice Gattefosse, a French chemist working in his lab in the early 1900's, spilled boiling water on his hand. He quickly shoved his red throbbing hand into a beaker of lavender oil, and when the hand healed much sooner than mishaps of this kind usually do and without infection, he became interested in essential oils. One of the discoveries he made was that most of these natural oils have antiseptic properties superior to the antiseptic chemicals in use at that time. Gattefosse was the first man to coin the term "aromatherapy" and wrote a book on the subject (*Aromatherapie*, 1928). He was more interested in the cosmetic use of essential oils than in the internal use and wrote in his book, "the French chemists are concerned that the natural complexes should be utilized as complete building units without being broken up. Dermatological therapy would thus develop into 'Aromatherapy,' or a therapy employing aromatics, in a sphere of research opening vistas to those who have started to exploit it."

Gattefosse outlines the importance of using essential oils for their own sake and not to adulterate them with synthetic chemicals; he feels this is the main point of aromatherapy, but unfortunately most chemists have become strong believers in synthesizing natural substances and using the individual components of oils rather than the whole essence. True aromatherapy is, as Gattefosse points out, the use of the whole essence, or when combining oils, the combination of whole essences. When you purchase aromatherapy oils, read the label to be sure that the whole essences are used and that no synthetic chemicals are in the oil. Also be sure that the base for the oils is natural (i.e., jojoba, peanut, and sunflower oils, etc.). Aromatherapy massage creams should also be natural, and the base should be an essential fatty acid base.

Robert B. Tisserand wrote an excellent book (*The Art of Aromatherapy*, New York City: Inner Traditions International, Ltd., 1977), in which he recounts the history and use of essential oils and describes in detail twenty-nine essences with a list of their properties. He also has a chapter on yin and yang (see also **THE EAST AND WEST OF IT, THE YIN AND YANG OF IT** in this book).

Today skin care clinics use aromatherapy mainly for relaxation, but it is also an important part of a facial or hair treatment because herbal essential oils facilitate cellular nutrition and the reproduction of cells. Aromatherapy steam on the hair encourages hair growth and is a natural treatment for dull, dry, lackluster hair (see **THE NATURAL METHOD** in this book).

Some of the essential oils with agreeable odors and stimulating qualities are camomile (the one most often used in facial steamers), nutmeg, fennel, mint, ginger, sassafras, lavender, marjoram, rosemary, and sage.

The astringent essential oils tend to contract the skin and they are often used in the facial salon for people with large pores or oily skin. They are used alone, combined in an astringent tonic or toner, and are put into a facial steamer. The astringent oils are comfrey root, horse chestnut, lettuce, nettle, rhubarb, sandalwood, sumac, strawberry leaves, elm leaves, lemon, lime, orange, grapefruit, magnolia bark, sage, shepherd's purse, witch hazel, and alum root (the strongest astringent of all).

The antiseptic agents used for inhibiting or destroying bacteria are clove, heather, olive, sassafras, peppermint, eucalyptus (used today for congestion and throat problems), lavender, sandalwood, and thyme.

The aromatherapy oils that have a stimulating effect are eucalyptus, ginseng, rosemary, magnolia bark, mistletoe, wintergreen, fennel, thyme, lavender, spearmint, and sandalwood.

The skin is calmed and soothed by the following aromatherapy oils: almond, hollyhock, balm, lettuce, whitepond, lily root, comfrey root, camomile, pansy, jasmine, marjoram, aloe, jojoba, and ginseng.

Herbal oils with an excellent cleansing action are lovage root, lemongrass, geranium leaves, milfoil, and witch hazel.

Some aromatherapy oils that are emollients and can be used to soften and soothe the skin are almond, comfrey root, figs, aloe, hollyhock, marshmallow, jojoba, and olive leaves. Some essential oils that help to moisturize the skin are orange blossom, rosewater, rose hips, camomile flowers, rose petals, white willow bark, aloe vera, jojoba, and olive.

Aromatherapy oils that are healing agents include peppermint, camomile, rosemary, comfrey root, pansy, milfoil, elder flowers, lovage, aloe, primrose, jojoba, and wild daisy.

Aromatherapy Facial Massage

In this book are diagrams on a natural facial massage in the chapter on **The Natural Method of Skin Care** in which I give you a complete step-by-step skin care system that takes you from cleaning to moisturizing. Acupuncture points and aromatherapy (essential oils) are the basis of the facial massage used in **The Natural Method**. The steaming of the skin also uses aromatherapy when camomile or some other essential oil or misture of essential oils is put into the steam and also when the essential oils are massaged into the skin. This method is the ultimate in an aromatherapy facial treatment, and I have found that it has superb results on the skin.

The following essential oils have been suggested for the skin types listed: **normal skin** can benefit from avocado, grape, lemon, peach, wheat germ, jasmine, neroli, lavender, aloe, and camomile. **Dry skin** can benefit from avocado, carrot, melon, aloe, wheat germ, sunflower, jojoba, primrose, figs, almond, and olive. **Oily skin** can benefit from cabbage, lemon, strawberry, witch hazel, ginseng, eucalyptus, camphor, and pear. Blemished skin can be helped by grape, cabbage, camphor, juniper, and bergamot oil. **Mature skin** can benefit from aloe, apple, banana, wheat germ, and jojoba oil.

Aromatherapy Hair Care

In this book is a detailed chapter on *The Natural Method of Hair Care*, which features aromatherapy in the form of massaging and steaming the scalp with a hot jojoba oil treatment. The following essential oils have been used for hair care with good results: **greasy hair with dandruff** can benefit from henna (the non-coloring extract), cedarwood, cypress, juniper, kelp, rosemary, sage, witch hazel, primrose, and jojoba oil. Tisserand also suggests an aromatherapy mixture for dandruff: cedarwood, 7 parts; cypress, 10 parts, and juniper, 10 parts. He suggests that this mixture be diluted 3% in vegetable oil. Tisserand also has some aromatherapy oils on the market in a jojoba oil base.

The herb American Bearsfoot (*polymnia uvedalia*) has been suggested as a hair treatment for dry hair. The liquid extract of the herb is combined with lanolin and rubbed into the hair as a scalp treatment. Kelp is also considered a skin and hair treatment because of the presence of silicon which is an important food for the roots of the hair. An ample supply of silicon is believed to help prevent hair loss.

Another substance important to hair is the amino acid cystine which contributes to the strength of each hair strand (known as the cystine bridge). The cystine bridge can be destroyed by cold wave solutions and hair color. In aromatherapy, two herbs are very high in both silicon and cystine: coltsfoot (*Tussilago farfara*) and horsetail (*Equisetaceæ*). These two herbal oils should be used in hair tonics, creams, lotions, and shampoos. The oil or extract of coltsfoot and horsetail can be rubbed into the scalp for growth and repair.

Aromatherapy Body Care

The use of essential oils to massage the body goes back thousands of years. When massage is combined with essential oils, the benefits of both are greatly enhanced. I have always wondered why chiropractors do not use essential oils and creams with essential oils in their work and include a steamer or vaporizer. Another form of massage is the Swedish soft tissue massage first introduced in the nineteenth century by a Swedish professor named Ling who used various types of movements such as kneading, stroking, hacking, and cupping. A deeper massage is included in this system by using the thumbs (*petrissage*). The thumbs are also used to stimulate various points in acupressure. In stroking or *effleurage*, a slow gentle, rhythmic movement of the whole hand is used in an upward direction toward the heart. If done properly the stroking is almost a continuous movement without pause. When the pressure is strong, it has a deeper effect on blood circulation and muscular tissue, but when the pressure is lighter, it has an effect on the nervous system which is both pleasant and relaxing. Kneading, which is done with the whole hand in a squeezing and rolling motion, is almost never used in facial massages and very seldom in aromatherapy body massages.

Shiastu, the Japanese word for "finger pressure," is a cross between regular massage and acupuncture (acupressure). When it is combined with the use of essential oils, you have *shiatsu aromatherapy*. It works on the principle of *ch'i* (life force) and yin and yang; the massage is given to stimulate the energy flow within the body and the meridians in the body. This is a vigorous massage and can be painful because it is done along the meridians of the body.

The true aromatherapy massage uses neither the Swedish system nor the *shiatsu*; instead, it uses massage as a method to aid the penetration of the essential oils, to stimulate or relax the body, to treat the skin topically and the body via the pilo-sebaceous apparatus, and to treat via the acupuncture (acupressure) method with the principals of *ch'i* (see the chapter **DOES THE SKIN REALLY ABSORB AND USE NUTRIENTS?** in this book).

For the essential oils to penetrate, the skin should be clean and the lymphatic system should be free from congestion. Lymphatic stagnation causes aching muscles, cellulitis, obesity, swollen glands, and skin problems. Fasting can reduce toxicity and the stagnation of the lymphatic system, and an aromatherapy massage can help get the lymph flowing and free the congestion. The pores must be open for a good massage, so aromatherapy steam is often used and steaming towels (as in the Natural Method facial), but a friction massage will also begin the circulation needed for a good aromatherapy massage.

Before you apply the essential oil, give a fairly vigorous friction massage to the whole area with the palms. I believe in aromatherapy steam and feel that you can aim the steam at the area you are about to massage just as you do in a facial and then friction massage the area under warm steam (which includes an essential oil). If you don't use steam, then proceed with the friction massage. Pour the aromatherapy oil or cream into the palms and work between palms (use only as much as you need). Gently *effleurage* the whole area; that is, use a gentle, slow, rhythmic movement with the flat palms of the hands in an upward motion. If you are massaging the back, begin at the waist and move upward, and then move around to the head of the client and go downward the same way. Any good massage method can be combined with aromatherapy oils, creams, and steam. Never pour aromatherapy oils or creams directly on the skin but apply them to your hands, spread between your hands, and then massage onto the person's skin. This method ensures an even application of the oil or cream onto the client's body.

Aromatherapy oils for external use have two basic parts: the essential oil or essential oils and the carrier oil which is generally a plant oil. Many various vegetable oils can be used. If you are going to compound your own aromatherapy oil, one easy-to-get oil is a simple safflower oil. To the vegetable oil, add between 1% and 3% essential oil or essential oil mixture. To keep your aromatherapy oil from becoming rancid, do not mix the essential oils with the vegetable oil until you are ready to use it. You can, however, preserve the aromatherapy oil naturally (to a certain extent) by using some natural vitamin E to prevent oxidation of the oils. Some commercial vegetable oils contain the synthetic antioxidants BHA and BHT, so it is best to buy cold-pressed vegetable oils from a health food store for your base. Read the label to be sure it does not contain a synthetic preservative. Because the aromatherapy oil goes into your skin, both the carrier oil and the essential oils must be completely natural.

One superb oil to use as your carrier oil is jojoba oil, which is really more of a liquid wax than an oil. It has the one drawback, however, of being very expensive and difficult to obtain. You can get pure jojoba oil from your health food store in two ounce or four ounce bottles, and, if you wish, you may add your essential oil mixtures to this oil.

There is also the temptation to add more than 3% essential oil to your carrier oil, but do not do this. Essential oils are very strong, and more is not better. There is an allergic reaction to some essential oils by some people, though it is rare. When the correct amount of essential oil is used (2-3%), there is very little possibility of allergic reaction even to those natural essential oils that have been found to be more likely to cause allergic reactions. Of course, if you are allergic to an essential oil, you should stop using it.

Here are some of the carrier oils I suggest. I have used all of them at one time or another, and I like various ones for various reasons. *Peanut Oil* - This one is used all over the world as a massage oil and can act as a good natural base for your aromatherapy oil formulas. *Sunflower Oil* - This is a fine oil that is slightly more oily on the skin than peanut and leaves a smooth natural sheen when the massage is finished. *Avocado Oil* - This is an oil that is nourishing to the skin and is also a good carrier for the essential oils. *Wheat Germ Oil* - The only drawback to this oil is its very distinctive odor, but I have found that it works very well if combined with other carriers. It nourishes the skin and is also a natural preservative, due to its vitamin E content. *Jojoba Oil* - This oil is a superb carrier because, unlike other vegetable oils, it never becomes rancid. You must keep in mind, however, that the essential oil that you put into the jojoba oil can turn rancid. In order to naturally preserve your aromatherapy oil, add 10% wheat germ oil to your finished formula. This will keep it fresh for a longer period.

Here, step-by-step, is how to make an aromatherapy oil. We will formulate, for example, a massage oil for hair loss. Measure out 1 fluid ounce jojoba oil. Measure out the essential oils in a separate container thus: 20 drops juniper oil, 14 drops lavender oil, and 14 drops rosemary oil. Pour the jojoba oil into the essential oil mixture. This will give you approximately 3% essential oil to jojoba oil. To this add 90 drops wheat germ oil as a preservative. Put this mixture into a bottle and cap tightly. To use: apply to tips of fingers and massage well into scalp daily. You could also add coltsfoot and horsetail for the cystine content.

The above aromatherapy treatment is considered a massage oil because you massage it into your scalp, but a facial oil is also a massage oil. The ideal mixture for a facial massage oil is 1% or 10 drops essential oil for every ounce of vegetable oil. Skin tonics, which can be massaged onto the skin like a lotion or sprayed on the complexion in an atomizer spray, should be compounded of 5 drops of essential oil to every 100 grams of water. To steam the skin, or to add essential oils to a vaporizer, the same is true: 1 to 5 drops essential oil to every 100 grams of water in the steamer or vaporizer. If you want to put essential oils in a tub of hot water, add 5 or 10 drops to the tub of hot water.

Here is how you make a skin tonic water. Use only distilled water. Put one pint mineral water in a clean container. Combine the following oils in another container: 4 drops bergamot, 10 drops jasmine, 10 drops geranium, 7 drops rose, 6 drops lavender, 7 drops cypress, and 10 drops juniper. Pour this combined aromatherapy oil mixture into the pint of distilled water.

To use: shake well to mix oils with water. Apply to cotton and wipe face to remove any soap film after washing face. You can also spray on the skin as an herbal mineral water spray. Keep this formula refrigerated when not in use, and check it for mold occasionally.

Aromatherapy Massage Oil and Bath Mixture

Arthritis and Rheumatic Pain Massage Oil Formula. Measure out 1 ounce jojoba oil in a clean container. Add 90 drops of wheat germ oil to the jojoba oil. Add the following drops of essential oils to the jojoba and wheat germ mixture: 14 drops camphor, 14 drops eucalyptus, 14 drops rosemary. To use: massage oil on painful areas. If it seems too strong, you can add up to ½ ounce more jojoba oil. You can also increase strength and penetration by massaging oil on painful areas after a hot bath (which opens pores and increases the penetration of the oils).

Muscle Toner and Mild Aches Massage Oil Formula - Measure out 1 ounce jojoba oil in a clean container. Add 90 drops wheat germ oil to the jojoba oil. Add the following essential oils to the jojoba and wheat germ mixture: 20 drops geranium, 10 drops lavender, and 8 drops marjoram. This can be used as a general massage oil.

Massage Oil for Cellulitic Skin - Measure out two ounces jojoba oil in a bottle. Add the following oils to the jojoba oil: 10 drops birch, 10 drops ivy, 10 drops horse chestnut, 10 drops bladderwrack, 50 drops aloe juice. Shake well to mix. Add 180 drops wheat germ oil to the finished formula. Shake well before using.

Bath Oil for Cellulite - This formula is used right before you massage with anti-cellulite oils or creams. The amount shown is added directly to the bath water. Measure out ¼ ounce jojoba oil in a clean container. Add the following oils: 2 drops fennel, 4 drops juniper, 1 drop rosemary, 4 drops bladderwrack or ivy. Pour into hot bath and relax for twenty minutes or so. Massage affected areas with anti-cellulite skin oil formula.

Massage Oil for Wrinkled, Dry, Chapped, or Scaled Skin - Measure out 1 ounce jojoba oil. Add 90 drops wheat germ oil. Add the following essential oils: 4 drops geranium, 2 drops rose, 5 drops sandalwood, 10 drops horsetail, 5 drops cone flower, 4 drops ginseng, 5 drops St. John's Wort.

Freshener, Sedative, and Healing Massage Oil for Dry Delicate Skin - Measure out 1 ounce jojoba oil in a bottle. Add 90 drops wheat germ oil. Add the following essential oils to this mixture: 10 drops aloe, 10 drops mallow, 5 drops marigold, 5 drops camomile, and 5 drops linden tree oil.

Aromatherapy Ointment for Cuts and Bites - Combine 2 ounces jojoba oil with ½ ounce beeswax. Melt this mixture and add the following oils to the hot mixture: 12 drops bergamot, 6 drops eucalyptus, 12 drops lavender, and 90 drops wheat germ oil. Stir well, put into jar, and allow the ointment to cool in the refrigerator.

I have suggested jojoba oil in these formulas, but any vegetable oil can be used. You could also use vaseline to make an ointment instead of the beeswax and jojoba mixture, but vaseline is a mineral oil product and will decrease absorption. I have found that natural extracts do not work well in petrochemical and synthetic chemical bases. Keep it natural!

The perennial problem with natural substances is that they are almost impossible for consumers to obtain. Unfortunately, synthetic chemicals are more available and cheaper than natural extracts, and therefore few manufacturers are really interested in using or selling natural extracts (except as a label eye-catcher). We have listed the addresses of a few manufacturers and distributors of essential oils in our "Resources" Section at the back of this book. The unique aspect of working with essential oils, however, is that you can leave an oil out or put in another one, and you will still have an aromatherapy product.

Thalassotherapy: Aromatherapy From The Sea

Thalassotherapy is the name given to the art of using sea water and sea plants for therapeutic results. The word originally referred to taking a sea voyage to cure an illness. The French physician Bonnardiere coined the phrase from the Greek *thalassa*, meaning "sea." Dr. Bonnardiere's advice to his patients was to get some sea air for maintaining good health, and it is true that many people still have a desire to get away to a sea resort for their health. Sea water therapy is used for rehabilitation, arthritis, and even complexion improvement, and many Europeans spas cater to those who go to the sea for their beauty and health. The shores of France, England, West Germany, Belgium, Spain, Italy, Yugoslavia, and the Soviet Black Sea are lined with spas where complete facials are given based on thalassotherapy skin care products, sea water baths, jet sprays of warm sea water, seaweed wraps for treating cellulite as well as aches and pains, and internal sea herb drinks.

Why are people attracted to these spas? Many return year after year. The fact is that thalassotherapy really works. In England the use of thalassotherapy for arthritis pain was also found effective for reducing the lumps of toxic fat called cellulite.

Dr. Raymond Denniel has explained how he thinks sea extracts work when applied externally in combination with other herbal extracts. "They [seaweed essential oils] have specific properties, but all share one common attribute: the ability to pass through the cutaneous [skin] barrier, which up to now was a difficult obstacle to cross for chemical molecules no matter how elaborate they are. These essential oils act as vectors for the diverse ions contained in algaes, by increasing the speed of their penetration and perhaps their fixation around certain organs. In effect, it was proven that following an application to the skin, the essences are found in the bloodstream within minutes or fixed on one of the organs to which it was destined" (*Aesthetics World*, 3 [August 1982]).

There are over 20,000 varieties of seaweed, but some of the most used species include *Fucus*, *Ascophyllum, Laminaria, Chondria, Crispus,* and *Lithotamia*. They contain alginic acid, amino acids, polysaccharides, iodine in organic and inorganic combinations, minerals (magnesium, potassium, and calcium), and vitamins (A, B, C, D, etc.). Seaweed contains all the nutritional elements contained in the sea, and this is the reason that spas and cosmetic products are using thalassotherapy as an important basis for their treatments and products.

France has developed a method of removing the essential oils from seaweeds with a process called *crybroyage*, a form of cryogenics, which lowers the temperature of the seaweed cells to 50° C. and literally explodes the plant cell walls to release the active essential oils. These essential oils are used in various cosmetic products and are even more popular as thalasso-therapy massage creams for weight loss and cellulite. It is possible to combine the seaweed anti-cellulite extracts with the earth's herbal anti-cellulite extracts to create a thalassotherapy-aromatherapy massage cream with excellent slimming action containing, among other ingredients, seaweed complex, arnica, birch, ivy, escin, horse chestnut, and camomile. *Crybroyage* or *microburst* (as it is often called to suggest the "bursting out" of the essential oils) seaweed extract products will stimulate circulation, attract oxygen from the skin's lower levels and enhance its absorption, and, by combining the treatment with steam (such as a bath, moisturizer, or mask), increase capillary action.

Bladderwrack (*Fucus vesiculosis*), one of the algaes found on submerged rocks in the northern seas where it drifts from the Strait of Gibraltar, is used in the manufacture of kelp. The thallus of this seaweed is used to make a glycolic extract which contains 0.1% iodine; this is used to make a massage cream for cellulite. It is also used in foam baths along with other sea herbs to give the effect of a bubbling sea bath. Some authorities believe that bladderwrack can reduce obesity by stimulating the thyroid gland, and in 1750, a jelly was made to rub on the body and reduce obesity through massage. Dr. Russell used bladderwrack jelly in this manner and also was reported to be successful in dispersing scrofulous tumors by rubbing in the oil of bladderwrack and then rinsing the areas with sea water. Dr. Duchesne-Dupart (1862) found, while experimenting on cases of chronic psoriasis, that weight was reduced with bladderwrack without injuring the health. Seaside chemists sell *Sea Pod Liniment*, which is the juice of the bladderwrack in their own secret formulas. Tablets made from bladderwrack are said to be excellent treatments for obesity.

Agar-agar, a seaweed with strong jelling characteristics, is often used as the base to make "sea products," and bladderwrack is often added to this jelly to make cosmetics that soothe the skin and condition the hair.

Laminaria digitata is an interesting species of seaweed in many ways. I have found that it works very well in moisturizers and skin creams because of its ability to attract moisture. *Laminaria* are strong and tenacious, from two to twelve inches long and an inch or more wide. If you store this seaweed for years and then take it out and let it absorb moisture, it will expand to its original size as if it had never been stored. One reason that this seaweed is such an excellent humectant is that *laminaria*, like all plants that grow immersed in water, have thin cells so that water can be freely exchanged and the special pores (*stomata*) aid in this exchange process. But seaweed also have the capacity to conserve water in that they contain cells that are coated with a mucilage that restricts evaporation.

The algaes, red, green, and brown, have many uses and surprises. From red algae, for example, both pectin and carrageen (thickening agents) are obtained for use in foods and cosmetics. One species of green algae, *Trentepohlia*, provides us with an indication of atmospheric pollution because of its sensitivity to gases. The brown algae is the most prevalent; it gets its brown color from a pigment (*fucoxanthin*) which masks the green chlorophyll. The brown algaes (i.e., *Hormosira banksii, Lessonia fuccescens, Pelvetia canaliculata, Sargassum Fucus,* and *Sargasso*) are exposed at low tide which is why they can wind up wrapped around your ankles or on rocks. They are covered with a mucilage, and the swollen bulges in the stems are the *vesicles* where male and female gametes form. The genetic material (DNA) which occurs in humans as chromosomes within the cell nuclei is a direct fusion of genetic material in the seaweed, and this material, plant DNA, is present in the essential oils of seaweed.

It is remarkable how similar plant skin is to human skin. Both are comprised of 90% water which indicates the importance of this compound to plants as well as to all living organisms. The surface of plant tissue (leaves) is covered with a protective wax just as our own skin is covered with an oily substance which acts as an acid mantle. Also, the plant has pores (*stomata*) just as human skin does, and in each case these pores permit the organism to breathe. The outer skin of humans is called the epidermis, which in plants is called the cuticle. The plant cuticle is basically a sponge whose pores are filled with wax. The plant's inner skin is called the cutin; below this layer are pectin and a cellulose cell wall. This structure is comparable to our own collagen and collagenic fibrils. In plants, the pectin is interwoven with the outer cell walls allowing flexibility (similar to human soluble collagen). On the surface of the plant, the wax is visible as a "bloom" but is also in the pores, again as is the sebum of human skin. In each case, the wax has a similar function--to hold in moisture. If you removed this coating, large amounts of water would evaporate. The cuticle of the plant controls the exchange of water and nutrients between the plant and its environment. Just as with our own skin, the plant allows a certain amount of water to evaporate on the surface to prevent overheating in strong sunlight. More specifically, the plant skin has developed guard cells that allow the pores of the plant to vary their shapes. In a humid state, the pore is fully open, but in a dry state, the pore closes to retain its moisture and, at the same moment, it increases its wax coating. This can keep the plant alive for a while, but in time it would die. Similarly, on a hot day our own sweat glands release as much as three gallons of water to keep us cool.

Plant and human skin resemble one another both in function and structure; it is therefore not surprising that the balance elements found in seawater and sea herbs are very similar to the chemical make-up of human plasma. Many of the nutrients found in both sea herbs and land herbs are nutrients needed by the skin, hair, and internal organs. The concentration, however, of these trace elements in seaweed is ten times greater than that of earth-grown herbs. Thus, the use of seaweed extracts in health and beauty products, either alone or in combination with algae or earth plant extracts, superbly nourishes the body. We could call this aroma-therapy-algotherapy-thalassotherapy (if it weren't such a long name) because these extracts enhance human functions that are similar to their own.

Avocado Oil

The avocado pear (*Persea Americana*) grows on a tree that reaches a height of about sixty feet; it is native to tropical America, including Mexico and Central America. The Mexican avocado is grown in southern California, and the larger West Indian avocado is grown in Florida.

Avocado oil, obtained from the pulp of the fruit, stands almost alone in contrast to other commercial vegetable oils in that, when used in cosmetics, it does not serve simply as an oil base but is also considered an active ingredient. The active ingredients in one kilogram of avocado oil are approximately 20,000 I.U. vitamin A, 40,000 I.U. vitamin D, 300 I.U. vitamin E, 2% protein, 6-9% carbohydrates and sugars, amino acids, glycerides of oleic, linoleic, and palmitoleic acids, and between 20-40 grams of unsaponifiable substances (Unsaponifiable means that the substance can't be decomposed into an acid, alcohol, or salt).

The therapeutic value of avocado oil was formerly judged by its vitamin content, but more recent studies attribute avocado's benefits to its unsaponifiable substances. Parasitic skin damage and eczemas benefit from the use of avocado preparations because of these substances, and the oil also accelerates crusting and the skinning over of wounds. Recently, cosmetic formulators are also considering avocado oil for hair care treatments due to the sterols contained in the oil, but ancient herbalists have traditionally used avocado to stimulate hair growth. The combination of the unsaponifiable substances and the phytosterols gives the oil a high spreadability and the cosmetics containing avocado oil not only cover a large area but are easily absorbed by the skin.

Various forms of sclerodermas (*sclero*, hardening or thickening; *derma*, skin) have been treated and improved by topical application of the unsaponifiable substances in avocado oil during long-term treatment. It is believed that this improvement is due to the softening effect these substances give to hardened and inelastic tissue. The pulp and the oil can be used to create massage creams, muscle oils, and hair products. A pharmaceutical preparation from avocado seed oil has been patented for use in the treatment of sclerosis of the skin, pyorrhea, arthritis, and other skin conditions. (H. Thiers, *Neth. Appl. 6,601,888, 1966*).

Calendula Oil

Calendula blossoms (*Calendula officinale*) have been praised by herbalists of the past for every imaginable injury and damage to skin tissue. Slow healing wounds, burns, sunburns, eczemas, tears or cuts, abrasions, chapped or chafed skin areas, inflamed mucous membranes, and bedsores have all been successfully treated with a poultice of calendula blossoms. According to phytotherapeutic (*phyto* - plant) literature, success has been observed with accelerated closing of wounds, the rapid subsiding of an inflammatory reaction, and the renewing of healing tissue in the case of serious burns. In ancient times, calendula was also used for beautifying purposes, especially for toning the skin.

Calendula extracts exert the following overall effects: they stimulate the formation of new tissue, their anti-inflammatory properties are soothing to the skin, and they gently promote blood circulation. The oil must be extracted by a gentle process in soya oil, and no synthetic solvents should be used.

Carrot Oil

Carrot seed oil is obtained by steam distillation and carrot root oil is obtained by solvent extraction. Both oils are high in beta carotene and vitamin A. The oil has about 3.3 million I.U. per kilogram of pro-vitamin A; in addition to carotene and carotenoids, the oil also contains tocopherols (vitamin E). Though carrot oil is used mostly as a fragrance component in soaps, detergents, creams, lotions, and perfumes, the root oil can also be used in sunscreens due to its high content of carotene and vitamin A.

Carrot oil is used as a flavor ingredient in many major food products as well as alcoholic and non-alcoholic beverages in low levels of about 0.003%. It is also a natural food color because of the yellow carotene content. When mixed with the green extract of nettles, the yellow carrot oil creates a natural cosmetic color of green that is also beneficial to the skin. Very little of this lovely mixture is needed in a facial cream or body lotion, but it contributes to an excellent moisturizing cream in the correct formula.

It has already been well-documented that vitamin A or its provitamin carotene is indispensable to the body in maintaining its metabolic processes. If the vitamin A balance in the body is disturbed, several functional disorders such as night blindness, eye diseases, bone malformation, and so forth, can develop. Dermatologically, such vitamin A deficiencies show up as thickening skin, excessive drying, elevated pigmentation, the formation of wrinkles, and the defective function of the sebaceous and sweat glands. Hair growth is also impaired by a deficiency of vitamin A, and the growth cycle of the hair is disturbed to the extent that loss can set in. Vitamin A exerts a direct influence on the *epithelium* (any body covering, e.g., skin or the covering on internal membranes), and a deficiency will show up here before any other organ is affected. The skin thus is an indicator for an orderly vitamin A balance (which is also true of certain other vitamins and minerals such as zinc).

Taken internally, provitamin A is converted into vitamin A in the liver and intestines with the aid of enzymes and therefore exerts the same biological factors as vitamin A. When carrot oil is used in a cosmetic, provitamin A is similarly converted into vitamin A in the sebaceous gland cells of the skin. Studies have demonstrated that well-known vitamin A deficiency symptoms of the skin can be compensated by percutaneous applications of cosmetic preparations containing carrot oil. As little as 0.5% and as much as 5.0% can be used in cosmetics for the skin and hair with positive results.

External application of products containing carrot oil accelerates the formation of new cells. It protects the external layers of the skin and counteracts cornification of skin and hair follicles. It stimulates the secretion of sebum and perspiration, without increasing these secretions above normal. The skin is thereby protected from scaling and the hair from becoming brittle.

Carrot oil gives best results to skin that does not secrete sufficient sebum, such as dry, chapped, and scaling skin, but because of carrot oil's general beneficial skin and hair properties, it can be used on non-problem hair and skin with protective benefits.

Castor Oil

Just in the name of the castor oil plant are several millennia of history and a whole world of geography! The castor oil plant (*Ricinus communis*) is native to India where it has several ancient Sanscrit names, of which the most ancient is *Eranda*. The botanical name *Ricinis* means dogtick which describes the markings of the seeds of the plant, but the name *castor* was given to the plant in Jamaica, where it was called *Agnus castus*, although there is a European plant called this which has no similarities to the castor oil plant. The seeds form in a pod that when dry are crushed between huge rollers. The crushed seeds are then placed in hempen cloths and pressed in an hydraulic press. The oil obtained from the press is mixed with water and boiled; the mucilaginous matter is strained and then bleached in the sun. A pressing of the seeds yields 25-35% oil, which is remarkably stable and does not turn rancid easily. The oil is exported from Calcutta, but can also be obtained from Brazil and China. The Chinese have a method of removing the medicinal properties from castor oil which makes it suitable for other purposes.

The main objection to castor oil taken internally is its taste and the fact that it can produce a nauseous feeling when taken, but as an herbal medicine castor oil is highly regarded, especially as a laxative for children and the aged, but it should not be used in cases of chronic constipation. How castor oil works is unknown, but in India, when mixed with citron ointment, it has been used for years as a topical application for leprosy.

Castor oil has some use in cosmetics for lipsticks, hair grooming products, ointments, creams, lotions, transparent soaps, and suppository bases. It has an excellent lubricating quality and has been used for years in China, India, Egypt, and Europe for sores and abscesses. Because castor oil has excellent absorption qualities, care should be taken when mixing it with other ingredients as they will be quickly absorbed into the body with the oil. Castor oil has triglycerides of ricinoleic acid, linoleic acid, oleic acid, stearic acid, and dihydroxystearic acid. These fatty acids make the oil soothing to the skin and the presence of hydroxy acid gives the oil its characteristically high vicosity.

Leading You Down The Primrose Path

The evening primrose (*Oenothera biennis*) has yellow flowers that open only in the dark. The old saying that you are "following the primrose path" means that you are leading a life of irresponsible hedonism, but I am going to take you down the primrose path for a different purpose. We are going to find out about that yellow flower that can cure brittle nails, treat eczema, moisturize the skin, break up psoriasis lesions, condition the hair, help arthritics, hyperactive children, alcoholics, women with premenstrual syndrome, schizophrenics and multiple sclerosis patients. Evening primrose oil sounds like a medicine show snake oil, but there is research that indicates that it could be helpful for all the various problems that I have listed. Remember one thing as we walk along the primrose path, however: some of the benefits of evening primrose oil I know from my own research, but some are simply the published results of researchers, some of whom have used animal experiments which are never reliable.

In early 1981, people began going into health food stores to buy the oil of evening primrose flowers in capsules because some researchers had documented claims that it would do a great variety of things. I had been working with this unique oil for cosmetic purposes for some time, but now it was being sold as a health aid. The first run on evening primrose oil was due to its reputation as a diet aid. It was said that people who took as little as 0.6 to 5.0 milligrams would lose weight even if they didn't change their diet, and even if they didn't lose weight, they didn't gain any weight. I had one unique call from a woman who said that she had lost twenty-five pounds by taking evening primrose oil for skin problems. It worked on her skin problem, she said; in fact, it made her skin beautiful, but she lost weight as well. Other people have told me that they lost no weight at all. I am always suspicious of weight loss products and don't accept the weight loss claims for evening primrose oil. On the other hand, if you took it and lost weight, then it works for you.

One company in England called Efamol, Inc., manufactured evening primrose oil and distributed it through the General Nutrition Stores and a distributor called "Health Under the Sun" in the United States. Other companies packaging evening primrose oil include Evening Primrose Oil Company of England and Naudicelle, Ltd., in Canada. As the popularity of this oil grew, more and more manufacturers have entered the evening primrose business, but it is an expensive oil. One of the least expensive prices I could find was $17.75 per pound wholesale.

Evening primrose oil is extremely high in essential fatty acids, commonly known as the vitamin F complex, consisting of linoleic acid, linolenic acid, and arachidonic acid. Linoleic acid is the one most commonly found in the food we eat, and the other two fatty acids can be synthesized from it, provided certain vitamins and minerals are present. An approximate analysis of evening primrose oil is 65-75% linoleic acid, 8-10% gamma-linolenic acid (GLA), 9-26% oleic acid, and 0-6% other fatty acids. Linoleic acid you will recognize as one of the essential fatty acids mentioned above, oleic acid is a common constituent of many animal and vegetable fats, but what on earth, you ask, is gamma-linolenic acid? Dr. David Horrobin, one of the early researchers working with evening primrose oil, published scientific papers claiming that the evening primrose oil is beneficial due to the high GLA content in the oil which occurs naturally in only one other source: mother's milk. Drinking evening primrose oil or mother's milk is not the only way the body has to obtain this very important substance. GLA is normally formed in the body as part of the process of manufacturing prostaglandins, hormone-like substances which contribute to the control of every organ of the body. Evening primrose oil, with its high GLA content, supplies to the body one of the ingredients essential for prostaglandins (PGs), thus seeming to speed up the manufacturing process by eliminating one of the steps. The process of synthesizing GLA and hence PGs is interrupted in many people because they are consuming the wrong kinds of fats. Saturated fats will destroy the essential fatty acids, as will heat and exposure to air; the presence of these factors will inhibit the production of PGs. Other inhibitors to the production of GLA are the consumption of alcohol and dietary deficiencies of pyridoxine (B_6), niacin (B_3), ascorbic acid (C), or zinc, which are also necessary to the PG-producing process. The difficulty could also be genetic and not related to any of the other difficulties. But whether you get your GLA from evening primrose oil, mother's milk, or an abundance of linoleic acid in your diet, the GLA will not go on to produce PGs if the other nutrients are not present.

What do the prostaglandins do? It is not known exactly what all the PGs do because there are so many of them, but an example of one is PGE_1, which has already been proven to prevent thrombosis, lower blood pressure, open up blood vessels, and relieve the pain of angina. Dr. Ulf von Euler of Sweden and Dr. M. W. Goldblatt, working independently, discovered PGs and their effect on reducing blood pressure in the 1930's. Because it was thought at that time that the body could easily produce PGs, little was done with their discoveries, but we know now that this is not always true, and if your intake of the correct essential fatty acids or any of the other nutrients needed for the process is deficient, your body will also be deficient in PGs.

PGs also have quite a bit to do with brain activity as certain amounts are concentrated in areas of the brain and stimulate the release of substances known as neurotransmitters. The neurotransmitters can trigger the release of a whole slew of biochemicals which have specific behavioral or biochemical effects which make loops and reflex arcs similar to a switchboard except that there are an infinite number of "area codes." The PGs' effect on brain activity is probably the reason that an intake of GLA (in evening primrose oil) has decreased hyperactivity in children, and this effect is also being investigated as a means to slow down the degenerative process of multiple sclerosis.

But GLA is only one of the ingredients in the manufacture of PGs. The three series of PGs are based on the essential fatty acids linoleic acid, arachidonic acid, and alpha-linolenic acid. These parent compounds are then acted on by enzymes; linoleic acid becomes GLA and then PGE_1, arachidonic acid becomes PGE_2, and alpha-linolenic acid becomes eicosapentaenoic acid (EPA) and then PGE_3. However, the production of PGE_1 and PGE_3 may be deficient and cause an excess of PGE_2. And, because some of the characteristics of PGE_2 are opposite those of PGE_1, (for example, PGE_1 inhibits blood clotting, while PGE_2 accelerates it), unhealthy conditions such as blood clots and high blood pressure may result. If all this seems extremely confusing to you, perhaps the table on the following page will be helpful.

The relationship between PGE_1 and PGE_2 is very important, and there has been research to support the idea that PGE_1 limits the amount of PGE_2, and that a deficiency of PGE_1 permits overproduction of PGE_2 with unpleasant results. In 1981 Dr. John R. Vane of Wellcome Research Laboratories in England discovered that aspirin blocked the last step in the body's synthesis of PGE_2, which suggests that this class of PGs is involved in pain, inflammation, and fever. Aspirin thus works negatively to prevent the formation of PGE_2 without stimulating the production of PGE_1 which would naturally control the amount of PGE_2 present in the body. PGE_2 has also been linked to the improper function of certain lymph cells (T-suppressor

Prostaglandin Synthesis From Essential Fatty Acids

Linoleic Acid	Arachidonic Acid	Alpha-Linolenic Acid
$\longleftarrow$ pyridoxine (B$_6$)		
Gamma-Linolenic Acid		
zinc $\longrightarrow$		
Dihomogammalinolenic Acid		Eicosapentaenoic Acid
$\longleftarrow$ ascorbic acid		
$\longleftarrow$ niacin (B$_3$)		
PGE$_1$	PGE$_2$	PGE$_3$

This chart makes it clear that we can form the PGs without supplemental GLA (found in evening primrose oil) in any of the EFA series, but the researchers' idea is that GLA may speed up the process or perhaps be for those who cannot form the GLA within their own bodies. It could also be postulated that if we had an intake of arachidonic acid or eicosapentaenoic acid, we could bypass a step in the PG$_2$ and PG$_3$ producing process. Here is another chart that shows in what foods the various precursor fatty acids are found:

LINOLEIC ACID — This is the most abundant fatty acid. It is found in most vegetable oils and organic meats.

GAMMA LINOLENIC ACID — This is a less common fatty acid and is found mostly in two places: mother's milk and in the oil of the evening primrose flower.

DIHOMOGAMMALINOLENIC ACID — The only place this fatty acid can be found is in human milk.

ARACHIDONIC ACID — This acid is found in meats, some dairy products, and some seaweeds.

ALPHA-LINOLENIC ACID — This acid is found in linseed oil and dark green vegetables.

EICOSAPENTAENOIC ACID — This acid is found in oils from marine fish (one trade name is MaxEPA™).

(Also see articles in this book on fatty acids, eicopentaenoic acid, and octocosanol.)

lymphocytes) which in turn causes the synthesis of more PGE$_2$. The improper function of these lymphocytes limits the immune system's control and also decreases its ability to attack foreign bodies. The increase in the PGE$_2$ level results in defective cells and damage by the immune system's attack on its own body. Diseases that demonstrate this are rheumatoid arthritis, eczema, inflammatory bowel disease, and multiple sclerosis. Researchers believe that the two problems, that of defects in T-suppressor lymphocytes and the excessive formation of PGE_2, can be corrected by an increase in the class of PGs known as PGE_1. Because the production of PGE_1 limits the amount of PGE_2 available to the body, it has been suggested that evening primrose oil could be taken, accompanied by the nutrients the body needs to synthesize PGE_1 (vitamins B_3, B_6, and C), instead of steroids or aspirin since these substances might cause a degenerative problem in the long run by upsetting the PG balance and synthesis in the body. Horrobin, Lovell, and Burton suggest that the correct approach to improve the function of T-lymphocytes and reduce the synthesis of PGE_2 is through nutritional means by increasing the intake of linoleic acid and GLA, thereby encouraging the increase of PGE_1 within the body. This would be a natural treatment for many inflammatory diseases and a natural immune system control (Lovell, C. R., Burton, T. F., and Horrobin, D. F., "Treatment of Atopic Eczema With Evening Primrose Oil," *Lancet*, January 1981; also, Zurier, R. B. and Ballas, M., "Prostaglandin in E_1 Suppression of Adjuvant Arthritis," *Arthritis and Rheumatism*, 16 [1973], 251-258).

There is also a chance that some forms of cancer are associated with a loss of the body's ability to synthesize PGE_1, and it has been suggested by Horrobin and others that an increase in the intake of GLA by doses of evening primrose oil may help this problem.

Shortly before a pregnant woman delivers, there is an increase in certain PGs that bring on this delivery. The use of PGs to induce labor after an otherwise normal pregnancy has gained approval in the United Kingdom, and the United States is conducting clinical trials for PG-induced birth. A related problem that has recently received a good deal of publicity is premenstrual syndrome, which is a condition that some women experience up to ten days before menstruation. The symptoms of this are weight gain, bloating, breast pain, and irritability. Some women with severe PMS have reported relief by taking doses of evening primrose oil.

I sent evening primrose oil and a cream containing evening primrose oil to the Feingold Institute for Hyperactive Children, and they found some children were helped by the cream applied topically as well as as by an intake of the oil. The Hyperactive Children's Support Group in England conducted extensive surveys (as did the Feingold Institute) and found that hyperactive children are deficient in the essential fatty acids, especially GLA. Both institutes found an improvement in preliminary experiments with evening primrose oil. The Feingold Institute has been in the forefront in pointing out that synthetic chemicals increase the problem of hyperactivity in children, and diet is the key to improvements in behavior and function. A majority found that evening primrose oil had better results when applied topically instead of taken orally, probably due to the efficiency of the pilo-sebaceous apparatus (See **DOES YOUR SKIN REALLY ABSORB AND USE NUTRIENTS?** in this book).

Vaddadi and Horrobin reported on weight loss produced by evening primrose oil in *IRCS Medical Science* in 1979. Twenty-two persons who were within ten percent of their ideal body weight neither lost nor gained more than five pounds. Of sixteen who were more than ten percent above their ideal body weight, eleven lost weight with an average of nine pounds, and five showed no change. The subjects took a 0.6 milligram capsule four times per day, and some took one eight times per day. The subjects' diet was not regulated, although some of the subjects said that they were less hungry. Of the eleven subjects who lost weight, the four subjects who took eight capsules a day lost eighteen, twenty-two, twenty-four, and twenty-eight pounds within the eight week period.

Prostaglandins are also potent regulators of blood pressure. They dilate the blood vessels, increase cardiac output, increase blood flow to most organs, and some have an extraordinary anti-clotting effect. PGE_1 can lower cholesterol, and this fact makes evening primrose oil and other essential fatty acids vital when we consider the recent studies linking high cholesterol to certain fats in the diet. PGs in proper amounts and in correct balance, which is controlled by the body if the intake of primary fatty acids is sufficient, are vital in maintaining a healthy cardiovascular system. GLA is converted by the body into PGE_1, and this prostaglandin is the secret to a healthy heart. Horrobin and others believe that supplementing the diet with evening primrose oil drastically reduces the chances of developing heart disease.

The first evening primrose plants to be exported to Europe gained the name of "King's Cure-All," but the list of modern diseases we've just discussed make evening primrose oil sound like a contemporary cure-all, and our list is not complete. In modern herbal medicine, an infusion of the root is taken as a remedy against headache, and today the evening primrose oil has been extolled as an excellent remedy for a hangover. Perhaps the oil will reduce the effects of alcoholism in some individuals, and, due to the biochemical relationship that has been discovered between alcoholics and hyperactive children, for the same reason that it helps these children: deficiencies in PGE_1. Alcohol intake produces an elevation of PGE_1 in the brain, and it is this elevation that causes the intoxication, not the alcohol itself; this brief elevation is followed by a more extended deficiency in PGE_1 which is the cause of the hangover. Many researchers believe that alcoholism is a chemical need within the body, and this need can be genetic and biochemically induced. It is possible that some people feel the need for a certain level of PGE_1 within the brain, and they discover that alcohol elevates this level. If this theory is true, the intake of GLA in evening primrose oil could be a therapy to rehabilitate alcoholics, a preservative agent from the physical damage caused by alcohol, and a potential preventive to keep the alcohol-sensitive individual from becoming an alcoholic. An essential fatty acid diet designed to increase PG production would be far superior to chemical drug methods in the treatment of alcoholism.

The topical use of evening primrose oil, like other fatty acids, has shown promising results as well. In a shampoo it moisturizes dry hair and scalp and, in the same manner as jojoba oil, reduces the excessive flow of oils without drying out the hair. I have prepared a special conditioning spray using evening primrose oil that makes the most difficult snarls and tangles disappear, thereby reducing hair damaged by grooming. It also lays down a non-greasy luster without using lanolin as a topical agent, which is most often used in tangle-free sprays, luster-izing sprays, and cream rinses.

By combining evening primrose oil with other essential fatty acids in a natural cream base, you can have a light natural moisturizer for the complexion and the body. Many studies in medical research centers have demonstrated that evening primrose oil is excellent for treating the inflammation, redness, and itching of eczema. I have found that an evening primrose oil cream does this same job and also have found great success by using evening primrose oil in a baby lotion to be used for infant eczema and diaper rash.

Several report success using primrose oil on the skin disease psoriasis, but they are not scientific studies. Here is how the oil was used on psoriasis: ten to fifteen minutes before a shower, the subjects applied pure primrose oil directly to the lesions, which caused an intense itching as the hard scales were softened. The subjects then got into the shower and washed all the oil from the skin which reduced the itching somewhat. A rough towel was used to "massage" the scales. A body lotion containing evening primrose lotion was applied to the lesions. This method did seem to loosen hard scales which allowed treatment of the lesions. Used on a daily basis, the oil increasingly reduced the itching to the point where there was no more itching when it was applied. I am not sure whether or not this is a good long-term treatment, but I think it is good for at least a short time as it loosens up and washes away heavy scales which then allows an ultraviolet treatment of pink skin rather than heavily crusted lesions. The main problem in treating psoriasis with evening primrose oil is that it smells very strongly and may leave a ring in the bathtub if not well washed afterwards, but these difficulties are minor. A medical study following these ideas might prove very interesting. One girl who used the evening primrose psoriasis treatment had great success and claimed she was able to go out in a bathing suit because the scales cleared completely. There is no way of knowing, however, whether she had psoriasis or some type of eczema.

Jojoba Oil

The jojoba (pronounced *ho-ho-ba*) plant suffers from a geographical misnomer because its official name, *Simmondsia Chinensis*, designates the herb as being from China although the plant is American and Mexican. Patches of jojoba are scattered throughout the Baja penninsula south of California, the southern half of Arizona, the California desert east of Los Angeles and San Diego, and along the 1000 miles of the western half of Mexico's mainland. Few plants could survive the temperatures that reach 115⁰ F. (46⁰ C.), the sparse rainfall (less than five inches per year in some areas), and poor soil. Jojoba, however, has a built-in suvival mechanism because it needs no water during the summer when the rain almost never falls. During this time the pores of the plant (*stomata*) are completely sealed by a wax thereby reducing the evaporation that would shrivel any other plant. This unique coating is not only a moisture-retention agent but also insulates the plant from the low nighttime temperatures of the desert. This wax is concentrated in the jojoba beans which are harvested in quantities up to twelve pounds per bush. The jojoba survives a hostile environment with a life span of over 100 years.

In 1769 the famous emplorer-missionary Junipero Serra found the Indians who lived along the Baja California coast cooking with oil taken from the seeds of a bush they called "ho-ho-wi." Serra wrote it as "jo-jo-ba," which is how the plant came to be called. The mistaken Chinese heritage came about in a different way. In 1822, the British naturalist H. F. Link landed in Baja and observed the Indians cooking with jojoba, massaging their hair and bodies with jojoba, and even feeding their livestock with the seeds. The naturalist gathered several of the plants to take back to England with him, but he was going on to China first, which is how the American-Mexican plant got its Chinese tag. The boxes of jojoba plants got mixed with the Chinese plants, and the jojoba was designated a Chinese species.

I got involved with jojoba in my labs in 1972, and at that time jojoba was hard to come by and extremely expensive. I recall at the time that the only jojoba cosmetics were two shampoos, one created at the Laboratorios Jojoba in Mexico and the other by Four D Marketing in the United States. But the price for jojoba oil was an outrageous $225-$275 per gallon, which meant that a good jojoba cosmetic had to retail for about $20.00. The high price limited its appeal as a cosmetic ingredient; nevertheless, I was so impressed with this remarkable plant that I created a shampoo, conditioner, and complexion oil from the jojoba oil and a facial mask from the jojoba meal left over after the oil had been removed from the seeds, which I found superior to any other herbal or facial mask.

Its increasing popularity as a cosmetic ingredient led many manufacturers to add products containing jojoba to their lines, and one company (Wickhen Products, Inc.) to create a synthetic jojoba oil. Like most synthetics, however, it does not have the same positive results as natural jojoba oil, but many cosmetic manufacturers probably use the synthetic copy due to the high price of the natural oil. Another method cosmetic companies use to cut corners with jojoba oil is to ferment jojoba meal (what remains of the bean after the oil has been removed) for ninety days to produce a tincture that they add to their jojoba products. Sometimes they add both the tincture and the oil, but if this is the case, they add the tincture high on the ingredient list and the oil much farther down. This too obviously cuts down on the expense, but the benefits of the jojoba oil, based on its 97% unsaturated waxy esters, are not there.

Jojoba oil offers the cosmetic industry an almost colorless, odorless oil with remarkable resistance to oxidation and rancidity. Its antioxidation characteristics make it a good natural stable carrier for plant hormones, natural pesticides, and herbal extracts. I have also found that jojoba oil is both a waterproofing agent and a softener of leather which indicates that it can aid in the moisturization of skin and also lay down a protective film. Its cosmetic uses are just beginning to be discovered (or re-discovered), and yet these applications do not begin to suggest the range of this versatile plant.

Tom Janca, President of Janca's Oil and Seed Company, Inc., began in the early 1970's to cold press jojoba beans. He has expanded his business into not only supplying cosmetic manufacturers with jojoba oil, but also industry with jojoba products for high-speed machinery lubrication. "It is a fine light lubricant and an anti-corrosive coating for tools and equipment. In pharmaceuticals it has proven invaluable in reducing foaming in the production of penicillin and recently was researched as a tumor reductive and an anti-viral agent" (Tom Janca, *Liquid Gold from the Desert*, Mesa, Arizona, 1976). These applications of the jojoba bean in cosmetology, industry, and medicine, however, are useless if the plant is not accessible for processing and distribution. And here, too, Tom Janca was among the first, by underwriting beginning jojoba growers.

The development of an Indian jojoba industry was financed by the Office of Arid Land studies at the University of Arizona in the summer of 1972. More than 87,000 pounds of jojoba seeds were harvested, and members of the San Carlos Apache Indian tribe harvested more than 75,000 pounds on their land in Arizona alone. In the summer of 1975, more than 1,600 Indians harvested the seeds from jojoba growing wild on their reservations. By 1977, over 700 acres of jojoba were harvested by Indian cooperatives in Arizona and California. This land, which was left to the Indians because it was unproductive and of little commercial value, turned out to produce liquid gold for its Indian owners.

The growth of the jojoba industry is of benefit to the Indians, but it also benefits an endangered species--the great sperm whale. People who are concerned with the disappearance of this species will like the fact that jojoba oil can replace sperm whale oil and is actually superior to sperm oil. The "Save the Whale" slogan is a perfect tag for the use of jojoba oil. About thirteen barrels of jojoba oil (6½ tons of seeds) can replace the oil obtained from the head of one sperm whale, yet in the face of adverse public reaction, the fleets of ships armed with helicopters, radar, and harpoons with explosive grenades hunt the whales with a tenacity that can be compared to the ruthless men who beat baby seals to death. A sperm whale is killed every twenty-nine minutes; the whale meat is almost inedible, but the oil is extremely valuable commercially. Even now you can read a cosmetic label with spermaceti, and this wax, which is made with sperm oil, is used in cleansing creams, deodorants, emollient creams, lotions, shampoos, and nail enamel removers. Yet jojoba oil is so similar to sperm oil that it could be nicknamed "desert whale oil." Jojoba can be hydrogenated (the process by which vegetables oil is "hardened" into margarine) to produce a sparkling crystalline white solid just like spermaceti that has a wide array of uses, ranging from waxes for polishing cars to bright burning candles that do not sag in hot weather (as most waxes do). By combining jojoba with sulfur chloride, substances with unique properties ranging from oils to rubbery solids are formed that can be used in the manufacture of printing inks, lubricants, varnishes, synthetic rubber, and even linoleum. Jojoba is versatile, increasingly accessible, and morally beneficial.

Jojoba has the following potential uses: *liquid wax* - this list comprises most of the uses already mentioned, including cosmetological, industrial, and food preparation uses. In pharmaceuticals, it is a suitable carrier or coating for some medicinal preparations, stabilizer of penicillin products, inhibitor of tubercle bacilli, potential treatment for acne, and has historical use as a hair restorer; *meal (after oil is extracted)* - this meal can be used as a fertilizer if high nitrogen content can be utilized; I have also used jojoba meal in a facial mask for its high protein content and its light scrubbing action on the skin; *seed hulls* - this can be used as a mulch-soil additive to enrich soil that is low in organic matter, also as a ground cover to reduce evaporation, erosion, or weed growth; *jojoba shrub* - the shrubs are good browse for cattle, deer, sheep, and goats; it is already used as an ornamental plant throughout the Southwest; *hydrogenated wax* - combined with other waxes, hydrogenated jojoba wax makes superior candles that burn with an almost smokeless flame; it can be substituted for candellia wax and carnauba wax; in textiles, it is a good sizing for yard goods and can be used to make polishing waxes for floors, furniture, and automobiles; also as a protective coating on fruit, food, and paper cups; to mask ingredients in vitamin tablets; also for lipsticks; *liquid wax sulfurized* - in this form, jojoba is a suitable replacement for sperm whale oil; it also has potential industrial applications as mentioned above; *jojoba alcohol and acid derivatives* - these products can be used to prepare disinfectants, surfacants, detergents, driers, emulsifiers, resins, plasticizers, protective coatings, fibers, corrosion inhibitors, and bases for creams and ointments.

Jojoba's benefits, however, begin with your body, and it's important to understand what this substance is chemically. Jojoba oil, which comprises 40-60% of the jojoba bean, is actually not an oil at all; it is rather a polyunsaturated liquid wax composed of straight-chain alcohols free of the glyceride esters usually found in vegetable oils. It occurs naturally as a liquid oil but can be used to create a natural jojoba cream or butter.

As I write this, there is a new cream being made with jojoba oil, jojoba butter, ozone, and perhaps jojoba wax (hydrogenated with chromium). This cream is said to be an excellent antiseptic jojoba cream. Since many people say that jojoba oil is a good acne treatment, such an antiseptic cream would be a possible treatment for acne. It is, at this time, in the experimental stages, and the creator is preparing a patent.

Jojoba oil is also a no-calorie vegetable oil. The lipase enzymes used by the human body to hydrolyze vegetable oils and animal fats in the stomach so that they can be digested will not hydrolyze jojoba oil. Due to this fact, jojoba oil passes through the digestive system largely unutilized. This makes it an obvious diet aid because it will not hydrolyze within the body and adds no calories.

Cosmetic Uses of Jojoba - The best way to discuss the hair and skin care uses of jojoba oil is to base it on actual clinic and salon use. At the **Aubrey Natural Hair and Skin Care Clinic**, one of the hair treatments we perform uses a hot jojoba oil treatment for the scalp. First we apply warm jojoba oil directly to the scalp with a cotton swab. We massage this treatment into the scalp and then steam the hair under an aromatherapy steamer. This is simply a facial steamer with a hood so that the steam is directed over the hair. Next, we apply a jojoba, aloe, and yucca shampoo to the dry hair. It is best to apply shampoo to dry hair when there is a hot oil treatment on the hair rather than to wet the hair first so that the oils and excess sebum are removed more efficiently. Then we wet the hair and shampoo it. We lather twice and then rinse the hair with an herbal rinse made with rosemary and sage. Our last step is to apply a jojoba butter cream conditioner to the damp hair. We allow this to remain on the hair for about five to ten minutes, then rinse the hair well for a full minute to get all the oils and conditioner out of the hair. I have seen this treatment work wonders for the worst hair conditions, including hair loss and greasy hair with dandruff.

Jojoba oil is more effective if it is used in sufficient amount, and obviously the pure, warmed jojoba oil treatment directly on the scalp is very beneficial. You can gauge the content of the jojoba oil in a product by reading the label. Most cosmetic products will have various synthetic preservatives and detergents, such as methyl and propyl paraben, triethanolamine (TEA), and sodium lauryl sulfate. If the jojoba oil appears on the label before these chemicals, then it has more jojoba oil, but if it appears after these chemicals, then you are getting only an infinitesimal amount of jojoba oil. There is also no way to know if the jojoba oil is natural or synthetic. For example, one popular jojoba, aloe, and yucca shampoo has an ingredient list thus: Coconut Oil, Olive Oil Castile, Jojoba Oil, Aloe Vera, Yucca Root, Citrus Seed Extract, Vitamins C and E. This shampoo is high in jojoba oil and also uses natural soaps (the coconut and olive oil castile soap). It has no water in the formula and is preserved naturally with citrus seed extract and vitamins C and E. This shampoo is rather expensive, which a good jojoba cosmetic has to be because although jojoba oil is no longer $275 per gallon, it is still an expensive ingredient, and any cosmetic with a beneficial amount of jojoba oil is not going to be cheap. Let's contrast this jojoba shampoo with another one sold in health food stores. Its ingredients list is as follows: Water, Sodium Lauryl Sulfate, Cocamide DEA, Blue-Green Algae, Distilled Fermented Jojoba (a trade name for the fermented jojoba was used), Glycerine, Jojoba, Biotin, Fragrance, Sodium Chloride, Citric Acid. The shampoo is a green color, but what makes it green? Blue-green algae would not color it the beautiful cosmetic green that it is. Only a natural or synthetic dye could do this, and no dyes or colors are listed on the label. Also, if you're after jojoba oil, you may be out of luck! A little logic tells you that the shampoo is almost all synthetic chemicals (i.e., sodium lauryl sulfate and cocamide DEA). The DEA stands for "diethanolamine," which, like TEA and the "sulfate" in sodium lauryl sulfate, may be contaminated with nitrosamines which are believed to be carcinogenic. By using hair and skin care products that contain TEA, DEA, or sodium lauryl sulfate, greater amounts of these carcinogenic sustances can be absorbed into your body through your skin than by eating foods containing nitrites and nitrates such as bacon, ham, hot dogs, etc. The jojoba oil is listed just before biotin, another very expensive substance, that sells wholesale for about $5.50 per gram. Obviously, the shampoo doesn't contain a gram of biotin. Let's say they put in $1/16$ of a gram (which costs about 34¢), then how much jojoba is in the product, or for that matter, how much fermented jojoba is in the product, since both are before the biotin which is far less than a gram? A little label reading can tell you just how much of the expensive ingredients are in that expensive cosmetic.

Jojoba's therapeutic effects can be traced back to native American Indian lore. The Spanish observed the Indians using jojoba for medicine, as well as for cooking and cosmetics. In Mexico Dr. Javier Gomez has spent years researching the effects of jojoba oil on hair loss, but these studies are not considered scientifically acceptable because they are based on folk remedies that date from pre-Columbian times. However, when hair loss is related to the sebaceous glands, jojoba oil can help because it works on the human scalp just as it does in its original plant environment to moisturize and protect the skin. As the sweat glands remove waste from the skin and act as a cooling agent, the sebaceous glands lubricate, soften, and provide an acid mantle for the skin as well as leave a coating that protects from microbial attack. The sebum contains 22% waxy esters, but jojoba contains 97% pure waxy esters (unsaturated). A jojoba oil treatment lays down a film which acts as a medium for attracting and holding in moisture and also to regulate the flow of sebum in the scalp. Even if you don't have a hair loss problem, jojoba oil, jojoba shampoo, and jojoba conditioner will lubricate the hair shaft so that you get conditioning without a greasy feel. These treatments all help prevent split ends, and we have found in our clinic and field studies that they are very good for permed and over-processed (salon damaged) hair.

Many people feel when they read the fantastic list of uses for jojoba that they are being hyped with just another medicine show snake oil. Quite often natural herbal substances are touted as cure-alls, and the consumer hears about these substances and creates a demand for them and their healing properties. The natural substances are then either synthetized or exploited in non-natural formulas that inhibit their effectiveness as herbal remedies, and these products are subsequently discarded as leftover superstitions from a gullible past. This reaction has taken place, to a certain extent, with jojoba oil, but the many uses of this "liquid gold" have been proven. Jojoba oil, like any natural ingredient, only comes to life in the hands of a good compounder and imparts its vitality to you. By using products with jojoba oil not *spermaceti* on the label, we can feel that we are helping to protect the sperm whale.

St. John's Wort Oil

St. John's Wort (*Hypericum perforatum*) has a unique name. The name of the herb comes from the traditional date of gathering these yellow flowers--the eve of St. John the Baptist's day--to ward off evil. In fact the Latin name of the plant, *Hypericum*, is derived from the Greek and means "over an apparition," which is a reference to the belief that the herb was so obnoxious to evil spirits that one whiff would cause them to fly away--superstitious aromatherapy!

St. John's Wort Oil is listed in the German Pharmacopeia as an all-purpose herbal remedy from antiquity to the present time. It is an aromatic and an astringent and reduces inflammation and soothes nerves. It has been used in all pulmonary complaints, bladder problems, suppression of urine, dysentery, worms, hysteria, nervous depression, and jaundice. The oil is made from an infusion of the flowers in olive oil. St. John's Wort has been used externally for a treatment of a wide variety of problems and injuries. The main medical indications are rheumatism, gout, lumbago, sciatica, ulcers, hemorrhoids, bruises, sprained muscles, open wounds of all kinds, and burns. Success with using St. John's Wort Oil has been reported in phytotherapeutic literature. In the case of rheumatic complaints and inflammations of tissue (contusions), the inflammatory reaction is reduced. Open wounds close faster than with other treatments. Burns also respond well to the oil in that both the inflammatory reaction and the susceptibility to inflammation are reduced. The main active ingredient in St. John's Wort Oil is *hypericin*, which has inflammation-inhibiting, nerve-soothing, antiseptic properties.

In the cosmetic field, preparations with St. John's Wort Oil are used for the care of skin which is extremely sensitive, nervous, or has a tendency to allergies. I have found that combining this oil in a product can reduce allergic reactions to many common topical sensitizers, and by combining it with allantoin and other herbal extracts, a superior moisturizer can be compounded with inflammation-inhibiting and hydrating action on the skin.

Tocopherol Oil and Wheat Germ Oil

Tocopherol oil is prepared by diluting natural mixed tocopherols--or vitamin E--with soya oil, whereas wheat germ oil is obtained by cold-pressing fresh-milled wheat germ, the vital force of the wheat berry. The physical difference between tocopherol oil and wheat germ is that the tocopherol is light-colored and odorless while the wheat germ oil is ivory to medium brown in color and smells strongly of grain.

The fundamental physiological significance of tocopherol is that it is an antioxidant; it inhibits the oxidation process, thereby reducing the number of free radical oxygen molecules that break loose in biochemical reactions that can damage other molecules and cells. The oxygen consumption in the musculature and in the liver is particularly reduced. Also, substances which are easily oxidized during metabolism (vitamin A, for example) are protected from a too-rapid oxidative degradation. Vitamin E is also involved in regulation of the pituitary function and intervenes in the autonomic nervous centers. Percutaneously applied creams and lotions containing tocopherol oil improve the circulation of the blood in the peripheral vessels and strengthen the connective tissue. There is also a positive influence on the formation of skin cells. This has been documented by the application of vitamin E to cuts and the resulting healing of the cuts with improved cell structure. It has also been documented that vitamin E protects the skin fat from decomposition by oxygen through its antioxidative power.

Natural mixed tocopherols can be obtained from alfalfa, almond oil, coffee oil, fennel oil, and mint oils. Wheat germ oil is, however, the best source of vitamin E and octacosanol as well as a complex of substances such as provitamin A, vitamin F, lecithin, and sterols. Wheat germ is a depot for various biologically active substances, and contains the ingredients necessary for the development and growth of the new plant in a naturally balanced complex. It has a high content of oil and fat-soluble active substances which is a valuable starting material for high-grade vegetable oils. Because it is of embryonic origin, it is an ideal composition for cellular improvement creams (See **CELLTHERAPY** in this book), and the content of fat-soluble vitamins, sterols, and plant hormones make it a good topical cosmetic ingredient. Wheat germ oil must be obtained by cold pressing, however, because chemical or thermal influences destroy the native structure of the active ingredients. Synthetic chemicals also destroy the biologically active components in any cosmetic containing wheat germ oil.

The essential oils I have discussed can be found in many cosmetics, and you can use them to make your own cosmetics which will have a phytotherapeutic value to your skin and hair. In recent decades, vegetable active substances have become of interest to some cosmetic compounders, and herbal extracts are, as I have pointed out, used by massage therapists, aestheticians, and in spas for the care of skin, hair, and body. The terms aromatherapy, thalassotherapy, and phytotherapy suggest methods and areas where herbal extracts are used. The more natural the combined extracts, the more beneficial, and it is important to avoid natural substances that have been chemicalized in synthetic formulas. Also, it has been recognized that neither synthetic active substances nor individual active substances isolated from plants are of the same value as the total complexes extracted from the herbs. Synthesis or isolation cannot include the numerous natural accompanying substances with their unique synergistic properties. It is the total complex of the herb, root, bark, or flower that creates a unique completely natural hair, skin, or body product.

organitoons

CHAPTER VII

Charting The Hair and Skin Care Herbs
Or
What Do Arnica, Betulla, Ivy, Horse Chestnut, and Bladderwrack Have in Common?
Or
Betulla Sounds Like What You Don't Want To Happen To Your Hips

Betulla does sound somewhat fattening, but if you call it by its common name birch, it sounds slimming, which is how it's used in anti-cellulite creams, along with arnica, ivy, horse chestnut, and bladderwrack. Spas in Europe use a mixture of these herbs in a whirlpool bath to sweat away pounds, in lotions to massage away pounds, and under plastic wraps to squeeze away pounds. Do they work? The answer is yes--and no. There is a temporary displacement of liquid build-up in the fat cells, and the lymph build-up of waste material is also reduced with massages and hot tubs. Arnica, ivy, horse chestnut, and bladderwrack are the classic anti-cellulite herbs, and a quick look at our chart will tell you this. Men with pot bellies have been known to put these anti-cellulite creams to work under a tight stomach wrap. Perhaps you recall seeing the fighter Muhammed Ali with one of these wraps around his middle when he was in training to reduce the fat cell build-up. Plastic-wrapped thighs, well-creamed with anti-cellulite cream, have become the sign of many society women, just as leg warmers declare their wearers to be dancing buffs. These herbs in creams, steams, rubs, and wraps do work for a while, but their effects are not eternal. Exercise and a modified diet are both necessary to do away with cellulite for good. There is no miracle in these herbs, and none of the herbs we have charted can deliver miracles. These charts simply deliver herbs. You supply the miracles.

The Greek physician Hippocrates (468-377 B.C.), regarded as the father of modern medicine, knew the properties of 300 medicinal herbs, but today probably not even thirty modern physicians know camomile flowers from elder blossoms. (The former is an aromatic, anti-spasmodic, and antiseptic; the latter, a diuretic, laxative, and purgative. Camomile flowers have white petals with yellow centers, and elder blossoms have tiny white flowers). Yet herbs and other natural substances make up a great portion of what is now condescendingly termed traditional medicine that was used successfully for thousands of years. Many of us forget the so-called miracle drugs and other examples of modern medicine such as mass immunization have almost nothing to do with the increase in life span in technologically advanced countries; this improvement can be traced to simply better diets and flush toilets and is not particularly a credit to the modern medical profession. Further, when one considers the rate of increase in diseases that seem to be lifestyle-related, such as heart disease and some forms of cancer, any advancements the medical profession have made have been lost in a miasma of general ill-health. One herb chart more or less will not reverse this trend away from synthetic drugs and back to herbs, but it will make this valuable information available to consumers who may not have considered the health-giving aspects of "green medicine."

Herbal remedies are prepared in six ways: 1) **Infusion** - This is a tea. A teaspoon of the leaves, flowers, and stems is covered in a cup of boiling water and then left, with a cover, to steep for about ten minutes. Honey is frequently added to improve the flavor. The herb is strained off and the tea is taken hot in quantities from one to four cups. **Decoctions** - The roots, twigs, berries, seeds, and bark are used. One ounce of herb per cup cold water is put into an enamel or stainless steel pot and boiled for twenty to thirty minutes. The liquor is strained off and taken as the infusion. **Juice** - The juice is extracted from plants by cutting them into tiny pieces and crushing them. **Cold Compresses** - dip a cloth into an herbal infusion, decoction, or juice and apply to the skin. **Poultice** - The plant is crushed into a pulp and applied, either cold or hot, on the affected area. Sometimes it is wrapped in gauze or cheesecloth. If applied hot, the pulp is heated, put into a hot damp cloth, and applied. Poultices are ideal for inflammation, bruises, wounds, and abscesses. **Ointments or creams** - Boil the plant until its properties are extracted. Strain and add some vegetable oil (safflower, olive, jojoba, etc.). Return to heat and simmer until water has been absorbed into the mixture. To make an ointment, add beeswax until the desired consistency is obtained. To make a cream or lotion, add yogurt or cetyl alcohol (natural fatty acid alcohol) until the desired emulsion has been obtained.

Here is a glossary of herbalists' terms you will find used in this chart:

Alkaloids - These are natural amines (nitrogen-containing compounds) which have pharma-cological properties. They are usually of plant origin. They are almost insoluble in water (though their salts may be soluble in water) and are therefore mixed with alcohol. Examples include cocaine, nicotine, atropine, and quinine.

Alterative - An agent that gradually produces a change towards good health.

Analgesic - Relieves or stops pain.

Anesthetic - Reduces pain and causes an absence of sensation.

Anodyne - Relieves pain.

Anthelmintic - Destroys or expels intestinal parasites. See **VERMIFUGE**.

Anti-coagulant - A substance which prevents clotting.

Anti-convulsive - A substance that relieves or prevents convulsions.

Anti-emetic - Relieves vomiting.

Anti-inflammatory - Relieves inflammation. Also sometimes called "anti-phlogistic."

Anti-paralytic - An agent that works to relive paralysis.

Anti-periodic - An agent that acts against periodic diseases such as intermittent fever.

Anti-pruritic - An agent that relieves itching.

Anti-pyretic - Prevents fever and is an anti-rheumatic and anti-neuralgic agent.
Anti-scrobutic - An agent that prevents or cures scurvy (such as ascorbic acid).
Antiseptic - Destroys or inhibits bacteria.
Anti-spasmodic - Relieves or checks spasms.
Anti-tussive - An agent that relieves coughing.
Aperient - Causes bowel movements.
Aphrodisiac - Arouses sexual desire.
Aromatic - A substance with an agreeable odor or stimulating qualities.
Astringent - Makes organic tissue contract.
Balsams - These are healing or soothing agents. They are mixtures of resins that contain large amounts of benzoic acid or its esters. Examples are *Balsam Tolu, Balsam Peru, Styrax* and *Benzoin Gum*. The *Oregon Balsam* and *Copsiba Balsam* are not true balsams as they contain no benzoic acid, cinnamic acids, or their esters. The balsams are often used cosmetically in hair conditioners, as skin soothers, and as preservatives.
Bitter - Properties which promote movement of saliva and gastric juices to increase appetite and digestion.
Calmative - Agent that has a calming or tranquilizing effect.
Cardiac - Agents that affect the heart.
Carminative - Relieves gas from the intestines.
Cataplasm - This is a poultice.
Cholagogue - An agent for increasing the flow of bile into the intestines.
Coagulant - Causes clotting.
Counter-irritant - Agent to produce an irritation to counteract an irritation elsewhere.
Demulcent - Soothes irritated tissues, particularly mucous membranes.
Depressant - Agent which reduces nervous activity.
Depurative - Agent that purifies the blood or an organ (detoxifies).
Dessicant - Drying agent. Also **EXSICCANT**.
Diaphoretic - Agent that produces perspiration.
Digestive - Helps digestion.
Diuretic - Increases the flow of urine.
Elixirs - These are clear hydroalcoholic liquids intended for oral use. Homeopathic medicine makes use of elixirs. They usually have sweetener added to the simple solution.
Emetic - Causes vomiting.
Emmenagogue - Promotes menstrual flow.
Emollient - Agent that when used externally has a softening and soothing effect on the skin.
Essential Oils - Also called volatile oils, ethereal oils, or essences. They are complex mixtures of a wide variety of compounds such as alcohols, ketones, phenols, acids, ethers, aldehydes, esters, oxides, and sulfur compounds among others. They usually represent the odoriferous principals as well as the medicinal properties of the plant.
Expectorant - Promotes the release of mucus from lungs and air passages.
Febrifuge - Reduces or stops fever.
Glycolic - This is the semi-thick to light olific extract of the plant (see **ESSENTIAL OILS** and **GLYCOSIDES**).
Glycosides - Sugar containing compounds which when hydrolyzed yield one or more sugars. Their two main components are glycone and aglycone. The former is the sugar component and the latter is the non-sugar component. The glycosides are vital in plant life and also are an important source of drugs such as digitalis, sennosides, ginseng glycosides, and rutin.
Hemostatic - Halts bleeding.
Hepatic - An agent that works on the liver.

Lactagogue - Substance which stimulates the breasts to produce milk. Also **GALACTAGOGUE.**
Laxative - Causes bowel movements.
Lipases - These are lipolytic enzymes that can hydrolyze fats or fixed oils into glycerol (see **GLYCOLIC**) and fatty acid components.
Lipids - These are the fatty materials soluble in solvents such as alcohol but not in water. They include fatty acids, fats, waxes, and fixed oils.
Moisturizer - Agent that when used externally acts to raise skin or scalp moisture content.
Mucilaginous - Emits soothing qualities to irritated skin or swollen areas.
Nephritic - A medicine which acts on the nervous system to calm the nerves.
Oleoresins - These are mixtures of resins and volatile oils. They can occur naturally, like gum turpentines and balsams or are extracted from a plant with a solvent, like paprika and ginger.
Pectoral - Relief for chest and lung ailments.
Phototoxic - Describes a substance that increases sunburn response of the skin to ultraviolet light without any allergic effect being involved.
Poison - A substance that has a destructive effect on living tissue.
Powdered Extract - To prepare a powdered extract, the natural extract is diluted with appropriate diluents such as lactose, dextrose, sucrose, or starch, and anti-caking agents are added such as calcium phosphate and magnesium carbonate. This mixture is dried and then ground into a powdered form.
Proteases - These are proteolytic enzymes which act on proteins by hydrolyzing specific peptides. An example is *bromelain* (pineapple protease) and *papain* (papaya protease). They are used as meat tenderizers, to relieve inflammation and bruises, and as skin softeners in cosmetics.
Purgative - An agent that causes bowel relief.
Refrigerant - Reduces excess body heat.
Rhizome - Part of a plant: a rootlike stem.
Rubefacient - Produces reddening of the skin: a mild irritant.
Saponin - These are glycosides with sterols or triterpenes in the non-sugar fraction (aglycones). One of their activities is the ability to form foam (suds) when shaken. This foam-forming action makes them ideal in beverages such as root beer and in soaps or shampoos. Examples include quillaya bark and yucca root (which are used in shampoos), and sarsaparilla.
Scrofulous - Pertaining to lymph and tubercular disorders, also characterized by inflammation of the joints. The word "scrofulous" formerly carried a connotation of moral degeneration, as the disease with which it was connected--tuberculosis--was associated with filth, poverty, and promiscuity.
Sedative - Agent which has a direct effect on a particular disease.
Spermatorrhea - Involuntary discharge of semen without sexual intercourse.
Stimulant - An agent that excites or quickens the activity of physiological properties.
Stomachic - Agent that stimulates, strengthens, and tones the stomach.
Styptic - A plant that can contract organic tissue, e. g., as an astringent.
Tenesmus - Painful straining, particularly to empty bowel or bladder, usually without success.
Tonic - Strengthens and stimulates the system.
Vasoconstrictor - Substance that narrows blood vessels, thus raising blood pressure.
Vasodilator - Substance that dilates blood vessels, thus lowering blood pressure.
Vermifuge - Destroys worms.
Vesicant - Substance that produces blisters.
Waxes - Plant waxes are the esters of fatty acids with alcohols. They have a high molecular weight and are straight-chained. They are used extensively in cosmetics.

Herb Name Synonyms Folk Use	Parts Used	Typical Substances	Cosmetic Use	Properties & Other Uses	Similar Plants	Extracts	Comments
ABSINTHIUM (*Artemisia absinthium*) SYN: Wormwood, Absinthe, Armoise FOLK MEDICINE: Used as aromatic bitter for anorexia and as digestive tonic for gall bladder disorders.	Leaves & flowering tops	Volatile oil, azulene, thujone, pinene, camphene, thojyl alcohol, absinthin, ketopelenolide, carotene (0.05%), ascorbic acid (0.26%), tannins (7.7%), essential oils.	Oil used as fragrance in soaps, creams, lotions, perfumes	Bitter tonic, Emmenagogue, flavor for vermouth (0.024%). Maximum use in food is about 0.006%.	Wormseed and other *Artemisia* species. Marijuana (similar psychological action because of the thujone & tetrahydrocannabinol).	Glycolic	In perfumes: maximum 0.25%; in soaps, 0.01%. Approved by FDA for food if thujone-free. Average maximum amount used 0.024%.
ACACIA (*Acacia senegal*) Gum arabic, Egyptian thorn	Stems & branches	Sugars, acids (glucuronics), calcium, magnesium, potassium, sodium	Used in hairsprays, wavesets, as a thickener and filmforming agent for masks. Suspending and emulsifying agent.	Demulcent, mucilage, nutritional, possible hypocholesterolemic, suspending and emulsifying agent. Trochisci, syrups, and jujubes.	Gum tragacanth, kordofan gum, mogadore gum, Indian gum, quince seeds	Gum	1 to 4 drachms of gum creates a syrup. Gum can be dissolved in water and strained (1 in 8.75).
ACONITE (*Aconitum napellus*) SYN: Wolfsbane, monkshood, Jacob's chariot, friar's cap FOLK LORE: "Even a man who's pure at heart and says his prayers at night can become a werewolf when the *wolfsbane* blooms, and the moon is full and bright."	Whole plant	Alkaloids (0.2 to 1.5%) consisting of aconitine, picraconitine, aconine, and napelline. Also aconitic acid, itaconic acid, succinic acid, malonic acid, fructose, maltose, melibiose, mannitol, starch, fat & resin.	No longer in use. The British used a tincture of aconite in 1914 to make liniment (mixed with belladonna), but this can be absorbed into the skin & cause poisoning.	A fast-acting poison. As little as 2 mg. is fatal. "The bane of wolves may be used to ward off werewolves."	Belladonna (deadly nightshade)	Crude extract	Due to toxic nature, no percents are given.
ADDER'S TONGUE (*Erythronium americanum*) SYN: Serpent's tongue, dog's tooth, yellow snowdrop	Leaves & bulbs	Constituents of plant have not been analyzed.	Used as a poultice and applied to swellings.	Emollient and antiscrofulous properties; an emetic.	Plants in the lily family	Glycolic	Used as a soothing and healing agent at 1:1 extract to water.

Herb Name Synonyms Folk Use	Parts Used	Typical Substances	Cosmetic Use	Properties & Other Uses	Similar Plants	Extracts	Comments
AGAR-AGAR (*Gelidium amansii*) SYN: Japanese isinglass	The dried mucilage after boiling seaweed.	Not fully determined. Free amino acids, sugars, and polysaccharides. Glose (a powerful gelatinizing agent).	Used as emulsion, suspending agent, and gel. Gives a smooth, soft feel.	Hydrophilic--used in fruit, meat, fish as gel filler or gel binder. Maximum level of use is 0.4%.	Other algaes: *agal, gigartina speciosa, euchema spinolum, algin*.	Mucilage is dried to powder form.	Thickener and gel. Use according to product.
AGRIMONY (*Agrimonia eupatoria*) SYN: Church steeples, cockleburr, sticklewort	Entire plant	Volatile oil obtained by distillation, tannin 5%.	Its ability to contract tissue is used for large pores and for skin eruptions, acne, and oily skin.	Astringent, tonic, diuretic, French tea, eye wash, yellow dye, wound healer, and gargle.	Peruvian bark, hemp agrimony, water agrimony, boneset, eupatorium, gravel root.	Glycolic, essential oil	Fluid extract 10 to 60 drops as needed in cosmetic formula.
ALFALFA (*Leguminosae*) FOLK MEDICINE: As a nutrient to increase vitality and weight.	Aerial parts	Saponins (2 to 3%), soya-sapogenols, vitamins A, B, C, D, and E. Triacontanol (which is a plant growth regulator and increases the growth of corn, rice, and barley), flavones, enzymes, calcium, amino acids.	Used in peelable face masks. Reported use in treating skin conditions including radiotherapy.	Antifungal properties, estrogenic activities, cholesterol lowering properties. Used as cattle feed and sprouts for health food enthusiasts.		Crude and extract	

Herb Name Synonyms Folk Use	Parts Used	Typical Substances	Cosmetic Use	Properties & Other Uses	Similar Plants	Extracts	Comments
ALOE & ALOE VERA (*Aloe barbadensis*) SYN: Bitter aloe, cape aloe, cape, curacao aloe FOLK MEDICINE: Used as a stimulant and an anti-spasmodic; in Chinese medicine to treat headaches. It's been called "burn first aid," or "medicine plant" for centuries. When fresh gel is squeezed from the leaf, it relieves burns and sunburns and promotes healing. Used directly on skin as moisturizer, for yeast infection in genital areas, and for anal rashes, etc.	Leaf	Contains carthartic anthraglycosides (barbaloin), a glucoside of aloe-emodin. Range: 4.5 to 25% aloin. Aloe vera gel contains glucomannan, a polysaccharide similar to guar and locust bean gums. Also galactose, xylose, and ararinose (polysaccharides); steroids, organic acids, enzymes, amino acids, "biogenic stimulators," saponins, wound healing hormones, antibiotics, and minerals.	Celltherapy creams, moisturizers, sun screens, refreshing lotions, and tonics.	Emollient, demulcent, sunscreen, food. Maximum levels of about 0.02% in alcohol (186 ppm) and non-alcohol (190 ppm) in laxative.	Refreshers: camomile, mallow, linden Dehydrated skin: coneflower, horsetail St. John's Wort, walnut Sun screen: St. John's wort, Walnut, PABA, Willow Bark	Glycolic extract, aloe fluid, aloe dry extract	Aloe-emodin like buckhorn has been said to have anti-cancer activity (J. M. Kupchan, A. Karim, *Lloydia*, 39, 223, 1976). Sometimes guar and locust bean gum is mixed with aloe vera to increase its glucomannan and viscosity. Fresh leaf extract can be used to ensure quality.

Herb Name Synonyms Folk Use	Parts Used	Typical Substances	Cosmetic Use	Properties & Other Uses	Similar Plants	Extracts	Comments
ALLSPICE (*Pimenta officinalis*) SYN: Pimento, Jamaica pepper, British pimento water (British pharmacopoeia): Oil of pimento: 1 fl/oz Alcohol 12 fl/oz Distilled water 20 fl/oz (Deleted--Talc: 1 oz)	Fruit & shell	Major component is pimento or eugenol (60 to 80%); methyleugenol, cineole, caryophyllene, protein, lipids, carbohydrates, vitamins A, B₁ (thiamine), B₂ (riboflavin), B₃ (niacin), C, and minerals.	Fragrance oil (spicy & exotic odor). Used in islands as after shave and splash.	Aromatic, antiperiodic. Used in alcoholic beverages, dairy desserts, candy, baked goods, etc. Highest food use is 0.025%.	Carolina allspice or sweet bush (*calycanthis floridus*)	Essential oil oleoresin, berry and leaf oils. Allspice N.F. Official F.C.C.	Aromatic carminative at dose of 0.05 to 0.2 ml.
ALMONDS SWEET--*Amygdalus communis, var. dulcis* BITTER--*Amygdalus communis, var. amara* FOLK MEDICINE: In Chinese medicine, kernels of apricot, peach, and almonds contain tumor treatment. This is known today as the anticancer drug Laetrile.	Kernels	Both oils contain 35 to 55% fixed oil. In bitter almond oil, there's 3 to 40% amygdalin, but only trace or none at all in sweet oil. Protein (18-20%), emulsin, prunasin, daucosterol, sterols, calcium oxalate, zinc, copper, and tocopherols (vitamin E). Also fatty acids: palmitic, stearic, lauric, myristic, oleic, and linoleic.	Excellent emollient for chapped hands (sweet) and used in lotions and creams. For cosmetics use only sweet oil.	Essential oil emollient.	Apricot kernels (*p. armeniaca*). See APRICOT OIL.	Essential oil	Sweet almond oil is used in doses of up to 30 ml as laxative. Oil is used in lotions, creams, and ointment bases.

Herb Name Synonyms Folk Use	Parts Used	Typical Substances	Cosmetic Use	Properties & Other Uses	Similar Plants	Extracts	Comments
ALTHEA ROOT *(Althaea officinalis)* SYN: Marshmallow root, mallards, mauls, schloss tea FOLK MEDICINE: Used for over 2,000 years in Europe both internally and externally as a wound healer, for coughs, sore throats, stomach troubles, and in ointments for dry or chapped skin.	Leaves, root, and flowers	The mucilaginous polysaccharides form 6.2 to 11.6% and are composed of L-thamnose, D-galactose, D-galacturonic acid. Contains sugar, fats, tannin, asparagine, calcium oxalate, pectin.	Used in moisturizing and astringent formulas as a soothing agent. In hand and body creams.	Emollient, demulcent. Used in some foods at very low level of 0.002% (20 ppm).	Other plants of mallow family	Crude extracts	In France the tops and leaves are eaten as a spring salad for their property in stimulating the kidneys.
AMBRETTE SEED *(Abelmoschus moschatus)* SYN: Musk seed, musk mallow FOLK MEDICINE: Used as stimulant and antispasmodic; Chinese medicine for headaches.	Seed (oil)	The floral musk odor is due to ambrettolide and (2)-5-tetradecen-14-olide. Also contains phospholipids, palmitic and myristic acids.	Gives pleasant non-animal musk fragrance to sophisticated perfumes, soaps, creams, and lotions. Use level is 0.12%.	Aromatic, antispasmodic	Musk type plants	Essential oil	A musk for those who don't like the animal musk essential oil.
ANGELICA *(Archangelica officinalis)* SYN: Garden angelica, European angelica FOLK MEDICINE: The Chinese use ten angelica species to make "dang-gui," a drug for female ailments for thousands of years.	Roots, leaves, seeds	Contains 0.3 to 1% volatile oil: linolool, bornpol, acetaldehyde, anselicin, osthfenol, anselicin, osthfenol, archangelicin, etc. Also resins, starch, plant acids, essential fatty acids, sugars.	Has soothing effect on nerves of the skin when applied topically. Has fragrance use.	Diaphoretic and expectorant. Bergapten & xanthotoxin, etc., like bergamot oil, can be phototoxic. The seed oil is not phototoxic. Also exhibits antibacterial and antifungal properties.	Bergamot	Crude extracts and oil. Root and seed oil are N.F., U.S.P. and F.C.C.	The bergapten, xanthotoxin and the other coumarins have been shown to be effective in treating psoriasis.

-87-

Herb Name Synonyms Folk Use	Parts Used	Typical Substances	Cosmetic Use	Properties & Other Uses	Similar Plants	Extracts	Comments
ANNATTO (*Bixa orellana*) SYN: Arnotta, annotta, achiote, and achiotillo	Dried pulp of fruit	Contains bixin and norbixin, which are carotenoids but have no vitamin A activity.	Used as color	Used as annatto color for foods in about 0.25% maximum.	Carrot oil	Crude oil and water soluble extracts	Can lose color strength with storage.
APRICOT (*Prunus armeniaca*)	Kernels (oil)	Apricot kernels yield 40 to 50% fixed oil similar to almond and peach kernel oil. Contains olein, glyceride of linoleic acid. Also amygdalin used in Laetrile.	Has softening action on the skin. Used in soaps, lotions, creams, and fragrances.	Essential oil emollient	Almond oil	Essential oil	
ARAROBA (GOA) (*Andira araroba*) SYN: Goa, chrysarobin, bahia powder, Brazil powder, vouchapoua araroba	Medullary substance of stems and branches	Contains several substances but owes its power to chrysophanol-anthranol. Contains quinone and chrysophanic acid which is also found in buckhorn berries (*Rumox eckolianus*).	Astringent, skin treatment (Goa can stain clothing yellow or brown, but the stains can be removed with benzene).	Herbal treatment for acne, eczema, and psoriasis. It is a gastro-intestinal irritant.	Cabbage tree (*Andira inermis*)	Powder	In India and South American, goa has been esteemed for the treatment of psoriasis, ringworm, and itching. The action of Goa on the skin is not germicidal; it has a chemical affinity for the keratin elements of the skin. I have used goa in a face moisturizer for oily-type skin and in an amino acid gel for acne and oily skin with great success (non-staining).

Herb Name Synonyms Folk Use	Parts Used	Typical Substances	Cosmetic Use	Properties & Other Uses	Similar Plants	Extracts	Comments
ARISTOLOCHIA *(Aristolochia clematitis)* SYN: Birthwort, Dutchman's pipe	Green parts and root	Main constituent is aristolochine. It has never been carefully analyzed.	Can be used in amounts up to 20% in skin care creams for skin regeneration (celltherapy).	Anti-inflammatory, anti-paralytic, antiperiodic, aphrodisiac	Snakewort, aloe, echinacea	Glycolic	Aristolochia is a well-tried medicinal with wound-healing, granulating, and epithelizing effects. This extract increases the body's own defensive powers and eliminates skin damage due to organic dysfunction.
ARNICA *(Arnica montana)* SYN: Mountain tobacco, leopard's bane FOLK MEDICINE: Has been used as a diaphoretic, diuretic, stimulant, and vulnerary.	Roots & flowers	Contains up to 1% of a viscous volatile oil composed of fatty acids: palmitic, linoleic, myristic, and linolenic acid; vitamins A, B, C, and D; triterpenic alcohols, phytosterols, carotenoids, & flavonoids.	Flower extract is used for hair tonics, lotions, creams, massage lotions for cellulitis. Also for perfumes and topical treatments for bruises and sprains.	Essential oil stimulant, coadjutant in the treatment of cellulitis. Limited food use.	Stimulant extracts similar: ginseng, nettle, rosemary, sage Coadjutants for cellulitis similar: birch, ivy, horse chestnut, bladderwrack	Glycolic essential oil	Arnica is also used in deodorants along with calendula extract and vitamin E to reduce body odor. Do not use over 0.5% in cosmetic formulas.
AVOCADO *(Persea americana)* SYN: Alligator pear, avocato, ahuacate FOLK MEDICINE: The pulp has been used as a hair pomade to stimulate hair growth; used for wounds, as an aphrodisiac, and emmenagogue. Indians used the seeds for dysentery and diarrhea.	Pulp oil (avocado oil) and seed oil	Pulp oil consists mainly of glycerides of oleic acid, sterols, amino acids, and vitamin D (more than in milk). Mexican avocado leaves contain 3.1% of an essential oil that is 95% estragole and 5% anethole.	The pulp oil is used as a massage oil, in creams, lotions, and hair products. The seed oil has been patented for use in treatment of sclerosis of the skin. Pulp is used in face creams.	Essential oil. Pulp has been used for thousands of years as food; a good source of vitamin D and potassium.		Glycolic essential oil	A condensed flavanol isolated from avocado seeds has been reported to have anti-tumor activity against Sarcoma 180 and Walker 256. This flavanol is known as 4,8-Biscatechin (M. M. DeOliveira, An. Acad. Brasil Cienc., *Chem. Abstr.*, 75, 1973).

Herb Name Synonyms Folk Use	Parts Used	Typical Substances	Cosmetic Use	Properties & Other Uses	Similar Plants	Extracts	Comments
BALM OF GILEAD (*Commiphora opobalsamum*) SYN: Popular buds and balsam poplar buds FOLK MEDICINE: Used for minor aches and pains; for colds and coughs; topically on sores, cuts, and bruises.	Resinous juice of the bark	Contains 2% volatile oil, resins, salicin, populin; phenolic acids, chalcones, and others.	Topical use for cuts, sores, and bruises. Little use in cosmetics though balsams are used in hair conditioners (i.e., balsam of tolu).	Stimulant, expectorant, anti-pyretic, anti-rheumatic, analgesic.	Balsam Peru, balsam tolu	Glycolic liquid (juice); oil obtained is about $1/_{10}$ the amount of juice.	Major use of this herbal extract is in cough syrups with white pine, wild cherry bark, bloodroot, and spikenard root. Salicin (the glucoside or salicyl alcohol) is medicinal.
BALSAM OF PERU (*Myroxylon perairae*) SYN: *Tolufera pereira* FOLK MEDICINE: Reportedly used in treating cancer (J. L. Hartwell, *Lloydia*, 33, 97; 1970).	Oleoresinous liquid	Contains 50 to 60% high-boiling volatile oil called cinnamein and 20 to 28% resin which is mainly benzoic and cinnamic acid esters (traces of styrene, vanillin, coumarin).	In perfumes (maximum 0.8%); also in soaps, creams, and lotions.	Antiseptic, aromatic oil	Balsam tolu	Glycolic liquid	In recent years, balsam Peru and balsam tolu are in hair conditioners.
BALSAM TOLU (*Myrospermum toluiferum*) SYN: *Balsam tolutanum* FOLK MEDICINE: Reportedly used in treating cancer (see above).	Oleoresinous liquid	Contains cinnamic and benzoic acids and volatile oils composed of these acids and their esters with small amounts of terpenes.	In hair conditioners, soaps, creams, lotions, and perfumes (maximum 0.1% in soaps and 0.2% in perfumes).	Antiseptic. A few people may be allergic to balsam tolu. Used in cough medicines, lozenges, etc. Used to compound benzoin tincture.	Balsam Peru	Glycolic liquid	Balsam tolu is most popular in hair conditioners for its fragrance and mild antiseptic qualities.

Herb Name Synonyms Folk Use	Parts Used	Typical Substances	Cosmetic Use	Properties & Other Uses	Similar Plants	Extracts	Comments
BASIL, SWEET (Ocymum basilum) SYN: Basil FOLK MEDICINE: Used for head colds and as a cure for warts. Widely used as a medicinal herb in China and India (Basil comes from the Greek basileus--king--because of its royal fragrance)	Herb	The volatile oil contains d-linalool, methyl chavicol; also protein (14%), carbohydrates (61%) and high concentrations of vitamins A and C.	Fragrance ingredient in perfumes, soaps, and hair products.	Antiwormal activity. Used as a spice and in chartreuse liqueur. Oleoresin used in major food products in low levels of 0.005% or lower. Can be used as insect repellent on the skin.	Basil rush, wild basil	Essential oil oleoresin	The basil plant is sacred to both Krishna and Vishnu and is held in high esteem in every house in India. Every good Hindu goes to rest with a basil leaf on his breast. This is his passport to the Elysian fields.
BEARSFOOT (Polymnia uvedalia) SYN: Uvedalia, leaf cup, yellow leaf cup	Root	Complete analysis not known, but probably contains fatty acids, some quinone and maybe chrysophanic acid.	Known as a treatment for hair loss and is used in many hair ointments and lotions.	Anodyne, laxative, and stimulant. It is valued for the treatment of malaria.		Essential oil (fluid extract)	To use as a hair tonic, formulate with an herbal alcohol or witch hazel. To use as a hair growth lotion, mix with jojoba oil or lanolin.
BEET JUICE, RED (Beta vulgaris, Chenopodiaceae) SYN: Spinach beet, sea beet, garden beet, mangel wurzel	Root	Betalains (quaternary ammonium amino acids) are the coloring agents in red beet juice. High in glucoses and fine sugars that are very wholesome. A treacle principle in the glucose renders it even more nutritious.	Used to a limited extent as a color in cosmetics.	Used to color foods to a limited extent. Used as a food and health juice. In Russia, used to make borsch.		Juice	The red color is stable at pH 4.5 to 5.5, but outside this range the color is altered, due to the destruction of betalain at about pH 3.3.

Herb Name Synonyms Folk Use	Parts Used	Typical Substances	Cosmetic Use	Properties & Other Uses	Similar Plants	Extracts	Comments
BEESWAX *(Apis mellifera)* SYN: White beeswax, yellow beeswax FOLK MEDICINE: In Chinese medicine, beeswax is dissolved in hot wine and taken as a treatment for diarrhea, hiccups, and pain.	Wax obtained from honeycombs	Yellow and white beeswax contains 71% fatty acid esters. One substance in the wax, myricyl alcohol, has been shown to be a plant growth stimulator, and has increased yields of tomato, cucumber, and lettuce.	Thickener, emulsifier, stiffening agent in ointments, cold creams, lotions, lipsticks, etc. Also used to remove hair by beauty salons.	Also used in foods as thickener, emulsifier, and flavor ingredients (use levels are low; the maximum is 0.05%).	Jojoba wax	Wax	White beeswax is obtained by bleaching yellow beeswax with peroxides. It is on the FDA G.R.A.S. (Generally Regarded As Safe) list, but some people are allergic to beeswax.
BENZOIN *(Styrax benzoin)* SYN: Benzoin gum, gum benjamin, Siam benjamin, Sumatra benzoin	Resin from bark	Chiefly contains cinnamic and benzoic acid esters. Sumatra benzoin has 70 to 80% of these acid esters and Siam benzoin contains 60-80% and 12% free benzoic acid.	Can be used as face lotion astringent and antiseptic. Benzoin tincture is used as a skin protectant and styptic on small cuts. Also as preservative. Used in soaps, creams, and lotions up to 0.8%.	Antioxidant, preservative, astringent. Certified as natural flavor. Use level is low maximum 0.014%.		Resin oleoresin tincture	Chief product is benzoic acid used as sodium benzoate in beverages. Tincture of benzoin (B.P. and U.S.P.) is ½ to 1 drachm.
BERGAMOT *(Monarda didyma)* SYN: Scarlet monarda, oswego tea, bee balm	Herb	Thymol is the main substance, though this oil is also obtained from *Monarda puctata*.	Fragrance used in soaps, lotions, creams, and perfumes.	Oswego tea is made from the leaves.	Mint, horsemint, similar also to bergamot orange oil	Essential oil	The whole plant has the "bergamot orange" fragrance.

Herb Name Synonyms Folk Use	Parts Used	Typical Substances	Cosmetic Use	Properties & Other Uses	Similar Plants	Extracts	Comments
BERGAMOT OIL (*Citrus bergamia*)	Peel of fruit	Three hundred compounds are present in the peel oil from this fruit. 60% linalyl acetate and 11 to 22% linalool, alcohols, bergamotene, terpenes.	Extensively used in perfumes and eau de cologne. Also in creams and lotions. Used 0.25% in cosmetics and 3% in perfumes.	Due to the presence of bergapten and xanthotoxin (5-methoxypsoralen and 8-methoxypsoralen) it is phototoxic. Effective in the treatment of psoriasis (see **PSORIASIS** in this book).		Oil of peel	Though this oil is on the FDA's G.R.A.S list for use in food as a flavor, there are allergic reactions to it.
BETULLA (*Betula pendula*) SYN: White birch, bouleau, berke, bereza	Leaves and bark	The essential oil contains tannis, a triterpenic pentacyclic derivative (*betulin*) and saponins high in methyl salicylate (98%) which gives it anti-inflammatory properties. Leaves contain betulorentic acid.	Used in shampoos, lotions for greasy hair, astringent lotions, creams for oily skin, and body massage lotions for cellulite. Also as a fragrance material.	Astringent, mild skin purifier, coadjutant in treatment of cellulitis. When used in foods, the highest level used is 0.1%. Anti-inflammatory, anti-pyretic, analgesic.	Astringents similar: witch hazel, rhatany Skin purifiers: rosemary, sage Cellulite: ivy, escin, horse chestnut, bladderwrack	Birch glycolic extract	
BISTORT (*Polygonum bistorta*) SYN: Osterick, snakeweed, Easter mangiant, adderwort, twice writhen	Root stock	Never been carefully analyzed. Contains 20% tannin, starch, gallic acid, and gum.	One of the strongest astringents, but is not used in cosmetics though it would be superior to alcohol and acetone.	Astringent, styptic	Witch hazel, rhatany, betulla	Root extract	The European white birch (*Betula pendula roth*) is used for psoriasis, eczema and other skin problems.

Herb Name Synonyms Folk Use	Parts Used	Typical Substances	Cosmetic Use	Properties & Other Uses	Similar Plants	Extracts	Comments
BLADDERWRACK (*Fucus vesiculosis*) SYN: Fucus, sea-wrack, kelp-ware, quercia marina	Thallus	Alginates, iodine, mineral salts, sugars, amino acids, fucosterol.	Foam baths, creams, gels, massage lotions for cellulite. Has soothing properties for skin.	Soothing, coadjutant in external treatment of cellulitis. A valuable fertilizer.	Other seaweeds are similar. *Laminaria digitata* is a superb moisturizer. Also kelp.	Glycolic extract (0.1% iodine) and fluid extract	In 1862 bladder-wrack was found to be a good weight reducer. Fucol is a "cod liver oil" obtained by roasting bladderwrack with a bland oil.
BOIS DE ROSE OIL (*Aniba rosaeodora*) SYN: Rosewood oil, cayenne rosewood oil	Bark	Major component is linalool (90-97%), cayenne bois de rose oil, Brazilian oil.	Used to obtain natural linalool or linalool acetate used in perfumes. Also used in soaps, creams, lotions, and perfumes in maximum amounts of 1.2%.	Fragrance used in some foods in maximum amounts of 0.003% (24.9 ppm).	Plants with linalool.	Glycolic extract from wood.	
BONESET (*eupatorium perfoliatum*) SYN: eupatorium, feverwort, thoroughwort, agueweed FOLK MEDICINE: Tonic, febrifuge, diaphoretic, emetic, and for skin rashes.	Herb	Contains flavonoids, triterpenoids, triterpenes, sterols, and resins.	Little or no commercial use in cosmetics. Used by herbalists for skin problems.	Stimulant, febrifuge, laxative, diaphoretic.		Crude extracts, not readily available.	
BORONIA ABSOLUTE (*Boronia megastigma*)	Flower	Contains ionones, eugenol	Used in expensive perfumes.	Aromatic, flavor. Used in fruit type flavors.		Essential oil	The ionones are reportedly allergenic.
BRYONY (*Tamus communis*) SYN: Black bryony, blackeye root, bryonia	Root	Never been carefully analyzed.		Cathartic. Can be poison if taken internally.	European bryony, white bryony	Crude extracts	Externally applied, the powdered root, mixed with water into a paste, removes freckles.

Herb Name Synonyms Folk Use	Parts Used	Typical Substances	Cosmetic Use	Properties & Other Uses	Similar Plants	Extracts	Comments
BUCKTHORN, ALDER *(Rhamnus frangula)* SYN: Frangula, buckthorn, arrow wood, black dogwood FOLK MEDICINE: Laxative and tonic. Used in cancer treatment as a component of the Hoxsey cancer cure (J. L. Hartwell, *Lloydia*, 34, 103, 1971).	Bark	Contains 3 to 7% anthraquinone glycosides, tannis, flavonoids, and anthraquinones.	Extract is reported to be useful in sunscreen products.	Tonic, laxative, cathartic	Common buckthorn, sea buckthorn, others	Crude extracts	A fluid extract of the bark is an excellent laxative and far milder than the commonly used *cascara sagrada* which has taken its place.
BUTCHER'S BROOM *(Ruscus aculeatus)* SYN: Kneeholy, knee holly, kneeholm, Jew's myrtle FOLK MEDICINE: It was recommended by Dioscorides and other ancient physicians as a diuretic.	Rhizome	Essential oil resins, saponins (1.8% saponosides).	For delicate and sensitive skin.	Diaphoretic, diuretic, skin-lightener, anti-redness, astringent	Similar astringents: birch, escin, witch hazel, rhatany Similar sedatives and lighteners: marigold, camomile horse chestnut, linden tree	Glycolic extract	
CADE OIL *(Juniperus oxycedrus)* SYN: Oil of cade, juniper tar, oil of juniper tar FOLK MEDICINE: Has been used for years on problem scalps and for hair loss. Reportedly used for cancers (J. L. Hartwell, *Lloydia*, 33, 288, 1970).	Branches and wood	Contains cadinene, cadinol, p-cresol, guaiacol, viridiflorol, etc.	Used as a topical for treatment of eczema, wounds, and parasitic skin. Also used in anti-dandruff shampoos, creams, and ointments. Used as fragrance in soaps and perfumes (0.2% in fragrances).	Analgesic, anti-pruritic, essential oil		Cade oil N.F., juniper tar oil, essential oil	Though cade oil has actions similar to evening primrose oil, it is not similar.

Herb Name Synonyms Folk Use	Parts Used	Typical Substances	Cosmetic Use	Properties & Other Uses	Similar Plants	Extracts	Comments
CAJEPUT OIL (*Melaleuca leucadendron*) SYN: Cajuput, punk tree, paper bark tree. FOLK MEDICINE: Used for colds and headaches, aching muscles, arthritis, various skin problems and treatment tumors (see CADE OIL).	Leaves & twigs	Contains 14 to 65% cineole, pinene, phenone (10%), terpineol, nerolidol, and traces benzaldehyde and valeraldehyde.	Used as fragrance component in soaps, creams, lotions, and perfumes (Max. 0.4% in perfumes).	Carminative, stimulant, diaphoretic, antimicrobial, and antiseptic.		Essential oil	
CALAMUS (*Acorus calamus*) SYN: Sweet flag, sweet root, sweet cinnamon, sweet myrtle, sweet sedge FOLK MEDICINE: Used for over 2,000 years in China to treat arthritis, strokes, epilepsy, and skin diseases. When chewed it is said to kill the taste for tobacco and clear phlegm from the throat.	Root	Contains asarone, asarylaldehyde, calamene, linalool, calamol, calameone, eugenol, methyl eugenol, azulene, pinene, cineole, camphor, etc.	Used mainly as a fragrance in soaps, creams, lotions, perfumes (0.4%).	Considered toxic and not approved for food use. May be carcinogenic (D. L. J. Opdyke, *Food Cosmet. Toxicol.*, 15, 623, 1977).	*Calamus draco*	Essential oil	Should not be confused with calamine lotion which is a mineral not an herb.
CALENDULA or MARIGOLD (*Calendula officinalis*) SYN: *Caltha officinalis*, golds, marygold	Flowers, herb leaves	Carotenoids, oleanolic acid, mucilages, essential oil.	Freshening tonics, after-sun products, softening hand creams, and sensitive skin lotions.	Stimulant, demulcent, softener, freshener.	Sedatives: camomile, mallow, linden tree Skin brightener: witch hazel, horse chestnut, butcher's broom	Glycolic liposoluble extract	Calendula has recently been used in deodorants.

Herb Name Synonyms Folk Use	Parts Used	Typical Substances	Cosmetic Use	Properties & Other Uses	Similar Plants	Extracts	Comments
CAMOMILE or CHAMOMILE German camomile: *(Matricaria chamomilla)* Roman camomile: *(Anthemis nobilis)* SYN: Wild chamomile FOLK MEDICINE: German and Roman camomile have been used since ancient times for colic, diarrhea, toothache, arthritis, and skin problems. Camomile has also been traditionally used to color hair.	Flowers, herb	German camomile contains volatile oil (0.25 to 1.9%); flavonoids (apigenin, apiin, rutin, luteolin, and puercimeritrin); plant acids and fatty acids, a polysaccharide with d-galacturonic acid, choline, amino acids, etc. Chamazulene and "blue" chamazulene in some species (rare). Roman camomile contains up to 1.75% volatile oil; 0.6% bitter sesquiterpene lactones; flavonoids (apigenin, apiin, quercitrin); coumarins, choline, fatty acids.	Both camomiles are used in cosmetics including bath oils, hair dyes (for blond hair), shampoos, sun protection creams, face masks, and creams. On the skin camomile has a sedative and emollient effect and acts as a normalizer for rough skin.	German camomile has bacterial and fungicidal properties against gram-positive bacteria. Chamazulene, a major component, has pain-relieving, wound-healing, anti-spasmodic, anti-inflammatory, and anti-microbial properties. Roman camomile is emetic. Three sesquiterpene lactones have been reported to have anti-tumor activities *in vitro* against human tumor cells (M. Holub and Z. Samek, *Collect. Czech. Chem. Commun.*, 24, 1053, 1977).	Similar sedatives: marigold, butcher's broom linden tree Similar emollients: aloe, mallow Similar skin normalizers: cone flower St. John's wort oil	Camomile glycolic extract; camomile liposoluble fluid extract; azulenic essential oil	Camomile is used in perfume formulas at up to 0.4%. "Blue" camomile is very rare and high in azulenic content. It has a much different fragrance from the "yellow" variety of camomile. Blue camomile is also very expensive.
CAMPHOR *(Cinnamonum camphor)* SYN: Laurel camphor, gum camphor	Gum from tree	The chief constituent of the oil is borneene.	Tiny amounts can be used in after-shave lotions and antiseptic and cooling skin creams.	Antiseptic, stimulant, anti-inflammatory.	Menthol, eucalyptus	Oil of camphor	Camphor relieves irritation of the sexual organs and is useful against yeast infections combined with menthol and eucalyptus in topical creams.

-97-

Herb Name Synonyms Folk Use	Parts Used	Typical Substances	Cosmetic Use	Properties & Other Uses	Similar Plants	Extracts	Comments
CANANGA OIL *(Cananga odorata)*	Flowers	Contains B-caryo-phyllene, benzyl acetate, benzyl alcohol, farnesol, borneol, methyl salicylate, benzaldehyde, saf-role, linalool, eugen-ol, etc. (over 100 compounds).	Used as a fragrance in soaps, creams, lotions, and perfumes. It is popular in men's fragrances. Used at a max. level of 0.8% in perfumes.	Essential oil also used as flavor in food.	Ylang-ylang oil *(canangium odoratum)*	Essential oil	
CARAWAY *(Carum carvi)* SYN: Caraway seed, caraway fruit, and carium FOLK MEDICINE: Used as an antispasmodic, car-minative, expectorant, and stomachic; also to relieve menstrual discomfort.	Fruit or leaves	Contains 4 to 7% volatile oil, 15% lipids, 20% protein, mannan, and flavonoids.	The oil is used in toothpaste, mouthwash, soaps, creams, lotions, and in perfumes at 0.4% level.	Essential oil, anti-spasmodic, carmina-tive, stomachic. Us-ed in foods, espe-cially baked goods.		Caraway oil N.F.	In Shakespeare's *Henry IV,* Squire Shallow invites Fal-staff to a hot roast-ed dish of caraways. The custom of serv-ing a saucerful of caraway with roast-ed apples is still kept up at Trinity College, Cambridge, and at some of the old London livery dinners just as in Shakespeare's day.
CARDAMON *(Elettaria cardamomum)* SYN: *Amomum car-damomum; Alpinia car-damomum;* cardamon seeds	Dried ripe seeds	Up to 10% volatile oil, 10% protein, 10% fixed oil, 20 to 40% starch, magnanese, and iron.	Used as fragrances in soap, creams, lotions, and sham-poos. Used in per-fumes 0.4%.	Carminative, stimulant		Essential oil	In China the species *Amomum carda-momum* is used in herbal medicine.

Herb Name Synonyms Folk Use	Parts Used	Typical Substances	Cosmetic Use	Properties & Other Uses	Similar Plants	Extracts	Comments
CARRAGEENAN (*Chondrus crispus*) SYN: Carrageen, chondrus, carrahan, and Irish moss. FOLK MEDICINE: Considered as a demulcent and a nutrient. Also used for coughs, bronchitis and intestinal problems.	Dried plant	Carrageenan is a sulfated straight-chain galactan of d-galactose and 3,G-anhydro-D-galactose. It contains a gelling fraction (K-carrageenan) and a non-gelling fraction.	It is used in cosmetics as a binding agent, emulsifier, and stabilizer; used as such in toothpaste, hand lotions, and creams.	Anti-coagulant, hypotensive, immunosuppressive. Used in foods extensively.	Locust bean gum and other types of seaweeds.	Powdered extract	Some carrageenan is believed to be toxic though the food grade is considered safe. Tests have shown that carrageenan lowers blood cholesterol.
CARROT OIL (*Daucus carota*) SYN: Carrot, wild carrot, and Queen Anne's lace. FOLK MEDICINE: Used in China to treat chronic dystentery and as an anthelmintic.	Dried fruit and root	Contains carotol, daucol, limonene, B-bisabolene, B-elemene, geraniol, geranyl acetate, B-carotene and vitamin A (as well as other substances).	Though used primarily as a fragrance and coloring agent in cosmetics, it is very useful in sunscreens as a source of B-carotene and vitamin A.	Soothing, diuretic, emmenagogue. Used as a food color.		Glycolic: seed oil or root oil	Carrot oil used in skin lotions exhibits usefulness for dry as well as oily skin. Also useful in anti-acne skin treatments.
CASSIE ABSOLUTE (*Acadia farnesiana*) SYN: Sweet acacia, husiache, and popinac.	Flowers	25% volatile oil composed mainly of benzyl alcohol, methyl salicylate, geraniol, and over 40 other compounds.	This absolute is used in high-cost perfumes; also used in bath oils for dry skin.	Anti-spasmodic, aphrodisiac, food flavoring.		Essential oil	Root has supposedly been used in Venzuela to treat stomach cancer (J. L. Hartwell, *Lloydia*, 33, 97, 1970).
CASTOR OIL (*Ricinus communis*) SYN: *Rincinus palma christi*, castor bean, and castor seed oil. FOLK MEDICINE: Castor oil has been used since ancient times in India, Egypt, and China as a carthartic.	Seeds	Contains mostly triglycerides of ricinoleic acid (90%); other fatty acids are linoleic, oleic, stearic, and dihydroxystearic acids.	Used in lipsticks, hair grooms, ointments, creams, and lotions.	Cathartic, anti-sticking agent, solvent. Used in candy as hardening and anti-sticking agent.		Oil	The main objection to castor oil is its nauseous taste and the sickness often produced after its use. Its largest use is industrial.

Herb Name Synonyms Folk Use	Parts Used	Typical Substances	Cosmetic Use	Properties & Other Uses	Similar Plants	Extracts	Comments
CATECHU (Black & Pale) *(Catechu nigrum & uncaria gambier)* FOLK MEDICINE: Both types of catechu have been used to stop nosebleeding, also for treating sores and ulcers; reported use in treating cancer (J. L. Hartwell, *Lloydia*, 33, 97, 1970).	Heart-wood, leaves & twigs	Black catechu contains 2 to 20% l- and dl-catechin; up to 50% catechutannic acid. Pale catechu contains 30 to 35% d- and dl-catechin and catechutannic acid (24%).	Both types are used as astringents.	Astringent, antibacterial. Tannic acid is considered toxic.		Essential oil	
CEDAR LEAF OIL or CEDARWOOD OIL *(Thuja occidentalis)* SYN: Cedar oil, white cedar, thuja oil FOLK MEDICINE: Used as ointment or decoction to treat arthritis, coughs, fever, and skin rash. Has been used in treating condyloma and cancers (J. L. Hartwell, *Lloydia*, 33, 288, 1970).	Leaves, twigs, & wood	Contains thujone, isothujone, l-fenchone, borneol, l-bornyl acetate, dl-limonene, camphor, myrcene, terines, etc.	Usually used as fragrance ingredient in soaps, shampoos, creams, lotions, bath oil, and perfumes.	Expectorant, stimulant, and counter-irritant.	Other wood oils (pine wood, etc.)	Essential oil	Due to its high thujone content, the oil is poisonous in large quantities.
CENTAURY *(Cantaurium arythraea)* SYN: European centaury, bitter herb, feverwort FOLK MEDICINE: Used as a stomachic, febrifuge, and sedative.	Herb leaves	Bitter glucosides, alkaloids, phenolic acids, fatty acids, and triterpenes.	Due to its soothing and astringent properties, it is useful in skin care products. Used in lotions to remove freckles, spots, and skin blemishes.	Bitter tonic, sedative, anti-pyretic.	Canchalagua (Centaury herb of Chile)	Glycolic	This herb was used in ancient Egypt to treat hypertension and for kidney stones. J. L. Hartwell reported in *Lloydia* (1969) that it has been used to treat cancers.

Herb Name Synonyms Folk Use	Parts Used	Typical Substances	Cosmetic Use	Properties & Other Uses	Similar Plants	Extracts	Comments
CHAULMOOGRA (*Taraktogenos kunzii*) SYN: Chaulmugra, chaulmogra FOLK MEDICINE: Has been used internally and externally for skin diseases, scrofula, arthritis, eczema, bruises, sprains, and open wounds.	Oil of seeds	Contains chaulmoogric acid, palmitic acid, glycerol, phytosterol, and fatty acids.	Used in ointments, lotions, and creams for the treatment of psoriasis and eczema.	Sedative, anti-irritant, healing	The allied species *Glynocardia odorata* and *Hydnocarpus*	Oil	When applied topically to psoriasis, the oil breaks up lesions much the same as goa, but will not stain as does goa. In Great Britain, the fatty oil is known as gynocardia oil; in the U. S., it is known as *oleum chaulmoograe*.
CHICLE (*Manilkara zapota*) SYN: Sapodilla	Latex in the bark, pith, and leaves	Contains 15 to 20% hydrocarbons that are polyisoprenes, 55% yellow resin, and a gum composed of xylan.	This is a useful natural gum for hair dressings and hairsprays.	Used in chewing gum (20%) with sugar, corn syrup, and flavorings.		Gum	The trade name "chicklets" is based on this tree gum.
CHINA (*Smilax china*) SYN: Smilax, China shrub FOLK MEDICINE: Used in China since 1535 for gout and skin problems.	Herb	Contains steroids, smilagenin, sitosterol, glycosides, and saponins.	Used in herbal medicine for skin diseases.	Diaphoretic, tonic. When mixed with alum, a yellow dye is produced; when mixed with sulfate of iron, a brown dye is produced.	Sarsaparilla	Glycolic	This plant should not be confused with the "china" used in homeopathy which is Peruvian bark.

Herb Name Synonyms Folk Use	Parts Used	Typical Substances	Cosmetic Use	Properties & Other Uses	Similar Plants	Extracts	Comments
CINCHONA (Red & Yellow) Red: *(Chinchona succirubra)* Yellow: *(Chinchona calisaya)* SYN: Red bark, red Peruvian bark, cincho ruba, yellow bark, jesuit's bark, Peruvian bark, fever-bark, China bark. FOLK MEDICINE: Used for malaria, fevers, indigestion. Used in China to treat hangovers.	Bark	Contains 16% quinoline alkaloids consisting mainly of quinine, quinidine, cinchonine, and cinchonidine. Also tannins, bitter glycosides, resins, and waxes.	Used in hair tonics to stimulate hair growth and control oiliness. Also in gels for aging and troubled skin.	Stimulant, anti-malarial, anti-pyretic. Quinine from red cinchona is used in tonic water.	Other stimulants for skin: arnica, ginseng nettle, rosemary, sage	Glycolic	See pp. 1-2 regarding the Countess of Chinchon and fever-bark.
CINNAMON *(Cinnamomum zelanicum)* SYN: Ceylon cinnamon, and Saigon cassia.	Bark, leaves	Up to 4% volatile oil, tannins, resins, mucilage, gums, sugars, calcium oxalate (two insecticidal compounds cinnzelanin and cinnzelanol.	Cinnamon leaf oil is used as a fragrance and in mouth-washes, toothpastes, and gargles.	Antiseptic carminative anti-fungal. A food spice.		Glycolic	
CITRONELLA OIL *(Cymbopogon nardus)*	Dried grass	Citronellal, geraniol, citronellol, linalool, monoterpene, hydrocarbons (limonene, pinene, camphene, etc.), phenols, and alcohols.	As fragrance material in soaps, hair tonics, disinfectants, and perfumes.	Anti-bacterial, anti-fungal.		Essential oil	Some people are allergic to citronella oil.
CLOVE OIL *(Suzygium aromaticum)* SYN: *Eugenia aromatica*	Buds, stems, & leaves	The buds contain 15 to 18% volatile oil, the stems only 4 to 6%, and the leaves 2 to 3%. Contains glucosides, sterols, and esters.	Clove leaf oil is used in perfumes. Clove bud oil is used in dentifrices, creams, lotions, and perfumes.	Carminative, anti-emetic, counter-irritant		Essential oil	This oil is, of course, known to reduce the pain of toothache.

Herb Name Synonyms Folk Use	Parts Used	Typical Substances	Cosmetic Use	Properties & Other Uses	Similar Plants	Extracts	Comments
COCOA *(Theobroma cacao)* SYN: Theobroma FOLK MEDICINE: Cocoa butter was used to treat wrinkles around the eyes and mouth.	Seeds	Contains over 300 volatile compounds, hydrocarbons, monocarbonyls, esters, lactones, proteins (18%), fats (cocoa butter), amines, theobromine (0.5 to 2.7%), etc.	Cocoa butter is used as a suppository, ointment base, emollient, skin softener, and protectant.	Also used as a food flavoring ingredient.		Cocoa powder, butter, and syrup	Some people are allergic to cocoa butter.
COLTSFOOT *(Tussilago farfara)* SYN: Horseshoof, ass's foot, foalswort	Leaves, flowers, & roots	Contains phytosterol, tannin, silica, amino acids (cystine), dihydride alcohol, and faradial.	Due to the cystine and silica content, it is used in hair care products.	*Tussilago* means "cough dispeller" (a tobacco made with it helps coughs). Used in cough drops with horehound, marshmallow, and ivy.	Horsetail	Glycolic	Coltsfoot is high in cystine and silica—excellent for the hair. A tobacco can be made by combining coltsfoot, buckbean, eyebright, betony, rosemary, thyme, lavender, and camomile.
COMFREY *(Symphytum officinale)* SYN: Comfrey, knitbone, knitback, slippery root, boneset FOLK MEDICINE: Used to treat a wide variety of ailments: diarrhea, dysentery, coughs, etc.	Roots & leaves	Root contains 0.75 to 2.55% allantoin, pyrrolizidines, lithospermic acid, mucopolysaccharides (29%), glucose, fructose, d-glucoronic acid, tannins, carotenes, glycosides, saponins, etc.	Comfrey root and its extract, allantoin, are used in a wide variety of cosmetics.	Anti-inflammatory, astringent, demulcent, emollient, hemostatic, expectorant.		Glycolic; powdered as allantoin	The healing and emollient properties of this herb can be used in many products. The mucopolysaccharides and allantoin can be used in celltherapy.
CONEFLOWER *(Centaurea cyanus)* SYN: Bluebottle, bluebow, blue cap, bluet. FOLK MEDICINE: This herb was known as a tonic, stimulant, and emmenagogue, also an active wound healer. The blue juice from the herb was used as a water color.	Flower	The blue extract of cornflower is cyanin and contains many flavones. Contains 3,5-diglucoside, and gallo-catechin known for their antiseptic and astringent action. Also various flavonoids and amino acids.	In France an eyewash is made with cornflower water (called *eau de casse-lunettes*). It is excellent in toners, astringents, and healling or celltherapy creams.	Used in pot-pourri to give a lovely blue color.	Blessed thistle	Glycolic	The Latin name of this species refers to the goddess Floral; the name of the genus is derived from the centaur Chiron who taught mankind the healing virtue of herbs. Hence, this is a healing herb.

Herb Name Synonyms Folk Use	Parts Used	Typical Substances	Cosmetic Use	Properties & Other Uses	Similar Plants	Extracts	Comments
CORN SILK *(Zea mays)* SYN: Stigmata, maydis, and zea. FOLK MEDICINE: Used as diuretic in urinary problems. In Chinese medicine it is used to treat diabetes and hypertension.	The long styles and stigmata of the pistils called "corn silk."	Corn silk contains 2.5% fats, 0.12% volatile oils, 3 to 8% gums, 2.7% resin, 1.5% glucosides, 3.8% saponins, vitamins C and K, etc.	Used in face powders	Diuretic, hypoglycemic. Also used as flavoring in some foods.		Powdered extract	
CUCUMBER *(Cucumis sativa)* SYN: Cowcumber	The whole fruit peeled and unpeeled	Cucumber contains up to 96% water. The seeds are similar to pumpkin seeds.	Used in facial creams, lotions, and cleansers.	Astringent, soothing properties.		Crude pulp & juice	The juice of a cucumber mixed with glycerine and rosewater in equal parts is excellent for sunburns.
ECHINACEA *(Echinacea angustifolia)* SYN: Black sampson, coneflower	Roots	Large amounts of inulin, inuloid, sucrose, bulose, betaine, phytosterols, and fatty acids.	Used in creams and lotions. Used for greasy skin as gel or lotion.	Texturizer, firming agent, co-adjutant in treatment of wrinkles.	For firming: horsetail ginseng Skin texturizing: camomile St. John's wort	Glycolic essential oil	Used in combination with aristolochia and aloe in celltherapy.
ELDER FLOWERS *(Sambucus nigra)* SYN: Black elder, pipe tree, hylder, hylan tree	Bark, leaves, flowers, & berries	Essential oil composed of fatty acids (66%) and alkanes (7%), sterols, flavonoids, flavone glycosides, phenolic acids, rutin, pectin, etc.	In Europe elder flower water is used for eye and skin lotion. Flower essential oil is used in perfumes.	Diuretic, astringent, laxative, diaphoretic.		Glycolic essential oil	Used combined with other herbs in hair and skin products. Known for elderberry wine and elderberry tea.
ELECAMPANE *(Inula helenium)* SYN: Elf dock, wild sunflower, scabwort.	Root	Contains 1 to 4% volatile oil including alantolactone (elecampane camphor), azulene, inulin, sterols, etc.	Used in soaps, creams, lotions, and perfumes.	Diuretic, tonic, diaphoretic, antiseptic, astringent.	Spikenard, samphire	Glycolic (essential oil)	A natural blue dye can be extracted from the root. A distilled water of the leaves is an excellent face wash.

Herb Name Synonyms Folk Use	Parts Used	Typical Substances	Cosmetic Use	Properties & Other Uses	Similar Plants	Extracts	Comments
ELM, SLIPPERY *(Ulmus fulva)* SYN: Red elm, moose elm, Indian elm. FOLK MEDICINE: For coughs, colds, sore throats. A pinch of the powdered bark on a tooth kills pain.	The inner bark	The mucilage in the cells of the bark is similar to that found in linseed. Contains starch, calcium, & gums.	Used as thickener and in creams and ointments.	Demulcent, emollient, nutrient, expectorant, diuretic. Wide use for coughs, bronchitis. The bark will preserve oils from becoming rancid (antioxidant).	*Fremontia california* has similar properties but is not related to slippery elm.	Glycolic, mucilage, and powdered bark.	An herbal ointment can be made by combining 3 oz. marshmallow leaves, 2 oz. slippery elm bark powder, 3 oz. jojoba wax or beeswax, 16 oz. jojoba butter or lard.
EUCALYPTUS *(Eucalyptus globulus)* SYN: Blue gum tree, stringy bark tree FOLK MEDICINE: Used as antiseptic, febrifuge, and as expectorant in respiratory ailments. Also used for burns, wounds, & ulcers.	Oil of the leaves	Contains 0.5 to 3.5% volatile oil, tannins, polyphenolic acids, flavonoids, wax, aldehydes, etc. 70 to 85% eucalyptol gives it cooling, antiseptic properties.	Used as fragrance in soaps, creams, lotions, and perfumes. Also used in liniments, cleansers, and bath oils for spas. When used in creams it reduces itching of yeast infections.	Antiseptic, expectorant, antibacterial. Used in small amounts in some foods, cough drugs, & eucalyptol candy.	Menthol	Essential oil	This is an excellent oil in skin care and in bath oils, but it must be used in tiny amounts (less than 1.0%). It can be toxic in large amounts, although it is non-irritating and non-phototoxic to the skin.
EYEBRIGHT *(Euphrasia officinalis)* SYN: Euphrasia	Herb	The precise constituents are unknown. Contains a tannin called euphrasia-tannin acid, mannite, glucose.	Classically used as an eye lotion and eye wash.	Tonic, astringent, used in British herbal tobaccos for coughs.	Bartsia	Fluid extract	1 teaspoon eyebright extract and 1 teaspoon goldenseal make an eye lotion for eye disorders.

Herb Name Synonyms Folk Use	Parts Used	Typical Substances	Cosmetic Use	Properties & Other Uses	Similar Plants	Extracts	Comments
FENNEL (*Foeniculum vulgare*) SYN: Fenkel, sweet fennel, and finocchio	Seeds, leaves, & roots	Seeds contain 1.5 to 8.6% volatile oil; 9 to 28% fixed oil composed of oleic acid, linoleic acid, and high concentrations of tocopherols, flavonoids, protein (16 to 20%), sugars, vitamins, minerals (calcium and potassium).	Fennel and sweet fennel oil are used as a fragrance in soaps, shampoos, lotions, creams, and perfumes.	Carminative, antibacterial, cytotoxic properties; weight loss properties.		Oil extract	The ancient Greeks called this herb *marathron*, from *maraino*, to grow thin. The seeds, leaves, and root are used in drinks for weight loss. Milton in *Paradise Lost* says: "Grateful to appetite, more pleased my sense/than smell of sweet fennel."
FENUGREEK (*Trigonella foenum graecum*) SYN: Foenugreek, Greek hay.	Seeds	Contains simple alkaloids, choline, gentianine, trigonelline, saponins, flavonoids, lysine, tryptophan, vitamins A, B₁, and C.	Used in soaps, creams, lotions, and perfume bases. In Java, it is used as a hair growth tonic.	Used in foods and in spices. A good source of sapogenins for the manufacture of steroid hormones.		Liquid and spray-dried form	Fenugreek was first introduced in Chinese medicine during the Sung Dynasty (1057 A.D.) for kidney ailments, hernia, impotency.
FRANKINCENSE (*Boswellia thurifera*) SYN: Olibanum	Gum from bark	65% resins, 6% volatile oil, 20% water, soluble gum, bassorin 8% and alibanoresin.	Used as a fragrance material.	Stimulant. Principally used for incense.	Balsam (tolu or peru)	Resin	In ancient Egypt, the kohl used to paint the eyelids was made from charred frankincense.
GERANIUM OIL (*Pelargonium gravedens*) SYN: Algerian geranium oil, bourbon geranium oil	Leaves & stems	High in herbal alcohols such as citronellol, geraniol, linalool, and ketones, aldehydes, menthol, & acids.	Rose geranium oil is widely used as a fragrance component in soaps, creams, lotions, and perfumes.	Anti-fungal and anti-bacterial activities *in vitro*. Some use in foods.		Essential oil	Some people are allergic to geranium oil.

-106-

Herb Name Synonyms Folk Use	Parts Used	Typical Substances	Cosmetic Use	Properties & Other Uses	Similar Plants	Extracts	Comments
GINGER *(Zingiber officinale)* SYN: Common ginger, Nigerian root. FOLK MEDICINE: Used as carminative, diaphoretic, and appetite stimulant. Used for thousands of years in China for many ailments including baldness and arthritis.	Root	Contains 1 to 3% volatile oil and pungent principals (gingerols and shogaols); 6 to 8% lipids (triglycerides, phosphatidic acid, lecithins, fatty acids); protein (9%); starch (50%); vitamins (especially niacin and A); minerals; amino acids; resins; zingerone; etc.	Ginger oil is used as a fragrance material in some cosmetics. Also used in herbal cosmetics such as men's products, bath oils, body rubs.	Numerous pharmacological properties including stimulating the vasomotor and respiratory centers. Lowers serum and hepatic cholesterol. Carminative properties. Antitussive, non-irritating, non-sensitizing, non-phototoxic. Food use.		Ginger oil, powdered root, and oleoresin	I have used ginger in bath oils, sports rubs, and other products. It is "warming," and soothing to tired, sore muscles. It also has anti-oxidative activities in foods.
GINSENG Oriental ginseng *(Panax ginseng)* American ginseng *(Panax quinquefolius)* SYN: Chinese ginseng, Korean ginseng, seng and sang, man root, man's health. FOLK MEDICINE: Many uses. Oriental ginseng has warming properties, but American ginseng has cooling properties.	Root	There are many types and grades of oriental ginseng. It contains many saponins; volatile oil; sterols; starch; sugars; pectin; vitamins (B$_1$, B$_2$, B$_{12}$, nicotinic acid, pantothenic acid, and biotin); choline, fats, minerals (zinc, copper, manganese, calcium, iron, etc.); polyacetylenes; and others.	Used in creams, gels, tonics, and masks; reactivating and wrinkle creams for the skin. Excellent in hair tonics and shampoos.	Stimulant, toner, reactivating agent; reduces stress, and lowers blood sugar. Used as tea and in capsule form.	Plants with similar use for wrinkles: horsetail coneflower St. John's wort Plants with similar use as hair stimulant and tonic: arnica peruvian bark nettle rosemary sage.	Ginseng glycolic extract; ginseng fluid extract (both have 1% saponosides as ginsenoside); ginseng dry extract (has 10% saponosides as ginsenoside).	Liquid ginseng can be used in hair and skin care products in amounts from 2 to 10%. Powdered ginseng can be used up to 2% in products.

Herb Name Synonyms Folk Use	Parts Used	Typical Substances	Cosmetic Use	Properties & Other Uses	Similar Plants	Extracts	Comments
GOLDENSEAL (*Hydrastis canadensis*) SYN: Orange root, yellow root, Indian tumeric, eye balm FOLK MEDICINE: Used for hemorrhoids, nasal congestion, sore gums, itchy scalp and dandruff, and acne.	Root	Contains iso-quinoline alkaloids (good dandruff treatment); hydro-stine (1.5 to 4%); berberine (0.5 to 6%), chlorogenic acid; lipids; satu-rated and unsatu-rated fatty acids; resins; sugars; starch.	Limited cosmetic use, but has history as topical for acne, dandruff, & sore eyes.	Anti-convulsive, an-tiseptic, hemostatic, diuretic, laxative, and tonic. Used as herbal tea.	No plants offer the hydrastis extract but goldenseal.	Crude extract (fluid and tincture) and hydrastine salts.	Berberine, an alkaloid in golden-seal is similar to hydrastine used in uterine problems and for menstrual pain. Other drug uses.
GRAPEFRUIT OIL (*Citrus paradisi*) SYN: Shaddock oil, citrus preservative Recent dermatological studies: grapefruit oil was found non-irritating, non-sensitizing, and non-photo-toxic (D. L. J. Opdyke, *Food Cosmet. Toxicol.*, 12, 723, 1974).	Peel & seed	The peel oil and seed oil contain monoterpenes; limo-nene (90%); sesqui-terpenes; aldehydes; citronellyl; nootka-tone; ketones; ber-gaptens; 7-methoxy-8-2-formyl-2-methyl-propyl; other substances.	Grapefruit oil from the peel is used as a fragrance in soaps, lotions, creams, and perfumes. Grape-fruit seed oil is used as a preservative in cosmetics.	Seed oil has been used for herpes and skin problems in South America and in water to destroy bacteria. Used as weight reducer in capsules.	Other citrus oils	Grapefruit oil and naringin extract.	I have created a preservative using grapefruit seed oil with other natural extracts. Excellent preservative action and non-toxic. The preservative action is due to various esters. This is the best natural preservative.
GUAR GUM (*Cyamopsis tetragonoloba*)	Endosperm of seed	Contains 80% guaran (a galacto-mannan); 5 to 6% protein; 10 to 15% moisture; 2% fiber; 0.5 to 0.8% ash.	Used as a binder and thickener in lo-tions and creams.	Lowers the serum and liver choles-terol. Used as a thickener and stabilizer in foods. An appetite suppressant.	Gum arabic, gum tragacanth	Powdered ex-tract for various viscosities.	
GUAIC WOOD OIL (*Bulnesia sarmienti*) SYN: Champaca wood oil	Bark	Up to 72% guaiol, bulnesol, and guaioxide.	Used as fixative, modifier or fra-grance oil in soaps, creams, lotions, and perfumes.	Used as flavor com-ponent in foods and beverages. Non-irritating, non-sensitizing, non-phototoxic.		Oil	

-108-

Herb Name Synonyms Folk Use	Parts Used	Typical Substances	Cosmetic Use	Properties & Other Uses	Similar Plants	Extracts	Comments
HAWTHORN *(Crataegus oxyacantha)* SYN: May, may-blossom, whitehorn, ladies' meat, cuckoo's beads	Dried haws or fruit	Amygdalin crataegin, & other constituents.	Can be used in creams, lotions, and hair tonics as astringent.	Cardiac, diuretic, astringent, tonic.	Other plants of the order *rosaceae: c. aronia, c. odoratissima, c. azarole.*	Glycolic	
HEARTSEASE *(Viola tricolor)* SYN: Wild pansy, love-lies-bleeding, love-in-idleness, loving idol.	Herb: leaves, flowers, & seeds	Main constituent is violin (an emeto-cathartic substance), resin, mucilage, sugar, salicylic acid).	A strong decoction of the syrup is recommended for skin problems.	Tonic, expectorant, demulcent, cathartic. Medical journals say it is valuable for a cutaneous disorder called *crusta lactes* or "scald head".	Violet	Glycolic	Love-in-idleness is still used in Warwickshire as love charm (heartsease). It was used by Puck in *A Midsummer Night's Dream* as a love charm.
HENNA *(Lawsonia alba)* SYN: Henna, Ac-khanna, Egyptian privet, Jamaica mignonette FOLK MEDICINE: Leaves have been used for centuries in Middle East, Far East, and North Africa as dye for nails, hands, hair, clothing, and for treating skin problems, headaches, jaundice, etc.	Flowers, leaves, stems, root. (Only leaves have coloring principal).	Contains 0.55 to 1.0% lawsone (2-hydroxy-1,4-naphthoquinone), 5-10% gallic acid and tannin, 11% sugars and resin. Lawsone is the active color principal. It is not in the bark, stem, or root-just in the leaves.	Used in hair care products as dye, conditioner, and rinse. Dye can turn hair "orange" unless mixed with indigo and other dyes.	Lawsone has antifungal (fungicidal and fungistatic) activity against alternaria, aspergilus, absidia, penicillium, and other species. Only 0.1% (1000 ppm) is active as fungicide. The gallic acid and 1,4-naphthoquinone also have anti-bacterial activities.		Crude	Henna is mixed with indigo and logwood to obtain different shades. For long-lasting results, a pH of 5.5 must be obtained (i.e., citric acid added). The non-coloring henna makes an excellent ingredient for shampoos and neutral rinses.
HONEYSUCKLE *(Lonicera caprifolium)* SYN: Dutch honeysuckle, goat-leaf (Fr. *chevrefeuille*)	Flowers, seeds, leaves.	There is little uniformity in composition, and its constituents have not been analyzed.	Used for its fragrance & cleansing properties. A popular soap in France ("Le Petit Marseillais") contains honeysuckle (Available in American health food stores as "Honeysuckle Vegetal Soap").	Expectorant, laxative, diuretic, antispasmodic, and emitico-cathartic properties	There are 300 species of *Caprifoliaceae.*	Glycolic (essential oil)	Culpepper says: "Honeysuckles are cleansing. It is an herb of Mercury and therefore for the lungs. It is a cure for asthma and take away the evil of the spleen . . .in an ointment it will clear the skin."

Herb Name Synonyms Folk Use	Parts Used	Typical Substances	Cosmetic Use	Properties & Other Uses	Similar Plants	Extracts	Comments
HOPS *(Humulus lupulus)* SYN: European hops, common hops FOLK MEDICINE: Used for treating diarrhea, insomnia, and nervous conditions.	Flowers	Contains 0.3 to 1.0% volatile oil; 3-12% bitter principals (i.e., humulone, cohumulone, etc.). Glycosides, rutin, phenolic acids, tannins, lipids, estrogen.	Used in skin creams and lotions in Europe for its skin softening properties.	Antimicrobial sedative, estrogenic properties. Used is some foods at maximum levels of 0.072%.		Crude and essential oil	Hops contain phytohormones responsible for toning and calming nervous skin. "A pillow of hops brings calm sleep."
HOREHOUND *(Marrubium vulgare)* SYN: Marrubium, horehound, and white horehound FOLK MEDICINE: An ancient well-known treatment for sore throat, colds, and coughs.	Herb	Contains 0.3 to 1.0% of a bitter called marrubiin (a diterpene lactone); alcohols; 0.29% choline; 0.3% betonicine; volatile oil; resin, tannin, wax, fat, sugar.	Little commercial cosmetic use though an ointment with horehound syrup is good for wounds.	Diuretic properties, also a source of natural sweeteners. Expectorant and tonic.	Hyssop (also contains marrubiin)	Crude extract	A simple tea made of horehound is excellent for the common cold.
HORSE CHESTNUT *(Aesculus hippocastanium)* SYN: Ippocastano, robicastanie	Seeds	Escin and other triterpenic saponins, purinic derivatives, amino acids, B vitamins, and flavonoids.	Tonics, lotions for reddened or sensitive skin, protective creams and gels for the hands. Products for cellulitis.	Decongestant, mild astringent, skin lightener, coadjutant in treatment of cellulitis.	Lighteners: marigold Sedative: camomile butcher's broom, linden tree Cellulitis: birch, ivy, bladderwrack	Glycolic extract (with 1% escin)	
HORSETAILS *(Equisetum aruense)* SYN: Shave-grass, bottlebrush, pewterwort. FOLK MEDICINE: Used to stop bleeding, as external ointment, and internal tea.	Herb	High in silica (silicic acid 7%), starch, sulfur, saponins, malic and oxalic acids, flavonoids, fatty acid esters, amino acids (cystine).	Tonics, lotions, creams to prevent wrinkles, hair products to prevent hair loss and greasy hair.	Texturizer, elasticizer, diuretic, astringent	For hair: coltsfoot Texturizer and Plasticizer: coneflower, ginseng Rough skin & wrinkles: marigold, St. John's wort	Glycolic	I have used horsetail combined with coltsfoot and ginseng for the scalp. Scalps that are low in silicic acid, sulfur, and cystine have higher hair loss.

Herb Name Synonyms Folk Use	Parts Used	Typical Substances	Cosmetic Use	Properties & Other Uses	Similar Plants	Extracts	Comments
HYSSOP (*Hyssopus officinalis*) SYN: Common hyssop FOLK MEDICINE: Used in treating sore throat, coughs, and colds.	Herb	Contains 0.3 to 2% volatile oil, hyssopin (a glucoside), 5 to 8% tannin, fatty acids, hesperidin, diosmin, marrubiin, resin, and gum. Contains over 50 unidentified compounds.	Used externally as a diaphoretic (in baths) and in treating skin irritations, burns, and bruises. Used as a fragrance in soaps, creams, lotions, and perfumes at 0.4% maximum.	Hyssop extracts have been used to treat herpes simplex virus (E. C. Herrmann, J., and L. S. Kucera, *Proc. Soc. Exp. Biol. Med*, 124, 874, 1967) Nonirritating, nonsensitizing, non-phototoxic.	Horehound (also contains marrubiin). Balm oil of lavender.	Oil	The fine odor of hyssop essential oil is valued more than oil of lavender. It is also used in a liqueur known as chartreuse. Bee's honey from hyssop is the finest honey!
IMMORTELLE (*Helichrysum angustifolium*) SYN: Helichrysum, everlasting FOLK MEDICINE: Used as an expectorant, diuretic, and conditions such as burns, bronchitis, psoriasis, migraine, and allergies.	Flowers and flowering tops	Contains 0.075 to 2% volatile phthalides, helipyrone, triterpenes, wax, flavonoids, caffeic acid, nerol, geraniol, linolool, eugenol, and others.	The absolute is used as a fixative and fragrance in perfumes. Extracts are soothing and moisturizing. Can be useful in sun protection products because of UV absorption properties.	Expectorant, antitussive, antiinflammatory, antiallergic agent, UV light absorber, and diuretic. Used for burns, psoriasis, headache, migraine, and allergies.		Extracts and oils	Immortelle (everlasting) oil has anti-microbial properties *in vitro* against *Staphylococcus aureus, Escherichia coli,* and *Candida albicans.*
INDIGO (*Indigofera tinctoria*) SYN: *Pigmentium indicum* FOLK MEDICINE: Used as a natural dye.	Herb	Not completely analyzed.	Used as a blue color in cosmetics. It is calming to the scalp.	At one time used as medicine to produce nausea and vomiting but is no longer in use as such.	Similar sedative plants: marigold, camomile, butcher's broom	The blue dye is obtained from a yellow chemical known as indocan. On fermentation it turns blue.	Indigofera is synthesized and known as indigotine. Often mixed with henna to produce a variety of hair color shades.
IVY (*Hedera helix*) SYN: Ivy, climbing ivy FOLK MEDICINE: Used as food for cattle. Flowers were used for dysentery and removal of sunburn.	Leaves, berries	Saponins (mainly ederin), chlorogenic, caffeic acids, and flavonoids.	Used in foam baths, creams, and for packs or massage lotions for cellulitis.	Sedative and coadjutant for cellulitis.	Similar anti-cellulitis herbs: birch, horse chestnut, and bladderwrack	Glycolic	

-111-

Herb Name Synonyms Folk Use	Parts Used	Typical Substances	Cosmetic Use	Properties & Other Uses	Similar Plants	Extracts	Comments
JASMINE *(Jasminum officinale)* SYN: Royal jasmine, Italian jasmine, poet's jessamine, and common jasmine. FOLK MEDICINE: In China numerous *jasminum* species are used for hepatitis, cirrhosis of liver, skin problems, abdominal pain, headaches, and insomnia.	Flower	The aroma of jasmine essence is made up of over 100 compounds. Benzyl acetate is the highest concentration. Also linalool, jasmonates, jasmolactone, and jasmonic acid.	The strong aroma of jasmine is widely used in cosmetics and perfumes. Maximum use in perfumes is 0.3%.	In Western culture the essential oil is used as a calmative and as an aphrodisiac.		Essential oil	In China jasmine is known as *Moli* and the Hindus call it "Moonlight of the grove." This yang herb is used in aromatherapy massages. I've used it in many cosmetics.
JUNIPER BERRIES *(Juniperus communis)* SYN: Genévrier, ginepro, enebro, common juniper berries FOLK MEDICINE: Used as carminative and diuretic. Also to treat colic and gastrointestinal infections. The steam is used for bronchitis.	The ripe, dried fruit and leaves	Berries contain 0.2 to 3.42% volatile oil. Also sugars (glucose and fructose), glucuronic acid, l-ascorbic acid, gallotannins, geijerone, and others.	Oil is used in soaps, creams, lotions, and perfumes. Also used for skin problems such as acne and eczema. Makes an excellent water for toning the skin.	Diuretic, antiseptic, astringent, and carminative. In foods it is used as a flavor component in gin.		Essential oil	This yang herb, like jasmine, has many uses. The product known as cade oil or juniper tar oil is used in France for chronic eczema.
KARAYA GUM *(Sterculia urens)* SYN: Sterculia gum, Indian tragacanth, kadaya	Dried exudation from trunk of tree	Contains a polysaccharide with high molecular weight (9,500,000 m.). The chemical structure is complicated and has not been determined.	Used as a thickener and suspending agent in lotions, creams, and hairsetting products.	Used in foods as a binder and to prevent ice crystals in sherberts, ice creams, etc.	Other gums such as gum arabic, gum tragacanth.	Powder of various particle sizes	Karaya gum is able to swell in cold water up to 100 times its original volume.

Herb Name Synonyms Folk Use	Parts Used	Typical Substances	Cosmetic Use	Properties & Other Uses	Similar Plants	Extracts	Comments
KELP (Fucus vesiculosus) SYN: Seaweed, bladder-wrack, fucus, and seawrack	Entire plant	Alginates, iodine in organic combination with mineral salts, sugars, amino acids, and vitamins A, C, B complex, and E.	Used in foam baths, creams, gels, and massage lotions for cellulitis.	Due to its high iodine content kelp is used for obesity and to normalize the thyroid.	There are various seaweeds used in cosmetics today (see BLADDER-WRACK).	Glycolic	The soothing pro-perties of kelp are similar to aloe and mallow.
LABDANUM (Cistis ladaniferus) SYN: Ambreine, rockrose, gum cistus, ciste, and cyste. FOLK MEDICINE: Used as an expectorant and for diarrhea.	Leaves and twigs	Labdanum gum con-tains volatile oil, paraffins, and resins. The oil con-tains over 120 compounds.	Oil is used as fix-ative in soaps, creams, lotions, and perfumes.	Also used as flavor-ing in foods.		Oleoresin and oil	
LAVENDER (Lavandula angustifolia) SYN: True lavender and garden lavender FOLK MEDICINE: Used internally and externally for many ailments, in-cluding flatulence, spasms, colic, headache, sprains, acne, sores, and toothache.	Flowering tops	Contains 0.5 to 1.5% volatile oil, tannin, coumarins, flavonoids, triter-penoids, etc.	Lavender oil is used in antiseptic oint-ments, creams, and lotions. It is a wide-ly used fragrance material.	Analgesic, anti-convulsive, anti-spasmodic, car-minative, sedative, tonic, and stomachic.	Other yang oils are jasmine and juniper berries.	Essential oil (lavender and lavandin)	This yang oil is non-toxic, non-irritating, and is not phototox-ic. It is used in aromatherapy.
LEMON OIL (Citrus limon) SYN: Lemon oil, cedro oil	Rind, juice, oil of peel or seed	Contains 90% monoterpenes (main-ly limonene, sabinene, pinene, and myrene). Also linalool, octanol, nonanol, citropten, geranoxypsoralen, and waxes.	Used as a fragrance in soap, creams, lo-tions, and perfumes.	Used in pharma-ceuticals as a flavor-ing, and in foods. The waxes have an-tioxidant properties.	Other citrus oils (orange, lime, grapefruit and bergamot).	Oil	The seed oils of citrus (especially grapefruit seed) have antioxidant and antibacterial properties.

Herb Name Synonyms Folk Use	Parts Used	Typical Substances	Cosmetic Use	Properties & Other Uses	Similar Plants	Extracts	Comments
LEMON GRASS (*Cymbopogon citratus*) SYN: West Indian lemongrass, Madagascar lemongrass, cochin lemongrass, etc. FOLK MEDICINE: Used in Chinese medicine to treat colds, headache, stomache ache, and rheumatic pain.	Leaves	Contains volatile oil (0.2 to 0.4%), an unknown alkaloid, saponins, hexacosanol, and others. Fragrance comes from citral (65 to 85%), citronellic, linalool, geraniol, etc.	Used as a fragrance component in soaps, creams, lotions, and perfumes.	Anti-microbial, analgesic, anti-pyretic, and anti-oxidant properties. Non-irritating, non-sensitizing, non-toxic.		Essential oil	Lemongrass is used as a starting material for the synthesis of vitamin A.
LICORICE ROOT (*Glycyrrhiza glabra*) SYN: Italian licorice, Turkish licorice, glycyrrhiza, and sweet wood.	Dried runners and roots	The major active principal is glycyrrahizinic acid (1 to 2%). Also flavonoids, isoflavonoids, licoflavonol, licoricone, glycyrol, amines, gums, wax, and many aromatic chemicals.	Used only as an aromatic in cosmetics, but can be used as an anti-inflammatory in lotions and creams. Has been successful with contact dermatitis.	Estrogenic activities, anti-ulcer, mineralocorticoid, anti-inflammatory, anti-allergic, inhibition of tumor growth (I. F. Shavarev, Vop. Izuch, Ispolz. Soludki, SSR, *Akad Nauk USSR*, 167, 1966).		Crude extracts	
LITMUS (*Roccella tinctoria*) SYN: Lacmus, orchella weed, dyer's weed.	The whole plant, for its pigment	Contains resins, wax, starches, gum, tartrate and oxalate of lime, chlorine, and the color principals are acids or acid anhydrides.	Could be used for color but is not used at present.	Used to make litmus papers for measuring pH		Liquid	Used to make blue and red litmus paper.
LOCUST BEAN GUM (*Ceratonia siliqua*) SYN: Carob bean gum, carob gum, locust gum	The seed of carob	Similar to guar gum with a different d-galactose chain.	See GUAR GUM.	See GUAR GUM.	Guar gum	Powdered extract	Guar gum and locust bean gum are often used together.

Herb Name Synonyms Folk Use	Parts Used	Typical Substances	Cosmetic Use	Properties & Other Uses	Similar Plants	Extracts	Comments
LILY-OF-THE-VALLEY (*Convallaria magalis*) SYN: May lily, convallaria, our lady's tears, ladder-to-heaven, Jacob's ladder	Flowers, leaves, whole herb	Contains two glucosides (convallamarin and convallarin), volatile oil, tannin, salts, etc.	Can be used as aromatic material in cosmetics but to get a strong fragrance, many infusions are needed.	Cardiac tonic and diuretic. Action of drug.		Essential oil	The crystalline powder of the active principals acts upon the heart like digitalin.
LIME OIL (*Citrus aurantifolia*)	Whole crushed fruit or juice of fruit, peel, and seeds.	Contains large amounts of d-limonene, pinenes, camphene, citral, linalool, bergapten, bergamottin, and others.	Lime oil is used as a fragrance and fixative in soaps, creams, lotions, and perfumes (up to 1.5%).	Non-irritating, non-sensitizing, and non-phototoxic to human skin.	Other citrus	Distilled lime oil	
LINDEN TREE (*Tilia cordata*) SYN: Tiglio, linden	Flowers	Essential oil with major constituent being farnesol. Also flavonoids, gallic and catechnic tannins.	Eye tonics, after-sun lotions, emollient lotions for sensitive skin, foam baths, feminine hygiene products	Refreshener, sedative	Similar refresheners: aloes, camomile, marigold, and mallow	Glycolic	Up to 5% linden can be used in hair and skin care products.
LOVAGE (*Levisticum officinale*) SYN: Old English lovage, smellage, smallage, and maggi herb. FOLK MEDICINE: Used as a diuretic, stomachic, expectorant, and for skin problems.	Root, leaves, seeds, stems	Contains from 0.5 to 1.0% volatile oil, angelic acid, resins, (a coloring principal called ligulin), phthalides, glucoside, gum, and resin.	Used as a fragrance component in soaps, creams, lotions, and perfumes (maximum 0.2%).	Used as a flavor component in foods and beverages. Non-irritating, non-sensitizing.	Angelica	Essential oil	Lovage oil can be used to test the purity of water. A drop of lovage oil in pure water turns a fine crimson red, but if the water is not pure, the red changes to blue.

Herb Name Synonyms Folk Use	Parts Used	Typical Substances	Cosmetic Use	Properties & Other Uses	Similar Plants	Extracts	Comments
LUPINS *(Lupinus albus)* SYN: Lupin, wolfsbohne FOLK MEDICINE: Used as a diuretic and emmenagogue.	Seeds, herb	Contains a glucoside called lupinin, a crystalline (magolan), dextrin, lupanine, others.	Used in soaps, creams, lotions, and as an external treatment of ulcers.	Anthelmintic, diuretic, emmenagogue.		Crude extract	In 1917 a lupin banquet was given: the table had a lupin tablecloth; lupin beefsteak roasted in lupin oil, lupin bread, lupin cheese, and lupin coffee were served; and hands were washed with lupin soap.
MAGNOLIA *(Magnolia acuminata)* SYN: Cucumber tree, blue magnolia, swamp magnolia, sassafras FOLK MEDICINE: Used for rheumatism, malaria, and as a laxative.	Bark, stem, root, blossoms	Contains a crystalline principal magnolin, bitter glucosides, and others.	Used as a fragrance material in soap, lotions, creams, and perfumes.	Mild diaphoretic, tonic, and aromatic stimulant.		Essential oil	It is said that if the bark is chewed it cure the desire for tobacco.
MALLOW, BLUE *(Malva sylvestris)* SYN: Common mallow, mauls. FOLK MEDICINE: Used for coughs, colds, for urinary organs.	Leaves and flowers	Flavonoids, anthocyanines, chlorogenic, galacturonic acid, tannins, starch, mucilage, pectin oil, asparagin, cellulose.	Tonics, lotions, emollient lotions and creams, bath products, mouth washes.	Softener, smoother, emollient	Marsh mallow, musk mallow, sea tree mallow, other mallows (also see **ALTHEA ROOT**)	Glycolic	I have used marsh mallow for astringents, and blue mallow as a skin ointment. A "clay mask" of mallow is a skin softening mask.

Herb Name Synonyms Folk Use	Parts Used	Typical Substances	Cosmetic Use	Properties & Other Uses	Similar Plants	Extracts	Comments
MINTS: **PEPPERMINT** *(Mentha piperita)* **SPEARMINT** *(Mentha viriois)* **CORNMINT** *(Mentha arvensis)* **PENNYROYAL** *(Mentha pulegium)* FOLK MEDICINE: Peppermint, spearmint, and their oils are used as stomachics and anti-spasmodics, and for nausea, sore throat, colds, headaches, toothaches, and cramps. The Japanese menthol plant and Chinese peppermint oil have high quantities of menthol. The Japanese have used menthol for over 200 years and even carried it with them in a tiny silver box. Rats dislike peppermint: in ancient times, rags soaked with peppermint oil were stuffed into rat holes.	Herb	Peppermint yields 0.1 to 1.0% volatile oil composed mainly of menthol, menthone, and menthyl acetate. Spearmint yields about 0.7% volatile oil consisting of carvone, dihydrocarvone, phellandrene, limonene, menthone, menthol, and piperitenone. Cornmint yields 1 to 2% volatile oil with a high concentration of menthol (70 to 95%), menthone, menthyl acetate, isomenthone, thujone, and piperitone. Pennyroyal yields about 1% of a volatile oil known as pulegiom with a ketone of pulegone.	The mints are used mostly as flavoring and fragrances in cosmetics, e.g., flavoring for mouthwashes and lip gloss and fragrance for soaps, shampoos, rinses, creams, lotions, and perfumes. Spearmint and cornmint have a maximum use of 0.4% and 0.8% respectively as fragrance materials.	Mints are used in foods. Spearmint oil is popular in chewing gum (about 0.132%), and peppermint is popular in candy (about 0.104%). Menthol is extracted from cornmint by freezing, which reduces the amount of menthol from 90% to 55%. Allergic reactions to menthol include itchy skin, rash, headaches, but good results with menthol have been obtained with colds, sore throats, coughs, and skin care. Menthol is strong and should be used in small amounts (5.967 ppm or less). Pennyroyal, in ancient times, was known for its water purifying qualities. Pliny the Elder has written about the power of pennyroyal to drive away fleas, and the herb's Latin name *(pulegium)* refers to the Latin word *pulex* for fleas.	Other mints: marsh mint *(mentha sativa)* wild water mint *(mentha aquatica)* curled mint *(mentha acrispa)* bergamot mint *(mentha citrata)* Egyptian roundleaf mint *(mentha rotundifucia)* horse mint *(mentha sylvestrias)*	Essential oil	I have used the various mints in many unconventional cosmetics, e.g., in mint hair rinses which are cooling and antiseptic; in unique bath oils with ginger and eucalyptus; in a non-hardening clay mask with sea extracts. The mints are stimulants, antiseptics, anesthetics, as well as cooling and soothing. Men's shaving and skin care products can make good use of the mints. My most successful skin cleansers and astringents utilize the mints.

Herb Name Synonyms Folk Use	Parts Used	Typical Substances	Cosmetic Use	Properties & Other Uses	Similar Plants	Extracts	Comments
MUSK SEED *Hibiscus abelmuschus* SYN: Ambretta, Egyptian alcée, bamia moschata. FOLK MEDICINE: The Arabians mix the seeds with coffee for their strong exotic aromatic flavor. Seeds are also said to be an aphrodisiac.	Seeds	The seeds of this evergreen shrub contain a fixed oil, a colored resin, and albuminous matter.	Used for its albuminous extract to make "skin milk" used for dry itchy skin. It can be used to create a vegetarian musk oil fragrance.	Anti-spasmodic, stomachic, nervine, and as a breath sweetener.		Essential oil	
MYRRH *(Commiphora myrrha)* SYN: Balsamodendron, myrrha, mosmol, mirna, didthin, bowl FOLK MEDICINE: Used as stimulant, antiseptic, expectorant, antispasmodic, emmenagogue and stomachic.	The oleo-resin from the stem	Contains 1.5 to 17% volatile oil composed of herrabolene, limonene, dipentene pinene, eugenol, comic, resins, cholesterol, and 60% gum.	Myrrh is an excellent astringent and can also be used in mouthwashes and gargles. Also as a fragrance in soaps, creams, lotions, and perfumes (0.8%).	Used as a flavor in foods and beverages. It also has anti-microbial activities, is non-sensitizing, non-irritating, and non-phototoxic.		Crude extracts	I have used myrrh for many years in hair and skin care products.
NETTLE *(Urtica urens)* SYN: Common nettle, stinging nettle	Herb, seeds	Contains formic acid, mucilage, mineral salts, ammonia, carbonic acid and water. Also phytosterols (scalp treatment), amino acids, protein, vitamins.	Used in hair and skin products. Said to stimulate hair growth if juice is applied to scalp. Used in hair tonics, skin creams, and astringents.	As a medicinal food, it is high in phosphates and trace minerals such as iron. Nettle juice is a recognized homeopathic tonic.	Plants with similar hair tonic effect: arnica, ginseng, rosemary, sage, Peruvian bark.	Glycolic	I have used nettle in hair tonics, skin astringents, and even to make a "beautiful green color" for cosmetics.

Herb Name Synonyms Folk Use	Parts Used	Typical Substances	Cosmetic Use	Properties & Other Uses	Similar Plants	Extracts	Comments
OATS (*Avena sativa*) SYN: Common oats, white oats, panicle oats, groats	Seeds	Starch, gluten, albumin, protein, sugar, gum oil, and salts.	Popular as a facial mask combined with other ingredients. Used in soaps, lotions, and creams for its cleansing action. Said to remove "brown spots."	Nervine, stimulant, anti-spasmodic.		Powdered extract	Herbalists suggest boiling oats in vinegar and applying the mash to "age spots" and freckles.
OLIBANUM (*Boswellia carteri*) SYN: Frankincense and olibanum gum. FOLK MEDICINE: Used since antiquity as incense in India, China, Egypt, and the Catholic Church. Called Frankincense. Used in ancient Egypt to make embalming oil for their dead.	Oleogum from bark of tree	Contains 3 to 10% volatile oil with 20% gum, and 5 to 8% bassorin. High content of boswellic acid.	It is used as fixative or fragrance in soaps, lotions, creams, and perfumes (0.8%).	Used is some foods as maximum level of 0.001%. Non-irritating, non-sensitizing, not known to be phototoxic. Strong analgesic effect. Antioxidative properties on fats and oils. A natural replacement for BHA.		Crude extrct as olibanum oil	
OLIVE OIL (*Olea Europea*) SYN: Olea, olea lancifolia, olea oleaster, olivier FOLK MEDICINE: One of the oldest trees is the olive tree. The branch means peace. It was used in the diet and burned in the sacred temples.	Oil of fruit, leaves, bark	The gum-resin contains benzoic acid and olivile. Mannite is found in the leaves. Also the palmitin, triolein, archidic esters, oleic acid, and other fatty acids.	Olive oil soap is made by mixing olive oil with salt. Warm olive oil is believed to be good for the scalp. Also used in shampoos, conditioners, and moisturizers.	Leaves are astringent and antiseptic. Bark and leaves have febrifugal qualities. Oil is demulcent and laxative.	Cottonseed oil, rape oil, sesame oil, and poppy-seed oil are often used as adulterants.	Oil	Olive oil mixed with witch hazel is a good hair tonic for dry, dull hair. It also relieves stings and burns.

Herb Name Synonyms Folk Use	Parts Used	Typical Substances	Cosmetic Use	Properties & Other Uses	Similar Plants	Extracts	Comments
ORANGE OIL **Bitter** *(Citrus vulgaris)* **Sweet** *(Citrus aurantium)* SYN: Citrus oil, bitter orange, Seville orange, sweet orange. FOLK MEDICINE: Used as carminative in treating dyspepsia.	Fruit, flowers, peel	Bitter peel contains 1 to 2.5% volatile oil, naringin, rhoifolin, lonicerin, hesperidin, and other flavonoids, rutin, vitamins A, B, C, carotenoid, pectin, citrantin, etc. Sweet peel contains 1.5 to 2% volatile oil, many of the above substances, and vitamin E.	Neroli and petitgrain oils are used as fragrance materials in soaps, creams, lotions, and perfumes.	Anti-inflammatory, anti-bacterial, anti-fungal, anti-hyper-cholesterolemic.	As anti-bacterial similar plants are: grapefruit oil lemon oil pine needle oil lime oil	Oils are U.S.P. and N.F.	I have used citrus seed extracts in cosmetics for their preservative qualities for over a decade with good results.
PAPAIN *(Carica papaya)* SYN: Vegetable pepsin	Latex from unripe fruit	Papain is similar to bromelain and ficin, but as an enzyme it contains no carbo-hydrates. Contains 212 amino acids, organic salts, fur-maric acid, malic acid, dihydroxyfur-maric acid, and others.	Used in some face creams and cleansers as a "face lift" and skin softener. At one time was used for wounds, sores, ulcers, and psoriasis (topical).	Widely used as meat tenderizer (sometimes com-bined with brome-lain or ficin). Also used in beer to hydrolyze proteins.	Bromelain, ficin	Various grades of powdered extract	Chymopapain is be-ing studied for use in the treatment of lower back pain.
PARIS HERB *(Paris quadrifolia)* SYN: Herba Paris, true love, one berry	Entire plant	Contains a glucoside called paradin.	A cooling ointment is made from the seeds and juice for skin problems and inflammations.	Poison and narcotic. Should be used in-ternally with great caution as overdose is fatal. Tiny amounts have been used for bronchitis, coughs, colic, heart palpitations.	Other species: *Paris polyphylla*	Glycolic	The seeds and ber-ries have a nature similar to opium. In Russia the leaves are used for the in-sane. It is also used as an antidote against mercury and arsenic.

Herb Name Synonyms Folk Use	Parts Used	Typical Substances	Cosmetic Use	Properties & Other Uses	Similar Plants	Extracts	Comments
PARSLEY *(Petroselinum crispum)* SYN: Garden parsley and common parsley FOLK MEDICINE: Used to treat jaundice, menstrual problems, asthma, coughs, indigestion, gallstones (as tea) and eaten as breath freshener (garnish).	Roots, seeds	Contains 2 to 7% volatile oil and 22% fixed oil high in petroselinic acid (octadecenoic acid) and palmitic, myristic, stearic, oleic, linoleic, myristolic acids. Also proteins, vitamins A and C, and sugars. Also furocoumarins and myristicin.	Used as a fragrance component in soaps, creams, lotions, and perfumes (0.2% maximum).	Highly nutritious with pharmacological properties; laxative, hypotensive, anti-microbial, and tonic. Contains some furocoumarins which are phototoxic. Used in some forms.	Coriander (known as Chinese parsley)	Flakes, oil, oleoresin	A chemical in parsley, myristicin, is believed to be a psychedelic.
PATCHOULY OIL *(Pogostemon cablin)* SYN: Patchouli oil FOLK MEDICINE: In Chinese medicine, patchouly is used for colds, headaches, nausea, and stomach pain.	Dried leaves	Contains 1.5 to 4% volatile oil comosed mainly of patchouli alcohol, norpatchulenol (both give the oil its odor), cinnamaldehyde, benaldehyde, eugenol, etc.	Extensively used as a fragrance component and as a fixative. Also used for bad breath in mouthwash.	Used as a food flavor. Used for insecticidal activity against insects in stored grains. Antimicrobial and bactericidal properties.		Essential oil	
PECTIN	Obtained from the cell walls of plants, the peel of citrus, and apple pomace	Pectin contains dextrose, sodium citrate, potassium carbonates, lactates, and other sugars and salts.	Used as a thickener and film-forming agent in beauty masks. Also in creams and lotions as a thickener and combined with kaolin.	Largest use is in jams, jellies, and preserves.	Other gums: algin, guar, etc.	Various grades of powder extract. Some are N.F.	Pectin has cholesterol-lowering properties and is not digested.

Herb Name Synonyms Folk Use	Parts Used	Typical Substances	Cosmetic Use	Properties & Other Uses	Similar Plants	Extracts	Comments
PINE BARK, WHITE *(Pinus strobus)* SYN: Eastern white pine FOLK MEDICINE: Used for centuries by American Indians for coughs, colds, congestion, and as a poultice to treat wounds.	Bark	Mucilage coniferin, coniferyl alcohol, diterpenoids, volatile oil, and others.	Other pines are used as fragrance materials in cosmetics. Some such as white pine are used in rubs and turpentine liniments. Pine tars are used in bath oils.	Used in some cough syrups.	Various pine species	White pine bark extract	There are more than 33 species of pines that have medicinal properties.
PINE NEEDLE OIL *(Pinus sylvestris)* SYN: Swiss mountain pine	Needles	Contains monoterpene; hydrocarbons (d-limonene, camphene, murcene, etc.); sesquiterpenes, alcohols, etc.	Dwarf, Scotch, and Siberian pine oils are used as a fragrance in soaps, creams, lotions, and perfumes (maximum 1-2%). Popular in bath oils.	Anti-microbial, anti-viral, anti-bacterial, non-phototoxic.	Various pine needles	Oil, N.F.	Siberian pine needle extract has the most pleasant fragrance.
PIPSISSEWA *(Chimaphila umbellata)* SYN: *Pyrola umbellata.* wintergreen, king's cure, love-in-winter, rheumatism weed, ground holly FOLK MEDICINE: Used as tea for bladderstones, externally for sores and blisters. Used for diabetes, diminishes lithic acid in urine, and as replacement for uva-ursi herb.	Dried leaves	Main ingredient is arbutin gum and other glycosides, flavonoids, ursolic acid, methyl salicylate, resins, tannins, gums, starch, sugar, etc.	When the bruised leaves are applied to the skin, they act as a vesicant and rubefacient, which is very efficacious for skin problems.	Astringent, diuretic, antiseptic action on urine, tonic, bacteriostatic properties. Used in some foods.	Pyrola, wintergreen	Crude extract	

Herb Name Synonyms Folk Use	Parts Used	Typical Substances	Cosmetic Use	Properties & Other Uses	Similar Plants	Extracts	Comments
PRIMROSE OIL, EVENING *(Enothera odorata)* SYN: Tree primrose, evening primrose flowers FOLK MEDICINE: Has been used for dyspepsia, torpor of the liver, and female complaints.	Bark, leaves, seeds	A mixture of essential fatty acids, and said to be the only source of GLA, or gamma-linolenic acid (besides mother's milk).	Recently used in shampoos for dry hair, in lotions and creams for dry skin and eczema, and in hair conditioners.	Astringent, sedative, recently used for premenstrual syndrome and for its GLA content.	Another species: *Enothera biennis* and a white-flowered species grow in the Nilghiri Hills in India.	Crude oil	Large section on **EVENING PRIMROSE OIL** in Chapter VI ("Aromatherapy").
QUILLAIA *(Quillaja saponaria)* SYN: Soapbark, soap tree bark, quillaya, ke-li-ya, murillo bark, panama bark	Dried inner bark	Contains 9 to 10% triterpenoid saponins consisting of glycosides of quillaic acid (quillaja sapogenin); tannin; calcium oxalate; sugars; starch; others.	Used in shampoos for its foaming and anti-dandruff properties. Relieves itching and psoriasis scales.	Anti-inflammatory, anti-microbial, expectorant, but due to hemolytic and gastrointestinal irritation it can be toxic if taken in large amount internally. Used in foods as a foaming agent (root beer) as is yucca root (maximum use is 0.01%).	Yucca	Crude powdered and fluid extracts; saponin extracts	I have used quillaia for many years in cosmetics with good results. The powder should not be inhaled during manufacturing, but once in a liquid state, it's non-irritating.
ROSE OIL *(Rosa alba)* SYN: Bulgarian otto of rose, Bulgarian rose oil, French rose absolute, and rose de mai absolute	Flowers	Rose oil contains geraniol, citronellol, nerol, B-phenethyl alcohol, geranic acid, and eugenol which constitutes 55 to 75% of the oil.	Rose oil and rose water are used as fragrance components in soap, creams, lotions, and perfumes (oil is used maximum 0.2% in perfumes). Rose-water and glycerine are used together as a skin moisturizer.	Rose oil and absolute are used as flavor ingredients in foods for their fruit-type flavor (use is 2 ppm maximum).		Rose oil is N.F.; Rose-water is N.F.	In India rosewater is used to make an excellent yogurt drink.

Herb Name Synonyms Folk Use	Parts Used	Typical Substances	Cosmetic Use	Properties & Other Uses	Similar Plants	Extracts	Comments
RHATANY *(Krameria triandra)* SYN: rhatanhia, mapto, red rhatany	Dried root	Tannins (krameria-tannin), rhatanine (methyl-tyrosine), lignin, gum, starch, mineral acids, others.	Astringent, lotions, and creams. Used in bronzers as suntanning agent.	Astringent, restorer, tonic. Used for dystentery, sore throats, and as astringent wash.	Similar for suntanning: aloes, St. John's wort, walnut Astringents: birch, witch hazel	Glycolic	Rhatany glycolic extract is used in amounts from 2 to 10%.
ROSEMARY *(Rosemarinus officinalis)* SYN: Polar plant, compass-weed, compass plant, rosmarino FOLK MEDICINE: Used in China for centuries to treat stomach pains, headaches, and tension. Herbals suggest rosemary mixed with borax to prevent baldness.	Herb, root	About 0.5% volatile oil; flavonoids (diosmetin, hispidulin, etc.); rosmarinic acid; carnosic acid; oleanolic acid; tannins, others.	Widely used in cosmetics as a purifier, toning agent, and as a fragrance material (maximum 1%).	Anti-microbial activities, analgesic activity, non-irritating, and non-sensitizing.	Other skin purifiers: sage Toning agents: arnica, Peruvian bark, ginseng, nettle	Glycolic extract	I have used rosemary for almost two decades in cosmetics with great success in amounts from 0.5 to 2%.
RUE *(Ruta graveolens)* SYN: Herb-of-grace, herbygrass, garden rue FOLK MEDICINE: Used as an emmenagogue, anti-spasmodic, hemostatic, and vermifuge in Chinese medicine. It is also used for colds, fevers, toothache, and insect bites.	Herb	Contains a volatile oil (0.1%), rutin (2%), various alkaloids, bergapten, psoralen, and other coumarins.	Rue oil is used as a fragrance ingredient in soaps, creams, lotions, and perfumes (0.15% maximum in perfumes). Rue oil is also the source of 2-undecanone, a valuable perfume chemical (methyl-nonyl acetaldehyde).	Used as a flavor component in foods (maximum 2 ppm).	Other plants with bergaptens	Crude oil is N.F.	Since furocoumarins have phototoxic properties, these extracts can be used to treat psoriasis.

Herb Name Synonyms Folk Use	Parts Used	Typical Substances	Cosmetic Use	Properties & Other Uses	Similar Plants	Extracts	Comments
RUTIN SYN: Quercetin-3-rutino-side, rutoside, eldrin.	The glycoside from various species of ferns.	Can be obtained from eucalyptus leaves, fiola flowers, buckwheat, various ferns.	Can be used in cosmetics for its anti-inflammatory and anti-phototoxic properties.	Main biological ac-tivity is the decrease of capillary permeability.		Pure rutin (formerly N.F.)	Rutin is considered non-toxic and has shown the ability to inhibit skin cancer in animals (B. L. Vanduuren, et. al., *J. Natl. Cancer Inst.*, 46, 1039, 1971).
SAGE (*Salvia officinalis*) SYN: Garden sage, true sage, Balkan sage. FOLK MEDICINE: Is used as a tonic, digestive, antiseptic, astringent.	Leaves	Contains 1.0 to 2.8% volatile oil; picrosalvin, carno-sol, salvin, carnogic acid, flavonoids, camphor, thujone, tannis, others.	Used as a skin purifier and toning agent in shampoos, creams, lotions, gels, masks for greasy skin, wrin-kled skin, and as a fragrance compo-nent (0.8% maximum).	Phenolic agents in sage give it anti-microbial activity especially against *staphy-loccus aureus*. It is non-irritating, non-sensitizing, non-phototoxic.	Similar skin purifiers: rosemary Toning agents: arnica, Peruvian bark, ginseng, nettle	Sage oil	I have used sage oil for many years in cosmetics with good results from 0.5 to 1.0%.
ST. JOHN'S WORT (*Hypericum perforatum*) SYN: Iperico, millepertuis, johanniskraut FOLK MEDICINE: Used as aromatic, and for blad-der problems, catarrh, and bedwetting in children.	Herb tops and flowers	Volatile oil (terpenes and sesquitepenes); tannis, flavonoids (hyperin, rutin); hypericin; others.	After-sun oils, creams, lotions, tonics, for reddish or chapped skin, for wrinkles, and as healing agent.	Texturizer, purifier, astringent, soothing agent.	Other healing agents: marigold, camomile, coneflower Astringents: birch, witch hazel, rhatany Pre-sun and after-sun: aloe, walnut, horse chestnut, butcher's broom	St. John's Wort Oil	I have used St. John's Wort oil in many cosmetics with excellent results (up to 2.5%).

Herb Name Synonyms Folk Use	Parts Used	Typical Substances	Cosmetic Use	Properties & Other Uses	Similar Plants	Extracts	Comments
STORAX (*Liquidambar styraciflua*) SYN: Liquid storax FOLK MEDICINE: Used as an antiseptic, expectorant, and for treating wounds and skin problems.	Balsam of bark	Contains cinnamic acid; styracin; phenylpropyl cinnamate; styrene; various alcohols (phenylpropyl, benzyl, ethyl); vanillin; others.	Storax oil is used as an ingredient to make benzoic tincture, also as an antiseptic and antimicrobial for preserving cosmetics.	Used in foods, as a flavoring and fixative (0.001%).	Balsam tolu, benzoic gum.	Storax oil is official in U.S.P.	
STRAWBERRY (*Fragaria vesca*) FOLK MEDICINE: Used for dysentery. The once-famous Antioch drink was prepared with stalks to be drunk on the nativity of John the Baptist.	Leaves, fruit	Cissotanic, malic, citric acids, sugar, mucilage and an unknown aromatic oil (similar to musk, rose, and violet).	The oil of the leaves or fruit can be used for their astringent action in cosmetics.	Laxative, diuretic, astringent		Oil	A cut strawberry rubbed over the face immediately after washing will lighten the skin and remove a slight sunburn.
SUNFLOWER OIL (*Helianthus annus*) SYN: Marigold of Peru, sola indianus, chrysanthemum peruvianum FOLK MEDICINE: Seeds were made into infusion for relief of whooping cough. They have been used in Russia for malarial fever, even where quinine has failed.	Seeds	Seeds yield 50 to 60% oil. Contains tannis (helianthitanic acid); inulin; levulin; essential fatty acids; others.	Sunflower seed oil is used as an emollient in soap, creams, and lotions. It is a good base for massage oils and lotions.	Diuretic and expectorant properties.		Sunflower seed oil	

-126-

Herb Name Synonyms Folk Use	Parts Used	Typical Substances	Cosmetic Use	Properties & Other Uses	Similar Plants	Extracts	Comments
THYME *(Thymus vulgaris)* SYN: Common thyme, garden thyme, and French thyme FOLK MEDICINE: An infusion or tincture of thyme was used for acute bronchitis, laryngitis, coughs, gastritis, and to improve appetite.	Herb	Contains 0.8 to 2.6% volatile oil consisting of phenols, monoterpene hydrocarbons, linalool, thujan, thymol, carvacrol, others.	Used in ointments or creams to treat fungal skin infections. Also used in toothpastes, soaps, creams, lotions, and perfumes (0.8%).	Thyme oil has anti-spasmodic, expectorant, and carminative properties; anti-microbial on both bacteria and fungi (due to thymol and carvacrol). Non-irritating, non-sensitizing, and non-phototoxic.	Marjoram, rosemary, sage, oregano, and other plants of mint family have similar anti-oxidative properties.	Thymol and thyme oil	
TRAGACANTH *(Astragalus gummifer)* SYN: Gum tragacanth, gum dragon	Gummy exudation of branches	Consists of 20 to 30% water, soluble fraction of tragacanthic acid and arabinogalactan; acetic acid; bassorin; polysaccharides; others.	Used in creams and lotions as an emulsifier and binding agent; in hair sets as a film-former, and in toothpastes.	Used in foods as an emulsifier and in confectionaries.	Gum arabic	Flake, powder, ribbon in various grades. Meets U.S.P and N.F. standards.	
VANILLA *(Vanilla planifolia)* SYN: Bourbon vanilla, Réunion vanilla, Tahiti vanilla	Unripe fruit	Contains vanillin and over 150 other aromatic chemicals.	Vanilla extract N.F. is used as a fragrance in soap, lotions, creams, and perfumes. Mixed with almond it is used as a "baby fragrance."	Used as a flavor in foods and beverages.		Crude extract and tincture is N.F.	

Herb Name Synonyms Folk Use	Parts Used	Typical Substances	Cosmetic Use	Properties & Other Uses	Similar Plants	Extracts	Comments
WINTERGREEN OIL (*Gaultheria procumbens*) SYN: Checkerberry, teaberry, or gautheria oil.	Leaf	Wintergreen oil contains mainly methyl salicylate (about 98%).	Wintergreen oil is used in body rubs, bath oils, toothpaste, mouthwash.	It has a "heating" and "warming" action on muscles and skin. Tonic, stimulant, astringent, and aromatic.	Sweet birch oil, *betula lenta*, peppermint oil, menthol.	Oil is U.S.P.	
WITCH HAZEL (*Hamamelis virginiana*) SYN: Hamamelis water, winter bloom FOLK MEDICINE: Used internally to treat diarrhea and externally to treat mouth and throat irritations, hemorrhoids, eye inflammations, insect bites, burns, and skin irritations.	Bark, leaves	Tannins (Hamamelitannin); essential oil (aldehydes and carboxylic acids); gallic acid; saponins; choline; resins; flavonoids; others	Used as an astringent in creams, lotions, gels, face tonics, aftershaves, fresheners, and masks.	Astringent and hemostatic properties. Witch hazel water is 15% alcohol.	Similar astringents: birch, rhatany Skin lighteners: horse chestnut, butcher's broom	Glycolic extract, hamamelis water	I have used witch hazel in many cosmetics.
YARROW (*Achillea millefolium*) SYN: Milfoil, common yarrow, nosebleed, and thousand leaf FOLK MEDICINE: Tonic, carminative, astringent. Used for loss of appetite, stomach cramps, flatulence, gastritis, external bleeding of all kinds, wounds, sores, and skin rashes.	Herb	Contains 0.1 to 1.4% volatile oil which has azulene (51%); pinenes; borneol; cineole; camphor; other compounds. Also flavonoids (rutin); sterols; alkanes; fatty acids and sugars.	Extract can be used in bath oils for soothing effect on the skin, and in creams and lotions.	Used in bitters and vermouths, and herb tea mixes. Anti-inflammatory, non-phototoxic.		Crude extract	

Herb Name Synonyms Folk Use	Parts Used	Typical Substances	Cosmetic Use	Properties & Other Uses	Similar Plants	Extracts	Comments
YLANG-YLANG OIL (*Cananga odorata*)	Flowers	Contains linalool, geraniol, sesquiterpenes, methyl eugenol, hexanoic, and others.	Used as fragrance material in soaps, creams, lotions, and perfumes (maximum is 1%).	Used in foods as flavor component (5.03 ppm). Non-sensitizing, non-phototoxic, non-irritating.		Essential oil	
YUCCA (*Yucca schidigera*)	Leaves	Contains steroidal saponins (sarsasaponin, tigogenin). Little else is known of the chemical composition.	Used in shampoos for foaming ability and in soaps.	Hemolytic properties. Non-toxic. Used in foods such as root beer and frothy drinks (618 ppm).	Quillaya bark, sarsaparilla	Yucca extract	

organitoons

S. Meadows

Mucopolysaccharides, Glucosaminoglycanes, Hydroxyproline, Eicosapentaenoic Acid, and Other Natural Tongue-twisters, Or

If Peter Picked a Peck of Potent Pipissewa, And A Pint of Periwinkles, Pomegranates, Pelargoniums, and Polypods For His Pop's Poke, How Many Potent Pipissewa, Periwinkles, Pomegranates, Pelargoniums, and Polypods Did He Pick?[1]

If you've read my chapter on "Charting the Herbs," you will have realized that the various components of herbs contain complex chemical names. Ambrette seed extract contains a chemical called (2)-5-tetradecen-14-olide, and the wonderful aloe vera plant contains glucosaminoglycanes and anthraglycosides. What is this stuff? Obviously many of us would not buy a cosmetic that contained a word on the label like 1,10-epoxynobilin, because it sounds like a new glue that would hold the broken chrome bumper on our car until the car was a pile of rust. This chemical, plus 3-epinobilin, 3-dehydronoblin, 7-hydroxycoumarin, and apigenin-7-apiosylglucoside are all listed as some of the components of a well-known herb called camomile. We would all quickly buy a camomile shampoo or camomile rinse or camomile bath oil, but if these chemical tongue-twisters were on the labels of these products we may, rather than try to understand what the chemicals are and where they came from, simply buy another brand of camomile shampoo that didn't have things like 7-hydroxycoumarin or the epoxy chemical on the label. Of course, the camomile shampoo that didn't list these chemicals would still have them in it if it contained real camomile. The chemicals contained in natural substances are a mystery to most chemists. I know this to be true since I've played the "Natural Tongue-Twister" game with them at chemical conferences and seminars.

"What do you think of the anti-microbial activity of chamazulene?" I ask innocently. "Do you think it's been around long enough to be as good as methyl and propyl paraben?"

"What was that?" Chemists always ask you to repeat things because they want to appear loftily absent-minded, but really it's a strategy they use to think up some kind of response that will make them seem more intelligent.

"The preservative chamazulene, is it as good as the parabens?"

"Does Dow Chemical make it?"

"No, it's made in Germany."

"In Germany, you say. Ah, they're doing some interesting things with preservatives. That was chamazulene?"

"Yes, and it's combined with en-yn-dicyloether and umbelliferone which is excellent against gram-positive bacteria such as *Staphylococcus aureus* and *Candida albicans*."

[1]He picked 320 ounces, or 20 pounds.

"Made in Germany, you say?"

"Well, 'made' is not the correct word. It's grown in Germany. The German camomile flower extract has it in it."

"Oh, it's a plant. What are you, some kind of 'organic' chemist?"

To be perfectly fair, if somebody asked me what en-yn-dicyloether was I'd draw a blank too, but if he or she told me it was in a flower I'd be pretty interested. I already accept the fact that nature creates within its own universe the chemicals it needs to survive. They are there for the herbs, and they are there for us as well.

The hardest thing for modern chemical technology to accept is that everything in nature ages and eventually passes away. The example of my little talk with the chemist illustrates how our technocrats have been programmed to think synthetically. What could a flower possibly produce, they think, that couldn't be better produced by Dow Chemical or a similar chemical mega-corporation? However, this is both an economically limited way of thinking and a "we are the gods of the universe" syndrome.

It is economically limited because by usurping nature and synthesizing everything we get immediate gains but lose overall. We have said to ourselves, "We can't accept the limits of nature. We can't tolerate Nature's clock. Everything must meet our calendar and our deadline. We will preserve and protect our natural resources through chemical intervention." We didn't consider the fact that nature had a purpose in its natural cycle, and that within the chemistry of plants, for example, there is a synergism we don't know and can't understand. By altering that natural chemistry and that evolutionary synergism we destroy the very essence of what the purpose of the plant might be.

We have created stronger and stronger chemicals to put into our land, water, air, and plants based solely on our distorted idea of economic gain. Food and cosmetics have been so chemicalized that they can last on a shelf or in a hot warehouse for years, but this does not mean that they are safe, or pure, or fresh. The products prepared in this way may look good, but the aging process, the rotting process, still goes on. We can look at it, and it looks good; we can even gaze at it under a microscope, content that it passes this penetrating gaze, but it is still under the natural clock. It is rotting. We even color the natural products so they look fresh and pure, and we add fragrances to cover up the smell of decay, but within the natural substances the process still takes place. By attempting to distort the decaying process of living things, we destroy what I call the "natural essence." The paltry attempt of science to make nature better by extending the natural life-span of the natural substances succeeds in destroying whatever the life-force of the natural substance is, and at the same time we alter our own environment and our own bodies.

I believe that by chemicalizing our land and plant world we have chemicalized ourselves. The breakdown of our own immune systems evident in such diseases as cancer and AIDS may be due to this chemicalization on every level. It is not simply biochemical: it is also psychological, ecological, and economical.

Well over a century ago an Indian chief said, "There is no quiet place in white man's cities, no place to hear the leaves of spring or the rustle of insect's wings. The white man does not seem to notice the air he breathes . . . like a man dying for many days, he is numb to the stench. What is man without the beasts? If all the beasts were gone, man would die from great loneliness of spirit, for whatever happens to the beasts also happens to man. All things are connected."

The herbs, if unchemicalized, have an essence for us that is unique and can't be duplicated. I've pointed out some of the chemicals that make up some of the herbs, but these are just names that in no way explain how or why the herbs work. Camomile, regardless of the chemical tongue-twisters, is still camomile. Although we talk about some of the recently discussed herbal structures we are not interested in their complex chemical structure, but what they will do for us. What magical qualities do these substances give us? However, isolating the substance from the plant for use in a product may not be ideal because the whole essence of the herb is far superior to the derived complex.

I find it very exciting that most of the "new discoveries" of therapeutic value to the hair and skin are really "old discoveries" being revived in the 1980's. The American Society of Pharmocognosy (a non-profit scientific organization) includes specialists who discover, identify, analyze, and test natural products in relation to their medicinal value. Yet outside of this excellent organization, there are botanists, chemists, pharmacologists, and a new breed of "herbal cosmetic chemists" who are interested in medicinal plants and the exciting investigation of the vegetable kingdom. This work is done in the research library, the lab, the woods, fields, jungles, and, in my own case (in addition to these places), in the research clinic for natural hair and skin care. This is where products are made completely of roots, barks, herbs, and bio-organic substances, used on the hair and skin, and then observed for their positive results.

In the third edition of the *Cosmetic Ingredient Dictionary* (Cosmetic, Toiletry, and Fragrance Association, Washington, D. C., 1982), there are 150 herbal extracts listed for use in cosmetics, and in the *Encyclopedia of Common Natural Ingredients* (by Albert Y. Leung), it is suggested that more than 500 natural ingredients are currently used in foods, drugs, and cosmetics.

Some people aren't aware that long chemical names, what I call the tongue-twisters, are sometimes extracted from natural products. For example, the alkaloid from the ancient Indian snakeroot is known chemically as 3,4,5-trimethoxylbenzoyl reserpate. Obviously, just to look at this odd chemical name (which could be anything) leads to the sweeping generalization that "everything comes out of a test tube today." It is hard to defend our society from this derogatory remark because, as we look around us at our "plastic world," this sweeping statement has some validity, but a little knowledge of the ancient and natural origins of these synthetic-sounding tongue-twisters can help dispel this attitude.

When the Pennsylvania Radiology Department found that aloe vera gel was more effective in treating radiation burns than any man-made chemical, they were only re-discovering what ancient Egypt knew in the early dynastic period (3100 B. C.). Nonetheless, our society hailed the use of aloe vera gel as an exciting and new discovery. It was a "new-old" discovery because although I assume that radiology was not known, as such, to the ancient Egyptians, the hot sun and the fierce sunburns must have led to their need for aloe vera gel. I must also add that radiology was cradled here as well since the transmutation of elements by the ancient Egyptian alchemists has been translated into radioactivity by modern science.

What has happened since the growth of the chemical industrial complex and the end of the agricultural era is a movement to a more plastic, synthetic environment and with this has come the computer-dependent society. There are good aspects to this, since we can now store and quickly gather massive amounts of information, data, records, and more. However, this age has also created a synthetic mind, so to speak, which does not resemble the scientist-adventurer who went into the woods, jungles, fields, and water in search of roots, barks, plants, weeds, flowers, and fungi in a hands-on investigation of the mystical power of these natural substances. The new researcher pushes buttons on a computer, which gathers the knowledge that is then fed to him on sprocketed sheets of paper, rather than just holding a root in his hand and squeezing the juices into a beaker as the ancient alchemist once did. The electrical connection is quicker than the organic connection, and we have become a society that is not only synthesized, but one that wants to travel at the speed of light too. What has become known as "hands-on experience" and the "natural-organic connection" is often viewed with disdain or skepticism but not all knowledge is contained in computers, and the damage done to the earth and its inhabitants by the radiation of this new technology cannot heal itself, so the gel must be squeezed from the aloe vera plant to soothe the damage done.

Not all civilizations have forgotten the discoveries of their forefathers. Unlike the Western world, China did not discard herbal medicines for chemical drugs. Their natural remedies maintain an unbroken tradition that is almost as mystical as ancient Egypt's heliopolitan and hermapolitan traditions: the principles of yin and yang. Today, China leads the world in the formulation of herbal concentrates by manufacturing pills, tablets, and capsules based on the yin and yang of ancient herbal therapy. In the United States, however, the FDA and the medical establishment regard this practice with disdain, and even go so far as to label it as "charlatanism" or "faddism." Thus, herbal extracts, which are usually sold by mail or in health food stores, are labeled "herbal tea capsules" and considered innocuous herbology by the medical establishment.

The new herbal concentrates are made as you would make a traditional tea, although sometimes alcohol is used in place of water to improve the extraction. After filtering out the cellulose, starch, and other inert ingredients, the extract is dried to form a very concentrated powder. This goes into a gelatin capsule. Herbs such as ginseng, dong quai, eleuthero, and foti are part of a huge import business for the Orient and are made into capsules in the U. S. or used in the formulation of cosmetics.

A standard decoction or infusion of one ounce of herb to every pint of water (one fluid ounce or two tablespoons), is used in formulating herbal tea extracts. For a tincture, four ounces of herb for every pint of alcohol is used, and some of the other fluid herbal extracts consist of multiple extraction procedures. I have combined all the different procedures to get the essence of various botanicals for a strong "green medicine" extract.

Modern suppliers of herbal extracts are able to produce materials that are consistent in quality, but this art depends on carefully selecting the herbs as well as the extraction method (or solvent used). I am a purist and avoid some of the common solvent systems, such as propylene glycol, butylene glycol, or ethoxidiglycol, whenever possible.

Not only are herbal extracts a "new discovery," but various elements within the extract itself are coming under the researcher's eye for drug, food, and cosmetic use. Below and on the following pages are some natural tongue-twisters that you may have heard and wondered what they are as well as some that you've probably never seen before. After reading this chapter you will probably decide that although these words look and sound complicated, they are only man's names for nature's substances. Nature is the supreme chemist, and humankind will never learn all of nature's secrets.

ACIDOPHILUS *(as•e•dof'•e•les)*

There is a fungus called *Monilia abrican* that can grow in the intestines, vagina, lungs, mouth, fingers, and under the fingernails which can produce a yeast-like infection (see *Candida* below). Within our bodies we have important intestinal flora which, if destroyed, allows unfriendly fungi such as *Monilia abrican* to flourish. One of the problems with taking antibiotics is that the friendly flora will be destroyed and can cause unfriendly bacteria to go unchecked. Bad breath (from the intestines) is one of the symptoms of *Monilia abrican*, and it is useless to use a mouthwash or breath freshener against this problem. The problem can be solved by eating yogurt or acidophilus culture *(Lactobacilli acidolphili)* which acts to restore friendly bacteria (See also page 8 for acne treatment with acidophilus).

Mycologists, scientists who specialize in fungi, say fungi are plants yet they contain no chlorophyll, can't make their own food, and require oxygen to survive. Some scientists see them as a third kingdom (i. e., animal, plants, fungi). Fungi are found in diverse environments. They thrive in cool to tropical climates: they're in the air, on our skin, inside our bodies, in dead leaves, in water, in citrus fruit, and in leftover food.

When these "unfriendly fungi" are inside our body we have "friendly bacteria" along with our immune system to deal with them. This is also true of our intestinal flora which protects us against fungi that are not friendly.

After you've been on antibiotics it is advisable to include acidophilus in your diet. Acidophilus culture is incubated in cow's milk, goat's milk, and carrots.

ALLANTOIN *(e'•lan•tewen)*

Quite often when you read a soap or cosmetic label you will see the word *allantoin*, and if you are curious you will wonder what it is and what it does. A business acquaintance of mine, S. B. Mecca, has probably done more scientific papers on allantoin than anyone else, and as chemical director of Schuykill Chemical Company, he is not simply a "book chemist," but also works at the lab bench. Through Mr. Mecca's writing and my own work creating products with allantoin (as well as testing it in actual skin care facial work), I find that it is another "new-old" discovery from the world of herbs really worth talking about.

One herbal source of allantoin is comfrey (*Symphytum officinale*), a unique herb that probably has more uses than any other herb. Joseph Kadans lists well over twenty uses in his book *Encyclopedia of Medicinal Herbs* (Arco Publishing Company, Inc., New York). Old country people have called it "knitbone" because the combination of mineral salts in the herb were considered irreplaceable for healing fractures; however, the positive effects on the skin, hair, and scalp are what particularly interest us. Sores or ulcers on the outside of the body can be relieved with a poultice made of the crushed green leaves of comfrey. A salve concocted from comfrey leaves promotes healing since comfrey forms a protective coating and helps the body's ability to form new skin (in burn cases). Since comfrey has a large protein content, it can even be used to make a highly nutritious drink by combining fresh comfrey leaves with unsweetened pineapple juice (liquified). The reputation of comfrey as a vulneray (wound healing agent) is now known to be due to the allantoin content. Allantoin was first isolated in 1912 when C. J. Macalister prepared extractions of comfrey root. He noticed a brilliant crystalline substance, which upon chemical analysis proved to be glyoxyldiureide, or what we now call allantoin. Allantoin is also found in wheat germ, rice polishings, sycamore leaves, the bark of the horse chestnut tree, dog urine, and human urine (in trace amounts).

The positive action of allantoin as a wound healer has been compared to urea by some researchers, but as Mecca has pointed out, urea is definitely inhibitory to wound healing, whereas allantoin has many positive actions. Urea tends to dry and cake on the skin, which prevents close contact, but allantoin creates an occlusive bond on the skin. Allantoin is also a valuable cell-proliferant, thereby stimulating healthy tissue formation which indicates that it is excellent for all skin care products. Allantoin is also a chemical debrider of necrotic tissue, which serves to clean up dead skin cells, yet it is bland, stable, non-toxic, soothing, and non-irritating. This in itself is unique for a substance that can clean up the skin since most products use harsh solvents to do this job. I have used allantoin with great success in sun protection creams (where it is soothing to the skin after UV exposure), in lip protection balms (where it heals chapped lips and encourages healthy skin regrowth), in deodorants (where it reduces the possibility of skin rash and irritation), in a selenium shampoo where it is soothing to the scalp and has a positive healing and cleansing action to dead skin cells), and in amino acid acne products (because of its healing action).

Allantoin also works with amino acids to improve absorption from shampoos into the hair. Allantoin and methionine combine to reconstitute the protein content of damaged hair. It has also been found to be effective in shampoos for seborrheic dermatitis. It helps remove scales and crusts, and clears the scalp of oiliness. It has an anti-pruritic modality which prevents aggravation of the condition due to scratching, activates the healing process, and is non-sensitizing, non-irritating, and non-toxic.

CANDIDA *(can'•did•e)*

No, this isn't a play by George Bernard Shaw about the superiority of a woman named Candida and the inferior men in her life. *Candida* is a strain of yeast known as *Candida albicans*. In some ways *candida* has beneficial actions within our body, working as a silent partner to our immune system. *Candida* is found in mucosal surfaces of the intestinal and urinary tracts. If you are lucky enough to have a strong immune system, then *candida*'s proliferation is kept minimal so that it is a friendly fungus. Of 169 adults, 163 studied supported *candida* colonies in mucosal surfaces and in skin tissue (S. S. Lorenzani, Ph.D., "Candida Albicans," *Let's Live Magazine*, 51 [April 1983]).

When we have too much *candida* in our systems (usually due to our immune system's inefficiency), many problems can result: heartburn, colitis, gastritis, diarrhea, gas, constipation, headaches, depression, hay fever, sinus problems, earaches, asthma, food and chemical sensitivities, and, the best-known symptom, vaginal yeast infections.

Avoiding antibiotics, immunosuppressant, and oral contraceptive drugs is important, but a yeast-free diet and an individualized program of vitamins, minerals, food concentrates, and digestive enzymes may also be beneficial. In addition, cytoxic testing, which helps determine food sensitivities, is needed (this is not the scratch test often given by allergists, which is only 20% accurate and not accurate for foods at all).

Since I am discussing skin and hair care in this book, let's talk about yeast vaginitis, the common yeast infection. This shows up as a rash and/or severe itching of the vaginal canal. Forty per cent of vaginal infections can be attributed to *candida*. There may be a "cottage cheese-like" discharge or no discharge at all. The discharge can be observed in a saline solution under a microscope for the characteristic budding yeast and hydrae forms (the use of potassium hydroxide on the slide makes the presence of the organism more obvious). This infection can be transferred through sexual intercourse from one person to another. In men, the infection appears as a rash, redness, and severe itching. There are topical treatments to stop the itching and combat the yeast organism. Bear in mind, however, that the symptom is a message to you that your diet needs altering and vitamin-mineral supplementation is needed.

A vaginal suppository called mycostatin, or a cream containing this chemical, is often prescribed by a physician and used for two weeks or more (*Medical and Health Annual Encyclopedia*, London: Britannica, Inc., 1977, pp. 405-406). A natural topical treatment can be used by applying a cream or using a cleanser that contains menthol, eucalyptus, camphor, and aloe vera gel in the formulation (see **RESOURCES SECTION** on skin cleansers). This treatment is to be used on the external vaginal area only. Application of this cream may stop the itching and discomfort, though it may not stop the infection. Nevertheless, cleaning the area with this type of cream cleanser is important for men and women with yeast infections.

Method: dampen the genital area with warm water and work the cleanser over the entire area. Rinse well and repeat. Clean the infected area twice daily and even more often if needed. Consult a physician if the problem doesn't clear up within a week. Again, a cytoxic test can indicate the foods to avoid as far as the allergic reaction to *candida* is concerned.

EICOSAPENTAENOIC ACID *(i•ko'•sap•en•te•no•ik as •id)*

What is this mile-long word, and why does it need to be part of our diet? Not too long ago many health food vitamin manufacturers were getting this oil into capsules to sell to health food retailers, and at almost the same moment that EPA was showing up in capsules all over the U. S., another oil known as evening primrose oil was being marketed in health food stores. Both evening primrose oil and EPA are precursors to the remarkable biochemical regulators within our body called prostaglandins (PGs). When we eat foods that contain essential fatty acids (EFAs) such as linoleic acid, the body chemistry ideally converts the linoleic acid into gamma-linolenic acid (GLA), then into di-homo-gamma-linolenic acid, and finally to PGE[1]. It is postulated, however, that some people cannot manufacture PGs from the EFAs in their diet or that they consume inadequate amounts of EFAs and that they can benefit from supplementation of evening primrose oil and eicosapentaenoic acid. Consequently, a product called Max-EPA™ (a trademark of Seven Seas Health Care, Ltd., Hull, England) and a non-trademarked series of products called Evening Primrose Oil began saying that their products were a good way to facilitate the production of prostaglandins within the body.

EPA comes from the oils of cold water fish such as salmon, mackerel, and sardines. Through their food chain (beginning with phytoplankton), the fish can convert linolenic acid to EPA and DHA (docosahexenoic acid). Both are long-chain fatty acids.

The main attraction to these fatty acids is that studies have shown that they may contain substances that lower blood fats and thereby reduce the risk of cardiovascular disease. The consumption of the EPA capsules is also based on the study of Eskimos in Greenland, who have a low incidence of heart disease because the fats they consume are long-chain unsaturated members of the EPA family (See **EVENING PRIMROSE OIL**).

ETHOXYLATE PHYTOSTEROLS *(eth•oxs´•e•lat fi•to•ster´•ols)*

This is a long tongue-twister for a simple, natural substance: soya sterol. It really opens the door for me to suggest that soya is an excellent high protein medium, and can be used in place of animal protein. Soya can, and is, being used in shampoos, soaps, night creams, day creams, and body lotions. I personally have used both soya and milk protein (lactalbumin) with great success in many skin, body, and hair products. Soya gives a soft, silky feel to the hair whether it is used in a shampoo or conditioner. In the proper formula (using glycol-proteins), it is excellent for damaged, dry, chemicalized, or brittle hair.

The soya sterols are incorporated into skin cleansing products for their natural emulsifying properties, and in addition, they improve the feel of the skin. Soya sterols can also have the same results in moisturizers and body lotions. It is believed that when used in shampoos and conditioners they have the effect of straightening the hair, as well as reducing the electrostatic effects of what many people call "flyaway" hair.

GLUCOMANNAN *(gloo•co•man´•an)*

Glucomannan, another of our natural tongue-twisters, is an example of an "old" but "new" dietary fiber which is extracted from the konjac root (cultivated in Japan). The eating of the konjac root goes back more than a thousand years when herbalists taught people that this fiber would regularize bowel movements, block the absorption of poisons and toxins, and produce a feeling of satiety. Konjac was used in various foods, not for taste, but because it was known to be good for the body and clean out the digestive tract. Today, this extract from the konjac root (glucomannan) is processed as a food supplement mainly for dieting and as a fiber to regulate the activity of the intestinal tract. When glucomannan is taken with a glass of water, it absorbs water in the digestive tract. It swells and becomes jelly-like, thereby producing a full feeling and repressing the appetite. At the same time it regularizes the activity of the intestinal tract, absorbs excess food and toxic substances, and softens the feces for more efficient bowel movements. Some health food stores have glucomannan dietary fiber in packets and capsules (which sometimes contain pectin and alginic acid). This extract of the konjac root is manufactured in Tomioka City, Japan, by a company called Tsuruta Shokuhin Co., Ltd. They process the konjac root with water rinsing and parching with an instantaneous drying procedure, and package the product in two ways: (1) konjac flour for Japanese cooking, and (2) refined glucomannan as a dietary fiber. I cannot personally compare it to other natural fibers, nor do I know whether or not it is a good supplement for weight loss, although I have heard that it is excellent for this purpose. As far as attracting moisture to the skin, I have not found it to be any better than more easily obtainable herbal extracts.

HYALURONIC ACID *(hi•a•lu•ro'•nik as'•id)*

Hyaluronic acid is a mucopolysaccharide (we discuss this tongue-twister in this chapter) found in animal tissues. It is one of the many components found in skin cells and in our connective tissues. This acid is a natural polymer which holds cells together and lubricates joints. It is found in the skin (along with other mucopolysaccharides) and in the synovial fluid. Hyaluronic acid works with an enzyme called hyaluronidase which breaks down the molecular structure of hyaluronic acid so it has increased permeability in the tissues (including skin tissue).

The mucopolysaccharides and polysaccharides have found use in skin and hair care products for their ability to leave the skin smooth and moist. It has been suggested that hyaluronic acid is a "water reservoir" for skin cells and binds up to 40,000 times its weight in water. Some cosmetic manufacturers add hyaluronic acid to cosmetic products, but this specific polysaccharide is no more moisturizing than a good vegetarian mucopolysaccharide which can be found in simple aloe vera gel. There are also other excellent hydrolyzers of the skin such as pantothenate, a B vitamin. If you leave a jar of pantothenate overnight with the lid slightly ajar it will, overnight, collect a mass of water beads.

Don't worry too much whether or not a cosmetic label says hyaluronic acid because if the label says mucopolysaccharides it also contains hyaluronic acid. The mucopolysaccharides work together synergistically, and if the manufacturer has included just hyaluronic acid in his formula, he is using it for the "buzz word" advertising effect it will have on consumers and not for the benefit to their skin and hair. I have found that hyaluronic acid is no more effective than mucopolysaccharides nor is it more moisturizing than vitamin E and panthenol.

HYDRO-OCCLUSIVE™ MASK *(hi'•dro o•klu'•siv mask)*

This tongue-twister can be broken down into two parts: hydro, which means water, and occlusive, which suggests a gentle adhesion to the skin that facilitates absorption and moisturization. Hydro-occlusive (a trademark of Aubrey Organics, Tampa, Florida) describes a method of deep moisturization utilizing an herbalized mineral water and a natural film mask of honey and the dermal proteins collagen and elastin. The water activates the mask and causes the nutrients (as well as any other moisturizing treatments you have put on under the mask) to be absorbed deep into the skin. However, hydro-occlusive can also describe any method of moisturization that uses water, or substances (such as herbal extracts) that are soluble in water because the water is readily absorbed into the skin and carries any substances dissolved in it deep into the skin.

Occlusion is an old curative art which was used by herbalists and Indians hundreds, in fact thousands, of years ago. The American Indians used leaves from various plants to create an occlusive wrap for bruises or skin wounds. The treatment frequently brought miraculous relief, even by today's modern medical standards.

Today one well-established medical treatment for psoriasis uses occlusion: the patient applies cortisone cream or any cream or oil that will break up the crusty lesions and then wraps the area in plastic wrap. What happens is that the plastic wrap causes the pilo-sebaceous apparatus to work more effectively, thereby absorbing the treatment cream or oil beneath the lesions, below the epidermal layer. (See "**DOES YOUR SKIN REALLY ABSORB AND USE NUTRIENTS?**") The lesions or scales soften and wash away or even dissolve, leaving the skin treatable by UV rays. A modern adaptation of this treatment is to use photosensitizing agents to get more results from the UV rays.

In the cosmetic field the researchers at the Secol Corporation decided to create a hydro-occlusive mask with nutrients built into the "film" medium and activated by water. I had already used thin plastic wrap, and also clay and herbal masks, to get this effect for some years, but Secol accomplished it by combining protein (in this case, dermal proteins) with sorbitol to create a film or gelatin substance and adding honey to thicken and bind the mixture. The problem with Secol's mask, however, is the limitation of the mask formula itself because it does not utilize the many phytodermatologicals available. The masks contain either collagen and elastin, vitamin E, panthenol, or clay. They also have a mask that supposedly removes blackheads; however, this is a professional mask and is not readily available to the consumer. One version of Secol's Hydro-Occlusive Mask with collagen and elastin is sold in many health food stores.

The moisturizing benefits of occlusive masks have been studied by the Essex Testing Clinic, Inc., in Verona, New Jersey, who conducted a series of smoothness studies using facial masks containing various substances. They found that the B vitamin, panthenol, was probably the best of all the tested nutrients as far as topical appearance, but that vitamin E has a similar hydration effect, almost as great as the B vitamin. The test of vitamin E had the additional effect of smoothing fine lines, and the smoothing effect lasted well beyond the four hour study. The Essex Testing Clinic conducted their smoothing and moisturizing tests on 57 subjects, 6 male and 51 female, ranging in age from 20 to 70. They had no toxic reactions to the natural substances used.

A test of smoothness and moisture was also conducted by the Xienta Institute for Skin Research using the Sampson technique and the Goldschmidt and Kligman technique. In this technique the subjects are studied to determine the normal patterns of dermatoglyphic markings. The skin is either studied with a fluorescent dye or left unstained. Areas under study are photographed during the tests. Peter T. Pugliese, M. D., who was the principal investigator, found that a combination of vitamin E and panthenol produced the best effect on the skin. He noticed a decided smoothness and moist look to the skin with reduced lines. "The obvious physical effect requires rather profound physiological changes which suggest that the mask is quite effective in both hydration and debridement," observed Dr. Pugliese.

I have found that it is not a specific natural substance but a combination of substances that will give a desired moisturizing effect. That is why an isolated substance such as hyaluronic acid is not as effective as a good natural mixture of polysaccharides, or a combination of panthenol and vitamin E. The best moisturizing and regenerating substance I have found, though, is a mixture of water-soluble herbal extracts and vitamins. Here's my mixture: red vine, St. John's wort, arnica, witch hazel, horse chestnut, and ivy (these extracts are anti-blotchiness and anti-varicose treatments). I combine this with blue bottle, Roman camomile, feverfew, marigold and limetree (these are anti-inflammatory, softening, and desensitizing). This I combine with hops, rosemary, horsetail, pine-tree, and lemon (these extracts are anti-wrinkle, softening, and antiseptic). I combine this with cucumber, elder, mallow, and pellitory (*parientaria officinalis*). These are very softening to the skin and natural emollients. This mixture of herbs is combined with vitamin E, pantothenate, and a mixture of seaweed extracts. I have termed my mixture "vegacell therapy" because it contains no animal substances. All the extracts are water-soluble--no oils are used.

In hydro-occlusive treatments both the method of application and the naturalness of the formula are extremely important because these type of treatment is so efficient that it transports whatever is dissolved in the water into the skin. If the treatment contains chemicals this could be very harmful to your skin and to your health. If used with natural, beneficial substances, however, the hydro-occlusive process can help reduce the aging process of the skin: it is an essential part to natural skin care. I have included a "pattern" for making your own hydro-occlusive mask in this book as well as the various ways you can use this technique to benefit your skin (See **NATURAL METHOD OF SKIN CARE**).

HYDROXYPROLINE *(hi•drox•i•pro'•len)*

Hydroxyproline is the collagen-specific amino acid which plays an important role in joining together the various elements of our collagen fibrils (of which the mucopolysaccharides are one). It is formed when its precursor proline is utilized for the synthesis of proto-collagen and is then modified by taking in hydrogen and oxygen to form hydroxyproline.

The collagen-specific hydroxyproline and the essential fatty acids (EFAs) work together to keep our skin healthy and youthful, at least as far as its collagen is concerned. The EFAs play a vital role in the body's enzymatic activities, and we also have a dietetic need for them because they cannot be duplicated by the body. For example, a decrease in the blood level of two EFAs, linoleic acid and arachidonic acid, will result in eczematic symptoms. A deficiency in any of the EFAs will result in a deficient synthesis of prostaglandins, which is another tongue-twister but an important one. Some prostaglandins (PGs) are important inflammation mediators, such as PGE_1 and PGE_2. These PGs supply a special secretion of natural substances that are known as lymphocytes, which retard hypersensitivity, and release hydrolase and other lysosomial enzymes. But the EFAs cannot be utilized in the body without proline; that is, the proper use of the EFAs depends on the health of your collagen.

That was quite a complicated link of words, but it places well into focus exactly how the EFAs work within our collagen. So what? If I eat good foods, get plenty of rest, and get fresh air and exercise, won't all this fall into place? No, because the quality of our food, rest, air, has been compromised by chemicalization and our civilized stressful way of life. For example, hydrogenated or rancid fats may interfere with the absorption of the essential fatty acids. And, the UVs in the sun age your skin, including of course your collagen, all year round, especially in the summer.

Our body and outer skin are designed to develop and deal with our surrounding environment. The problem is that we find ourselves in a continually changing and degenerating environment. The body which was designed to deal with a clean, natural environment is desperately trying to cope with a dirty, synthetic environment. The aging process is definitely accelerated by the chemicalized world in which we live. This statement is not just a "scare tactic" but a fact of life: the struggle to live longer and reflect a healthy appearance is being reduced from the outside in. I have found that by topical care of the skin and hair (scalp) with the elements utilized within the body, you can change the hair and skin in a positive fashion. Most cosmetics that go on our skin and in our hair create an illusion or certain "look," but there are also cosmetics that can help you retain a healthy appearance and are health-augmenting instead of health-debilitating. If the cosmetics contain the various elements, or some of the various elements that I am setting forth in this book then you will be giving your body care and protection from the outside to the inside as well as looking your best (See also **ESSENTIAL FATTY ACIDS, EVENING PRIMROSE OIL, COLLAGEN,** and **ALOE VERA**).

KERATIN *(ker'•a•tin)*

We see more and more products for the hair and skin that contain keratin. The basis of compounding cosmetics with this sulfur-containing fibrous protein is that our hair and skin contain keratin. Soft keratin, which has a low cystine content, is the type contained in the skin and sloughed off, removing parasites and micro-organisms with it. Hard keratin, which is high in cystine, is the type of keratin which makes up our hair. It is for this reason that we see more and more keratin shampoos and keratin conditioners. Originally keratin shampoos and conditioners made claims of hair growth but since these products did not grow hair the claims were altered. Keratin shampoos and conditioners were then labeled as products to thicken and texturize the hair.

The amino acid composition of hair keratin is as follows: alanine 2.8%, arginine 8.8%, aspartic acid 3.8%, cystine 18.0%, glutamic acid 13.4%, glycine 4.1%, histidine 1.2%, isoleucine 4.7%, leucine 6.4%, lysine 1.8%, methionine 0.6%, phenylalanine 2.4%, proline 4.3%, serine 10.5%, threonine 8.5%, tryptophan 1.0%, tyrosine 2.2%, and valine 5.5%. I list the amino acids because there are two prevailing justifications that cosmetic manufacturers give for keratin shampoos and conditioners: (1) the amino acid content is unique in keratin and can be used by the hair; and (2) since keratin is produced by the ribosomes within the epidermal cells (in contrast to other dermal proteins such as collagen and elastin), the unique structure makes it a valuable additive to hair care products. However, the way in which keratin as an ingredient is used in most hair care products sold today does not justify either of the two reasons listed above.

Keratin can be obtained from wool or feathers, both of which are almost identical in amino acid structure to human hair. Wool has one additional amino acid that human hair lacks, ammonia-N (1.1%), and feathers have one amino acid missing (in relation to hair and wool)-- tryptophan. The big difference in amino acid structure is that of cystine: human hair contains more cystine (18%) than any other type of keratin. Wool keratin contains 10.3% keratin, and feather keratin contains only 6.8%. Obviously, keratin from wool is the best non-human source and keratin from feathers the least desirable source when based on amino acid structure. However, these distinctions are unimportant because most of the keratin shampoos sold contain a form of keratin without cystine. They extract the cystine because it smells "medicinal," plus it can be profitably put to use in other ways. Although the odor of cystine is far from pleasant, it can be masked partially by fragrances or essential oils. What is interesting about the removal of the cystine from keratin "protein" hair care products is that for your hair cystine is the most important amino acid in keratin. In fact, this is the amino acid that acts as a bridge in the structure of your hair and it is the amino acid destroyed by cold wave solutions and other chemicals. When this bridge is reduced, the hair is damaged and hair loss can often result thereafter. Removing the cystine from the keratin protein in shampoos greatly reduces any positive conditioning it may have for your hair.

In addition, much of the conditioning benefits from keratin "protein" hair care products does not come from the keratin but from other protein sources. Cosmetic manufacturers must add other proteins to their keratin "protein" hair care products because the FTC has a rule that in order to make a protein claim, the shampoo must have a minimum molecular weight of 1,000. Since keratin does not meet this minimum, most keratin shampoos contain other types of protein to bring up the molecular weight. So, in reality, your keratin shampoo is just another protein shampoo with some keratin in it, even though it may lack cystine (which is vital to proper care for damaged hair). Topically applied amino acids do have conditioning benefits and help repair damaged hair, but they lack film-forming and texturizing properties which enhance the feel of the hair. These basic conditioning qualities are supplied by other kinds of protein besides keratin.

I have compounded shampoos and conditioners with cystine and know that the manufacturer, retailer, and consumer must be prepared for a "vitamin-like" odor, and also be aware that the label should state that the keratin "protein" hair care product contains cystine. Your keratin shampoo/conditioner that makes all kinds of promises will probably do a limited job of texturizing the hair. It is best to look for a completely natural protein shampoo which could contain soya protein or any other type of protein. Whether or not it contains keratin, at this point in time, is of little value to your hair and/or skin, unless it contains more than a minute amount of cystine.

MUCOPOLYSACCHARIDES *(mu•ko•pol•i•sak'•e•rids)*

The dermis is composed of 79% collagen, 11% lipids, 7% mucopolysaccharides, 2% elastin, and 1% carbohydrates. This makes each of these various elements of some importance to the skin as topical skin care treatments.

We've discussed collagen, lipids, and elastin in various parts of this book so we can take a close look at that natural tongue-twister, mucopolysaccharides. These substances are also know as glucosaminoglycanes, which is as much of a tongue-twister as mucopolysaccharides. "Muco" means mucoid (a biochemical found in the connective tissues or a mucoprotein yielding carbohydrates and amino acids if hydrolyzed). "Poly" means many. "Saccharides" are organic compounds containing sugars. I will call them MPs for short. MPs are produced in the body by glucose and are composed as hyaluronic acid, condroitin sulfate, and dermantan sulfate. As the skin ages, the amount of hyaluronic acid decreases from 70 to 30%; condroitin sulfate reduces from 20 to 3%. At the same time the skin decreases in water content and shrinks somewhat. This means the skin is less moist (i.e., dry) and has less flexibility. MPs have the ability to act as a binding agent for water, and this is the job of their gel-like structure in water that fills the space between the collagen fibers. Hyaluronic acid, for example, can bind from 5 milliliters up to 4 liters of water per gram. (See the discussion of **HYALURONIC ACID** in this chapter).

MPs not only regulate the water content of the connective tissues, but they also restrict other solutes and act as a sieve for passage of large molecules. A very important role of MPs is to prevent the conversion of soluble collagen to insoluble collagen. We have seen in the discussion of collagen in this book that when collagen becomes insoluble (cross-linked), the skin becomes taut and wrinkled. On aging, the ratio of MPs to collagen decreases which demonstrates why the skin is dry, because the MPs act as a sheath for the collagen fibers as well as a lubricant. If collagen fibers are reconstructed without MPs, they are much more rigid and tend to be cross-linked.

Hydrolyzed mucopolysaccharides (HMPs) offer the smallest MP molecule which allows a better penetration through the skin. HMPs offer increased skin moisturization and skin elasticity. A combination of HMPs with collagen increases the effect of the collagen as a moisturizing agent. By combining HMPs in a celltherapy cream the skin has increased moisturization and the newer skin that replaces the dead skin cells is better moisturized and has increased turgor, or plumpness. When HMPs are combined with extracts of arnica, cucumber, elder, ivy, and mallow, a skin tonic is created that gives the skin a soft, moist, healthy tone.

OCTACOSANOL *(ok•te•co'•san•ol)*

Not content to stop with the fish and the primrose path, we turn to the fields of wheat. There we can find wheat germ oil and a substance derived from wheat germ known as octacosanol. This is a natural substance which is not vitamin E but is believed by some resarchers to be a critical factor in our physical fitness. Studies have shown that wheat germ oil concentrate (high in octacosanol) has shown erogenic activity, or improvement in oxygen utilization when exercising. Wheat germ oil, as well as the wheat germ itself, has already been well-established as an important part of topical hair and skin care.

SELENIUM & GLUTATHIONE *(se•le´•ni•um & glu•ta´•thi•on)*

Probably the first shampoo on the market to contain the mineral selenium was Selsun Blue Shampoo (by Abbott Labs), or at least it was the first to have a national advertising campaign about the values of selenium for dandruff control. It has been documented in several monographs and books as an aid in keeping youthful elasticity in tissues (anti-aging factor), in alleviating hot flashes and menopausal distress, in helping in the treatment and prevention of dandruff, and, as a natural antioxidant (with Vitamin E), in possibly neutralizing certain carcinogens as well as providing protection from some cancers.

In the plant world selenium is found in wheat germ, bran, onions, tomatoes, and broccoli. In the animal world it is found in tuna fish (best source listed). As a mineral supplement it is available in microgram doses of 25 to 200 mcg., though if sufficient natural foods containing this element were eaten, you would get enough in your diet. The problem here is that selenium is easily destroyed by food processing techniques. Adding synthetic chemicals will change its structure and void its nutritional value. Selenium is even more valuable and stronger as a nutrient when it is combined with vitamin E (as it is naturally in wheat germ) because the two are synergistic. Vitamin E working alone is considered an excellent antioxidant, but when combined with selenium the two together are more powerful than the sum of their equal parts. Selenium is part of the natural enzyme glutathione peroxidase, and as the name implies, its job in your body is to break down peroxides so that they do not become elements destructive to the connective tissues.

Besides controlling dandruff and itching, selenium has also been found to reduce the age-related loss of hair pigment due to damage of the melancytes (pigment cells) in the hair follicles. It is not known whether or not topical application in conditioners and shampoos will help this problem, but selenium supplements have helped color loss. Hair care products that contain selenium can be slightly drying to the hair and scalp, so it is advisable to use a hair conditioner with a selenium shampoo. This is because selenium acts to prevent scalp lipid autoxidation and eliminate scalp itch and dandruff. However, I found that some heads of hair didn't have the drying effect and still got the benefit of the anti-dandruff action. I have found that some fatty acids or essential oils can be combined with the selenium-amino acid-vitamin shampoo to reduce the dryness. One other natural substance that works with selenium besides Vitamin E is the amino acid cystine (See **KERATIN** in this chapter).

Putting aside our discussion of selenium for hair care, there are many new ideas being put forth about selenium as an anti-cancer agent. No more than a few years ago, selenium was ignored (look in some old nutrition books and you may not even find it mentioned). Today we are aware that many trace minerals serve a purpose, and sometimes a powerful health purpose. Selenium will not cure cancer, nor will it arrest the development of cancer, but it will play a role as a protector against cancer. One thing researchers are becoming aware of is that selenium works to prevent certain types of cancer. Cancers of the tongue, esophagus, stomach, intestine, rectum, liver, pancreas, larynx, lung, kidney, prostate, bladder, lymph glands, breast, thyroid, and uterus all seem to respond to selenium. Obviously, this micromineral is a powerful one when we consider that our bodies only contain .2 of a part per million selenium, which is almost the lowest mineral content in the body (molybdenum, arsenic, chromium, gold, mercury and lithium are found in lesser amounts).

Let's think a minute about glutathione. This is a sulfur-containing amino acid that contains three component aminos called l-cystine, l-glutamic acid, and glycine. One unique thing about this combo is how fast it is absorbed orally. Work I have done with the amino acid complex (combining sulfur-containing amino acids and essential fatty acids) leads me to believe that topical absorption and use is possible.

As pointed out above, selenium works with glutathione peroxidase and breaks down the peroxides that would otherwise cause cross-linkage of your collagen. Glutathione, which was discovered in 1921 by a biochemist named Hopkins, not only prevents (along with selenium) the oxidation of synthetic or hydrogenated oils in your body but has this same action (and others) on your skin. I have been utilizing the amino acid to reduce oxidation of lipids and other oils on the skin as well as the oils in the products. Glutathione, along with vitamin E, is a natural antioxidant. You may wonder why this natural nutrient (or other natural substances) is not frequently used as a natural preservative and a therapeutic agent for skin (double service, so to speak), rather than a synthetic preservative (which is almost always the usual choice of cosmetic chemists).

This subject matter may seem new to you, and as you read about glutathione in magazines and books today, it does seem like a new subject; however, it is not new. Amine-type antioxidants have been known to the cosmetic industry for years. H. S. Olcott and H. A. Mattill published "Antioxidants and the Autoxidation of Fats" in 1936 (*J. American Chemical Society*, 58:204), and they discussed glutathione and other amines.

There is obviously a link between amino acids and essential fatty acids, which has been a link that I have used for many successful effects on the hair, scalp, and skin. For example, an amino acid complex made up of sulfur-rich amino acid concentrates (cysteine, cystine, methionine, glutathione, etc.) is suitable for greasy and blemished skin, as well as for scalps that have an excessive secretion of sebum (i.e., oily with dandruff). I created a gel made with minerals and these amino acids which if rubbed on the skin in an oily area immediately creates a dry smooth area. Of special significance in cosmetology is the experimental evidence that on percutaneous application, sulfur-containing amino acids are absorbed by the skin (scalp) and incorporated in the hair (and as we have pointed out above, cystine has a regenerative effect on hair keratin) providing for the intromolecular structure of keratin on which the elasticity of the hair depends (See also **AMINO ACIDS**).

SPIRULINA AND OTHER BLUE-GREEN ALGAE *(spi•ru•li'•na)*

Food from the sea is a dream which may in time be a necessity if world famine due to crop failure occurs. Many researchers think food from the sea is impractical, though in some countries such as Japan, seaweed and algae are well-recognized and accepted food products. I have found that seaweed extracts have many benefits for the skin and hair. For example, a seaweed known as laminaria contains an extract which when applied to the skin leaves a smooth, soft, moisturized skin texture. I have used it along with other seaweed and algae extracts for skin care products. There's also a seaplant native to Hawaii (algae extract) which is completely harmless, edible and when applied to the body gives the skin a soft, smooth, fresh, emollient non-sticky feel. An algae extract like aloe vera gel may be a cosmetic product in itself, but can also be used as a part of skin and hair care products, e. g., the hydroglycolic extract of sea ware (*Yhalles*), which is high in carragahenin, iodides, ergosterol (provitamin D_2), and amino acids. Sea ware is believed to be beneficial for weight control and accelerates the exchanges in cellular tissue (anti-cellulitic) when used externally in massage creams. Bladderwrack (*Fucus vesiculosus*) is a seaweed of the Northern Atlantic Ocean which is believed to be soothing, moisturizing, and a coadjutant in external treatment of cellulitis. Land plants whose extracts have properties similar to bladderwrack and sea ware are arnica, birch, ivy, escin, horse chestnut, and for soothing properties, aloe and mallow. In addition to using sea plant extracts in cosmetics I have also used the salts derived from sea water in spa products (bath oils) which are excellent in whirlpool tubs and hot tubs. A spa bath liquid made with sea salts and algae extracts creates an effervescence like the sea shore, and this spa treatment is also suitable for mildly irritated skin conditions as well as soothing to dry eczema and psoriasis. After you've been in a spa bath containing these algae, seaweed, and sea salts, the body feels relaxed and soothed. The skin is left with a thin layer of extremely minute crystals (called the Frenkenhauser film) which accounts for reflex therapy and tonic effect of the iodic brine bath. (See also **THALASSOTHERAPY** in Chapter 6).

Some people have the idea that algae is bad for you, but this is a misconception as we've seen by the many uses in hair and skin care products discussed above as well as the use of algae as foods and nutritional supplements. Algae are simple plants that grow in ponds, rivers, oceans, and even in the soil. In the water they serve as food for fish and water animals. Kelp, for example, is a well-known algae that has long been used as a food product and nutritional supplement sold in health food stores. Kelp is high in silicon, which is believed to keep skin from wrinkling and sagging, which in turn is why seaweed creams, lotions, and cleansers are popular. Silicon is also an important food for the root of the hair, so an ancient folk remedy was to boil kelp in water and use the water as a hair tonic, massaging it well into the hair. Kelp as a food contains vitamin A, vitamin B complex, vitamin C and vitamin E, calcium and sulfur. Kelp is said to help relieve anemia due to the presence of iron and copper which helps the body to obtain a sufficient supply of red corpuscles. (Red corpuscles are essential in order for the blood to absorb oxygen from the lungs which is one of the causes of anemia.) The high iodine content of kelp has made it a valuable food for cases of obesity mainly because of the normalizing effect on the thyroid gland. Folk medicine suggests that an ounce of kelp (powdered) be put into a pint of hot water. This is allowed to steep and a cup is taken twice a day. Most people who take kelp tablets find that one ten-grain tablet or two five-grain tablets daily are sufficient for good results.

There are two types of blue-green algae that have found favor with people who buy nutritional supplements at health food stores: spirulina and chlorella. It has been said that spirulina is the higher grade of the two because it is easier to assimilate by the body. Another trade-marked brand of blue-green algae designed as *alphanae-klamathomenon flos-aquae* (there's a tongue-twister for you) which is found in upper Klamath Lake in Oregon has been researched by Victor H. Kollman, Ph.D., who states that the nutritional value of this blue-green algae for 1500 mg is as follows: provitamin A (beta-carotene) 1000 IU, thiamine (B_1) 0.04 mg, riboflavin (B_2) 0.07 mg, pyridoxine (B_6) 0.06 mg, cyancobalamin (B_{12}) 0.65 mg, ascorbic acid (C) 5.00 mg, niacin 0.55 mg, choline 7.00 mg, pantothenic acid 0.65 mg, calcium 53.00 mg, phosphorus 8.00 mg, iron 2.00 mg, and magnesium 0.30 mg. The trace elements found in this blue-green algae are boron 13 mcg, cobalt 2 mcg, copper 50 mcg, manganese 38 mcg, potassium 75 mcg, sodium 3 mcg, titanium 0.21 mg, and zinc 0.21 mg. The amino acids percentages are as follows: arginine 11.7%, histidine 3.8%, isoleucine 6.0%, leucine 8.0%, lysine 4.6%, methionine 1.8%, phenylalanine 5.0%, threonine 4.6%, tryptophan 1.4%, valine 6.5% for the essential amino acids; asparate 8.7%, glutamate 11.1%, glycine 5.0%, proline 4.0%, serine 4.0%, and tyrosine 4.1% for the non-essential amino acids. People who take this blue-green algae as a food supplement usually take two 250 mg capsules with each meal daily which gives them the nutritional vitamin and mineral supplementation as outined above. Some people take the supplement as a powder sprinkled on their food (about one or two teaspoons daily).

Some of the statements Dr. Kollman has made about the supplement (which is called Blue-Green Manna™) is that it will burn off excess pounds, and the body will return to a stable body weight. "This permits a gradual equilibrium of weight and eliminates the need for continual dieting. In essence, the Blue-Green Manna sets the body's weight regulator to normal," says Dr. Kollman. "The rate of metabolism is either increased or decreased to maintain the individual at a constant optimal level."

The amount of testimonial evidence for the benefits of blue-green algae is vast. People suffering from allergies, Alzheimer's disease, arthritis, cardiovascular problems, herpes, headaches, high blood pressure, Hodgkin's disease, leukemia, nervous tension, obesity, psoriasis, sickle-cell anemia, stress, and ulcers have supposedly been helped by blue-green algae. Of course, people saying or being reported as saying that they are "cured" or that they have improved due to a product is shaky evidence at best. No tests have been conducted to show that blue-green algae is anything other than a food supplement which delivers a wallop of nutritional values.

- - - - - - - - - - - - - -

I have found these tongue-twisters to be important substances for creating skin and hair care products. There is more research being done using these various substances from the many celltherapy night cream and cellular repair creams to cellulite creams applied under body wraps. Whether or not they do the "magic" claimed is another matter. Selenium used in shampoos does seem to reduce dandruff; collagen and mucopolysaccharides do seem to make skin softer, smoother, and healthier than mineral oil moisturizers; allantoin (from comfrey root) is a good healing agent to the skin and helps reconstitute the protein and moisturize dry damaged hair; so as time goes on these long tongue-twisting names may become second nature to us as we see them used more and more on cosmetic labels.

CHAPTER IX

How To Make A Natural Cosmetic In Ten Easy Lessons

Or

Mother Nature May Have Some Surprises For You

If making a natural cosmetic is so easy, as I say in the heading to this chapter, then why aren't lots of cosmetic manufacturers making all-natural cosmetic products? The answer is deceptively simple: it's easy only if you know how to do it, and there's no school or book (until this one) that will tell you how to do it. In fact, the best way to learn how to make a natural cosmetic is to spend a day with me, and that is how I will write this chapter. I also promised you to do it in ten easy lessons, but this may not turn out to be quite as easy as I suggested. That's why I have my "or" in the chapter head. That's my escape clause.

I work on new products on either Saturday or Sunday when there's nobody in the lab. Sometimes I work late at night (after hours) when there's nobody in the lab. The reason why I do this is it's the way I work best. I don't want any phones to ring and bother me, and I also don't want anybody to come over and say, "What's that awful brown stuff?" I also have a habit of stretching out. I can't work in a tiny little spot like many chemists (although I admire those who can). I tend to jump from one thing to another and try a hundred different variations at the same time (which is also why I have to stretch out).

Before I ever go into the lab I do book research. I research every single herb or natural ingredient I plan to put into a product. This book research is hard to do because it requires reading everything in print and sometimes talking to herbalists who have hands-on knowledge of the herb or natural substance. Remember, I don't have a book like this one you're reading. Also, most books include synthetic chemicals or petrochemicals with their herbs and natural ingredients, and most supposedly "country" or "kitchen" cosmetics say to mix this or that with petroleum jelly, etc. So as I hit the books I have to be an editor and throw out the synthetic chemicals suggested. After all, if we're going to make a natural cosmetic we don't want to start off by making a cosmetic that is, instead, almost natural.

Some of the books I read are not herb books, or even chemistry or cosmetic books. Some of my ideas come from plays. There's quite a bit to learn about herbs, for example, from Shakespeare. One product I made came from a macrobiotics master named George Ohsawa and a discussion we had concerning the use of ginger and its role in herbal medicine. Not only did this discussion lead to an excellent bath therapy product but it also led to a sports rub

I made many years later. This takes me to the first rule which is probably the hardest: **LEARN ALL YOU CAN ABOUT THE INGREDIENTS YOU INTEND TO PUT IN A PRODUCT.**

Why is this the hardest rule? I think it's because people simply don't read as much as they did at one time, and we often rely too much on various forms of electronic information which are incomplete and often too general in nature. How could I get what Ohsawa was going to tell me out of a computer terminal? Of course, I may get a reference that says "rosemary tea is good for the brain cells" (or I may not), but when Ophelia says, "Rosemary, that's for remembrance" it becomes clear to my mind that rosemary was thought of by ancient herbalists as good for the memory. The herb does have some chemical constituents that have a beneficial effect upon the brain and the nerve cells. Poor Ophelia didn't use it soon enough because she goes mad and throws herself into the river. A little reading tells you that rosemary is good for other parts of the head: the hair, the skin, the nose, the throat. It makes, for example, an excellent tea for a migraine headache. A heaping teaspoon of the dried herb in a pint of boiling water with lemon juice (one half lemon) and honey will make the headache go away. This same tea is the finest tranquilizer, and the soothing effect on the nerves transmits itself to the stomach for upsets of that type. Rosemary is also the original woman's herb and not just in name: ancient legend says that it will flourish in gardens only where the woman is the head of the household.

I make a study of the various ingredients which I plan to put in a product before I ever start working on it which I think is just as important as the actual compounding. Creating a new natural hair and skin care product is like creating a play or a novel. You have to do all your research and know all there is about the characters in your creation. I even give my project a name just like a writer gives his play or novel a name. I write it up at the top of my formula: Jojoba Hair Conditioner. Then I put down the various possible ingredients. The leading character is jojoba oil. I may also want to put some aloe vera in this hair conditioner so that ingredient name goes down as well. I make notes on the formula sheet about the things I've learned about the jojoba plant. One note may say, "This conditioner should be thick so it can be squeezed onto the hair and worked through the hair and into the scalp." This becomes one of my objectives. I also know that my "main ingredient character" comes in other forms. There's a jojoba wax and a jojoba butter as well as a jojoba oil. Due to my knowledge of this oil I know I can thicken the product with jojoba butter and jojoba wax. Most cosmetic chemists will think about all the various synthetic thickeners on the market, but it doesn't make sense to create a product called Jojoba Hair Conditioner and then thicken it with some synthetic chemical mixture. Which do you think would make a better thickening agent and a richer formula in a product called Jojoba?

This takes me to my second rule: **DON'T PUT SYNTHETIC CHEMICALS INTO YOUR NATURAL FORMULAS.** This rule is easier for a non-chemist to follow than a chemist. A chemist's business is chemicals: natural and synthetic. He has often been trained that man-made chemicals are superior to natural chemicals and that there's no difference. The chemist also is not top man on the totem pole in the cosmetics business. He answers to the men and women in that industry who make more money and have more pull: the marketing people. They are always interested in the more synthetic considerations: e. g., the color of the product. "Should Jojoba Hair Conditioner be green which is the color of herbs?" they ask themselves. "Most conditioners on the market are yellow...a bright yellow. We don't want to look too different, so we should color the product yellow? What about the fragrance?" And on and on.

So you see, the chemist gets lost in the shuffle. Even if he is one of those few unique chemists who wants to create a natural product he will have to do what he's told by the product management group. This is one of the main reasons that large cosmetic manufacturers make inferior products. It's the reason they make products that cause us to break out in a rash, or why they have to recall products because they contain toxic chemicals. The truth is "No Mass Produced Cosmetic is Natural." In fact, even the products labeled as "natural" are usually not natural (as we've said before!). This is the reason why if you asked a cosmetic chemist if he could make a completely natural product he would say "no." He doesn't think you can do it; he isn't paid to even want to do it; and HE could never do it in his lab. Chances are, too, he was an urban kid who went off to an urban university to study chemistry, and all his knowledge of ingredients came not from a "farm mentality" but from a city environment and chemical tech sheets.

What about the chemicals that are already added to many natural raw materials before you get them? Quite often natural raw materials will contain some of the chemicals you'd never use yourself, and, to make matters worse, the companies who sell them don't have to tell you what they do to process their natural substances so you can't always know all there is to know about every material you use. What you can do, however, is try to avoid this as much as possible by working out an arrangement with these companies. Tell the company from whom you buy herbal extracts that you want them without anything added that's synthetic. I've had pretty good luck with this straightforward arrangement. You can't tell the whole world how you want it to operate, but you can make sure you are not adding to the already over-burdened chemical assault on our environment and our own bodies.

The third rule in making a natural cosmetic fits well with the other two rules: **LEARN ALL THERE IS ABOUT SYNTHETIC CHEMICALS USED IN COSMETICS, FOODS, AND DRUGS.** Yes, you should know about what you're going to avoid because this will help you know more about what you want to replace it with (if you want to replace it with anything). Quite often I get ideas for a natural cosmetic based on a mass-produced synthetic cosmetic. I usually wind up throwing out half of the chemicals used in the product and replacing them (or not) with natural substances that not only perform the same function in the product but have positive action on the hair and skin as well. Let me give you an example. There's a certain mass-produced complexion product by a large well-known cosmetic firm. It's a firming lotion. Many women who use it claim it is excellent for making lines less noticeable on the skin. Here are the ingredients as listed on the bottle: SD alcohol 40, castor oil, water, glycerin, corn oil, BHA, BHT, fragrance, wheat germ glycerides, and retinyl palmitate. If I wanted to make a similar firming lotion, the chemicals I would get rid of first would be the BHA, the BHT, and the fragrance materials (the rest of the formula is natural: the retinyl palmitate is a form of vitamin A). The formula doesn't really need the BHA and BHT (strong synthetic antioxidant preservatives) because the alcohol content will work as a preservative on its own. I would, however, replace the SD alcohol with witch hazel which is an excellent firming base and is not as harsh as the alcohol. The rest of the formula is natural, but I'd probably include some herbal extracts that are known for their firming action.

A knowledge of the many synthetic chemicals along with a knowledge of the many natural substances gives you an ability to create products that are not only natural but are far superior to the mass-produced products now sold at highly inflated prices. The example of the synthetic firming lotion is a good one. It retails for $16.50 for a two ounce bottle, but it can be made naturally for half that price: a good quality natural firming lotion for $8.25 retail. But don't think the synthetic lotion is more expensive than the natural one because the ingredients cost more: far from it. In fact, it is the other way around. The synthetic lotion manufacturer spends almost all his money on the lovely pink box with gold graphics and white enamel raised lettering, but then what does all that have to do with firming your skin?

Did you ever go into a department store and read all the ingredients labels on a specific product type? If you have, you will notice they're pretty much alike. Moisturizers, for example, are made with the key ingredient "mineral oil" or some other petrochemical, and this is the top ingredient in practically all of them. Yet, these moisturizers and "antiaging formulas" never do anything for your skin and hair, much less perform the miracles they claim. This brings me to my fourth rule: **CREATE A NATURAL COSMETIC THAT DOES SOMETHING FOR THE HAIR AND SKIN.** You're probably thinking right now "Easier said than done," but it really isn't that hard if you've followed the other rules because already you've become "naturalized" instead of "synthesized." You see, all those cosmetics that look alike also work alike (i. e., not very well) because they aren't natural and they aren't original. Packaging and price are the major differences among them, but each has its own "buzz word" or gimmick to make you think it's unique. Many, many stores and consumers eat this up. For example, the flamboyant heart surgeon Christiaan Barnard (who performed the world's first heart transplant in 1963) has a "celltherapy" type cosmetic called "Glycel" which is claimed to slow the aging process. It is said this product will retail for $150 per ounce. When this "medical elixir fountain of youth" was announced in November 1985, the company representing Dr. Barnard said they already had orders of over $4 million from 400 outlets including Bloomingdale's, Marshall Field's, Saks Fifth Avenue, Bullock's, Neiman-Marcus, and I. Magnin. The main claim made for "Glycel" is that it substantially increases the process of healing or regeneration. Supposedly the company that manufacturers Dr. Barnard's cream keeps a farm where they raise a special breed of sheep for the purpose of slaughtering them and getting their cell extracts to use in their beauty product line. The name of the company is Alfin, and they will have nine "barnyard" products ranging from a $30 skin cleanser to a $195 kit of five basic items. When you buy these products you will be leading a lot of sheep to slaughter. "Cellular rejuvenation" is far from being an idea originating with Barnard's barnyard: Dr. Vladimir Filatov discovered this process in the 1930's when he used celltherapy topically on burned patients to heal them. Let me show you exactly how EASY it is to create a simple natural moisturizer that works much better than those selling at outrageous prices. Of course the natural moisturizer you will make will not contain mineral oil or propylene glycol or some other gimmicky chemical that actually makes the skin drier and ages it in the long run. You will make your celltherapy without killing sheep, cows, or monkeys. Also, it will not have all those synthetic chemicals which actually negate any regenerative effects the cellular extract creams may have. So let's go on and lock the lot of them in Barnard's barnyard with their sheep and make our own superb celltherapy.

First, purchase yourself an aloe plant at the garden store or use one you already have at home. Don't buy any of those bottled aloe vera gels because they probably all have chemicals in them you want to avoid. Carefully cut off an aloe leaf and open it by sectioning the leaf to get to the semi-thick plant gel inside. Use a spoon to scrape out this gel and put it in a clean glass container. If you can, get about two ounces of the gel. Since aloe vera is almost 99% water, you don't need to add water to the gel. It has the finest natural active water you can find at any price in its magical gel!

The next step is to add some herbal extracts. There are some herbs that have been tested for their healing powers (remember, this is the big claim made by the Barnyard people for cell improvement) and you will add these superb herbs (or as many of them as you can) to the pure aloe vera gel. Don't forget though that pure aloe vera gel on its own has healing and cell improvement powers (see **ALOE VERA** in this book).

The following plants have anti-inflammatory activity and healing properties: Calendula (*Calendula officinalis*), Roman Camomile (*Anthemis nobilis*) Wild Camomile (*Matricaria chamomilla*), Linden or Limetree (*Tilia chordata*), Corn Flower or Blue Bottle (*Centaures cyanus*), and St. John's Wort (*Hypericum perforatum*). More information about these herbs is available from the herb chart in Chapter 7. To add them to your natural moisturizer, go to a health food store or any store that sells herbs or herbal teas and get each of the herbs listed in either loose tea form or tea bag form. (You may have to special order some of them--see **RESOURCES SEC-TION**). There are two ways you can obtain a hydroglycolic extract of these herbs. Either boil them with distilled water (no tap water, please!), or you can boil them in glycerine. Use equal parts of each herb and bring them to a boil in a pan. Very carefully strain through cheesecloth until there are no plant parts. Add exactly one ounce of the extract to one ounce of the aloe vera gel. Keep this natural moisturizer bottled, tightly closed, and in the refrigerator. When you use this product around the eyes, mouth, and even as a hand lotion, you will find out it has all those $35, $75, and $150 cellular creams and lotions beat. You will also know that it's really natural and free of all the chemicals that you don't need on your skin (including those they leave off the label).

Don't worry too much if you can't get all six of the herbs on my list for your hydroglycolic extract because each one of the herbs alone has been found to have the same beneficial properties. Calendula alone, for example, contains provitamin A, vitamin D, oleanolic acid, and many other ingredients found to be cellularly active. If you use them all or just one you will still have a better moisturizer than you can get out of Barnard's barnyard or at department store skin care outlets. Prove it to yourself first by reading the ingredients labels on those high priced skin care products, and then prove it more so by making your own.

Many, many cosmetics cite studies and scientists to "prove" the miracles they guarantee, but beware of manufacturers' overstated claims and spectacular promises. These researchers have been hired, after all, by cosmetic companies, and it's therefore somewhat difficult to credit their results. Herbs and other natural ingredients, on the other hand, have been used since ancient times, both as cosmetics and treatments for disease. By a method of trial and error, primitive people acquired knowledge to determine the medicinal value of roots, herbs, barks, and juices. Though the discoveries were by accident, they were passed on to successive generations. In this book when we draw on this knowledge we are not making a chance discovery, and we need not run animal tests (which don't prove anything anyway).

This does not mean, though, that herbs are not studied by modern scientists: far from it. Dr. Albert M. Fleishner, Ph. D., tested the cellular rejuvenating benefits of the six herbs we recommend for your homemade moisturizer in an experiment for International Sourcing Inc., Ridgewood, New Jersey. He mixed the hydroglycolic extracts of the six plants with an 0.5% hydrocortisone cream. (Why he uses hydrocortisone--a non-healing agent--in an experiment to study healing we can only speculate except that this substance has been recently released by the FDA for over-the-counter use in 0.5% concentration.) In the experiment Dr. Fleishner introduced abrasions on the skin of five volunteers (three male, two female) using a one-half inch scalpel. He scraped the skin a predetermined number of times then placed the hydrocortisone cream without the plant extracts on some abrasion areas; he placed cream with the plant extracts on other areas, and he allowed other areas to go untreated. The abraded skin was considered healed when it became indistinguishable from the surrounding skin. In all five volunteers the cream containing the six plant extracts caused healing to occur an average of 16% more rapidly (3.4 days) than the skin not treated (control group). The cream without the plant extracts accelerated the healing time an average of only 3% over the control. Since hydrocortisone is not a healing agent, the slight increase in healing time of the cream not containing plant extracts can be attributed to the cream itself.

Though Dr. Fleishner told me he considered his study more of a panel research lab experiment, he was being modest. Many cosmetic manufacturers make claims based on animal studies (which aren't scientific at all), and the human studies used are no more or less accurate than Dr. Fleishner's study. For example, I can easily cite the New York University study that said 30% of the bald men grew hair with the application of a drug called minoxidil, yet when I personally recreated this study with minoxidil, absolutely none grew hair. Dr. Fleishner's study is far more accurate, and when I reran the study I found that the herbs did accelerate healing time. I also found on using these herbal extracts in various products the hydrocortisone is not needed at all. The herbal extracts work just as well in an essential fatty acid absorption base and also in the simple aloe vera base I describe on previous pages. I've also used these herbs in creams and skin care products for almost two decades and in that time I've had a chance to observe the results of herbal formulas of this type on many people of various ages and occupations. The long term good results are far superior to even the lab tests which are often used to make claims.

My fourth rule (to create something beneficial for the hair and skin) doesn't need inconclusive animal tests to back it up. Animal testing is unscientific, innacurate and only believed by the very gullible, the pseudo-scientist who places his own dogma above human and animal life, and I suppose those men and women who shop at the exclusive department stores buying over-priced and over-packaged dream concoctions. Remember, though, that everyone in this researcher-to-manufacturer-to-retailer-to-consumer chain is looking for gain: the scientist to sell his research services, the manufacturer and the retailer to sell lots of merchandise, and the consumer to find the one dream cream that will be his or her fountain of youth. I can tell you, though, consumers who buy based on advertising hype and slanted studies are buying a dream which eventually turns into a reality of aging, sagging skin. This leads me to my next rule and a good one: **ONE NATURAL PRODUCT IS NOT A PANACEA, BUT TWO MAY BE A SOLUTION AND A METHOD.**

This is a strange-sounding rule, but if you get to know all the various cosmetics: creams, lotions, astringents, shampoos, cleansers, and so forth you will soon realize that one magic product does not exist. Just as everything in nature works together so do the natural substances that go into a skin and hair care product. Similarly, ONE PRODUCT alone will not improve your hair and skin, but several products working together can. As you become acquainted with **The Natural Method of Hair Care** and the **The Natural Method of Skin Care** you will quickly learn that the only way to give appreciable long term improvement to your hair and skin is with a method--not a one-product panacea. A shampoo for dry hair will make your hair a little less dry, but a good conditioner, hair rinse, and a hot jojoba oil treatment will really make a difference. Moisturizing your skin will make it smooth and less dry, but to properly care for skin, you need to clean it (both daily with a good cleanser and weekly with a deep cleansing mask), tone it, and moisturize it. When I create any new product I am always thinking of not only how the combined ingredients within the formula will work together, but also how the new product will work with other products.

My sixth rule is to **ACCEPT A NATURAL PRODUCT AS A NATURAL PRODUCT AND DON'T TRY TO MAKE IT LOOK OR ACT LIKE A SYNTHETIC PRODUCT.** Today consumers have been raised to think the way merchandisers want them to think. A product should look perfect . . . whatever that means. Merchandisers and the cosmetic advertising people conspire to produce technicolor visions removed from reality: perfect red apples without a speck, polished and glimmering, and Florida oranges, bright orange with a perfect high gloss wax job. They sell shampoo with a pearl floating slowly inside a bottle of impossibly green gunk. They see a gorgeous model turning her head in slow motion as her hair creates a golden trail of light: "Her hair is soft, lovely, natural . . . She uses Emerald Green Shampoo now with the magic of aloe vera." They see a man in a white coat who looks a little like me: gray hair at the temples, touches of gray in a full professor-type beard, and steel-rimmed glasses. Of course, next to him on the desk is a microscope and a bottle of Hair Saver Shampoo. "Your hair has a pH of 4.5 and every time you use an alkaline shampoo you damage your hair a little bit more. Look at these four bottles of shampoo: I'm going to perform the acid test by dipping litmus paper into each of them. Brand A turns the paper blue: it's too alkaline. Brand B turns it blue, and Brand C is also alkaline. Ah, Brand D doesn't change the litmus paper! Let me turn the bottle around so you can see--Hair Saver Shampoo!'' Never mind what these ads say: pH balanced shampoos contain harsh synthetic detergents that dry out the hair and do all the other bad things the man in the white coat warns you the non-pH balanced brands do. And, to work their litmus paper trick they put in a lot of acid and a chemical called triethanolamine (TEA) that has been discovered to be sometimes contaminated with nitrosamines. Ad men learned a long time ago that a little bit of pseudoscience goes a long way and they know how to sell through fear. Nature, however, doesn't fit into these advertising slogans, and the merchandisers really care little about what one chemical or another does because they operate under the theory of "don't confuse me with the facts."

When I started compounding natural cosmetics almost twenty years ago (actually longer since I helped my mother make big blocks of brown soap that you can't buy any more), this sixth rule came to me naturally. I made a shampoo out of the bark of a tree called the quillaya tree. I didn't have merchandising men there to advise me so when the shampoo came out a brown color I didn't think anything about it. When it didn't have a perfumy smell, I didn't do anything to correct it. It was brown and had a woodsy kind of fragrance. It didn't billow with suds either. If you dropped a pearl in the bottle of shampoo, it would disappear into the brown bark color, and its alkaline pH would scare away the litmus paper freaks. Rule number six was important: I didn't do anything to change the way the natural ingredients went together. Some batches came out thicker than others, and some came out browner than others, but it was still the same natural bark shampoo. People who like and understand natural substances used it and raved about it. Some people who'd been using all kinds of shampoos and knew nothing about what is synthetic and what is natural loved it and told their friends that this product was "their discovery." A few people complained, "It doesn't suds like other shampoos . . . sometimes it's thick and sometimes it's thin . . . " etc. If a merchandiser or ad man had heard these complaints, he'd hit the panic button and holler, "Get that crazy chemist in here!" Yet, most of the people who made these complaints kept on using the product because they realized the problems were minor and did not affect how the product worked on the hair. I've found that by NOT changing the natural product and by NOT using thickeners, emulsifiers, artificial colors, etc., the product was a better product, superior in every way, and it easily met the criteria of rule number four because it did something positive for the hair and skin. Don't be afraid to write "Shake Well Before Using!" on bottles because these four little words are far safer than the chemicals they've come up with to replace them.

My seventh rule sounds like a summation of all the other rules: **IT'S WHAT'S INSIDE THE BOTTLE THAT COUNTS.** This is the only way to make a good natural product. Everything you do must be gauged to what goes inside the bottle. I know there are people who buy products based on the packaging design and even based on a famous designer's name on the box. They will also pay more than all that is worth. If you must buy a famous box, buy it, but throw away the synthetic stuff inside, and then nail up the box on your wall. However, if you want to make a superior quality natural product, don't bother with the part that ends up in the trash. A famous name, a famous face, a pretty package: none of these are important next to the all-important juice in the bottle. In fact, nine out of ten times if you buy a product based on these priorities you will get an inferior and over-priced product. Even the models used by the advertising agencies to sell these products won't use them and frequently use natural products instead. "My hair and skin are my most important assets," they declare. "Why should I compromise them with synthetic junk?"

In 1983, for example, Catherine Deneuve looked at people across the country from their television sets: "Take a closer look," she said as the camera moved in to spread her beautiful face across the screen. "This year I'll be forty . . . I've got nothing to hide." She was peddling a skin care product, but it WILL NOT make your face like Deneuve, nor did it make Deneuve's face like Deneuve. Other women are selling "line-killing" moisturizers and "face lifting creams": Isabella Rossellini (the late Ingrid Bergman's daughter) is pushing Lancome; Lynda Carter is pushing Maybelline, and you can hear the voice of Roberta Flack singing "The first time ever I saw your face . . . " over an Oil of Olay commercial. Oil of Olay contains the following ingredients: water, mineral oil, potassium stearate, sodium stearate, cholesterol, cetyl palmitate, butyl paraben, sodium carbomer 934, potassium carbomer 934, propyl paraben, methyl paraben, sodium laurate, potassium laurate, castor oil, sodium myristate, potassium myristate, myristeryl alcohol, cetyl alcohol, sodium palmitate, potassium palmitate, stearyl alchol, fragrance, and FD & C Red No. 4. These largely synthetic chemicals are not the elements of love and yearning that we hear in the commercial, but if the song makes you say "Olé" for Oil of Olay . . . Ad hype, famous faces and voices cost dearly so you'll pay dearly for the chemical mix that make you dream you'll look like Deneuve at forty, or fifty, or sixty. Mary Kay openly admits her ad budget for skin-care products jumped from $1 million to $10 million in 1983 (Gay Pauley, UPI, New York, September, 1983). *Advertising Age* estimated that Oil of Olay spent $26 million in advertising in 1982. Whitehall Labs has projected spending $8 million for Youth Garde in 1983. None of the advertising budgets have anything to do with the juice in the bottle. They all spend millions on hype and pennies on what you actually pay for: the product.

There's an economic side to this obsession with packaging and advertising. Of the consumer's dollar, sixty cents goes to the manufacturer and forty cents to the retailer. The juice in the bottle--the actual ingredients that go on your skin and hair--cost around eight cents, and this is an average figure. Sometimes the juice costs less. Eleven cents goes to packaging; ten cents to advertising; nineteen cents for wages and administration; two cents to interest and other expenses. The manufacturer's costs are then around fifty cents, leaving him or her with a profit of ten cents. (Margaret Allen, *Selling Dreams: Inside the Beauty Business*, Simon and Schuster, 1981). These figures are hardly accurate if you consider the quality of a product according to a natural measurement. The eight cent figure may buy mineral oil or some other petrochemical but will not buy a good quality natural ingredient. When Margaret Allen came up with the title *Selling Dreams*, she was, in just two words, telling you exactly what you pay for, those elements that surround the bottle, although the only reality is what goes inside the bottle.

I've received letters from designers who call themselves "artists" and they always advise me to spend more on the package . . . to make my packaging more appealing. I've had advertising executives and their artists come into my office with their drawings, slogans, and story boards. No one ever asked me about the ingredients; they never asked me what would be good for their hair and skin; they were never curious about the most interesting plant names: quillaya bark, yucca root, jojoba oil, St. John's wort oil. All they were interested in was spending money on packaging and slogans and ads, no matter what the product does or what it contains. Advertising and packaging designers have an inflated idea about the importance of their jobs. When you buy a product for ten dollars and two of them go for the packaging and ads, what have you got? Are you going to rub the gold foil label into your scalp or massage it into your complexion? Do you really think that because your ten dollar product has a famous designer's name on the bottle that you can rub that into your skin and scalp and come out looking like that? Let's face it: when you spend two bucks for packaging and hype you're sending out the message that you're a sucker. What happens to that fancy box with its expensive design and the bottle with the gold cap? You finish off the juice (if you do) and you drop it into the fancy little bathroom trash can with the plastic bag inside; you twist the bag and drop it into your trash can outside, and a huge truck comes along and crunches it. Wouldn't it be far more intelligent to spend two dollars of the ten dollars on the juice inside the bottle and the eighty cents on the package and advertising? That is how I do it: the other way around. I've even experimented with my idea of top quality ingredients and plain packaging to prove to myself that it really is *the juice in the bottle that counts*. I dressed up one of my natural products with fancier packaging and of course had to raise the price. Consumers who used the product did not appreciate the change. Some consumers who had used the product in the simpler package swore it had been changed and that it was no longer as good, although new consumers who had never used the product before accepted it. It's important to note that the product did not increase in sales due to the fancier package. I think those who say the color of a product (artificially dyed) or a fancy package will make the consumer feel the product is better are condescending to the consumer. Only if the product REALLY IS BETTER will the consumer think it is better. Clever packaging will attract consumers and this outside element may make a sale; however, the consumer must pay dearly for this. My seventh rule is the better way. Eventually more and more consumers will use good natural quality products in plain packaging because word of mouth advertising is, in the long run, the best kind. Over the years, consumers have complimented me on the packaging I helped create for the natural products I compounded. They liked the clean white bottles, the simple green lettering, and the ingredients labeling. Always write ingredients in language the consumer will understand. Don't put the Latin name of a plant down in order to be fancy or obscure. *Millerpertuis* may sound fancier because it's French, and the Latin *Hypericum* may be more appealing than St. John's Wort Oil, but it obscures a simple direct communication of what you have in the product. I think some products can use a little more fancy packaging, especially if they are gift type products such as perfumes and colognes (which are costly for their essential oils anyway), but for the most part stay with the rule and the idea that IT'S THE JUICE IN THE BOTTLE THAT COUNTS.

My eighth rule is to PUT CONSUMERS FIRST. You'd think this is an obvious rule and one that any good manufacturer would follow, but the old saying "the customer is always right" hasn't been followed since the day after it was written. Since then it's been replaced with *caveat emptor:* let the buyer beware. When I say to put consumers first, I don't mean put the retailer first because that would NOT be pleasing consumers. When a retailer buys from a manufacturer he isn't thinking of consumers, and when a manufacturer sells to a distributor or retailer he isn't thinking of consumers. The distributor is after product lines that are easy to sell, well-advertised, and give him a good deal. The retailer is looking for pretty much the same thing. If it's a department store you will deal with a buyer, and a buyer often knows less about a product than consumers who will buy that product in the buyer's store. They only ask questions: "Will you be advertising in *Vogue* or *GQ* or where?" If, as a cosmetic company, you're so busy trying to please the wholesaler, the department store, and the buyer you will never please consumers or, for that matter, even create a product consumers will like or need. Oh, I know consumers will still buy it and lots of them will even buy it again and again, but as time goes on fewer and fewer will buy the product. This is the reason why most companies (especially cosmetic manufacturers) will tell you that a product has a life of only about three years. After three years, they say, you have to re-package. Some manufacturers do a little repackaging and use the phrase: new and improved. This insults consumers by telling them they've been buying an old inferior product until now. If they thought the old product was good, why did they need to "new and improve" it? These are all tips that tell us consumers aren't considered in any way. If the manufacturer really thought consumers were important why would they use the same FD & C colors year after year when they've been proven over and over to be carcinogenic? If a "new and improved" product has a synthetic dye added to it, doesn't that make it new and worse? If cosmetic manufacturers really cared about consumers would they still be putting formaldehyde into their products knowing it is highly toxic? In order to put consumers first manufacturers must think just like consumers: not buyers, not wholesalers, not sales people. Think as you would think as a consumer.

The first person who uses any product I have worked on is me. I use it first because I have to like it. Sometimes I even go into a store where my products are sold and buy one and use it. I do this quite often when I'm out of town. I could take one with me but it wouldn't be the same. I go into the store and pick it up. I look at the price. I look at the other products, the competitors on the shelves around it, and I look at their prices. I read the ingredients on all of them. I do it like a good consumer though. I don't open the bottles and pour some into my hand and then put the bottle back on the shelf. There are inconsiderate consumers just as there are inconsiderate manufacturers and retailers.

This discussion of pleasing the consumer brings me to my ninth rule: **DON'T MAKE OR SELL ANY PRODUCT YOU WOULDN'T USE YOURSELF**. I guess this is another way of saying "please the consumer." As I was saying above, I am the first one to use every product I make. I'm as enthusiastic about the latest product I made as I am about the first. In fact, my first product, a bath product, was made for myself. It was a mixture of herbs that I could pour into a tub of hot water and soothe the aches and pains and the cold New York-New Jersey wind and rain that goes clean to the bone. At first I made bottle after bottle for myself. Then I began making a few bottles for my friends. Anybody who told me they had a bad back or headaches at night was a candidate to get one of my bottles. I got a great deal of satisfaction when they told me how well it worked. I remember giving a truck driver a bottle for himself because he said he couldn't get to sleep at night. He gave some of it to his sister who had horrible pains in her back, legs, and hands. He came by my office a few days later with actual tears in his eyes. Here was this big tough truck driver with moist eyes telling me his sister had the first trouble-free sleep she'd had in months. I asked him how he was sleeping. "That's another thing," he replied. "This stuff makes you sleep like a baby."

I don't want this product to sound like a wonder drug because it will not cure anything. Problems or pains and headaches usually indicate that there's a more serious problem than a bath product can help. This product pleased me, though, and I made it to please me, but by doing so I made a product that pleased others. From that day on I always had my first tough test: I have to like it before anybody else gets to like it. I've had many salespeople tell me the same thing. "If I don't like something I have trouble selling it." Now, of course, if you're selling hair color and you don't color your hair you won't like it or dislike it, but in that case you can learn to recognize superior products. You can read and compare. I know of some retailers who won't carry anything in their store that they don't like and use themselves. If they don't like coloring their lips they won't carry any kind of lip color. If they have dry hair and the shampoo is for oily hair they won't carry it. "I tried it and it made my hair drier," they'll complain. So you see I have to temper my rule a little bit, but it's still a good rule and for the most part you can't go wrong following it whether you're a retailer, a wholesaler, a manufacturer, or a consumer who is about to give a gift to a friend.

My tenth and last rule is to **REMEMBER MOTHER NATURE IS YOUR FRIEND**. Mother Nature does have surprises for you. Whether you set out to create a few natural products for your own personal use or want to know what natural products to buy to express your feeling for a natural way of life; whether you want to distribute or manufacture natural products, you are always going to have a partner: Mother Nature. I know quite a bit about her because she's been my partner for a long time. Whoops! I'm being arrogant now, so I'd better put this differently: "I know a little about Mother Nature, but she always has a few surprises for me." Remember, though, if you take from the earth, you have to give back to it. There are many ways of doing this. You can try your best to educate people about the environment and how important it is to care for it. You can do this on several levels. It can be a simple direct person-to-person level; it can be through an article or a book; it can be by joining a group and getting signatures to prevent dumping and chemicalization; it can be by speaking out against animal testing; it can be by being aware and making others aware. Even in natural cosmetics that's the way I see it. If you use a natural cosmetic, and it really helps a skin or hair problem you had or if it just makes you feel good about yourself, you owe nature a return. You bought the product or made it yourself and used it, but that dollar didn't really go to the silent partner: Mother Nature. You still owe her. Always pay your partner back even if she's your silent partner.

organitoons

GLUE ON NAILS HAVE BECOME RIDICULOUS—
MAYBE EYE LASHES WILL CATCH UP!

CHAPTER X

Paint Your Face, Color Your Eyes, and Dye Your Hair

Or

Color Me Dead

You look just as beautiful the way you are without all those cosmetics. People let the fashion industry tell them what to do. Think for yourself.

These are some of the statements Ralph Nader made to the group of women watching him on the Phil Donahue Show one day. He smiled at them, and they smiled back with their made-up faces, their carbon-black lashes fluttering slightly, and a smear of red on their lips so that all the mouths looked the same in their false intensity of red.

Nader had a few more remarks about the high price of cosmetics, and how it wasn't controlled by the FDA so that a product had to do damage before it was removed from the marketplace. He didn't stay on this subject, though, because obviously most of the women there used make-up. Nader had learned through the years that taking on the cosmetic and fashion industry was not as easy as taking on General Motors. Women like Nader, but they see him in his plain gray suit (the same one he's worn for many years), and they know he doesn't wear Ralph Lauren scent because he wouldn't be impressed by the rehash of the Marlboro man on TV who sells men's perfumes today. They're not really impressed by Nader's refusal to allow the cosmetic and fashion industry to dictate to him what he should wear or use.

When Nader talks about the cosmetic industry he usually gives a quick comment on the dangers of chemicals in cosmetics, but for the most part he talks economics. Why in heaven's name are the women paying all that money to paint up? Nader is puzzled by it. Year after year he had fought this industry that spends more on TV than any other advertising group (even car ads don't outdo them), but he gets nowhere. However, if Nader had known (or read about) Henri de Mondeville (1260-1325), he might have realized that trying to reform the cosmetic industry is a losing battle. Henri was a powerful physician in France, and he began the separation of cosmetics and medicine with the puritanical cry "All this [make-up] goes against God and righteousness: it is not the treatment of illness but something that goes outside of this with the intention of concealment and disguise." Henri sounds like a religious fanatic to today's ears; furthermore, he failed to defeat the painted, powdered face, although he learned to tolerate them because, as a physician, he had many rich women patients. He finally said, with his best bedside manner, "The favor of women cannot be overestimated."

Although artificial colors are dangerous (as are some natural substances that color) and suspected carcinogens, I think women will go on using them as long as the cosmetic industry goes on manufacturing with them. After all, if a woman wants to give her cheeks the flush of health with an unhealthy brew of propylene glycol, methyl p-hydroxybenzoate, wax, etc., blended with an aluminum lake color called D & C Red No. 3 or 4 or 6, why shouldn't she? Why shouldn't she flutter her black lashes made that way by spitting on a brush and smearing them with carbon black, triethanolamine stearate, wax, paraffin, lanolin (and even mercury as a preservative)? Why not have a rainbow of eye lids: blue, green, brown, pink, and even silver created with finely ground aluminum powder? Nader and Henri aside, it is obvious that painting various parts of the body is here to stay, and there have always been cosmetic manufacturers ready to cater to the public's every whim. When some showed concern about their health, the cosmetic industry introduced "natural make-up." It isn't natural, of course, but it contains some natural ingredients. Then there is also the "no make-up look" or "the natural look," which uses synthetic dyes, although there are natural mineral and herbal colors if you want a real "natural look." High fashion models may not like these natural colors, which tend to be softer than their synthetic counterparts, but many women do.

Many women put make-up on their skin out of habit, a habit that was originally engendered by a sense of inferiority. "I'll never be as beautiful as this model, but maybe if I put make-up on the way she does, I'll fool somebody into thinking I am." The make-up habit can also begin from a feeling of duty. "My [boss, husband, co-workers, fellow subway riders--fill in the blank] expect me to look a certain way, and I've got to put make-up on to fulfill their expectations." Finally, the urge to make-up is fed by the individual woman's sense of self: the make-up mask has become more real than the real woman's face. "Maybe I'll feel better [or younger or happier or sexier or--fill in the blank] with my make-up on."

One woman told me, as we gave her a facial to improve her skin, that she felt naked without her make-up. Afterwards she wanted us to put make-up on over the facial. To apply synthetic make-up--which ages the skin--after a facial seems self-defeating, and it is. Yet isn't that the first thing an aesthetician does to you after your facial? One high priority I have always included in the formulations for skin care products is ingredients to reduce the damage of synthetic make-up on the skin because I know that many people are going to use skin care products and then put make-up on the skin. However, a good skin care program, along with good eating and exercise habits, defeats the need for the make-up mask. When the skin is healthy and clear, you don't need a foundation base. You also won't need a blush because you'll have your own natural color. You won't need lipstick because your lips will be their own individual shade of pink or red. You won't need eyeshadow because the tone and beauty of your skin will naturally make your eyes beautiful. Yet isn't the use of color a fashion consideration and aren't there times when you want a skillful application of color to the face?

The answer to both these questions is, of course, yes. And, in addition, I must admit that many men are attracted to a woman who knows how to make herself appealing or romantic with the use of make-up. Most women, though, who are skilled at putting on make-up are also skilled at taking care of their skin and in fact spend more time without make-up on than they do with make-up on their skin. The purpose of make-up is to attract. Yes, it has a sexual or romantic purpose. This is the reason make-up was created, and it's the way you see it advertised. Yet, paradoxically, many men, it is said, also want a woman to look natural. This message was communicated to the cosmetic industry by the advertising industry some years ago, and the natural or "unmade-up look" came into being. What is the "natural look"? This face has no heavy rouge on the cheeks, and even if a blush is used, it looks almost transparent on the skin. The cheeks, have a very natural rosy blush. The eyebrows are not darkened. The lips have a very, very slight red or pink look to them (not bright red). If an eyeshadow is used, it is very subtle. There is absolutely no overall make-up used. If the skin tends to be uneven in color, a powdered "translucent base" is brushed on the skin. What is interesting is that all these make-ups can be obtained without an artificial color mix or synthetic chemicals. There's another consideration: women look better with this type of approach. Here is what is done: 1. A complete facial is given; 2. Natural herbal or mineral powders are used to accent the cheeks, lips, etc.; 3. The whole effect is set with a mineral water spray on the skin. In the chapter called *The Natural Method of Skin Care*, this natural make-up method is given step by step. The woman who said she "felt naked without make-up" was given this simple natural make-up look, and she had to admit she looked better without the paint on her skin. She said, too, that her skin had never felt that good.

There are *seventy-six* D & C colors listed in the Cosmetic, Toiletry, and Fragrance Association's (CFTA) Cosmetic Ingredient Dictionary, and about nineteen FD & C colors. The term D & C stands for Drug and Cosmetic and FD & C stands for Food, Drug and Cosmetic. The former is used only in drugs and cosmetics, and the latter can be used in foods as well. When the term "Ext. D & C" is used, it means the color can only be used in products that will be used externally and not around mucous membranes (i. e., lips). All these colors are certified by the government for use in approved amounts and for the uses indicated.

What does "certified" mean? Quite often we think that if it is "certified" it must be safe and good. Obviously this is not what "certified" means since the FDA has six colors thought to be carcinogens which they have never removed from the "certified" list, but admit that they are suspected carcinogens. The FDA to keep the cosmetic industry happy will keep delaying action on the colors for as long as they can. The very first color be be suspected as a carcinogen was FD & C Red No. 40. This red was used to give maraschino cherries and lollipops their bright red look. Red No. 40 is a color classed chemically as a monoazo color. There are other monoazo colors such as FD & C Red No. 4 and FD & C Yellow No. 6. If the monoazo Red No. 40 was a carcinogen, then were the other monoazo colors such as Red No. 4 and Yellow No. 6 also carcinogens? Various colors have links with the class of chemical they belong to, and sooner or later if one is found to be toxic, then another will also be found to be toxic.

It has been said that no other government has so carefully guarded the colors that may be used in cosmetics as has the United States. The manufacturer must submit samples of every batch to be analyzed for purity before certification, and the official lot-test number must accompany the colors through all subsequent packagings. The process of manufacturing certifiable pure colors is a highly specialized branch of the dyestuff industry, and many precautions and controls are needed to eliminate or exclude objectionable metallic impurities. In coal-tar colors the maximum amounts of lead and arsenic permissible are 10 ppm (FD & C colors), and 20 ppm for the D & C and Ext. D & C colors. You would think that if the government is truly concerned with keeping a tight rein on color certification that suspected carcinogens would be immediately removed from the market, but that isn't the case. The certification was not set up to consider the danger of the color itself, but to protect that color from metal contamination (i. e., lead and arsenic). Synthetic colors have many adverse effects on the body, but certification has never addressed these problems.

Naturally occurring coloring matter and inorganic pigments are not certified. They do not come under the jurisdiction of the coal-tar regulations because approval is not necessary for their use. This does not mean they're safe, only that they are not government certified and regulated. With the natural colors the burden of proof of purity rests with the user, and manufacturers who make natural colors available to the cosmetic industry usually give an analysis as to the purity (i. e., the content of lead, arsenic, or materials known to be injurious). If all this certification really goes on, what is the difference between natural colors and the synthetic coal-tar approved coloring materials? The key can be found in the the government's phrase "the burden of proof rests with the user." If you are damaged by a toxic reaction to FD & C Red No. 40 (before it was removed from the market), you can't sue the government because they betrayed your trust in their certification process. Can you sue the manufacturer who used the Red No. 40 in a product? Well, you can sue, but you stand little chance of winning. The manufacturer will say he or she met all the government's certification regulations, and the government will say the color had no contaminates. If a new toxic reaction becomes evident because of one of the chemicals in the color (as was true of Red No. 40), then it was an unknown for which neither the government nor the manufacturer will take responsibility. This is known as "passing the buck," and it leaves the consumer, as usual, carrying the "burden" alone.

If one considers the test of time a reliable barometer of safety, then natural colors certainly pass the test, while synthetic colors have been in use only since the turn of the century. In May 1900 the Secretary of Agriculture appointed Bernard C. Hesse to perform a study on the use of coal-tar dyes in the coloring of foods. Hesse was chosen because he had been associated with a leading dyestuff manufacturer in Germany. He subsequently presented seven colors as being harmless: Orange No. 1, Indigotine (a synthesized version of the indigo herb), Naphthol Yellow, Ponceau 3R, Amaranth, Erythrosine, and Light Green SF Yellowish. Hesse conducted pharmacological tests to assure the U. S. these dyes were safe. Over the years seven more colors were introduced: Tartrazine (yellow) in 1916, Yellow AB in 1918, Yellow OB in 1918, Guinea Green B in 1922, Fast Green FCF in 1927, Ponceau SX (a red) in 1929, and Sunset Yellow in 1929. Before the Federal Food, Drug, and Cosmetic Act in 1928 went in effect, Brilliant Blue FCF, the last coal-tar color to be permitted, was introduced.

Certified colors are classed into two groups according to their chemical structures. *Nitro dyes* are FD & C Yellow Nos. 1 and 2 (the former known as Naphthol Yellow S). *Azo dyes* form the largest group of colors. They are synthesized by coupling a diazotized primary amine with a chemical capable of coupling. The azo group is separated into four other groups: unsulfonated pigments, unsulfonated dyes, insoluble sulfonated pigments, and soluble sulfonated dyes. I won't give you the various chemical formulas for nitro and azo dyes, but if you're interested they can be obtained from the FDA or a book on dyes. The important thing for us to know is that almost all the colors have a chemical link as they belong to either the "yellow" nitro group or they belong to the azo group. If Red No. 40 is a carcinogen, then so are the others in that azo group, or, to be more specific, in the "monoazo" group.

Most people are now aware from various human studies as well as *in vitro* studies that the synthetic colors aren't safe and that certification that they contain no metal contamination will not make them safe. What about the natural colors?

There are many, many natural colors. Two of the simplest are cherry juice and beet juice. Both are red and completely safe. They are far safer than FD & C Red Nos. 3, 4, and 40. Another red color, and one of the best established, is carmine, but many people shun it because it comes from the insect world. Cochineal is a tiny insect which lives on a cactus in Mexico, the Canary Islands, and Central America. The insect contains a red coloring matter known as carminic acid. Its use goes back as far as 1239, and it is a safe coloring substance. If you want to protect the insect world, however, you wouldn't like the use of carmine in food, drugs, and cosmetics. Since the arrival of coal-tar dyes, very little carmine is in use. It is debatable whether the "Save the Cochineal" movement (if there is such a movement) has improved the environment with the use of FD & C dyes, but there is no question that millions of laboratory animals have died to "prove" the safety of synthetic dyes.

Annatto is a red waxy material surrounding the seeds of the *Bixa orellana*, a shrub found in Central America. The carotenoid, Bixin, forms red-brown crystals, and, when precipitated by acids, has a deep red color. If you dilute it you can get a creamy yellow color, which is used in cheese, ice cream, and other foods.

Saffron is the dried stigma of *Crocus sativus*, a plant cultivated in Spain, Greece, France, and Iran. The coloring agent is the glycoside crocin which is a yellow powder that goes easily into water.

Alkanna root, from the plant *Alkanna tinctoria* indigenous to Asia Minor and Southeastern Europe, contains a coloring agent that is brownish red, but when mixed with metals becomes blue.

Probably the best-known natural color is indigo, from the plant *Indigofera tinctoria*. The characteristic blue color develops during fermentation. Indigo has been used as a dye since Phoenician times and even today millions of pounds are grown and exported from India.

Simple nettles, if fixed in a solvent such as alcohol, will give a bright green color. Mineral colors give us the reddish-brown of hematite, the ultramarine blues and pinks, the white zinc, and other shades from white to black (from clay).

Coal-tar dyes are not used over natural coloring substances because they are safe, far from it. They are used, first, because they are certified (which is dubious since this process has not proven to protect the public), cheap, and convenient. (For example, formulas specifying synthetic dyes are passed from chemist to chemist which keep them in use.) Recently, synthetic colors have been suspected of many health problems and allergic reactions. Children with motor problems and learning difficulties are put on diets free from synthetic colors because of the allergic and toxic reactions the coal-tar dyes seem to have on children. Many health-conscious individuals avoid the FD & C and D & C colors in foods and cosmetics. This is a wise decision.

An avocado face cream which is avocado green due to FD & C Green No. 3 is decidedly inferior to a natural, uncolored cream. The fake green cream is a cheat to consumers by insinuating that it's just so chock full of avocado that it just has to be green when in reality the avocado is probably way down on the ingredients list next to the fake avocado fragrance. The motivation to add synthetic colors is another part of the synthetic mind-set we've discussed in other chapters. But when you buy the avocado green dream cream you may be buying a problem for yourself that will cost you more than a whole case of avocado cream. Again, read the label and avoid the coal-tar dyes. Remember they are not certified to build better health; they are not certified to be nutritious (which they aren't); they are not certified to be free of allergic reactions; they aren't certified to be non-cancerous. All you know is that you won't get arsenic and lead in high concentrations. If, however, everything we eat and put on our bodies has synthetic colors in it, can we assume that the 10 ppm and 20 ppm of lead and arsenic could become a concern? Sorry, the certification does not cover how many coal-tar colors are used in products. The certification was, in short, a control for manufacturing standards, NOT on the cause-and-effect ratio when you use products with artificial coloring in them. We often seek a government agency to protect us, but the only protection is your own concern: your own certification is the best certification.

As this book went to press, the Public Citizen Health Research Group (PCHRG) is applying legal pressure to have ten color additives removed from the market. Since 1960, when the controversial Color Additives Amendment to the original Food, Drug, and Cosmetic Act was passed, the FDA has repeatedly deferred de-listing some FD & C colors, even after they have been demonstrated to be potentially carcinogenic; they do not say, however, that these colors are safe. The PCHRG filed a law suit against Margaret Heckler and FDA Commissioner Dr. Frank Young to remove ten color additives from the market due to cancer studies. These colors are D & C Red Nos. 8, 9, 19, 33, 36, and 37; FD & C Yellow Nos. 5 and 6; D & C Orange No. 17; FD & C Red No. 3. The FDA used the Cosmetic, Toiletry, and Fragrance Association (CFTA) to intercede for them and keep these colors on the market in previous legal actions by the PCHRG. Obviously, the FDA is more concerned about the manufacturers than about the actual safety of the additives. Many people erroneously believe that the FDA and the

Certified Color Regulations are there to protect the consumer, but it takes action from the consumers themselves to attempt to keep the FDA on the straight and narrow. The purpose of the CTFA is to protect the cosmetic manufacturers and their chemical counterparts and not the consumer. Figure 3 at the end of this chapter illustrates the "loophole" the cosmetic industry has tunneled for certain colors indispensable to certain types of products, like hair colors and sunless tanning products. A close perusal of Figure 1 shows how closely the synthetic colors are related to each other. Figure 2 shows the wide range or origin shared by noncertified colors: animal, vegetable, mineral, and laboratory-synthesized. "Color Me Dead" is the coloring book that would be appropriate for the FDA to publish in view of the fact that although they first announced that synthetic colors were potentially carcinogenic, they nevertheless fought (with the CTFA) to keep them on the market. Avoid them.

Synthetic Color Additives for Cosmetics

FDA NAME	TRADE AND OTHER NAMES
FD & C Blue No. 1	Brilliant blue FCF; food blue 2
D & C Blue No. 4	Alphazurine FG; Erioglaucine
D & C Brown No. 1	Resorcin brown
FD & C Green No. 3	Fast green FCF; food green 3
D & C Green No. 5	Alizarin cyanine green
D & C Green No. 6	Quinizarin green SS
D & C Green No. 8	Pyranene concentrated
D & C Orange No. 4	Orange II
D & C Orange No. 5	Dibromoflorescein
D & C Orange No. 10	Diiodoflorescein
D & C Orange No. 11	Erythrosine yellowish Na
D & C Orange No. 17	Permatone orange
FD & C Red No. 3	Erythrosine; food red 14
FD & C Red No. 4	Ponceau SX
D & C Red No. 6	Lithol rubin B
D & C Red No. 7	Lithol rubin B Ca
D & C Red No. 8	Lake red C
D & C Red No. 9	Lake red C Ba
D & C Red No. 17	Toney red; Sudan III
D & C Red No. 19	Rhodamine B
D & C Red No. 21	Tetrabromofluorescein
D & C Red No. 22	Eosin YS; eosine G
D & C Red No. 27	Tetrabromotetrachlorofluorescein
D & C Red No. 28	Phloxine B
D & C Red No. 30	Helindone pink CN
D & C Red No. 31	Brilliant lake red R
D & C Red No. 33	Acid fuchsin D; napthalene red B
D & C Red No. 34	Deep maroon; Fanchon maroon; Lake Bordeaux B
D & C Red No. 36	Flaming red
D & C Red No. 37	Rhodamine B stearate
FD & C Red No. 40	Allura[1] red; food red 17
D & C Violet No. 2	Allizurol purple SS
Ext. D & C Violet No. 2	Alizarine violet
FD & C Yellow No. 5	Tartrazine; food yellow 4
FD & C Yellow No. 6	Sunset yellow FCF; food yellow 5
D & C Yellow No. 7	Fluorescein
Ext. D & C Yellow No. 7	Naphthol yellow S
D & C Yellow No. 8	Uranine
D & C Yellow No. 10	Quinoline yellow WS; food yellow 13
D & C Yellow No. 11	Quinoline yellow SS
FD & C Lakes	
D & C Lakes	
Ext. D & C Lakes	

[1]Trademark of Buffalo Color Corp.

FIG. 1

Non-Certified Color Additives to Cosmetics

FDA NAME	TRADE AND OTHER NAMES
Aluminum powder*	
Annatto★	Annatto extract; Bixin; *Bixa orellana* L. extract; natural orange 4
Bismuth citrate*	
Bismuth oxychloride*	Pearl white
Bronze powder*	
Caramel★	Burnt sugar; natural brown 10
Carmine✓	Carminic acid lake
Beta-carotene★	Carotene; natural yellow 26
Chromium hydroxide green*	Cosmetic green
Chromium oxide greens*	Cosmetic green
Copper powder*	Copper, metallic powder
Dihydroxyacetone[1]	1,3-Dihydroxy-2-propanone
Disodium EDTA-copper*	Copper Versenate–
Ferric ammonium ferrocyanide*	Cosmetic iron blue; iron blue
Ferric ferrocyanide*	
Guaiazulene★	Azulene; in greatest concentration from camomile
Guanine✓	Pearl essence; 2-aminohypoxanthine
Henna★	from plant *Lawsonia alba* Lam.
Iron oxides*	Cosmetic black, brown, umber, and ochre
Lead acetate*	
Manganese violet*	Manganese ammonium pyrophosphate
Mica*	Muscovite
Potassium sodium copper* chlorophyllin (chlorophyllin-copper complex)*	

* Inorganic (metal or mineral)   ★ Herbal   ✓ Animal   [1] Synthetic chemical   Fig. 2

Loophole Color Additive List

This is a chart showing how some coloring ingredients are allowed to remain on the market for use in certain products, sometimes despite evidence demonstrating their toxicity.

Bismuth citrate	Scalp hair coloring only
Dihydroxyacetone	"Sunless tanning" products
Disodium EDTA-copper	Shampoo coloring
Henna	Hair coloring. This is an herb used for thousands of years. Henna is also an excellent hair conditioner.
Lead acetate	Scalp hair coloring only.
Potassium sodium copper chlorophyllin (chlorophyllin-copper complex	Dentifrice coloring only (in combination with other substances)
Silver	Fingernail polish color

Fig. 3

CHAPTER XI

The Advantages and Dangers of UV Rays

Or

Here Comes the Sun!

One of the biggest scares of the 1980's is skin cancer due to sun exposure, and of course many studies support the fact that the sun ages the skin by altering the skin's collagen, causing cross-linking of the collagen in the connective tissues. More sun protection creams and lotions with an SPF 15 rating have been sold during this period than any other time previously, and every major company has a sunblock labeled SPF 15. A few are even marketed with higher SPF numbers though the FDA doesn't recognize any protection higher than SPF 15. One company markets a gadget on the end of their suntan lotion so you could "dial" the SPF you wanted.

Exactly what is the SPF, or Sun Protection Factor, and which SPF is right for your skin? The Sun Protection Factor (SPF) is defined as the UV energy required to produce minimal erythemal doses (MED) on the skin protected with a sunscreen product. Most sunscreen products use one of the B-complex vitamins known as para-aminobenzoic acid, or PABA. It has also been found that a combination of willow bark extract and cuttle fish oil, like PABA, acts as an excellent light absorber in the burning range of UV rays. The amount of PABA in a formula can range from 1% to 5% or more depending on the desired SPF.

The SPF system works as follows: SPF 2 to under 4 gives minimal protection, permits suntanning, and is used only on those skin types that tan easily and never burn. SPF 4 to under 6 acts as a moderate skin protector. It permits some suntanning and can be used by those who tan moderately easily and usually do not burn. SPF 6 to under 8 gives extra sun protection and permits limited tanning. SPF 8 to under 15 gives maximum protection from sunburn and permits little or no suntanning. SPF 15 and higher is considered a "sunblock" and permits no tanning.

How much sun you can safely take (before you sunburn) varies from one individual to the other. A pale individual with blue eyes and blond hair may burn easily in the sun and would be at risk in getting sun cancer. This is also true of a pale-skinned person with red hair. No matter what your skin type, get a safe tan gradually. People who burn easily should begin the summer with a good protection lotion with an SPF 8, and only after they have been in the sun several times (gradual exposure) can they use a product with an SPF 4. Most people should began sun exposure for short lengths of time with protection (SPF 8) and then go to a more minimal protection.

When you sun, try to avoid the middle of the day when the sunburning rays UV-C and UV-B rays are the strongest. The sun emits three types of UV, or ultraviolet, rays: UV-A, UV-B, and UV-C (See fig. 2). UV radiation is in the region of the electromagnetic spectrum consisting of wavelengths ranging from 100 nanometers (nm) to 400 nm. UV-A is 320-400 nm or long-wave; it's also called "black light." UV-B ranges from 290-320 nm; it's known as the middle wave and can cause sunburning. UV-C is 100-290 nm: a short wave with germicidal activity. UV-C can cause very serious burning of the skin and skin cancer with short exposure. Luckily, we are protected from UV-C by the ozonosphere (See fig. 1), which is a special layer of oxygen (O_3) that has three atoms to the molecule. It has been suggested that the ozone layer has been damaged due to the wide use of aerosol sprays, and perhaps the increased number of people with skin cancer due to the sun is a result. This is, however, speculation.

When you choose a suntan lotion, be aware that many suntan lotions, oils, and creams contain chemicals that do not give good skin protection even though they may contain PABA and may have what looks like a good SPF number. For example, chemicals such as mineral oil (5% or more), propylene glycol (5% or more), alcohol (20% or more), sodium hydroxide, triethanolamine, and color, fragrance, and many preservatives will cause allergic reactions on the skin, will dry skin, and can even reduce the protection given by the lotion. Remember, mineral oil is phototoxic, so any product containing mineral oil (or one of its many derivatives) will actually increase the sun's burning rays on your skin. Alcohol, besides being very drying on the skin, goes into the skin very quickly, as well as any sun protection ingredient that's dissolved into it, and so any suntan product with an alcohol base should be avoided. Isopropyl palmitate, dimethicone (a silicone agent), petrolatum PEG 15 cocoate, and other heavy creams can cause a rash on the skin or a "cosmetic acne" which look like tiny white grains or bumps on the skin.

You have probably seen "sunless tanning" products on the market, and whether they're health food store brands or drugstore brands, they all have one ingredient in common: dihydroxyacetone, or DHA. Sunless tanning products do NOT tan the skin; instead, they dye it brown. DHA is not a desirable cosmetic ingredient because it can leave the skin with an orange or yellowish tinge when the desired tan is a brown or bronzy-brown. If products with DHA in them are used frequently they may discolor the hair as well as the skin. In addition, the use of these products, which generally do not have an SPF rating, may fool users into believing they don't need protection from the sun (Tom Conry, *Consumer's Guide to Cosmetics*, New York: Anchor Press, 1980, pp. 287-288). One of the ingredients in the DHA is acetone (a major ingredient in nail polish removers), and this is known to be very toxic. Though some astringents contain this chemical, most cosmetic manufacturers are removing it from their products due to its toxic nature.

Another sunless tanning product is canthanaxin, which is taken by pill and produces a reddish-yellowish skin tone. It can be purchased in some health food stores and by mail. Its safety is completely unknown, and at the time of this writing, there were reported various reactions to both DHA and canthanaxin, though no tests have been conducted on the drugs. In addition, the tanning pills do not contain any sun protection ingredients in them, so consumers who insist on tanning from the inside out must be sure to use sun protection creams when out in the sun.

There is, however, a natural way to increase your tan. It was introduced in 1986 in Switzerland and found its way to the United States (used by major producers of sun care products). I have developed a "before sun" and "after sun" product using this method.

Vitamin B_2 (riboflavin) is combined with an amino acid known as tyrosine and is included in sun care formulas at levels of 5%. Although less of this combination will decrease tanning time, more will not increase it. This natural combination accelerates the tanning process by increasing the production of melanin in the skin; this tan is your own individual natural color,

OZONOSPHERE
UV–C
UV–B
UV–A

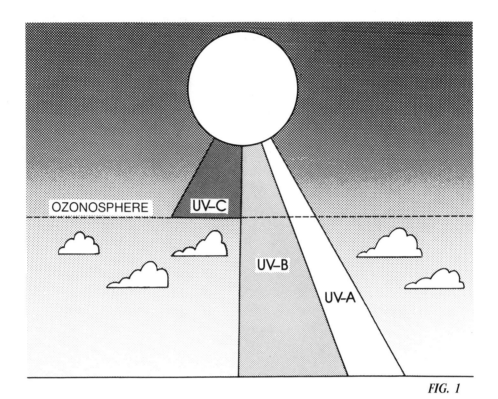

FIG. 1

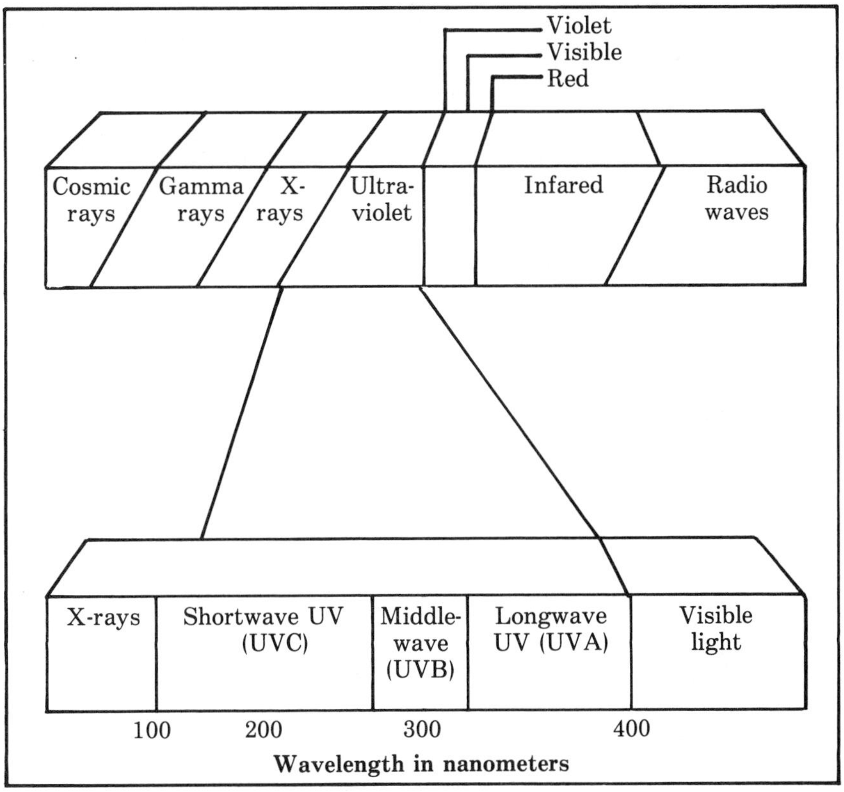

Violet
Visible
Red
Cosmic rays
Gamma rays
X-rays
Ultra-violet
Infared
Radio waves
X-rays
Shortwave UV (UVC)
Middle-wave (UVB)
Longwave UV (UVA)
Visible light
100
200
300
400
Wavelength in nanometers

FIG. 2

unlike synthetic "staining" tans from dihydroxyacetone or canthanaxin. For three consecutive days before going into the sun the "tan accelerator" is applied. When in the sun the body produces melanin more efficiently than usual, and the result is a faster and deeper tan. Perhaps this combination could be utilized in a hair care product to darken gray hair.

The "tan accelerator" must be used with another sun tan lotion with an SPF. Other natural moisturizing and antiaging ingredients that work well in these products are *Rosa Mosqueta* rose hip seed oil, shea butter (from the African butter plant), jojoba butter, St. John's wort oil, horsetail and coltsfoot. Adding these substances will not only accelerate tanning and maintain the tan longer but also reduce the UV aging of the sun caused by sun exposure.

Some other ingredients to look for in a good quality sun protection lotion or cream are aloe vera gel, collagen, jojoba oil (rather than mineral oil), or jojoba wax (both of which reduce the easy wash-off of the sun protection), allantoin (from comfrey root), panthenol or B_5 (which is a natural skin hydrator), and a base made from coconut fatty acid or some other natural substance instead of mineral oil, PEG, or isopropyl palmitate. A light cream-lotion is better than a thick heavy lotion or oil. Aloe vera and allantoin help soothe sun-damaged skin, and collagen helps re-build it.

After coming out of the sun, a moisturizer should be used, or pure aloe vera gel can be applied to the skin. When in the sun it is best to wear sunglasses that have UV 400-coated lenses. This special coating is not found in most commercially sold sunglasses, but the UV 400 coating is more than 99% effective in protecting the eyes from both UV-A and UV-B rays.

Treatment of Psoriasis with UV Rays

A combination of UV-A rays and psoralen-melanizing drugs called PUVA is a photo-chemotherapy treatment for severe psoriasis (i. e., involving 30% or more of the skin). The treatment involves the combination of a photo-sensitizing pill (usually methoxsalen) and the exposure of the infected areas with UV-A rays. The primary developer of PUVA therapy was Dr. Thomas Fitzpatrick of Harvard Medical School, and it was approved as a treatment by the FDA in May 1982. This type of treatment can't be used on patients who have had a history of skin cancer, who are pregnant, with previous arsenic intake, with previous ionizing radiation therapy, sensitivity to the sun, heart or blood pressure problems, or patients with eye problems (particularly cataracts). About 90% of the patients treated with PUVA will have a remission as long as one year.

Be Sensible About The Sun

Despite sun cancer fears, suntanning is here to stay. You can, however, if you use a good natural sun protection cream, keep your skin looking healthy AND tanned. To bronze your body to a dark brown year after year is not good for you, but, then neither is no sun at all, nor are synthetic bronzing products an adequate alternative. Remember (and this final statement also takes us into our next chapter): the sun is yang, the moon is yin, and a balance is in order or you'll get burned.

CHAPTER XII

The East Of It, The West Of It, The Yin and Yang Of It

Or

Does the Acupuncture Face Lift Really Work?

I carry a package of acupuncture needles with me along with a tiny cocktail straw to act as the "blow-gun" for tapping them into my body. I know how to erase a headache, neckache, backache, and even a toothache by tapping the needles into certain points. Does this sound dangerous? Some people carry bottles of aspirin or Valium around. If you think about it, the tapping of a tiny needle about the size of a horsehair into the body is far safer than the drugs people pop down their throats. Choosing pills over needles is our cultural bias. Nevertheless, I must now introduce my disclaimer: go to a qualified physician who has a knowledge of acupuncture. Don't do as I do: do as I suggest.

I became interested in acupuncture many years before Richard Nixon went to China and physicians began going there to learn the art of the needles. I learned acupuncture from a Chinese doctor and an American doctor and also read books about it. Western physicians, however, still do little work with acupuncture, and this is because it is not explainable. Eastern medicine does not, like Western medicine, feel the need to explain. The need to know "why" something helps the sick, "why" certain herbs work, and the need to prove through testing (first on animals) the "why" and "how" of any substance or technique is not part of the Eastern philosophy. It is peculiarly Western and most apparent in the United States. We test everything. We disapprove or approve based on the tests, and yet the tests are always inaccurate (or can be proved by other tests to be inaccurate). Still, we base much of what we do, indeed, of what we believe, on tests and statistics. Even what we see on TV is based on this.

The Chinese care nothing for our "why." What this means is that if a physician is going to accept and use acupuncture, he or she is going to be put in the position of accepting a whole different way of looking at the body, without knowing, in the Western way, why. Yin and yang, the complementary opposites on which Chinese medicine is based, is an essential difference between East and West. The chart on the following page shows some of the basic differences between yin and yang. Medically speaking, there are five yin organs: heart, lungs, spleen, liver, and kidneys. These organs store but do not transmit. There are six yang organs (which transform but do not retain): gall bladder, stomach, small intestine, large intestine, bladder, and Triple Warmer. The Western physician must also accept the five fundamental substances:

YIN AND YANG CHART

	YIN	YANG		YIN	YANG
Tendency:	Expansion	Constriction	Attitude:	Gentle	Active
Position:	Outward	Inward	Shade:	Dark	Bright
Structure:	Space	Time	Construction:	Interior	Exterior
Direction:	Ascent	Descent	Action:	Psychological	Physical
Color:	Blue	Red			
Temperature:	Cold	Hot	Catalyst:	Water	Fire
Weight:	Light	Heavy	In the Body:	Interior	Surface
Factor:	Water	Fire		Chest and Abdomen	Spine and Back
Atomic:	Electron	Proton			
Element:	Potassium	Sodium		Cloudy or dirty body fluid	Clear or clean body fluid
	Oxygen	Hydrogen			
	Phosphorus	Arsenic		Blood	Energy (Ch'i)
	Calcium	Chlorine			
Biological:	Vegetable	Animal		Nourishing (Ch'i)	Protecting (Ch'i)
Agricultural:	Salad	Cereal		Liver	Gall bladder
Sex:	Female	Male			
Nerves:	Ortho-sympathetic	Para-sympathetic		Heart	Small intestine
Birth:	Cold season	Hot season		Pancreas	Stomach
Movement:	Feminine	Masculine		Lung	Large Intestine
Taste:	Hot, Sour, and Sweet	Salty and bitter		Kidney	Bladder
Vitamins:	C	D, K		Percardium	Triple Warmer
Season:	Summer	Winter	In Disease:	Chronic and non-active	Acute and virulent
	Cloudy day	Clear day		Low temperature. Patient feels cold to the touch.	High temperature. Patient feels hot to the touch.
	Darkness	Light			
	Moon	Sun			
	Spring	Autumn			
Shape:	Thin, Plump	Wiry, Heavy		Moist	Dry
Hair:	Curly, Light	Straight, Dark		Retiring	Advancing
Complexion:	Pale, yellow	Tan, red		Lingering	Hasty

chi, blood, jing, shen, and other elemental substances not specifically named but which represent a variety of elements, e. g., saliva and perspiration. He must also accept the five phases (sometimes wrongly translated as five elements): wood, fire, earth, metal, and water. The Chinese, who think in terms of processes rather than in terms of substances, could never accept our concept of testing and statistics. In turn, Western physicians may approve of acupuncture, but they will never understand why it works.

Phases, changes, and processes give an entirely different understanding of what we call substances and elements. Wood (like a tree) is associated with growth; fire is the peak of activity (including incipient decline); metal is associated with decline; water with rest and incipient growth; and earth, which links all the others together, is both a beginning and an end.

Chinese herbal medicine, which is accepted even less than acupuncture by Western doctors, is also based on yin and yang and the temporal cycles. In China this ancient art of healing is still practiced by the barefoot doctors of China who work in a most unique way. You pay your doctor's fee as long as the doctor keeps you well and healthy, but if you become sick you pay the doctor nothing. It is in the doctor's interest to keep you well. Of course, if you fail to follow the doctor's advice you may have to pay him for treatment.

I explained this unique method of medicine to a woman who worked in a hospital. She was aghast. "Why, people like me who are never sick would be paying the doctor all the time."

"That's true," I explained, "but people who are well can afford to work and pay the doctor. Besides, it's a very nominal sum. Think of how the insurance-medical system works now: it's unfair. Many seriously ill people without medical insurance have all their money wiped out by medical expenses. And, whether you're sick or well, you must still pay your medical insurance premiums. It seems far more logical to give the money directly to the doctor, and make him or her responsible to keep you healthy."

The barefoot doctor explains the laws governing yin and yang to his patient in a simple direct way. "I will be telling you how to keep in balance: a good balance of yin and yang," he may say, "All things have different qualities but are still products of one infinity, yet everything is constantly changing. All antagonisms are complementary, yet no two things are identical. Every condition has its opposite: either yin or yang. The extremity of any condition is equal to its opposite. It can be so cold that the moisture on your face turns to a sheet of ice, and it can be so hot that there is no moisture at all on your face and it is red and raw. Whatever has its beginning also has its end." This is hardly what your family physician will discuss with you, but Chinese medicine has less to do with symptoms than Western medicine because the primary purpose of the Chinese doctor is to keep his patient well, and health is more than the absence of disease. Western physicians only treat the disease, not the patient (though this has been changing somewhat in recent years).

Oriental medicine has never been completely explained in any book (including this one) because it is based on the Chinese system of thought called the Tao. The word Tao has two major meanings: the absolute-eternal nature of all being and non-being and "the path" or "the way." We follow the path, or Tao, in order to recognize our unity with the Great Tao, the absolute-eternal. This explanation is useless, however, because it's just words. The major text of Taoism, *Tao te Ching*, starts with these words: "The Tao that can be expressed with words is not the Great Eternal Tao." Similarly, our yin and yang chart on the preceding page is interesting but hardly illuminating, and if I told you "this is this" or "that is that," I wouldn't be correct. Su Wen, a Taoist master said:

"There is yin within the yin and yang within the yang. From dawn until noon the yang of heaven is the yang within the yang; from noon until dusk the yang of the heaven is the yin within the yang; from dusk until midnight the yin of heaven is the yin within the yin; from midnight until dawn the yin of heaven is the yang within the yin."

What this tells you in simple terms is that the qualities of yin and yang are relative, not absolute. A careful understanding of yin and yang takes years of study, and in the field of Oriental medicine it is so important that I'd say no Western doctor understands (even those who've studied it) because a Western doctor does not seek the path nor recognize unity with the Great Tao. For example, the surface of the body is our skin, and all Western physicians discuss it based on anatomical studies by dissecting animals and dead humans. The Chinese believe the body must remain intact, even after death, so it's amazing to us how much the Chinese know about the human body without anatomy classes. Western technology, however, has barely begun to catch up with Chinese traditional knowledge: for example, the Russian technique of Kirlian photography, which records patterns of life energy with high-voltage electromagnetism, duplicates in its photos of the human body the acupuncture meridians.

Again, the example of how a Western doctor sees our skin is not the same in Chinese medicine. The surface of the body is yang; the interior is yin, and this relationship remains constant within the body: the surface of every organ is always yang, and the interior is yin down to the individual cells that compose it. A gas is sometimes yang, and a solid is yin; but among gases the more rarefied are yang, and the denser are yin. Life and death are yang; growth and storage are yin. If only yang exists there would be no birth; if only yin, there would be no death, and the life of every organism depends on the correct balance of its various components. An "S" shape within a circle is used to represent yin and yang because it is a continuous flow with no beginning and no end.

Yeh Ch'ing-Chiu, a master of Chinese medicine, explains yin and yang in this way:

> "As heaven has its sun and moon, its order of stars, rain and wind, thunder and lightning, so man has two eyes, a set of teeth, joy and anger, voice and sound. The earth with its valleys, rocks and stones, trees and shrubs, weeds and grasses, has its parallel on the human body in the shoulders and armpits, nodes and tuberosities, tendons and muscles, hairs and down. The four limbs correspond to the four seasons, the twelve joints with the twelve months. The pulse is of twelve different kinds to agree with the twelve rivers. The human skeleton has 360 bones for the simple reason that there are the same number of degrees in a circle."

Acupuncture works whether or not you understand the philosophy of Chinese medicine and yin and yang. Why isn't more acupuncture practiced in America? It is unlikely that the medical system in the United States is ignorant of acupuncture because of the many nations now involved in the practice of acupuncture.

Mark Duke (author of *Acupuncture--the Chinese Art of Healing*) asked the news editor of the American Medical Association (AMA) weekly newsletter some years ago why more acupuncture isn't used by physicians since it obviously works and has since 1600 B. C. The AMA answered:

> "We don't understand it and we don't know anything about it. We know that it exists and that it has for a long time. But it has not come up so far in this part of the world. Remember, we are an association of doctors, not a research or licensing organization. Acupuncture ranks with Oriental folklore, but it can't be called medicine. There is a very heavy psychological element in it, possibly involving self-hypnosis. Is there any real scientific basis for it? It doesn't really matter. You know, if it helps you with the discomforts of an ailment, you don't really care whether it's scientific or not."

Mark Duke noticed that the AMA either did not classify acupuncture as medicine so he asked who might practice acupuncture in the United States. "It would be the practice of medicine," the editor said, "So it would have to be licensed, that is, it would have to be done by licensed physicians."

The AMA is practicing a double standard on acupuncture: on the one hand, they don't want anyone but licensed physicians practicing it, but on the other, they classify it as folklore and don't teach it in medical schools. Therefore, it is unlikely that many physicians will use acupuncture on patients (just as a lack of nutritional knowledge prevents many physicians from utilizing nutritional treatments with patients).

Remember the woman who was surprised at the preventive medicine and non-medicine of China? Her husband told me that he had a bad leg. He didn't know what was wrong with it. He was limping. This man was a scientist--a chemist. He first went to a specialist who couldn't help him. Then a friend told him about an Oriental doctor who practiced acupuncture, and the chemist went to him. The acupuncturist said he'd heal his leg with ten treatments. After ten treatments with moxabustion (a form of acupuncture that uses burning herbs to stimulate the needles), the chemist was walking again without a limp. His leg was back to normal.

"I told the M. D. about my success," he told me.

"That was a waste of time," I said in my usual cynical manner. "What happened?"

"He laughed and wasn't at all interested."

If acupuncture were to become common in the United States, the average doctor's income would fall, and surgeons and anesthesiologists would be the ones most damaged since acupuncture completely replaces general anesthesia. In many cases, surgery isn't needed. With the use of acupuncture, the 15,000,000 pounds of aspirin sold every year would drop drastically. The almost two billion prescriptions (and a half billion refills) would be greatly diminished as drugs are completely replaced by acupuncture and Chinese herbal medicine. The life-sign monitoring devices, which make up 20% of the cost of an operation, would no longer be needed. Hospital stays would be reduced by up to 30% due to the elimination of chemical anesthetics.

The United States is one of the few countries that refuses to study acupuncture or offer research grants to understand it better. Thus, an individual wishing this effective and non-invasive method of treatment may not be able to easily find an acupuncture practitioner.

Chinese medicine has been associated with spectacular examples of longevity. One example is Li Ch'ing Yuen, who was born in 1678 in the mountains of southwest China. At the age of eleven he ran away from home with three travelers who were in the herbal trade. Yuen learned about herbal medicine, acupuncture, yoga, meditation, Tai Ch'i Chuan, and the Tao from his three teachers as they traveled through China, Tibet, and Southeast Asia. As Yuen became older he was recognized as a master of herbal medicine, well known for his excellent health and amazing vigor. One day when Yuen was fifty he met a much older man who, in spite of his age, could outwalk Yuen. The old man told Yuen that if he walked briskly every day and consumed a bowl of soup made with an herb known as *Lycium chinensis* he would soon attain a new vigor and have the health of a young man.

Li Ch'ing Yuen began following his new master's advice, but the tradition of the Chinese is to always seek and learn, and to learn from those older who have lived longer and know more about life. When Yuen was about sixty years old, he heard of an old Taoist sage who was five hundred years old and lived in the mountains. Yuen begged the sage to teach him his secrets. The sage saw that Yuen was sincere and he began teaching him. He taught him the secrets of Taoist Yoga (*Nei Gung*, the inner alchemy), and he taught Yuen to take daily doses of *Panax ginseng* and *Radix polygonum*. Yuen ate little meat or root vegetables and limited his consumption of grains. His diet consisted mostly of herbs and above-ground steamed vegetables. Yuen was married fourteen times, and lived through eleven generations of his own descendants (numbering almost two hundred). He died in 1930. Li Ch'ing Yuen's case is rare, but it has been authenticated, and Oriental lore is full of tales about men and women living to be ages unimaginable by us.

The use of Chinese herbals in cosmetics is not as developed in the East as it is in the West, and even in the case of royal jelly, bee pollen, and ginseng (which are used in many cosmetics) their hair and skin care use was developed in Europe and the U. S. One of the topical and internal mixtures for the care of the skin is known as the *Siler Combination* or *Ching-shang-fang-feng-tang*. It is a classic Chinese treatment for acne, eczema, acne rosacea, and various skin problems. It can be used internally as a tea or externally as a facial tonic. Here is the herbal mixture:

Angelica 1 part, Chih-ko 1 part, Cnidium 1 part, Coptis 1 part, Forsythia 1 part, Gardenia 1 part, Licorice 1 part, Mentha 1 part, Platycodon 1 part, Schizonepeta 1 part, Scute 1 part, Siler 1 part. To this *Ching-shang-fang-feng-tang* mixture add Coix, 1 gram. This herb improves the tone of the skin. You may also add Rhubarb, 0.5 gram. This herb prevents constipation from the use of siler. You can add up to 1 gram of Rhubarb if needed.*

A combination of herbs known as *Tang-kuei-shao-yao-san* is used for pale complexions and pigmentation problems as well as freckles and melasma. Chinese herbalists also say that this mixture of herbs is excellent for various body pains, improves circulation, and is for people with poor physical strength. Here is the combination: Alisma 1 part, Atractylodes 1 part, Cnidium 1 part, Coix 1 part, Peony 1 part, Tang-kuei 1 part.*

Another combination known as *Kuei-chic-fu-ling-wan* is for people with freckles and melasma, but it is also used in China for menstrual irregularities. Here it is: Cinnamon 1 part, Hoelen 1 part, Moutan 1 part, Peony 1 part, Persiica 1 part.*

Most of us would like to live to be 252 years old as Li Ch'ing Yuen did, so here is one of the Taoist Longevity tonics that young Li probably took as tea for his whole life. The name of this tonic is Ching, Ch'i, Shin Longevity tonic. The name refers to the great Chinese classic, the *I Ching*, or *Book of Changes*. Ch'i is Life Energy, and Shin is the higher spirit which manifests itself in love. Here's the combination of herbs for this classic tonic: Asparagus 1 part, Ginseng 1 part, Ho Shou Wu 1 part, Lycium 1 part, Schizandra 1 part.*

Writing a book like this requires clear thinking and energy. You can't be a "muddle brain" and put it all together. There's a Chinese tonic for this called Ma Huang Tonic Of Clear Thinking. Ma Huang is the key to this formula. If you leave Ma Huang out of the formula you get a very gradual sharpening of the memory and sound sleep, but with Ma Huang the effects are more immediate. This is used for those who are involved in strenuous mental activity or if you're writing a book. Here's the formula: Astragalus 1 part, Ginseng 1 part, Lycium 1 part, Ma Huang 1 part (optional for immediate results), Red Dates 2 parts, Schizandra 1 part, Suk Gok, 1 part, Tang Kuei, 2 parts.*

Chinese philosophy also says that balance is important and the perfect balance between yin and yang is ideal. There is an herbal tonic that is known as the "Balanced Tonic" or Yin and Yang Tonic. This tonic tones the muscles, but is also said to promote beautiful skin. The barefoot doctors of China say that if this tonic is consumed regularly, it will strengthen the constitution and lengthen life. Here it is: Astractylus 1 part, Atractylus 1 part, Cinnamon 1 part, Ginseng 1 part, Licorice 1 part, Ligusticum, Paeonia 1 part, Poria 1 part, Rehmannia 1 part, Tang Kuei 1 part.*

* Total herb weight for herbal tonic recipes should come to no more than sixteen ounces, except where otherwise specified.

These are some of the Chinese herbal formulas that have been handed down from generation to generation, but don't think you can use them to cure what ails you. If you're sick, you had best consult a physician, and if you can find a Chinese doctor (barefoot or no), he may know what can be done for you by using herbs and acupuncture.

I conclude this chapter with a chart of Chinese medical herbs. It is fairly complete, though I have left off things like Ti-Lung (Earthworm), Lung-ku (Dragon Bone), Hsieh-yu-tan (Human Hair), Tsan-chu (Toads), Tsan-shu (Toad Secretion), Hsiung-tan (Bear Gall), and Lu-chiao (Deer Horn). Not everything in Chinese philosophy and medicine is perfect, and the killing of a deer to get his horn in order to treat the blood or circulation, when so many herbs suit this purpose, or the eating of a scorpion (Chuan-hsieh) for a nerve tonic seems excessive. I have also excluded Hua-shih (Talc) because recent studies have shown it to be a carcinogen, and I have excluded some of the minerals such as ferrous sulfate and red mercuric sulfide because many minerals have poisons in them.

Acupuncture Face Lift

The two finest methods to reduce wrinkles and tone the facial muscles for a youthful, clear, healthy skin are the **Natural Method of Skin Care** used with the **Natural Method Massage** (See **PART III** for a complete description). A useful adjunct to these two methods, however, is the Acupressure Face Lift that stimulates the meridian points on your face and other parts of the body that are skin care points in acupuncture treatments. It is ideal to use the three methods together. Do it daily.

There are a few acupuncture practitioners who give cosmetic acupuncture face lifts, and some give acupressure face lifts. Some aestheticians use acupressure during facial massages, and this is a system we always include as part of the **Natural Method of Skin Care**.

You don't actually need dozens of needles in your face, arms, legs, feet, and back to get the benefits of an acupressure face lift. A medium pressure applied with a blunt pointed object for about ten seconds with a clockwise circular movement to the meridian points will yield excellent results. Alternate between adjacent points so that both points receive the acupressure equally.

The best time to do the face lift is right after you've done your facial. Don't do this after you've just eaten and don't do it when you're tired. Put aside some time at the beginning of your day or in the early evening. The first acupressure face lift you give yourself will take about twenty minutes, but when you learn the points you can do it in much less time.

The methods of stimulating the points is to use a medium pressure and a circular clockwise movement as you press. Move from left to right and stimulate the points opposite each other. For example, start at point 1 on the left of your forehead and then go to point 2 on the right side of your forehead, etc.

To apply pressure, you can use your fingertip, your thumb, the knuckle of your index finger, or a blunt smooth object such as the end of an eyebrow pencil or artist's brush (See Fig. 1).

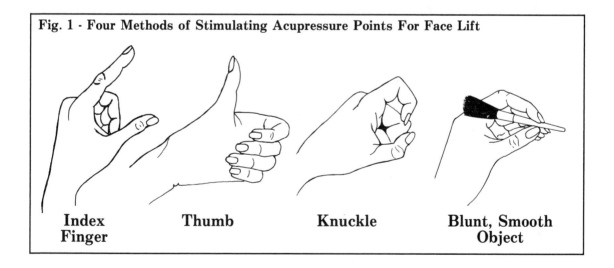

Fig. 1 - Four Methods of Stimulating Acupressure Points For Face Lift

Index Finger   **Thumb**   **Knuckle**   **Blunt, Smooth Object**

In fig. 2 on the following page, you will see all the acupressure points. From Fig. 3 to Fig. 6, you will see exactly how to give your face this acupressure treatment. The additional points in Fig. 7 to Fig. 9 are important because they are for the skin and important for the rest of the body.

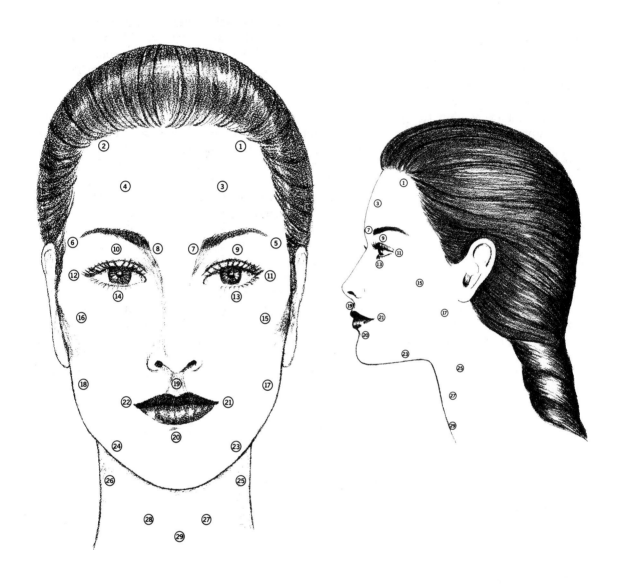

Fig 2. Acupressure Points On the Face

It is best to start at the top left point on the head just below the hair line. Apply a medium pressure at this point with the end of an eyebrow pencil or artist's brush. Rotate as you stimulate the point. Then move to the spot on the right and apply the pressure slowly rotating (clockwise). Now move on to the next point down to the left, and apply pressure with rotation. Then move to the right, etc. There are twenty-nine points on the face and neck. We have numbered them in the order in which you will stimulating them from 1 through 29.

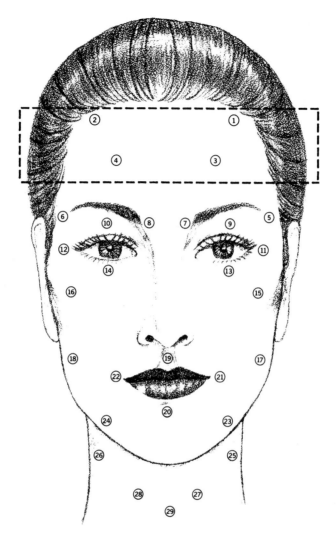

Fig 3. Acupressure Points On the Forehead

This is where you start as you progress across and downward with your face lift treatment. I will discuss the specific points and what they represent as "treatment points" in acupuncture though we are concerned with them as a dermatology-beauty treatment. I will refer to the points by number (this is also the same number applied to how you follow one point after the other. These numbers are for our use here and do not refer to other numbers that might appear on other acupuncture charts).

Points 1 and 2 are not only stimulating to the skin and soften lines along the forehead, but are similar to classic acupuncture points on the back of the neck, in the webbing between the thumb and forefinger, and on the spine, atop the third lumbar vertebra often used to relieve headaches, pain, and migraine. These are the points I often use to stop a headache. See other diagrams for acupressure points on other parts of the body.

Move on to points 3 and 4. These serve the same function as 1 and 2 and complement them. As you move through these four points, stimulate each point for about ten seconds, that is, ten circular moves of the point. When you have stimulated 1 through 4, you have tightened the skin on the forehead area.

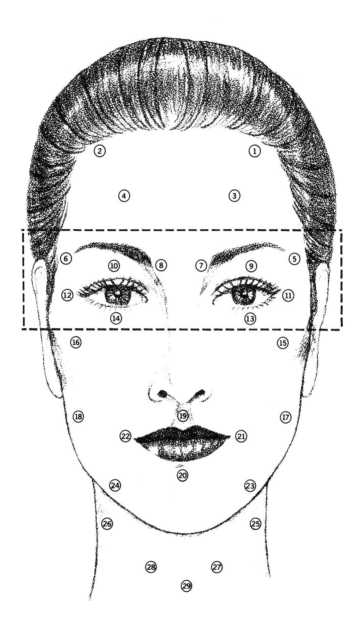

Fig. 4 - Acupressure Points in the Eye Area

Starting at point 5 on the outer edge of the left eyebrow, stimulate this point and move to point 6 on the outer edge of the right eyebrow. Move to point 7 on the inner edge of the left eyebrow, and then move the short distance to point 8 on the inner edge of the right eyebrow. Points 9 and 10 are just below the eyebrow close to the center of the eye, just beyond the notch that can be felt in the skull opening. Stimulate these areas more gently and with great care where the skin is more delicate. The points in the eye area will reduce lines around the eyes. Points 9 and 10 are also indicated for treatment of allergy, the lower back, neck, and sinusitis. Move on to points 11 and 12, then points 13 and 14.

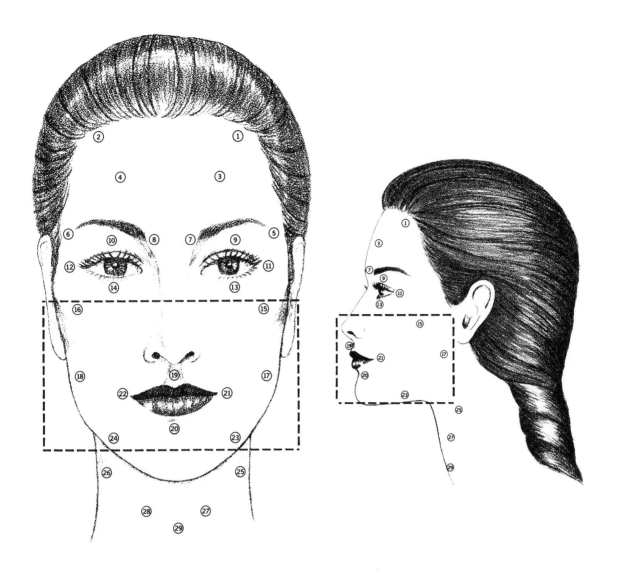

Fig. 5 - Acupressure Points in the Mouth Area

Start with point 15, which is on the high part of the cheek bone area in line with the center of the ear, then move to point 16. Proceed to point 17, which is slightly below the ear. Move to point 18 on the other side.

Go to point 19 which is midway between the nose and upper lip, and on to point 20 which is just below it. Point 29 is also the sneezing control center, so if you have a fit of sneezing, you can stimulate this point. Move on to to points 23 and 24 which are on the edge of the jaw line.

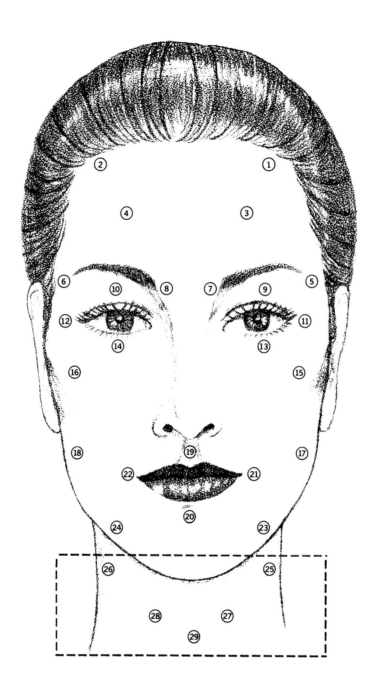

Fig. 6 - Acupressure Points on the Neck

Go to point 25 on the left side of the neck and then to point 26 on the right side of the neck. Move to the front of the neck to point 27 then 28, and finish with point 29.

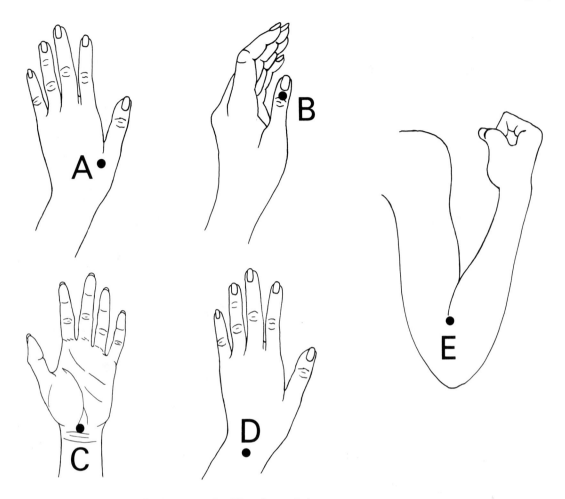

Fig. 7 - Acupressure Points on the Hands and Arms

There are quite a few more points which are located on other parts of the body that have quite a bit to do with the skin. These additional points will complete the perfect skin care treatment. I will letter these points beginning with "A" so there will be no confusion with the numbered points.

In the webbing between the thumb and forefinger is point A, and it is one of the most important points in acupuncture and acupressure. This is in the same location on your left and right hands. This is the first place I stimulate when I have a headache. It is a sedation point and relaxes the entire body.

Between the nail and the first joint of the thumb, just behind the nail on the side farthest from the other fingers, is a very delicate spot we will call point B. Again I use this to get rid of a headache along with the various other points.

On the most prominent crease of the inner wrist, in a direct line with the middle finger is point C. This is an important point for the skin, and in acupuncture and G-Jo (The Chinese word for first aid), it is used to treat eczema (along with other points).

Point D is on the back of the arm about two thumb widths above the most prominent crease of the upper wrist, and in line with the middle finger. This is another skin care area.

Point E is on the extreme end of the outer crease of the elbow. This point along with point A is used to treat acne. Point E is another skin care point.

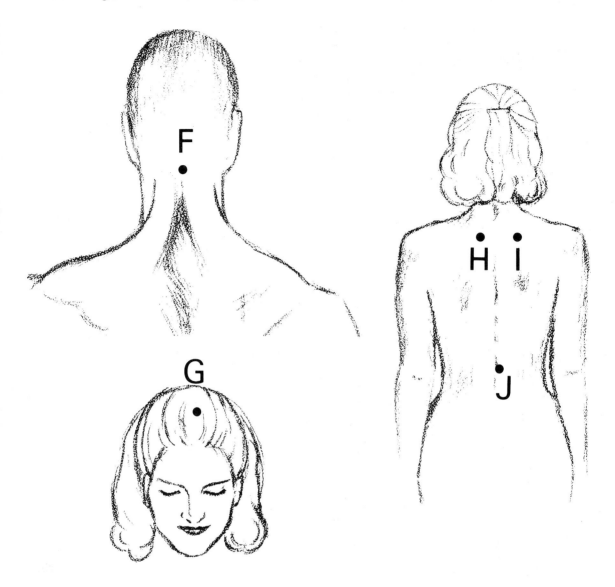

Fig. 8 - Acupressure Points On Other Parts of the Body

There are two points on the head that are great for neck stiffness and headaches, and I'm giving them to you so you can stimulate them anytime you feel tense, have a sore, stiff neck, or headache. They can be combined with points A and D. On the back of the neck, at the center, where the spine joins the skull (cervical atlas) is Point F. Put your hand back there now and locate the spot. Remove your fingers and slowly rotate your head. How relaxed it is! Point G is at the top center of the head midway between the ears. This is a very delicate point and should never be used on a child. Locate it with your fingers. Now press firmly and massage this spot. It's relaxing as is Point F.

There are three points on the back which are also very relaxing, and again I use them for headache, tension, and insomnia. Points H and I are on the back about one thumb length on either side of the spine, slightly below a line between the tips of the shoulders and Point J is on the spine, atop the third lumbar vertebra in line with the waist.

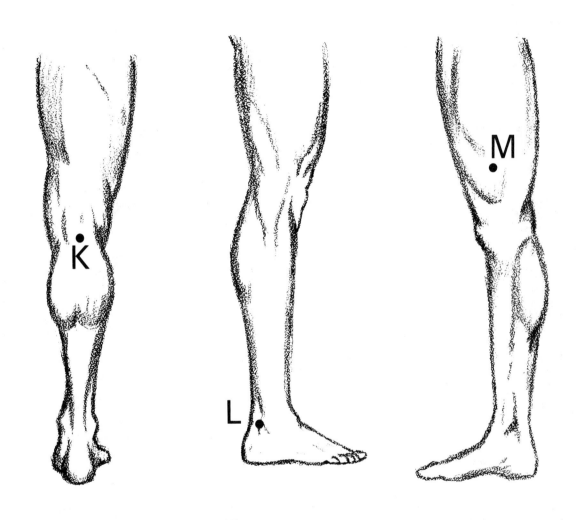

Fig. 9 - Acupressure Points on the Legs and Feet

Point K is in the center of the crease at the rear of the knee. This point is not to be used if you have varicose veins. K is a stimulating point for skin care problems, as well as a reliever of lower back pain, tension, etc.

Point L is another skin care point for the face as well as a general pain control center. It is located in the hollow behind the crown of the outer ankle.

Point M is the width of about two thumbs above the top of the kneecap, in the inner thigh, in line with the crown of the inner ankle. This is a skin treatment area and has been used for the treatment of acne.

Chinese Medicinal Herbs

COMMON NAME *Scientific Name* Chinese Name	Parts Used	Medicinal Uses
ACANTHOPANAX *Acanthopanax gracilstylus* Wu-chia-pi	Root epidermis	Anti-rheumatic, restoring vigor and sexual potency
ACHYRANTHES *Achyranthes bidentata* Niu-hsi	Root	Diuretic, emmenagogue, mucilaginous demulcent
ACORUS *Acorus gramineus* Shia-chang-pu	Rhizome	Stomachic for dyspepsia
AKEBIA *Akebia quinata Decne* or *Clematis armandi* Mu-tang	Stem	Diuretic, anti-inflammatory
ALISMA *Alisma plantago* Tse-hsieh	Tuber	Diuretic, diaphoretic
ALTAICA *Anemone altaica* Chiu-chieh-chang-pu	Rhizome	Stimulant, expectorant, detoxifier
ALUM $KAl_3(SO_4)_2 12H_2O$ Ming-fan	Mineral	Astringent, hemostatic, vermifuge detoxifier
ANEMARRHENA *Anemarrhena asphodeloides* Chih-mu	Rhizome	Anti-pyretic, expectorant
ANEMONE *Anemone cernua* Pai-tou-weng	Root	Anti-diarrheic

Chinese Medicinal Herbs Con't COMMON NAME *Scientific Name* **Chinese Name**	Parts Used	Medicinal Uses
AQUILARIA *Aquilaria agallocha* Shen-hsiang	Wood	Stomachic in gastralgia, colic, nervous vomiting
ARCTIUM *Arctium lappa* Niu-pang-tzu	Fruit	Diuretic, anti-pyretic, expectorant, anti-inflammatory
ARECA *Areca catechu* Ta-fu-pi	Fruit rind	Diuretic
ARECA SEED *Areca catechu* Pin-lang	Seed	Astringent, vermifuge (tapeworms)
ARISAEMA *Arisaema amurense* Tien-nan-hsing	Tuber	Analgesic, anti-spasmodic, vermifuge (tapeworms)
ARTEMSIA (Mugwort) *Artemisia vulgaris* Ai-yeh	Leaves	Hemostatic, stomachic
ASAFOETIDA *Ferula assafoetida* Ah-wei	Gum-resin	Vermifuge, sedative, anti-spasmodic digestive
ASARUM *Asarum sieboldi* Hsi-hsin	Herb	Analgesic, sedative, expectorant
ASPARAGUS *Asparagus cochinchinensis* Tien-men-tong	Root	Diuretic, expectorant. Yin tonic with sweet-bitter taste.
ASTER *Aster tartaricus* Tzu-wan	Root	Anti-tussive, expectorant

Chinese Medicinal Herbs **COMMON NAME** *Scientific Name* **Chinese Name**	Parts Used	Medicinal Uses
ASTRAGULUS *Astragalus hoantchy* Huang-chi	Root	Tonic, diuretic, anti-pyretic. Energy tonic. Sweet taste
ATRACTYLODES *Atractylodes ovata* Tsang-chu	Rhizome	Aromatic, tonic, chronic stomach and intestinal problems
AURANTIUM *Citrus aurantium* Chu-pi	Fruit rind	Stomachic, digestant, diaphoretic, expectorant, anti-tussive, anti-emetic
BAKERI *Allium bakeri* and *A. macrostemon* Hsieh-pai	Bulbus	Smooth the ch'i
BAMBOO *Phyllostachys nigra* Chu-ju	Stem with outside skin removed	Refrigerant, anti-pyretic, anti-tussive
BAMBOO SAP *Phyllostachys nigra* Chu-li	Sap	Expectorant, anti-tussive
BELAMCANDA *Belamcanda chinensis* Yeh-kan	Rhizome	Expectorant, anti-pyretic, stomachic, purgative
BENINCASA *Benincasa hispida* Cogn. Tung-kua-tzu	Seed	Diuretic
BIOTA *Biota orientalis* Po-tzu-jen	Seed	Tonic, sedative, lenitive
BLACK CARDAMON *Elettaria cardamonum* I-chih	Seed	Stomachic, tonic for stomach pain, weak bladder, spermatorrhea

Chinese Medicinal Herbs Con't **COMMON NAME** *Scientific Name* **Chinese Name**	Parts Used	Medicinal Uses
BLETILLA *Bletilla striata* Pai-chi	Rhizome	Nourishes the muscles, hemostatic
BLUE CITRUS PEEL *Citrus medica* Ching-pi	Fruit rind	Aromatic, stomachic
BORNEOL *Dryobalanops aromatica* Ping-pien	Crystal	Anti-inflammatory, anti-spasmodic, sedative, anti-tussive
BOS *Bos taurus* Niu-huang	Calculus	Anti-toxin, cardiotonic, anti-pyretic, sedative, diuretic
BRASSICA *Brassica alba* Pai-chieh-tzu	Seed	Emetic
BROUSSONETIA *Broussonetia papyrifera* Chu-shih-tzu	Fruit	Stimulant, diuretic, eye tonic
BRUCEA *Brucea javanica* Ya-tan-tzu	Seeds	Vermifuge
BUDDLEIA *Buddleia officinalis* Mi-meng-hua	Flower	Eye tonic for night blindness, weak eyes, cataracts
BULRUSH *Typha angustata* Pu-huang	Pollen	Hemostatic, diuretic, astringent, dessicant, vulnerary.
BUPLEURUM *Bupleurum chinense* Chai-hu	Root	Anti-pyretic, late or infrequent menstruation

Chinese Medicinal Herbs Con't **COMMON NAME** *Scientific Name* **Chinese Name**	**Parts Used**	**Medicinal Uses**
CALAMUS GUM *Calamus draco* Hsieh-chieh	Resinous secretion	Astringent, hemostatic, analgesic (See also **HERB CHART**).
CAPILLARIS *Artemisia capillaris* Yin-chen	Herb	Diuretic, anti-pyretic in jaundice
CARTHAMUS *Carthamus tinctorius* Hung-hua	Flower	Uterine astringent in painful menstruation
CASSIA SEED *Cassia tora* Chueh-ming-tzu	Seed	Various eye and liver disorders
CATECHU *Acacia catechu* Erh-cha	Resin	Astringent, refrigerant, anti-diarrheic (See **HERB CHART**).
CELOSIA *Celosia argentea* Ching-hsiang-tzu	Seed	Eye tonic
CHIN-CHIU *Gentiana macrophylla* Chin-chiu	Root	Anti-pyretic, diuretic, dessicant
CHRYSANTHEMUM *Chrysanthemum morifolium;* *C. indicum* Chu-hua	Flower	Sedative, refrigerant in headache, influenza
CIMICIFUGA *Cimicifuga dahurica* or *C. foetida* Sheng-ma	Root	Anti-pyretic, sedative, analgesic
CINNAMON *Cinnamonomum cassia* Kuei-chih or Kuei-pi	Ramulus or Bark	Aromatic, stomachic, astringent, tonic, analgesic, or stimulant (See also **HERB CHART**).

Chinese Medicinal Herbs Con't COMMON NAME *Scientific Name* Chinese Name	Parts Used	Medicinal Uses
CHAENOMELES *Chaenomeles lagenaria* Mu-kua	Fruit	Astringent in diarrhea, analgesic in painful joints, gout, chlolera
CHERRY BARK *Prunus yedoensis* Ying-pi	Bark	Astringent, anti-tussive
CHIH-KO *Citrus kotokan* Chih-ko	Ripe fruit	Excessive sputum, visceral distention abdominal swelling
CHIH-SHIH *Poncirus trifoliata* Chih-shih	Unripe fruit	Stomachic for dysentery, anti-diarrheic
CISTANCHE *Cistanche salsa* Jou-tsung-jung	Herb	Aphrodisiac, tonic in spermatorrhea and impotence
CITRUS *Citrus nobilis* Chen-pi	Fruit rind	Stomachic, digestant, expectorant, anti-tussive, vermifuge
CLEMATIS *Clematis chinensis* Wei-ling-hsien	Root	Analgesic, rheumatism, anti-pyretic, diuretic
CLOVE *Eugenia caryophyllata* Ting-hsiang	Flower	Aromatic, carminative, anti-emetic, aromatic, stomachic. (Also see **HERB CHART**).
CLUSTER *Amomum cardamomum* Pai-tou-kou	Fruit	Aromatic, stomachic, with anti-emetic action.
CNIDIUM *Cnidium officinale* or *Ligusticum wallichii* Chuan-chiung	Rhizome	Sedative, analgesic, emmenagogue

Chinese Medicinal Herbs Con't **COMMON NAME** *Scientific Name* **Chinese Name**	**Parts Used**	**Medicinal Uses**
COIX *Coix lachrma-jobi* I-yi-jen	Seed	Refrigerant, diuretic, anti-rheumatic
COPTIS *Coptis chinensis* Huang-lien	Root	Bitter stomachic, digestive, anti-dysenteric
CORDYCEPS *Cordyceps sinensis* Tang-chung-hsia-tsao	Fungus	Hemostatic, expectorant, aphrodisiac astringent, sedative
CORNUS *Cornus officinalis* Shan-chu-yu	Fruit	Astringent, tonic in impotence, spermatorrhea, lumbago, vertigo, night sweats
CORYDALIS *Corydalis ambigua* Yen-hu-suo	Tuber	Sedative, anti-spasmodic, analgesic in headache, menstrual cramps
CRATAEGUS *Crataegus pinnatifida* Shan-cha	Fruit	Digestant, anti-diarrheic
CROTON *Croton tiglium* Pa-tou	Seed	Violent purgative
CURCUMA *Curcuma longa* Yu-chin	Rhizome	Aromatic, stomachic, cholagogue, hemostatic
CUSCUTA *Cuscuta japonica* Tu-szu-tzu	Seed	Tonic in impotence, spermatorrhea, prostatitis
CYANCHUM *Cyanchum stauntoni* Pai-chien	Root	Anti-tussive, expectorant

Chinese Medicinal Herbs Con't **Common Name** *Scientific Name* **Chinese Name**	Parts Used	Medicinal Uses
CYNOMORIUM *Cynomorium coccineum* Suo-yang	Stem	Tonic, aphrodisiac, spermatorrhea
CYPERUS *Cyperus rotundus* Hsiang-fu	Tubercles	Aromatic, stomachic, emmenagogue, sedative, analgesic
DANDELION *Taraxacum officinale* Pu-kung-ying	Herb	Stomachic, cholagogue, lactagogue
DENDROBIUM *Dendrobium nobile* Shih-hu	Herb	Salivant, sedative, promotes glandular secretions
DIANTHUS *Dianthus superbus* Chu-mai	Herb	Diuretic, emmenagogue
DICHROA *Dichroa febrifuga* Charng-shan	Root	Anti-malarial, anti-pyretic
DIGENEA *Digenea simplex* Che-ku-tsai	Herb	Vermifuge
DIOSCOREA *Dioscorea batatas* Shan-yao	Root	Nutrient tonic, digestant in chronic intestinal inflammation and diarrhea
DIPSACUS *Dipsacus asper* Hsu-tuan	Root	Tonic, analgesic, hematic
DOLICHOS *Dolichos lablab* Pai-pien-tou	Seed	Astringent, stomachic, digestant, vermifuge

Chinese Medicinal Herbs Con't COMMON NAME *Scientific Name* Chinese Name	Parts Used	Medicinal Uses
ELSHOLTZIA *Elsholtzia cristata* Hsiang-ju	Entire herb	Stomachic, carminative, diuretic
EPIMEDIUM *Epimedium macranthum* Yin-yang-huo	Herb	Aphrodisiac
ERIOBOTRYA *Eriobotrya japonica* Pi-pa-yeh	Leaves	Anti-tussive, expectorant
EUCOMMIA *Eucommia ulmoides* Tu-chung	Bark	Tonic, hypotensor with sedative and analgesic effects
EUPHORBIA *Euphorbia pekinensis* Ta-chi	Root	Purgative, diuretic
EURYALE *Euryale ferox* Chien-shih	Seed	Tonic and astringent in spermatorrhea analgesic in neuralgia, joint pains
EVODIA *Evodia rutaecarpa* Wu-chu-yu	Fruit	Stomachic, carminative, stimulant, uterotonic
FENNEL *Foeniculum vulgare* Hui-hsiang	Fruit	Carminative, stomachic, stimulant (See **HERB CHART**)
FLAVA WAX *Apis chinensis* Huang-la	Wax	Internal hemostatic, astringent
FORSYTHIA *Forsythia suspensa* Lien-chiao	Fruit	Anti-pyretic, anti-inflammatory

Chinese Medicinal Herbs Con't **COMMON NAME** *Scientific Name* **Chinese Name**	**Parts Used**	**Medicinal Uses**
FRAXINELLA *Dictamnus dasycarpus* Pai-hsien-pi	Peel	Anti-pyretic
FRAXINUS *Fraxinus rhynchophylla* Chin-pi	Bark	Astringent, stomachic
GALANGA *Alpinia officinarum* Kao-liang-chiang	Rhizome	Stomachic for indigestion, stomach pain, chronic intestinal inflammation
GAMBIR *Uncaria rhynochophylla* Tiao-teng	Spines	Sedative, anti-spasmodic in infantile nervous disorders
GARDEN BALSAM *Impatiens balsamina* Chi-hsing-tzu	Seed	Expel effused blood, expectorant
GARDENIA *Gardenia florida* Chih-tzu	Fruit	Anti-pyretic, hemostatic, anti-inflammatory for jaundice
GASTRODIA *Gastrodia elata* Tien-ma	Root	Tonic in vertigo, headache, muscle and nerve pain, rheumatism
GENDARUSSA *Gendarussa vulgaris* Chieh-ku-tsao	Herb	Anti-rheumatic drug for bone-setting
GENKWA *Daphne genkwa* Yuan-hua	Flower	Diuretic, stomachic, anti-tussive
GENTIANA *Gentiana scabra* Lung-tan	Root	Stomachic

Chinese Medicinal Herbs Con't COMMON NAME *Scientific Name* Chinese Name	Parts Used	Medicinal Uses
GINGKO *Ginkgo biloba* Pai-kuo	Seed	Astringent, sedative, anti-tussive in asthma
GINSENG *Panax ginseng* Jen-sheng	Root	Tonic, stimulant, asphrodisiac, indicated in nervous exhaustion, indigestion, palpitation, impotence, asthma (see also **HERB CHART**).
GLEDITSIA *Gleditsia sinensis* Tsao-chiao	Fruit	Stimulant, expectorant
GLEHNIA *Glehnia littoralis* Pei-sha-sheng	Root	Expectorant, anti-tussive
HOELEN *Poria cocos* Fu-ling	Fungus	Diuretic, sedative, treatment of oliguresis, insomnia
HO-SOU-WU *Polygonum multiflorum* Ho-sou-wu	Root	Blood tonic
HOUTTUYNIA *Houttuynia cordata* Yu-hsing-tsao	Herb	Diuretic, urinary, antiseptic
INDIGO *Indigofera tinctoria* Ching-tai	Pigment	Anti-inflammatory, anti-pyretic (See also **HERB CHART**).
INULA *Inula japonica* Suan-fu-hua	Flower	Expectorant, stomachic

Chinese Medicinal Herbs Con't COMMON NAME *Scientific Name* **Chinese Name**	Parts Used	Medicinal Uses
JUJUBE *Zizyphus sativa* Ta-tsao	Fruit	Nutrient tonic, sedative in insomnia, nervous exhaustion
JUNCUS *Juncus communis* Teng-hsin-tsao	Pith	Diuretic, anti-inflammatory
KAKI *Diospyros kaki* Shih-ti	Calyx	Lower ch'i, treat hiccoughs
KAN-SUI *Euphorbia kansui* Kan-sui	Root	Diuretic, expectorant
KAOLIN Hydrated aluminum silicate Chih-shih-chih	Mineral	Astringent
KAO-PEN *Ligusticum sinense* Kao-pen	Root	Sedative, analgesic
LAMINARIA *Laminaria japonica* Kun-pu	Herb	Alterative
LASIOSPHAERA *Lasiosphaera nipponica* Ma-po	Fungus	Astringent, anti-inflammatory, anti-tussive, hemostatic
LEONURUS *Leonurus sibiricus* I-mu-tsao	Herb	Emmenagogue, diuretic, vasodilator

Chinese Medicinal Herbs Con't **COMMON NAME** *Scientific Name* **Chinese Name**	**Parts Used**	**Medicinal Uses**
LEPIDIUM *Lepidium apetalum* Ting-li-tzu	Seed	Expectorant, diuretic
LICORICE *Glycrrhiza uralensis* Kan-tsao	Root	Demulcent, expectorant, emollient in peptic ulcer (see **HERB CHART**).
LILY *Lilium japonicum* Pai-ho	Bulb	Nutrient, anti-tussive, expectorant
LINDERA *Lindera strychnifolia* Wu-yao	Root	Aromatic, stomachic
LITHOSPERMUM ROOT *Lithospermum erythrorrhizon* Tzu-tsao	Root	Anti-pyretic
LONGAN *Euphoria longana* Lung-yen-jou	Aril	Nutrient tonic in nervous exhaustion, insomnia
LONICERA *Lonicera japonica* Chin-yin-hua	Flowers	Diuretic, refrigerant, anti-inflammatory, anti-diarrheic
LOPHATHERUM *Lophatherum gracile* Tan-chu-yeh	Herb	Diuretic, refrigerant
LORANTHUS *Loranthus parasiticus* Sang-chi-sheng	Entire plant	Tonic, anti-inflammatory, lowering blood pressure agent
LOTUS PEDUNCLE *Nelumbo nucifera* Lien-fang	Peduncle	Hemostatic

Chinese Medicinal Herbs Con't **COMMON NAME** *Scientific Name* **Chinese Name**	**Parts Used**	**Medicinal Uses**
LOTUS SEED *Nelumbo nucifera* Lien-tzu	Seed	Tonic, diarrhea
LOTUS STAMENS *Nelumbo nucifera* Lien-hsu	Stamens	Astringent
LUDWIGIA *Ludwigia octovalvis* Shui-teng-hsiang	Root and stem	Anti-pyretic, diuretic
LYCIUM BARK *Lycium chinense* Ti-ku-pi	Root epidermis	Anti-pyretic, anti-tussive in pulmonary tuberculosis
LYCIUM FRUIT *Lycium chinense* Kou-chi-tzu	Fruit	Nutrient tonic in diabetes mellitus, pulmonary tuberculosis
LYGODIUM *Lygodium japonicum* Hai-chin-sha	Spore	Anti-inflammatory, diuretic, helps difficulty in passing urine
MADDER *Rubia cordifolia* Chien-tsao	Root	Emmenagogue, hemostatic
MAGNOLIA BARK *Magnolia officinalis* Hou-pu	Bark	Anti-spasmodic, stomachic, antiseptic (See also **HERB CHART**).
MAGNOLIA FLOWER *Magnolia liliflora* Hsin-i	Flower	Tonic, analgesic in sinusitis, inflammation of the nose, head cold, headache, vertigo (See also **HERB CHART**).
MA-HUANG *Ephedra sinica* Ma-huang	Stem	Bronchial asthma, hay fever, inflammation of the trachea

Chinese Medicinal Herbs COMMON NAME *Scientific Name* Chinese Name	Parts Used	Medicinal Uses
MALT *Hordeum vulgare* Mai-ya	Fruit	Stomachic, digestant
MALTOSE *Oryza sativa* Chiao-i	Fruit	Tonic
MASTIC *Pistacia lentiscus* Ju-hsiang	Resin	Analgesic, sedative, anti-tussive, expectorant
MEL (HONEY) *Apis cerana* Feng-mi	Honey	Astringent, demulcent, anti-diarrheic, analgesic
MELO PEDICEL *Cucumis melo* Tien-kua-ti	Pedicel	Expectorant, emetic
MENTHA *Mentha arvensis* Po-ho	Leaves	Stomachic, carminative, stimulant, diaphoretic. (See **HERB CHART**).
MORUS *Morus alba* Sang-pai-pi	Root epidermis	Anti-tussive, expectorant in asthma, bronchitis, cough
MORUS BRANCH *Morus alba* Sang-chih	Branch	Anti-rheumatic, diuretic
MORUS FRUIT *Morus alba* Sang-chen	Fruit	Tonic
MORUS LEAVES (MULBERRY) *Morus alba* Sang-yeh	Leaves	Influenza, headache

Chinese Medicinal Herbs **COMMON NAME** *Scientific Name* **Chinese Name**	**Parts Used**	**Medicinal Uses**
MOMORDICA *Momordica cochinchinensis* Mu-pieh-tzu	Seed	Dispel swelling, detoxifier
MOUTAN *Paeonia moutan* Mu-tan-pi	Root bark	Anti-pyretic, emmenagogue, for infections of the digestive tract
MUME *Prunus mume* Wu-mei	Unripe fruit	Stomachic, anti-pyretic, astringent
MYRISTICA *Myristica fragrans* Jou-tou-kou	Fruit	Dispel swelling, stimulant
MYRRH *Commiphora myrrha* Mo-yao	Resin	Dessicant, stomachic, anti-spasmodic. (see also **HERB CHART**).
NUPHAR *Nuphar japonica* Chuan-ku	Root	Hemostatic, astringent
NUTGALLS *Rhus chinensis* Wu-pei-tzu	Galls	Astringent, styptic
OPHIOPOGON *Ophiopogon japonicus* Mai-men-tong	Root	Anti-tussive, expectorant, emollient, anti-scrofulous
ORANGE PEEL *Citrus reticulata* Chu-hung	Exocarp	Expectorant
ORYZA *Oryza sativa* Keng-mi	Seed	Tonic, stomachic

Chinese Medicinal Herbs COMMON NAME *Scientific Name* Chinese Name	Parts Used	Medicinal Uses
PEONY *Paeonia lactiflora* Shao-yao	Root	Gastric disorders, intestinal antiseptic, expectorant, emmenagogue
PAI-WEI *Cyanchum atratum* Pai-wei	Root	Diuretic, anti-pyretic
PERILLA & PERILLA FRUIT *Perilla frutescens* Tzu-su-yeh & Tzu-su-tzu	Leaves and fruit	Anti-tussive, stomachic, antiseptic
PERSICA *Prunus persica* Tao-jen	Seed	Anti-tussive, sedative in hypertension
PEUCEDANUM *Peucedanum dercursivum* Chien-hu	Root	Analgesic, anti-pyretic, expectorant
PHARBITIS *Ipomoea hederacea* Chien-niu-tzu	Seed	Cathartic, diuretic, vermifuge
PHASEOLUS *Phaseolus calcaratus* Chih-hsiao-tou	Seed	Diuretic, dispel effused blood, anti-pyretic, detoxifier
PHELLONDENDRON *Phellodendron amurense* Huang-po	Bark	Stomachic, antiseptic, externally as anti-inflammatory in skin diseases
PHRAGMITES *Phragmites communis* Lu-ken	Rhizome	Stomachic, anti-emetic, anti-pyretic
PHYTOLACCA (Pokeberry) *Phytolacca esculenta* Shang-lu	Root	Diuretic

Chinese Medicinal Herbs **COMMON NAME** *Scientific Name* **Chinese Name**	Parts Used	Medicinal Uses
PINELLIA *Pinellia tuberifera* Pan-hsia	Tuber	Anti-emetic, sedative, anti-tussive in nausea, upper respiratory pain, hiccoughs, chronic stomach pains
PIPER (Long Pepper) *Piper longum* Pi-pa	Fruit	Aromatic, stomachic, analgestic
PLANTAGO *Plantago asiatica* Che-chien-tzu	Seed	Diuretic, expectorant
PLATYCODON *Platycodon grandiflorum* Chieh-keng	Root	Expectorant
POLYGALA *Polygala tenuifolia* Yuan-chih	Root	Expectorant, cardiotonic, kidney tonic
POLYGONATUM *Polygonatum canaliculatum* Yu-chu	Rhizome	Tonic
POLYGONUM *Polygonum aviculare* Pien-hsu	Herb	Diuretic, vermifuge, anti-diarrheic, anti-inflammatory
POLYPORUS *Grifola umbellata* Chu-ling	Fungus	Arrests local hemorrhages
PRUNELLA *Prunella vulgaris* Hsia-ku-tsao	Inflorescence	Alterative, anti-pyretic, diuretic in gout

Chinese Medicinal Herbs COMMON NAME *Scientific Name* Chinese Name	Parts Used	Medicinal Uses
PSEUDO-GINSENG *Panax pseudoginseng* San-chi	Root	Hemostatic, analgesic
PSORALEA *Psoralea corylifolia* Pu-ku-chih	Seed	Tonic, stimulant
PUERARIA *Pueraria thunbergiana* Ko-ken	Root	Anti-pyretic, refrigerant
PUERARIA FLOWER *Pueraria thunbergiana* Ko-hua	Flower	Anti-pyretic, refrigerant
CHIANGHUO *Notopterygium* Chiang-huo	Rhizome	Diaphoretic
QUISQUALIS *Quisqualis indica* Shih-chun-tzu	Fruit	Vermifuge
RAPHANUS *Raphanus sativus* Lai-fu-tzu	Seed	Stomachic, expectorant
REHMANNIA *Rehmannia glutinosa* Ti-huang	Rhizome	Cardiotonic, diuretic, hemostatic in diabetes mellitus
RHUBARB *Rheum palmatum* Ta-huang	Rhizome	Stomachic in inflammation and diarrhea
ROSA FRUIT *Rosa laevigata* Chin-ying-tzu	Fruit	Carminative, astringent tonic

Chinese Medicinal Herbs **COMMON NAME** *Scientific Name* **Chinese Name**	Parts Used	Medicinal Uses
ROYAL JELLY Feng wang	Bee secretion	Yin and energy tonic
RUBUS *Rubus chingii* Fu-pen-tzu	Fruit	Astringent
SAFFRON *Crocus sativus* Fan-hung-hua	Stigma	Improve the circulation, anti-pyretic
SALVIA ROOT *Salvia miltiorrhiza* Tan-sheng	Root	Female tonic in the absence of menstruation, vaginal bleeding, stomach pains, breast inflammation
SANTALUM *Santalum album* Tan-hsiang	Wood	Aromatic stomachic, carminative, analgesic in nervous stomach pains
SAPPAN-WOOD *Caesalpinia sappan* Su-mu	Wood	Hemostatic, astringent
SARGASSUM *Sargassum fusiforme* Hai-tsao	Herb	Diuretic, used for iodine deficiencies
SAUSSUREA *Saussurea lappa* Mu-hsiang	Root	Treatment of asthma, stomachic
SCHIZANDRA *Schizandra chinensis* Wu-wei-tzu	Fruit	Tonic, stimulant, anti-tussive
SCHIZONEPETA *Schizonepeta tenuifolia* Ching-chieh	Whole herb	Diaphoretic, anti-pyretic

Chinese Medicinal Herbs COMMON NAME *Scientific Name* Chinese Name	Parts Used	Medicinal Uses
SCIRPUS *Scirpus martimus* San-leng	Rhizome	Emmenagogue, analgesic, laxative
SCROPHULARIA *Scrophularia ningpoensis* Hsuan-sheng	Root	Cardiotonic, anti-pyretic, anti-inflammatory
SCUTE *Scutellaria baicalensis* Huang-chin	Root	Stomachic, anti-pyretic, expectorant
SEGETUM *Cirsium segetum* Hsiao-chi	Herb	Dispel effused blood, cool the blood, hemostatic
SESAME *Sesamum indicum* Hu-ma-tzu	Seed	For constipation; as nutrient tonic for nerve pathlogies
SETARIA *Setaria italica* Su-mi	Seed	Nourish the spleen, digestive, stomachic
SIEGESBECKIA *Siegesbeckia pubescens* Hsi-chien-tsao	Herb	Analgesic, anti-rheumatic
SILER *Siler divaricatum* Fang-feng	Root	Anti-pyretic, analgesic
SMILAX *Smilax china* Tu-fu-ling	Root	Alterative, diuretic in syphilis, gout, skin disorders, rheumatism. (See **HERB CHART**)

Chinese Medicinal Herbs COMMON NAME *Scientific Name* Chinese Name	Parts Used	Medicinal Uses
SOJA *Glycine max* Tan-tou-shih	Preparation	Anti-pyretic
SOPHORA *Sophora flavescens* Ku-sheng	Root	Bitter stomachic, astringent in dysentery, intestinal disorders
STAR ANISE *Illicium verum* Pa-chiao-hui-shiang	Fruit	Stomachic, stimulant
STEMONA *Stemona sessilifolia* Pai-pu	Root	Anti-tussive, lice-killer
STEPHANIA *Stephania tetranda* Fang-chi	Root	Anti-pyretic, diuretic, analgesic for arthritis, low back or muscular pain
SULFUR Processed mineral sulfur Liu-huang	Mineral	Vermicide, laxative
TANG-KUEI *Angelica sinensis* Tang-kuei	Root	Emmenagogue, sedative, analgesic
TANG-SHENG *Codonopsis tangshen* Tang-sheng	Root	Tonic in anemia, chronic intestinal inflammation and weak stomach tone
TEA *Thea sinensis* Hsi-cha	Leaves	Cardiotonic, central nerve stimulant, diuretic, intestinal astringent
TERMINALIA *Terminalia chebula* Ho-tzu	Fruit	Astringent, hemostatic, anti-diarrheic, anti-tussive

Chinese Medicinal Herbs COMMON NAME *Scientific Name* Chinese Name	Parts Used	Medicinal Uses
TETRAPANAX *Tetrapanax papyrifera* Tung-tsao	Pith	Diuretic, lactagogue
THLASPI *Thlaspi arvense* Pai-chiang	Herb	Anti-pyretic, detoxifier, improve circulation, dispel pus, expectorant, diaphoretic
TOKORO *Dioscorea sativa* Pi-hsieh	Root	Diuretic
TRAPA *Trapa natans* Ling-chueh	Fruit	Tonic, anti-pyretic
TRIBULUS *Tribulus terrestris* Chi-li	Fruit	Tonic, astringent
TRICHOSANTHES ROOT *Trichosanthes kirilowii* Kua-lou	Root	Anti-pyretic
TRICHOSANTHES SEED *Trichosanthes kirilowii* Kua-lou-tzu	Seed	Anti-tussive, expectorant, emollient for skin swellings
TSAO-KO *Amomum tsao-ko* Tsao-ko	Fruit	Digestive, expectorant
TSAO-TOU-KOU *Alpinia katsumadai* Tsao-tou-kou	Seed	Stomachic
TUHUO *Angelica laxiflora* Tu-huo	Root	Anti-spasmodic, analgesic, diaphoretic, diuretic

Chinese Medicinal Herbs **COMMON NAME** *Scientific Name* **Chinese Name**	**Parts Used**	**Medicinal Uses**
TUMERIC *Curcuma aromatica* Chiang-huang	Rhizome	Dispel effused blood, emmenagogue, analgesic
VISCUM *Viscum album* Hu-chi-seng	Entire plant	Lowers blood pressure, lactagogue, anti-inflammatory
VITEX *Vitex rotundifolia* Mian-ching-tzu	Fruit	Sedative, analgesic
WHEAT *Triticum aestivum* Fu-hsiao-mai	Fruit	Sedative, anti-pyretic
WISTERIA *Wisteria florabunda* Tzu-teng-liu	Gall	Stomachic, anti-inflammatory
WU-TOU *Aconite carmichaeli* Wu-tou	Root	Anti-spasmodic, sedative, analgesic
XANTHIUM *Xanthium strumarium* Tsang-erh-tzu	Fruit	Anti-pyretic, anti-spasmodic, diaphoretic
ZANTHOXYLUM *Zanthoxylum piperitum* Chuan-chiao	Fruit	Stimulant, tonic, stomachic, carminative, diuretic
ZANTHOXYLUM *Zanthoxylum simulans* Chiao-mu	Seed	Diuretic, edema and swelling
ZIZYPHUS *Zizyphus jujube* Suan-tsao-jen	Seed	Nutrient tonic, sedative, insomnia, neurasthenia

organitoons

ANIMAL TESTING DOESN'T WORK
FOR ANIMALS OR HUMANS!

CHAPTER XIII

Love Thy Neighbor

Or

Animal Testing May Be Hazardous To Your Health

The world is not a series of fragmented subjects to be studied but is part of the entire universe of which man is both part and whole. Fragmentation and scientific experimentation cause us to lose sight of the validity of our own thinking.

Hermann Hesse

If a group of beings from another planet were to land on earth, beings who considered themselves as superior to you as you feel yourself to be to other animals, would you concede them the rights over you that you assume over the other animals?

George Bernard Shaw

I was first made aware of animal testing as a boy when I read Bernard Shaw, but not until later, as an adult, did I realize through my research while writing a biographical drama about Shaw (to be published soon) that the England of the late 1880's was not much different than England and America of the early 1980's. The senseless animal torture that goes on in the name of science is only questioned by the most unique thinkers and superior individuals, and today, just as before, they alone still speak and write against this.

For Shaw the 1880's were made up of concern for animal rights, but also human rights, including women's rights and the rights of the poor. Today in my 1980's, all these same things still exist, but many of us also have a profound concern for nuclear and chemical contamination that has so nearly accomplished the devastation of the planet; therefore, I add these rights to Shaw's list: the right to a clean, peaceful, chemical-free planet. Obviously, we are too late to put right what we've already done to our earth, but it isn't absolutely too late to set new standards, new priorities. Because I am an optimist, I believe we will do this. This keeps me going and keeps me writing and gabbing to anybody who will listen. My voice is not as dynamic as Shaw's in his day, but today there aren't many well-known individuals who are as outspoken and eloquent as he was. Shaw consistently put his reputation on the line for every issue he pursued, not because he felt secure in his position as a popular dramatist, but because of his feelings, his humane instincts. He did the same thing for women's rights, poverty, war, and social reform, and many times he was vehemently criticized for doing so. Then and now, many people consider him either a crackpot or an ignorant "big mouth" or a cynic; however, he was none of these. He was, in fact, more knowledgeable of the evils he criticized than those who were directly involved; just as today, most men and women who seek to make the dangers of animal testing clear to the public know more about the science of that dubious work than the people torturing and mistreating the animals in the name of science.

Greg Tozian, a correspondent for *Organica News* in Europe, interviewed members of Parliament in London and members of the BUAV (British Union for the Abolition of Vivisection). Parliament member Roger Gale defended animal testing by saying, "There are some people who'd like to see a unilateral ban on all animal experiments. There are woolly-headed idealists who say the LD/50 test is not effective. Well, the Lethal Dose 50 test may not be particularly humane. But where do you stop? The LD/49 . . . the LD/48, right on down to one? Some people want to stop all toxicity testing. But it's not practical. If you buy a tube of lipstick and your toddler eats it, because two-year-olds are wont to do these things, and the lipstick is toxic, then that child dies. You're not going to buy a product that says, "This product not properly tested." And at the moment, there's no toxicity test that is effective that doesn't use animals" (Greg Tozian, "Organica in Europe," *Organica*, Vol. 5, No. 17, 1986).

This quote is wrong in every way possible and points to the scare tactics used by animal experimenters. First, animal testing is NOT proper testing because it only establishes the "safe to sell" limits for the chemical being tested. It cannot establish an amount of chemical that is safe for all people all the time, or even some people some of the time; the numbers scribbled on the testing sheet represent only a twisted economic shorthand to satisfy manufacturers, chemical buyers, and bureaucrats. The description of the toddler eating the tube of lipstick has NOTHING to do with animal testing: it's a classic example of the scare tactics used by those who push animal testing. The child survived because it didn't have a toxic reaction to the chemical mix, not because it was made safe through animal testing. Those same animal tests, as you will read in this chapter, contributed to the death of those toddlers when these supposedly effective tests said that hexachlorophene was "safe," and those same animal tests caused death and horrible birth defects when thalidomide was considered safe due to animal tests. The "woolly-heads" that Mr. Gale speaks of are himself, and he is, in fact, though not an idealist, a neophyte in the deathly cause-and-effect brought on by animal testing.

The most absurd thing Mr. Gale said, however, was that "you'd go a long way to find a lab technician in this country [England] who would let an animal suffer." How very, very silly! That's exactly what animal testing does: torture and then kill. The reporter (Tozian) didn't let Mr. Gale off the hook, however; he asked him what he thought of the BUAV's successful legal action against the British government's Royal College of Surgeons in which the RCS was found guilty of causing unnecessary suffering to a monkey under the noses of governmental inspectors. Gale responded that this abuse was the exception to the rule. This is a spokesperson in London in 1986, not Shaw's London of 1886, and the animal testing continues. In fact, the BUAV points out that there's an estimated three and one-half million animals used in lab experiments in the United Kingdom every year to unleash thirty to forty thousand drugs on the market of which only two hundred and twenty are of any real benefit. ("Every Six Seconds An Animal Dies in A British Laboratory," *BUAV Newsletter*, London, 1986).

Animal testing is NOT the only method of testing, and there are more effective tests. This chapter is dedicated to Shaw and the many others who decry this inhumane practice.

This is a hard chapter to write. It isn't hard to write for want of facts. The facts on animal testing are disturbing and horrendous to normal humans. It isn't hard to write because I can't write how I feel about it. All the blood-curdling details can be obtained from the various animal rights and anti-vivisection societies, and these horrific facts I have known since I was old enough to understand what animal testing really meant. No, this chapter is hard to write because it forces me to reconcile conflicting memories of myself as the science student seeking approval and the unspoiled child who encountered cruelty and indifference in an educational system he had been taught to revere.

My exposure to vivisection began, as it does for many young people, with my first biology class. Every young person comes to the requirement of cutting up a frog in order to pass biology even though this senseless act teaches no biology, and the time would be much better spent learning a reverence for life instead of an obvious irreverence for living things to prove yourself worthy of a passing grade. I got an A in biology and indeed, throughout a portion of my life I followed this example by reading and accepting all kinds of animal tests to set forth this theory or that theory because it was expected for the grade and for approval. Yes, I got that first A in biology. I did cut up the frog. I did label everything. I had no difficulty doing it. I got the A, but I learned nothing about biology doing it.

This first lesson was not a lesson concerning anatomy, unlike what we are told. Anatomy is already well-established and illustrated in excellent texts on the subject, and there are even motion picture films from which one can learn anatomy before actually taking a class on this subject at university. Even though I did not feel right about cutting up the frog, even though I knew it was wrong inside myself (in my heart, which scientists agree exists, and in my soul, which scientists have proven to their satisfaction does not exist), even though it was detestable, even though it was intellectually demeaning, I did it. Getting the A, after all, meant approval and entrance to the world of science which I intensely desired. My peers would approve; my instructor would approve; my parents would approve, and this was the only way I could see to progress to greater scientific knowledge; nonetheless, inside, I did not feel right about it. Yes, inside my heart, inside my "non-existent soul" and inside my mind, I knew it was wrong.

I remember the days leading up to that biology class. Some boys were quiet about it (as I was). Some laughed gleefully and taunted the girls: "Tomorrow we cut up the frog. Yeah, tomorrow you're going to pass out or throw up." Some worried if they could do it the way the teacher wanted to get a good grade. I don't recall a single person saying, "Why are we doing this?" I know I didn't say it because if you were a boy and said you didn't want to cut up the frog, or even were to question it, you were labeled a sissy or even a "homo" as some boys suggested. On one level, this butchering of the frog was a rite of passage that demonstrated to me that we humans were more powerful than animals, that we could, and indeed, could be required to injure another living being, and that we could be ostracized for NOT doing so; on another level, this act of cutting up the frog showed that this was what scientists did, and this was how they were supposed to learn things. A "true scientist" cuts up the frog, I learned, because he is told to do so, but also because he can.

This is why this chapter is hard to write, because most scientists have learned to compromise, to accept, and to believe that animal testing is accurate and scientific. They have not grown beyond the first day of dissecting the frog. They have not been able to join the ranks of the greatest scientists and thinkers of our day and, indeed, of past centuries as well: Leonardo da Vinci, Voltaire, Johann Wolfgang von Goethe, Ferdinand Schiller, Arthur Schopenhauer, Victor Hugo, Henrik Ibsen, Richard Wagner, Alfred Tennyson, John Ruskin, Leo Tolstoy, Cardinals Manning and Newman, Mark Twain, G. B. Shaw, Mahatma Gandhi, C. G. Jung, Clare Booth Luce, Albert Einstein, Albert Schweitzer, Sigmund Freud, Joseph Wood Krutch, Nancy Newhall, J. A. Rush, Anna Kingsford, Hans Ruesch, E. B. de Condillac, Mary Wollstonecraft, Rachel Carson, Jeremy Bentham, Charles Darwin, Tom Regan, Mary and Percy Shelley, St. Francis of Assisi, Richard Serjeant, St. Jerome, William Blake, Samuel Butler, Cleveland Amory, Susan B. Anthony, Elizabeth Stanton, Horace Greeley, Lord Shaftsbury,

Henry S. Salt, Henry Bergh, Jean-Jacques Rousseau . . . the list is too long to go on, but there is no doubt that these men and women (and so many others) are better examples of great scientists and thinkers than the likes of J. H. Draize, the inventor of the Draize test, which is a completely unscientific and misleading test as to the safety of chemicals in cosmetics when they come in contact with the eye.

Now I will make the statement that will single me out as being a non-scientist and will make animal-testing scientists label me, if they are kind and patronizing, as "out of my discipline," or, if they are unkind, as " a stupid, superstitious vitalist." I accept their labels (whatever they are), and here is my statement:

ANIMAL TESTING DOES NOT WORK. IT IS OFTEN A "PUT-UP JOB." IT NEVER PROVES ANY SUBSTANCE IS SAFE TO BE USED BY HUMANS OR OTHER ANIMALS. ANIMAL TESTING IS NOT ONLY INHUMANE, IMMORAL, AND UNSCIENTIFIC, BUT ALSO THE LOWEST FORM OF GREED AND EGOTISM.

Some years ago after I cut up the frog I read an article by Bernard Shaw in which he said that laboratory experiments on animals were "put-up jobs." He described the Russian experimenter Pavlov and his treatise on conditioned reflexes using dogs as follows:

"Pavlov's book told of experiments where Pavlov had cut half the brains of several dogs out, and he pierced their cheeks and dragged their tongues through them to study salivation. He tortured and frustrated the dogs until their discomfort and misery left them dead or of no use. And from twenty-five years of this sort of thing all that the world would learn was how a dog behaved with half its brains out, which nobody wanted to know, and what was perhaps more important, what sort of book a psychologist could write having any brains at all! The press gravely applauded Pavlov's discovery that a dog's mouth watered when it heard the dinner bell. If the fellow had come to me I could have given him the same information in less than twenty-five seconds without tormenting one single dog."

Shaw made this statement in 1880, after H. G. Wells had written an impassioned eulogy on Pavlov's treatise. Wells was angry at Shaw's logical analysis and declared that if he were standing on a pier in a storm with Shaw and Pavlov struggling in the waves, and he, Wells, had only one lifebuoy to throw to them, he would throw it to Pavlov and not to Shaw. This Wellsian statement so amused Shaw that he stated he was concerned about this because Pavlov had taken the unpardonable liberty of presenting such a personal resemblance to himself that their photographs were indistinguishable, and there was a very good chance that Wells would throw the lifebuoy to the wrong person, thereby saving the anti-vivisector instead of the vivisector (Hesketh Pearson, *GBS: A full Length Portrait*, New York City: Harper & Brothers, 1942).

Actually, in fairness to Wells, Shaw pointed out that he first came to the realization that laboratory experiments were "put-up jobs" through reading Well's early novel, *Love and Mr. Lewisham*, in which the hero of the book claimed to be a genuinely scientific discoverer because his laboratory was the world, where he could not control the events nor manufacture the cases, whereas the laboratory researchers did nothing else except cook the expected results, or suppressed them when they were not the intended results.

At the time when Shaw attacked the lab experimenters he was labeled hopelessly unscientific (even by his friends H. G. Wells, Sir Almroth Wright, and J. B. Haldane), and he made matters worse when he came to the defense of Frances Power-Cobbe, who had written a book on the horrors of vivisection, which had been attacked by an eminent medical vivisector as containing errors. Shaw replied, "The question is not whether or not the book contains errors. If you knew anything about science you would know that no book ever published, including the Bible and all the scientific treatises, is free from errors, or ever will be. The question is whether or not you are a scoundrel: that is, a person who acts without regard to moral laws."

The vivisectors and animal experimenters, and most of today's scientists, contend that moral considerations are not pertinent, if through animal testing human disease can be eliminated, but is this the real reason for animal testing? Absolutely not.

Many, many synthetic substances--among them drugs, cosmetics, food additives, and household cleansers--are approved for use through animal testing, with tests like the LD/50 in which animals are force-fed the substance under scrutiny until they die. Then the amount in proportion to the body weight is dutifully recorded and distributed in technical sheets by the manufacturer. This kind of testing in no way duplicates everyday human use: it's so blatantly, to quote Shaw, a put-up job. Coal tar dyes (discussed in Chapter Ten) used in foods, drugs, and cosmetics are an excellent example of the fallacy of this process. The original safety standards for these colors were based on--you guessed it--animal tests. The colors were certified and declared safe, but time has proven, of course, that they are not. Yet, as with so many of the products and chemicals being tested today, the real consideration is not, and should have never been whether or not these colors are safe based on animal tests, but whether or not we need them at all! Is it important to color a cosmetic pink, a lollypop red, a soda pop green if it's lime-flavored and yellow if it's lemon? Is it important to color dog food or baby food? The thought process behind artificial colors has nothing to do with whether they are safe or not: it's completely economic, and the animal tests performed with these colors only certify to manufacturers that they are *safe to sell.*

The Public Citizen Health Research Group (PCHRG) announced in their newsletter and press releases dated December 17, 1984, that the same dyes that were once found safe in animal tests were not safe and were a danger to the public. For example, FD & C Red No. 3 caused thyroid tumors, chromosomal damage, and allergic reactions; FD & C Yellow No. 5 caused allergic reactions, thyroid tumors, lymphocytic lymphoma, and chromosomal damage . . . on and on the list goes about the dangers of the FD & C and D & C dyes. Weren't these colors already proven safe and yet here was another test to prove they were not safe?

I am sorry to say, as much as I know these chemicals are dangerous and do not belong in our drugs, foods, or cosmtics, that even the tests presented by the PCHRG are animal tests and therefore not only unscientific but immoral. Even the well-meaning PCHRG falls into the trap of the young biology student cutting up the frog to get his A and his approval; they turn to the animal tests to have the dyes removed from the market that were put there by animal testing to begin with. The trap is obvious: another test by another group of scientists who favor the dye makers or the FDA or CTFA will have animal tests to show that the PCHRG animal tests are wrong. It is sad but true that we begin to believe in the validity of these senseless unscientific animal tests, and what is worse, we believe that they mean that something is safe to eat, drink, or rub on our skin or into our hair.

Many years ago a chemical called hexachlorophene was presented as "safe to use" with animal tests, and this chemical became commonly used as a germicide agent in soaps, cleaners, shampoos, etc. One of the soaps containing this chemical was used on infants in a hospital: some became brain-damaged, and some died due to this chemical which was subsequently removed from the market. The key to these animal tests was that this chemical was declared safe, but in reality it was only *safe to sell*, not safe to use. Thalidomide is one of the most dramatic examples of the stupidity of believing in animal testing. The animal testers declared that it was the most harmless tranquilizer in the whole history of modern therapeutics. After three years of animal tests thalidomide was put on the market (*Time Magazine*, February 23, 1962). Thalidomide was invented by a pharmaceutical company in West Germany, and they declared that the animal tests had been particularly thorough and extensive, and it was described as the best medicament for pregnant women and breast-feeding mothers because it could damage neither mother nor child. Results: 10,000 children or more born throughout the world deformed;

some with fin-like hands, stunted or missing limbs; deformed eyes and ears; lung disease; and a great many died shortly after birth. When the first few cases of damage due to this drug appeared, the animal tests resumed but didn't confirm the suspicion, and made researchers believe that the drug was safe, and it continued to be sold and used. Many researchers force-fed the drug to dogs, cats, mice, rats, and as many as 150 strains and substrains of rabbits. It was safe, they said. One strain of white New Zealand rabbit was tested and had a few malformed babies, and eventually a few malformed monkeys appeared. What did the researchers think of this? They immediately pointed out that malformations, like cancer, *could be obtained by administration of practically any substance in high concentration, including sugar and salt, which will eventually upset the organism, causing trouble* [Editor's italics].

After a long criminal trial (over two years) the pharmaceutical company was acquitted. Many medical authorities appeared at the trial to say that animal tests could never be conclusive for human beings. The medical authorities making this statement had built their careers and reputations based on animal experimentation, including the testimony of 1945 Nobel laureate biochemist Ernst Boris Chain, who co-discovered penicillin with Fleming and Florey. Professor Widukind Lenz, who had conducted thalidomide tests on primates who subsequently delivered malformed offspring, testified that there was no animal test capable of indicating that human beings would react in an identical fashion to the animal tested (Hans Ruesch, *Slaughter of the Innocent*, New York: CIVITAS Publications, 1978)).

Because animal tests do not prove a chemical is safe to use, only that it is safe to sell, they are irredeemably an economic consideration rather than a scientific one. For example, the first thing a chemical salesperson does when he or she calls on a manufacturer is to show the tech sheet showing the animal tests that have been conducted to demonstrate that the chemical is safe, or that it has certain attributes that you can use as a sales pitch in marketing products. The chemical is safe to sell . . . safe to advertise . . . safe to hype . . . but no animal tests address themselves to the issue of whether it is safe for humans to use in their everyday lives, or even if it will perform as claimed. The claims made for all manner of things from vitamins to foods to drugs to cosmetics are usually based on animal tests which are not only unscientific but can, in some cases, be as dangerous to you as the tests were to the animals experimented on. Remember, the researcher is paid by the manufacturer, and this relationship does not always produce unbiased results. Even if the researcher is honest, the animal tests don't work and therefore are not only unreliable but dangerous.

In October 1984, John Hopkins University conducted a two-day seminar that stated that live animals were unnecessary to toxicity testing. To most of us, this is obvious. Evidently there are some who still believe that animal testing is necessary, even in view of the relative lack of success these tests give which means that more and more animals must be used to supposedly prove a medical or chemical point that a substance is safe. The animal testers who feel that the variability of toxicity responses of rodents with humans and that the phylogenic differences between rodents and humans compromise toxicity testing turn to increased numbers of animal tests or the use of animals of a higher phylla such as dogs, cats, pigs, and primates. What this tells us is that there is none so stupid as the animal testers and their advocates. They have learned nothing from the tragedy of hexachlorophene or thalidomide it would seem, but that is not the case. To even accept these tragic incidents is to say animal testing not only doesn't work but is a danger to humanity.

Another form of testing that is being is developed is called *in vitro*, which translated literally means "in the glass" or "test tube." One ocular irritancy test is currently available from the Preventive Diagnostics Corporation. The researcher simply mixes his chemical or product into a clear solution (trade name EZ-I-TOX); if the solution becomes cloudy, it indicates that irritancy is possible. The company claims 84-90% correlation with the Draize animal test.

Another *in vitro* test for skin irritancy was introduced at the December 1982 Society of Cosmetic Chemists (SCC) meeting in New York by Dr. Shigeru Yamamoto (director of the Yamamoto Skin Clinic in Osaka, Japan). Dr. Yamamoto pointed out that cosmetic ingredients (including petrolatum) which show gene-damaging potential are most likely to produce irritation or allergy on human skin. Gene damage, he stated, is directly proportional to the peroxide content of fats and oils; therefore, skin irritation also increases in proportion to the peroxide content. Dr. Yamamoto claimed he was able to prevent such irritancy with petrolatum with a refining process he developed, by repeatedly passing the substance through activated charcoal. To evaluate the cosmetic ingredients he used and the results of his refining methods, he used *in vitro* testing, no animal tests. We are pleased that Dr. Yamamoto is not using animal tests, but find it amazing that anybody would bother to attempt to "refine" a mineral oil product that can cause gene damage and allergic reactions when there are other oils that cause none of these allergic reactions in most humans. Nevertheless, only as the results of researchers such as Dr. Yamamoto become accepted will truly safe skin-irritancy testing techniques develop.

"Alternative" is the word attached to procedures like *in vitro* and other non-animal forms of product testing, and this word bothers me. It isn't because I'm not in favor of these procedures. I certainly am, and I hope they progress and improve. The ethical reasons in favor of *in vitro* testing is obvious, but it is far superior scientificially as well. There is far less chance of error when non-animal tests are conducted, and much greater accuracy when individual cells are scrutinized for mutations rather than when junk is shoved down a helpless animal's throat (as in the LD/50 test) or dripped in a rigidly held rabbit's eyes. The reason why this word "alternative" bothers me is that it suggests that animal testing works and that we must therefore find an "alternative," that non-animal testing is a sort of side road from the mainstream, accepted, tried-and-true formula for our health and general safety. The truth is that animal testing was not used by Hippocrates, father of Western medicine and the author of the oath that's on every doctor's wall. Hippocrates instead advocated hygiene and a simple diet, both of which strengthen the natural immune power of the body to heal itself. His motto was: *Vis suprema guaritrix*: nature is the supreme healer. Hygiene and diet are modes of therapy that were later neglected when Galen, a passionate vivisector, and his treatises became the only medical authority the medieval church would accept. Galen's misconceptions, such as his dismissal of hygiene as pagan superstition and the poisonous nature of fruit, which are based on his experiments with live animals, contributed to poor health in Western civilization for over fifteen centuries. Further, our current "vogue" of animal testing was pre-dated by thousands of years of medical knowledge and research in Asia, India, and the Middle East, yet we generally choose not to benefit from that knowledge. It's presumptuous of us to think that our modern age of Western medicine is more humane, more scientific, and more devoted to progress than any previous one, and for every advancement the vivisector can claim is due to his "speciality" I can point to a dozen disasters it has caused. The purpose of finding other testing methods is because **animal testing does not work; it has failed; it is dangerous and unacceptable.** Instead of establishing a scientific standard for non-animal forms of testing to imitate ("alternative"), animal testing is the dead-end back alley off the road to medical progress from which we must return.

The true scientist has a saying which is part of the scientific method: if it doesn't work once, then it doesn't work at all. This is as important as the pure scientist who discovers without any pre-conceived ideas. Animal testing has failed enough, damaged enough human and non-human animals, released into our environment chemicals that have done irretrievable damage, and built within the soul of the physician a lack of sensitivity to pain, suffering, and death to make it the worst possible form of scientific measure.

"The spiritual malady which rages in the soul of the vivisector is in itself sufficient to render him incapable of acquiring the highest and best knowledge. He finds it easier to propogate and multiply disease than to discover the secret of health. Seeking for the germs of life, he invents only death."
-Anna Kingsford, Britain's first female physician.

There are no lower or higher animals. It seems to me that the most brilliant men and women throughout history have been aware of this, just as every species is aware that the term "animalistic" more easily fits man than almost any other creature. The chemicalization of our land, water, air, and our cruelty to animals in the name of scientific advancement is the reason other animals fear man. We are not content with the destruction of our earth and our animal neighbors so we are now planning to take our war machines into space. I cannot help but feel that this hunger for destructive devices to aim at our own species, with whom we cannot communicate, is somehow linked to the chemicalization, the animal experimentation, and the total disregard of the natural order that our greed and avarice has unleashed. The true link to survival is our link to nature and the entire animal kingdom: preserving this is the way to preserve our own lives.

Sometimes when I am sitting quietly with my dog I wonder what he thinks, as man's best friend, of the lack of friendship we show each other and our animal neighbors. Jesus said that the meek would inherit the earth. If what He says is true, only the other species will survive. I hope it will change.

ORGANIZATIONS DEDICATED TO THE ETHICAL TREATMENT OF ANIMALS

Friends of Animals, Inc.
11 West 60th Street
New York, New York 10023

Society for Animal Rights
900 First Avenue
New York, New York 10022

United Action for Animals
205 East 42nd Street
New York, New York 10017

American Anti-Vivisection Society
1903 Chestnut Street
Philadelphia, Pennsylvania 19103

The Fund for Animals, Inc.
140 West 5th Street
New York, New York 10019

American Vegetarians
Post Office Box 5424
Akron, Ohio 44313

American Vegan Society
Box H
Malaga, New Jersey 08328

Animal Liberation, Inc.
319 West 74th Street
New York, New York 10023

Vegetarian Activist Collective
616 - 6th Street
Brooklyn, New York 11215

Beauty Without Cruelty*
175 West 12th Street
New York, New York 10012

Argus Archives
228 East 49th Street
New York, New York 10017

National Anti-Vivisection Society
100 East Ohio Street
Chicago, Illinois 60611

People for the Ethical Treatment of Animals
P. O. Box 42516
Washington, D. C. 2000

*Not to be confused with "Beauty Without Cruelty Cosmetics," a U. S. cosmetic manufacturer.

IN THE UNITED KINGDOM

Royal Society for the Prevention of Cruelty to Animals
105 Jermyn Street
London, SW1

Farm and Food Society
4 Willifield Way
London, NW11 7XT

Compassion in World Farming
Copse House
Greatham
Liss, Hampshire

National Anti-Vivisection Society
51 Harley Street
London W1N 1DD

The Scottish Society for the Prevention of Vivisection
10 Queensferry Street
Edinburgh EG2 4Pg
SCOTLAND

Fund for the Replacement of Animals in Medical Experiments (FRAME)
312A Worple Road
Wimbledon, London SW20 8QU

The Vegetarian Society
Parkdale, Dunham Road
Altrincham, Cheshire,
& 53 Marloes Road
Kensington, London W8.

The Vegan Society
47 Highlands Road
Leatherhead, Surrey

Beauty Without Cruelty*
1 Calverley Park
Tunbridge Wells
Kent TN1 2SG

British Union for the Abolition of Vivisection
16A Crane Grove
Islington, London N78LB

CHAPTER XIV

Preservatives

Or

Nothing Lasts Forever

Preservatives are deadly by definition because they attempt to interrupt the life cycle which naturally ends in decay. They're deadly, too, because they're part of the synthetic mind set that says we're above nature; we can control nature; we know more than nature. They're deadly because they lull us, with their co-conspirators, colors and fragrances, into believing preserved products have been protected from putrefaction, but this of course is not true: the decaying process goes on because THIS IS A NATURAL PROCESS. In cosmetics a combination of color, fragrance, and preservative covers up the obvious indications of this decay. The color hides the visual decay; the perfume hides both the chemical smells and the smell of degrading due to the bacterial growth. The preservative slows the process of decay--but nothing can stop it.

From the sarcophagi of the pharaohs to the pristine bottles of shampoo stored in the warehouse year after year after year, the use of preservatives demonstrates our unsuccessful effort to conquer the microorganism and our unwillingness to accept death. Yes, I'm getting a little philosophical here because the use of preservatives is so pervasive that no one has ever stopped to think why we have them and what they're supposed to be doing, and before I can explain how preservatives are toxic, we must realize why they are toxic. In the case of preservatives this is especially important because preservatives don't work: they do not protect us from microorganisms because there are more microorganisms than there are us, and we'd all be dead from chemical intervention long before there was an end to the infinitely adaptable microorganism.

This is one time when I will not begin by saying "natural" is better than "synthetic". Both natural and synthetic preservatives are deadly because if they weren't, they wouldn't be doing their job. Natural preservatives are, as I discuss below, not as strong or as toxic as synthetic ones; in a natural formulation, I believe they are far superior. The ideal situation would be, of course, to use no preservatives, but we do not live in an ideal world, but rather a compromised world where we must choose what degree of compromise we can tolerate. We must, however, understand the choices.

Many naturally-oriented consumers have a double standard about preservatives: on the one hand, they'll buy foods with the words "NO PRESERVATIVE" on the labels, and they will religiously shun BHA or BHT (synthetic antioxidants) when they show up on labels as food additives. Yet, on the other hand, if they read in a book that BHT may extend their lifespan, they'll buy it straight up in pill form. Similarly, they will demand all-natural cosmetics but then anxiously suggest synthetic preservatives to keep them from "going bad."

We're told preservatives are necessary for three reasons: 1) because they're safe to use in foods, drugs, and cosmetics; 2) because they're the most effective way to limit microbial growth in products; and 3) because they're necessary to protect us from microorganisms. None of these three statements are true. First, the tests are animal tests and are therefore inconclusive for humans (the tests never prove safety). Second, preservatives are NOT effective. They don't stop microbial growth, and they build up a false belief in consumers and manufacturers alike that products will last forever. Third, the chemicals used to preserve are more toxic than the bacteria they're supposed to kill, and more harm has been caused due to chemical reactions than to bacterial contamination.

To give you a little historical background--preservatives go back thousands of years. In fact, the first preservatives were not thought of as "preserving" but rather as "cleansing" and "disinfecting" substances. Thus soap is the first preservative because it has been used for over 4500 years. The first preservatives, however, were probably mercury compounds (sublimates), whose use dates back to 2637 B. C, and herbal alcohols such as benzyl alcohol (a constituent of jasmine), but, like soap, these natural chemicals were not thought of as "preservatives" but as "cleansing" and later "disinfecting." In 1774 chlorine, a powerful disinfectant, was discovered, followed by sodium hypochlorite in 1789 and chlorine dioxide in 1925. Iodine was first discovered in 1812 and used in 1816. Phenol was discovered in 1842 and used in 1867; the discovery of three phenolic compounds followed: cresol (1842), chlorocresol (1906), and bis-Phenols (1906). Although sodium benzoate was introduced in 1875, its chemical relations, PHB esters and phenylmercuric compounds, were not used as preservatives until 1924 and 1936 respectively. Quaternary ammonium compounds were first described in 1856 and used in 1916. Though formaldehyde was described in 1867 it was not used until the first of the century (1900). Sorbic acid was first used in 1939, and chlorhexidine in 1954.

Animal toxicity evaluation of preservatives supposedly screen for two types of toxicity: local and systemic. These tests have failed. However, using their own animal tests, I will discuss the safety of some of the preservatives and demonstrate the discrepancy between animal tests and human tests. These substances were tested by the Draize Test on rabbits and humans for twenty-one days under Saran Wrap to arrive at the threshold of irritation. The values given for irritation are 1 (most irritating) to 12 (least irritating). Salicyclic acid was 3 for humans, and 1 and 2 for rabbits (this is very similar); benzoic acid was 2 for humans and 1 and 2 for rabbits (very irritating to both species); formaldehyde was 4 for humans and 10 and 8 for rabbits (far more irritating to humans); diethyltoluamide was 1 for humans and 3 for rabbits; triethanolamine scored 8 for humans and 9 and 7 for rabbits. As you can see, in some cases the humans had a greater irritation response (formaldehyde and diethyltoluamide) and sometimes less (salicyclic acid). Yet, what do these tests tell us? They tell us that these chemicals are irritating to the humans and rabbits tested. They tell us little else. According to this test, of which I am suspicious, formaldehyde was less irritating than benzoic acid, but simply look at these two chemicals yourself. Just smell them. Formaldehyde will almost knock you off your feet with just one whiff, but not benzoic acid, or for that matter, salicyclic acid. Can it be that formaldehyde is really the mildest of the three? I would hardly need tests to arrive at the fact that these chemicals are toxic. As a matter of fact, men and women who work with these materials know how strong they are from the smell alone. If formaldehyde is rated as a 4 and salicyclic acid as a 3, and benzoic acid as 2, then does this mean that formaldehyde, which is used to preserve cadavers from parasites, is the mildest, safest, and most desirable of the three? (M. Steinberg et al, "A Comparison of Test Techniques Based on Rabbit and Human Skin Responses to Irritants With Recommendations Regarding the Evaluation of Mildly or Moderately Irritating Compounds," in *Animal Models In Dermatology*, ed. H. I. Mailbach, New York: Churchill Livingston, 1975).

In previous chapters we have already pointed out the disastrous results (death and brain damage) of hexachlorophene (an antimicrobial preservative) to infants, but you can still find this substance in products; the registered trade names of this chemical include hexachlorophene, G-11, Hexosan, and Gamophene. This phenolic compound was tested with the classic animal tests and found safe to use, but we now know that it is not safe. What they did know at the time of testing was that it had a high absorption-resorption coefficient and accumulated in the *stratum corneum*; in other words, it could be easily absorbed into the skin and penetrate into the body and would build up in the outer layer of the skin. What they obviously didn't know was that it was neurotoxic to humans. The FDA now regulates its use, and here is how the EEC (European Economic Community) guidelines read: maximum dose for cosmetics is 0.1%, but not to be used in preparations for children, not to be used for intimate hygiene, not to be used for babies or children under the age of three years. The animal tests didn't protect the babies who died from the neurotoxicity so the "new guidelines" quoted here were based on human reactions, i. e., the babies who died or got brain damaged. In other words, because animal tests didn't work, the babies became the guinea pigs and were tested on without their consent. This may seem ghoulish, but this is how the system works, and no animal test can protect us from the specific toxic reactions of our own species. Further, since hexachlorophene, a phenolic compound, is dangerous, then aren't all the others a potential danger? If the preservative tends to be absorbed into the skin and collect in the *stratum corneum*, could there be potential dangers not appearing in animal studies, because animal studies didn't pick up the original danger with hexachlorophene? Here are other phenolic compounds used to preserve cosmetics, and you may be surprised at the chemicals you see on this list: amyl gallate, BHA, BHT, 2,5-di-tert-butyl hydroquinone, nordhydroguaiaretic acid (NDGA), butyl p-hydroxybenzoate, dihydroxyphenol, gallic acid, guaicol, methyl p-hydroxybenzoate, propyl gallate, propyl p-hydroxybenzoate, phenoxetol or phenonip (which is a trade name for a blend of phenoxetol and p-hydroxybenzoic acids), and the parabens (methyl paraben, ethyl paraben, propyl paraben, butyl paraben, and benzyl paraben). We don't often think of BHA and BHT as phenolic compounds, but they are classed as PHB esters, i. e., p-hydroxybenzoate esters. Through this, we can see that BHA and BHT, butyl, methyl, and propyl benzoic acids, and hexachlorophene are all linked because they are all phenolic compounds and all potentially harmful.

Cosmetic preservatives may be some of the most dangerous chemicals in this field, because they are required to work for a longer period than an ordinary disinfectant.

"Unlike disinfectants and many antiseptics, which may act quickly and powerfully, often against specific organisms, to accomplish their tasks in a short period of contact, preservatives must act steadily and effectively against a wide range of microorganisms over a long period of time. The fast kill of a successful antiseptic may, in fact, be a disadvantage for a cosmetic preservative because such lethal effects against microorganisms usually coincide with toxic or irritant properties toward all living tissues." (Rosen, W. E. and Berke, P. A. "Germall 115--A Safe and Effective Preservative." *Cosmetic and Drug Preservatives*, New York: Kabara and Dekker, Inc., 1984).

Perhaps, without knowing it, the writers quoted above were discussing the slow and long-range kill rather than the fast and immediate kill. First, it has not been established that any of the chemicals they discuss are safe, and to call the imidazolidinyl urea (Germall 115) a safe and effective preservative is more sales hype than science (but this is the problem with animal-tested products). Even if it is slightly more safe than the methyl and propyl paraben, for example, the recommendation is to include the parabens as helpful in the "slow, long-range" kill the writers suggest. It seems, in any case, a lot of chance-taking to protect a product.

The reason preservatives are added, we're told, is to protect the consumer from invisible disease-causing bacteria, but they're not very effective in performing this function. First, most microorganisms will not survive or propagate in a product, and if they do it will be obvious as the product will show this. When products become contaminated (especially with fungi) the growth begins on the edge of the cream, where separation takes place, and gradually spreads on top of the surface. This can happen in a matter of months as the product is being used, or it can occur on the shelf before the product is taken home.

But even if the "juice in the bottle" is completely free from microorganisms, there are "bugs" in the packaging. Although collapsible tubes and bottles with small openings have less bacteria than jars, flexible bottles, and products that are handled are easily contaminated. To assume that even a synthetically preserved product does not contain microorganisms is silly because they're already present in the caps that are put on the products. Even if the caps are submerged in alcohol there are microorganisms under the cap linings where the alcohol bath never goes.

Natural cosmetics are NOT more susceptible to microorganism invasion than synthetics. In a sense microorganisms feed on "synthetic junk" just as some humans do. In all cosmetics, it is usually the water phase that supports this growth. Oil-in-water products have been found to have a more pronounced growth of bacteria than the water-in-oil: the more water content, the more bacteria. Emulsions, then, will develop more microorganism growth than single phase systems. However, single phase, or non-emulsion products will also develop microorganism growth depending on pH, osmotic pressure, surface tension, and oxygen tension of the product.

A specific example of how microorganisms grow in synthetic, preserved products is "semi-natural" shampoos, many of which use synthetic surface-active-agents (surfactants) which support microorganism growth even in the presence of preservatives such as methyl and propyl paraben. The microorganisms are able to split ester linkages of some nonionic and anionic surfactants. It was believed that the chemical structure of these surfactants controlled susceptibility to attack by bacteria, but certain bacteria are able to oxidize terminal methyl groups to carboxyl groups. Alkyl sulphates, sulphonated fatty acids, amides, esters, polyethelene glycols derivaties and alkyl phenoxypolyoxyethanols are all attacked, sooner or later, by microorganisms (Yu-chih Hsu, *Nature*, 207:385, 1965).

The parabens have been held up by the various cosmetic manufacturers as the ideal preservatives. Remember, however, their safety has been "proven" only by animal tests, and there are allergic reactions to these preservatives even in tiny amounts. You will notice that many shampoos and soaps contain the parabens, even though they have been found to be incompatible with anionics, nonionics, and proteins. This means the parabens in a synthetic surfactant shampoo don't work (i. e., a shampoo that contains sodium lauryl sulfate, sodium laureth sulfate, etc.), and they will not work in any protein product. The other possibility is that they are used in much higher amounts than are claimed in order to be effective. Like many preservatives, they're also not safe since allergic reactions have been linked to the parabens. Gram-negative bacteria (the type of bacteria that may cause disease) have been found in cosmetics preserved with the parabens, so obviously the inclusion of the parabens may have appeared to protect the product, but obviously didn't protect either the product or the consumer (Goldman, C. L., *Drug, Cosmet. Ind.* 117:40, 1975). I have seen "natural" protein shampoos that contain the parabens as a preservative, but a combination like that neither works, nor is it "natural." Also, sooner or later, enlightened consumers realize they're being had with "half-natural" products and will no longer buy them. What's ironic in this situation is that these preservatives weren't doing their job to keep the products fresh, despite their major purpose to reassure the manufacturer.

Imidazolidinyl urea compounds, with the trade name Germall 115, were introduced in the early 1970's and heralded as, like the parabens, a safe and effective preservative. However, quite often Germall 115 is combined with methyl and propyl paraben. Most cosmetics that use all three mix 0.3% Germall 115, 0.2% methyl paraben, and 0.1% propyl paraben. The pattern we see here is yet another preservative that may or may not protect the product, that is called safe to the consumer (by animal tests which don't work), that is called much safer and more effective than the parabens, but what happens? It is mixed with the parabens to be effective, and instead of one unsafe, ineffective preservative, we have three.

Cell growth is a fact of nature and the ideal preservative does not exist, at least one that can be considered safe. The first requirement of any preservative is that it be free from toxic or irritant effect at the concentrations used on the skin, mucous membranes, and indeed, the gastro-intestinal system as well as the entire body, through the blood. After all, preservatives are absorbed into the body and often accumulate in the *stratum corneum* (see **HEXACHLORO-PHENE** above). A rash can occur due to this accumulation quite a bit later since the preservative is an allergen and a poison. If the preservative is so effective that it can destroy almost any bacteria, then obviously the beneficial bacteria on the skin can be destroyed. The effect of cosmetic preservatives on our immune system is not known, but we can't assume that a preservative is safe based on animal studies. What we can assume is that we are probably much safer and more healthy without the preservatives though the products may go bad. I have found, and indeed, time has shown that most of the natural preservatives found in plants are safe and not sensitizers to most people. They have always been present in nature and are therefore recognized by our immune system. The main argument against natural preservatives is that they aren't strong enough. Indeed, this is probably true, but then that is exactly why the natural and milder preservative is better.

I have for almost the past two decades prepared cosmetics without preservatives and with various natural preservatives. When I first began creating cosmetics in 1968, I used no preservatives at all, or at least, no substances as preservatives though some of the herbals used in the products had natural preservative qualities. At times the products would spoil and had to be replaced without charge to the consumer. This was a cost I had decided to bear in order to leave preservatives out of the products. I manufactured small batches and shipped directly to stores so that a product would not be warehoused. One amazing fact is that a shampoo I made contained no added preservatives at all (except those naturally in the herbals used), but it held up on the shelf just as well as shampoos which contained the parabens and even formaldehyde. I even ran tests on the shampoo against well-known brand shampoos that were mass-produced and the bacterial content was not any more pronounced than the synthetic shampoos with the preservatives. During the years that followed I got very few returns from spoiled products (less than 1%) and no returns for allergic reactions. This cannot be said of the preserved cosmetics, though it isn't simply the preservatives in the cosmetics that cause physical problems; it is also other chemicals that have nothing to do with preserving the product.

Some years later I had to make more different cosmetics, and I felt I had to preserve my products to protect the shelf life, but I didn't want a preservative that could possibly cause allergic reactions. I also wanted a natural preservative that I felt comfortable with using.

My friend, Dr. Jakob Harich, who is president of Chemie Research and Manufacturing Company, Inc., in Florida, sent me a sample of a natural preservative he had developed in South America from grapefruit seeds and the fruit itself. I was the first cosmetic researcher to begin testing Dr. Harich's unique natural product. He had told almost unbelievable stories about the powers of this simple oil. They were of a medical or physiological nature and not cosmetic. He was aware that I had already used large amounts of ascorbic acid (vitamin C) and tocopherols (vitamin E) to preserve cosmetics. I was also using citrus oils because they have antimicrobial activities. Lemon oil and lemon petitgrain oil also contain components in the waxes that have antioxidant properties. In the lemon oil is a chemical called benzanthracene which has microbial properties; lime oil also has these properties. Though these oils can be phototoxic and are even used to treat psoriasis, if the oil is distilled, it is non-sensitizing, non-irritating, and non-phototoxic.

Dr. Harich's grapefruit oil consists of 80% grapefruit seed oil and 20% grapefruit pulp. It is prepared with a complex infra-red and UV radiation process which retains the trace elements extracted from amino acid groups, ascorbic acid, peptides, fructose, glucose, sucrose, lactose, maltose, etc. I found it was an excellent preservative and, of course, far more natural than the parabens or other chemicals used to preserve cosmetics. I ran many tests on grapefruit seed extract (not animal tests) and found that it was not only compatible with natural ingredients and protein (which the parabens are not), but that it was not a sensitizer. I was able to utilize the grapefruit oils in my own natural preservative consisting of vitamins A, C, and E, combined with the other citrus extracts I was already using.

Although I was the first cosmetic compounder to use citrus seed extracts (including the simple but effective grapefruit seed extract), and it was apparent that formulas made in this way were successful and safe, few other cosmetic manufacturers used it. The few who did use it were more knowledgeable about my work and the general concept of natural cosmetic manufacturing. The Cosmetic, Toiletries, and Fragrance Association (CTFA) finally let the preservative be printed in their "recognition dictionary," though most cosmetic manufacturers still use the synthetic chemicals. I have never found the need for approval from the CTFA and only see their cosmetic ingredient dictionary as another reference work compiled from the technical sheets of chemical manufacturers. When you make natural products and are against artificial colors and animal torture (called testing), the CTFA can hardly be considered a friend.

There are many preservatives from nature that can be used to increase the shelf life of cosmetics, but there must first be a desire to create that kind of cosmetic. It's obviously a waste of money to put citrus seed extracts into a synthetic cosmetic, so you can say "no synthetic preservatives" if the rest of the product is largely synthetic. Worse, it gives the NO PRESERVATIVE-seeking consumers a false sense of security, while bombarding them with FD & C colors, synthetic detergents, and artificial fragrances. If the manufacturers' aim is to protect the consumer, they wouldn't include any of these substances.

A natural product should be natural. The use of preservatives has become the "label watch" for those who avoid chemicalization of their foods and cosmetics. Although there are other chemicals that are synthetic and damaging to our environment and ourselves, it seems the preservative must suffer the position of being the riskiest ingredient, which we have sadly found to be true. However, the consumer need not settle for the chemical additive or feel it's there for their protection because that isn't the reason. The preservative does not preserve you: it is there for economic purposes, for mass production and warehousing. To sell preservatives to consumers under any other auspices is to deceive them. Most cosmetics (with the exception of child-proof caps) are made today for dumb consumers who don't know enough to throw out a two year old half-used tube of moisturizer. It's unnatural to assume that things should last forever. Food spoils and we have to throw it out. The cosmetic may spoil, too, and we may have to throw it out. Just as a potato chip is better without BHA and BHT, so is a natural and organic cosmetic better without methyl and propyl paraben, formaldehyde, and hexachlorophene. Nothing lasts forever.

Glossary of Preservatives

ACETONE CHLOROFORM - The registered names for this preservative are chloreton, chlorbutol, methaform, and sedaform. This is an alcohol with a camphor-like odor. It is sold to cosmetic manufacturers as crystals. It is slightly soluble in water; very soluble in alcohol, propylene glycol, and glycerine. Propylene glycol is often used as a solubilizing agent for acetone crystals. **This chemical has acute oral toxicity.** Labels containing this product should have a warning: **Contains Chlorobutol.** Acetone can be absorbed into the skin and is a strong sensitizer. Many allergic reactions. Chemical Name: *1,1,1-Trichloro-2-methylpropane-2-ol.*

ADERMYKON - The registered names for this preservative are Mycil, Adermykon, Chlorphenesin, and Geophen. This is an alcohol that is supplied as a white crystalline powder. It has no odor. It is soluble in water (less than 1%), and propylene glycol (PG) is used to act as a solubilizer. It is synthesized by condensing equimolar amounts of *p-chlorophenol* and *glycidol* with *tertiary amine* or *quaternary ammonium salts.* It is considered a topical fungicide. It is used in amounts of 0.5% in cosmetics. It causes skin rashes, dry scaly skin, and allergic reactions. It is considered to be low in toxicity (animal tests). Chemical Name: *3-(4-Chlorophenoxy)-1,2-propanediol.*

ALKYLTRIMETHYLAMMONIUM BROMIDE - The registered trade names of this preservative are Arquad, Cetavlon, Cetab, Micol, and Dodigen 5594. This is a quaternary compound. It is supplied as crystals. It is soluble in water at 10% and completely soluble in alcohol. **This chemical is toxic.** It is inactive and incompatible in the presence of soaps, anionics, nitrates, metals, proteins, and blood. Often used in deodorants at about 0.05 to 0.1%. Chemical Name: *Alkyltrimethylammonium Bromide* and *Cetrimonium Bromide.*

ASCORBIC ACID - This is an organic acid known as vitamin C. It occurs naturally in many plants, especially citrus fruits. It can be used as a food and cosmetic preservative due to its antioxidant qualities. The fat-soluble form of vitamin C, ascorbyl palmitate, works better in emulsions and cosmetic oils than ascorbic acid, which is water-soluble. Ascorbic acid and ascorbyl palmitate are supplied as a white powder. Completely non-toxic. Topical use will not irritate the skin. Large amounts are needed to preserve some cosmetics, but this antioxidant works well when combined with tocopherols and vitamin A (which is known to improve the appearance of the skin and helps protect from viral and bacterial disease). The combination of ascorbic acid and ascorbyl palmitate protects both the water phase and oil phase of a cosmetic from microorganisms. Chemical Names: *Ascorbic acid* and *ascorbyl palmitate.*

BENZALKONIUM CHLORIDE - The registered trade names of this preservative are Zephirol, Roccal, Dodigen 226, and Barquat MB-50. This is a quaternary compound (cationic). It is supplied as a white or yellowish powder. It is very soluble in water (50%) and in alcohols. **This chemical has been shown to be highly toxic. It is a primary skin irritant. There are warnings not to breathe this powder into the lungs.** It is incompatible and inactive with anionics, soap, proteins, plastic, rubber, citrates, metals, and nitrates. It is used in hair conditioners (cationic type), in conditioning shampoos (cationic types), and deodorants (maximum amount used is 0.1% to 0.5%). Chemical Names: mixture of *Alklydimethylbenzylammonium chloride* and *N-dodecl-N,N-dimethylbenzylammonium chloride.*

BENZOIC ACID - The CTFA name for this preservative is benzoic acid or sodium benzoate. It was first described by H. Fleck in 1875, but has probably been used via the herb *benzoin* in earlier times. It is an organic acid found in nature in berries, roots, and herbs. It is supplied in tablet form or as a white powder. It is soluble in water (at 20° C.), and in alcohol. It is limited to an acid medium for antimicrobial activity. In oil-soluble emulsions benzoic acid separates from the water phase into the oil phase and only the amount left in the water phase is effective. There is a loss of activity in glycerols, so a solubilizing agent will probably not make it more effective in the water phase. It is not compatible and is inactive in proteins, gelatin, nonionics, and quaternary compounds. It is used as a preservative agents in foods (especially beverages) and in pharmaceuticals (acceptable daily intake is 0-5 mg/kg body weight per day. It is used in cosmetics as 0.1-0.2% with a maximum use of 0.5%. A toxic dose on the skin is 6 mg/kg. **Acute oral toxicity and skin irritations.** Lab animals have been murdered by feeding them 80 mg/kg in animal food over a three month period. Mice and rats have stunted growth by feeding them 40 mg/kg in food per day for seventeen months). Chemical Name: *Benaene carboxylic acid.*

BENZYL ALCOHOL - The CTFA name for this chemical is benzyl alcohol. This is a natural alcohol found in jasmine and other plants. It is soluble in water at 1 g to 25 ml water, in ethanol and 94% alcohol. It is supplied as a liquid and has a sharp burning taste. It slowly oxidizes to benzaldehyde and dehydrates at a low pH; inactive and not compatible with nonionics. It is used in injectable drugs, ophthalmic products, and oral liquids. It is used in internal products at 0.5 to 2.0% and in cosmetics at 1.0 to 3.0%. **Note: It has a high percutaneous toxicity.** As a toxicokinetic, it metabolizes into hippuric acid. Chemical Names: *Benzyl Alcohol, Benzenemethanol, Phenylcarbinol,* and *Phenylmethanol.*

BENZYL CARBINOL - This preservative is also known as Phenethyl Alcohol. It is a natural alcohol found in natural essential oils such as rose, hyacinth, and aleppo pine. It is supplied as a colorless liquid with a floral rose type odor, but bitter and burning to the taste. About 2 ml will dissolve in 100 ml water with vigorous mixing, and it is soluble in alcohol at 1:1 ratio. It is not stable in oxidants and is inactive in nonionics. It is manufactured by reducing the ethyl phenylacetate with sodium in alcohol. It is toxic internally at 1.79 g/kg; skin toxicity at 5-10ml/kg; irritates the eyes (human) at 0.75%. Animal tests make the claim that it is non-sensitizing in concentrations of 1-2%. Chemical Name: *2-Phenylethanol, β-phenylethyl alcohol.*

BISULFITES AND SULFITES - These are inorganic acids. The sulfites are white powders and the bisulfites are clear to semi-clear solutions. They are not stable in solutions. Some of the sulfites are soluble in water. **The bisulfites and sulfites are toxic.** Humans suffer headaches, nausea, or diarrhea at doses lower than 4 g (body weight 50 mg/kg). Lab animals fed 0.5-2% bisulfite in food showed injuries to the nervous system within a year; those fed 0.25% had diarrhea but no other toxic effects. Neither the human or animal tests show these preservatives to be safe. They are used at 0.2% in cosmetics and as a food preservative and disinfectant in the food industry (especially in wines) at 1-2%. Chemical Name: *Inorganic sulfites and bisulfites.*

BORIC ACID - This is a mineral acid. It is a white crystalline powder and is odorless. It is soluble in water at about 1 g per 18 ml cold water and 4 ml boiling water. Soluble in alcohol (18 ml) and in glycerol (4 ml). It is not compatible and inactive with alkali carbonates and hydroxides. The point at which this substance becomes toxic to human life is 1-3 g for babies, 5 g for children, and 15-20 g for adults. Boric acid should not be used in baby cosmetics and in baby powder. It can be used in medical eyedrops, astringents, antiseptics, and for foot powders. It can be used around windows and doors as a bug repellent. Chemicals Names: *Boric acid, boracic acid,* and *orthoboric acid.*

BROMOCHLOROPHENE - This is a phenolic compound. It is sold as a white powder. It is not very soluble in water (0.1%) but is soluble in alcohols: ethanol (95%), isopropanol (4%). The best bactericidal activity is at alkaline values (pH 8); also bactericidal at pH 5 or 6. It is unstable in light and inactive in blood and milk. **Acute oral toxicity. Also bear in mind that this is a phenol and must be viewed with suspicion.** Does it have a high absorption-resorption coefficient? Does it accumulate in the *stratum corneum*? Is it potentially neurotoxic? The answers are not known, but this chemical could cause problems as can other phenolic compounds. Chemical Name: *3,3-Dibromo-5¹-5¹-Dichloro-2,2¹-dihydroxydiphenylmethane* and *Bromophene.*

5-BROMO-5-NITRO-1,3-DIOXANE (BRONIDOX L) - This is an active ingredient in propylene glycol and a compound known as o-Acetal, o-formal. It is a clear to semi-clear solution. It is soluble in ethanol at about 25%, in isopropanol at just over 10% and in water at 0.46% (wt/vol). Freely soluble in propylene glycol and vegetable oils, but insoluble in paraffin oil. It is unstable at a pH of 5 and at temperatures above 50° C. It is corrosive to metal containers and will eat right through them. It is used as a preservative for technical products and is suggested at only 0.1% by European Economic Community (EEC) in cosmetics. **Very toxic.** In concentrations of 0.5%, it is a skin irritant (though the irritation didn't occur when suspended in olive oil). Human patch tests of 0.5% caused irritation to the skin and 0.25% in petroleum jelly showed irritation. Cutaneous resorption also occurs with metabolites in the urine. (Guinea pigs did not show this sensitization to this chemical, but we are not guinea pigs. After a few doses, some rats died.) This chemical is incompatible with and destroys the amino acid cystine and should not be used on the hair. Chemical Name: *5-Bromo-5-nitro-1,3-dioxane.*

BRONOPOL - This is an alcohol in the form of a white crystalline powder. It is soluble in water at 22-25%, ethanol at 25%, isopropopanol at 50%, and in various glycols. It is stable in water solutions at a low pH or temperature. Has a long storage rate (up to two years) with no decomposition. The trade name is Bronopol. It is inactive and not compatible with cystine, thioglycolate, thiosulfate, and metabisulfite. **This chemical is toxic.** Bronopol causes human skin irritation (0.25%). Guinea pigs did not show irritation to the chemical at first, but after three tests, two out of the ten guinea pigs became sensitized. I suppose if you're a guinea pig there's a chance you may be harmed. If you're a human you may be harmed. If you're a stupid human you will allow it on or in your body because eight guinea pigs were okay. Rats were murdered in the lab with 160 mg/kg bronopol, and this was called "acute dermal toxicity." Rabbits had their eyes filled with 0.5% bronopol solution for four successive days. They were finally irritated (blinded?) with a 5% solution. Rats contacted gastrointestinal lesions, respiratory distress, and some died with doses of 80 and 160 mg/kg. This chemical is used in household products (fabric softeners and detergents) and pharmaceutical products. It is used in cosmetics in concentrations of 0.01 to 0.1%, in face creams, shampoos, hair dressings, mascaras, and bath oils. Chemical Name: *2-Bromo-2-nitro-propane-1,3-diol.*

CA 24 (CHLOROACETAMIDE) - This is a compound known as Acidamide, and it is synthesized from ethyl chololacetate and ammonia. It contains 70% chloroacetamide and 30% sodium benzoate. It is a white crystalline powder and is odorless; it is soluble in 20 parts water and in 10 parts alcohol. It is compatible with anionics, cationics, and nonionics (which means it could be used in shampoos). It is incompatible with strong acids and alkalis upon saponification. The antimicrobial activity of this chemical is increased in the presence of sodium lauryl sulfate and sodium laureth sulfate. Humans have had allergic reactions to the chemical after 24, 48, and 72 hours of use (0.1% water solution). (It is said that lab animals showed no toxic reactions from 1% to 10% solutions.) This chemical is used in shampoos and bath lotions in concentrations of up to 0.3%. The EEC says label must have warning: Contains Chloroacetamide. Chemical Names: *2-Chloroacetamide, CA 24.*

CAPTAN - This is a phthalimid derivative sold under the trade names Vancid 89 RE and Advacide TMP. This chemical is phenolic. Phthaleins are formed by treating phthalic anhydride with phenols. Captan is sold as crystals. It has no odor. Almost insoluble in water; in ethanol 0.29%. It is compatible with nonionics, anionics, and cationics at a pH of 7 (neutral pH). **We must regard this product as toxic due to the presence of phenol** (See Phenoxetol, Hexachlorophene, PHB Esters, Parabens, etc.). Used in soaps and shampoos 0.5%. Used as agricultural fungicide. Chemical Name: *N-(Trichloromethyllthio)-4-cyclohexene-1,2-dicarboxi-mide.*

CARVACROL - This is a phenolic compound. Supplied as a liquid with a thymol type odor. Slightly soluble in water and freely soluble in alcohol. It is synthesized by the chlorination of a-pinene with t-butyl hypochlorite. **This product is toxic.** It is used in cosmetics at 0.1% concentrations. Chemical Names: *Isopropyl-o-cresol, 1-methyl-2-hydroxy-4-isopropylbenzene, p-cymenol.*

CHLOROBUTANOL - This is an alcohol. It is supplied in crystals and has a camphor-like odor. It is slightly soluble in water, very soluble in ethanol, propylene glycol, and glycerin. Trade Names: Chloreton, Chlorbutol, Methaform, and Sedaform. It decomposes by alkalis and heat. Incompatible with some nonionics and alkalis. It is unstable in some plastic containers (polyethylene, PVC). **This product is toxic.** It is used in cosmetics in concentrations up to 0.5%, but is prohibited in aerosol dispensers. Warning must appear on label: Contains Chlorobutanol. Chemical Name: *1,1,1-Trichloro-2-methylpropane-2-ol.*

p-CHLORO-m-CRESOL - This is a halogenated phenolic. It is supplied as crystals or a white powder. Odorless. It is soluble in water at 1 g to 260 ml at 20° C., but more soluble in hot water; freely soluble in alcohols, fixed oils, terpenes, and aqueous alkaline solutions. Solutions with this chemical turn yellow in light and after contact with air. Inactive with nonionics. **Phenolic-containing products should be considered as toxic.** Used as topical antiseptic, disinfectant, preservative in pharmaceuticals. Used in protein shampoos and in baby cosmetics at 0.1 to 0.2%. Trade Names: BP, PCMC, Preventol CMK. Chemical Names: *4-Chloro-m-cresol, PCMC, 4-chloro-3-methylphenol.*

CHLOROPHENE - A phenolic compound prepared by the chlorination of o-benzylphenol. Supplied as crystals. Soluble in water at 25° C., 0.007%; in propylene glycol 80%; isopropanol 85%; ethanol 70%. It is incompatible with nonionics, quaternary compounds, and proteins. It has a very limited antimicrobial activity. Used in cosmetics at 0.2%. **Due to the presence of phenolic compounds it should be regarded as toxic.** Trade Names: Santophen 1, Septiphene, Chlorophen, and Ketolin. Chemical Names: *2-Benzyl-4-chlorophenol, 4-chloro-2-(phenylmethyl)phenol,* and *chloro phene.*

CHLOROTHYMOL - This is a phenolic compound. It is supplied as a crystalline powder. One gram dissolves in 100 ml of water, 0.5 ml ethanol. Trade Name: KM 6. It is incompatible with nonionics. Synthesized by the chemical reactions of sulfuryl chloride on thymol. Thymol and chlorothymol are both used as local antifungal agents (i. e., foot powders and other dusting powders). Thymol on its own is not irritating to most people, but when combined with chloride it is very irritating to the mucous membranes. This preservative has been found to be a primary skin irritant. Chemical Names: *4-Chloro-5-methyl-2-(1-methylethyl)-phenol, 6-chloro-4-isopropyl-1-methyl-3-phenol, 6-chlorothymol (4-chlorothymol)*.

CHLOROXYLENOL - This is a halogenated phenolic compound snthesized by treating 3,5-dimethylphenol CL2. It is a crystalline powder and has a phenolic odor. One gram can be dissolved in 3 liters of water at 20° C., and it is more soluble in hot water. Also soluble in alcohol, terpenes, fixed oils, and alkaline solutions. It is incompatible with many cationics and nonionics. This mixture is sixty times more potent than phenol and has a greater antimicrobial acivity than p-chloro-m-cresol; however, it is said to be less irritating than phenol or cresol. Trade Name: Ottasept. It is listed in *The British Pharmacopoeia* (1976), registered with the EPA and FDA. This preservative used in cosmetics from 0.5% to 2%. Used in deodorant soaps, hair conditioners, and children's cosmetics. A test on guinea pigs shows no sensitization. Human use? Who knows? I rank it as **toxic**. If you want to accept all those EPA and FDA registrations as "safety factors," then it's your choice. I don't trust men in white coats who issue safety standards based on chemicalizing guinea pigs. The statement "non-sensitizing to guinea pigs," and then the statement "less irritating than phenol or cresol" is enough to make me pass on any product with this on the label. Chemical Names: *4-Chloro-3,5-xylenol, 4-Chloro-3,5-dimethylphenol, p-Chloro-m-xylenol,* and *PCMX*.

CLOFLUCARBAN - This preservative is known as a carbanilide compound. It is supplied as a white crystalline solid. It is insoluble in water, but is soluble in organic solvents. It is not stable in alkaline solutions. Incompatible with proteins. Compatible with nonionics, anionics, and cationic compounds. Trade Name: Irgasan CF3. Used as a disinfectant and in cosmetics in aerosols (0.2%); deodorants and soaps (1.5%). **This chemical is toxic.** Chemical Names: *N-(4-Chlorophenyl))-N¹-(4) chloro-3-(trifluromethyl)phenyl]-urea, 4,4¹-Dichloro-3-(3)fluormethyl)-carbanilide,* and *Halacarban*.

COSMOCUL CG - This preservative is a cationic. It is supplied as a clear yellow liquid and is odorless. It is incompatible with anionics and compatible with nonionics and cationic products. T ais **product is toxic.** (In lab tests rainbow trout were murdered with 10 ppm. Wistar rats showed retardation of growth after ninety days on 6.2 ppm.) This is a primary skin irritant. It is used as a disinfectant, preservative for technical products, and in cosmetics 0.2 to 1.0% of 20% solution. Trade Names: Cosmocil 20% solution, Vantocil IB. Chemical Name: *Polyhexamethylene biguanid hydrochloride.*

DANTOIN 685 - This preservative is a nonionic compound containing formaldehyde (19%) and N-acetal. It is supplied as crystals of which 19% are formaldehyde. It is soluble in water and alcohol. It is stable at low temperatures (below 85° C.), and the formaldehyde is split off at a pH of 6 in water solutions. **This is highly toxic, as are all formaldehyde solutions.** It is used in shampoos at 0.2% and in deodorants. At this level it is actually free formaldehyde. The cosmetic industry can list it on their label with the CTFA adopted name of MDM hydantoin, but this does not tell the consumer who wishes to avoid formaldehyde that THIS IS FORMALDEHYDE. Trade Name: Dantoin 685. Chemical Names: *l-(Hydroxymethyl)-5,5-dimethylhydrantoin, 1-(Hydroxymethyl)5,5-di methyl-2,4-imidazolidinedione,* and *Monomethyl oldi-methylhydantoin.*

DIBROMOPROPAMIDINE - This is a benzamidine compound. It is supplied as white crystalline. Freely soluble in water (50%) but may decompose after prolonged storage. It is active at 5-8 pH, but as the pH increases the antimicrobial activity also increases. **This is a toxic chemical.** (Lab mice were murdered with intravenous doses of 10 mg/kg and were murdered with subcutaneous amounts of 300 mg/kg. Guinea pigs had skin irritations at 0.05 g/100 ml.) Used in cosmetics at 0.1%. Trade Name: Brolene. Chemical Name: *4,4¹-(Trimethylenedioxy)-bis-(3-bromobenzamidine)diisethionate.*

2,4-DICHLOROBENZYL ALCOHOL - This is an alcohol. It is supplied as a yellowish crystalline powder. Soluble in water at 20° C. (0.1%) and other glycols and solvents such as ethanol and isopropanol. It is incompatible with some anionics and nonionics. It has a broad spectrum of activity and destroys yeast and other molds. Used in combination with Bronopol and Germall 115. **This chemical is toxic and a danger to the environment.**

(Lab mice murdered at 2.3 g/kg; rats murdered at 3.0 g/kg; rainbow trout murdered at 18.9 ppm within twenty-four hours; mallard ducks murdered with 2.5 mg/kg; guinea pigs had swelling, inflammation and blistering with slightly higher than 1% solutions within four hours.) Trade Names: Dybenal, Myacide SP. Chemical Names: *2,4-Dichlorobenzyl alcohol* and *2,4-DCBA*.

DICHLOROPHENE - This is a phenolic compound. It is supplied as crystals. Not very soluble in water; 1 g soluble in 1 g ethanol. Bactericidal effect better at acid pH of 5. Not effective at pH of 6 or 7, but more effective at pH of 8. It is inactive with blood, serum, and milk. **This is a toxic chemical.** The EEC suggests cosmetic concentrations of 0.2% in soaps with maximum use of 1%. Warning on the label: Contains Dichlorophene. (In animal tests, rats were murdered at 2.69 g/kg, and mice at 1.2 g/kg.), Little human information. Does it have an absorption/resorption coefficient? Does it accumulate in the *stratum corneum* as do other phenolic compounds? It is potentially neurotoxic? Trade Names: G-4, Preventol GD, Dichlorophene, DCP. Chemical Names: *5,5'-Dichloro-2,2'-dihydroxydiphenylmethane, 2,2'-Methylene-bis-(4-chlorophenol)*.

DICHLORO-M-XYLENOL - This is a halogenated phenolic compound. It is supplied as a white powder. One gram is soluble in 5 liters of water. It is incompatible with nonionics, quaternary compounds, and proteins. **This chemical is toxic.** (See cautions on other phenolic compounds.) Used in baby cosmetics and soaps at 0.1%. This is called a substitute for phenol in the CTFA dictionary. Chemical Names: *2,4-Dichloro-3.5,-xylenol, DCMX*.

DIMETHOXANE - This is an o-Acetal compound and a dioxin. It is supplied as a clear liquid and has a mustard-like odor. It is soluble in water and has a broad pH range. It hydrolyzes in aqueous solutions and is stabilized with alkali. Compatible with non-ionic emulsifiers. Discolors in the presence of amines and amides. **Dioxin products are toxic and a danger to the environment.** (Lab rats died with 1.9 ml/kg.) It is used to preserve cutting oils, resin emulsions, water-based paints, and is a gasoline additive. In cosmetics it is used 0.1%. Trade Name: Dioxin CO. Chemical Names: *6-Acetoxy-2,4-dimethyl-m-dioxane, 2,6-Dimethyl-1,3-dioxan-4-ol-acetate*.

DIMETHYLOLDIMETHYLHYDANTOIN - This is a nonionic compound with 17.7% formaldehyde. The CTFA Dictionary lists it as DMDM hydantoin. This does NOT tell consumers who wish to avoid formaldehyde that this is a formaldehyde product. As with most formaldehyde pro-

ducts it has a broad spectrum of activity against bacteria, but higher concentrations are needed against fungi. It is often combined with parabens and inorganic salts such as *5-chloro-2-methyl-4-isothiazoline-3-one and 2-methyl-4-isothiazoline-3-one* (Kathon CG). It is a liquid with a formaldehyde odor. Soluble in water. Compatible with anionics, cationics, nonionics, and proteins. **This is a toxic chemical.** (Acute oral toxicity for female rats--death at 3.8 g/kg; male rats--death at 2.7 g/kg. Dermal toxicity to lab rabbits at 20 g/kg. No recorded lab animal skin irritation. Patch test with 50 persons of 4000 ppm supposedly gave no sensitization.) Used as a preservative in detergents. Used as a preservative in shampoos, cream conditioners, hand creams, and against yeast and molds at 0.4%. Use: 0.15 to 0.4%. The EEC limit is 0.2%. Trade Names: Glydant, Dantoin 55% solution, and DMDMH-55. Chemical Names: *Dimethyloldimethylhydantoin, 1,3-Dimethol-5,5-dimethylhydantoin*.

ETHANOL - This alcohol is derived by the fermentation of sugar and starch. It is a clear liquid with a burning taste. It is miscible with water, acetone, and glycerol. Due to the fact that it absorbs water it can be very drying to the skin, hair, and scalp. Adjunct: glycerols and vegetable oils reduce drying effect on skin. As a preservative it is effective at concentrations of 15 to 20%. It is a disinfectant in concentrations of 60 to 70% with a bactericidal effect within 45 seconds. It is tolerable at daily doses of 80 g, but more than this is toxic. The acceptable intake has been recorded at 7 g/kg per day. (The lethal dose to lab rats was 13.7 g/kg; guinea pigs 5.5 g/kg; and rabbits 9.5 g/kg.) A 50% solution of alcohol provokes a delayed allergic reaction on the skin. Some people are allergic to alcohol and must avoid it. Used in cosmetics such as skin lotions at 15%, but these skin lotions should include natural oils to reduce drying effects of alcohol on the skin. Also used in astringents, acne treatments, hair rinses for oily hair, fast-evaporating skin lotions, and as a general disinfectant.

FORMALDEHYDE - This is an aldehyde compound. Methanol is sometimes added to formaldehyde at 15% to prevent polymerization. It is a colorless liquid and strong reducing agent. The odor is strong and inhalation over a prolonged period is probably carcinogenic. At one time it was removed from use in cosmetics by the FDA, but is now in use in shampoos at 0.1 to 0.2%. The EEC requires a label warning if the formaldehyde content is greater than 0.05%. Label must say: Contains Formaldehyde) but this is not a U. S. requirement). **Formaldehyde is acutely toxic by inhala-**

tion, internal dose, or topically. (Lab rats fed this chemical died at 800 mg/kg; guinea pigs at 260 mg/kg. Lethal toxicity subcutaneously in mice at 300 mg/kg; dogs 800 mg/kg. Lethal inhalation by rats at 250 ppm in four hours; cats 800 mg/kg was lethal.) OSHA (Occupational Safety and Health Administration) has set a permissible exposure to vapors at 3 ppm. Topical exposure to formaldehyde has demonstrated that 4 out of 9 people exposed to it will get a toxic reaction. (For lab rats inhaling this chemical for six hours a day for five days and within twenty-four months, there was a 43.2% tumor frequency). [1.5% formaldehyde solution]. Inhaling 15 ppm caused 2.4% tumors. Mutagenicity: chromosomal aberrations in bone marrow). Trade Names: Formalin and Formol.

FORMIC ACID - This is an organic acid and the strongest of the fatty acids. It has a pH of 3.5. This fatty acid was observed by Fischer in 1670, in ants. It is a colorless liquid with a pungent odor (threshold limit is 5 ppm). Soluble in water. It is only active in acid products. **Very toxic.** Avoid all contact with skin. A 10 g dose is dangerous, and 50-60 g is lethal. An acceptable daily intake is said to be 0-3 mg/kg daily, but why take a chance? (Many lab animals fed lethal doses at 1.25 g/kg.) Cosmetics use EEC maximum: 0.5%. Has been used as a food preservative since 1865 in the form of sodium, potassium, or calcium formate, but is not allowed in the United States. Chemical Name: *Formic Acid.*

GERMALL II (DIAZOLIDINYL UREA) AND GERMALL 115 (IMIDAZOLIDINYL UREA) - Germall II is a white free-flowing powder, completely water soluble with a wide pH range. Germall II is Diazolidinyl urea and Germall 115 is Imidazolidinyl urea. The antimicrobial activity of Germall II is better than Germal 115. When used in amounts of 0.5%, gram-negative and gram-positive bacteria are inhibited and sometimes killed. Neither of the Germall products have a good antifungal activity and must be combined with PHB esters (parabens). These chemicals are compatible with anionics, nonionics, and proteins. Germall 115 releases formaldehyde over 10° C. **These chemicals are toxic.** (Acute oral toxicity to lab rats at 5.2 g/kg; mice at 7.2 g/kg. Rabbits had severe edema and erythemas [redness and irritation] on abraded skin. Mice had fetoxic reactions at 300 mg/kg.) Cosmetic uses 0.1 to 0.5% in combination with parabens. Trade Names: Germall II, Germall 115, Biopure 100, Euxyl K 200. Chemical name: *N, N¹-methylene-bis-[N¹-[1-(hydroxymethyl)-2,5-dioxo-4-imidazolidinyl] urea.*

GLUTARALDEHYDE - This is a dialdehyde compound. It is an oily liquid stabilized with ethanol or with hydroquinone. Slightly soluble in water. Inactivated by ammonia or primary amines. Glutaraldehyde is strong compared to formaldehyde. A 2% solution is ten times as effective as a bactericide than a 4% solution of formaldehyde. Ths antimicrobial activity works best at a neutral to alkaline pH. **This is a toxic chemical.** Contact dermatitis in humans. (Lab rats lethal dose is 60 mg/kg.) Used in cosmetics at 0.02% to 0.2% (of 50% solution). Trade Names: Ucarcide, Alhydex. Chemical Names: *Glutaraldehyde, glutardialdehyde, 1,5-Pentandial, Dioxopentane.*

GLYCERYL MONOGLYCERIDE - This is distilled monoglyceride (90% mono content). The fatty acid content gives this chemical a waxy solid powder or paste-like appearance. It is soluble in water after melting at 86° C. Compatible with most emulsifiers; inactivated by sodium lauryl sarcosine and some nonionics. Active against gram-positive bacteria, but not against gram-negative bacteria (the harmful sort) except when combined with EDTA, lactic acid, parabens, etc. A good antifungal activity against molds and yeasts, and against lipid-coated viruses such as herpes I and II. A mild sensitizer to some individuals. Used 0.5% in deodorants, soaps, powders, medicated shampoos, hand and foot care products, dental and gum care products. A good grade antimicrobial agent which is approved as an emulsifier in foods by the FDA (21 CFR GRAS 182.4505). Also used as a base lotion for pharmaceuticals. Trade name: Lauricidin. Chemical Name: *Glyceryl monolaurate (alpha and beta forms).*

HEXACHLOROPHENE - This is a phenolic compound. It is supplied as white crystals. Almost insoluble in water; soluble in alcohol, propylene glycol, polyethelene glycol, olive oil, and cottonseed oil. Due to the death and brain damage of infants, this product must carry a warning on label when used: Not To Be Used on Babies. **Acute oral toxicity, neurotoxic to humans, high absorption-resorption coefficient. This substance accumulates in the stratum corneum.** (Lab rats were murdered with 59 mg/kg doses.) Used in cosmetics at 0.1% (New EEC Guidelines). Trade Names: Hexachlorophene, G-11, Hexosan, and Gamophen. At one time the trade name for a topical disinfectant cleanser was pHisohex (no longer on market due to toxic reactions). Chemical names: *2,2-Dihydroxy-3,3¹,5,5¹,6,6¹-hexachlorodiphenyl methane, 2,2¹-Methylenebix[3,4,6-trichlorophenol].*

HEXAHYDROTRIAZINE - This is an N-Acetal compound. It is a yellow liquid, soluble in water, alcohol and acetone. Stable in alkaline solutions and compatible in anionics and nonionics. **This is a toxic chemical.** Humans who are sensitive to formaldehyde can have a severe reaction to this chemical. Contact dermatitis often occurs. Various allergic reactions. (In lab tests rabbits were blinded and/or sustained irritations of the eyes. Lab rats were murdered with 1200 mg/kg, and mice were murdered with 950 mg/kg in food. Acute dermal toxicity to lab rats who were murdered with 5 ml/kg.) Environmental toxicity: rainbow trout were murdered with 69.5 ml/liter within 96 hours. Use in cosmetics at 0.3% maximum use allowed by EEC. Trade names: Bacillat 35, Grotan BK, Bakzid 80, KM 200. Chemical names: *Tris-hydroxyethylhexahydrotriazine, Hexhydrotriazine.*

HEXAMETHYLENETETRAMINE - This is a Formaldehyde N-Acetal compound. Supplied as crystals, granules, or powder. One gram dissolves in 1.5 ml water or 12.5 ml alcohol. The pH of aqueous solutions must be at least 8.4, as this chemical has a formaldehyde split with an acid pH (below 7). It is synthesized by reacting formaldehyde with ammonia in water solutions. This chemical is toxic. Carcinogenicity: Injections into lab animals caused sarcoma. The acceptable daily intake of this chemical has been suggested as 0-0.15 mg/kg daily. It is used as a preservative for hides, an agent for hardening phenol-formaldehyde resins; a corrosion inhibitor for steel and as an antibacterial agent. It is used in cosmetics at 0.2% for lotions and creams and if used in concentrations higher than 0.05% a warning should appear on label that says: Warning: Contains Formaldehyde. Trade Names: Aminoform, Formid, Uritone, and Cystamin. Chemical Name: *1,3,5,7-Tetraazatricyclo [3,3,1,1³⁷]decane.*

HEXAMIDINE ISETHIONATE - This is a Benzamidine compound. Supplied as a powder. Soluble in water and alcohol, not in oils. It is incompatible with chloride and sulfate ions, anionics, and proteins. **This is a toxic chemical.** Used in cosmetics at 0.1%. Used as a topical antiseptic. Trade Names: Hexamidin, Desomedine, Esomedina, and Hexmedine. Chemical Names: *1,6-Di(4-amidinophenosy)-n-hexane, p,p¹-(hexamethylenedioxy)-dibenzamidine-bis-(Beta-hydroxyethane sulfonate), 4,4¹-hexamethylene dioxybenzamidine and salts.*

HEXETIDINE - this is an n-Acetal compound. A colorless liquid that is insoluble in water and soluble in alcohol. This is a toxic chemical. High acute oral toxicity (when fed to lab rats they were murdered 1 g/kg). This chemical is widely used in mouthwashes (1 mg/ml) for its local anesthetic, antibacterial and oral disinfectant effects. In pharmaceuticals 100 mg hexetidine in 100 ml of solution is used against *Candida albicans* infections. Trade Names: Hexetidine, Hextril, Hexatidine. Chemical Names: 5-Amino-1,3-bis-(2-ethylhexyl)-5-methyl-hexahydropyrimidine, 1,3-bis-(2-ethyl hexyl)hexahydro-5-methyl-5-pyrimidine.

n-HEXANE - This is a cationic compound supplied as a white crystalline powder. It is soluble to some extent in water, soluble in alcohol, glycerol, propylene glycol, and polyethelene glycols. To be effective at low concentrates, this chemical is usually combined with parabens, chlorocresol, and B-phenoxyethanol. It is unstable at high temperatures (above 70° C.) and incompatible with anionics, various gums, natural soap, and sodium alginate. **This is a toxic chemical.** Acute oral toxicity (lab mice were murdered at 2 g/kg). Human studies show allergic reactions to this chemical. It is used in concentrations of 0.01 to 0.1% in cosmetic creams, toothpaste, deodorants, and antiperspirants. Trade Names: Hibitane, Novalsan, Rotersept, Sterilon, Hibiscub, and Arlacide. Chemical Name: *Bis(p-chlorophenyldiguanido)hexane.*

p-HYDROXYBENZOIC ACID BENZYL ESTER (PHB ESTERS) - This is a benzoic acid ester that is widely used in cosmetics under the names methyl paraben, propyl paraben, ethyl paraben, and butyl paraben. These preservative agents were first used in 1924. Supplied as a white crystalline powder, they are odorless. They are often used in shampoos, but are incompatible with anionics, nonionics, and proteins; however, products preserved with the parabens (even in high concentrations) have been found to contain microorganisms, although the product may appear to be bacteria-free. Soluble in water at 20° C. and soluble in solvents. Different PHB esters have differing antimicrobial activity. These are toxic chemicals. Acute oral toxicity. (In lab tests the "higher animals" are more sensitive. Dogs were murdered with the following paraben doses: methyl 3.0 g/kg, ethyl 5.0 g/kg, propyl 6.0 g/kg, and butyl 6.0 g/kg. Subchronic toxicity to rabbits of these chemicals at 300 g/kg was toxic, but, as you can see, the lethal dose for dogs and cats was far, far lower. Since these chemicals are not effective in the presence of protein, they cannot be used in most skin care products (i. e., collagen, elastin, placenta, hydrolyzed animal protein, keratin, etc.). Trade Names: Solbrol, Nipagin, Nipasol, Nipakombin, Nipabenzyl. Chemical Names: For PHB esters: *Esters of p-hyroxybenzoic acid, PHB esters.* For Nipabenzyl: *p-Hydroxybenzoic acid benzyl ester.*

8-HYDROXYQUINOLINE - This is a quinoline compound. Quinoline occurs in coal tar and is obtained by oxidation of aniline and glycerol (this process is also used to make artificial colors). It is supplied in the form of a yellow (sulfate) or white (sulfate-free) crystalline powder as a preservative. It is almost insoluble in water (except for the sulfate-free form), but it is freely soluble in alcohol. Acute intraperitoneal toxicity. Phototoxic. Carcinogenic (some coal tar FD & C colors have been found to be carcinogenic via animal tests) due to presence of coal tars. This chemical is used as a topical antiseptic applied to the skin as potassium hydroxyquinoline sulfate skin creams or lotions (0.05 to 0.5%). Not to be used in products for children under three years old. Warning on label: Not For Sun Protection Products. Trade Names: Bioquin, Chinosol, and Quinosol. Chemical Names: *8-Hydroxyquinoline, Phenoxypyridine.*

IRGASAN DP 300 - This is a diphenyl ether compound (also known as a biphenyl) which is derived from coal tar. It is supplied as a white crystalline powder. Soluble in water at only 0.001%; ethanol 70%; propylene glycol (100%) and in vegetable oils (60-90%). **This is a toxic chemical.** Carcinogenic, because coal tar chemicals are believed to be cancer-causing agents; phototoxic; Environmentally toxic because hydrocarbons pollute the air, water, and land. (Acutely toxic: lab rats murdered at 4.53 to 5 g/kg; dogs murdered at 5 g/kg.) This chemical is used in cosmetics at 0.1-0.3% in shampoos, soaps, and deodorants. Trade Names: Irgasan DP 300, Triclosan. Chemical Name: *2,4,4ʹ-Trichloro-2ʹphydroxydiphenylether.*

4-ISOPROPYL-3-METHYLPHENOL - This is a phenol substance. Supplied as a colorless white powder or white crystals. Soluble in water (0.03 to 0.04%). More soluble in alcohols. It is incompatible with nonionics and quaternary compounds. **Due to the presence of phenolic compounds it should be regarded as toxic.** (Lab mice were murdered at 5 g/kg). EEC recommends use of only 0.1% in cosmetics. Trade name: Biosol (a product from Osaka, Japan). Chemical Names: *3-ethyl-4-(1-methylethyl)-phenol, 4-Isopropyl-m-cresol, 4-Isopropyl-3-methyl-phenol, 0-Cymen-5-ol.*

LIQUAPAR - This is a blend of p-hydroxybenzoic acid esters. A white emulsion consisting of 50% total parabens (See **PARABENS** above).

OXADINE A - This is an amine substitute: Dimethyl oxazolidine compound. Completely water soluble. Unstable below pH 5.0. Compatible with cationic, anionic, and nonionic systems. **This is a toxic chemical.** It is used in protein shampoos and hand creams at 0.05%-0.2%. Trade Name: Oxadine A. Chemical Name: *4,4-Dimethyl-1, 3-oxazolidine.*

PARAFORMALDEHYDE - This is a polymerized formaldehyde. It is supplied as a white crystalline powder. **This chemical is toxic.** Trade Names: Triformol, Formagene, Foromycen. Chemical Name: *Polyoxymethylene* (See **FORMALDEHYDE** for toxicity data).

PHENONIP - This is a blend of p-hydroxybenzoic acid esters and like PHB, the parabens, and phenoxyetol, it is toxic. (See PHB and parabens for toxicity data.) Trade Name: Phenonip. Chemical Names: Mixture of 14.5% methyl; 5.7% ethyl; 2.4% propyl; 2.4% isobutyl; and 2.4% n-butyl parabens in 69.6% 2-phenoxyethanol.

PHENOXYETOL - This is a phenolic deriative. Supplied as an oily liquid. **It is toxic.** See PHB esters for details. (Murdered rats at 1.3 g/kg.) Trade Names: Dowanol EPH, Phenyl Cellosolve, Phenoxethol, Phenoxetol, Arosol, and Phenonip. Chemical Names: *2-Phenoxyethanol, Ethylene glycol monophenyl ether.*

PHENYLMERCURIC ACETATE - This is an organic mercurial cationic. This is supplied as tiny prisms which is only soluble in water at 1 part to 600 parts. It is soluble in hot ethanol. It is not compatible with iodine compounds, sulfides, thioglycolates, anionics, halogenics, ammonia. It is compatible with nonionic emulsions. It is made by heating benzene with mercuric acetate. **Highly toxic.** Mercury is a deadly poison. (Lab animals have developed kidney disease when this mercuric compound was put into their food.) It is a primary skin irritant. It is used in eye cosmetics and can enter the body through the eyes or the tender skin around the eye area. The EEC limits maximum concentration at 0.003% and requires a label warning: Contains Phenyl-Mercurial Compounds. Trade Names: Advacide PMA 18, Cosan PMA, Mergal A 25, Metasol 30, Nildew AC 30, Nuodex PMA 18, Nylmerate, and Troysan. Chemical Names: *Phenylmercuric acetate, PMA, acetoxyphenyl mercury.*

o-PHENYLPHENOL - This is a phenolic compound. Supplied in white flaky crystals. Almost insoluble in water. Soluble in methanol and propylene glycol. Incompatible with nonionics, glycols, quaternary compounds. (Lab rats murdered with 2.48 mg/kg.) Trade Names: Doxicide 1, Preventol O. Chemicals Names: *O-Phenylphenol, 2-phenylphenol, o-hydroxydiphenyl, OPP, o-hydroxybiphenyl.*

PIROCTONE OLAMINE - This is a pyridone derivative. It is supplied as a yellowish fine powder. It is stable in a pH range of 5 to 9 at 80° C. for a few days. It is soluble in water at 0.2% (wt/wt) and in water that contains synthetic detergents (from 1-10% wt/wt). This chemical is compatible with ingredients often used in hair care products such as anionic, cationic, and amphoteric synthetic detergents. It is incompatible with many natural essential oils. **This chemical is toxic.** Though it showed an average toxicity in animal tests (lab rats murdered at 8.1 g/kg; lab mice at 5.0 g/kg), little is really known about this chemical mixture. It is reported (by manufacturers) to have a ''good'' skin tolerance in animals and humans; however, its actual use is not needed. It is used, for example, in anti-dandruff hair tonics and shampoos, but we have safe natural ingredients for this. The use for rinse-type cosmetics is 0.5 to 1.0%, but in products that remain in the hair or on the skin, the amount used is 0.05 to 0.1% (wt/wt). The problem here is absorption into keratin, but this problem has barely been touched on (excuse the pun). Trade Name: Octopirox. Chemical Name: *1-Hydroxy-4-methyl-6-(2,4,4-trimethylpentyl)-2(1H)pyridone ethanolamine salt.*

PROPAMIDINE ISETHIONATE - This is a benzamidine compound. It is supplied as crystals, or granular powder. Solubility in water is 1 part to 5 parts, in alcohol 1 part to 32 parts. It is not stable in the presence of natural phospholipids (such as lecithin) or amino acids. These substances eliminate the possible antibacterial action and may cause adverse reactions. Even blood decreases the activity this chemical may have on microorganisms such as *Staphylococcus aureus* and *Escherichia coli*. This chemical can be considered toxic due to the incompatibility with natural and human substances. (Lab mice were murdered with 42 mg/kg internally and 55 mg/kg topically.) This chemical is reported to be for topical use only in cosmetics at 0.1%. Chemical Names: *4,4-Diaminodiphenoxypropane, p,p¹-(trimethylenedioxy)dibenzamidine-bis-(B-hydroxyethane sulfonate), 4,4¹-diamidino-α, ω-diphenoxypropane isethionate.*

PROPIONIC ACID - This is an organic acid synthesized by the fermentation of bacteria of the genus *Propionibacterium*. It is an oily liquid with a pungent rancid odor. Is active in the pH range 3.5 to 4.5. The preservative is used mainly as an antimicrobial agent. It is a primary skin irritant. (Lab rats were murdered at 2.6 g/kg). Used in cosmetics at 2%, and as a preservative for foods. Used in breads to prevent ropiness at 0.15 to 0.4%. Long range toxicity is unknown, but it causes irritation

of skin and mucous membranes. Trade Name: Mycoban. Chemical Names: *Methylacetic Acid, Ethylformic Acid.*

QUATERNIUM-15 - This is a quaternary adamantane. Supplied as an off-white powder. Soluble in water, alcohol, and glycols. Has a broad pH range of 4 to 10. It is unstable above 60° C. When used in cosmetic creams, it makes them yellowish in color. Compatible with anionics, nonionics, cationics, and proteins. This chemical is more effective against bacteria than it is against molds and yeasts. This is one of the most used quats. **It is toxic.** The main reactions are skin rashes and allergic reactions due to hexammonium chloride. (Lab rats murdered with doses of 0.94 to 1.5 g/kg and to mice 40-80 g/kg; guinea pigs had skin reactions above 2%). Trade Names: Dowicil 200, Dowicide Q, and Preventol Dl. Chemical Names: *Cis isomer of 1-(3-chlorallyl)-3,5,7-triaza-1-azonia-adamentane-chloride, N-(3-chloroallyl)-hexammonium chloride.*

SALICYLIC ACID - This is an organic acid that occurs as esters in several plants. It was first synthesized in 1874 by Kolbe, but the synthetic chemical (formed by heating sodium phenolate with carbon dioxide) is not the same as the plant esters. It is supplied as a crystalline powder. When it is heated it decomposes to phenol. Soluble in water at 1 g to 460 ml (at room temperature) or 15 ml boiling water; in alcohol (2.7 ml); in glycerol (60 ml). Solubility can be increased in water by the addition of sodium phosphate, borax, alkali acetates, or citrates. This chemical is incompatible with iron salts, ether, lead, and iodine. **This chemical is toxic.** Salicyclic acid is quickly absorbed into the body. It is toxicokinetic due to its slow secretion and cumulation. Though used as a food preservative, it is now forbidden in some countries. (Lab rats were murdered at 891 mg/kg and rabbits at 1300 mg/kg.) It is used in cosmetics at 0.025-0.2%. Listed not to be used in children's products (3 and under). Chemical Names: *O-hydroxybenzoic acid, 2-hydroxybenzoic acid.*

SODIUM IODATE - This is an iodine compound. Supplied as a white crystalline powder. Soluble in water at 1 g to 11 parts water (at room temperature) or 9 parts boiling water. Not soluble in alcohol. It has a broad antimicrobial spectrum. **This is a toxic chemical.** (Dogs were murdered in the lab with 200 mg/kg.) It causes skin and mucous membrane irritation. Used in cosmetics at 0.1% only for rinse-off products. Chemical Name: *Sodium iodate.*

SODIUM PYRITHIONE - This is a cyclic thiohydroxamic acid and a pyridine derivative. First synthesized by Olin Chemical in 1948. It is a white to yellowish powder. Soluble in water, 53%, and in alcohol, 19%. It is inactive in the presence of nonionics. Has a chelating effect on metal ions. **This chemical is toxic.** (Lab rats murdered at 875 mg/kg and mice at 1172 mg/kg.) Allergic reactions. Used in cosmetics at 250 to 1000 ppm. EEC maximum is 0.5% for rinse-off products only. Trade Name: Sodium Omadine and Pyrion-Na. Chemical Names: *Pyridine-1-oxide-2¹-thiolsodium salt, Sodium-2-pyridinethiol-1-oxide.*

SORBIC ACID - This is an organic acid. It is found in the berries of the mountain ash *Sorbus acuparia* (as parasorbic acid). It was first isolated in 1859 by A. F. Hofmann. It was originally an organic preservative, but today it is synthesized by condensing crotonaldehyde and malonic acid in pyridine solution. (Do not confuse Sorbitol with this chemical. Sorbitol is a natural humectant.) Sorbic acid is supplied as a crystalline needle-like granular. It is soluble in water at 30°, 0.25%. Potassium sorbate, a white powder, is soluble in water at 20° C., 138 g to 100 ml water, 1.2%. Calcium sorbate, a white powder, is soluble in water. This preservative is incompatible with nonionics. **This chemical is toxic.** (Lab rats showed reduced body weight, thyroid gland, liver, and kidney problems over a two year period.) This product is used in cosmetic creams and lotions as an antifungal preservative. Trade Name: Sentry. Chemical Name: *2,4-Hexadienoic Acid, 2-Propenyl Acrylic Acid.*

TETRABROMO-O-CRESOL - This is a phenolic compound. Synthesized by bromination of o-cresol. (Cresol is a poisonous isometric phenol occurring in coal tar. Bromine is a corrosive and toxic liquid similar to chlorine. It is used as an additive for the manufacture of anti-knock gasoline.) This preservative is supplied as a buff-colored powder. Almost insoluble in water, but soluble in alcohol. **This is a toxic chemical.** (Lab rats were murdered with 1.1 g/kg and mice with 0.8 g/kg.) It is a primary skin irritant and irritating to the mucous membranes. Used in deodorants at 0.3% and shampoos at 0.5 to 1.0%. Trade Name: Rabulen-TL. Chemical Name: 3,4,5,6-Tetrabromo-o-cresol).

THIMEROSAL - This is an organic mercurial anionic. Supplied as an off-white crystalline powder. One gram soluble in 1 ml water or 8 ml ethanol. **This is a toxic chemical.** Mercurial compounds are deadly poisons. The EEC has limited its use to eye make-up, and the warning--Contains Thimerosol--must appear on the label. EEC use limit: 0.007%. A high percentage of people have been allergic to this chemical in studies in Sweden. Trade Names: Merfamin, Merthiolate, and Merzonin. Chemical Name: *Ethylmercurithiosalicylate.*

TRICLOCARBAN - This is a carbanilide compound prepared from 3,4-dichloraniline and 4-chlorophenylisocyanate. Supplied as white layers or plates. Not very soluble in water, but soluble in acetone and glycols. Incompatible with nonionic, phosphatides, and proteins. Compatible with anionics and cationics. **This is a toxic chemical.** Chemical is not to be used in maternity units or on infants as cases of methemoglobinemia have been reported. (Lab mice were murdered at 0.6 g/kg and lab rats at 3.6 g/kg.) Human skin toxicity similar to phenols with low blood levels and TCC in the *stratum corneum*, with some penetration into the epidermis. This chemical is used in soaps, antiperspirants, and skin cleansing products at about 0.2%. Chemical Name: *3,4,4¹-Trichlorocarbanilide, TCC, N-(4-chlorophenyl)-N¹-(3,4-dichlorophenyl)urea.*

UNDECYLENIC ACID - This is an organic acid similar to that which is in our own perspiration. It is a zinc salt with the chemical name undecylenic acid monoethanolamide-di-sodium-sulfosuccinate. It is supplied as a liquid or crystals. Insoluble in water; soluble in alcohol Compatible with boric acid and salicylic acid. **This is a toxic chemical.** It is a primary skin irritant. (Lab rats murdered at 2.5 g/kg.) Used in cosmetics as an anti-dandruff agent (1%) for shampoos. EEC suggests use of only 0.2%. Trade Names: Declid, Renselin, and Sevinon. Chemical Name: *10-undecenoic acid.*

USNIC ACID - This is an antibiotic produced by *Cladonia stellaris, Usnea barbata*, and other lichens. Supplied as a yellow powder. Soluble in water, 0.01%, and alcohol 0.02%. **This is a toxic chemical.** (Lab rats were murdered at 30 mg/kg; mice at 25 mg/kgd. Also subcutaneous toxicity to mice at 700 mg/kg.) Used in antiacne formulas at 0.1-0.3% and in deodorants at 0.2%. Also used as a local therapeutic agent. Chemical Name: *2,6-Diacetyl-7,9-dihydroxy-8,9b-dimethyl-1, 3(2H,9bH)-dibenzofurandione.*

ZINC PYRITHIONE - This is a cyclic thiohydroxamic acid. This zinc complex was first synthesized by Olin Chemical in 1980. A white to yellow powder. Soluble in water at 15 ppm (pH 8). Incompatible with EDTA, nonionics, and metal ions. Is not stable when used with cationics and amphoterics. **This is a toxic chemical.** (Lab rats murdered at 200 mg/kg, mice at 300 mg/kg. Doses in food were toxic above 10 ppm. Irritating to rabbits' eyes.) This chemical is a primary skin irritant. Used in cosmetics at 250 to 100 ppm for gels, creams, talcum powder, and shampoos. EEC guideline is 0.5% maximum, for rinse-off products only. Trade Names: Zinc Omadine, Vancide. Chemical Names: *Zinc bis-(2-pyridinethiol-1-oxide) bis-(2-pyridylthio)zinc-1,1¹-dioxide, bis-[1-hydroxy-2(1H)-pyridinethionato-O,S]-(T-4)zinc.*

As you look at the glossary of preservatives used in cosmetics it will become obvious to you that I say that almost all of them are toxic, or have features in their chemical mix that would make it wise to avoid them. This may seem to you that I am biased against synthetic chemicals and simply make the blanket statement that "they're all toxic." This is not true. It looks that way simply because the cosmetic and chemical industry makes it seem as if all these chemicals are NOT toxic and are, in fact, safe. This is not a book, after all, to forward the sale and use of synthetic chemicals in cosmetics: I am biased, as you well know, towards natural substances. But I'm not the only one who's biased--don't suppose that the scientists who work in the chemical industry creating these chemicals nor the cosmetic chemist who put them into products are objective scientists. First, all the "safety" of these chemicals is based on animal testing which is not scientific. Also, many chemical textbooks give the impression that chemicals are apparently safe based on some animal tests and then ignore other animal tests which disagree with the "safety standard" they wish to set as well as leaving out the "in-use" studies. As a rule, human tests are only carried out if the animal experiments do not provide translatable results. This means that if the animal test is considered unsatisfactory by the animal experimenter then they will proceed on the human tests. The key is "translatable results." What does this mean? It means that the testing results must meet some criteria set by the chemical testers who are, by the way, the same industry that wants to sell the chemical: an important point. My bias is based on the intuition that natural substances are better and safer than synthetics, backed up by my years of experience working with them AND centuries of research before me. Their bias is economically-based, i. e., "let's prove it's safe so we can sell it." They have no years of research to back up their position that synthetic chemicals are safe, quite the contrary. The track record of chemical manufacturers is dismal, and as soon as one chemical, like hexachlorophene, is shown to be deadly, they grind out a dozen related compounds that "pass" the animal tests and are sold to cosmetic manufacturers and then to you as "safe."

For example, you will notice that phenol preservatives similar to hexachlorophene are listed in our glossary. They have passed the same animal tests as were conducted on hexachlorophene. In animal experiments hexachlorophene murdered rats at 59/kg. Let's compare this to the animal experiments on other phenolic or hexachlorophene-type preservatives. O-phenylpheno murdered lab rats at at 2.48 mg/kg. Dichlorophene murdered lab rats at 2.69 mg/kg. Phenoxetol murdered lab rats at 1.3 g/kg. 4-Isopropyl-3-methylphenol (which is called a substitute phenol) killed lab mice at 5 g/kg. It is obvious from these figures that these other phenolic compounds may be far more toxic than hexachlorophene, just by looking at animal tests alone. But the synthetic apologists always say the same thing at this point: "But only a tiny amount of these chemicals is added to products. That makes them safe." This is absolutely untrue. Again, let's compare the deadly hexachlorophene in the amounts used to other phenolic compounds.

Hexachlorophene is used in cosmetics at 0.1% which is the latest EEC guidelines since the infant deaths and brain damage due to this chemical. Dichlorophene is used in 0.2% (this is the amount originally used by hexachlorophene), and it can be used up to 1%. Phenoxetol is used at 0.5% to 2% (in combination with the parabens). O-phenylphenol is used at 0.2% 4-isopropyl-3-methylphenol (the phenol substitute) is used at 0.1% which is the same as the new guidelines for hexachlorophene.

You could consider most of these uses as tiny amounts (with the exception of the 1% and 2% uses for dichlorophene and phenoxetol), but obviously when strong poisons are used on humans in any amount, some toxic reaction may occur, perhaps even a deadly reaction. And, once chemicals have been approved as "safe" by the FDA, only a tragedy like that which occurred with hexachlorophene can get them taken off the market. Are you willing to be the guinea pig?

The glossary of chemicals I present here is not quite like the ones you'll find in other research books because I've established that they are TOXIC instead of SAFE. Many details are left out of various source materials about preservatives, which may or may not be an obvious "cover-up" on their part, but is nevertheless inappropriate for a consumer-oriented presentation. For example, formaldehyde has been found to cause cancer in laboratory animals. In a human study, OSHA (Occupational Safety and Health Administration) has estimated the risk that exposure to the LEGAL LIMIT of formaldehyde causes cancer at 71 to 620 workers for every 100,000 workers exposed. However, information in technical books on formaldehyde suggest it is not a carcinogen. None contain the obvious human statistics based on the OSHA findings. The National Cancer Institute (NCI) released a study that said formaldehyde causes cancer among 1.3 million workers who are exposed to it in more than 50,000 factories. The NCI said that this was expected compared to the general United States population. The NCI dismissed formaldehyde exposure as a cause of cancer based on the fact that some people exposed to higher amounts didn't get it. The former director of epidemiology for the National Institute for Occupational Safety and Health (NIOSH) was shocked at the NCI saying formaldehyde didn't cause cancer. He said, "Thirty-two per cent is a lot of excess death, and I think the NCI study needs to be studied" (*The Washington Post*, March 7, 1986). The scientists perform their studies, and then argue about the results. Meanwhile, workers are exposed to this chemical, cancer rates increase, and everyone ends up paying. These arguments among scientists and manufacturers have made our preservative glossary complicated, even more than in chemical directories, but this is unavoidable. I have tried to compile it so you can see the chemicals, what they are, what their trade names are, and how they link together.

The chemists who manufacture cosmetics don't really understand these chemicals and all the possible side effects or toxic possibilities because they are sold to them as being safe. On the other hand, no cosmetic chemist is going to admit he doesn't understand them any more than he's going to admit that animal testing is completely fallacious.

Cosmetic chemists are not a bad lot. They have homes and children, and they too are consumers. They try to please their boss who manages or owns a cosmetic company. I'm sure some of them go home and their dog greets them at the door, happy to see them, and their cat rubs against their legs and purrs. There is no reason for them to think that the increased chemicalization is due to a cosmetic. Cosmetics make you feel better about yourself if they do nothing at all, and some do improve the hair and skin. Cosmetic chemists only put in enough preservative to protect the product from going bad, and they will tell you (some of them) that this protects the consumer.

The fact is, cosmetic chemists, for the most part, aren't a creative bunch, and they will usually "follow the leader," and the leader is the chemical salesperson who, speaking for the chemical industry, tells them of all the advantages of a certain chemical. The salesperson will show them the LD50 and LD60 tests. This is the guideline of how much you can use in a cosmetic, because they have, after all, killed the animals at a level that sets the toxic dose. The salesperson will explain that the effective use of the chemical is very, very much lower than the toxic dose.

In reality, the cosmetic chemist doesn't care about all this and finds it boring reading. The cosmetic chemist will check with his friends who work with other cosmetic companies and find out how much or how little is used by them. The cosmetic chemist will also put various amounts in the product and put it to an "oven" test and observe at what level the product is protected. Then the amount of chemical needed goes into the product to "protect the product." Whether or not it is over-used depends on the individual chemist. More than likely, rather than use more than the supposedly safe amount, the cosmetic chemist will again take the lead from the suggestions of the chemical industry and combine several preservatives until the product can sustain a long shelf-life.

The cosmetic chemist is a victim in the same sense that the consumer is a victim. He or she must put in the chemicals and support animal testing (either silently or vocally) as the criteria of safety. The cosmetic chemist has to keep his or her job, and it means accepting a strange array of chemicals or be considered strange as a chemist by your peers. The consumer is the victim in the sense that he or she must also accept the chemicals put into foods and cosmetics because there is little choice.

I have attempted to present a choice for those who do want a choice, and this is done by awareness. There are still some products (foods and cosmetics) that use none of the many chemicals, and by being able to understand the chemicals you can avoid them. Perhaps you may have to alter your lifestyle slightly and take on a more natural look, but in the long run you will be healthier.

It is in the power of each individual, as a consumer, to control chemicalization by avoiding and denouncing. In the past few years we've seen the power of the consumer to make the animal tester uneasy in his or her work, and many consumers are buying natural foods and cosmetics. They may not be perfectly natural, but they are more perfect than unnatural.

organitoons

CHAPTER XV

Anatomy Of A Natural Product,

Or

Putting It All Together

This chapter was going to be called "Summing Up Part I," but I think it's a waste of time to sum anything up. I hate it when they sum up the news because either I got it or I didn't. I hate it when they do an "instant replay" because I either saw it or I didn't. If I were going to make Chapter XV a "summing up" chapter, then I wouldn't bother writing all the other fourteen chapters. Instead, I'd just sum it up all right here and save myself (and the reader) a lot of work. Let's make this last chapter easy (or hard, depending on your perspective) and create a product, but not a fictitious product. Let's create a real product. In other words, instead of talking about natural products, we'll actually make one, and we'll make one that works!

Trade Secrets and All That

I'm sure some of you are asking yourselves, "If this is really a successful product, then what's keeping me from making up a batch and selling it myself? Why not, if he's going to give me his formula?" You're absolutely right, and there are literally hundreds of small cosmetics manufacturers right now that began in someone's kitchen and grew. It does seem reasonable, but it's not quite so simple. It's easy to copy the formula of "Oil of Olay," for example, but what about all those TV and magazine ads that sell it? And, all those consumers who swear it works for them will never believe your copy is as good as--or even identical to--the original-- even if it is. I know this is true because I've done it. Let me tell you the ABC story.

When I was working for a well-known cosmetic company, we took three bottles of the same hair product. It wasn't "almost the same": it was the same. We made a batch big enough to fill several bottles labeled A, B, and C. We called all three the same name: "Super Soft Hair Conditioner." We then made up a test sheet that asked our respondents several questions. Which conditioner made their hair feel softest? (A, B, C) most manageable? (A, B, C) Which conditioner had the best fragrance? (A, B, C) best appearance? (A, B, C) Which hair conditioner do you like best? (A, B, C) Not one consumer said they liked all three conditioners equally. Not one consumer said that all three made their hair feel the same, and even an obvious question like "which has the best fragrance?" received a variety of answers. More people liked A, but a few were going for B and C. Does this mean it doesn't matter what's in a product? No, it only means that you can't duplicate a product and expect it will do as well as the original because of consumers' expectations. It may do worse, and it may be better.

Despite the drawbacks I've outlined above, in the cosmetics business there are what is known as "knock-off artists," and I've known quite a few in my day. They work on the idea of copying a product and selling it for less. This is especially prevalent in the part of the cosmetics business known as Professional Sales Division or Salon Division. These are the beauty manufacturers who sell to beauty salons through beauty distributors. Many of them are always looking for a "hot idea" to take to beauty distributors so their sales people can go into salons and say, "Look at this, Mary Jane, it's going to do wonders for your client's hair, and you can charge an extra dollar per treatment." If one of these "hot ideas" makes it, then the "knock-off" men copy it and go to the distributor and say "This is just like XYZ. But there's one big difference. It costs less and you make more!" Whole beauty manufacturing businesses have been built on the good old "knock-off" theory.

A good illustration of this is a hair conditioner on the market that's been there for years. It's a balsam hair conditioner made by a well-known cosmetic manufacturer. When they began manufacturing it, they made, by their own admission, one major mistake: they called it "Balsam Hair Conditioner," which is a name that can't be trademarked. It was a big-selling instant conditioner with a nice *balsam tolu* fragrance that they launched by selling on the professional beauty salon level as described above. Then, two salesmen who worked for the big cosmetic manufacturer left and went to a custom filler and made their own "Instant Balsam Conditioner." They sold it for less and got it into salons and retail stores, and after a while, everybody was making a balsam conditioner. (Mind you, all this took place before the FDA regulation that required manufacturers to print ingredients on the label.) With these hair conditioners, however, there was NO trade secret involved because all the products were based on the same chemicals: stearalkonium chloride or stearyl dimethyl benzyl ammonium chloride. To put it into simpler terms, all the manufacturers used (and still use) the same chemicals that go into fabric softeners. The balsam was there only for the lovely fragrance. It was a "hot word!" Here are the trade secrets for most hair conditioners on the market today: fabric softeners and perfume. Pretty tacky, huh?

We always recommend using an astringent after cleaning your skin. What do you think is the "trade secret" of the various astringents on the market? It's SD 40 alcohol. This type of alcohol is used because it has very little "alcohol" odor to it and can be easily perfumed. A few brands (mostly labeled "for oily skin") contain acetone or isopropyl alcohol. A few contain witch hazel but will still contain alcohol. I picked a few at random and listed the top three ingredients.

Chanel Lotion Vivifiante contains water, alcohol, and witch hazel. It is pink in color and has a perfume oil. It is expensive. Clinique Clarifying Lotion No. 2 contains SD alcohol 40, water, and witch hazel. It is also pink, but contains no perfume oil. It is also expensive. Lancome Tonique Fraicheur contains water, alcohol, and PEG-8 (a petrochemical). It is also pink. Like the Chanel product, it has a French name, and that makes it expensive. Frances Denney pHormula ABC contains water, glycerin, and witch hazel distillate. It is pink and has perfume oil. The only inexpensive toner I could find that was pink was Max Factor Skin Freshener which contains water, SD alcohol 40, and propylene glycol. Pink astringents may be all the same in the bottle, but they have different prices and different scents. One brand is called a non-alcoholic freshener. That brand is Stage Ten Lemon E Toner which contains water, witch hazel, and oleth-10 (this is the polyethylene glycol ether of oleyl alcohol). It has a lemon fragrance and is not colored pink. It is colored yellow. It is not as expensive as the pink ones.

When it comes to the juice in the bottle, there are NO trade secrets because there are no shortcuts and no miracle ingredients manufacturers pull out of their hats to save your skin and hair. Mother Nature is the only trade secret that counts for anything, but she's more expensive and more trouble than most cosmetic manufacturers are willing to expend. For example, I make an astringent by boiling herbs in water and combining them with witch hazel. This is a superb trade secret, and I can tell everyone about it because no cosmetic company is going to boil herbs in water. They aren't even going to bother with the herbs. Their idea of herbs is a perfume oil with an "herbal odor" which isn't even made out of herbs. The "knock-off" men can't copy my herbal astringent because not even an expert chemist can figure out which herbs are used (unless he reads the label), and then he's not going to boil those herbs and strain them dozens of times to make an astringent. Here's how to make an herbal astringent that's not at all harsh and is completely natural. None of the big cosmetic manufacturers can make it better than you can.

Aubrey's Homemade Herbal Astringent

Water, 16 ounces
Witch Hazel, 16 ounces (32 ounces, see below)
Nettle, 2 tablespoons
Coltsfoot, 1 tablespoon
Camomile, 2 tablespoons
Benzoin Gum, 2 tablespoons
Elder Berries, 2 tablespoons
Marshmallow, 2 tablespoons
Comfrey, 1 tablespoon
Fennel, 1 tablespoon
Eucalyptus Leaves, 1 tablespoon
Peppermint Leaves, 1 teaspoon
Lavender Flowers, 1 tablespoon
Calendula Blossoms, 2 tablespoons
Orange Blossoms (Optional, if available)
Aloe Vera Gel, 2 ounces
Glycerin, 2 tablespoons (Optional, see below)
Pressed Lemon Peel Oil, 4¼ teaspoons

Whether or not you have a gift for cosmetic chemistry, you can create this superb astringent, and when you're through, you will discover that you've made a better one than all those big cosmetic chemists who bring in up to fifty thousand dollars per year.

Measure out 16 ounces of witch hazel and 16 ounces of water in a clean stainless steel pot (don't use aluminum). Have all your herbs and measuring spoons handy. Combine the 16 ounces of water with the 16 ounces of witch hazel (total 32 ounces), and put it on the stove to boil. Allow the water-witch nazel mixture to heat. While the mixture is heating, measure out all the herbs into the water. If you don't have any orange blossoms you can leave them out of the formula. I get mine fresh from my orange trees. The rest of the herbs can be obtained from herbal suppliers or from your health food store. You can order as little as a pound of each from a supplier (see **RESOURCES SECTION** in this book).

The lemon peel oil must be cold-pressed essential oil of the highest quality. After all, why avoid all the chemicals, then wind up with chemical solvents in the lemon oil? If you can't find a good quality cold-pressed lemon oil, then peel two lemons. Cut them into strips and allow them to boil with the rest of the herbs. Do not use lemon juice or lemon pulp. Only use the skins or get the natural peel skin oil from an aromatherapy oil supplier.

As soon as you've added all the herbs, and the brew begins to boil, take it off the heat, and let it cool to lukewarm. Now you have to strain this herbal brew into a clean quart container, but you're going to strain it first just the way the "old herbalists" did hundreds of years. They didn't have fancy strainers, and don't bother to buy one. I don't use one when I make hundreds of gallons of herbal astringent!

Take a small face towel (use one you don't mind getting stained) or a section of cheesecloth. Drape this over the empty quart container. Pour a small amount of the herbal brew into the towel. Now drape it together with the herbal brew inside and twist so the liquid is squeezed into the container. Squeeze hard and get all the herbal liquids out of the herbs. Throw away the damp herbs and pour more into the towel. Squeeze again until you've strained all the liquid through the towel into a clean container.

When you've squeezed it all out you will have about 12 liquid ounces (you lost about 20 ounces during the boiling and squeezing process). If you wind up with more, good for you!

To this liquid, add your 2 ounces aloe vera gel. I suggest you get the best quality aloe vera gel you can. Don't buy any that has any other chemicals in it. If you can't find a good natural aloe vera gel, then buy a plant and scrape out the liquid inside the leaf until you have 2 ounces. You now have 14 ounces of herbal astringent. It should be fairly free from herbal sedimentation (although a little is all right because it will eventually settle on the bottom and doesn't make the product unpleasant in any way. It's even a sign that you've got a really natural product and not some synthetic alcohol mix! The color of this herbal astringent is a medium dark brown, like an herbal tea. The fragrance is not "perfumy." It's refreshing and even elegant!

Try using it to wipe your face after you clean it. Your skin is left in superb condition: refreshed, toned, and not harshly dry and perfumed as with all those high and low-priced name brand cosmetic toners and astringents.

There's only one way to get a better herbal astringent than this one, and that is to buy the one I make. Absolutely no manufacturer of cosmetics goes to this trouble to make any natural product.

Now that you have Aubrey's Homemade Herbal Astringent, you can alter it for various skin types. The formula as you've just made it is for most skin types, and it's a good all-around skin toner. It isn't too "drying," and there's no alcohol (except the amount in the witch hazel, which is about 15%, and this has been buffered with water). You may not need to do anything else to it unless your skin is extremely oily or extremely dry. Here is how to alter it:

Three Herbal Astringent Variations

All Skin Types	*Oily Skin Types*	*Dry Skin Types*
Leave this one just as it is.	Add 16 oz. witch hazel to this one.	Add 2 tablespoons glycerine to this one.
This will now be 4.6 oz. The color is a natural dark amber brown.	This will now be 20.6 oz. The color is a light amber.	This will now be 5.1 oz. The color is a natural dark amber brown.

You don't need to add a preservative of any kind to this product (and after Chapter XIV, I can't imagine that you'd want to). If you wish, you can keep your astringent in the refrigerator to be sure it retains its freshness.

Before you use an astringent, you wash your face. You can use a soap or you can use a facial cleanser. The problem with using a soap is it simply isn't good for your face, and is far, far less sanitary than either a liquid soap or a facial cleansing cream. If you do want to use a soap, find a cake of good quality vegetarian soap because the animal tallow is awful on the skin and leaves a film.

Most expensive well-known brands of facial cleansers are still based on the way Galen first made his *ceratum refrigerans* in 150 A. D. (See Chapter II, pp. 20-22) by combining oils, water, and beeswax. What I mean to say is that Galen's cold cream was a prototype. Today no matter how much (or how little) you pay for a facial cleanser, you'll be paying for mostly water, mineral oil, and some kind of wax. Let's look at the first few ingredients in some well-known high-priced facial cleansers.

The first three ingredients in Estee Lauder Whipped Cleansing Cream are mineral oil, purified water, and beeswax; this is a high-priced blue-green colored mineral oil product. Jergen's All Purpose Face Cream consists of mineral oil, deionized water, and beeswax; this is a pink-colored mineral oil product, but it costs less money. Pond's Lemon Cold Cream has mineral oil, water, and beeswax; it is a low-priced mineral oil product that smells like lemons. Lancome's Galatee Milky Creme Cleanser contains water, mineral oil, and isopropyl myristate. (Isopropyl myristate is a partly natural, partly synthetic fatty acid used in cosmetics to reduce their greasy feel; allergic reactions and toxicity unknown). It has no artificial color but has perfume oil. It is expensive. Another "famous name" is Diane von Furstenberg's Creme Cleanser Facial Spa with water, mineral oil, and propylene glycol (synthetic hydrocarbon glycerine). It is moderately priced but elaborately named. Noxema Complexion Lotion contains water, propylene glycol, and stearic acid. (Stearic acid is a white, waxy fatty acid from tallow, butter acids, animal fats, or vegetable oils. It is used in cosmetic creams for the pearliness and firmness provided and may cause allergic reactions.) The Noxema product contains no artificial color but does contain perfume oil. It is lower in price than the others. Flori Robert's Anti-Oil Lotion contains water, sodium lauryl sulfate, and oxtoxynol. This cleanser does not contain mineral oil or propylene glycol. The face is cleaned with sodium lauryl sulfate (a very harsh synthetic detergent), but while it may be used as a "non-oily" cleanser, it doesn't clean the face well and SLS is very drying to the skin. It is moderately priced. Dorothy Gray 2-Minute Magic Moisturizing Cleansing Lotion contains water, mineral oil, and ozokerite (synthetic wax). It is not colored and contains perfume oil. It is low-priced.

All of these facial cleansing creams or lotions work on the principal of using mineral oil to wipe away dirt, grime, and make-up. None are natural, and they don't really get the skin clean. All you have to do to prove this to yourself is use them, then take a clean white cloth, and wash your face with soap. Look at the cloth; look at your skin. What you will notice is that your skin was not clean until you cleaned it with soap. Mineral oil, propylene glycol, wax, petrolatum, or even the sulfates will not clean the skin properly. So all these petrochemical mixes are not only extremely over-priced for what they are, but they also don't work. The petrochemicals lay on top of your skin. If you insist on using them, at least use your herbal astringent to get them off your skin. In fact, when you use these petrochemical cleansers, it is the astringent that is really doing the cleaning job.

To do a good job, the cleanser should clean with a soap or natural oil and mildly exfoliate the skin. The skin should be totally clean when you're through, but not "harshly" clean and that's why most cake soaps don't work: they're too harsh.

It's more difficult to make your own cleanser, but you can do it with the old Galen formula of 56% olive oil, 24.5% beeswax, and 14.5% water. You can even refine this formula by using almond oil, rosewater, and borax, which is a naturally-occurring mineral that reacts with the beeswax to form a stable emulsion (see page 22). I make a facial cleanser without mineral oil or wax by combining natural castile soap (olive oil type) into a fatty acid cream base. I put in many herbal extracts such as eucalyptus and menthol oils, rosemary, sage, camomile, myrrh, etc. Even though I don't use beeswax to make a cleanser (mine uses an herbs and fatty acid emulsion), it is the best medium to make a good natural emulsion. Yellow beeswax contains 71% fatty acid esters, 1% cholesteryl esters of fatty acids, 0.3% coloring matter, 0.6% lactone, 1% free alcohols, 14.5% free wax acids, 10.5% hydrocarbons, and 1.1% moisture and minerals. Many modern cosmetic manufacturers are using paraffin wax and ozokerite mixed with mineral oil rather than beeswax. Some cosmetic companies object to the odor of beeswax, but it isn't an unpleasant odor. Adding rosewater is a natural way to cover up the beeswax odor.

The borax is mixed with the other ingredients and put into the melted beeswax to create an emulsion. The amount of borax used is around 5% to 6% of the weight of the beeswax. The amount of borax and combined beeswax in a formula can range from 5% to 17%, but from 5-12% will give a softer cream. As you increase the ratio of borax to wax, the cream will stiffen.

NATURAL ALMOND FACIAL CLEANSING CREAM FORMULAS

	A	B	C
Almond Oil	42.0%	50.0%	72.5%
Beeswax	12.0%	5.0%	6.5%
Vitamin E Oil	0.5%	0.5%	0.5%
Astringent	44.0%	44.3%	
Soap chips	0.5%		
Borax	0.5%	0.2%	
Rosewater	0.5%		
Cocoa Butter			20.5%
	100%	100%	100%

Here are three natural facial cleansing formulas using almond oil. Though almond oil may be more expensive than mineral oil, it is far superior in every way. Instead of using water in Formulas A and B, I have used the astringent we made earlier. This will make the formula superior to even supposedly "natural" facial cleansers. With all the herbals and natural oils, this is an exquisite facial cleanser, and so much better than the mass-produced brands. Here's how you make it:

FORMULA A: Heat the almond oil, beeswax, and vitamin E oil together to about 70° C. Dissolve the borax in the astringent and add the rosewater and soap chips. Heat the water mixture to 70°C. Slowly add oil mixture to the astringent mixture with thorough agitation. Pour the mixture into a clean jar at 45° C.

FORMULA B: Heat the almond oil, beeswax, and vitamin E oil together to about 70° C. Dissolve the borax in the astringent and heat to 70°. Slowly add oil mixture to the astringent mixture with thorough agitation. Pour the mixture into a clean jar at 45° C.

FORMULA C: This is a non-water liquifying facial cleanser which is used by people with dry skin, though many people with oily skin will also find it effective. Melt the beeswax first. Add the almond oil, vitamin E oil, and cocoa butter to the melted wax. Stir thoroughly and pour into jar to cool.

Formulas A and B are emulsion-type cleansers which use the borax-beeswax system. Formula C is not an emulsion and utilizes the beeswax only as a thickening agent. This is an oil-liquefying cleanser.

You can also make a natural facial cleanser that does not use the borax-beeswax system by utilizing fatty acid esters and various absorption bases. Jojoba wax can also be used to make a natural cleanser as well as jojoba oil and jojoba butter combined with jojoba wax. Here is a unique facial cleanser using jojoba products and our astringent base. This is a good cleanser for acne and blemished skin but is not drying to the skin.

Jojoba Facial Cleanser

Jojoba Oil	38.0%
Jojoba Butter	12.0%
Jojoba Wax	5.0%
Glycerine	5.0%
Astringent	40.0%
	100.0%

Combine the jojoba oil, jojoba butter, and jojoba wax and melt together to 70° C. Heat the glycerine and astringent together to 70° C. Slowly add the oils to the water with rapid stirring. Agitate until cooled to about 45°C. Pour into jar and allow to cool.

There are many oil-soluble emollients which can be used to make facial cleansers and moisturizing creams and lotions. Let me list the natural ones. I will, of course, exclude the hydrocarbon oils and waxes which we want to avoid for our skin's sake.

WAX ESTERS - Beeswax, Candelilla, Carnauba, Jojoba, Lanolin.

STEROID ALCOHOLS - Cholesterol, Lanolin Alcohols.

FATTY ALCOHOLS - Cetyl, Lauryl, Oleyl, Stearyl.

TRIGLYCERIDE ESTERS - African Butter (Karite or Shea Butter), Jojoba Butter, Cocoa Butter, Various Animal and Vegetable Fats and Oils.

PHOSPHOLIPIDS - Lecithin.

POLYHYDRIC ALCOHOL ESTERS - Glycerin, Sorbitol, Mannitol.

FATTY ALCOHOL ETHERS - Cetyl, Oleyl, Stearyl.

HYDROPHILIC LANOLIN DERIVATIVES - (Natural Types).

Emollient Waxes and Oils to Avoid

The following oil-soluble emollients are either synthetic or they are hydrocarbons or petrochemical mixtures which are more irritating to the skin; you may wish to avoid them because they aren't natural (and there are so many natural alternatives they aren't needed).

WAX ESTERS - Spermaceti (sperm whale oil, outlawed in United States).

POLYHYDRIC ALCOHOL ESTERS - Mono and Di-Fatty Acid Esters of Ethylene Glycols, Diethylene Glycol, Polyethylene Glycol (PEG), Propylene Glycol, Polyoxyethylene Sorbitol and Sorbitan (Tweens).

HYDROCARBON OILS AND WAXES - Mineral Oil, Petrolaum, Paraffin, Ozokerite, Ceresin, Silicone Waxes, Silicone Oils.

The hydrocarbons and silicons are widely used in cleansers and moisturizers for the skin and hair. They are, in fact, the major vehicles used in cosmetic emulsions, and when they remain on the skin for some time, they do cause the skin to hydrate temporarily; however, the moisture supplied from the underlying tissues is prevented from evaporating to the environment by the hydrocarbon barrier. This can cause edema and subsequent irritation. Petrolatum, for example, has poor washability and is greasy. Hydrocarbon oils and waxes are barriers to penetration by the most effective emollients and afford no softening or plasticizing of the upper epidermal layers. Prolonged use of mineral oil removes sebum from the skin and should never be used in a moisturizing product or "celltherapy" type skin treatment. This is also true of the other hydrocarbons listed above. While the hydrocarbons (and silicone oils) are non-polar, the natural emollients are polar and exhibit varying degrees of hydrophilic-lipophilic characteristics. Their affinity for the skin is well-known, and they are the substances of choice for hair and skin care products. The only problem is that the natural substances aren't used in mass-produced cosmetics; they are out of favor with cosmetic chemists. When these natural emollients are used, they are too often combined with the undesirable synthetics and hydrocarbons.

KARITE BUTTER

Under Triglyceride Esters above, I have listed African butter (karite or shea butter), jojoba butter, and cocoa butter. All three can be used in moisturizing formulas for the skin and conditioning formulas for the hair. Let's consider karite butter, my favorite of the three, and learn a little about it. Although it has not been extensively used in cosmetics, I have been utilizing it in formulas for several years.

I used it when I developed a shampoo for a company called Nyaanza Naturals in 1981. It was called African Butter Shampoo and was the first time karite butter was utilized in a shampoo for dry and damaged hair, but I had also used it in skin care products before that. The damage many people inflict on their hair with straighteners or permanents or corn-rowing is helped by this karite butter product. I also included the karite butter in hair conditioners to treat damaged hair. Karite butter is superior to both cocoa butter and jojoba butter in this respect.

I first began learning about karite butter when a man with the company Sederma in Meudon, France, sent me a jar of it to use in various formulations. I took just a bit on the tips of my fingers and applied it to the skin. It was amazing how soft yet non-greasy it left the skin. It is called African butter because it comes from the nuts of the genus *Butyrosperum Parkii Kotschy*, a tree which grows in Central Africa. The natives gather the tiny almond-like berries from the trees and extract the slightly greenish-yellow butter which is known as karite butter and in the CFTA as shea butter.

The natives of Central Africa used karite butter for food as well as body care, and in Japan the butter is a replacement for regular dairy butter in foods. Vegetarians use it as a replacement for dairy butter in cooking. One variety of the tree, *Mangifolia*, which grows in the rich silicate clay soil of the Ivory Coast, stands out as exceptional due to the amount of unsaponifiable material contained in its karite butter. The *Mangifolia* variety of karite butter contains:

Triglycerides	50%
Diglycerides	4%
Monoglycerides	2%
Fatty Acids	5%
Unsaponifiables	8%
Waxy Esters	7%
Unknown Substances	24%

The African butter tree is fifteen meters high and one meter in diameter. Its berries look like green plums and are a dark green when ripe. These berries are harvested in June and July, and the pits are removed and dried for several months. These pits contain up to 50% lipids which are extracted by crushing the pits and boiling them in water. The lipids rise to the top and are recovered during cooling. A more modern method of removing the lipids so that a high quality butter can be obtained is to press the pits at a controlled temperature. In order to get the important unsaponifiable substance out of the karite plant, the pits are roasted before pressing which assures a higher yield of unsaponifiables and a lower acidity.

Any plant oil or fat is to a major extent composed of esters of glycerol with saturated fatty acids. There are small portions of heterogenous mixtures in these plant substances which are not transformed into soap by alkali. They are called unsaponifiables. Usually plant oils are poor in unsaponifiables in their lipid fractions. Soy bean and avocado are often used in cosmetics for moisturization, etc., because they both have a relatively large amount of unsaponifiables. Obviously coconut oil, which is used to make most natural soaps, has the least amount of unsaponifiables which is why it makes a good cleansing soap. Karite butter is the highest in unsaponifiables. A chart below shows the amounts of these important substances in various plant lipids.

PLANT OIL	UNSAPONIFIABLES IN PERCENTS
Karite	3.5 - 11%
Avocado	2.0 - 6.0%
Soy Bean	0.5 - 1.5%
Sesame	1.0 - 1.5%
Rice	1.0 - 3.0%
Flax	1.0%
Carrot (Grains)	1.5%
Carrot (Root)	0.2 - 0.5%
Olive	0.6 - 1.2%
Peanut	0.2 - 0.9%
Castor Oil	0.3 - 0.8%
Coconut	0.1 - 0.3%

These unsaponifiables found in karite butter are also higher than avocado and soy bean in important natural plant hydrocarbons though not as high in phytosterols; however, karite does contain a substance known as *Stigmasterol*, which is the sterol known as the "anti-stiffness factor" (W. J. Van Wagten-donk and R. Wulzen, *Vitamins and Hormones*, Vol. 8, New York: Academic Press, 1950). This may explain why it has long been used in Africa with astonishing results as a massage balm for tired sore muscles, rheumatism, burns, and light wounds. It is for this reason that I utilize this butter in massage creams and oils. The butter has a nourishing effect and seems to induce a state of self-protection in the cells through its stimulating action on the metabolism. Clinical observations suggest that karite butter increases local capillary circulation which in turns increases tissue re-oxygenation and improves the elimination of metabolic waste products. A natural anti-oxidation agent, B-amyrine (along with tocopherols), protects the double bond of the oil as a whole and the unsaponifiable compounds in particular.

Another asset natural to karite butter which I like is its protection against the ultraviolet rays that cause sunburn. The tests show that karite butter on its own without PABA prevented burning when exposed to UV rays (J. M. Lwoff and J. R. Boissier, *Journal de Pharmacologie*, 1 [35, 1970]). Another asset has to do with the elasticity of the skin and the prevention of weals, which is an unusual skin condition technically known as "dermagraphic skin" in which if the skin is marked, it raises into weal-like lines. Karite butter also helps anti-elastase problems of this kind. (A. M. Robert, M. Miskulik G. Godeau, and L. Robert, *Gazet Medicale de France*, 18 [January 10, 1975]). This means karite butter is a valuable addition to moisturizers and celltherapy creams for the reduction of wrinkles. Its high linoleic acid content makes it ideal for dry skin, dermatitis, dermatoses, sunburn, burns, redness, ulceration, irritation, and chapping.

I have used karite butter in solar products at a level of 5-10%; in soaps (a French vegetarian soap) in 2-3%; moisturizers and anti-wrinkle products at 5-7%; massage products at 5-10%; lip balms at 5-10%; celltherapy-type products at 1-5%; shampoos at 2-3%; and, because it is a non-toxic and gentle ingredient, in baby and extra-sensitive skin products from 5-7%.

We've put together several possible natural astringents and facial cleansers. Now we need a good natural moisturizer so we can complete our own natural skin care line of products and disregard all the junk cosmetics (which give you no choice at all).

An emollient is a material that prevents dryness and offers relief from dryness. It also protects the skin from sun damage and damage due to make-up and other synthetic chemicals on the skin. A good emollient will prevent and eliminate rough and flaky skin. In time, it will create a flexible and smooth surface on the skin and even soften fine lines (not including character lines and scars). The cleanser and astringent we have suggested here and the ingredients suggested with which to make them have emollient properties so that when you are cleaning and toning your skin you are getting some natural emollient action. It is, however, the moisturizer that really does the good. A good emollient cream or lotion will moisturize and hydrate the skin. This is also one of the important functions of the astringent (toner) because as it removes any soap or oil films left on the skin, it also hydrates the skin.

Today there are many complex moisturizers and they can incorporate any of the following categories of ingredients: emollients, barrier agents, healing agents, humectants, emulsifiers, preservatives, perfume oils, and coloring agents. To make it easy we will eliminate two categories you NEVER want in your skin care products: perfume oils and coloring agents, also most preservatives and some emulsifiers (See **CHAPTER 14** on preservatives). All the other categories of ingredients usually have positive assets (See **CHAPTER 4** for a preliminary discussion of these categories, especially humectants and emollients, and their role in absorption bases).

The most outstanding emollients are phospholipids, phytoglycols (plant oils), fatty acids, fatty alcohols, fatty acid esters, plant sterols, lanolin, and lanolin derivatives. I like the first three and have found them to make fine creams and lotions. I won't bother to discuss all the emollients, but since it's a good idea to know some of the positive results you'll get from the best ones, I'll talk about my favorites.

Phospholipids are substances whose molecule contains fatty acids, glycerol, a nitrogenous base, and phosphoric acid. These compounds are found in living cells in the human and plant world. A balance of phospholipids and sterols is important to a healthy skin, and, indeed, the health of all cells. There is a balance in the phospholipids and cholesterol (a sterol) which must be maintained for healthy skin. As skin cells die as part of the natural process of keratinization, this balance is upset, and if the phospholipid-cholesterol balance is not restored, new cells will not regenerate or will regenerate more slowly. One well-known phospholipid is lecithin, and only 1% or 2% is needed to give superb emolliency. Lecithin also is a natural emulsifier and surfactant.

Fatty acids are widely used in hand creams and lotions, and with good reason. They are excellent natural occlusive agents, but unlike other occlusive emollients (such as the hydrocarbons), they are non-greasy and form a thin film on the skin that is not objectionable. In fact, the thin film has many advantages. It can act as a slow-absorbing agent when combined with other ingredients; it is an excellent barrier agent. One of the most used fatty acids is stearic acid. Quite often a fatty acid is made consisting of about 45% stearic acid and 55% palmitic acid (triple-pressed) and combined with a liquid phase of oleic, linoleic, and myristic acids. I have been combining various fatty acid bases for two decades, and they make the finest natural products. However, when many cosmetic chemists use the fatty acids, they make the unfortunate mistake of blending them with hydrocarbons and various synthetic oils and fats.

There are many qualities of fatty acids, and some are better than others. It is only with experience that knowledge is attained on how to create natural products of a superior quality with fatty acids. For example, while fatty acids are mild and can be used in cosmetics without a problem, some pose various problems. Evening primrose oil, which is high in the fatty acid gamma-linolenic acid (see **CHAPTER 6** for complete discussion of EPO), must be used in small amounts in topical hair and skin care products because it can be irritating to some people; yet it can help skin problems such as eczema and psoriasis if used undiluted directly on the affected areas. Oleic acid has a tendency to become rancid easily. Both oleic and linoleic acids can be irritating to some people's skin (both are present in high amounts in evening primrose oil) and are absorbed very quickly into the skin. Thus, they are rather limited in their emolliency abilities. However, if a fatty acid blend is accomplished properly, there is no more versatile emollient.

Fatty acid esters are also used extensively in creams and lotions. They have a low viscosity and lay an oily film on the skin that is not objectionable. They are not greasy and tacky to the touch, and their hydrophobic nature make them a good choice for emollients. However, I don't care for the synthetic and hydrocarbon fatty acid esters (also known as polyhydric alcohol esters) because they can be irritating to the skin. They are propylene glycol monostearate, ethylene glycol monostearate, and polyethylene glycol monostearate. These are considered emulsifiers as well and are used in many, many mass-produced (and so-called "natural") cosmetics. Glycerin and sorbitol are natural emulsifiers I consider far superior to the poly esters and poly glycols.

Fatty alcohols are used in some lotions, creams, and soaps. Fatty alcohols are important to the hardening rate of soaps. As emollients, fatty alcohols produce a good occlusive film which hydrates the skin. They also have a high melting point sufficient to leave a pleasant non-greasy film on the skin. Cetyl and stearyl alcohols are the best and can be used in low concentrations of 0.2% for a smooth, velvety feel.

Barrier agents are used primarily in creams to protect the skin from chemicals and detergents. Protective hand creams, for example, can be used by garage mechanics or printers who come in contact with irritating chemicals, grease, and ink. The usual barrier or protective agent should be non-irritating, easy to apply and remove, relatively imperceptible on the skin; it should adhere well to the skin and form a flexible and non-cracking film. Sunscreens are a particular type of protective agent which screen the skin against UV rays, and I have made several of these. In addition, I have created a barrier agent, a balm, for snow, wind, sleet, and reflected sun (from water or snow). This is a protective agent that both repels water and helps prevent damage from UV rays. Natural gums can be combined with fatty acids and fatty acid esters to make this type of skin care product.

I think a healing agent is important to moisturizing day and night creams because it can reduce skin sensitivity and at the same time heal chapping, scratches, and dry skin problems. I have found that natural herbal agents are the best ingredients of this type. One of the most outstanding is allantoin, which is a crystal obtained from comfrey root or glyoxylic acid. Allantoin can be used in small amounts of 0.01% to 0.1% (See **ALLANTOIN** in **CHAPTER 8**). Herbal healing agents such as the hydroglycolic extracts of calendula blossoms, camomile flowers, linden, corn flower, and St. John's wort also have a important place in moisturizers and celltherapy creams and lotions. Another classic healing agent is aloe vera gel, which is actually three categories in one: healing agent, humectant, and emollient.

The humectant ingredient in your moisturizer is important both to your skin and to the consistency of the product in the tube or jar because it controls the moisture exchange between the product and the air. A humectant may be used in a facial mask, for example, to keep it moist and easy to use in the jar but will allow the mask to dry on your skin for the "drawing action" expected. Mass-produced (and so-called "natural") cosmetics use propylene glycol for their humectant, which is a bad choice because it's a petrochemical that gives many problems on the skin. Ingredients such as glycerine (vegetable glycerol) and sorbitol are excellent natural humectants. However, because propylene glycol yields a cream of a firmer and more stable consistency and consumers have been conditioned to believe that this sort of cream is richer and therefore more desirable, it continues to be used by a large majority of cosmetic manufacturers. This is a choice consumers must make in selecting a hair and skin care product. The natural cosmetic may not be the consistency they have come to expect as "best," or even perfectly smooth, but is this visual element more important than the ingredients that go on your skin and hair?

There are many moisturizers and night creams on the market. Today a vast amount of them claim to contain some type of "magic ingredient" that promises it will take away or prevent wrinkles and help you retain a youthful look. Even though all these claims are made, let's take a quick look at some of the better-known mass-produced and high-priced skin moisturizers. You will notice that they all, regardless of the price, contain mineral oil (instead of a good quality herbal oil or botanical glycerol) or propylene glycol or petrolatum or urea or some hydrocarbon or synthetic chemical mix. PLEASE NOTE: the ingredients have absolutely nothing to do with the price you pay. Although the top three ingredients of the products listed below are in many cases similar, the prices of these moisturizers vary widely.

The well-known and fairly low-priced moisturizer known as "Oil of Olay" contains water, mineral oil, and potassium stearate. It is colored pink and has a perfume oil (see page 150).

"Revlon Eterna 27 All-Day Moisture Lotion" contains water, propylene glycol, and urea. It is not artificially colored but contains perfume oil.

Adrien Arpel Bio-Cellular Creme suggests "celltherapy" with its product name but contains the two usual petrochemicals at the top of the ingredients' list: water, mineral oil, propylene glycol. It isn't artificially colored but has perfume oil.

When Coco Chanel was at the height of her designing powers, petrochemicals and synthetic chemicals had not yet brought about so many junky, high-priced cosmetics. "Coco Creme No. 1 Skin Equilibrium Supplement" has a beautiful package which speaks well for the memory of Coco Chanel but an ingredients list that fits in with the vulgar *hoi polloi* of synthetic moisturizers: water, propylene glycol, dicaprylate/dicaprate and isostearyl neopentanoate. It is not artificially colored but contains perfume oil. It's expensive.

Avon Rich Moisture Face Cream contains water, propylene glycol, and SD alcohol 40B. It's artificially colored yellow and contains perfume oil. A fairly low price.

Coty Equation One Perfect Ounce Maximum Cream sounds like a scientific equation, but the usual dream-cream petrochemicals are here: water, mineral oil, and petrolatum. It is artificially colored pink and contains perfume oil.

Redken pH Moisturizing Skin Balancer wears the company's usual "pH balanced" slogan, but contains the usual water, mineral oil, and emulsifying wax NF (a hydrocarbon wax).

Jovan Oil of Mink may contain the animal oil obtained from those little furry animals some people murder for their skins, but the top three chemicals are water, mineral oil, and octyl dimethyl PABA.

I could go on and on listing ingredients in the various moisturizers, rejuvenation creams, eye creams, hand and body lotions, but they contain the usual hydrocarbons and synthetic chemical mixes which you want to avoid if you want a gentle natural moisturizing product. I've only listed the first three principal ingredients, but a complete reading of the various labels will reveal other chemicals, including artificial coal tar dyes, solvents, and preservatives.

Now let's make our own natural moisturizer, and I can assure you it will be better and, of course, far more pure and fresh than all the high, medium, and low-priced synthetic mixtures. All you will be missing are the chemicals, the pretty package, the gold caps, the designer names, and the high prices. You will, however, have a healthier skin and the knowledge that you're doing a much better job for yourself than a whole fleet of cosmetic chemists and marketing mavens.

In Chapter 9 ("How To Make A Natural Cosmetic in Ten Easy Lessons"), I describe how to make your own celltherapy lotion with herbs (see page 147). It's a simple formula and far superior to all the mass-produced moisturizers. The information in this chapter introduces various natural emollients and humectants so you can be as original as you want in making a natural moisturizer.

As we make these moisturizers we will, once again, use the basic "astringent water" you made at the beginning of the chapter. Let me explain why we aren't using regular water to make the facial cleanser and moisturizer. The herbal astringent you made contains excellent herbals, and they will help you create an excellent moisturizer. Be sure to make up a large batch of herbal astringent since you're using it here as a base.

LANOLIN MOISTURIZING CREAM

Oil Phase:

Almond Oil	12.0%
Lanolin	1.0%
Beeswax	10.0%
Vitamin E Oil	0.5%

Water Phase:

Borax	0.5%
Glycerine	2.0%
Astringent	74.0%
	100.0%

This is a simple moisturizing cream based on almond oil, with just 1% lanolin. Combine the oil phase and heat to about 80° C. while mixing. Combine the water phase and heat to about 80° C. while mixing. Add the water phase to the oil phase at 80° C. while mixing. Continue to mix until the product cools to 40° C. Pour into clean jar.

JOJOBA AND ALOE MOISTURIZING DAY & NIGHT CREAM

Oil Phase:

Jojoba Wax	10.0%
Jojoba Oil	25.0%
Jojoba Butter	10.0%
Vitamin E Oil	.5%

Water Phase:

Aloe Vera	20.0%
Glycerine	5.50%
Astringent	29.0%
	100.0%

Combine the oil phase and heat to about 70-73° C. while stirring. Combine the water phase in another container and heat to about 70-73° C. while stirring. When both phases are about 73° C., slowly add the oil phase to the water phase while continuing to stir. Stir until cooled to 30° C., then pour into clean jar. This unique cream is for dry skin. The jojoba blend is for the amelioration of dry skin, and the water phase with the herbal astringent is a skin tonic. The absorption is fairly rapid, but a lovely sheen is left on the skin. Though jojoba does not become rancid like other vegetable oils, I have included vitamin E oil as an antioxidant.

NIGHT REPAIR CREAM

Oil Phase:

Almond Oil	10.0%
African Butter	10.0%
Vitamin E Oil	1.0%
Jojoba Oil	5.0%
Beeswax	2.0%

Water Phase:

Aloe Vera Gel	50.0%
Glycerine	5.0%
Astringent	17.0%
	100.0%

Combine the oil phase in a container and heat to 80° C. while stirring. Put the water phase into a container and heat to 80° C. while mixing. Continue to mix until the product cools to 40° C. Pour into clear jar for use.

HERBAL BEAUTY OIL BLEND

Almond Oil	2.50 oz.
Wheat Germ Oil	.50 oz.
Jojoba Oil	.50 oz.
Avocado Oil	.50 oz.
Sunflower Oil	.50 oz.
Vitamin E Oil	.50 oz.
Aloe Vera Gel	2.00 oz.
Glycerine	1.00 oz.
	8.00 oz.

This excellent blend of herbal oils can be used as a massage oil, a beauty oil, and a make-up remover. It is gentle and nourishing to the skin. The vitamin E oil nourishes the skin and is a natural antioxidant, as is the wheat germ oil. There are many beauty oils on the market, and though the mass-produced ones are made with mineral oil, you can get any number of natural ones in health food stores. In the herbal blend I make I also include evening primrose oil, macadamia nut oil, lavender oil, panthenol, aloe vera oil, and essential fatty acid oils, most of which can be difficult to obtain. The formula above has only easy-to-get oils.

To make, simply combine the first six oils in a clean container. Heat to about 70° C. Combine the aloe vera gel with the glycerine in another container. Heat to about 70° C. Slowly pour the aloe-glycerine mixture into the oils while stirring. Stir until cooled to about 45° C. Pour the mixture into an applicator bottle (with a toggle cap for easy pouring). Even though this oil is preserved with vitamin E and wheat germ oil it is a good idea to keep it in the refrigerator when not in use. If the oils tend to separate (due to the water content of the aloe vera gel), simply use the good old emulsion system invented in 30 B. C.: shake well before using.

SUN PROTECTION OIL WITH SPF 15

Almond Oil	2.50 oz.
Vitamin E Oil	.50 oz.

Jojoba Oil	1.00 oz.
Aloe Vera	2.00 oz.
Glycerine	1.25 oz.
PABA Powder	.50 oz.
Panthenol Powder	0.25 oz.
	8.00 oz.

Combine the three oils in a container and heat to 70° C. while stirring. Combine the aloe vera, glycerine, and PABA powder in a container and heat to 70° C. while stirring. Be sure all the lumps of PABA powder and panthenol powder are thoroughly mixed into the solution. Slowly pour the aloe-PABA mixture into the oils while stirring. Allow to cool to 45° C. Pour into an applicator bottle for use. If the mixture tends to separate because of the water in the aloe vera, shake well before using. The PABA can be obtained from a vitamin supplier or simply mash PABA tablets into powder to add to the formula, although the tablets may contain undesirable excipients and fillers: the pure powder is better. The SPF 15 is probably exceeded by the amount of PABA in the formula; however, you will want to test this product out on your own skin by using it on one arm and a mass-produced suntan oil on the other arm. If you adjust the PABA to a higher amount, reduce the almond oil to a lower amount. The aloe vera gel in this formula is soothing to the skin, but if you want a pure oil with no water content, use aloe vera oil.

SUN PROTECTION LOTION WITH SPF 15

Oil Phase:	
Almond Oil	38.0%
Jojoba Oil	5.0%
Beeswax	2.0%
Vitamin E Oil	.5%
Water Phase:	
Aloe Vera Gel	10.0%
Glycerine	5.0%
PABA	10.0%
Astringent	29.5%
	100.0%

Combine the oil phase in a container and heat while stirring to 70° C. Combine the water phase in a container and heat while stirring to 70° C. Slowly add the oil phase to the water phase at 70° C. while stirring and continue to stir until it cools to 45° C. Pour into applicator bottle. You will want to test this sunscreen on yourself to arrive at whether or not the PABA is adequate for your needs. Adjust as needed. If you want a lower SPF, add less PABA; for more SPF add more PABA.

SUN PROTECTION BUTTER WITH SPF 15

African Butter	2.5 oz.
Almond Oil	1.0 oz.
PABA Powder	0.5 oz.
	100.0%

Heat the almond oil and add the PABA powder to it. Stir until the PABA is completely in solution. Melt the African butter in a separate container. Add the almond oil-PABA mixture to the African butter. Put in jar hot and allow to harden in refrigerator. This gives superb protection from UV rays. You can lower the PABA for a lower SPF and a tanning butter. Experiment on skin to attain protection factor for your skin type.

- - - - - - - - - - - - - - -

These products are all natural. I have excluded any synthetic chemicals, including hydrocarbons, from the formulas. I have not used emulsifiers so perhaps shaking the products will be needed when you use them. How do they compare to products you can buy in supermarkets, drug stores, and department stores? They are far, far superior, much better for your skin and the environment as well. How do they compare with the various brands of natural products you find in health food stores? They are just as good and in some cases better, though some natural products contain more costly and exotic ingredients. I am, quite naturally, in favor of the products I have developed, but since I have created well over a hundred natural hair and skin care products, I don't fear that you'll simply make your own and never partake of a few of my natural products. If you get hooked on making your own cosmetics, and friends begin saying (as you hand out your natural works of art), "I'd like to buy some," and you begin pouring your mixtures into bottles and labeling and shipping and printing up flyers (well-researched and utilizing ideas from this book, of course), and you even run ads in magazines that say "At Last A Truly Natural Hair and Skin Care Line . . . Read Labels" with your cosmetic company name at the bottom (something like Mother Nature and Associates), it is THEN I want you to remember me with a little token of thanks (in the form of a check every month), because after all, Mother Nature was my partner first!

Part II

A to Z Guide to Natural and Synthetic Chemicals in Cosmetics

or

Mother Nature's Cosmetic Dictionary

A to Z Guide
To Natural
and
Synthetic Chemicals
In Cosmetics

Webster, Noah, (web'ster), n., 1782-1843, U. S. lexicographer and writer. If Webster's name appeared in his own dictionary under the definitions, this is what you'd learn. His name has become a household word for definitions, meanings of words, and proving you're right and somebody is wrong when playing Scrabble. The dictionary in this book is a bit different. It will, of course, have far fewer words than Mr. Webster's effort, but it will imitate Mr. Webster in that it will give you a lot of information without disguising it with chemical jargon. Technical terminology IS necessary in the interests of brevity, but we will, insofar as it is feasible, explain terms to you as they occur. For example, if you look up the term sodium lauryl sulfate in a Webster's unabridged dictionary, you will learn that this chemical is the crystalline sodium salt $CH_3(CH_2)_{10}CH_2OSO_3Na$ of sulfated lauryl alcohol; also a mixture of sodium alkyl sulfates consisting principally of this salt as an anionic detergent, wetting agent, emulsifying agent. You will have learned quite a bit, once you understand the terminology, which we will explain. "Anionic," for example, refers to the negative charge the substance forms in a water solution, and a "detergent" is formed by the reaction of sulfate with oil, while soap is the result of an alkali reacting with an oil. A wetting agent makes water wetter, while an emulsifier acts as a chemical "binding agent" to hold an oil and water or water and oil mixture together. You will know it's a lauryl, which means it has some fatty acid in it, and, in fact, the Cosmetic Toiletry and Fragrance Association's (CTFA) *Cosmetic Ingredient Dictionary* lists it as "the sodium salt of lauryl sulfate . . ." (Second Edition, ed., Norman F. Estrin, Ph.D., Washington, D. C.; CTFA, Inc., 1977). You will also learn there are many other names for sodium lauryl sulfate, and which manufacturers are associated with the other names. What you will not learn, from either of these two dictionaries, however, is that sodium lauryl sulfate is a synthetic detergent, frequently passed off as a "coconut derivative" by so-called natural cosmetic companies, and used in shampoos, face soaps, toothpastes, etc. "Originally," states *Harry's Cosmeticology*, a standard cosmetology textbook, "the standard alkyl radicals . . . were derived from natural oils and fats . . . Gradually, however, these natural materials are being supplanted by petrochemical derivatives" (Ralph G. Harry, revised by J. B. Wilkinson, et al., Sixth Edition, London: Leonard Hill Books, 1975).

This is not an advertisement for Mr. Webster's dictionaries; his definitions do, however, offer more usable information than most dictionaries, and you can learn as much and in many cases more than from special interest dictionaries (including the CTFA's work). My dictionary is not intended to compete with Mr. Webster's fine work or the more commercial work of the CTFA (which has its place as a buying guide for cosmetic manufacturers). Instead, I decided to make it a special guide for people who want to know more about the various chemicals, both natural and synthetic, used in cosmetics; a guide they can use as a personal reference and for more detailed information about various ingredients. This information is for the more naturally-oriented individual who seeks to know if something is, for example, "drying to the hair." Mr. Webster couldn't be bothered with that, and the CTFA wouldn't want to say that whether it was true or not.

Some of my definitions are "short and sweet" or "short and sour," whichever the case may be, and some ramble on and on and on. After all, if you asked me about some ingredient I may go into a discussion, and I may not. That's how this is written. I may point out that a certain ingredient has murdered a hundred rabbits or I may say it causes skin rashes. I've carefully researched the ingredients and had experience with many of them in the lab and in the hair and skin care salon, even in utilizing them as an ingredient in a product. The main concern in my definitions, however, is that you learn about the various substances from a more personal "I can use it" or "I'd rather avoid it" knowledge.

Some chemicals are not mentioned in this dictionary because they are covered in other parts of the book (e.g., preservatives are discussed in Chapter 14; specific herbs in the herb chart and in other parts of the book).

A, VITAMIN - A fat soluble vitamin that can be obtained from the following food sources: fish liver oil, liver, carrots, green and yellow vegetables, eggs, milk and dairy products, margarine, and yellow fruits. Vitamin A works to counteract night blindness, rough and dry skin (including mucous membranes). It is an antioxidant and prevents vitamin C from being oxidized too quickly in the body. Some studies have found that amounts of vitamin A over 100,000 units daily over a period of months can be toxic.

Discussion - The cosmetic uses of this vitamin may be more outstanding than most other vitamins. The oil from carrots, which is high in vitamin A and provitamin A, has been used in combination with vitamin C, vitamin E, and grapefruit seed extract as a cosmetic preservative with great success originally by Aubrey Organics and later on by other natural cosmetic manufacturers (See **GRAPEFRUIT SEED OIL**). It has been reported that an intake of 50,000 units of vitamin A and 50 mg daily of zinc cleared some forms of acne. Topically vitamin A has been used as an acne treatment. Retinoic acid, or vitamin A acid, which is classified as a drug, is used to treat acne though some people are allergic to the treatment and their skin is made worse than before.

This acid has also been used to treat aging skin based on the positive cell action of RA in the shedding of skin cells (L. M. Milstone, J. McGuire, and J. F. LaVigne, "Retinoic Acid . . ." *J. Invest. Dermatol.*, 79/4, 1982). Vitamin A deficiency reduces the mucopolysaccharides in the skin, which profoundly accelerates the skin's aging process (K. A. Latif, I. Amla, P. B. Rama Rao, "Studies on Skin and Urinary Mucopolysaccharides . . ." *Discipline of Biochemistry and Applied Nutrition*, Mysore [India]: Central Food Technological Research Institute, 1982). Vitamin A has also been used in the treatment of psoriasis. Twenty patients with psoriasis were treated with the vitamin A derivative etretinate. Four out of seven patients improved. Side effects were dose-related and included skin problems as well as abnormalities of the blood lipids and liver (R. P. Kaplan, D. H. Russell, and N. J. Lowe, "Etretinate therapy for psoriasis . . ." *J. Am. Acad. Dermatol.*, 8/1, 1983). Topical benefits of vitamin A include its normalizing, water barrier, and anti-keratinizing properties and its role in maintaining soft and plump skin. Vitamin A also is useful in the treatment of seasonal or environmental skin problems caused by heat, dryness, pollution and UV exposure and is an excellent ingredient in after-sun products as well. The amount of vitamin A to include in cosmetic products is 5,000 to 8,000 IU/gram.

Chemical Type -Can be synthetic or natural, derived from animal or vegetable sources. Cod liver oil and carrot oil are two common sources for vitamin A.

Cosmetic Use - Used in skin creams for skin that is weak in the secretion of sebum or that is dry, chapped, or scales easily. Used for aging skin, in sun protection creams, and after-sun products.

Toxicity - Vitamin A is non-toxic in topical use, though some vitamin A derivatives have side effects.

ABIETIC ACID - This is an organic acid from wood rosin. Turpentine (from rosin) contains up to 50% abietic acid.

Discussion - In Chinese medicine, rosin has been used for centuries to treat rheumatism, stiff joints, toothache, boils, and sores.

Chemical Type - Can be natural or synthetic.

Cosmetic Use - Turpentine is used as an ingredient in many ointments and as a fixative for perfumes.

Toxicity - The toxic effects of turpentine include erythema, urticaria, headache, insomnia, coughs, vomiting, and contact allergenic reactions. It also has antimicrobial activities.

ABRASION - When the skin is scraped but not cut.

Discussion - Certain plant extracts have been found to increase the healing of such excoriations by 16% compared to creams without these herbal extracts (which only increased healing time by 3%). The skin was abraded and treated with creams containing the herbals and creams without the herbals (human tests). The herbal extracts used for increased healing were Roman camomile, St. John's wort, blue bottle, feverfew, calendula, and limetree.

ABRASIVES - The most used abrasives are calcium carbonate (chalk) and dicalcium phosphate dihydrate in toothpaste. An abrasive should buff and polish the teeth without scratching them. Chalk has a higher pH and more aftertaste than phosphate. Abrasives are used in skin cleansers and scrubs, but great care should be taken so the skin is not harmed. Meals and powdered herbs can be used; pumice and clay can be used, but the exfoliation action must be gentle.

ABSOLUTES - This is the named applied to pure essential oils which are obtained from plants (generally flowers) and used in products as natural fragrance additives. When used for the care of the body as in aromatherapy, they are simple "essential oils."

ABSORPTION BASE - This is a mixture or compound that acts as a carrier for ingredients and at the same time increases the absorption of these

ingredients by the skin (usually via the pilo-sebaceous apparatus).

Discussion - The earliest evidence of absorption bases and the therapeutic action of introducing substances into the epidermis is 1809, but the use of absorption bases probably goes back to the beginnings of cosmetics in ancient Egypt. A modern example of an absorption base is DMSO (dimethyl sulfide), a solvent that is so quickly absorbed that if you applied DMSO to your foot, you could detect its oyster-like taste in your mouth within minutes. Of course any ingredient combined with DMSO would also be taken into the body as well. (One episode of the TV show *Quincy* illustrated this capacity. Quincy solved a murder based on the victim's saying - just before he died - that he had the taste of oysters in his mouth, although he hadn't eaten any oysters. From this Quincy eventually deduced that the murderer had painted a mixture of DMSO and poison on the steering wheel of the car driven by the victim just before he died.) Lanolin is another absorption base, although some people are allergic to this substance. One early absorption base was a mixture of 10% lanolin alcohols, 55% lanolin, 34.5% water, and 0.5% essential oils (Germany, 1880). A natural absorption base I have created and used for some time consists of essential fatty acids (EFAs), aloe vera, and vitamins A, C, and E. Mineral oil does not absorb well into the skin and is not a good absorption base. Many essential oils (from herbs) make excellent absorption mediums.

Chemical Type - May be natural or synthetic. Obviously, a natural absorption base is safer because the purpose of the base is to be absorbed into the body.

Toxicity - An absorption base may be toxic or non-toxic depending on the substances used.

ACEROLA - The fruit of a small tree *(Malpighia glabra)* known as the Barbados cherry. They have a tart flavor and are high in vitamin C (1 to 4.5% compared with 0.05% in the orange). Also contains 4,300 to 12,500 IU vitamin A (per 100 grams) compared with 11,000 IU vitamin A in 100 grams of carrots. The other vitamins (thiamine, riboflavin, and niacin) are the same as other fruits. Acerola doesn't have a specific cosmetic use, but it is an excellent source of vitamins C and A.

ACETIC ACID - An organic acid found in vinegar, also in human sweat.

Chemical Type - Can be natural or synthetic.

Cosmetic Use - Solvent, rubefacient, astringent, styptic, and acidifier.

ACETONE - A colorless volatile liquid sometimes used in astringents, nail polish, nail polish removers, preservatives, etc.

ACETONE Continued.
Chemical Type - Synthetic.
Cosmetic Use - Acetone is used in cosmetics as a solvent to dissolve and remove whatever debris may be on the surface of the skin or nail. In industry acetone is used in paints or to clean paintbrushes.
Toxicity - Extremely toxic. Acetone may be fatal with an oral intake of more than four ounces. Splitting of the keratin in nails, dermatitis, eye and lung irritation, and possible central nervous system disorders may also result from exposure to acetone.

ACETYLCHOLINE, AS PERSPIRATION INITIATOR - The cholinergic nerves release acetylcholine which induces perspiration. Sweating can be produced by the intradermal application of acetylcholine; however, it is not prudent to tamper with the cholinergic process since these glands are controlled by the sympathetic nervous system. The endings of the nerve fibers liberate acetylcholine as the body's chemical mediator between them and the sweat glands. The body utilizes sweat as a means of "cooling" and ridding itself of toxins. Also, the use of deodorants with aluminum to reduce perspiration may cause collection of "toxic reserves" in the glands resulting in rashes and irritation. Interference with acetylcholine may be a cause of Alzheimer's Disease. See **ALUMINUM CHEMICALS IN COSMETICS..**

ACID - A substance containing hydrogen replaceable by metals to form salts and capable of dissociating in an aqueous solution to form hydrogen ions. Also designated as having a pH of below 7.0 (the pH of water).

ACID COLOR - Large group of inorganic dyes including many FD & C and D & C colors. See **CHAPTER 10.**

ACID, AMINO - An inorganic acid containing an amine chemical group. Amino acids are linked together in specific ways to form polypeptides and proteins. Glycine, for example, is a simple amino acid.
Discussion - It has been suggested that the sulfur-hydrogen link called a sulfhydryl bond (also known as thiol compounds) is dependent on the thiol amino acid cysteine, believed by some researchers to be an important stimulant to the immune system which works with thiamine (B_1). Animal studies have suggested that the amino acids arginine and ornithine prevent the formation of tumors and that they also enhance the thymus and the lymphocytes. It is believed by some that the thymus gland, if large and healthy, will increase the lifespan due to the development of the immune system cells known as thymocytes. Interestingly enough, a large and healthy thymus is also associated with the study of classical music but not with other forms of music; hence, the old age many famous classical conductors, composers, and performers attain. We have not learned all there is to know about amino acids.

Chemical Type - Usually natural. What consumers need to watch for with amino acids in cosmetics is the overall naturalness of the formula and where the amino acid is listed in the ingredients list. Is enough amino acid included to make a significant contribution to the hair and skin's health, or is it down at the bottom next to the fragrance?
Cosmetic Use - The hair is made up of eighteen amino acids that form large condensed polymeric structures by the formation of amide links between the acid group of one amino acid and the amino acid of another group. Cystine is one of the important amino acids to the hair and forms the "cystine bridge" or "cystine bond." Quite often this bridge is destroyed by cold wave solutions, hair colors, toners, and bleaches, which causes heat breakage and sometimes hair loss. Other sulfur-containing amino acids important to hair and skin health are cysteine and methionine. These particular amino acids are essential to protein metabolism during which they give up their sulfur, thereby enabling the body to build its own amino acid model. Some of the better hair and skin care products contain the sulfur amino acids in their formulas.
Toxicity - Generally non-toxic.

ACID BALANCED - A pseudo-scientific advertising term used to sell shampoos and skin cleansers. The pH of hair and skin ranges between 4.5 to 5.5, and the pH of an "acid balanced" product has been adjusted to within this range (although a product's pH generally drifts over time and changes as soon as it is used on the hair or skin). The idea of an "acid balanced" product has been around for more than a decade and has not been proven to improve the hair or skin in any way, particularly since most "acid balanced" products use the same old synthetic chemicals. Further, when a substance is used on the hair or skin, its pH is adjusted by the body to fit within the optimum range fairly quickly as long as its pH is not too acid or alkaline. Our bodies are not fragile organisms that must be protected from every deviation in the environment. What is unfortunate about the "pH balanced" slogan is that it lures consumers into a false sense of doing something natural and better for themselves. Consumers must question this kind of advertising approach and not allow themselves to be distracted from the all-important ingredients list. See **CHAPTER 3.**

ACID, ESSENTIAL FATTY - Otherwise known as vitamin F, these substances cannot be manufactured by the body and must be consumed in the diet; they are linoleic, linolenic, and arachidonic acids.
Discussion - The essential fatty acids lubricate the body, aid in the transportation of oxygen to the cells, help coagulate the blood, combine with vitamin D to make calcium available to the tissues, regulate glandular activity, break up cholesterol deposits on arterial walls, maintain healthy

ESSENTIAL FATTY ACIDS Continued.
mucous membranes and nerves, assist in the assimilation of phosphorus, and help convert carotene to vitamin A. The more saturated fats are consumed in the diet, the greater the intake of essential fatty acids should be; this amount has been estimated by the National Research Council to be at least one per cent of the daily caloric intake, and should probably be higher. There are no known toxic effects of vitamin F; however, the essential fatty acids are highly perishable and are destroyed by heat, light, and exposure to air. Excellent sources for unsaturated fatty acids are raw wheat germ, raw sunflower seeds, butter, and cold-pressed vegetable oils. Keep these foods refrigerated!

Chemical Type - Natural and non-toxic.

Cosmetic Use - Essential fatty acids are used in the production of sebum, your skin's own natural oil, so including these substances in skin care products makes good sense. Plus, the essential fatty acids tend to be bateriostatic, i.e., they inhibit the production of bacteria. They're also readily absorbed by the skin (See **CHAPTER 4**). Essential fatty acids are found in the best hair and skin care products.

ACID MANTLE - The slightly acidic mixture of fatty acids and perspiration on the surface of the skin that helps protect from bacterial growth. There is disagreement as to whether the skin is protected by the pH of the acid mantle or the bacteriostatic nature of the fatty acids, which inhibits the growth of microorganisms. The acid mantle is temporarily destroyed each time you wash your face and remove the acidic coating but re-establishes itself quickly. Look for natural fatty acids and disinfecting herbal oils in your cosmetic products - they'll help protect your skin.

ACID RINSE - An acid rinse is useful for removing soap films from the hair after shampooing. A solution of vinegar and water or lemon juice and water is a natural acid rinse.

ACNE - An inflammation of the sebaceous glands due to retained secretions.

ACNE ARTIFICIALIS - Pimples occurring due to external irritants or drugs administered internally.

ACNE ATROPHICA - Vulgaris in which the lesions of the pimples leave a slight amount of scarring.

ACNE CACHECHTICORUM - Occurs in the subjects of anemia or some debilitating constitutional disease.

ACNE HYPERTROPHICA - Pimples in which the lesions, upon healing, leave conspicuous pits and scars.

ACNE INDURATA - Deeply seated pimples with hard tubercular lesions occurring chiefly on the back.

ACNE KERATOS - An eruption of papules consisting of horny plugs projecting from the hair follicles, accompanied by inflammation.

ACNE PUNCTATA - Appearing as red papules, usually accompanied by blackheads.

ACNE PUSTULOSA - Vulgaris in which the pustular lesions predominate.

ACNE ROSACEA - A form of acne, usually occurring around the cheeks and nose, due to congestion in which the capillaries become dilated and on occasion broken.

ACNE SIMPLEX - Simple, uncomplicated pimples.

ACRYLAMIDE/ACRYLATES/BUTYLAMINO-ETHYL/METHYLACRYLATE POLYMER - These are polymers and copolymers. Some are used as opacifiers in cosmetics (such as styrene, PVP, and methacrylates). Acrylates and other synthetic polymers are also used in shampoos. Cellulose polymer is used in nail lacquers. Acrylates cause various skin problems. When used in fabrics or cosmetics, allergic reactions occur. See **POLYMERS**.

ADDITIVES - A substance which is added to a product by the manufacturer of the product or by anybody during or after the product is made. An additive can be natural or synthetic.

ADENOMA SEBACEUM - A small tumor of translucent appearance originating in the sebaceous glands.

ADIPIC ACID - Polymers of adipic acid and diethylene triamine are sometimes used for permanent wave preparations (though polyvinylpyrrolidone is most often used). Also used in neutralizers for permanent wave solutions. Allergic reactions and eye problems are encountered from these polymers. See **POLYMERS**.

ADIPOSE TISSUE - Tissue where fat is stored, consisting of connective tissue in which the cells are distended with fat.

ADRENAL GLANDS - Adjacent to the kidneys, these endocrine glands produce adrenalin (the flight or fight hormone) and other regulatory hormones.

ADULTERATE - To falsify or alter; make impure by combining foreign substances with a natural one: a common practice in some cosmetics. To be sure of unadulterated products, read the ingredients label.

ADVERSE EFFECTS OF SUNLIGHT - It is now well-established that ultraviolet rays from the sun can adversely affect the skin. The major disadvantage is skin cancer. Using a sunblock with SPF 15 is advisable. It is not known if the intake of 1000 mg PABA will act to protect the skin from UV rays, but this has been suggested. The eyes can also be harmed by the sun, and glasses with a special 400 UV protective coating have been suggested, but some researchers say that any type of dark lenses work as well. See **CHAPTER 11**.

AEROSOL - The use of aerosol sprays began in the U. S. Army for various military and domestic uses. One of the earliest patents for aerosol use in cosmetics was granted to R. W. Moore in 1903 for a perfumery atomizer. Carbon dioxide was then used as the propellant. Billions of dollars have been made with the sale of aerosol hairsprays. In the 1960's George Barrie, president of Caryl Richards Beauty Products and later of Fabergé, introduced a low-priced line of aerosol hairsprays with two brands: Aqua Net (from Rayette) and Just Wonderful Hairspray (from Caryl Richards). Before Barrie, aerosol sprays were expensive (compared to pump bottles). Barrie installed a mass production aerosol line in one of his plants and introduced aerosol hairsprays for under $2.00. The aerosol can allowed Barrie to move from the beauty salon products field into the retail toiletries field. This same mass-produced aerosol technology was occurring simultaneously in other industries (paint, pesticides, cleansers, etc.). What we didn't know during these years is that aerosol propellants and various other chemicals were being released into our atmosphere the same as a smoke stack billows out toxic fumes. The propellants reduce the ozone layers in the stratosphere which protects us from UV rays (especially the harmful UVC rays). The simplest way to stop this airborne pollution and ozonosphere destruction is to use pump bottles. There are "fine mist" pump applicators that give a fine aerosol type spray pattern.

AESTHETICIAN - Also esthetician. A professional who works to clean and beautify the skin. A natural aesthetician uses only natural substances and methods to care for the skin.

AETT - Acetyl Ethyl Tetramethyl Tetralin. A fragrance oil widely used in the 1970's as a fixative or masking agent. Tests on laboratory animals found that AETT turned the inner organs of these animals blue. Further testing showed that AETT went on to result in damage to the brain, spinal cord, and other neuropathological conditions. Continued use resulted in death. Tests on humans reported that the chemical would be absorbed through the skin tissue. These frightening test results led the cosmetic industry to impose their own ban on the use of AETT. The FDA would neither ban the chemical nor remove products with AETT from the shelves.

AFFINITY - Chemical compatibility of two or more substances. Also the force that unites atoms into molecules.

AGING OF SKIN - Aging is a natural process, but at the same time, some apparent effects of aging are not all that natural. Aging manifests itself in the cross-linking process in the skin's dermal proteins (collagen, elastin, and reticulin), but natural skin care can reduce this process that results in dry and wrinkled skin. Avoiding UV rays by using sunblocks or creams with PABA will also reduce the destruction of collagen by cross-linking.

And, NOT using mineral-oil containing make-up on the skin will also reduce the aging of the skin caused by all make-ups. Or, you can use protective moisturizers or oils under the make-up to reduce the damage. Cigarette smoke ages the skin and should be reduced or avoided completely. Allowing dead skin cells to pile up on the skin also increases aging of the skin, but a natural daily skin care program will eliminate this problem. See **The Natural Method of Skin Care.**

Studies have shown that an external application of soluble collagen will improve the condition of the skin by encouraging the development of new collagen fibrils. The body also recognizes organic silica as collagen, and the application of a cream containing horsetail and coltsfoot herbs will encourage the development of new collagen fibrils. See **CHAPTER 4.**

ALBUMIN - Simple class of proteins that are soluble in water, coagulated by heat, and can be found in plasma (serum albumin), eggwhites (ovalbumin), and milk (lactalbumin), as well as vegetables and fruits. Albumin is used in cosmetics as a film-forming agent. See **LACTALBUMIN.**

ALCLOXA - CTFA name for aluminum chlorhydroxy allantoinate (also dialuminum tetrahydroxychloro allantoinate). Synthetic chemical containing allantoin used as a buffer and astringent. See **ALUMINUM CHEMICALS IN COSMETICS.**

ALCOHOL - A colorless volatile liquid obtained by distillation, either by the fermenting of carbohydrates (grain, molasses, potatoes, etc.) or hydration of ethylene. The first process produces natural alcohol; the second synthetic.

Discussion - Alcohol is antiseptic and cooling, but it is also drying to the hair and skin and should be used in minor amounts. In cosmetics alcohol should be natural, i.e., grain alcohol. Isopropyl alcohol is a petrochemical and should be avoided. Sometimes you'll see the term "SD alcohol + a number." This means the alcohol was "specially denatured" and has had chemicals added to it to render it poisonous to drink. The numbers refer to different chemicals appropriate to different kinds of products in which the alcohol is used. Avoid SD alcohols because while the alcohol might be natural grain alcohol, the chemicals added are not.

Chemical Type - Can be natural or synthetic.

Toxicity - Can be drying to hair and skin in too great amounts. Avoid synthetic alcohols, including "SD alcohols." See **SD ALCOHOLS.**

ALGINIC ACID - This acid, obtained from brown algae, has been used in cosmetics as a skin protector and to soothe skin. Allantoin (from comfrey root) serves the same purpose and is a better natural material for cosmetic use.

ALKALI - Substance with a pH above neutral (7.0).

ALKALOIDS - Alkaloids can be broadly defined as natural amines (nitrogen-containing compounds) which have pharmacological properties and which are generally of plant origin. They are widely distributed throughout the plant kingdom. Most alkaloids are insoluble or only slightly soluble in water, but their salts are water-soluble. Morphine, codeine, and cocaine are all alkaloids.

ALKYL SULFATES - Alkyl sulfates were developed in Germany when vegetable oils and fats were scarce, and detergents resistant to hard water were needed. These sulfates are used in most shampoos today, and though they aren't natural chemicals, they are often represented on cosmetic labels as being natural and derived from coconut oil. Originally alkyl radicals were derived from natural oils and fats such as coconut oil, palm kernel oil, soya oil, etc., but they gradually were supplanted by petrochemicals (*Harry's Cosmeticology*, 1975). The Germans first created these sulfates for their own use, but they soon were used throughout the world in cosmetics (mainly shampoos). They have an advantage of a long chain of 12-14 carbon atoms which give more foaming power; the natural coconut or other vegetable oil soaps have a shorter chain and therefore give less foaming. Two of the best known surfactants are sodium lauryl sulfate (SLS) and sodium laureth sulfate (SLE). It has been pointed out that these two sulfates are more irritating to the skin than natural soaps (Frost and Horowitz, *Principals of Cosmetics for Dermatologists*, London: C. V. Mosby, 1982). No matter what the chain length of the synthetic sulfate detergents, they are irritating. They also can, according to a report released by the FDA in 1978, combine with other chemicals and create the cancer-causing substance NDELA. This report was never released to the public and was only written up in trade journals. See **CARCINOGENS, NITROSAMINES, SODIUM LAURYL SULFATE**, and **SODIUM LAURETH SULFATE**.

ALKYLOAMIDES - These widely used cosmetic chemicals consist of fatty acids that can be divided into four major groups: 1.) diethanolamides (DEA) type; 2.) monoethanolamides (MEA) type; 3.) monoisopropanolamides (MIPA) type; and, 4.) ethoxylated or PEG alkanolamides. Some of their many uses include thickening, gelling, emulsifying, emolliency, skin and hair conditioning, foam boosting, foam stabilizing, cleansing, wetting, solubilizing, opacifying, lubricating, powder binding, skin protecting, anti-irritant properties, fungicidal properties, and superfatting. They are most commonly found in detergent formulations such as shampoos, bubble baths, and liquid hand and body cleansers. Their main drawback is that these fatty acid-alkanolamine compounds can become contaminated with nitrosamines. Although the formation of nitrosamine compounds can be blocked with the addition of vitamin C and vitamin E, most manufacturers of these fatty acid compounds don't do this.

Discussion - *Cocamide DEA* is the best known of the DEA series. They are made with coconut oil, whole coconut fatty acids, and stripped coconut fatty acids. The mixture can vary from equal parts of DEA and cocamide to two parts cocamide to one part DEA. An equal mixture of DEA and cocamide is often used because it creates a thicker looking product, but it is less water soluble than the 2:1 ratio. Both mixtures should have vitamins C and E added to them to prevent the growth of a nitrosamine agent.

Lauramide DEA is another well-known chemical in the DEA series of fatty acid mixtures. These are believed to be the best foam boosters in shampoos, bubble baths, and other detergent systems. They are made by combining lauric and myristic fatty acids with DEA. Again, vitamin C and vitamin E should be added to prevent the formation of a nitrosamine.

Myristamide DEA is the least-used of the DEA series because it is less effective in foaming and cleansing. It does, however, produce thicker products. Vitamins C and E should be added to prevent the formation of a nitrosamine.

Undecylenamide DEA is similar to the other DEA series above, but it has fungicidal and bacteriostatic properties due to undecylenic acid. It can be irritating to the skin and drying to the hair. Again, vitamins C and E should be added to prevent the growth of a nitrosamine.

Oleamide DEA will not give the same foaming results as the other DEA types, but is a good thickening agent. It also has some conditioning properties. Vitamins C and E should be added to prevent the growth of a nitrosamine.

Isostearamide DEA is used in shampoos and for its viscosity-building properties. It can reduce the irritating effects caused by some chemicals, and it is claimed that it is a hair conditioning agent and a skin emollient. Vitamins C and E should be added to prevent the growth of a nitrosamine.

Stearamide DEA is made from triple-pressed stearic acid which can add a pearliness to shampoos and is a thickening agent. It can be used as a non-anionic emulsifier in water/oil emulsions. It will supposedly reduce tension between the oil and water phases as well as increasing the emulsion's overall viscosity. Vitamins C and E should be added to prevent the growth of a nitrosamine.

Linoleamide DEA is known mainly for its thickening properties. When used in anionic detergents it forms a clear thick product, like a gel. The addition of vitamins C and E is suggested to block the possible formation of nitrosamines.

The first fatty alkanolamides discovered were the DEA type by Kritchevsky in 1937. He combined one mole of fatty acid with 2 moles of diethanolamine. Diethanolamine has also been combined with palm oil, soya, and tallow to create soaps.

Fatty acid monoethanolamides (MEAs) are also used as foam boosters in shampoos and other cosmetics. They can also be used as waxes. They are less soluble in water since they have only a single hydrophilic hydroxy group compared with the two

ALKYLOAMIDES Continued
hydroxy groups of DEA. A positive fact is that the fatty amides in MEA are purer in composition than those of DEA.

ALLANTOIN - Allantoin is widely reported to have healing, soothing, and anti-irritating properties. It can be extracted from urea (from the urine of most animals, including humans) or from herbs such as comfrey or uva ursi. See **CHAPTER 8.**

ALLERGY - A hypersensitive reaction to specific substances that develops in some persons. To avoid allergic reactions, use natural products and if you have a doubt as to whether you are allergic or not to a certain substance, be sure to patch test.

ALMOND MEAL - This is the residue that remains after the almond oil has been expressed. Usually only sweet almonds are used. Almond meal is an excellent meal to use for exfoliation. See **CHAPTER 6.**

ALOPECIA - A deficiency of hair; baldness. Partial baldness is called **ALOPECIA AREATA.**

ALUM - Used in medicine, dyeing, and technical processes, this substance is a double sulfate of aluminum and potassium. It is used in the food industry as a food starch modifier, in the manufacture of pickles, baking powder, gelatin, cheese, and other foods. In the cosmetic industry it is used in antiperspirants, powders, antiseptics, and detergents. It can cause allergic reactions, infection of the skin or hair follicles, and irritation of the lungs when inhaled. Also known as aluminum sulfate. See **ALUMINUM CHEMICALS IN COSMETICS.**

ALUMINUM CHEMICALS IN COSMETICS - There are so many aluminum chemicals used in cosmetics that if the theory is true that aluminum compounds cause Alzheimer's Disease we are being prepared for this deadly disease under our arms with the use of aluminum chlorohydrate in deodorants, on our teeth with aluminum fluoride in toothpaste, and on our skin with alumina in astringents. Many researchers warn you not to use aluminum cooking utensils, but little is said about the aluminum that enters our bodies through the skin. It obviously does. Certainly there is a greater chance of aluminum entering the body through cosmetic use than by the frying pan. We are aware that the aluminum chemicals used in cosmetics are toxic and cause various allergic reactions. Read labels and avoid the various aluminum chemicals used in cosmetics. The measure of neurotransmitters in the brains of Alzheimer's victims showed a deficiency of acetylcholine. Chemicals or drugs that interfere with the action of acetylcholine will cause problems with intellectual functions. Anticholinergics can produce a dementia-like state. Aluminum chemicals may disrupt the normal activity of acetylcholine, and certainly an antiperspirant under the arms should be considered, along with other aluminum chemicals, as a danger to the normal function of the acetylcholine. Medical research is attempting to find a replacement for acetylcholine. See **ACETYLCHOLINE.**

AMBERGRIS - Secretion from the intestinal tract of the sperm whale. Some manufacturers have used it as a fixative in fragrances. Because whales are an endangered species, use of natural spermaceti is prohibited by law in this country.

AMIDES AND AMINES - Amides are derivatives of carboxylic acid, an organic acid like formic, acetic, and benzoic acids. The simple amides are considered to be derivatives formed by the placement of the carboxylic hydroxyl group by the amino group. When they are created the name is changed by dropping the "ic" or "oic" from the name of the parent compound and adding the suffix "amide." For example, formic acid, when replaced by an amino group, becomes foramide. Amides are strongly associated through hydrogen bonding and hence soluble in hydroxylic solvents (such as water and alcohol). They are also low-melting solids, stable, and weakly acidic. For these (and other) reasons, amides are often used in soaps or shampoos. One popular amide, cocamide, combines coconut fatty acid with the ammonium salts of carboxylic acid. The amide gives the coconut fatty acid a thicker appearance and an improved sudsing action. When amides are combined with soap bark (quillaya bark), a thick brown liquid with good sudsing action results. The soap bark on its own is very cleansing but has a low suds factor.

Amines are organic compounds that play a prominent role in biochemical systems because they are so widely distributed in nature as amino acids, alkaloids, and vitamins. Amines are present in substances as varied as adrenaline, thiamine (B$_1$), and novacaine. Nylon is an amine derivative. Amines are used in the manufacture of medicinal chemicals such as sulfa drugs and anesthetics. In cosmetics amines are often combined with synthetic chemicals and petrochemicals.

AMIF-72 - This is a synthetic chemical mixture to prevent spoilage proposed by the American Meat Institute Foundation. It contains 20% BHA, 6% propyl gallate, and 4% citric acid in propylene glycol. This mixture may replace the nitrates as antioxidants, but its possible toxicity is unknown. It is advisable to avoid using such synthetic chemicals. (See **BUTYLATED HYDROXYLANISOLE** and **PROPYL GALLATE.**)

AMINO ACIDS - See **ACIDS, AMINO.**

AMINOPHENOL - One of the amino-type permanent hair dyes in use since 1883. Aminophenol is used to produce medium brown, orange-red, and blond shades. Aminophenol is also used to develop photographs and to manufacture dyes, including those used for furs and feathers. This chemical has caused problems for its users since it was first introduced: contact dermatitis, skin sensitization, restlessness, convulsions, and depletion of oxygen in the blood. See **4-METHOXY-M-PHENYLENE-DIAMINE.**

AMMONIA - A familiar compound made from the elements nitrogen and hydrogen (NH_3). It is formed as the result of the decomposition of organic material and can easily be detected by its strong irritating odor. Amine (see above) is one of a group of compounds formed by combining ammonia molecules with metal ions such as calcium, strontium, and barium. Ammonia has a wide range of industrial uses. It is used, for example, in the production of nitric acid, ammonium salts, the sulfates (used in many shampoo chemicals), nitrate (used as a preservative in meats and occurring in shampoo chemicals), carbonate, chloride, and the synthesis of hundreds of compounds, including drugs, plastics, hair dyes, and permanent wave solutions.

Chemical Type - An inorganic gas. The chemical properties of liquid ammonia are of a solvent nature, and it is widely used as a glass cleaner or surface cleaner. Ammonia is synthesized in a process in which water gas is mixed with nitrogen and passed through a scrubber cooler to remove the dust and undecomposed material.

Toxicity - A very toxic material which should be avoided. Inhaling ammonia can be fatal. Topically ammonia causes serious skin problems and can be absorbed into the body. It has the same toxic reactions when it is used to manufacture various other compounds such as nitrate (which is now known to be a carcinogen). When used in wave solutions or in hair dyes it has caused a great variety of physical problems since it is a primary irritant. When used in shampoo chemicals it has many side effects (including dry hair, scalp lesions, hair loss, and the absorption of nitrate into the blood stream). This is a primary irritant. Avoid ammonia chemicals.

AMMONIUM CHEMICALS IN COSMETICS - It is difficult to say whether or not every ammonia chemical used in cosmetics has an adverse reaction. So much depends on the formula and purpose of the cosmetic as well as the content of ammonia. To date there have been so many allergic reactions to ammonium compounds it is fair to say the prudent individual should read a cosmetic label and avoid any cosmetic chemical containing ammonia. The problem is, of course, since ammonia is used to manufacture chemicals which are then given other names (such as sodium nitrate and the sulfates) that we can't know by simple label reading what chemical may contain ammonia or ammonium salts. Often a trade name may be given to an ammonium compound or raw material containing ammonia that we may be taking ammonia without being aware of it. When we eat bacon which contains nitrite (derived from nitric acid) or nitrate, we aren't aware that these are chemicals created with ammonia (including nitro- and nitroso- compounds). These compounds are used in meats and in cosmetics as liquid detergents, and when used on the skin or in the hair are absorbed in larger quantities than when eaten in meats (such as bacon). The best advice is to NOT use a cosmetic that contains a synthetic chemical or nitro-

or nitroso- compounds as well as sulfates or sulfites. For example, if you see the chemical sodium alkyl sulfate on a label you know that it contains ammonium salts because of the word "sulfate." The synthetic detergents used in shampoos, dishwashing liquids, laundry detergents, and soaps usually contain alkyl lauryl sulfates. Avoid ammonium chemicals as much as possible. Don't take them internally in foods or use them externally in cosmetics. Use gloves when you use a dish or laundry detergent, and don't lean over hot water and breathe in the fumes of detergents. Many allergies are due to these often simple contacts.

AMMONIUM CARBONATE - A powerful chemical used as a pH adjuster in many permanent wave preparations. It can sensitize the face, scalp, hands, and cause contact dermatitis.

AMMONIUM HYDROXIDE - Used in hair waving solutions, hair straighteners, and detergents, this highly caustic chemical can irritate the mucous membranes and even burn the skin. It is also used to remove stains, in refrigeration, and in the manufacture of explosives. Avoid putting this on your hair or skin at all costs.

AMPHOTERIC SURFACTANTS - Surface active agents possessing both a positive and negative charge, capable of reacting as either an acid or a base, depending on the rest of the formula. (Editor's note: according to *Harry's Cosmetology*, the correct term for this type of surfactant is "ampholytic," but the *CTFA Dictionary* and consumer books refer to them as "amphoterics," so we'll stick with their term for convenience's sake. What's in a word, right?) Amphoterics are sold to cosmetic manufacturers and hence, indirectly to consumers, as milder and better than the alkyl sulfate detergents discussed above. In fact, many shampoos combine an alkyl sulfate detergent and an amphoteric surfactant, like cocamide betaine. However, as you can see from the definition, "amphoteric" is an adjective that has nothing to do with what the substance actually IS. You can have a natural amphoteric or a synthetic amphoteric, and whether it's natural or synthetic is important, not what its pH or electrical charge is. In this respect, the amphoteric "debate" is rather like the "pH balanced" debate--- a tempest in a teacup for cosmetic chemists and marketing executives to carry on among themselves. As consumers we're interested in what a substance will actually do for the hair and skin, which has nothing to do with whether or not it's an "amphoteric surfactant." The truth is cosmetic chemists like amphoterics because they're easy to use, but that, like so many other aspects of a cosmetic's formula, has nothing to do with us. Look for natural soaps in your shampoos and don't settle for anything else.

AMYL ACETATE - Solvent used in nail polish. Acts as a central nervous system depressant and skin irritant. Inhalation of vapors harmful to respiratory system. Toxic. See also **BUTYL ACETATE** and **ETHYL ACETATE**.

AMYL DIMETHYL PABA - A PABA (para-aminobenzoic acid) ester mixed with amyl alcohol and used in sunscreen products. May cause eczema and allergic dermatitis. Partly natural and partly synthetic. Why use a partly natural PABA? Search out real natural PABA instead.

AMYLOPECTIN - A texturizing ingredient made from corn.

ANABOLISM - Constructive metabolism; the process of assimilation of nutritive matter into living substances.

ANAPHORESIS - The movement of electrically charged particles into tissues.

ANETHOLE - This substance is used in flavoring (especially toothpastes) and as an aromatic.
    Chemical Type - May be natural or synthetic. If natural, anethole is a mixture of anise and fennel essential oils. If synthetic, its chemical name is 1-methoxy-4-propenylbenzene, but there is no way for the consumer to know which form is in the product. Check the rest of the formula for naturalness.
    Toxicity - May be irritating to the skin or if ingested.

ANHYDROUS - Containing no water, e.g., anhydrous lanolin.

ANILINE - Discovered in Germany in 1873, aniline dyes are made from coal tar and used in permanent hair dyes. Coal tar is a suspected human carcinogen, and it (and its derivatives) should be avoided.

ANIONIC SURFACTANTS - "Anionic" refers to the negative electrical charge these surface active agents (detergents) have. These synthetic chemicals form the base detergent in most shampoos, mass-merchandised or so-called "natural."
    Chemical Type - Synthetic. NEVER natural.
    Cosmetic Use - Anionic surfactants are inexpensive for manufacturers but hard on consumers' hair. They make lots of suds so consumers think their hair is getting clean, but these harsh chemicals can strip hair of all natural oils and leave it dry and damaged. Some examples of anionic surfactants are sodium lauryl sulfate, TEA (triethanolamine) lauryl sulfate, ammonium lauryl sulfate, sodium laureth sulfate, TEA laureth sulfate, ammonium laureth sulfate, lauroyl sarcosine, cocoyl sarcosine, sodium lauroyl sarcosinate, sodium cocoyl sarcosinate, potassium coco-hydrolyzed animal protein, disodium oleamide sulfosuccinate, sodium dioctyl sulfosuccinate, sodium methyl oleoyl sulfate, and sodium lauryl isoethionate.
    Toxicity - A serious problem with these chemicals is that they may be contaminated with NDELA (N-nitrosodiethanolamine), one of the nitrosamines and a potent carcinogen, according to a 1978 FDA report. Shampooing the hair with a product contaminated with this substance can lead to its absorption into the body at levels much higher than eating nitrite-contaminated foods. Avoid these chemicals. See **NITROSAMINES**.

ANTI-BACTERIAL - Hostile to bacteria. This term differs slightly but significantly from **BACTERIOSTATIC**, which means to create an environment in which bacteria don't want to live without destroying them. Natural substances, such as herbal essential oils, tend to be bacteriostatic.

ANTI-DANDRUFF SHAMPOOS - Most contain colloidal sulfur, zinc pyrithione, salicyclic acid, or resorcinol, which are mixed into the usual harsh synthetic detergent base and preserved with the parabens. Selenium sulfide, jojoba oil, amino acids, indigofera, and aloe vera are natural dandruff treatments. Look for a mild soap base that will not be irritating to a dandruff-prone scalp.

ANTIOXIDANTS - These substances prevent the formation of free radicals in the body, i. e., chemically reactive molecules; also, the too-rapid oxidation of nutrients. These substances have received much publicity in recent years as potential life-extenders; they can be divided into several categories: vitamins, minerals, enzymes, amino acids, and synthetic chemicals, including some food additives. Vitamin A, Vitamin C complex (including ascorbic acid, rutin, bioflavonoids, and hesperidin), vitamin B complex (including thiamine, niacin, pantothenic acid, pyridoxine, PABA, inositol, and choline), and vitamin E are the antioxidant vitamins. The minerals include selenium and zinc. The enzymes, produced by the body, are superoxide dismutase (SOD) and glutathione peroxidase. Cysteine is the amino acid. BHA and BHT are the synthetic food additives.
    Chemical Type - Natural and synthetic.
    Cosmetic Use - Natural antioxidants, e.g., vitamins A, C, and E, can be used to preserve cosmetics, although usually we will see BHA or BHT used in this way.
    Toxicity - Avoid synthetic antioxidants.

ANTI-PERSPIRANTS - Substances or products that inhibit or prevent perspiration. This blocks the pores of the skin and can cause allergic reactions. See **ACETYLCHOLINE** and **ALUMINUM CHEMICALS IN COSMETICS**.

ANTISEPTICS - Against *sepsis*, or putrefaction and decay: also, inhibiting the growth of microorganisms. Many herbs have natural antiseptic action, which is preferable to the harsher synthetic antiseptics.

ARAROBA - Also known as **GOA**. See **CHRYSAROBIN** below. See also **ARAROBA** in the **HERB CHART**.

AROMATHERAPY - This is the art of using essential oils froms roots, barks, and herbs for treating the face and body. This art began in ancient Egypt, Persia, India, China, Greece, and Rome. In fact, the ancient Greek physician Hippocrates used aromatherapy massage, steaming and hot baths for many ills. Each herb has various

AROMATHERAPY Continued
therapeutic effects, whether they are inhaled, steamed, or massaged into the body. Essential oils have a vitalizing effect on the dermis and subcutaneous tissues to varying degrees.

ASTEATOSIS - A deficiency or absence of the sebaceous secretions.

ASTRINGENTS - Contracts tissue. In the **Natural Method of Skin Care**, the use of a natural herbal astringent is recommended after the skin is thoroughly cleansed to remove soap films and cellular debris.
 Chemical Type - Astringents may be natural or synthetic. We recommend a witch hazel based herbal astringent over synthetic astringents that may contain acetone or isopropyl alcohol. Read labels carefully.
 Cosmetic Use - Astringents tend to contract tissue and close skin pores. A natural herbal astringent with herbal extracts will also disinfect skin with herbal essential oils. Astringents are often recommended for the correction of oily skin, but a natural herbal astringent is excellent for toning all skin types.
 Toxicity - Check labels for synthetic ingredients, and avoid synthetic astringents.

ATHLETE'S FOOT - A fungus infection of the foot: epidermophytyosis.

ATOMIZE - To reduce to minute particles or to a fine spray. Generally used for application of various minerals, vitamins, and herbs to the skin.

AZINE - Type of synthetic color (acid-quinonoid type). Toxic. See **CHAPTER 10**.

AZO COLORS - The largest group of certified coal tar colors. These are synthetic. They are toxic. Avoid them. See **CHAPTER 10**.

AZULENE - An anti-inflammaory agent extracted in concentrated form from the camomile flower and used for its soothing qualities.

B

B COMPLEX VITAMINS - These water-soluble vitamins include B_1 (thiamine), B_2 (riboflavin), B_3 (niacin), B_5 (pantothenic acid), B_6 (pyridoxine), B_{12} (cyanocobalamin), biotin, folic acid, (PABA) para-aminobenzoic acid, carnitine (B^T), choline, and inositol.
 Chemical Type - Mostly natural.
 Discussion - Vitamin B Complex as a yeast extract contains natural B vitamins and secondary yeast components. It is used in cosmetics for the

application to skin with excessive secretion of sebum (greasy and blemished skin) and for enlarged pores. The B Complex can also be used in shampoos or scalp lotions for excessive secretion of sebum (the tendency to greasiness and dandruff). As a natural cosmetic raw material the B Complex should contain the following active ingredients per 100 ml: 25.00 mg vitamin B_1; 0.25 mg vitamin B_2; 1.80 mg vitamin B_6; and 1.40 mcg B_{12}. B Complex has an unpleasant medicinal odor and if used in cosmetics, an essential oil should be used to mask the odor. The amount used in cosmetics is between 0.5% to 2.0%. The higher amount will be absorbed into the body and utilized. Creams containing B Complex have been applied to the skin and give positive results on absorption for neuralgia, neuritis, and myalgia. Of all the B vitamins B_{12} is least easily absorbed and must be either injected or dissolved or chewed in the mouth. This vitamin can, however, also be absorbed topically and give positive results. B_6 deficiency causes nervous inflammation and various disturbances of the skin such as seborrheic dermatitis. There has been success in the appiication of B Complex creams or lotions to scaling of the skin and lesions. B_2 is important to the nails and skin. B_1 deficiency can result in acidosis of the blood which will affect the nervous system. Secondary symptoms are blemishes, vesicles, erythemas, and skin irritations. PABA is a superb sun protector. Panthenol (B_5) helps with hair loss and adds a thick feel to hair. Inositol is essential for cell respiration and helps strengthen the scalp. Biotin also helps promote hair growth and helps prevent hair dryness.
 Toxicity - Vitamin B Complex is not toxic, though megadoses of individual vitamins are not recommended, especially vitamin B_6.

BABY PRODUCTS - Hair, skin, and body care products specifically for babies. These generally include baby oil, shampoo, talcum powder, soap, and lotion.
 Discussion - Babies have been subjected to the same sort of synthetic cosmetic chemicals as adults, but they don't have a well-developed immune system and hence are prone to develop allergic rashes and other problems as a result. Mineral oil, harsh synthetic detergents, and asbestos-contaminated talc, preservatives, strong synthetic fragrances - these are only a few of the chemicals found in baby products. Babies need mild, natural soaps, pure vegetable oil (instead of mineral oil which can irritate infant skin), and an herbal lotion that can help disinfect and heal skin naturally.
 Chemical Type - Largely synthetic. Only a few natural brands of baby care products are available, and among these it's necessary to carefully choose products based on the ingredients label. Watch for products with evening primrose oil, which is an effective treatment for eczema.
 Toxicity - Synthetic chemicals are more toxic for small people than adults, so natural is very important here. Read labels!

BACTERIA IN COSMETICS - All cosmetic products contain some amount of bacteria. The method of controlling bacterial growth in cosmetics is by using a preservative. Many preservatives will not work in some cosmetic formulas. For example, the paraben preservatives are not compatible with protein and many shampoo formulas, but they're still used extensively in these products. The true purpose of the preservative in cosmetics is not to protect the consumer from bacteria, but to protect the shelf life of the cosmetic. For a detailed discussion of bacteria and preservatives, see **CHAPTER 14.**

BAKING SODA - Sodium bicarbonate. Known to relieve burns, itching, urticarial lesions and insect bites. It is often used in bath powders as an aid to cleansing oily skin and is a common component of many homemade cosmetics and food preparations.

BALDNESS - A condition in which the hair comes out of the head and does not grow back. When you are fifteen to thirty years old your hair grows faster but begins to decline at the age of thirty-five. From the ages fifty to sixty there is a sharp decline in hair growth and often baldness occurs. The growth of hair depends on the production of cells by mitosis at the sides of the papilla. There is an active growth cycle for the hair known as *anagen*. The *anagen*, or active period, lasts from eighteen months to several years. This active period decides how long the hair will be (though hair usually never grows longer than thirty-six inches) and sets up the actual life of the hair. It is believed that premature baldness can be genetic or caused by other reasons. The seasons also affect hair growth. The hair on your head grows faster from March to July and slows down from August to February. Hair on the back of the hands grows faster from October to May than from May to October. Shaving the hair does not make it grow faster nor does it increase the number of hairs. The use of creams or lotions on the face will not increase the growth of hair. Waxing the face or legs for the removal of hair tends to reduce hair growth, but continued irritation can stimulate the hair to grow. This has been observed in mentally deficient children who continue to irritate the wrist or hands by biting or sucking. This continued stimulation brought about a luxuriant growth of long, coarse, pigmented hair at the site of the irritation. Quite often bogus hair growing products instruct the user to "massage well into the scalp"; the stimulation of the area can cause some hair growth, but it will not prevent baldness and is only a temporary growth. There are many products advertised as "hair growing" or as "preventing baldness," but they don't work. One recent hair-growing drug known as minoxidil is no exception. Once consumers have begun using this particular drug on the hair, they must continue treatment for the rest of their lives or the hair loss is actually increased. The best prevention of hair loss is hair care. (See **NATURAL METHOD OF HAIR CARE**, Part III in this book, for ideas for saving your hair.)

BALNEOTHERAPY - The scientific medical study of bathing and its effects on the human body.

BALSAMS - Mixtures of *resins* that contain relatively large amounts of cinnamic or benzoic acid or their esters. Typical balsams are balsam peru, balsam tolu, styrax, and benzoin.

BARIUM SULFIDE - A toxic and caustic chemical in many cosmetic preparations, especially in hair relaxers. It can cause stomach and muscle cramps if swallowed. Less than a teaspoon can be fatal. It is also a suspected carcinogen. It is wise to carefully read the labels of any products that will curl or relax your hair's natural state since the chemicals used are altering the delicate balance of nature.

BARRIER CREAMS - Applied to the skin to provide a protective coating against chemical irritants.

BASAL LAYER - The layer of skin at the base of the epidermis closest to the dermis.

BEE POLLEN - High in pantothenic acid. European research suggests it may be helpful in combating the effects of radiation; however, it is not particularly valuable as a topical. As with so many other natural cosmetic ingredients, bee pollen has been included for advertising purposes in inferior synthetic cosmetic formulas. Including bee pollen in cosmetics is just another way of cashing in on the mystic aura of "beedom": don't mistake hype for quality.

BEESWAX - Obtained from the honeycomb of the honeybee, *Apis mellifera*, as well as other *Apis* species. Both yellow beeswax and white beeswax are used as thickeners, emulsifiers, or stiffening agents in ointments, cold creams, emollient creams, lotions, lipsticks, hair dressings, suppositories, and others. (See **CHAPTER 15** for a more complete discussion of beeswax.)

BEET POWDER - Natural color. See **HERB CHART.**

BEHENIC ACID - A crystalline mixture of fatty acids from seeds (e. .g, peanuts) used as an opacifier in cosmetics.

BENTONITE - Name comes from Benton, Montana. Soft, moisture-absorbing, clayey mineral, often of volcanic origin, containing montmorillonite as the essential mineral. Used as suspending agent, emulsifier, thickener, binder, and absorbent. Tends to form "gel" with liquid rather than dissolve as does kaolin. Also, bentonite's volcanic origin may cause some of its particles to have sharp edges. Used in inferior mask products. May be drying to the skin.

BENZALDEHYDE - Synthetic chemical used as an artificial almond oil, also as a preservative and solvent. It is irritating to the eyes, skin, and mucous membranes. It also has a narcotic effect, acting as a depressant to the central nervous system. Taken internally, it can be fatal.

BENZALKONIUM CHLORIDE - This quaternary compound can be found in many hair conditioners and creme rinses. It has been documented as lethal and is a common source of eye irritations. Used as an antiseptic and a germicide. (See **QUATERNARY AMMONIUM SALTS.**)

BENZENE - Petrochemical used as a solvent and manufacturing agent in cosmetics. Benzene vapors can be absorbed through the skin and cause irritation. It can cause depression, convulsions, coma, and death. Prolonged exposure to this toxic chemical has been suspected as a cause of leukemia.

BENZETHONIUM CHLORIDE - Common ingredient in many feminine hygiene products. It can sensitize and irritate the skin, possibly leading to allergic dermatitis. Also used as a preservative.

BENZIDINE - Potent carcinogen from which many hair dyes are derived. Workers exposed to this chemical have produced tumors. It is poisonous, easily absorbed though the skin, and has a host of deadly side-effects. This chemical was banned in 1971 in Japan, and the U. S. allegedly no longer uses benzidine or its derivatives in hair dye products.

BENZOIC ACID - Chemical preservative used in foods and cosmetics. Benzoic acid as used in cosmetics is not natural and is often combined with sodium bisulfite. In many countries the use of benzoates and sulfites is restricted. When used in cosmetics it is an irritant to the eyes, skin, and mucous membranes. When benzoic acid was fed to lab mice at only 1.1% levels, within thirty-five days brain damage, neurological disorders, and cancer resulted. Avoid this chemical!

BENZOIN - Balsamic resin obtained from various *Styrax* species. Benzoin gum is formed when the bark is incised; the exuded balsamic resin, which hardens on exposure to air and sunlight, is then collected. Benzoin, especially Siam benzoin, has antioxidative and preservative properties and is used in cosmetics for these purposes.

BENZOPHENONE 2 and 4 - Two yellowish synthetic powders used in many shampoos to retard color fading because of their ability to absorb ultraviolet light. Although they are on the FDA GRAS (Generally Regarded As Safe) list, they can be toxic if ingested.

BENZYL ALCOHOL - Aromatic alcohol used as a solvent in cosmetics. Is a constituent of many herbs, including balsam peru, canaga oil, cassie absolute, castoreum, cherry laurel leaves, jasmine, and storax. Benzyl alcohol, when synthesized or isolated from an herbal essential oil, may be irritating to the skin and mucous membranes.

BERIBERI - Inflammatory disease of the nerves, digestive system, and heart caused by a thiamine deficiency. Most vitamins were discovered through a deficiency disease; hence, our understanding of the roles vitamins play in health is based on their role in preventing sickness NOT promoting health.

BHA and BHT - Butylated hydroxyanisole and butylated hydroxytoluene. Synthetic antioxidants approved for use in food and cosmetics. Avoid. See **ANTIOXIDANTS** and **CHAPTER 14.**

BICHLORIDE - Compound having two parts or equivalents of chlorine to one of the other elements.

BIOCATALYST - Substance that acts to promote or modify some physiological process, especially an enzyme, vitamin, or hormone. Enzymes are also known as organic catalysts. (See **ENZYMES.**)

BIOCHEMISTRY - Study of living plants and animals; the study of chemical compounds and processes that occur in living organisms.

BIODEGRADABLE - Substance that is capable of breaking down chemically to parts that can re-enter the natural world without changing it.

BIOTIN - One of the B vitamins that helps dermatitis and hair loss. (See **B COMPLEX, VITAMIN.**)

BISMUTH CITRATE - Synthetic preservative. May cause skin irritation and can be absorbed through the skin.

BISMUTH OXYCHLORIDE - Synthetic substance used in a number of face powders, lipsticks, and eye shadows. Also used as a synthetic pigment for the manufacture of artificial pearls. It is not as damaging to your skin as some of the other ingredients in make-up, such as mineral oil, methyl paraben, or mercury, but it is still a possible cause of skin irritation. Mildly astringent.

BISMUTH SUBGALLATE - Synthetic antiseptic that may cause dermatitis.

BITHIONOL - Banned for topical use in 1969 by the FDA, this antibacterial agent could be found in many soaps, creams, lotions, shampoos, and make-ups. It was found to be a serious photosensitizing agent, and use of the chemical was aborted. Unfortunately, many of the products containing this chemical have long in-home shelf lives and stayed in use for a long period after the ban was initiated in 1969. Regulatory agencies' reluctance to publicize their mistakes, coupled with a lack of consumer awareness, often result in potential health hazards in the home. Read labels.

BLACKHEAD - Skin blemish resulting from oily secretion of sebum and dead cells that clog hair follicle. The plug darkens when it comes into contact with the air. Blackheads differ from whiteheads in that the follicle remains open to the air; a whitehead is covered with a layer of skin and is hence more likely to become infected. Deep cleansing of the skin can help prevent blackheads. See the **Natural Method of Skin Care** in Part III of this book.

BLEB - Blister of skin filled with watery fluid; a bubble, as in water or glass.

BLUE LIGHT - Therapeutic lamp used to soothe the nerves, and also heal and disinfect skin tissue.

BOIL - Subcutaneous abcess, or suppurating inflammatory sore forming a central core, caused by bacteria which enter through the hair follicle.

BOND - Molecular linkage between different atoms or radicals of a chemical compound usually effected by the transfer of one or more electrons from one atom to another, as represented by a dot or line between atoms shown in various formulas.

BOOSTER - An oxidizer used to enhance the chemical action of hydrogen peroxide. Percarbonate and ammonium persulfate are among the chemicals used.

BORAGE - The name borage comes from the Latin *borago*, a corruption of *corago*, which means "I bring heart," or "I bring courage." This herb, with its cucumber-like fragrance, makes a delightful cool, refreshing drink. (Steep the fresh herb in water, and add lemon, sugar, wine, and water.) Borage is used widely in France for fever and pulmonary complaints. On the skin it can be used as a poultice to soothe inflammatory swellings. Recently borage was found to be very high in gamma-linolenic acid (GLA); some borage oil has as high as 21% GLA (almost three times that of evening primrose oil) and more than black currant seed oil. Pliny the Elder says of borage that it makes men merry and joyful. Since GLA can help premenstrual syndrome, then the same can be said of women as well.

Cosmetic Discussion - Borage oil is soothing to the skin and has anti-aging properties. It can be combined with *Rosa Mosqueta* and alfalfa extract as a topical anti-aging oil for wrinkled dry skin.

BORATES - Generic term referring to salts related to boric oxide or ortho-boric acid. Borax, also known as pyroborate, diborate, or sodium borate, is used to manufacture glass, ceramic glazes, enamels, water-softening agents, flame-proofing materials, preservatives, and fluxes. It is used in cosmetics as an emulsifier. When combined with beeswax in a cream, the borax is usually about 6% of the weight of the wax. As the borax is increased, the cream will stiffen (See **CHAPTER 15** for borax in cosmetic formulas). Boric acid, also known as *acidum boricum*, or orthoborix acid, is used widely as an eyewash. It is also used as an antiseptic dusting powder. The borates are mineral, and the main deposits are found in California. Recent research has produced a borate substance harder than a diamond as well as boron hydrides used as rocket fuels.

BORON - This mineral makes up 0.001% of the earth's crust and is found in a few parts per million in sea water. It is vital to all forms of plant life in small amounts, but in large amounts is toxic to plant life. The mineral is second only to diamonds in hardness, but recent work has produced a borate substance harder than diamonds. Organic compounds of boron are numerous, including boric acid. (See **BORATES** above.)

BRAN - The fibrous outer coating of a wheat kernel. In cosmetics used in masks and baths for its calming and exfoliating effect.

BREWERS YEAST - High in protein and all the B vitamins, this powder is sometimes added to cosmetics for its nutritional value.

BROMELIN - Enzyme from the juice of the pineapple that hydrolyzes proteins. Used in cosmetics as a texturizer and keratolytic. Avoid if allergic to pineapples.

BROMIDROSIS - Condition in which the body secretes a foul-smelling perspiration.

2-BROMO-2-NITROPROPANE-1,3-DIOL - A synthetic preservative, much like TEA and DEA (triethanolamine and diethanolamine), in that it is easily contaminated to form the carcinogenic agent NDELA. Other names for this chemical include bronopol, onyxide 500, and BNPD. See **CHAPTER 14** and **NITROSAMINES**.

BRUCINE SULFATE - Poisonous alkaloid derived from the *Brucea antidysenterica* shrub used in denaturing alcohol.

BUBBLE BATHS - Chiefly designed for children, these largely synthetic detergent mixtures may irritate sensitive mucous membranes and, in fact, they sometimes say so right on the label. Read the label of any bubble bath you purchase and avoid any that contain harsh detergents.

BULLA - A vesicle or elevation of the epidermis containing a watery fluid. A large bleb or blister.

BUTANE - Liquid natural gas propellant; highly flammable. Dangerous.

BUTYL ACETATE - Solvent used in nail polishes as well as in the manufacture of many other products. It is a known central nervous system depressant and narcotic if inhaled. The vapors or fumes from nail polish cause nausea and are very flammable. There are cases of accidental poisoning recorded every year due to children drinking nail polish left within their reach. (See **ETHYL ACETATE**.)

BUTYLENE GLYCOL - Thick liquid used in hair rinses and conditioners. It is utilized as a humectant, although it may be irritating to the scalp. This substance is also used in the manufacture of polyester and cellophane.

BUTYL PARABEN - Another member of the paraben family of petrochemicals. It is commonly used as a preservative. In its pure form it is a white, crystalline powder. It is irritating to the skin and can cause sensitization reactions. (See **METHYL PARABEN** and **PROPYL PARABEN**, also **CHAPTER 14**.)

BUTYL STEARATE - Synthetic chemical found in face creams and other facial care products. It is a possible allergen and has caused strong acnegenic reactions. These reactions are termed *acne cosmetica* since they are a direct result of facial cosmetics.

BUTYROLACTONE - Synthetic chemical used as a solvent of resins in cosmetics, especially nail polish removers.

C

C, VITAMIN - Ascorbic acid plus a complex of other factors (rutin, hesperidin, and other bioflavonoids) present in fresh foods, especially citrus fruits. Vitamin C is an antioxidant and can preserve cosmetics both in the water phase and the oil phase (particularly in its fat soluble form ascorbyl palmitate). It plays an essential role in building collagen, the connective tissue that holds us together. The bioflavonoids help promote effectiveness of vitamin C and build capillary strength. (See also **ASCORBIC ACID** in **CHAPTER 14** on preservatives.)

C₁₂-C₁₈ ALCOHOLS - Long carbon chain fatty alcohols such as cetyl, palmityl, myristyl, stearyl, arachidyl, and oleyl.

CALAMINE - Pink powder made of zinc oxide with a small amount of ferric oxide used in lotions, ointments, and liniments. This is a traditional mixture that is soothing and healing to the skin, especially for itchy rashes such as poison ivy.

CALCIUM - This mineral makes up 3.64% of the earth's crust. Recently calcium supplements have been recognized as preventive nutrition for osteoperosis. Women have been advised to get 1000-1500 mg calcium daily. Often sodium compounds of calcium are used because they are less expensive (one-fifth to one-sixth the price of calcium). Check the label of calcium supplements for the salt content. In cosmetics various calcium are used as "whiteners" and in toothpastes as a polishing agent.

CALCIUM ACETATE - Calcium salt of acetic acid. This is a synthetic chemical used in cosmetics as an emulsifier and thickener.

CALCIUM ALGINATE - Calcium salt of alginic acid. Alginates are hydrophilic colloidal substances from certain brown algae. Alginic acid and its calcium salt are obtained from the following alginates: macrocystic, laminaria, and ascophyllum. Used in many food products and as a binding and disintegrating agent in tablets. Used as a film-former in peel-off masks; a suspending and thickening agent in cosmetic gels, lotions, and creams; and as a stabilizer for oil-in-water emulsion. Non-toxic.

CALCIUM CARBONATE - Naturally occurring salt found in limestone, chalk, and marble. Used as a pigment, pigment extender, in dentifrices and antiacids, and in making lime and whiting.

CALCIUM CHLORIDE - Used in road salt and antifreeze. In cosmetics it's used as an emulsifier and texturizer.

CALCIUM HYDROXIDE - Also known as hydrated lime or limewater, this caustic substance is used as an alkali and preservative.

CALCIUM SILICATE - Anticaking agent used in heavy manufacturing and cosmetics. May irritate lungs if inhaled.

CALCIUM SULFATE - Also called gypsum, this substance is a mineral mined in New York, Michigan, Texas, Iowa, and Ohio. It is used in cement and has been used to reduce the alkali in soil. The ancient Egyptians and Greeks used calcium oxide and lime to manufacture mortar. Calcium sulfate is used to make gypsum and asbestos ($CaMG_3CSiO_3)_4$. These products are carcinogens when breathed or absorbed into the body.

CANDELILLA WAX - Herbal wax obtained from various *Euphorbiaceae* species; used in lipsticks, creams, and as a substitute for rubber. It can be used with other waxes to harden them. See **WAXES**.

CANDIDA ALBICANS - Commonly known as a yeast infection, this fungus is usually present in the body in small amounts but can dominate other microorganisms. This imbalance leads to a variety of symptoms: exhaustion, intestinal gas, sugar cravings, alternating constipation and diarrhea, mood swings, depression, irritation, memory loss, dizziness, muscle aches, mysterious weight gain, vaginal or prostate itch.

CANTHANAXIN - Reddish carotenoid found in some mushrooms, shellfish, and flamingo feathers. Taken in large quantities, it will color the skin a reddish bronze. What it does to the rest of you while it's coloring your skin is unknown. We don't recommend it: too much sun is not good for your skin, but canthanaxin is not a safe alternative.

CAPRIC ACID - Low-melting crystalline fatty acid that occurs in fats and oils; called capric acid for its goatlike odor. Used in cosmetics as flavoring and aromatic.

CAPSICUM OLEORESIN - Resinous essential oil from the pepper family (i.e., cayenne pepper, sweet pepper), used as a rubefacient in cosmetics.

CARAMEL - Concentrated solution of heated sugar or glucose solution; used as natural color in cosmetics.

CARBON - Element number six on the periodic chart of elements. An element necessary for living things, a carbon atom is an essential part of an organic compound. However, for the purposes of this book, we consider only substances that are living or were once living to be organic. (See **IN SEARCH OF THE ORGANIC WORLD**.)

CARBOXYMETHYL HYDROETHYLCELLULOSE - Sodium salt of an ethylene glycol ether of cellulose gum. Used as an emulsifier, foaming agent, and stabilizer in cosmetics. Causes allergic reactions.

CARCINOGENCY IN COSMETICS - Substances in nature are carcinogenic as well as synthetic chemicals; in fact, the most pervasive natural carcinogens that unavoidably affect everybody are

CARCINOGENCY IN COSMETICS Continued
the various forms of radiation from the earth, the sun, and the rest of the universe. People are exposed to 200 millirams of atomic particle radiation each year from cosmic sources and even from radioactive elements in soils and rocks. There are also "atomic accidents" that account for the deadly human exposure on Earth and exposure to the sun's UV rays (See **CHAPTER 11**). Some carcinogens which occur naturally in plants are *Aflatoxin B₁* (toxin found in moldy grains) which has affected the livers of rats and rainbow trout but is not known to affect humans and ¹-*Asarone* (toxin found in Calamus root) which has caused cancer in the intestines of rats but is not known to affect humans. *Estragole* is a toxin found in the oil of tarragon which has caused tumors in the livers of mice though not humans; *N-Methyl-N-Formyl-hydrazine*, a toxin found in the false morel, has caused tumors in the liver and lungs of mice although the effect on humans is not known. Tobacco contains several toxic substances such as dimethylnitrosamine and benzo(a)pyrene, which have caused tumors in the livers of rats and are believed to be carcinogenic to humans. A toxic substance known as *Safrole* is found in the natural oils of some plants and has caused tumors in the livers of mice and rats but is not known to affect humans. The bracken fern contains unidentified toxins that have caused tumors in the bladder, intestine, and lungs of cattle, mice, and rats, but the effect on humans is not known. Russian Comfrey in tea has caused tumors in lab tests, but other types of comfrey are not known to do the same.

Pollution is another source of carcinogenic chemicals. One result of burning hydrocarbon fuels in power plants and auto engines is a measurable amount of a carcinogenic compound known as benzo(a)pyrene (BAP). Even though the air contains a certain amount of BAP expelled by volcanoes or synthesized by some plants or algae, the natural balance of nature can keep this contained by degradation with soil bacteria; the releasing of BAP into the air via burned hydrocarbons and into the water by soaps, shampoos, and various cosmetics is an "overload" which nature is not prepared to handle. Gourmets who enjoy tarragon vinegar (made from the tarragon plant) or consume the delicious mushrooms called the false morel should not be needlessly worried about the toxins they contain because it is far more likely that they can get cancer more readily from nitrosamines, known carcinogens found in most bacon or pork products in the form of sodium nitrite (put in meat to prevent the growth of the botulism-causing organism *Clostridium botulinum*). Nitrites are also detectable in some cosmetic chemicals and can be absorbed into the body; however, another souce of nitrites is the bacteria normally in salivary plaque and the gastrointestinal tract that also synthesize nitrites. In addition, nitrites combine with secondary amines in the stomach to form alkylnitrosamines which are active carcinogens. Ascorbic acid (vitamin C), however, competes with secondary amines for the nitrite and thereby reduces the

amount of nitrosamine. Another potent carcinogen found in cosmetics is n-nitrosodiethanolamine (NDELA), a combination of triethanolamine (TEA) or diethanolamine (DEA) and a nitrosating agent. NDELA has been found in many cosmetics from face creams to shampoos. The danger of nitrite contamination in cosmetics is that through using these cosmetics, more nitrites can be absorbed into the bloodstream than from eating nitrites as they are added to food. One solution to this contamination is for cosmetic manufacturers using TEA or DEA to at least include vitamin C in their formulas as a protection, but the best solution is to avoid using them altogether. We suggest you avoid any cosmetics that contain synthetic chemicals or petrochemicals (hydrocarbons) and in the case of the nitrite-contaminated cosmetics, look for ascorbic acid on the label and hope the vitamin C does its job. Avoiding synthetic chemicals in foods and cosmetics is your best bet, and even though there are carcinogens in nature, humans have created more carcinogens and burdened all of nature with chemicalization which may even cause more natural carcinogens.

While scientists use a sprig of the sassafras tree (high in *safrole*) to frighten consumers, they invented PVC and PCB's and atomic power which regularly cause cancer in the workers who are exposed to these chemicals. The carcinogens in nature I have outlined here are nothing compared to industrial chemicals, food chemicals, and cosmetic chemicals that contain carcinogens and other toxic substances. The prudent individual avoids synthetic chemicals and petrochemicals as much as possible and regards a cosmetic not simply as an innocuous substance applied to the skin and into the hair but an added burden to our environment and to our own bodies.

CARMINE - Natural red color from the dried female cochineal insect *Coccus cacti* (See **COCHINEAL**).

CARNAUBA WAX - (See **WAXES**.)

CARBOMER 934, 934P, 940, 941, 960, 961 - Synthetic emulsifier and thickener used in many cosmetics and toothpastes as well as industrial goods with a very acidic pH (3) in a 1% water solution. Can cause eye irritation. Potential allergen.

CAROTENE - Any of several orange or red compounds that occur in plants or in the bodies of plant-eating animals; beta carotene is the most common. They are precursors to vitamin A. Carrot oil is extremely high in beta carotene; it is an excellent oil for dry skin.

CASEIN - Protein specific to the milk of mammals.

CASTILE SOAP - Originally prepared from olive oil in much the same manner that soap is made from coconut oil. Castile soap now refers to a very mild soap; however, the finest grade of castile soap is still made with olive oil.

CATABOLISM - Chemical change which involves the breaking down of more complex molecules into simpler ones. It is often accompanied by a release of energy.

CATALYST - Substance having the power to increase the speed of a chemical reaction, or to cause an intended chemical change.

CATAPHORESIS - This is the forcing of medicinal substances into the deeper tissues of the skin by use of galvanic current from the positive pole towards the negative pole. It can be used to inject an astringent solution into the skin.

CATIONIC SURFACTANT - Surface active agent whose ions are positively charged in an aqueous solution. Quaternary ammonium compounds are cationic surfactants. See **ANIONIC SURFACTANTS, AMPHOTERIC SURFACTANTS,** and **SURFACTANTS.**

CELANDINE - One of traditional herbs used for the bleaching of hair.

CELLULAR EXTRACTS - Various extracts from the organs or tissues of animals (usually cows or sheep) which are put into facial moisturizing creams with the claims that these extracts will encourage rapid healing of tissue and encourage the growth of new healthy skin cells. One of the early pioneers in the use of cellular extracts was a Russian physician and biologist Vladimir Filatov. Dr. Filatov used the extracts from cutis, thymus, testes, ovary, placenta, and mammary glands. His original work was used on seriously burned patients to encourage healing and new skin growth. He also used the epidermal substances for eye transplant surgery and as a topical for the repair of burned skin. (Also see this section under **POLYMERS** for artificial skin.)

Discussion - Germany, Switzerland, France, and the United States have used cellular extracts in celltherapy treatments, and they have introduced several brands of "celltherapy type" creams to be used by women as a "wrinkle remover" and to "rejuvenate skin cells" for the purpose of "keeping the skin young." Quite often other dermal proteins are combined with the cell extracts such as collagen, elastin, and reticulin. Soluble collagen has been found to be absorbed into the skin, thereby encouraging the growth of new collagenic fibers. Many human tests (probably animal tests as well) showed a marked improvement in the skin and improved collagen from the use of collagen creams (See also **CHAPTER 4**). One company (Collagen Corporation, Palo Alto, CA) introduced a bovine dermal collagen called *Zyderm®* . This was called a "collagen implant" because the substance was injected under the skin at the site of acne scars, furrows due to facial gestures, creases and wrinkles due to age, scar tissue, and other skin imperfections. The surface texture was smoothed and the imperfections become less noticable. Treatments are followed with post-treatments of one to six month intervals because the injection does not permanently improve the skin but is resorbed,

leaving the skin in its original condition. This is an expensive treatment; the doctor's cost may be as high as $360 for six collagen implants of 1.0 cc. Cost to the patient depends on the dermatologist (prices may be higher at the time of publication).

In 1927 Dr. Paul Niehans, a Swiss physician, developed a therapy called "tissue transplantation." Dr. Niehans injected a dwarf with eosinophil cells from young calves into a dwarf's pituitary gland. The dwarf grew 12.5 inches. Dr. Niehans opened the Clinic La Prairie in Switzerland in 1931 to treat patients with tissue transplantation. He also used himself as a guinea pig by injecting animal cells into his body. He preserved the cells by lyophilization which is a process of removing all the liquid substances from the cells which leaves them dry and prevents oxidation. Dr. Niehans supposedly had famous patients such as Sir Winston Churchill, Dr. Konrad Adenauer, and Pope Pius XII. The purpose of the treatments at the La Prairie Clinic is not to make people look younger but to make them feel better. Whether or not it does this is not known. There is a superstitious belief that consuming an animal's "essence of life" will increase one's own life. This, after all, is the basis of these medical and cosmetic uses of animal organs and tissue. After the treatment, the patient is sent home and put on a diet of placenta extracts and vitamins, reinforcing these superstitions of the mystical value of consuming "the beginnings of the life force." In 1975 Dr. Fontaine of La Prairie proposed combining the cell extracts used in the injections with elastin and collagen to make a face cream. Dr. Nadja Avalle, a cosmetic chemist in Sion, Switzerland, was asked to compound the cell-therapy cream, and the clinic put out a cosmetic line. This celltherapy is supposed to be superior to other cell extracts because a special breed of black sheep is used. (These special treatment cosmetics are always based on some curious fiction; however, black sheep is a new one.) Only pregnant black ewes are killed to get the cellular extracts, again reinforcing the superstition of youth and increased life. The sacrificial lamb!

Recently, noted heart surgeon from South Africa, Dr. Christiaan Barnard, introduced his celltherapy which he reportedly developed in Switzerland (maybe it's the black sheep extract as well). Dr. Barnard put out ads discussing the fact that the quality of life is even more important than the length of life. The idea is that the celltherapy will make you look young and beautiful and give you a better quality of life. None of this works, of course, because the senseless murdering of animals, which are raised for this specific purpose of putting their tissue extracts into a face cream, will hardly give one a better quality of life.

Studies comparing the effectiveness of animal celltherapy creams versus herbal creams show that there is nothing special about the animal celltherapy creams. In fact, a few studies show that specific herbs compounded synergistically will increase healing time many times that of animal-containing creams or cortisone creams (16% more rapidly). Increased healing time is a

CELLULAR EXTRACTS Continued
good measure of healthy tissue (See Dr. Fleishner's study in **CHAPTER IX**).

Aubrey Organics is one cosmetic manufacturer who has created several products to replace animal extract cosmetics with herbals. Aubrey Hampton made some of the early celltherapy and collagen creams in the marketplace, but he also created a vegetarian celltherapy called Vegacell using over twenty-five herbal extracts in a synergistic formula. He also created a vegetarian collagen by combining herbs high in organic silica which is identified in the body as collagen. The company's skin care clinic studies suggested that the vegetarian replacements for celltherapy and collagen worked just as well as the various animal-containing tissue extracts. In fact, they had many qualities that were superior to the animal extract products. The main ingredient missing in these products besides the animal organs and tissue extracts is the element of superstition and the cosmetic manufacturing hype that suggests that dead animal parts will give youth and rejuvenation to the face.

It is also obvious when you read the label of the celltherapy creams that they contain the same synthetic chemicals that are present in most cosmetics. Many of the chemicals, especially the preservatives, are incompatible with the proteins and amino acids in the animal extract: this makes the mumbo jumbo of the advertising hype even more suspect. The protein is destroyed by the chemicals, and the skin is adversely affected by these chemicals; thus, this "cellular rejuvenation cream" slogan is reduced to meaningless ink on a very expensive bottle of glop. The best advice is still to read the label and select a moisturizing cream that is more natural and hopefully more vegetarian.

CELLULOSE GUM - Fiber combined with various synthetic chemicals to form white granules used as emulsifiers, stabilizers, and binders in cosmetics. Also sodium carboxymethyl cellulose. Related compounds are methylcellulose and the highly flammable nitrocellulose, which is related to gun cotton (the explosive) and is the staple ingredient in nail polish.

CERESIN WAX - See **WAXES**.

CETEARYL ALCOHOL - Mixture of cetyl and stearyl alcohols (fatty alcohols). May be natural or synthetic. Used as emollient, emulsifier, thickener, and as a carrying agent for other ingredients.

CETALKONIUM CHLORIDE - Quaternary ammonium salt used as an antiseptic and preservative. Toxic synthetic chemical. Avoid. See **AMMONIUM CHEMICALS IN COSMETICS** and **QUATERNARY AMMONIUM SALTS**.

CETAMINE OXIDE - Aliphatic amine oxide used as a stabilizer and emulsifier. May be irritating.

CETEARETH-3, etc. - Polyethylene glycol of cetearyl glycol. Synthetic emulsifiers and emollients used in cosmetics. Dessicates skin, allergic reactions.

CETRIMONIUM CHLORIDE - Quaternary ammonium salt used as a antiseptic and preservative. Synthetic, irritating, and toxic. Oral intake can be fatal. See **AMMONIUM CHEMICALS IN COSMETICS** and **QUATERNARY AMMONIUM SALTS**.

CETYL ALCOHOL - Solid alcohol consisting chiefly of n-hexadecanol. May be natural or synthetic. Used in cosmetics as an emollient, emulsifier, thickener, and as carrying agent for other ingredients.

CETYL LACTATE, MYRISTATE, PALMITATE, STEARATE - Esters of cetyl alcohol and lactic acid, myristic acid, palmitic acid, and stearic acid. May be natural or synthetic. Used as emollients and texturizers in cosmetics.

CETYLPYRIDINIUM CHLORIDE - Quaternary ammonium salt used as antiseptic in cosmetics. Synthetic, irritating, and toxic. See also **AMMONIUM CHEMICALS IN COSMETICS** and **QUATERNARY AMMONIUM SALTS**.

CHALK - Soft limestone of marine origin. See **CALCIUM CARBONATE** and **ABRASIVES**.

CHEILITIS - Form of dermatitis; cracking and drying of the lips. Caused by lipstick, primarily those containing large amounts of synthetic dyes (particularly eosin dyes which stain the lips), synthetic perfumes or other allergenic substances.

CHELATING CHEMICALS IN COSMETICS - Used to combat UV deterioriation in the color of cosmetics. Avoid synthetic chelating agents like EDTA. See **SEQUESTRANTS**.

CHEMISTRY - Study investigating the composition and interaction of existing compounds and elements, and the synthesis of natural and artificial compounds.

CHLOASMA - Irregular large brown patches on the skin, such as liver or age spots.

CHLORINATED CHEMICALS - Chlorine is disastrous to the hair and skin! Any cosmetic chemical that contains chlorinated chemicals should not be used. Aerosol cosmetics may be chlorinated as well as fluorinated. Shampoos sold as antibacterials and antidandruff may contain these chemicals. Of course, your swimming pool--all pools--contain chlorine. The results of swimming in a pool are dry hair and dry skin. When you swim in a pool, pull your hair back and protect it with a bathing cap. This is very important if you have colored hair as chlorine ruins hair dyes. After you come out of the pool, take a shower and shampoo your hair with a swimmers' shampoo to remove all traces of chlorine from the hair.

CHOLESTEROL - This is a steroid alcohol obtained from plants or animals. Human sebum (oils from the skin) is high in cholesterol and cholesterol esters (4.1%). Plant cholesterols are obtained from

CHOLESTEROL Continued
cocoa beans and myrrh; animal cholesterol from sheep wool. Cholesterol helps hold moisture within the skin.

CHOLINE - One of the vitamin B complex, usually found with inositol. Eggs and lecithin are high in this natural phospholipid which is essential to the metabolism of fats. (See **B COMPLEX VITAMINS**).

CHLOROFLUORCARBON 11, 12, 114, etc. - Propellant. May depress central nervous system and damage heart if inhaled. See **AEROSOL**.

CHLOROPHYLL - Green coloring matter of plants that is essential for photosynthesis. Used for its antiseptic, anti-fungal, and odor-absorbing qualities. Also used in very small amounts as a natural color.

CHLOROPHYLLIN - Chemically related to **CHLOROPHYLL** above, and used as a deodorant and color. Can contain heavy metals and synthetic additives.

CHLOROTHYMOL - Chlorine derivative of thymol (natural chemical in some essential oils but usually synthesized) used in mouthwashes as an antiseptic.

p-CHLORO-M-XYLENOL - Chlorine derivative of xylenol (coal tar chemical) Used as antiseptic and germicide in cosmetics. Allergic reactions. Phototoxic due to coal tars.

CHROMOSOME - Found in the nucleus of the cell, these rod or thread-like bodies contain chromatin, which carry the genes in all the cell nuclei of plants and animals.

CHRYSAROBIN - The *Andira Araroba* grows in Bahia, Brazil, and has yellowish wooden canals in which a powder is deposited as the tree ages. The powder is scraped out with an axe after the tree has been cut down. The yellow powder is mixed with splinters and other debris and must be sifted. The powder is ground, dried, boiled, and filtered once again. Even purified, the powder is irritating and permanently stains clothing. The powder is called Goa Powder and is a classic herbal treatment for acne, dry skin, eczema, psoriasis, and other skin diseases. The powder is used by adding only one gram to an ounce of carrying agent. It is applied to the infected areas but not to the other parts of the skin. One formula exists for treating acne and dry skin that will not stain. It has the following ingredients: witch hazel, water, amino acid complex, vitamin A, goa, mineral-herb complex (magnesium, zinc, burdock, ivy, lemon, sage, saponin, watercress), allantoin, and camomile. It is sold in health food stores as an acne and oily skin treatment. Goa can also be found in moisturizers for oily type skin. A treatment for hemorrhoids can be made by mixing 2% goa in a natural ointment. Goa should never be used full-strength on the face. See **ARAROBA** in the **HERB CHART**.

CICATRIX - Film of skin which develops over a wound and later contracts to form a scar.

CILIA - Hair which grows from the margin of the eyelids. Commonly known as eyelashes, cilia protect the eyes from dust and assist bacteria in locomotion.

CINNAMAL - Derivative of cinnamon bark oil, used in cosmetics as aromatic and flavoring.

CITRAL - Aromatic found in lemongrass and other herbs. Natural.

CITRIC ACID - Found widely in plants (e. g., citrus fruits), this organic acid is used as flavoring agent in foods and pharmaceuticals. In cosmetics citric acid is used as a preservative, acid, sesquestrant, and foam stabilizer.

CLAY - Used in face masks and recommended especially for oily skin because of its drawing properties. Deep cleansing and highly absorbent, clay can be drying if used too frequently. Kaolin or bentonite are the two clays most commonly used; bentonite, however, can scratch the skin due to its sharp edges and forms a gel consistency when mixed with liquid rather than a true cleansing clay mask. See **BENTONITE**.

COAL TAR - Thick liquid or semi-solid substance that is the by-product of the distillation process of bituminous coal. Though claimed by some to have healing properties, coal tar is allergenic and phototoxic. Avoid.

COBALT CHLORIDE - FD & C coal tar color. Probable carcinogen. Avoid.

COCAMIDE DEA or MEA or MIPA - Synthetic non-ionic surfactant frequently referred to as natural and "from coconuts" on the labels of health food store brand shampoos. The DEA, MEA, and MIPA stand for diethanolamine, monoethanolamine, and monoisopropanolamine; these substances can be contaminated with nitrosamines. Avoid these chemicals and be suspicious of so-called natural shampoos that contain them. See also **NITROSAMINES**.

COCAMIDOPROPYL BETAINE - Synthetic amphoteric surfactant frequently referred to as natural and "from coconuts" on the labels of health food store brand shampoos. A secondary surfactant used in combination with other, stronger surfactants (like sodium lauryl sulfate). Avoid this chemical and be suspicious of "natural" shampoos that contain them.

COCETH-6, -8 - Polyethelene glycols of coconut alcohol. Synthetic. Used as cleansers and emollients in shampoos.

COCHINEAL - Natural red dye obtained from the dried bodies of the female cochineal beetle *(Dactylopius coccus)* from Central and South America.

COCOA - See **HERB CHART**.

COCO-BETAINE - Synthetic amphoteric surfactant frequently referred to as natural and "from coconuts" on the labels of health food store brand shampoos. See **COCAMIDOPROPYL-BETAINE**.

COCOMIDO BETAINE - See above.

COCONUT OIL - This is an oil obtained from coconuts, those round hairy brown woody objects that grow on coconut palm trees. Coconut oil is used as an emollient and to make natural soaps through a saponification reaction with salts. Don't accept "from coconut" or "from coconut oil" derivatives in the natural cosmetics you buy.

COCOYL SARCOSINAMIDE DEA and COCYL SARCOSINE - Another synthetic "coconut" derivative used as a surfactant. See **COCAMID-OPROPYL-BETAINE** and **NITROSAMINES**.

COCOTRIMONIUM CHLORIDE - Quaternary ammonium compound used as an antiseptic and preservative. See also **AMMONIUM CHEMICALS IN COSMETICS** and **QUATERNARY AMMONIUM SALTS**.

COD LIVER OIL - Pale yellow fatty oil from the fresh livers of *Gadus morrhua* and *Gadidae* species of codfish. Extremely high in vitamins A and D.

COLD WAVING OF HAIR - Cold waving the hair is a method of waving the hair without externally applied heat. It began in 1930 with the "overnight cold wave process." Ten years later a fast cold wave process based on bisulfates was introduced, but it was quickly replaced with a thioglycolate cold wave lotion. This is the same chemical process in use today. It is also known as permanent waving and is given in salons, but heat is applied by hair dryer to speed up the process. The whole process is accomplished by altering the configuration of the hair while it is maintained in the curled position. Curler devices are used to change the configuration of the hair. There is a spiral rod used for winding the hair. The hair is divided into four to six sections. The sections are then divided into squares of one inch by one inch. The hair is grasped near the end and wound in a helical fashion. The ends are held in place on the curler with built-in elastic bands or a similar device. There are various sizes of curler rods and the quality of the wave is dependent on the dimensions of the curlers. Obviously, the amount of hair and the size of the curler will depend on how many turns the hair takes around the curler. One complete turn around the curler will yield one half-wave. A thin curler rod will produce more half-waves than a large rod. If there are too few half waves the permanent wave will be too loose, but too many half-waves will produce a tight, frizzy wave. The diameter of the curler varies from $\frac{1}{8}$ to $\frac{1}{4}$ inch. A large curler radius produces less strain on the hair than a small curler radius. If pin curls are made with cold wave solutions, the hair has a very loose look. The speed and quality of the wave also depends on the chemical reaction of the lotion in the hair. These chemicals, of course, affect the hair keratin in an adverse way. The term "over-processed hair" means that the hair has been adversely chemicalized by the wave solution. This leads to serious hair damage and in some cases baldness. Hair that is damaged or over-processed should be treated with a hair conditioner containing the amino acid cystine. This rebuilds the cystine bond or cystine bridge which has been destroyed by the wave solution.

COLLAGEN - One-third (70%) of the body's connective tissue of the dermis is made of collagen. Gerontologists have found that the aging process of the skin takes place in the connective tissue of the dermis. There are two types of collagen: 1. *SOLUBLE COLLAGEN* and 2. *INSOLUBLE COLLAGEN*. When skin is young it is soluble; when it has aged it is insoluble. Young connective tissue (a triple helix of amino acids) is made up of the soluble collagen which is non-crosslinked, i. e., its molecules are displaceable in relation to one another. This non-crosslinked or soluble collagen has a good capacity for absorbing moisture and is therefore capable of swelling. As the skin ages due to exposure to light, chemicals (make-up, coal tar dyes, chemicals that react adversely to protein), and diet, the soluble collagen becomes insoluble or crosslinked. The collagen is inflexible and the molecules are no longer displaceable in relation to one another. The connective tissue in turn loses its ability to absorb moisture and is also no longer capable of swelling. The skin becomes tight, dry, wrinkled, and aged.

The diagram on the next page illustrates the differences between the structure of collagen fibrils of healthy youthful skin with soluble non-crosslinked collagen and aging skin with insoluble crosslinked collagen (A more complete discussion of the dermal proteins can be found in **CHAPTER 4**).

Discussion - Extensive tests by various American and European researchers have concluded that topical application of collagen creams with a content of 10.0% soluble collagen (which should have the collagen-specific amino acid hydroxyproline in the amount of at least 12%) will arrest or compensate for collagen loss. Not all collagen meets this criteria, however. The skin can only utilize a collagen which is structurally intact, and even the presence of certain chemicals in a collagen-containing cream can render the collagen "insoluble" and unusable by the skin. Petrochemicals and hydrocarbons included in a formula with collagen renders the collagen (in any amount) insoluble. Many preservatives that are not compatible with protein such as methylparaben, propylparaben, ethylparaben, and butylparaben (the PBA esters) should not be used in a collagen cream. If you are going to purchase a collagen cream, check the label to be sure it contains no PBA esters. One of the labs that ran tests on soluble collagen (10% in a natural cream base) was Henkel International GmbH, Dusseldorf, West Germany. They found excellent absorption of collagen into the dermal protein, formation of new collagen fibrils, regeneration of the skin with a higher moisture content, and increased flexibility.

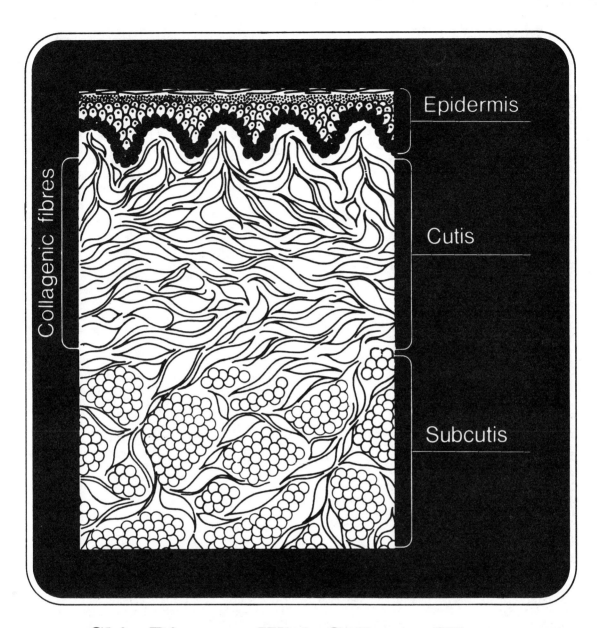

Skin Diagram With Collagen Fibers
**Example of Non-Cross-Linked
and Cross-Linked Collagen**

HEALTHY, YOUTHFUL SKIN   AGING SKIN

COLLAGEN Continued

It has been said that collagen and other dermal proteins can't be absorbed into the skin. This isn't true. Beneficial substances can be absorbed into the skin as well as toxic substances. The formula of a collagen cream (or for that matter any cosmetic) is all important. It is up to the consumer to check the label ingredients.

Can collagen be obtained or improved with other ingredients? Any of the dermal proteins seem to have a positive effect on the collagenic fibrils and the surface structure of the skin. It is even possible to increase the collagen and improve the skin with a vegetal substance like collagen. Organic silica (silica acid) which is found in the herbs wood horsetail *(Equisetum Sylvaticum)* and great river horsetail *(Equisetum Maximum)* is identified in the body as collagen. Organic silica can be taken in tablet form (obtained at health food stores) derived from these herbs, and it has been found to increase healing of bones and tissue. When it is used topically in a natural cream formula it has the same results as a soluble collagen cream. This offers vegetarians and animal rights advocates a vegetarian alternative to collagen for their skin.

Chemical Type - At present all collagen is natural and of bovine origin (usually from the skin), but some collagen is obtained from horse's hooves (this is an insoluble collagen). Vegetarian type collagen is obtained from the horsetail herbs as organic silica.

Toxicity - Collagen is not toxic.

COLLOIDAL SULFUR - Pale yellow dried mixture of sulfur and gum arabic.

COLLOIDON - Nitrocellulose in solution of ethanol and ether. Synthetic substance used to form protective film. May cause allergic reactions.

COLOCYNTH - Herbaceous vine from the Mediterranean region related to the watermelon; powerful carthartic is derived from this plant. Used as a denaturant in cosmetics. May cause skin reactions.

COLOGNE - Toilet water made of alcohol and aromatic oils. May be natural or synthetic.

COMEDO - Collection of oils and dead cells that clogs opening of hair follicle and oil gland duct in the skin; also known as blackhead. See also **BLACKHEAD**.

COMPOUND - Substance formed by a chemical union of two or more elements. A natural cosmetic compound uses no synthetic emulsifiers, thickeners, hardeners, sudsing agents, or binders.

CONCRETE - Water soluble, hydrocarbon soluble extracts prepared from natural materials by using a hydrocarbon-type solvent. They are primarily used in perfumery and in the preparation of absolutes.

CONTACT DERMATITIS - Skin damage caused by topical contact with chemicals. The two types of contact dermatitis are primary irritation and allergic sensitization. Primary irritation occurs at the time of exposure; its symptoms include itch-ing, swelling, and redness. If the concentration of the irritating chemical is high, then its effects may be corrosive, severely damaging several layers of skin. Allergic sensitization may take several exposures to develop, but once you've pinpointed a chemical as its cause, your reaction may be severe and may occur each time you are exposed to that chemical for the rest of your life.

COPAL - Resin obtained from tropical trees of the species *(Leguminosae)* or dug up as fossil. Used in cosmetics as a thickener. Natural.

CORN ACID - Mixture of fatty acids derived from corn oil and used in cosmetics as an emollient and thickener.

CORN OIL - Yellow semidrying fatty oil obtained from the wet milling of corn. Used in soft soap and as an emollient and thickener in cosmetics.

CORNSTARCH - Natural starch obtained from corn and used primarily as a thickening agent or powder. Its application is basically limited to the food industry, but it's used in non-talcum baby powders and as a filler, thickener, and anti-irritant.

CORN SYRUP - Stable solution of corn sugar consisting primarily of D-glucose. Used as a texturizer to coat hair and to pull chlorine from hair after swimming. Because of its acidic pH, corn syrup can be used to naturally lower alkaline pH while adding to the value of the overall formula.

CORRUGATOR SUPERCILLI - These muscles draw the eyebrows inward and downward, which results in vertical wrinkles at the root of the nose.

CORTISONE - Steroid hormone of the adrenal cortex. It is a powerful hormone that is also made synthetically for use in the treatment of disease. Prolonged use of cortisone can, however, lead to calcium loss in the bones, destruction of collagen, and a weakened immune system.

COSMETIC - The official FDA definition of cosmetic is "(1) articles intended to be rubbed, poured, sprinkled, or sprayed on, introduced into, or otherwise applied to the human body or any part thereof for cleansing, beautifying, promoting attractiveness, or altering the appearance, and (2) articles intended for use as a component of any such articles; except that such term shall not include soap." This term is generic and makes no distinction between natural preparations and synthetic ones, only that the intent of a cosmetic must be to somehow alter the appearance, while that of a drug is therapeutic.

COTTONSEED OIL - Pale yellow semidrying fatty oil obtained from cottonseed by solvent extraction or expression; high in glycerides of linoleic, oleic, and palmitic acids, and used as an emollient in cosmetics.

COUMARIN - Organic chemical found in tonka beans, lavender oil, and sweet clover, but can also be made synthetically. Used in perfumery and in the making of soap.

COUPEROSE - Word used by estheticians to describe a broken capillary condition of the skin.

CROSS BONDS - The holding together of the long chains of amino acids that compose the hair. These chains can be broken down by external environmental conditions, over-processing, or the use of harsh synthetic hair care products.

CUPRIC SULFATE - Synthetic color.

CUTANEOUS - Of, pertaining to, or affecting the cutis (deeper layer of skin), or any part of the skin.

CUTICLE OF HAIR OR SKIN - Outer layer of hair or skin.

CUTICLE REMOVERS - Harsh cosmetic products with an extremely alkaline pH; they contain corrosive substances such as potassium or sodium hydroxide. A safer alternative is to soften the cuticle with warm water and push them back with an orange stick or the fingernails of the opposite hand.

CUTIS - Dermis of the skin.

CYSTEINE - Sulfur-containing antioxidant amino acid that oxidizes to form cystine. L-cysteine is said to stimulate the immune system.

CYSTINE - Amino acid present in the hair protein keratin. Topical application of this amino acid may help strengthen the hair.

D

D, VITAMIN - Fat-soluble vitamin, chemically related to the steroids. Essential for healthy bones and teeth and the absorption of calcium. In sunny weather the body can produce its own vitamin D if the skin is exposed to the sun and there are oils present on the skin.

D & C COLORS - Colors (usually synthetic coal tar colors) approved for use in drugs and cosmetics; standards differ slightly from those for FD & C colors. Avoid coal tar colors. See **CHAPTER 10.**

DAMAR GUM - Gum extracted from east Indian pine of the genus *Agathis*. Used largely in printing inks and varnishes.

DANDRUFF - Clumps of cells which form on the scalp and flake off. Currently technological hair care aids for dandruff are usually harsh solvents that strip scalp in order to relieve the flaking. This can lead to the breakdown of the amino acid bonds in the hair. There are natural alternatives. See **CHAPTER 16.**

DEA (DIETHANOLAMINE) - Liquid amino alcohol similar to triethanolamine and used to alkalize cosmetics. May be contaminated with nitrosamines. Avoid this chemical. See **ALKYL SULFATES** and **NITROSAMINES.**

DEA-LAURYL SULFATE - Synthetic anionic surfactant used extensively in shampoos. May be contaminated with nitrosamines. This chemical does NOT come from coconuts. See **NITROSAMINES.**

DEA-LINOLEATE - Salt of linoleic acid plus DEA used as a cleanser. May be contaminated with nitrosamines. See **NITROSAMINES.**

DECOCTION - Dilute aqueous extracts prepared by boiling the botanicals with water for a specific period of time, followed by straining or filtering.

DECYL ALCOHOL - Colorless or light yellow liquid primary alcohol that may be made from coconut oil or synthetically; used in surfactants and perfumes. May be natural or synthetic.

DEHYDROACETIC ACID - Crystalline acid, used as a fungicide, bactericide, and plasticizer. Synthetic.

DEODORANT - In cosmetics, a product that reduces perspiration odor. Note that deodorants do not STOP perspiration; that is the role of an anti-perspirant.

DEODORIZED KEROSENE - Used as a solvent. This is a hydrocarbon. It's irritating, allergenic, flammable; there are plenty of natural alternatives. Avoid.

DEPIGMENTATION - Loss of color from skin.

DEPILATORIES - Extremely alkline cosmetics that destroy hair by breaking the chemical bonds that hold this strong fiber together. Chemicals this strong are also very irritating to the skin; the same chemicals that enter and destroy the hair can penetrate the skin and damage it. Chemical depilatories work in three steps. First, a strong detergent strips the sebum from the hair shaft, and adhesive chemicals hold the rest of the formula to the hair shaft for the time necessary to remove the hair. Second, swelling and accelerating agents cause the hair fiber to expand. Three, bond breaking chemicals like thioglycolic acid (as in permanent wave solutions) destroy the five chemicals bonds that hold hair together. Chemical depilatories are quite over-priced and may irritate the skin. Depilatory waxes can burn or irritate the skin and hair follicle. Avoid these products.

DERIVATIVE - When a particular substance or group of substances is removed from a "donor" substance, it is called a derivative. Derivatives are isolated from whole substances to obtain specific results. Quite often this is for the purpose of creating a drug to treat disease, but the derivative can also be used in a formula to enhance the end product. For example, amino acids can be derived from grains and combined with minerals such as zinc, magnesium, chromium, and phosphorus as chelates. The amino acids derivatives are, in this case, used for the specific purpose of helping the body assimilate the minerals. Though these amino acids could have a nutritional advantage as derivatives, in this case they are used to enhance the minerals by improving their assimilation by the organism.

A derivative should not be confused with a compound or a complex, nor should it be associated with the donor substance too closely. Allantoin can

DERIVATIVE Continued

be derived from comfrey (or uric acid), but it is not the same as these substances. Allantoin is used in cosmetics for its soothing and healing properties, but comfrey extract has these same properties because it contains allantoin as well as other constituents.

The words "derived from" can be misleading to consumers when used on a cosmetic label. For example, when chemicals such as sodium lauryl sulfate and triethanolamine appear on a cosmetic label followed by the words "derived from coconut oil," the consumer is led to believe that these synthetic chemicals must be natural and derived from coconut oil. They are not. Even if these synthetic chemicals contain some amount of coconut oil, they would not be coconut derivatives, but a synthetic detergent containing some amount of coconut oil. The misused "derived from" is probably used to make a consumer who wants a natural product believe that the synthetic chemical being used is natural. "Derived from" has become as misleading as the words "natural" and "organic" when written on products that aren't natural.

One school of thought is that whole substances are always superior to manmade derivatives. While there are probably reasons to use derivatives rather than the actual donor product, at the same time nature's whole substance may contain principals not found in a derivative.

DERMABRASION - Process by which skin is removed in varying amounts and depths by the use of mechanical brushes or sandpaper. A standard practice for removing scars and as a final treatment for *acne hypertrophica*.

DERMATITIS - Inflammation of the skin caused by allergic reactions. It is often caused by coming in contact with a cosmetic product that has numerous synthetic ingredients. Certain people may be allergic to natural substances as well.

DERMATOLOGIST - One who understands and has been trained in treating diseases of the skin, especially with drugs.

DERMIS - Sensitive layer of skin, protected by the epidermis, made up of connective tissue, muscle, and nerves; the corium, or true skin.

DETERGENT - Synthetic soap which may be made with a variety of chemicals. Detergents may lather better than soaps, but this is a superficial characteristic that has nothing to do with how it cleans. Detergents are frequently not biodegradable.

DIACETONE ALCOHOL - Used as a solvent in lacquer and in industry in hydraulic brake fluid. Oral intake is toxic, and it may be absorbed through the skin.

DIAMMONIUM CITRATE - Synthetic chemical used as a preservative, sesquesterant, and astringent in cosmetics.

DIAPER RASH - Inflammation of the buttocks caused by excessive exposure to urinary ammonia. Baby oil and vaseline, both commonly recommended remedies, contain mineral oil which can cause allergic reactions and prevent the skin from healing itself.

DIAPHORETIC - Substance causing perspiration.

DIATOMACEOUS EARTH - Also known as diatomite; consisting chiefly of the remains of diatoms, a form of algae that makes up planketon. High in silica. Diatomaceous earth is used as filter, adsorbent, abrasive, and insulating material. Excessive inhalation can cause lung irritation.

DIBROMSALAN - Synthetic chemical used as an antiseptic in cosmetics.

DIBUTYL PHTHALATE - Colorless, oily ester used as a plasticizer and solvent in cosmetics. Synthetic chemical.

DIET AND COSMETICS - Obviously what you eat has plenty to do with how you look as well as how you feel. The choice of a sensible diet can do wonders for your skin which will give it the healthy glow and texture that no cosmetic can. A muddy, dull-looking skin and dry, lackluster hair are often due to a bad diet, an excess of chemicalized foods, or synthetic chemicals in cosmetics. Cleansing the body from within is just as important as cleansing the body outside, as demonstrated in the following well-known biblical story. King Nebuchadnezzar chose four Hebrew boys for an experiment. They ate only grains and drank water for ten days. At the end of the ten days the four Hebrew boys appeared fairer and healthier than the children who ate the rich foods of the king's table. It may not be practical or desirable by everybody to eat only grains and vegetables, but these nutritious foods can be an important part of your diet. Fresh vegetables, fresh fruits, whole grains, beans, and herbal teas are the best sources of vitamins and minerals. Dandelions, for example, are found all over lawns, but few people know how high they are in vitamin A, vitamin C, riboflavin, and other nutrients. Other greens also contain these nutrients. A lack of vitamins A and C and riboflavin leads to a rough, scaly, wrinkled skin. Riboflavin helps prevent large pores; vitamin C is needed to help the blood carry oxygen to the skin cells, and vitamin A is known to keep the skin smooth and youthful in appearance. Another problem that will appear if you do not get enough riboflavin are blackheads (in the young usually) and wrinkles around the mouth (among older people). I believe every cosmetic should contain some amount of vitamins A, C, and E. Some will be absorbed into the skin and utilized by the skin cells and the blood. Even if only a small amount is utilized, the continual use will improve the skin and hair from the outside in as well as the inside out. Lack of essential vitamins and trace minerals will result in a muddy, pasty complexion. Proteins are important as are the essential fatty acids both of which

DIET AND COSMETICS Continued
retard the appearance of wrinkles. A diet heavy
in starches and sugar is acid-forming in the body
which contributes to premature aging of the body.
Salt is one of the worst chemicals you can use in
your diet. The skin already contains a large a-
mount of salt which is eliminated with the perspiration. Salt in your diet only increases this problem
and causes wrinkles and dry skin. Use no salt on
your foods. Here are the best nutritional sources
of the various natural substances we need to be
healthy: **PROTEIN:** Egg yolk, milk, meat and
chicken, seafood, cheese, brewer's yeast, wheat
germ, peanuts, and soybeans; **ESSENTIAL FAT-
TY ACIDS:** safflower oil, corn oil, soybean oil,
peanut oil, cottonseed oil, wheat germ, and nuts;
VITAMIN A: liver, fish liver oil, butter, cheese,
eggs, milk, carrots, and sweet potatoes; **VITA-
MIN B$_1$:** brewer's or torula yeast, wheat germ, rice
polish, whole grain breads and cereals; **VITAMIN
B$_2$:** same as vitamin B$_1$; **VITAMIN B$_5$:** brewer's
or torula yeast, wheat germ, wheat bran, liver,
blackstrap molasses; **VITAMIN B$_{12}$:** liver, milk,
eggs, cheese, and most meats; **BIOTIN:** brewer's
yeast, egg yolk, milk, and liver; **CHOLINE:** brains,
liver, kidney, brewer's yeast, and egg yolk; **FOLIC
ACID:** green vegetables, nuts, liver, and kidney;
INOSITOL: liver, brewer's yeast, wheat germ,
whole-grain breads and cereals, oatmeal, and corn;
NIACIN: brewer's yeast, liver, kidney, and wheat
germ; **PABA (PARA-AMINOBENZOIC ACID):**
liver, kidney, whole grain breads and cereals, and
brewer's yeast; **PANTOTHENIC ACID:** green
vegetables, brewer's yeast, liver, kidney, whole
grain breads and cereals; **BIOFLAVONOIDS:**
pulp and white inner rind of citrus fruits, black and
red currants, rose hips, apricots, and asparagus;
VITAMIN C: citrus ruits, guavas, ripe bell pep-
pers and rose hips; **VITAMIN D:** fish liver oils and
milk; **VITAMIN E:** unrefined vegetable oils, wheat
germ, whole grain breads and cereals, and nuts;
VITAMIN K: green vegetables; **BROMIDE:** green
leafy vegetables, whole grain breads and cereals,
seafood, liver, and kidney; **CALCIUM:** milk,
yogurt, cheese, and cultured buttermilk; **CHLOR-
INE:** green leafy vegetables; **CHROMIUM:** same
as bromide; **COBALT:** same as bromide; **COP-
PER:** green leafy vegetables, seafood, liver, whole
grain breads and cereals, kidney, dried fruits, and
egg yolk; **IODINE:** seafood, seaweed, or iodized
salt; **MAGNESIUM:** whole grain breads and cereals, nuts and soybeans; **MANGANESE:** same as
magnesium; **MOLYBDENUM:** same as bromide;
PHOSPHORUS: same as calcium; **SELENIUM:**
brewer's yeast, garlic, liver, brown rice, whole
wheat bread, and eggs; **SULFUR:** protein rich
foods, brussels sprouts, lentils, and onions; **ZINC:**
shellfish, liver, kidney, green leafy vegetables, and
nuts if grown in soil with adequate zinc deposits.
These are the elements important to your diet for
healthy hair and skin, and you must have some
amount of all of them. There are other foods that
have them, but the foods listed after each nutrient
will give you the highest amount.

DIETHANOLAMINE - Abbreviated to DEA.
Forms part of many synthetic chemicals used in
cosmetics. DEA may, like triethanolamine, be contaminated with nitrosamines. Used as an alkaliz-
ing agent, an antioxidant, a solvent, an emulsifier,
and a humectant in cosmetics. Avoid this
chemical. See **NITROSAMINES.**

DIETHYL PHTHALATE - Colorless, odorless
ester used as a solvent in perfumes and a plasticizer in nail polishes; also as an insect repellent
when clothing is saturated, and as a fixative. This
synthetic chemical can irritate the mucous membranes. Absorption through the skin can cause
depression of the central nervous system, leading
to unconsciousness and coma.

DIETHYLAMINE - Synthetic chemical used as
an alkali and a solvent in cosmetics. It killed rabbits when applied to their skin during laboratory
tests.

DIETHYLENE GLYCOL - Synthetic glycerine
used as a humectant, solvent, surfactant. Kidney,
liver, and CNS (central nervous system) damage
can result in oral doses of less than one ounce of
this toxic chemical.

DIGALLOYL TRIOLEATE - Synthetic chemical
from digallic acid and oleic acid (phenolic compound) used as a sun filter. See **CHAPTER 14.**

DIHYDROABIETHYL ALCOHOL - Chemical
derived from wood rosin and used as texturizer in
cosmetics. See **ABIETIC ACID.**

DIHYDROXYACETONE - Synthetic chemical
(containing acetone) used in quick-tanning products to dye skin brownish-orange. Substance can
also stain clothing. What it does when it is absorbed into the body is unknown. Approval by the
FDA is questionable since it alters skin and should
have a drug status.

DIISOCETYL ADIPATE - Synthetic compounds
of hexadecyl alcohol and adipic acid used as buffer.

DILAURYL THIOPROPIONATE - Synthetic
compound of lauryl alcohol and 3,3'-thiopropionic
acid used as antioxidant. See **PROPIONIC ACID.**

DIMETHICONE - This is a silicone fluid used to
give a smooth feel to a cosmetic cream or lotion.
Silicones were very popular during the 1960's, but
various allergic reactions and internal problems
due to their use make them questionable as a
cosmetic ingredient.

**DIMETHYL HYDANTOIN FORMALDEHYDE
RESIN** - The synonym of this compound is
DMHF, which is much less informative to consumers than its real name. Similar chemicals containing formaldehyde that are used in cosmetics
are listed in the *CTFA Dictionary* as DMDM
Hydantoin and MDM Hydantoin; unless you see
the chemical configuration of these chemicals you
will not know that they contain formaldehyde: a
sensitizer, an irritant, and a suspected carcinogen.
See **FORMALDEHYDE** and **CHAPTER 14.**

DIOCTYL PHTHALATE - Oily liquid ester used as plasticizer, solvent, and denaturant; it is an irritant and a CNS depressant. Dioctyl phthalate comes from phthalic acid, which is made by oxidizing benzene derivatives. See **DIBUTYL PHTHALATE** and **PHTHALIC ACID**.

DIPHENOLIC ACID - Aromatic alcohol used as a surfactant and intermediate in cosmetics. This synthetic phenolic compound is irritating to skin, eyes, and mucous membranes.

DIPHENYLENE SULFIDE - Phenolic compound used as an antiseptic.

DISINFECTANTS, AROMATICS AS - Disinfectants free the surfaces on which they are used from infection; they usually destroy vegetative matter and harmful organisms. Essentials oils (like lavender oil) sometimes have disinfectant properties.

DISODIUM MONOCOC-, LAURETH-, LAURYL-, MYRIST-, OLE-, AMIDOSULFOSUCCINATE - Synthetic fatty acid alcohols plus sodium and sulfosuccinic acid: what a mouthful! These synthetic substances are used as dispersants and surfactants.

DISPERSIONS - The incorporation of one set of particles into another set. This includes solutions, suspensions, and colloids.

DOLOMITE - Naturally occurring mineral consisting of calcium magnesium carbonate. Used as a food supplement and as an abrasive in cosmetics.

DOMIPHEN BROMIDE - Quaternary ammonium salt used as an antiseptic and preservative. See **QUATERNARY AMMONIUM SALTS**.

DROSERA - Herb of the genus *Droseraceae*, a bog-inhabiting, insectivorous group of low-flowering perennials or biennials; used in the medication of lung disorders and as an astringent in cosmetics.

DRAIZE TEST - Invented by J. H. Draize in 1959 and used extensively by the chemical and cosmetic industry to test the eye-irritancy levels of chemicals. Albino rabbits are used because their tear ducts are less efficient than those of other species and they cannot wash the irritating chemical away. During the testing, a head-holding device is used to keep the animal's body rigid to prevent it from shaking its head or scratching the eye that has been doused with the chemical. The chemical is dripped into one eye but not the other, so as to provide a control. Many millions of animals suffer every year with the Draize Test; the statistics of those tortured creatures are written on technical data sheets that are used to sell raw materials to cosmetic and other types of manufacturers. See **CHAPTER 13**.

DRUG - According to the FDA Federal Food, Drug, and Cosmetic Act (as amended), the term "drug" means (A) articles recognized in the official United States Pharmacopeia, official Homeopathic Pharmacopeia of the United States, or official National Formulary, or any supplement to any of them; and (B) articles intended for use in the diagnosis, cure, mitigation, treatment, or prevention of disease in man or other animals; and (C) articles (other than food) intended to affect the structure or any function of the body of man or other animals; and (D) articles intended for use as a component of any articles specified in clause (A), (B), or (C); but does not include devices or their components, parts, or accessories.

DRYNESS OF SKIN OR HAIR - Dry skin is flaky, dull-looking, and feels too tight; dry hair is lusterless, flyaway, and strawlike. Dryness of skin or hair can be caused by diet (insufficient essential fatty acids) or through hair and skin care products that strip away natural oils or inhibit the body's ability to re-oil itself after washing or shampooing. Essential fatty acids in the diet and in the cosmetics you use are an important part of any beauty program. Avoid harsh synthetic detergents in your shampoos and mineral oil or its derivatives (which lay greasily on top of skin and prevent it from re-oiling itself) in your skin care products.

DYSCHROMIS - Condition in which the pigmentation of the skin is abnormal.

E

E, VITAMIN - The most potent natural fat-soluble antioxidant around; vitamin E protects the fats in the body from uncontrolled oxidation and free radical damage. In cosmetics vitamin E protects the oil phase of moisturizers, lotions, and creams from oxidation; it is a natural preservative.

Discussion - We know that the tocopherols are well-known for their antioxidant properties and that the presence of vitamin E is necessary for the efficient utilization of oxygen in the tissues. There is also the probability that vitamin E is directly involved in biological oxidation. Vitamin E also has a protective action on vitamin A and other carotenoids as well as on unsaturated fatty acids. Is vitamin E useful in cosmetics? In her book *Selling Dreams*, Margaret Allen says, "There is no evidence whatsoever that the application of vitamin E cream will keep the skin young. Any improvement that we may think we see is probably psychological. From time to time other vitamins have been included in cosmetic products; as the extent to which the cream penetrates the skin is infinitesimal, such creams have neither a harmful, nor a beneficial, effect" (New York City: Simon & Schuster, 1981). On the surface of this statement there is much truth because the base of any skin care product can increase or decrease absorption

E, VITAMIN Continued

of vitamins or any other beneficial ingredient into the skin; however Ms. Allen's statement does not reflect this knowledge. Perhaps Ms. Allen wasn't aware that topical products have been used to treat heart disease, and that the vitamin content of the body can be altered by topical application. How successful the vitamin is for the purpose of skin or hair care is another matter, and again the formula is all-important. The blanket statement that this-or-that is not absorbed due to the size of the molecule shows a lack of understanding of topical application and the positive or negative effects of that absorption. Here is an update of the absorption of vitamin E.

M. Kamimura and Matsuzawa carried out a study on the absorption of vitamin E (as reported in *The Journal of Vitaminology*, 14:2 [June 10, 1968]). Alpha-tocopheryl acetate was applied to the surface of the skin followed by micro-radiographic studies to determine the conditions of absorption with the following discoveries: 1. Alpha-tocopheryl acetate is well-absorbed by the skin; 2. There are two paths of absorption from the surface of the skin to the dermis. The first is through the horny layer, the epidermis, and the line of separation between the dermis and epidermis. The second passes through the follicular canal and the interior of the hair follicles at the interior and exterior of the root envelopes and connective tissue envelopes. No path was found through the sebaceous glands and the ducts of the sweat glands; 3. Vitamin E has a great affinity for the small blood vessels. A short period after the vitamin E was applied to the skin, a large quantity was present in the hair papillae. Although a large quantity was seen in the sebaceous glands and ducts, very little was detected in the areas surrounding these systems, nor was the vitamin found in the sweat glands and ducts. Similarly, although vitamin E was not found in the fat cells, large quantities were observed in the intercellular septa. Degeneration of the collagen has been found to respond to topical application of vitamin E (especially when combined with pantothenic acid); topical application also reduced scar formation and the resolution of fibrotic tissue.

Chemical Type - Natural-source vitamin E is most reliably identified by the logo from the Natural-Source Vitamin E Association in Washington, D. C., because there is no one term that identifies vitamin E definitively as natural or synthetic. The "d-alpha" form of the tocopherol (note the "ol" spelling) is the purest form of vitamin E; however, it can be produced synthetically (in the lab) rather than isolated from natural sources. The "dl" form means the vitamin E is definitely synthetic, as only the "d" isomer occurs in nature. The "ol" ending means the tocopherol is the pure alcohol form, which has a tendency to combine with oxygen in the presence of light and air; the "yl" ending means the product is an esterfied and somewhat more stable form of vitamin E. The most common esters of vitamin E are tocopheryl acetate and tocopheryl succinate; the first is a liquid form, mixed with vegetable oil in gel capsules (which may become rancid on store shelves because esterfied vitamin E does not have much antioxidant activity), and the second is a dry form. Vitamin E exerts a protective antioxidant action on readily oxidized substances, including vitamin A and saturated oils. Only 100 to 200 parts per million are needed to provide stability to oils, emollients, and other cosmetics.

ECZEMA - Acute or chronic inflammation of the skin characterized by red, scaling, itching, and oozing lesions. Usually non-contagious. Most treatments for eczema (e.g., steroid creams) are synthetic and irritating to the skin. One natural treatment (internally and externally) found to help eczema is evening primrose oil.

EDEMA - Abnormal accumulation of clear, watery fluid in the lymph spaces of the connective tissue.

EDTA - This is an acronym for ethylene diamine tetra acetic acid. This synthetic chemical is used as a "complexing" agent in shampoos, i. e, it binds metallic ions so that the surfactants can work more effectively; also as an antioxidant. Other similar compounds are disodium or trisodium EDTA.

ENDOCRINE GLANDS - Organs producing secretions that flow through the bloodstream, rather than through ducts; glands that produce hormones, e. g. thyroid, suprarenal, and pituitary.

EFFLEURAGE - Stroking movement used in massage; light pressure.

EGG POWDER - Used as a protective film or protein. Some allergic reactions. Vegetarians may wish to avoid this ingredient.

EGG YOLK OIL - Emollient. See above.

ELASTIN - Dermal protein like collagen and reticulin, elastin is an excellent emollient ingredient when used in a natural formula. This is an animal by-product (usually bovine). There are herbal vegetarian alternatives. See **COLLAGEN** and **CELLULAR EXTRACTS**.

ELIXIRS - According to the U.S.P. definition, elixirs are clear, sweetened, hydroalcoholic liquids intended for oral use. They contain flavoring substances, and, in the case of medicated elixirs, active medicinal agents. Their primary solvents are alcohol and water, with glycerin, sorbitol, and syrup sometimes used as additional solvents and/or sweetening agents. They are prepared by simple solution or admixture of several ingredients.

EMOLLIENTS - Substances which prevent water loss of the skin. They can be natural substances or synthetic substances. Mineral oil, for example, is considered an emollient, but it is toxic and actually dries the skin. Vegetable glycerine is a natural emollient and is milder to the skin.

EMULSIONS AND EMULSIFYING AGENTS - A homogenous mixture of two incompatible substances; mayonnaise, for example, is an emulsion of oil and lemon juice. An emulsifying agent

EMULSIONS Continued
helps hold the incompatible substances together; in cosmetics, one example is soap which holds the dirt and oil from your skin in suspension until it is rinsed away. Most emulsifiers are synthetic chemicals. The best emulsifier is the old-fashioned saying "Shake well before using."

ENVIRONMENT - The world that surrounds us. According to the Gaia principle, all living things cooperate in making the environment possible. Far from being mere passengers on a cooling lump of rock, living things determine the environment by what we ingest and excrete. American Indians, and many other so-called primitive cultures, have believed this (that we are an integral part of "all that is") for thousands of years, but to western scientists this is a radical and somewhat subversive notion. Simply stated, it is this: most animals use oxygen and give off carbon dioxide; plants take in CO_2 and give off oxygen. We keep ourselves in balance and have since the beginning of life on this volatile planet. However, humankind's use of fossil fuels and our rapid rampant destruction of tropical forests threaten the CO_2-oxygen balance, creating the "greenhouse" effect. Get out your fan, folks: it's going to get hotter. Similarly, our pollution of the world with synthetic chemicals affects the environment; far from being a faddish notion, the use of totally natural, unprocessed products, whether food or cosmetics, makes conservative, long-term sense in terms of your health and the health of the earth. Those who question the superiority of natural substances over synthetic are either misguided nitpickers or have their own economic gain at stake.

ENZYMES - Protein that acts as a catalyst in some chemical reactions, sometimes called organic catalysts. The most commonly used enzymes in the food and drug industries are proteases, amylases, lipases, and pectinases.

EPIDERMIS - Outer nonsensitive layer of skin, consisting of numerous layers of cells, progressively more compressed and horny. Because of the pilo-sebaceous apparatus, however, the epidermis can be penetrated. (See page 41).

EPICHLOROHYDRIN - Volatile toxic synthetic substance used in making epoxy resins and as a solvent in cosmetics.

EPILATION - Removal of hair by the roots. This is done by various methods such as waxing, electrolysis, or simple tweezing.

EPSOM SALTS - Magnesium sulfate heptahydrate (originally from Epsom, England). In medicine it is used as a cathartic and a relaxing bath additive. In industry it is used to dye and finish leather and textiles.

ERYTHEMAL SOLARE - Sunburn.

ERYTHORBIC ACID - Isomer of ascorbic acid with $\frac{1}{20}$th of the vitamin C activity. Used as an antioxidant and preservative in cosmetics.

ESSENTIAL OILS - These are also known as volatile oils, ethereal oils, or essences. When exposed to the air, they evaporate at room temperature. They are usually complex mixtures of a wide variety of organic compounds (e. g. hydrocarbons, alcohols, ketones, phenols, acids, ethers, aldehydes, esters, oxides, sulfur compounds, etc.). They generally represent the odoriferous principles of the plants from which they are obtained. See **AROMATHERAPY**.

ESSENTIAL FATTY ACIDS - Linoleic, linolenic, and arachidonic acids; formerly called vitamin F. The essential fatty acids cannot be manufactured by the body but must be supplied from the diet. This complex of three fatty acids work together in the body, but the greatest biological activity is ascribed to linoleic acid. A deficiency of active fatty acids results in such bodily disorders as arrested growth, kidney and liver damage, anemia, and susceptibility to infections. Externally, eczemas and inflammations of the skin and hair, scaling, and hair loss appear. The skin is dry, withered and sallow. Hair and nails become dull and brittle.

Discussion - Numerous clinical studies make it apparent that the essential fatty acids have anti-infectious and bacteriostatic action. They inhibit the growth and metabolism of gram-positive bacteria *(staphylococci)* which allows an acceleration of the production of antibodies. This, of course, raises the defensive powers of the body against infections and inflammation. When vitamin F is used in topical cosmetic creams or ointments it gives the same advantages to the skin; as a skin protector against infections, eczemas, other skin diseases, and burns. On a longer term basis, vitamin F (in the form of capsules) lowers the cholesterol level in the blood and serves for prevention of arteriosclerosis.

Cosmetic Use - Vitamin F is recommended for use in moisturizers as applied for rough, dry skin and hair. It can be used in cosmetic products from 0.5 to 3.0%.

Toxicity - Natural essential fatty acids are not toxic. See **ACID, ESSENTIAL FATTY**.

ESTER - Esters are the product of a condensation reaction in which a molecule of an acid unites with a molecule of alcohol and elimination of a molecule of water. This is known as the esterification process. Esterification is any reaction in which at least one product is an ester. Some of the reactions occur between an acid and alcohol, between an acid anhydrase and an alcohol, between an acid and an unsaturated hydrocarbon, between an ester and an alcohol, between an ester and an acid, and between two esters.

ESTHETICIAN - Specialist who is devoted to skin care and is skilled in the treatment, beautification, and special care of the skin. See **AESTHETICIAN**.

ESTRADIOL - Usually synthetic female hormone in the form of a phenolic steroid alcohol. The esterfied form is used to treat menopausal symptoms. Cosmetics containing hormones may upset the body's hormonal balance.

ESTROGEN - Female sex hormone, also usually synthesized. See previous page.

ETHANOL - Alcohol from hydrocarbons. See **ALCOHOL** and **METHANOL**.

ETHANOLADMIDE & ETHANOLAMINE - Also known as monoethanolamine, or MEA. May be contaminated with carcinogenic nitrosamines. See **DIETHANOLAMINE**, **TRIETHANOLAMINE**, and **NITROSAMINES**.

ETHOXYDIGLYCOL - Solvent used in nail polishes and lacquer thinners. It can be a skin irritant.

ETHOXYETHANOL - Synthetic alcohol plus ethoxy, which is a hydrocarbon and a by-product of the natural gas industry. Absorption can produce kidney damage and CNS depression. Used as solvent.

ETHOXYETHANOL ACETATE - Ester of the above plus acetic acid; also synthetic. May depress the CNS. Used as solvent.

ETHYL ACETATE - Ester of ethyl alcohol and acetic acid; synthetic. May irritate the skin and depress the CNS. Used as a solvent in many industrial products, ethyl acetate is found in nail polishes and removers.

ETHYL ALCOHOL - Same as **ETHANOL**.

ETHYL PARABEN - See **PARABENS**.

EUCALYPTOL - Thick syrupy liquid that is the chief component of eucalyptus oil; also found in Levant wormseed and cajeput. Also known as cineole. Used for its antiseptic, flavoring, and aromatic qualities. See **HERB CHART**.

EUGENOL - Colorless aromatic liquid phenol found in many essential oils, especially cinnamon-leaf and clove oils; used in flavors, perfumes; in dentistry as a disinfectant and pain reliever.

EVENING PRIMROSE OIL - Essential oil of the yellow evening primrose flower; high in essential fatty acids, especially gamma-linolenic acid, which is a precursor to all-important prostaglandins. See **CHAPTER 6** and the **HERB CHART**.

EXCORIATION - To abrade a part of the skin so as to reach the flesh; stripping and wearing away of the skin; an abrasion.

EXCRETE - To separate and eliminate from the organic body; expel from the blood or tissues, as wasteful matter; for example, the excretions of the kidney and sweat glands.

EXTRACTS - These are generally, but not necessarily, concentrated forms of natural substances obtained by treating crude raw materials containing these substances with a solvent and then removing the solvent completely or partially from the preparations. Most commonly used: fluid extracts (liquid), solid extracts, powdered extracts (dry), tinctures, and native extracts.

FACE POWDERS - One of the safest forms of make-up because its ingredients are largely dermatologically innocuous; they do not clog pores, are fairly resistant to bacterial contamination, and do not need synthetic additives to the extent liquid make-ups do. Still, most face powders are not natural; they use synthetic color, talc (which can cause lung problems and may or may not be contaminated with asbestos), bismuth oxychloride, zinc oxide, titantium dioxide, and other synthetic chemicals. Natural ingredients such as rice starch, silk powder, hematite, allantoin (from comfrey root), and cinnamon (among others) work just as well with less irritation and allergic reactions.

FACIAL - Treatment of the face, usually done in the beauty salon with a whole variety of synthetic products whose ingredients are impossible to know because they are not listed for salon products. You can give yourself a **Natural Method Facial** at home with natural products. See **Part III, The Natural Method of Skin Care** in this book.

FATS - In chemistry, fats are a class of compounds that are solid, semi-solid or liquid; insoluble in water but soluble in ether; glycerides of one or more fatty acids; industrially obtained from rendered animal fat or oil seeds and fruit pulp; used as emollients in cosmetics.

FATTY ACIDS - "Saturated aliphatic monocarboxylic acids" is the chemical term for these organic oils found in vegetable and animal fats. They can be both saturated and unsaturated. Some saturated fatty acids are palmitic and stearic acids; some unsaturated fatty acids are oleic, linoleic, and linolenic acids. Fatty acids frequently occur in the form of esters and glycerides and are obtained by hydrolysis of fats or by synthesis. They are excellent emollients for the skin and an important part of the diet (especially in the form of essential fatty acids). See **ESSENTIAL FATTY ACIDS**).

FATTY ACID ESTERS - Esters of unsaturated fatty acids yield resins used in many industries. They are often used in compounding synthetic flavors and perfumes, and some are used in cosmetics. The alkyl salt of carboxylic acid is an example of a fatty acid ester. Esterification of fatty acids is a condensation reaction in which the molecule of an acid unites with a molecule of alcohol with the elimination of a molecule of water. Esters of fatty acids can be beneficial in some cosmetics, but there's the possibility of allergic reactions to some chemicals used in the esterification process.

FATTY ACID ESTERS Continued
Some fatty acid esters are natural and some contain synthetic chemicals. The following fatty acid wax esters are natural: beeswax, candellia, carnauba, jojoba, and lanolin. The following triglyceride esters are natural: shea butter, jojoba butter, cocoa butter. The following polyhydric esters are natural: glycerine, sorbitol, and mannitol (See **CHAPTER 11**).
Cosmetic Use - Fatty acid esters are used as emollients, thickeners, and emulsifiers.
Toxicity - None known.
FATTY ALCOHOLS - These are the alcohols of cetyl, lauryl, oleyl, and stearyl fatty acids. They're thick to semi-thick syrup-like liquids with high emolliency. sometimes used in hair and skin conditioners, creams, lotions, and conditioning shampoos. See **CHAPTER 15**.
FAVUS - A parasitic fungus disease that attacks the scalp of humans and is characterized by yellowish, dry incrustations resembling a honeycomb.
FERMENTATION - The chemical decomposition of organic compounds into a simpler compound through the action of enzymes or certain bacteria.
FERRIC CHLORIDE - Made by boiling iron in chlorine; used in medicine and cosmetics as a tincture or in a water solution; used as an astringent or styptic. Ferric chloride may irritate skin.
FERRIC FERROCYANIDE - Dark blue powder known as Prussian or iron blue. Exceedingly toxic.
FERROUS SULFATE - Astringent salt (from iron) used as an antiseptic in cosmetics and in treating anemia in medicine. It is a suspected carcinogen.
FINGERNAILS - Composed of keratin (a protein also found in hair) and consisting of a hard nail plate that rests on the bed of the nail. Both structures grow out of the matrix which is located at the bed of the nail. The hard nail plate is not living, but the nail bed contains blood vessels. The fold of skin at the base of the nail is called the cuticle. The fingernails have traditionally been decorated in various ways; long decorated fingernails are a sign of wealth and leisure since they are difficult to maintain in jobs requiring manual labor. Because the nail is so tough, nail polishes, nail polish removers, and cuticle removers are among the most caustic and damaging of cosmetics. There are practically no natural nail products.
FIXATIVES - Materials, usually high boiling and of a high molecular weight, that retard the evaporation of the more volatile components in perfume formulations.
FIXED (FATTY) OILS - Chemically the same as fats, but differing physically in that they are generally liquids at room temperature.
FLUORIDE - Compound of fluorine, an element. Fluoride, or one of its related compounds, is used in toothpastes as an antienzyme ingredient to retard tooth decay, and is added to the water supply.

FOLLICLE - A small cavity or depression in the skin containing the hair root.
FORMALDEHYDE - Colorless, pungent, irritating substance used as a preservative and disinfectant. A suspected carcinogen, formaldehyde forms part of many preservatives, such as the "hydantoins." See **CHAPTER 14**.
FORMALIN - Trade name for formaldehyde.
FRAGRANCE-FREE - Buzz words used on products to suggest that manufacturers have consumers' best interests at heart, i. e., fragrances make products allergenic, and fragrance-free products are more pure. However, the term fragrance-free is meaningless because a product is going to smell like its combination of ingredients, and some ingredients smell so noxious that something must be added to disguise the odor. A "no-fragrance" or "fresh" odor is the solution used by some "fragrance-free" products. The bottom line is, as always, don't buy a manufacturer's buzz words; read the whole label, look up the ingredients, and make up your mind on this, the most important part of the label.
FRECKLE - Yellow or brown spot on the skin, usually caused by sunlight.
FULLER'S EARTH - A variety of clay and fine siliceous material used for its moisturization ability. It can often be found as an ingredient in facial (mud) pack treatments.
FULLING - A treatment by massage therapists in which a person's limb is rolled back and forth between the therapist's hands.

G

GALEN - Physician of ancient Rome; the most famous physician (after Hippocrates) in antiquity. Galen was the inventor of cold cream which he called *ceratum refrigerans*, though some claim he got the idea from Hippocrates. Nevertheless, Galen's many treatises were translated and used as medical texts for fifteen centuries after his death. He was also the first physician to introduce animal experimentation and vivisection.
GAMMA-LINOLENIC-ACID - Fatty acid whose sole dietary source is evening primrose oil and mother's milk. See **EVENING PRIMROSE OIL** in **CHAPTER 6**.
GELS - A colloidal suspension of solid and liquid particles that exists as a solid or semi-solid mass.
GELATIN - Purified protein from animal sources used as thickener and film-forming agent.
GENES - The unit of a chromosome which transfers an inherited characteristic from parent to offspring.

GERANIOL - Fragrant liquid alcohol that occurs naturally in many essential oils such as geranium, palmarosa, and citronella oils; used as an ingredient in perfume.

GERMICIDE - Germ-killing substance.

GLAUBER'S SALT - See **SODIUM SULFATE.**

GLUCOSE - Simple sugar used as a thickener, anti-irritant and flavoring. Can be manufactured from the hydrolysis of starch and occurs naturally in foods, especially fruits.

GLUCOSE GLUTAMATE - Ester of glucose and the amino acid glutamic acid. Used as an humectant.

GLUTATHIONE - Sulfur-containing compound of glutamic acid, glycine, and cysteine that occurs in animal blood, tissues, and hair; glutathione plays an important role in the activation of some enzymes and the oxidation-reducing processes.

GLYCERETH - Polyethylene glycol ether of glycerine: this is another synthetic form of glycerine.

GLYCERIN - Glycerol or glycerine are two of the trade names for this sweet, syrupy alcohol that can be produced synthetically from propylene alcohol or naturally derived from vegetable oils. Glycerin is used as a solvent, plasticizer, humectant, emollient, and lubricant and has been used in cosmetics for thousands of years.

GLYCEROL - Trade name for glycerine.

GLYCERYL COCONATE, DILAURATE, ERU-CATE, HYDROXYSTEARATE, MONOSTEAR-ATE, MYRISTATE, OLEATE, RICINOLEATE, SESQUIOLEATE, STEARATE, TRIMYRIS-TATE, ETC. - These are esters of fatty acids combined with glycerine and generally used as glycerine is used. These are largely synthetic chemicals with perhaps a drop or two of some natural fatty acid in them. Glyceryl oleate is used as an emulsifier; glyceryl stearate SE acts as a texturizer in pasta products and an opacifier in shampoos, creams, and lotions.

GLYCINE - Amino acid. May be natural (from the hydrolysis of proteins) or synthetic (manufactured from the reaction of chloroacetic acid and ammonia). Used as a texturizer.

GLYCOGEN - Principal form in which carbohydrates are stored in animal tissues; animal starch that can be quickly converted to protein.

GLYCOL STEARATE - This ester of glycol and stearic acid is used as an opacifier, thickener, and pearlizing substance in shampoos, lotions, and cream and liquid detergents. It may be contaminated with up to 4% ethylene glycol. (See **GLYCOLS** below.)

GLYCOLIC ACID - An organic acid that occurs in unripe grapes and sugar beets, but usually manufactured from chloroacetic acid. Used as an acidifier in cosmetics. May irritate mucous membranes.

GLYCOLS - Glycerine is combined with alcohol to form a syrupy humectant. When used in make-up it helps the foundation adhere to the skin. One type, propylene glycol, is considered safe by the FDA and is used widely to formulate cough syrups and other drugs, but it is still a petrochemical and should be avoided. Some glycols are dangerous to use because they are absorbed into the skin: diethylene glycol and carbitol cause allergic reactions and can be considered toxic. Ethylene glycol has caused bladder stones and is a suspected carcinogen in bladder cancer.

GLYCOSIDES - Compounds containing sugar, which upon hydrolysis yield one or more sugars. They contain two components in their molecules: glycone and aglycone. Glycone is the sugar compound (e. g., glucose, arabinose, xylose, etc.), and aglycone is the non-sugar compound (e. g., sterols, tannins, carotenoids, quinones, etc.). Widely present in plants, they are a very important group of natural products and constitute a major class of drugs.

GLCYRRHIZIC ACID - Organic acid derived from licorice root. See **LICORICE** in the **HERB CHART.**

GRAPEFRUIT SEED OIL - The extracted oil of grapefruit seed can be used as a preservative in cosmetics. It works in both oil and water products. One processor of this extract (Dr. Jakob Harich, Chemie Research and Manufacturing) claims that grapefruit seed extract reduces bacterial infections in livestock when used as a feed additive, as well as eliminating the need for antibiotics. He also claims good results with grapefruit seed extract in the treatment of herpes, though this use is confined to South America where he has done extensive research. As a cosmetic preservative, grapefruit seed extract has been combined with various herbal and vitamin extracts by a natural cosmetic company with success for many years.

GREEN SOAP - Soap used in the treatment of skin diseases, especially acne, which is made from linseed oil and the hydroxides of sodium and potassium. It can often be found in a soft state or as a tincture (See **TINCTURE**).

GUAIAZULENE - Synonym for **AZULENE.**

GUANIDINE CARBONATE - Salt of guanidine, an alkali and humectant found in beet juice, vetch seedlings, and embryo chicks, but usually synthetically manufactured.

GUANINE - Natural pearlizing agent made from fish scales or ground-up pearls.

GUMS (ACACIA, ARABIC, BENZOIN, GUAR, DAMAR, KARAYA, LOCUST BEAN, ROSIN, TRAGACANTH) - Gums are hydrocolloids. They are polysaccharides of high molecular weight and can be dispersed in water. Some of the gums used as hair sets and natural thickeners are acacia, tragacanth, quince seed, and locust bean. They are superior to synthetic polymers (such as PVP) used in this way.

GUM RESINS - Also known as oleogums and used in some natural cosmetics. Some examples are myrrh gums, gamboge, and asafetida.

H

HACKING - A chopping stroke made with the edge of the hand during a massage.

HAIR - One of the filaments which grows from the skin of humans and animals which forms an extra thick covering on parts of the body, especially the head. Definitions of the individual parts of the hair follow. **HAIR BULB**: the lower extremity of the hair. **HAIR FOLLICLE**: the depression or cavity in the skin that contains the root of the hair. **HAIR PAPILLA**: a small cone-shaped elevation at the bottom of the hair follicle. **HAIR PILUS**: a slender, almost thread-like outgrowth on the body. **HAIR ROOT**: the part of the hair within the hair follicle. **HAIR SHAFT**: the segment of the hair that extends or projects beyond the skin.

HAIR COLORING - Artificially altering the shade or entire color of the hair. Prior to any hair coloring process, the advantages and disadvantages must be weighed carefully. Many hair dyes contain highly toxic chemicals.

HAIR TEXTURE - Density, general quality, and feel of the hair. Defined in such terms as fine, medium, coarse, dry, normal, oily, etc.

HALITOSIS - An offensive or foul odor emanating from the mouth.

HAMAMELIS WATER - *Hamamelis virginiana* is the Latin name for witch hazel; hamamelis water is a distillation with added water and alcohol. See **WITCH HAZEL** in the **HERB CHART**.

HECTORITE - A mineral that is one of the principal constituents of bentonite clay. See **BENTONITE**.

HELIOTROPINE - This is NOT the extract of heliotrope, as might be expected from the name, but a natural-sounding synonym for piperonal, a synthetic chemical that smells like heliotrope and is synthesized from piperic acid and isosafrole; used in perfumery, cosmetics, and soaps as an aromatic.

HELIX - The fleshy tip of the ear; the whole circuit of the external ear.

HEMATITE - A naturally-occurring color-imparting mineral used in ancient times as a make-up powder and now finding favor as a natural make-up product.

HENNA - See the **HERB CHART**.

HERB - A plant without woody tissue that withers and dies (to the root) after flowering. Herbal applications are found in the field of cosmetics, medicine, seasonings, etc.

HERPES - An inflammatory disease of the skin or mucous membranes characterized by clusters of vesicles that often spread. A contagious disease transmitted by direct contact.

HEXACHLOROPHENE - A white, free-flowing powder, essentially odorless, and used as a bacterial agent in soaps, cosmetics, and deodorants. Note: This highly toxic chemical was linked to infant deaths in the late 1960's and early 1970's. It was subsequently banned, but it had been termed "safe" and even "good for you" at the time, based on animal tests. The hidden toxicity of some chemicals may never be adequately determined until it is too late.

HEXYL ALCOHOL - Synthetic (hydrocarbon) alcohol used as an antiseptic and preservative.

HEXYLRESCORCINOL - Astringent derived from petroleum: a phenol. It is toxic and causes allergic reactions.

HISTAMINE - Substance produced by the body in response to allergens and subsequently detoxified by the liver.

HISTOLOGY - Study of anatomy of plants and animals as discerned under the microscope; a branch of anatomy.

HIVES - A condition in which there is an eruption of itching on the skin; urticaria.

HOMOGENOUS - The uniformity of a certain structure; having the same nature or quality.

HOMOGENIZER - Serving to produce a uniform suspension of emulsions from two or more normally immiscible substances.

HOMOSALATE - Synonym: homomenthyl salicylate. A synthetic chemical that replaces the phenolic compounds used in sunscreens. Poisoning has been reported when the chemical is absorbed into the skin.

HONEY - Sweet syrup made by various kinds of bees from flower nectar and stored in wax casings for food during the winter months. In cosmetics honey is used as an emollient and protective film. Unless you have an allergy to bee pollen there is no toxicity.

HORMONE - A secretion of an endocrine gland that is distributed in the blood stream or in bodily fluids to stimulate its specific functional effect in another part of the body. Such as substance can be produced synthetically. Hormones absorbed through the skin, such as estrogen, could have possibly harmful side effects.

HUMECTANT - A substance used to retain moisture. Some examples are glycerol and sorbitol. Using a natural humectant in a cosmetic product helps speed moisturization to the body without having to worry about the skin absorbing a synthetic chemical.

HYDROCARBON - Large group of chemical compounds that contains only carbon and hydrogen atoms; this group includes paraffins, olefins, acetylenes, and alicyclic and aromatic hydrocarbons; petroleum, natural gas, and coal products

HYDROCARBONS Continued
are all hydrocarbons. Most synthetic cosmetic ingredients are hydrocarbon derivatives (like mineral oil, propylene glycol, coal tar colors, etc.). Hydrocarbons from petroleum and its byproducts are potentially allergenic and phototoxic. They can be considered natural from the point of view that they were once ancient tropical vegetation squeezed over the centuries into oil; however, this is stretching the "natural" point beyond the point of logic and is more useful to the manufacturer of these chemicals than to you, the consumer. Hydrocarbons also occur naturally in essential oils, but these substances are part of Mother Nature's whole creation, not synthesized by man from petroleum products.

HYDROQUINONE - White crystals derived from benzene. Used in skin bleaches; also as an antioxidant and antiseptic. It is a phenolic compound and a potential skin allergen. Oral ingestion of less than one ounce may be fatal; ingestion of even tiny amounts can result in nausea and vomiting. See **CHAPTER 14.**

HYDRATE - Compound formed by the union of water with another substance. Hydrating the skin is also an important step in a facial treatment as when your skin is steamed or sprayed with the proper vitamins and minerals. See **Part III, The Natural Method of Skin Care.**

HYDROCHLORIC ACID - Also known as muriatic acid, this corrisive chemical is present in gastric juice (in dilute form) and is used in cosmetics as an oxidant and solvent. It is used in nail bleach. Even the inhalation of these fumes can irritate mucous membranes.

HYDROGEN - The lightest of the known elements (number one on the periodic table of elements). It is odorless, tasteless, and colorless; found in water and all organic compounds. It is also highly flammable.

HYDROGENATED OILS - Process by which hydrogen is added to oils to solidify them; hydrogenated oils may be stored for long periods of time without refrigeration. This process, however, destroys essential fatty acids and fat-soluble vitamins in the oils.

HYDROGEN PEROXIDE - H_2O_2; an explosive corrosive compound used as an oxidant, bleach, and antiseptic in cosmetics. It is a primary irritant and can cause blisters on the skin.

HYDROLYZED ANIMAL PROTEIN - Ingredient included in many shampoos for its ability to improve hair, "repair" split ends, and impart luster to the hair. Waste animal materials, such as pigs' feet or hides, are enzymatically or chemically broken down into protein fragments and added to cosmetic products in the form of a white powder or liquid. Though not a synthetic ingredient, it is a manufactured product and an animal by-product; also, chemical residues (as a result of incomplete reaction or careless manufacturing processes) may contaminate the protein.

HYDROCORTISONE - Hormone that occurs in the adrenal gland but is synthesized for medical use, particularly for application to broken-out or inflamed skin.

HYDROPHILIC - Having the ability to unite with or attract water.

HYDROTHERAPY - The scientific treatment of disease through the use of water.

HYDROXYPROLINE - Non-essential amino acid found in high quantities in pure soluble collagen.

HYDROXYAMINE HCL - Used as an antioxidant, this synthetic compound contains hydrochloric acid; may be severely allergenic and a skin irritant.

HYDROXYETHYLCELLULOSE - Synthetic polymer used as an emulsifier and plasticizer.

HYGIENE - System or practice designed to preserve, promote, and maintain personal health and cleanliness.

HYGROSCOPIC - Capable of absorbing moisture from the atmosphere; readily absorbing and retaining moisture.

HYPERIDROSIS - A state of excessive sweating.

HYPERSENSITIVITY - Abnormal reactions to drugs or other external substances.

HYPONYCHIUM - The portion of the epidermis upon which the nail-body rests under the free edge.

I

ICYTHYOSIS - An hereditary skin disease in which the skin becomes rough with diminished sweat and sebaceous secretion.

IMBRICATION - Cells arranged in layers that overlap one another; found in the cuticle layer of the hair.

IMIDAZOLINE DERIVATIVES - See **CHAPTER 14.**

IMPETIGO - A contagious skin disease (especially in children) marked by pustules which soon rupture and become crusted. It usually occurs on the face around the mouth and nostrils.

INCENSE - An aromatic gum, herb, or other substance that gives off an agreeable odor when burned.

INDOLE - Crystalline compound found in jasmine oil and civet; a product of the decomposition of proteins containing the amino acid tryptophan. Although indole has an unpleasant odor, it is used as a trace component in perfumes.

INFLAMMATION - The reaction of the body to irritation marked by redness, itching, swelling, heat, and pain.

INFUSIONS - See **DECOCTIONS.**

INGROWN HAIR - A hair that grows underneath the skin which may cause an infection.

INGROWN NAIL - The growth of the nail inward towards the skin instead of outward towards the finger or toe. It can cause pain and possibly an infection.

INORGANIC - Matter not related to, and lacking the structure of, living organisms. In chemistry it pertains to compounds which do not contain hydrocarbons but include the oxides and sulfides of carbon.

INOSITOL - B vitamin, usually associated with choline, that occurs naturally in lecithin (which the body produces). Inositol as part of lecithin helps metabolize fats and dissolves cholesterol. Although more inositol is found in the body than any other nutrient (except niacin), no minimum daily requirement for this substance in human nutrition has been established.

INSOLUBLE - Incapable of dissolving, or very difficult to dissolve; also, in reference to collagen, incapable of absorbing moisture. The collagen in cosmetics can be rendered insoluble by the presence of synthetic chemicals such as methyl and propyl paraben. This is also true of other natural ingredients when combined with synthetic chemicals.

IODINE - Non-metallic element that occurs in seawater, and plants and animals that grow in the sea. Iodine is necessary for correct functioning of the thyroid gland; when applied topically it has antiseptic benefits.

ION - Refers to the charge of an atom or a group of atoms. Positive ions are called cations, and negative ions are called anions.

IONIZATION - A term used in facial treatments to aid in the absorption of cosmetic products into the skin. By utilizing an electric current, the aesthetician can force positive ions through a moisturizing cream or lotion to assure deep penetration. If a good, natural moisturizer is used, ionization is not necessary.

IPECAC - Small evergreen shrub native to tropical forests of South America. The dried roots and rhizomes are used as an emetic in medicine and a denaturant in cosmetics.

IRON OXIDES - Rust; also jewelers' rouge; used as pigment, on magnetic tapes, and to polish glass.

IRRITANT - Substance that causes a negative skin reaction at the time and area that it is applied. A skin reaction to an irritant differs from that to a sensitizer in that an irritant causes approximately the same distress each time it is used, while the reaction to a sensitizer increases over time. See **SENSITIZER**.

ISOBUTANE - See **BUTANE**.

ISOPROPYL ALCOHOL - Synthetic alcohol made from propylene by means of sulfuric acid; used as a rubbing alcohol and as a source for acetone. Used as an antiseptic and solvent. Oral doses cause a variety of symptoms, including gastric, central nervous system, and mental disturbances.

ISOPROPYL MYRISTATE - A partly natural, partly synthetic chemical used as an emollient and lubricant to reduce the greasy feel due to the high oil content of other ingredients. Allergic reactions.

ISOPROPYL LANOLATE, LAURATE, LINOLEATE, OLEATE, PALMITATE, STEARATE, AND ISOSTEARATE - Esters of isopropyl alcohol and various fatty acids. Synthetic chemicals. Irritancy and allergic reactions are possible.

J

JABORANDI - Dried leaves from a South American rutaceous shrub; a source of pilocarpine, which is a diaphoretic and a treatment for glaucoma.

JALAP RESIN - Dried root of the Mexican plant *Exogonium purga*; a cathartic.

JAPAN WAX - See **WAXES**

JAUNDICE - An abnormal physical condition caused by bile pigments in the blood. It is characterized by yellowness of the skin and eyes, constipation, loss of appetite, and general weakness.

JUGLONE - Reddish yellow crystal obtained from green walnut hulls; chief compound in brown hair dye from walnuts.

K

KAOLIN - A fine white mineral clay that remains white after firing and is used in manufacturing high grade porcelain, paper, paint, cloth, soaps, and many powdered and covering cosmetics. It is an emollient agent with a dehydrating and astringent effect. Also known as China clay.

KARAYA GUM - See **GUM, KARAYA**.

KELOID - Originating in the connective tissue, this skin disease is marked by whitish, indurated patches surrounded by a pink or purple-like border. It is also characterized as a fibrous growth arising from irritations and usually a scar.

KERATIN - An insoluble albumoid (fiber protein) that can be found in horny tissues, such as hair and nails. High in sulfur, it is quite strong but subject to chemical penetration.

KERATOMA - A condition marked by a callous or a horny tumor. It is an acquired, thickened section of the epidermis.

KERATOSIS - A disease of the epidermis indicated by the presence of growths of the horny layer of tissue; a callous.

KEROSENE - Extremely flammable hydrocarbon used as a fuel and, in a deodorized form, in cosmetics as a solvent.

KNEAD - Term describing the process of working and pressng with the hands during a massage.

KOHL - A black powder relative to the East and used to darken the edges of the eyelids. It is made from the ash of frankincense.

L

LABELING - April 14, 1977, is the date the Cosmetic Labeling Act of 1977 passed, which requires that most cosmetics have to be accurately labeled. Exceptions include products packaged for salon use and soaps. Flavors, fragrances, and trade secrets are also exempt from the labeling law. Even so, the cosmetic labeling law marked a major step towards consumer awareness of what they wash into their hair and rub onto their faces.

LACTIC ACID - Naturally occurring acid in milk which produces pH levels like those of the hair and skin; also aids the Natural Moisturizing Factor of the skin. May be produced synthetically also, so look at the rest of the formula to see if natural or not.

LACTALBUMIN - A natural milk protein high in lactic acid and containing the eight amino acids. It was designated by the late Adelle Davis as the most perfect protein.

LAKE COLORS - Solid form of dye made by mixing liquid dye with an insoluble powder such as aluminum oxide. May be natural or synthetic, but usually synthetic (i. e., coal tar colors).

LANOLIN AND ITS DERIVATIVES - Fatty secretion from sheep's wool; a yellow, semisolid fat. If it contains water it is called hydrous lanolin; without water, it is called anhydrous lanolin. Used as an emulsifier, base, and an emollient. Lanolin alcohol is the fatty alcohol of lanolin; it is solid and used as an emulsifier and thickener. Lanolin oil has had the wax component removed and is used as a moisturizer. Lanolin is natural and is well absorbed by the skin. There are some reports of allergic reactions.

LANOSTEROL - Sterol derived from alcohol and used as an emollient. See **STEROL**.

LATEX - Liquid rubber, either from a rubber-producing plant or synthetic rubber (plastic or polymers) solution in water. Used as film-former.

LAURAMIDE DEA - White, waxy, non-ionic synthetic substance used in shampoos, bubble baths, and detergents as a surfactant and foam-builder. May be mildly irritating to the skin. Also may be contaminated with nitrosamines. See **DIETHAN-OLAMINE (DEA)**.

LAURETH 1-40 - Polyethylene glycol ether of lauryl alcohol. Synthetic surfactant and foaming agent.

LAURIC ACID - Mixture of fatty acids originally obtained from the European laurel but now obtained from coconut and palm kernel oils. Used to make soaps, esters, and lauryl alchol.

LAURYL ALCOHOL - Fatty alcohol often made from coconut oil and used to make anionic surfactants. May be natural or synthetic.

LEAD ACETATE - Inorganic salt made from lead monoxide and acetic acid; used as manufacturing agent in dyes, and as an inorganic color to dye hair, also formerly as an astringent. It is poisonous and a carcinogen.

LECITHIN - Naturally occurring mixture of stearic, palmitic, and oleic acid compounds found in plants in animals; high in choline and inositol (B vitamins). Used as an emulsifier and surfactant. Found in egg yolk and manufactured from soybean oil.

LENTIGO - Small spot of pigmentation on the skin, unrelated to sun exposure; may develop into a malignancy.

LETHAL DOSE (LD/50 or LD/60) - Animal test used to test toxicity of chemicals. In the test 100 or 120 animals are fed, force-fed, injected, or otherwise exposed to doses of chemical. The doses increase until half the animals are dead. These numbers are recorded and used to sell the chemicals. This test is inhumane and unscientific; it is a meaningless ritual of modern speciesism.

LEUCINE - One of the essential amino acids (i. e., an amino acid that cannot be manufactured by the body). It is found in hair and included in some amino acid shampoos.

LEUKODERMA - Skin abnormality characterized by a splotchy lack of pigment in bands or spots.

LIME - Calcium oxide, often occurring with magnesia. Caustic substance used as an alkali.

LIME WATER - See **CALCIUM HYDROXIDE**.

LINALOOL - Fragrant alcohol that occurs in many essential oils, especially bois de rose oil and coriander. Used as an aromatic.

LINOLEAMIDE DEA - Ethanolamide of linoleic acid, plus diethanolamine. Synthetic chemical that may be contaminated with nitrosamines.

LINOLEIC ACID - Essential fatty acid found in cold-pressed oils. This oil is essential for nutrition. Used as an emulsifier in cosmetics.

LIPASES - Lipolytic enzymes that hydrolyze fats or fixed oils into their glycerol and fatty acid components.

LIPIDS - Group of fatty substances that with proteins and carbohydrates constitute the structure of cells. The group includes fats, waxes, phosphatides, cerebrosides, and sometimes steroids and carotenoids. When used on the skin, they have a moisturizing and emollient action.

LIPSTICK - Waxy color applied to the lips that may be natural or synthetic. Lipsticks are usually synthetic, however, consisting of coal tar dyes and mineral oil waxes. These synthetic ingredients may cause irritation of the lips called cheilitis. Since lipsticks may be ingested as they wear off during the day, it's especially important that they be natural. Look for natural vegetarian waxes like (e.g., carnauba or candellia) and for natural colors like carmine or beet extract. PABA for sun protection is also an excellent ingredient in all skin care products.

LIVER SPOTS - See **CHLOASMA**.

LOCUST BEAN GUM - See **GUMS**.

LOOFA - Vegatable sponge that is the skeleton of the luffa fruit (family *Curcurbitaceae*). Usually long and cylindrically shaped, a loofa has a rough texture that is excellent for the body but somewhat too rough for the face. Also, a damp loofa makes an ideal environment for bacteria. Be sure to clean well before use.

LYE - Potassium or sodium hydroxide is the synonym for this strong alkali made by washing wood ashes in water which is sometimes used to make soaps. Lye is a caustic chemical used in drain cleaners because it dissolves organic matter; it is also found in hair straighteners, but it can burn the outer layers of the scalp and cause blindness.

LYSINE - One of the eight essential amino acids.

M

MAGNESIUM - Lightweight mineral occurring abundantly in nature and essential for nutrition, especially calcium and vitamin C absorption. See **DIET AND COSMETICS**.

MAGNESIUM ALUMINUM SILICATE - White flaky solid used as anticaking agent, filler, thickener, and stabilizer in cosmetics, especially antiperspirants, creams, and shaving creams. See **ALUMINUM CHEMICALS IN COSMETICS**.

MAGNESIUM CARBONATE - See **DOLOMITE**.

MAGNESIUM OXIDE - Also known as magnesia. Used as an inorganic color and abrasive.

MAGNESIUM SILICATE - Found in talc (natural source material) and used as anticaking agent.

MAGNESIUM STEARATE - Magnesium salt of stearic acid used as a filler in cosmetics.

MALIC ACID - Organic acid often found in herbs used as an antioxidant and alkali.

MANNITOL - Naturally sweet alcohol found in plants; used as a humectant.

MELANIN - Dark brown or black pigment found in varying amounts in animal or plant structures. May be derived from tyrosine or l-dopa (amino acids), believed to be a type of polymer related to indole.

MENSTRUUMS - These are solvents used for extraction such as alcohol, acetone, and water.

MENTHOL - This is the oleoresin from peppermint. It is an excellent counter-irritant and has soothing properties if used in amounts of 1% or less. See **MINTS** in the **HERB CHART**.

MERCURY, AMMONIATED - Used in bleaching cream for decades until pressure from Japan and consumer groups forced its removal. Phenylmercuric acetate is a highly toxic chemical used as a preservative in eye cosmetics, although it does not protect user from bacteria from products contaminated by use. The use of amalgam (silver and mercury mixture) used in dental fillings is also suspect as mercury vapor may be released during chewing. Mercury is a deadly poison, a heavy metal that accumulates in the body and may cause a wide variety of symptoms.

METALLIC SALTS - Used in men's hair restorers. They are the oldest known hair dyes and work by coating the hair with a metallic sheath that leaves the hair dull and dry-looking. Metallic salt dyes give inconsistent and unpredictable results; they are incompatible with permanent waves. Lead acetate is used in some hair restorers, which is toxic.

METHANAL - Trade name for formaldehyde.

4-METHOXY-M-PHENYLENEDIAMINE SULFATE - Coal tar color used in hair dyes. A known carcinogen that is being replaced by hair dye companies with a compound so similar that it is probably carcinogenic too. Coal tar hair dyes are even exempt from the portion of the Food, Drug, and Cosmetic Act (as amended in 1978) that defines "adulterated (i.e., poisonous or deleterious) cosmetics."

METHYL ACETATE - Ester of methyl alcohol and acetic acid. Synthetic chemical used as an aromatic and solvent. May cause dryness and dermatitis.

METHYL PARABEN - See **PARABENS**.

METHYLCELLULOSE - See **CELLULOSE GUM**.

METHYL SALICYLATE - The major constituent of wintergreen oil and sweet birch oil (around 98%), but may be produced synthetically. Watch for use of the essential oil (instead of the chemical name) on cosmetic labels. Used as flavoring, aromatic, local anesthetic, anti-inflammatory.

MICA - Group of silicate minerals that split into very thin sheet; somewhat shiny. Used in eye cosmetics to provide sparkle.

MILK PROTEIN - Also known as lactalbumin, lactalbumin is derived from milk whey and consists largely of casein. Used in a natural hair conditioner.

MINERAL OIL - Liquid mixture of hydrocarbons obtained from petroleum. Mineral oil is allergenic and phototoxic, but it is a cheap and almost unavoidable cosmetic ingredient. Tends to be heavy and greasy and cause the skin to become dry or develop clogged pores. Mineral oil (in any of its myriad forms) is NOT an ingredient in any good natural cosmetic.

MINERAL WATER - Water that is drawn from a natural mineral water spring, like Perrier or Evian, and which may have therapeutic properties. When mineral water is used in a product, be sure to check the rest of the ingredients listed to see if they are natural or not. Special "water" is a common buzz word advertising ploy and may disguise a largely synthetic product.

MINERAL SPIRITS - Flammable petroleum distillate, lighter than kerosene. Used as a solvent.

MINIMAL ERYTHERMAL DOSE - The amount of time in the sun that produces a sunburn; this may vary from skin type to skin type.

MINK OIL - Oil from minks. Another self-proclaimed miracle moisturizing ingredient. This animal oil is no better or worse than any other animal oil. Vegetable oils are just as good and don't kill any animals.

4 MMPD - This is the abbreviation for 4-methoxy-m-phenylenediamine sulfate.

MONTMORILLONITE - Clay mineral used in facial masks. See **BENTONITE** or **FULLER'S EARTH**.

MORPHOLINE - Amine made from ethylene oxide and ammonia; used as a solvent and emulsifying agent.

MOLE - Small raised spot, mark, or protuberance on the skin, usually pigmented.

MONOETHANOLAMINE (MEA) - Liquid amino alcohol used as an humectant and emulsifier in cosmetics. May be contaminated with nitrosamines. See **DIETHANOLAMINE, TRIETHANOLAMINE** and **NITROSAMINES**.

MUCOPOLYSACCHARIDES - Class of substances, widely distributed in the body, that bind with water to form the thick, jelly-like material that cements cells together and lubricates joints. The name "mucopolysaccharide" was coined by K. Meyer (Cold Springs Harbor Symposium in Quantitative Biology, 1938) to describe hexosamine-containing polysaccharides found in animal and plant cells. Mucopolysaccharides influence the metabolism of cells because all substances going from cell to cell must pass through them. Recently, mucopolysaccharides have become important in skin care formulations because of their ability to hold water. These substances hold more water because of the unique polymer matrix which is tightly bound by neighboring chains. They are also unique in a facial cream because unlike the chemical 2-Pyrrolidone-5-Carboxylic Acid (NaPCA) they will not cause skin dessication, rash, or irritation. How well do mucopolysaccharides in creams penetrate the skin? The simplest molecule of mucopolysaccharide that is able to penetrate the skin is laluramina. This is the essential element for proper use of mucopolysaccharides. (Also see **NaPCA**).

MUSK - Animal or vegetable substance used as a fixative in perfumes. Animal musk is obtained from a sac situated under the skin of the abdomen of the male musk deer; musk also is found in other animals, such as the musk-ox, the civet cat, and muskrat. Herbal musk may be obtained from musk seed (*Hibiscus abelmuschus*) or ambrette seed (*Abelmoschus moschatus*) or musk mallow or musk clover.

MUSTARD OIL - Bland oil obtained from black (usually) mustard seeds and used in soap-making and in salad dressings; also a pungent essential oil used in liniments and plasters. The mustard essential oil may be irritating to the skin.

MYRISTALKONIUM CHLORIDE - Quaternary ammonium salt used as a surfactant, antiseptic, and preservative. Made from myristic acid (See below). See **QUATERNARY AMMONIUM SALTS**.

MYRISTIC ACID - Fatty acid; also called tetradecanoic acid. Found in nutmeg, sperm oil, and coconut oil. Used in cosmetics as an emulsifier and foaming agent. The fatty alcohol from myristic acid is called myristyl alcohol.

MYRISTYL LACTATE - Ester of myristyl alcohol and lactic acid; used as an emollient.

N

NAILS - See **FINGERNAILS**.

NAIL POLISH REMOVER - Strong synthetic chemical mix consisting of a solution of acetone (or a related chemical) mixed with conditioning ingredients. Acetone is a highly flammable, volatile solvent that can dissolve many plastics. It may be fatal if swallowed. Conditioning ingredients in nail polish removers (which include petrochemicals like propylene glycol) do little to mitigate the strongly drying and degreasing effects of the acetone chemicals. The solution is simple, however: if you don't wear nail polish, you won't need nail polish remover. If you do wear nail polish, use nail polish remover as infrequently as possible to prevent the nails from becoming dry and brittle. There is little variation in the ingredients of nail polish removers, so be suspicious of high-priced brands.

1,5-NAPHTHALENDIOL, 2,3-NAPHTHALEN-DIOL & 2,7-NAPHTHALENDIOL - Coal tar derivatives used as diluents in cosmetics. They may irritate or dry skin.

1-NAPHTHOL & 2-NAPHTHOL - Coal tar derivatives used as dye intermediates; also as antiseptic and parasiticide. These substances may irritate the skin. They may be absorbed through the skin; oral doses larger than one teaspoon may be fatal.

NATIVE EXTRACTS - Botanicals extracted by a solvent or solvent mixture then concentrated under reduced pressure until all of the solvent is removed. They are usually of high potency from which one can derive solid, fluid, or powdered extracts of varying concentrations.

NATURAL - This is an abused word. It is most abused in the cosmetic field but also in the food industry. If we want a "natural product" we expect it not to contain synthetic chemicals. Read the label to be sure.

NATURAL COLORS - Derived from plants (such as indigo) or insects (cochineal beetle), natural colors are appropriate for use in natural cosmetics. Don't accept anything less.

NDGA (NORDIHYDROGUARIARETIC ACID) - Antioxidant used in trace amounts in cosmetics. NDGA may be made synthetically or from the creosote bush; it has caused kidney damage in animal tests.

NEAT'S FOOT OIL - Pale yellow fatty oil made from boiling the feet and shinbones of cattle. Used chiefly as leather dressing and fine lubricant.

NEROL - Aromatic alcohol found in a number of herbal essential oils, including immortelle, estragon, hops, labdanum, lemon petitgrain, lemongrass, orange, and rose. Essential oils containing high concentrations of nerol, geraniol, eugenol, beta-pinene,and furfurol have antimicrobial properties against *Staphylococcus aureus, Escherichia coli*, a *Mycobacterium* species, and *Candida albicans*.

NITRIC ACID - Inorganic acid used as an oxidizer and stabilizer in cosmetics. Corrosive liquid that can irritate skin, and inhalation can irritate lungs and bronchia passages. Oral doses can be fatal.

NITROCELLULOSE - Flammable synthetic substance (similar to gun cotton) used as an emulsifier and protective film in cosmetics, especially nail polish.

NITROSAMINES - Class of secondary compounds formed from secondary amines by nitrous acid. They have been found very carcinogenic in animal experiments. In 1978 Dr. David H. Fine (then working with the Thermo Electron Corporation in Waltham, Massachusetts) invented the Thermal Energy Analyzer which could detect N-nitrosamines in the environment. He and his group discovered that over 40% of cosmetics that contain triethanolamine (TEA) were contaminated with these potent carcinogens. Further research revealed that they can be absorbed through the skin into the body, and the contamination allowed nitrosamines to be absorbed in amounts far greater than eating nitrite-preserved food. The TEA or DEA reacts with a nitrosating agent to form NDELA; these nitrosating agents include sodium nitrite and bronopol (2-bromo-2-nitroprophane-1, 3-diol) and other C-nitrol compounds. These C-nitrol compounds are widely used as dyes and perfumes in cosmetics. Little is known about the problem, but more than one consumer publication has recommended avoiding any cosmetic that contains triethanolamine (TEA) or diethanolamine (DEA).

Discussion - More than 120 N-nitroso compounds have been examined for carcinogenic activity, and about 80% of them have been found to be carcinogenic to some degree (Magee, P. N., Montessano, R., and Preussmann, R., "N-Nitroso Compounds and Related Carcinogens," C. E. Searle, *Chemical Carcinogens*, [ACS Monograph 173], The American Cancer Society, 1976, pp. 491-625). One of those 120 compounds which has been found in many cosmetics is N-nitrosodiethanolamine (NDELA). NDELA is of concern in cosmetic products because it has been shown to penetrate human skin under normal conditions of topical application. The wide use of a chemical known as triethanolamine (TEA) in many cosmetic formulations is the main suspected chemical that creates NDELA, but there are many other chemicals believed to cause the NDELA contamination.

All amines and amides are capable of forming N-nitroso compounds. In cosmetic products two conditions will result in the creation of the nitrosating agents: 1.) the presence of the chemical capable of becoming a nitrosating agent; and 2.) the chemical state (e. g., pH) at which the reaction between nitrosating agent and amine or amide can take place. A cosmetic formula whose pH ranges between 3.4 to 4.5 and which contains any one of the chemicals listed in the table below has the potential of developing nitrosamines. A pH higher than 4.5 doesn't seem to generate substantial amounts of nitrosating agents, while a pH below 3.4 causes amines to protonate, rendering them safe from reaction from nitrosating agents. Therefore the formula of low pH and pH balanced shampoos, conditioners, and rinses should be free of the amines and amides to assure a parameter of safety. Quaternary amines and amine oxides also react with nitrites in an acidic medium to form nitrosamines.

The prevention of the formation of nitrosamines in cosmetics is to either 1.) eliminate the chemical that is the source of the nitrosating agent; and 2.) add an agent that prevents nitrosation reactions from occurring. One chemical to avoid is the chemical 2-bromo-2-nitropropane-1,3-diol because in aqueous solutions it forms nitrosamines. Another important chemical to avoid is sodium nitrite, but simply NOT putting sodium nitrite in a cosmetic formula may not protect the product from nitrosamines. Water and the aqueous formulations of cosmetic products can be a source of nitrite.

NITROSAMINES Continued

Although ion exchangers have been suggested to remove nitrite and nitrate from water, the ion exchanger resins contain minute amounts of nitrosamines as the resins are prepared with amines. Also, sodium nitrite is present in the seaming compound used in new drums and in the reconditioning process of used drums. The use of plastic and fiberboard drums can avoid this source of contamination, but this solution may not always be practical.

The conditions under which cosmetics are prepared and the raw materials stored may also contribute to nitrosamine contamination. Cosmetic raw materials in half-empty drums can become contaminated due to the nitrogen oxides in the air (a source of nitrosating species). The air that contains automobile exhaust and cigarette smoke is a great hazard to half-empty drums of cosmetic materials or drums of materials which are not tightly sealed. Of course, there should be no smoking in the areas where raw materials or finished products are kept, and delivery trucks should not let their motors run so that the exhaust pipes cause nitrogen oxide to contaminate the storage area. Half-empty drums of raw materials should be flushed with nitrogen or another inert gas to prevent contamination of raw materials. It is also a good rule to flush any new drum of raw material with inert gas, especially those materials shipped in metal drums.

The following antioxidant compounds potentially inhibit the formation of N-nitroso compounds, but both water soluble and fat soluble antioxidizing agents may be needed. The best choice is vitamin C in the form of ascorbic acid and ascorbyl palmitate. In the oil phase of the product ascorbic palmitate and tocopherol (vitamin E) can be used. The inhibitory action of ascorbic acid and ascorbyl palmitate against nitrosamines *in vitro* and *vivo* has been well established (Dahn, H., Loewe, I., and Bunton, C. A., "Uber die Oxydation von Ascorbinsaure durch salpetrige Saa. Teil VI: Ubersicht and Diskussion der Irgebnisse," *Helv. Chim. Acta.,* Vol. 42, 1960, p. 320. Archer, M.; Tannenbaum, S.; Fan, T. Y.; and Weisman, M., "Reaction of Nitrite with Ascorbate and Its Relation to Nitrosamine Formation," *Journal Natl. Cancer Inst.,* vol. 54, no. 5, 1975, pp. 1203-1205). I have used the combination of the water-soluble ascorbic acid and the fat-soluble tocopherol and ascorbyl palmitate with great success since 1969 and found them very effective in cosmetic formulations in both the aqueous and non-aqueous phases of a product. Synthetic antioxidants such as BHA and BHT have yet to be found to be effective blocking agents against nitrosamines. Phenolic compounds are also poor blocking agents because they can combine with a nitrosating agent to form a C-nitro compound. This may either liberate the nitrosating agent or be catalytic to nitrosamine formation itself.

Though the use of vitamin C and vitamin E may slightly discolor a cosmetic product, this is far more desirable than the presence of a nitrosamine.

Our advice: avoid cosmetics with the following chemicals that cause nitrosamine contamination and if any of them are used, read the label to see if vitamin C and vitamin E are in the products as a blocking agent.

NITROSATING AGENTS
2-bromo-2-nitropropane-1,3-diol
Cocoyl sarcosine
Diethanolamine (DEA)
Diethanolamine (DEA) plus any chemical
Imidazolidinyl urea
Formaldehyde
Hydrolyzed animal protein
Lauryl sarcosine
Monethanolamine (MEA)
Monethanolamine (MEA) plus any chemical
Quaternium-7, 15, 31, 60, etc.
Sodium lauryl (or laureth) sulfate
Sodium methyl cocoyl taurate
Triethanolamine (TEA)
Triethanolamine (TEA) plus any chemical

NITROUS OXIDE - Laughing gas. Used as a propellant in cosmetics. May cause depression of the central nervous system.

NON-ANIONIC SURFACTANTS - Surface active agents that produce an electrically neutral charge (i.e., neither ionic or cationic).

NONOXYNOL COMPOUNDS - A large group of ethoxylated alkyl phenols widely used as surfactants and dispersants. Phenols are toxic. Avoid these chemicals.

NUCLEIC ACIDS - Either of two groups of complex acids that determines the genetics of living things (DNA or RNA). These substances are added to cosmetics with the claim that they will "strengthen" the cellular rejuvenation of the skin, but don't buy this pseudo-scientific explanation.

NYLON - Synthetic fiber used to strengthen the effects of some cosmetics, e.g., nail polish.

OCCLUSIVE AGENTS - When used in cosmetics, occlusive agents are substances that hold strongly to the surface of the skin, increasing absorption and blocking access to the air. Examples of occlusive agents are plastic wrap and band-aids. Occlusive agents have been used for thousands of years to speed healing of wounds and as beauty treatments.

OCOTEA CYMBARUM OIL - Essential oil obtained by steam distillation of the bark of Brazilian trees *(Ocotea cymbarum)*. Used as a substitute for sassafras oil because of its high safrole content.

OILS - Viscous substances generally insoluble in water, obtainable from animal, plant, mineral, and synthetic sources.

OINTMENT - Semisolid preparation for the skin, usually with a fatty or greasy base.

OLEIC ACID - Fatty acid that is a common constituent in many animals and vegetables; also a common cosmetic ingredient. May be isolated from vegetable oils or produced from inedible tallow. When hydrogenated, oleic acid yields stearic acid.

OLEORESINS - Plant products consisting of essential oil and resin in solution. Oleoresins can occur naturally or be manufactured. One prepared oleoresin is ginger, and one example of a naturally occurring oleoresin is Oregon balsam.

OLETH-2 through 50 - Polyethylene glycol ethers of oleic alcohol used as surfactants. Synthetic chemicals.

OLEYL ALCOHOL - Fatty alcohol; an oily liquid unsaturated compound found in fish oils or manufactured from esters of oleic acid. Used to make surface active agents. See above.

OLFACTORY - Relating to the sense of smell.

OPACIFYING AGENTS - Substances used to change the appearance of cosmetics from clear to cloudy, e.g., titanium dioxide. Opacifying agents perform no useful function in skin and hair care but are added to "improve" the appearance of products.

ORGANIC - In today's chemistry, the term organic means the substance described contains a carbon atom. However, the definition in this book refers to the original definition as made by the Swedish chemist Berzelius: to be considered organic, a substance has to be, or once was, living. See **INTRODUCTION**.

ORIGANUM OIL, SPANISH - This oil (related to marjoram) has been found to be irritating to animals and nonsensitizing to humans. This shows how silly animal testing is. What if we tested this on humans for use in products for rabbits and mice? Does this proposal sound silly? Of course. Animal testing is silly, isn't it? Origanum oil *(Thymus capitatus)* is used as a fragrance component in cosmetics and as a flavor component in foods. May cause an allergic reaction, as do some natural ingredients.

ORRIS - As essential oil (from European plants of the genus *Iris*, especially *I. pallida*), orris is used as a flavoring and fragrance material. Orrisroot may also be powdered and used in sachets, tooth powders, and as a powder base.

OURICURY WAX - See **WAXES**.

OXALIC ACID - Strong poisonous acid used as a neutralizing, acidifying, and bleaching agent in the textile industry, also in the manufacture of dyes, and as an ingredient in rust removers.

OXIDATION - Chemical reaction caused by the combination of oxygen and another substance. Fire is an example of an oxidation reaction; so is rancid butter. Antioxidants inhibit oxidation; they protect the oil phase of cosmetics from combining with oxygen and becoming rancid.

OXYQUINOLINE - Aromatic alcohol, usually derived from coal tar, used as an antimicrobial. May cause allergic reactions.

OZOKERITE - See **WAXES**.

P

PABA - Para-aminobenzoic acid is a water-soluble B vitamin found in blackstrap molasses, bran, brewer's yeast, eggs, liver, milk, rice, organ meats, wheat germ, and whole wheat. The RDA is 50-60 mg per day, and it is not generally toxic. Some individuals, however, may have side effects with excessive intake on a regular basis. Topical toxicity is rare. Some individuals may have a slight "reddening" of the skin, but it is not a lasting reaction. This nutrient is important to the glands, hair, intestines, and skin. It facilitates blood cell formation, hair pigmentation (see **PANTOTHENIC ACID**).

Discussion and Cosmetic Use - PABA is well known for its ability to screen out the burning effects of UV rays, and though there are several substances known to do this job, PABA is still the choice for sun protection. PABA works best when combined with other sun protectors such as jojoba butter (and oil), African butter (karite or shea butter), aloe vera, willow bark extract, and cuttlefish oil. Though PABA is not easily washed away, it holds best to the skin if combined with fatty acid esters, sorbitol, or vegetable glycerine. PABA has been recorded as a nutrient that retards hair loss, prevents gray hair. It also, of course, can be used in shampoos and hair conditioners to prevent UV damage of the disulphide bond in hair (another cause of hair loss and breakage).

The salt of PABA, known as dimethylaminoethanol (DMAE) is an amino alcohol believed by some scientists to reduce the aging process by removing the accumulated toxic by-products of metabolism. It is believed that as we age the body has the inability to create digestive enzymes (known as lysosomes) and that PABA keeps the lysomal enzymes doing their job. When we see the "brown spots" on our skin known as "age spots" or "liver spots" it is a tissue result of toxic accumulation within the body. These toxins accumulate in brain cells where they interfere with cellular metabolism. It is believed that PABA combined

PABA Continued
with B_{12}, selenium, inositol, C, pantothenic acid, folic acid, biotin, niacin, and cystine can prevent hair loss.

PALM KERNEL OIL - White to yellowish fat obtained from palm kernels (such as the African oil palm). Palm kernel oil is similar to coconut oil and is used to make soap and margarine.

PALMITATE - Salt or ester of palmitic acid.

PALMITIC ACID - Also called hexadecanoic acid, this is a fatty acid that occurs in palm oil (hence the name) and most other fats and fatty oils. In the form used in cosmetics, however, palmitic acid may contain petrochemicals (such as propylene glycol) for enhanced emulsibility.

PALM OIL - Similar to Palm Kernel Oil.

PANTOTHENIC ACID - This is a B-complex water soluble vitamin. It is found in bran, brewer's yeast, broccoli, brown rice, carrots, cauliflower, cheese, eggs, fish, peas, legumes, lima beans, mushrooms, oats, organ meats, peanuts, royal jelly, salmon, soybeans, spinach, walnuts, wheat, wheat germ, whole grains, and liver. The RDA is 4-7 mg. It is not known to be toxic.

Discussion - Pantothenic acid (also known as vitamin B_5) works to assure proper function of adrenal glands, digestive tract, immune system, nerves, and skin. B_5 also facilitates antibody formation as a detoxifier; has antihistamine action; converts carbohydrates, fat, and protein into energy for the body; is an antistress nutrient; and stimulates growth and cortisone production. Pantothenic acid is needed for proper utilization of vitamin D.

Cosmetic Use - Pantothenic acid is one of the B vitamins attributed to the prevention of gray hair. It works with PABA, folic acid, and inositol. Several health writers have said they have seen fantastic color changes due to an intake of these B vitamins; two of the better known health writers who have written about this are Adelle Davis and Carlton Fredericks. It is obviously not from personal results that they make these statements (both have or had gray hair) but by observations of others or research. The actor Robert Cummings, however, had no gray hair and attributes this to the intake of these B vitamins.

My personal experience using pantothenic acid is for hair and skin care. Pantothenic acid is an excellent skin hydrator. If a beaker of pantothenic acid is left in a room with the lid slightly ajar, the next day the lid will be covered with moisture. It has this same effect on the skin and when used in skin moisturizers or complexion sprays, the skin is left smooth and moist. Pantothenic acid will not work, however, if the rest of the product contains chemicals that "dry out" the skin or hair. I have successfully formulated a mineral water spray for hydrating the skin by combining the following vitamins and herbals to the mineral water base: PABA, pantothenic acid, vitamins A, E, F, horse chestnut, fennel, hops, camomile, balm-mint, and yarrow.

The action of pantothenic acid on the hair is also interesting. It actually makes hair look thicker and fuller and gives hair body so that it can be used in hair groooming products and grooming sprays. Very little or even no "gums" or "resins" are needed in a hair spray using pantothenic acid.

PAPAIN - Proteolytic enzyme, which means a substance capable of causing proteins or peptides to break down into simpler substances (as in digestion). Papain comes from green papayas and is used to tenderize meat, to chill-proof beer, and as a digestive aid in medicine. It has been used in cosmetics to soften skin.

PARABENS - Para-hydroxybenzoic acid esters (methyl, propyl, butyl, etc.). Synthetic chemicals used to preserve cosmetics, but not effective with shampoos and products that contain proteins. Toxic and allergenic. For more information, see the preservatives glossary in **CHAPTER 14**.

PARAFFIN - Waxy crystalline mixture of hydrocarbons, usually derived from petrochemicals. Used as a thickener for cosmetics.

PATCH TEST - If you are concerned about allergic reactions to a cosmetic product, apply a small amount of the product to your inner arm, cover with a bandage, and leave it for twenty-four hours. If redness or soreness develops, you have an allergic reaction to some constituent of that product; if not, the product is probably safe for you to use.

PCMC & PCMX - Parachlorometacresol and parachlorometaxylenol are the names of these powerful phenolic anti-microbials used as preservatives. They are synthetic, and they are toxic. See **CHAPTER 14**.

PEACH KERNEL OIL - One of two oils: one obtained by expression called persic oil; one obtained by steam distillation; one aromatic toxic essential oil, very similar to bitter almond oil, obtained by steam distillation. Used as an emollient or aromatic in cosmetics.

PEARL ESSENCE - Also called guanine, this silvery coloring is sometimes obtained from fish scales (such as herring or bleak), or may be a synthetic translucent substance, such as crystallized mercuric chloride. Pearl essence has been used to add luster to face and eye shadow powders.

PECTIN - Natural thickener from vegetables or fruits, consisting of partially methoxylated polygalacturonic acids. Used in cosmetics as an emulsifier and thickener.

PEG COMPOUNDS - These are synthetic plant glycols, polyethylene glycols, polymers of ethylene oxide, and combinations of natural oils (such as castor oil) and these synthetic chemicals. We could go into each compound (and there are 33 pages of them in the CTFA cosmetic dictionary) and explain what they are, or we could save ourselves and you a lot of time and tell you not to use these chemicals because there are natural glycols that

PEG COMPOUNDS Continued
will do the job without polluting or contributing to the chemical manufacturing complex. PEG compounds are used as binders, solvents, emollients, plasticizers, bases, carriers, emulsifiers, and dispersants. They are used very widely in all sorts of cosmetics.

PENTAPOTASSIUM & PENTASODIUM TRI-PHOSPHATE - Inorganic salts used as emulsifiers, sequestrants, and dispersants. They may irritate skin and mucous membranes. They pollute our water and are toxic to marine life, therefore spoil the environment. Not biodegradable.

PERFUME - Fluid preparation for scenting; more concentrated than a cologne, may be natural or synthetic, but probably contains synthetics, unless you know the manufacturer to be dead-set against synthetic chemicals. Even high-priced French colognes and perfumes contain synthetic essential oils and fixatives. Allergic reactions.

PERMANENT WAVES - Cold process permanent waves were introduced in 1941 and have been extremely popular ever since, even though the chemicals used (highly alkaline thioglycolate compounds) are extremely toxic. Cold process permanent waves work by using enough thioglycolates to break the protein bond in the hair without destroying the hair itself, a tricky procedure. The hair's protein bond then reforms while the hair is rolled on curlers, and the permanent wave solution is neutralized. The hair is of course damaged and weakened by permanents and becomes more susceptible to UV and chemical damage. Worse yet, the strong detergents added to permanent wave solutions to degrease the hair and allow penetration of the thioglycolates into the hair shaft also enhance absorption of this corrosive, caustic chemical into the skin. People who get permanent waves should use a natural shampoo and conditioner daily. Hair loss is the eventual outcome. Avoid permanent waves if you want to keep your hair.

PEROXIDE - See **HYDROGEN PEROXIDE.**

PERSIC OIL - See **PEACH KERNEL OIL.**

PETROLEUM JELLY or **PETROLATUM** - Semisolid mixture of hydrocarbons derived from petroleum. Often well-meaning cosmetic consumer books and articles will point out the similarity among mass-merchandised cosmetics and state baldly, "since most moisturizing products are extremely similar, save yourself some money and buy plain old petroleum jelly." These writers are half right: yes, most moisturizers, lotions, hand creams, etc., are practically interchangeable, and most do consist of mineral oil, but petroleum derivatives are not good for your skin. They are allergenic; they smother your skin and cause skin irritation and acne; they do not absorb well into the skin, so any potentially beneficial ingredient that may be contained in the product also cannot be absorbed. These writers are also right in that petroleum jelly is cheap and readily obtainable, as are

most petrochemicals, but you'll be doing your skin (your largest organ) a big favor by avoiding petroleum jelly and all the other members of the petroleum chemical clan. All petrochemicals pollute our water and destroy marine life. Avoiding petrochemicals is essential for humans, animals, fish, water, land, and air. Don't use them.

pH BALANCED - See **CHAPTER 4.**

PHENACETIN - Also known as acetophenetidin, which is a white crystalline solid used as a analgesic and anti-pyretic; in cosmetics as an antiseptic. It can cause severe skin rashes and may be toxic if taken orally in amounts as small as one-quarter teaspoon.

PHENETHYL ALCOHOL - Fragrant liquid alcohol found in essential oils of rose and neroli, but usually synthesized; used in perfumes and as a preservative . Toxic.

PHENOL & PHENOLIC COMPOUNDS - Carbolic acid and related compounds, which are often used as preservatives in cosmetics. Toxic. See **CHAPTER 14** on **PRESERVATIVES.**

p-PHENYLENEDIAMINE - Solid crystalline substance used as an intermediate in aniline, coal tar hair dyes. Highly allergenic, a potential carcinogen. Used especially in dyes for dark shades and for some blond shades. Avoid this toxic chemical.

PHENYL MERCURIC ACETATE - See **CHAPTER 14** on **PRESERVATIVES.**

PHLOROGLUCINOL - Synthetic color which can be a severe skin irritant.

PHOSOPHOLIPIDS - Any of a class of fat-soluble organic chemicals present in the fat deposits of all living cells, e.g., lecithin.

PHOSPHORIC ACID - Clear, viscous liquid used as an antioxidant, sesquestrant, and acidifier in cosmetics. Corrosive to the skin and mucous membranes when used in a concentrated form.

PHYTOCOSMETIC - A cosmetic made exclusively of vegetal substances.

PHYTOTHERAPY - Using plants and herbs either internally or externally for therapeutic purposes.

PHYTODERMATOLOGY - Using herbal or plant substances for the treatment of the skin or manufacturing products with plant substances for skin care.

PICRAMIC ACID - Phenolic compound used as a manufacturing agent. It is a skin irritant that can be absorbed through the skin and cause death. Very toxic.

PINEAPPLE JUICE - See **BROMELEIN.**

PIPERONAL - Also called heliotropin and used extensively as a fragrance and flavoring material; may be obtained from safrole (the primary chemical in sassafras essential oil), but is usually produced synthetically. Piperonal may cause allergic reactions.

PITUITARY GLAND - Endocrine gland (meaning an organ that produces secretions distributed through the bloodstream rather than by way of ducts) in the brain that controls other endocrine

PUTUITARY GLAND Continued
glands, secretes substances that regulate growth
and development, the contraction of smooth muscle, renal function, reproduction, and affecting,
either directly or indirectly, most body functions.

PLACENTA - Organ in mammals (except mar-
supials and monotremes [echidnas and platy-
puses]) that unites the fetus to the mother and
which is expelled at birth. Bovine placenta liquid
(obtained from the mother cow between the third
and fourth month without chemical or thermal intervention) contains 56 bioactive substances yet
is free from estrogen. This is the kind of placenta
you want to look for in cosmetics (usually moisturizers or cell rejuvenation creams) that contain this
ingredient. Some placental creams may contain human placenta, or they may contain placental "af-
terbirth" substances, and this is not as desirable
as live, pre-birth placenta liquid. Like all natural
substances, however, placenta liquid works best
in a completely natural base; synthetic chemicals
(especially methyl and propyl paraben) inhibit the
effectiveness of these natural substances on the
skin.

PLASTER OF PARIS - See **CALCIUM
SULFATE**.

POLOXAMER COMPOUNDS - Polyoxethylene,
polyoxypropylene block polymers: synthetic
chemicals used as surfactants. Allergens and
pollutants. Avoid them.

POLYHYDRIC ALCOHOL ESTER - Fatty
alcohol esters that can be natural or synthetic;
they are used in cosmetics as emollients, humectant, emulsifiers, and moisturizers. Natural polyhydric alcohol esters include glycerin, sorbitol, and
mannitol. Synthetic ones include mono and di-fatty acid esters of ethylene glycols, diethylene glycol, polyethylene glycol (PEG), propylene glycol,
polyoxyethylene sorbitol and sorbitan (tweens).
There are usually no allergic reactions to the
natural polyhydric alcohol esters, but synthetic
glycols do cause allergic reactions.

POLYMERS - In botany the word polymerous
means that a flower will have many members; in
zoology, polymer means "composed of many
parts." A monomer is, of course, one, and when
several monomers or comonomers are combined
there is a polymerization. In chemistry a polymeric
compound is one that has the same elements combined in the same proportions by weight, but they
will differ in molecular weight. One is, in effect,
combining two or more molecules of one compound
to form a more complex compound with a higher
molecular weight. In the care of the skin,
polymerization has brought about important care
to seriously burned patients. Dr. I. V. Yannas of
MIT and Dr. J. F. Burke of Massachusetts
General Hospital in Boston created two different

forms of polymeric synthetic skin by using natural
substances. Collagen fibers were obtained from
cowhides and chemically bonded to
chondroitin-6-sulfate (a polysaccharide found in
cartilage and obtained from sharks). This polymer
was covered with a sheet of silicon rubber and applied to seriously burned areas of skin. This synthetic skin polymer gives a protective barrier to
the burned area and prevents infection and fluid
loss as well as providing mechanical strength.
Mesodermal cells from the body migrate into the
polymer creating more collagen and synthesizing
a new dermal layer (neodermis). Epidermal cells
also grow inward from the edge of the graft.
    There are several uses of polymers in cosmetics
as "wash-off" protection in sunscreens, as "binders" in skin creams, and in hair setting products.
Plastic fingernails are produced by polymerization
or copolymerization of monomers in the presence
of a polymer, a catalyst, and a polymerization
promoter.
    Some of the better known polymers are cellulose,
acetate, polystyrene, polyisobutylene, polyvinyl
acetone, and polyvinylpyrrolidone (PVP). Most of
the chemical polymers can be allergens to skin and
hair. PVP, for example, has been used in hair
sprays and wavesets and causes dry hair and scalp
which results in a "flaking" similar to dandruff.

POLYPEPTIDES - These are amino acid residues
or small proteins (like hormones or chemical mes-
sengers) that create a bond between adjacent amino acids. These bonds are called peptide bonds and
when this bond is broken, damaged hair is the result. One of the main bonds in hair is an amino acid
called cysteine. When hair is permed, colored,
straightened, braided, or chemicalized, the vital
cysteine bond is broken, thereby causing hair damage or loss. Some products (shampoos) and conditioners contain amino acids high in cysteine which
can help to repair this damage. The amino acids
(amine type substances) are connected in specific
ways to form polypeptides and proteins (see **AMI-
NO ACIDS**).

POLYSORBATES - These are fatty acid esters
which have been assigned various numerical values. They are used in many cosmetics to help dissolve oils in water; i.e., they act as emulsifiers.
Some authors have praised these substances for
their ability to grow hair and cure dandruff, but
they can be extremely drying to the scalp. Polysorbate 20 is also used as an anti-irritant in anti-sting
shampoos. If used in hair care cosmetics, the
polysorbates should be combined with essential
fatty acids, aloe vera, and other herbs to offset this
tendency.

POLYSTYRENE - Polymer of styrene, which may
be a liquid balsamic oil from the bark of the Asian
tree (genus *Styrax*) or synthesized. Used as a protective plastic film in cosmetics.

POLYVINYLPYRROLIDONE (PVP) - Petroleum-derived chemical used in hairsprays, wavesets, and in other cosmetics. It can be considered toxic since inhaled particles may cause problems in the lungs of sensitive people.

POTASSIUM - A chemical element, K, atomic number 19, atomic weight 39.102. It stands in the middle of the alkali metal family, below sodium (Na) and above rubidium (Rb) on the table of elements. (By the way, if you want to learn your entire table of elements you can get a record by Tom Lerher in which he sings the entire periodic table of the elements to a Gilbert and Sullivan tune: "I Am The Very Model of A Modern Major General." As a Harvard professor he knows the importance of cramming.) Potassium is similar to sodium in its metallic form. Potassium is an abundant element in the earth's crust accounting for 2.59% in combined forms of potassium. (Only oxygen, silicon, aluminum, iron, calcium, and sodium are more abundant.) Sea water contains 380 parts per million of potassium which makes it also the sixth most plentiful element in solution (exceeded by chlorine, sodium, magnesium, sulfur, and calcium). Potassium is a strong element that is even more reactive than sodium; the reaction to liquid acids is violent and verges on being explosive. Some potassium chemicals are used in cosmetics, but are not a desirable chemical to go in the hair and on the skin. Potassium hydroxide (also known as lye) is used in liquid soaps and potassium carbonate is used in making soft soaps (the saponification process used for many synthetic detergents). Potassium hydroxide is also known as caustic potash. In ancient times the saponification process for making soap was arrived at by burning sea weed and using the ash (or other herbs). Later table salt was used. Potassium lauryl sulfate is a synthetic detergent to avoid in shampoos, soaps, etc. Potassium alginate, potassium alum, potassium biphtalate, potassium borate, potassium bromate, potassium carbonate, potassium caseinate, potassium chlorate, potassium glycol sulfate, potassium iodide, potassium nitrate, potassium oleate, potassium persulfate, potassium phosphate, potassium silicate, potassium sorbate, potassium stearate, potassium sulfite, potassium thioglycolate, and potassium tripoly-phosphate are ingredients to avoid in cosmetics. Though the amount used in soap may not be toxic, the use of these chemicals and the allergic reactions are good reasons to avoid them when you see them on a cosmetic label. Remember that potassium is a reactive metal. WE are already aware of the chemical damage to our environment brought on by fertilizer mixes containing potassium chloride. Avoid all the potassium chemicals.

POTATO STARCH - Derived from potatoes and consisting of amylose and amylopectin. Used in cosmetics as a demulcent and emollient.

POWDERS, FACE - The safest form of make-up for the skin. It is a simpler kind of make-up, therefore is easier to make naturally, which means that fewer allergic reactions can be expected. It is less pore-clogging than oily liquid foundation make-ups and doesn't become as easily contaminated with bacteria (and needs fewer preservatives) than liquid make-ups made with oil or water. Look for a talc-free face powder, as prolonged inhalation of talc (even if not contaminated with asbestos) can lead to lung problems. Also, look for face powders with natural colors, not synthetic ones.

POWDERED EXTRACTS - Prepared from a native extract by dilution to a specified strength, followed by drying, usually under vacuum, to yield dry solids. These are then ground into fine powders or into coarse granules.

PREEN OIL - Comes from ducks' quills and has some moisturizing ability on the skin due to ducks' ability to repel water; preen oil is very similar to the skin's sebum. Now it can be manufactured by combining the same fatty acids contained in preen oil; this process can use natural or synthetic fatty acids, and a product can contain natural or synthetic preen oil.

PRESERVATIVES IN COSMETICS - See **CHAPTER 14.**

PREMENSTRUAL SYNDROME - Premenstrual syndrome (PMS) is a common condition that may affect a woman at any time from the onset of menstruation. As the prefix implies, PMS occurs before the period begins and should not be confused with menstrual discomforts. PMS begins any time from three to fourteen days before the period and then diminishes as the period begins. PMS also seems to recur at the exact time in the next menstrual cycle. Approximately 40% of menstruating women will have PMS and 10% will have a severe form of the condition.

Katharine Dalton, a British physician, introduced the term PMS in the 1950's and pointed out that about 150 different emotional and physical symptoms are associated with this condition. Hostility, depression, fatigue, aggression, diminished concentration, crying spells and changes in sexual drives are examples of the emotional symptoms. Migraine headaches, dizziness, blurred vision, acne, herpes lesions, hair loss, dark circles under the eyes, irregular heartbeat, asthma attacks, shortness of breath, diarrhea, constipation, bloating, cramps, rectal pressure, and water retention (swelling of hands, legs, breasts) are some of the physical symptoms associated with PMS.

Not all women will suffer from all these symptoms, though there can be a clustering of symptoms. One type of PMS, for example, may exhibit

PREMENSTRUAL Continued
mood changes, including varying degrees of anxiety, irritability, and depression. Perhaps there will be a craving for sweets, even in those who don't usually desire sweets. Very common PMS symptoms include aches and pains combined with irritability.

Due to the repetitive pattern of the symptoms, rather than the symptoms themselves, the condition is fairly easy to diagnose. There are no lab tests or hormonal evaluations to detect PMS; a chart of of the menstrual calendar is made, recording the PMS symptoms. The chart will clearly show the same occurrence, the same duration, and the same cessation. The drugs often used to treat PMS are natural progesterone tablets or suppositories, 200 mg. per day with a maximum dosage of 1,200 mg. per day. Dr. Dalton first treated the condition with natural progesterone. Because skin rashes and a delay of the menstrual period are side effects of natural progesterone, its safety has been questioned. In fact, some authorities maintain progesterone is an inactive substance and effects the alleviation of symptoms in women suffering from PMS only because of its psychological "placebo" effect. Synthetic progesterone (progestin) does not work at all, however, and may make the PMS worse.

Other drugs used to treat PMS are Bromocriptive which seems to reduce swelling and tenderness of the breasts by suppressing the hormone prolactin (from the pituitary gland). Antiprostaglandins (Motrin, Maprosyn, Anaprox) are often used. These chemicals inhibit prostaglandins within the body. The production of prostaglandins seems to be accelerated in those suffering from PMS. It is believed that the most natural and safest treatment is a combination of diet, food supplements, exercise, and evening primrose oil. This can be taken in the form of capsules (500 mg. per capsule) or by putting drops of the oil in grapefruit juice. Because evening primrose oil is quite acidic, it is not suggested that you put it directly into the mouth. The taste is NOT pleasant, and there may be a burning sensation. Fifteen drops of evening primrose oil equals about 500 mg (See also **EVENING PRIMROSE OIL**).

Nutritional treatment for PMS includes a high protein diet, very low in refined carbohydrates, low salt, low sugar, and NO coffee (except decaffeinated), tea, cola drinks, or chocolate. Coffee, team cola, and chocolate all contain chemicals called xanthines which stimulate the central nervous system; these substances can increase the severity of PMS symptoms. In addition, avoiding foods containing xanthines has been shown to alleviate or greatly lessen fibrocystic breast disease. Because a deficiency of B_6 (pyridoxine) or magnesium is another possible cause of PMS, supplementation of these substances is often suggested: 200-500 mg. pyridoxine daily may prove helpful, but too much (over 1,000 mg.) can be hazardous and lead to temporary symptoms of neurological disease such as unsteady gait, poor coordination, and numbness of the fingers and toes. The best

nutritional supplement possible is a chewable one that combines pyridoxine with other vitamins and minerals.

Stress may also play a role in causing PMS. Women in stressful jobs found that while on vacation, PMS symptoms disappeared. Biofeedback and a regular exercise program may be helpful in alleviating stress-related PMS symptoms.

PROPANE - A flammable gaseous paraffin hydrocarbon that occurs naturally in crude petroleum; used chiefly as a fuel but also as a propellant in aerosol sprays. Do not use an aerosol containing propane near an open flame. In fact, why use aerosols at all?

1,2-PROPANEDIOL - See **PROPYLENE GLYCOL**.

PROPYL ALCOHOL - Alcohol derived from petroleum.

PROPYL GALLATE - Antioxidant that has caused allergic reactions and skin irritations.

PROPYL PARABEN - See **PARABENS**.

PROPYLENE GLYCOL - Petroleum derivative; a sweet viscous liquid that attracts water. In cosmetics propylene glycol is widely used as an humectant, surfactant, and solvent. In industry, propylene glycol is used in antifreeze and hydraulic brake fluid. Because propylene glycol is a petroleum product, it causes allergic and toxic reactions. Although it is a synthetic chemical, it is used in many so-called natural cosmetics. Any product that uses propylene glycol, or one of its compounds, cannot be called natural.

PROLINE - Amino acid found in many proteins that form the body, including the skin.

PROTEIN - Any of a very large class of complex combinations of amino acids; the building blocks of living creatures, both animal and vegetable. Protein is an vital part of the diet. As Adelle Davis once said, "Since your body structure is largely protein, an undersupply can bring about age with depressing speed: muscles lose tone, wrinkles appear, age creeps in; and you, my dear, are going to pot." Every cell in your body is dependent on protein, and there are proteins in hormones, blood cells, the brain, enzymes, antibodies (our protection factor), and in every cell and organ of the body. Protein contains important substances called amino acids, and through the study of the effects amino acids have on the body we are able to look at the relationship of the timing of meals, sleep, and metabolism. We can also see the effect of protein on our hair and skin whether taken internally or applied externally. Though amino acids may not tell us about carbohydrate metabolism, they are like a sign post as far as how the body is working. A heavy protein meal eaten at 8:00 a.m. may lead to a very swift rise in amino acid levels, yet the same protein meal eaten at 8:00 p.m. may not raise amino acid levels in the blood and

PROTEIN Continued

there may be, in fact, a decrease in amino acid levels. Protein is also not utilized evenly around the clock which tells us how risky it is to advise people to take a protein supplement without knowledge of their lifestyles and diet, etc. People who work on rotating shifts may require more protein than those who have daytime hours. Protein foods are also important sources of vitamin A, thiamine (B_1), riboflavin (B_2), niacin, B_6, B_{12}, folic acid, pantothenic acid, and biotin. Protein as a food source is found mostly in meat, fish, eggs, and dairy products; however, vegetarians can get protein from plant sources. One ounce of meat, fish, or poultry is equal in protein to ½ cup of cooked beans, 2 tablespoons of peanut butter, 3 ounces of tofu (soybean curd), and 1½ ounces (3 tablespoons) of nuts or seeds. One ounce of meat is also equal to 1 egg, an ounce of cheese, and ¼ cup cottage cheese.

Cosmetic Use - Protein can be used with great success on the skin and hair. In 1937 the Stepan Company began combining proteins with higher saturated fatty acids, polypeptides, and amino acid complex for use in shampoos and conditioners for the hair. These proteins and protein derivatives had hydrophilic properties and when used in shampoos and conditioners left the hair clean and soft. They could, in fact, in the proper formulas, correct damaged hair. Protein combined with the amino acid cystine will correct damaged hair. One particular milk protein called lactalbumin has been quite successful in repairing damaged hair when used in a natural hair conditioner. Protein hydrolysates have low molecular weight polypeptide fractions and, when used in shampoos, are substantive to damaged or porous hair and can actually support claims of repairing the "split ends" of hair. This has been identified as a significant problem for women with long hair, women with perms, or who color or bleach their hair. The protein used in these cosmetics doesn't have to be hydrolyzed animal protein because, as we've reported, milk protein works as does soya protein. The role of proteins in the biosynthesis of collagen is well-known today, and the deficiency of proline (utilized in the production of collagen) can be detected as dry skin, wrinkled skin, and sclerosis. Topical application of protein combined with the cutaneous role of fatty acids such as linoleic, linolenic, and arachidonic acid can't be underestimated in the prevention of skin disease as well as the beauty and health of the skin (as well as the aging of skin). Just as a diet deficient in protein and fatty acids causes skin disturbances and a depletion of fats in tissues, there are positive results obtained through skin absorption of protein and fatty acid substances in cosmetics. As far as topical use of protein the skin can benefit with improved smoothness, softness, and resiliency.

PROTEASES - A class of enzyme that can break down protein, e.g., papain (from papaya) and bromelain (from pineapple). Used in cosmetics to soften skin and clear skin surface of cellular debris.

PSORIASIS - A disease of the skin marked by large or small crusty patches or lesions that can be on opposite elbows, knees, or ankles. It can cover the entire body and also appear on the scalp. It is believed to be an hereditary disease and is not curable. It is the result of a rapid and abnormal growth of skin tissue. It can be controlled by the use of UV light which slows down the proliferation of skin cells.

PSEUDOMONAS - Extremely virulent family of bacteria that can contaminate cosmetic products. Care must be taken in the production of cosmetics so that raw materials and finished products are not contaminated. Preservatives are inadequate to control this problem. Preservatives provide a false sense of security against bacterial contamination in consumers and manufacturers alike; there is no substitute for regular testing of finished products.

PUMICE - Volcanic rock that is extremely light because it is full of holes; hardened stone foam that is used whole to smooth calluses, or in powdered form as an abrasive in cleansers. Pumice can scratch the skin in this latter use; vegetable meals are more appropriate for this use.

PURCELLIN OIL - Trade names for synthetic preen oil (See **PREEN OIL** above). This is a combination of long-chain fatty acids esters which are similar to human sebum and lanolin; these fatty acid esters may be naturally derived or synthetically produced. Naturally-derived purcellin oil is a more humane product than preen oil which is taken from duck feathers.

PVP - See **POLYVINYLPYRROLIDONE**.

PYRETHRUM FLOWERS - Powdered extract from either *Chrysanthemum cinerariaefolium*, *C. coccineum* and *C. marshalli* (all of which belong to the genus *Chrysanthumum*). These extracts are potent natural insecticides.

PYRIDINE - Petrochemical that is both toxic and flammable. Used in cosmetics as a solvent, but is irritating to the skin and may be absorbed through the skin.

PYRIDOXINE - Vitamin B_6.

PYROCATECHOL - One of the constituents of black and pale catechu (*Acacia catechu* and *Uncaria gambir*); but is usually produced synthetically and used in cosmetics as an antiseptic and an antioxidant. In industry it is used as a photographic developer, as a developer in fur dyeing, and as an analytical reagent.

PYROGALLIC ACID - Synthetic chemical used in cosmetics in artificial dyes; also in photographic developing chemicals and in medicine to treat skin diseases.

Q

QUASSIN - Bitter crystalline principle of Jamaican quassia; used in cosmetics as a denaturant. Quassin is also an insecticide.

QUATERNARY AMMONIUM SALTS - These have been used as water repellants, fungicides, emulsifiers, paper and fabric softeners, antistatic agents, and corrusion inhibitors. There are a wide variety of these ammonium compounds. Their use in cosmetics, especially in hair conditioners and creme rinses, came from the paper and fabric industries as softeners and antistatic agents. They may give a soft feel to the hair and stabilize the hair rinse or conditioner's emulsion, but they damage the hair in the long run. The hair becomes dry and brittle. They are also allergenic. A mixture of complex lipids such as lecithin and acetylcholine can be accepted as a natural quaternary. Lecithin is a good replacement in hair rinses and conditioners for the caustic ammonium salts.

QUERCETIN - Flavonoid present in asparagus, catechu, dill, elder flowers, tarragon, eucalyptus, etc. The active principle of rutin (synonym quercetin-3-rutinoside).

QUERCITRIN - Flavonoid present in Roman camomile, eucalyptus, euphorbia, hops, immortelle, tea, and witch hazel. This flavonoid has reportedly cured influenza (Type A infections *in vitro* studies), increased the detoxifying activities of the liver, and shown antiinflammatory activity. It may be used in cosmetics as a natural color.

QUILLAIA - A large evergreen tree with shiny leathery leaves and thick bark. The powdered bark is a saponin concentrate also known as soap tree bark. The tree is known as *quillaja* (ki-li-ya) to the Indians of Peru and has long been used as a natural detergent. If inhaled the powdered bark can cause sneezing and chest congestion, but in folk medicine, the bark has been used for coughs and asthmatic conditions. Saponins have widely different pharmacological and biological activities: antiinflammatory, antimicrobial, antihypercholesterolemic, and cytoxic. Quillaia saponins are believed to be nontoxic and have been used in foods as a foaming agent in root beer and cocktail mixes (yucca saponins are also used for this purpose). Cosmetically, quillaia saponins have been used in some dermatological creams and in hair tonics and shampoos for treating dandruff, oily scalp, itchy scalp, and various scalp problems (See **HERB CHART**). In folk medicine quillaia has been used as a component in herbal douches and for athlete's foot.

QUINCE SEED - *Cydonia oblonga*; the dried seeds of which are used to thicken and emulsify cosmetics.

QUINOLINE COLORS - One of the class of coal tar colors.

R

RANCIDITY - Chemical decomposition of a substance, usually fatty, that causes it to smell "off" or rotten. It is better that a cosmetic smell rancid and be without synthetic preservatives and perfumes because then you'll know to throw it away. A synthetically preserved product can also become rancid, but because it is strongly perfumed and emulsified, its appearance may be deceptively unchanged. Rancidity is the result of oxidation, but natural antioxidants such as vitamins A, C, and E can safely slow this process.

RAYON - Produced from cellulose fibers, rayon is sometimes used in cosmetics to add fiber strength and shine.

RESINS - Natural products occurring either as plant exudates or preparations by alcohol extraction of botanicals containing resinous principles. They rarely occur in nature without being mixed with gums and/or oleoresins, and oleogum resins.

RESORCINOL - Aromatic phenol used as an antiseptic, preservative, and astringent; may be derived from resins such as galbanum or asafetida, but is usually produced synthetically. Exposure to resorcinol can cause methemoglobinemia (a blood disorder), convulsions, and death.

RETICULIN - Dermal protein sometimes used in "cellular" rejuvenation cosmetics. See **CELLULAR EXTRACTS** and **COLLAGEN**.

RIBOFLAVIN - Vitamin B_2, part of the vitamin B complex. See **DIET IN COSMETICS**.

RICE POWDER (STARCH)- Nontoxic powder used in face powders. See **POWDERS, FACE**.

RICINOLEIC ACID - Fatty acid found in castor oil. See **CASTOR OIL** in the herb chart.

ROSE *(Rosaceae)* - The rose was probably cultivated in Persia and brought to Mesopotamia, to Palestine and across Asia Minor to Greece who brought it to Italy. Horace writes about growing roses in beds and Pliny advises the deep digging of the soil for a better cultivated rose. Roses were cultivated in ancient Rome and the red rose of Provence *(Rosa gallica)* was of Roman origin. *Rosa,*

ROSE Continued

which means "red" in Greek (from the word *rodon*) suggests the Greek myth that the crimson-colored rose sprang from the blood of Adonis. The rose as a symbol can be found in many coats-of-arms, and the United States government chose the rose as the national flower in 1986.

Cosmetic Use - The first preparation of rosewater (by Avicenna) was in the tenth century, and between 1582 and 1612, the oil known as otto of roses was discovered. The ancient oil, *oleum rosarum,* was actually not a volatile oil, but a fatty oil perfumed with rose petals. A small amount of otto of roses has been produced in the south of France for the last 150 years and was an established industry before the French Revolution. French rosewater is superior to any developed elsewhere. The scientific study of the rose has been chiefly to improve the odor rather than the appearance of the flower or the medical or cosmetic uses of the oil. Oil of rose is a light yellow in color and has a strong odor of fresh roses. Otto of rose and rose oils in general can't be synthetically produced and even a supposedly artificial rose oil must contain some amount of natural rose oil. Synthetic rose oil is almost entirely deodorized by iodine, but natural rose oil holds its odor even in the presence of iodine. In Oxfordshire and Derbyshire, roses are grown for medical and cosmetic uses rather than for use in perfumes. Rose oil is non-irritating and non-phototoxic. Bulgarian rose oil has been reported to decrease urinary corticosteroids and serum ceruloplasmin (A. Maleev et al., *Eksp, Med. Morfol.,* 10, 149, 1971). Also see **HERB CHART.**

ROSE HIP

ROSE HIP - The prickly bushes or shrubs native to Europe, Asia, and South America have a ripe fruit called hipberries or rose hips. Rose hips contain high concentrations of vitamin C (ascorbic acid) ranging from 0.24 to 1.25%, which varies according to degrees of ripeness, climate, and other factors. Rose hips also contain carotenoids (0.01 to 0.05%), flavonoids (0.01 to 0.35%), pectic substances (3.4 to 4.6%), polyphenols (2.02 to 2.64%), as well as riboflavin, sugars, and plant acids. Various species of rose hips contain other compounds and demonstrate a wide variety of pharmacological activity.

The oil from the rose hips of one species, *Rosa aff. Rubiginosa* (popularly known as *Rosa Mosqueta*) has been analyzed extensively by South American researchers. This rose hip seed oil is extremely high in essential fatty acids: oleic 16%, linoleic 41%, linolenic 39% (unsaturated), palmitic 3%, and stearic 0.8% (saturated). Other fatty acids which have been identified are lauric, myristic, and palmitoleic. The high content of essential fatty acids in *Rosa Mosqueta* rose hip seed oil make it valuable in the synthesis of prostaglandins, the immune system, cell membrane improvement, and the growth of tissue. With its high amount of essential fatty acids, *Rosa Mosqueta* rose hip seed oil can be compared to evening primrose oil.

Cosmetic Discussion - *Rosa Mosqueta* Rose hip seed oil *(Rosa aff. Rubiginosa L.)* has a transparent red color and is classed as a drying oil. It differs from other herbal oils with a mild pH of around 5.1 and a rather low saponification number. *Rosa Mosqueta* rose hip seed oil has been used in dermatology treatments for skin burns, hypertrophic scars, hyperchromic scars, refractile scars, and cheloids. As a cosmetic, it has the positive effects of smoothing facial lines, wrinkles, hydrating, and slowing down new signs of aging. *Rosa Mosqueta* oil is contraindicated for oily skin and acne and should not be used on oily areas of the skin or on acne. An excellent night treatment that uses *Rosa Mosqueta* oil and cream for aging skin is as follows: clean skin; apply *Rosa Mosqueta* oil and massage in well; 3. apply *Rosa Mosqueta* seed cream over this. During the day use *Rosa Mosqueta* cream under make-up or as a skin smoother.

Discussion - The use of *Rosa Mosqueta* rose hip seed oil first came to my attention in the summer of 1986 when samples and technical information were sent to me from the University of Concepcion School of Dermatology in Chile. Dr. Fabiola Carvajal Montiel presented dramatic improvement of patients. One patient after three months of daily application of *Rosa Mosqueta* rose hip seed oil had fewer wrinkles and a smoother complexion. Wrinkles around the mouth and eyes were far less noticable and some seemed gone entirely. Another female patient with hypertrophic scars around the mouth, eyes, and on the forehead showed dramatic improvement after six months of *Rosa Mosqueta* oil treatment. A male patient of twenty-six years had extensive traumatic scars after an operation on the face. After four months the scars were almost non-existent. Whether or not the *Rosa Mosqueta* oil will work for everybody is not known, but it is an excellent skin care - and hair care - treatment, probably due to the fatty acids and the carotenoids. Whether or not every type of rose hip seed oil works the same is not known. The type used by Dr. Montiel was from the *Rosa Mosqueta (Rosa aff. Rubiginosa).* Dr. Montiel said that the oil helped patients with premature wrinkling and scars and increased moisturization. She recommended a two or three minute massage (to obtain good penetration). I have found that applying the oil and then the cream over it gives even better absorption; however, the cream should be made with a fatty acid base of a superior quality. No petrochemicals, mineral oil, etc., should be combined with the oil or cream as this would reduce absorption and affect the skin adversely.

Toxicity - *Rosa Mosqueta* rose hip seed oil has no known toxicity. It is not suitable for acne or for use on oily skin. The FDA considers rose hips as GRAS (Generally Regarded as Safe) for use as a nutritional or food supplement with *Rosa alba L., R. damascena Mill, gallica L.,* and their varieties. To date rose hip seed oil has not been animal tested, though it has been used on humans for skin treatments as outlined above and as a source for vitamin C. For more information about *Rosa Mosqueta,* see related chapter.

ROSEMARY *(Rosmarinus officinalis)* - Like lavender, rosemary is one of the plants that grows better in England than anywhere else. However, most of the rosemary oil used in commerce today comes from France, Spain, and Japan.

Queen Elizabeth of Hungary used rosemary oil in her now famous "Hungary water" which dates back to 1235. Hungary water was made by putting 1½ pounds of fresh rosemary tops into a gallon of white wine. This was allowed to stand for four days. The Queen of Hungary was partially paralyzed at one time, and she is said to have been completely cured by rubbing this water on her arms, legs, and feet. Rosemary and coltsfoot leaves are also said to be good when smoked for asthma and other problems of the throat and lungs.

Rosemary is used in hair tonics for its odour and to stimulate the hair-bulbs to renewed activity. Rosemary supposedly prevents premature baldness. Combining rosemary and sage makes an excellent hair rinse and wash.

The famous quote from Shakespeare's *Hamlet*, "There's rosemary, that's for remembrance" is based on the idea that rosemary is good for the brain and the memory. "As for rosemary," Sir Thomas More wrote, "I let it run all over my garden walls, not only because the bees love it, but because it is the herb sacred to remembrance, and therefore friendship."

According to *The Treasury of Botany*, rosemary could well be the symbol of women's rights: "There is a vulgar belief in Gloucestershire and other countries that rosemary will not grow well unless the mistress is 'master,' and so touchy are some of the lords of creation upon this point, that we have more than once had reason to suspect them of privately injuring a growing Rosemary in order to destroy this evidence for want of authority."

Rosemary also has a religious history. It was used in the wreath worn by a bride as a symbol of love and loyalty and as a New Year's gift (this allusion from Ben Jonson's plays). Rosemary was used by the ancients in place of more costly incense in their religious ceremonies. In Spain and Italy it has been considered a safeguard against witches and evil. The Spanish, who call it "Romero" or "The Pilgrim's Flower," revere Rosemary because it is one of the bushes that gave shelter to the Virgin Mary.

Rosemary oil is excellent for the skin and hair.

ROSEWATER - Aqueous dilution of the essence of roses first prepared by Avicenna in the tenth century.

ROYAL JELLY - Extremely nutritious substance secreted in the digestive tube of the worker bees and eaten by the male and worker bees for a few days and the queen bee her entire life. It has been pointed out that the queen bee, who eats only royal jelly, outlives all other bees. Health food stores like to point this out when they want to sell you some royal jelly, but it is as doubtful a premise as the one held by vivisectors that animal tests will protect consumers from chemicals. Royal jelly, in other words, is a hot commodity if you happen to be a bee. Also, don't forget that the queen stays on her throne making babies and being fed royal jelly by her workers until she grows even too big to get out of the throne room. She's a dictator but also a prisoner.

Health food hypers state that royal jelly is a great nutritional product because it contains a full range of amino acids, minerals, and enzymes. Royal jelly also contains Vitamins A, B_{12}, E, C, and pantothenic acid, but if you compare the cost with the amount of jelly necessary to get adequate amounts of these nutrients, you will find royal jelly is an expensive way to get your nutritional support. Another claim is that the female hormones contained in royal jelly are believed to stimulate the queen's fertility. Royal jelly has therefore been postulated as an excellent nutrient for women, and some women have claimed that royal jelly was an aid to helping them become pregnant after many years of being unable to do so, but this evidence is anecdotal at best. Another claim is that after an intake of royal jelly, the hair grows longer (about an inch a month) though the hair had stopped growing many years before: yet another hair growing substance! Some cosmetic manufacturers put royal jelly into face creams with the claim that the longevity of the queen bee can be transferred to your face. The few of these I've looked at contain the usual chemicals used in cosmetics and a microscopic amount of royal jelly. My feeling is that royal jelly moisturizer is, like all the other claims listed above, hype.

However, royal jelly has long been a part of Chinese medicine, usually mixed with tonic herbs such as *Astragalus, Codonopsitis*, and *Tang Kuei*, and this herbal tradition definitely has time on its side. One of the most popular liquid Chinese medicines is *Renshenfengwangjiang* which consists of royal jelly and ginseng. This is both a man's health and woman's health product, since the ginseng is yang and the royal jelly yin. Another Chinese medicine is called Ginseng-Bee Secretion (which is sold in Chinese herb shops and some health food stores), but it contains more than ginseng and royal jelly: ginseng 12%, royal jelly 2%, deer antler 5%, *Tang Kuei* 3%, *Astragalus* 7%, *Cordyceps* 4%, Licorice Root 5%, and *Polygonum Multiflorum* 2%. In considering the longevity and fertility claims for royal jelly, nevertheless, we must also consider that the Chinese claim aphrodisiac powers for deer antlers from young deer because of the role the antlers play in the deer's mating ritual, which has more to do with phallic symbolism than with human sexual reproduction. They fail to add, however, that the horns fall off, and the queen bee spends her relatively long life in a tiny space making babies. However, royal jelly will probably always be used in nutritional products and cosmetics, both here and in the Orient.

S

SACCHARATED LIME - Reaction product from the oxidation of glyconic acid followed by neutralization with lime; used in cosmetics as preservative and buffer.

SAFFRON - Crocus *(Crocus sativus)*, the dried stigmas of which are used as a deep orange-yellow dye and as an herbal medicine with stimulant, antispasmodic, and emmenagogue properties.

SALICYCLIC ACID - Also known as ortho-hydroxybenzoic acid, salicyclic acid is a crystalline phenolic acid found in nature (e. g., wintergreen oil, which consists of 98% salicyclic acid) but usually synthesized from phenol, sodium hydroxide, and carbon dioxide. Salicyclic acid is contained in aspirin (chemical name: acetylsalicyclic acid) which works as an antipyretic and analgesic by inhibiting prostaglandin production. In topical preparations, salicyclic acid is used as an antiseptic and preservative; also for its analgesic and antipyretic properties. Natural wintergreen oil is less likely to burn the skin than salicyclic acid.

SALT - Vital compound made of sodium and chloride (NaCl). Salts (either sodium or potassium) react with oils to form soaps.

SAMBUCUS - Species of plant native to temperate climates used in cosmetics; synonym elder. See **HERB CHART.**

SANDALWOOD - Small evergreen tree (genus *Santalum*) native to and cultivated in tropical Asia, processed by coarsely powdering and steam- or water-distilling the heartwood, yielding 3 to 5% sandalwood oil. Oil contains 90% or more of alpha- and beta-santalols, which accounts for its odor. This extremely expensive oil lends its distinctive fragrance to all kinds of cosmetics; it is used in Chinese herbal medicine to treat stomach ache, vomiting and gonorrhea.

SAPONINS - Glycosides occurring in nature (such as soap bark, soapwort, and sarsaparilla) characterized by foaming in water. They are used as foaming, emulsifying, and detergent agents in cosmetics.

SARSPARILLA - Saponin from one of the *Smilax* family; may come from Mexico, Central America, or South America. Formerly used to make sweetened carbonated beverage.

SASSAFRAS - American tree *(S. Albidum)*, the dried bark of which is used to make aromatic tea with diaphoretic and stimulating properties. Safrole, the major flavoring ingredient in sassafras, was found to cause cancer in animal tests (though lab animals probably don't drink sassafras tea).

SOAPWORT - European perennial herb *(Saponaria officinalis)* with coarse pink or white flowers and leaves that become soapy when bruised.

SODIUM - A chemical element, symbol Na, atomic number 11, and atomic weight of 22.9898. Sodium was named by Sir Humphrey Davy who isolated it by electrolysis in 1807. The largest use of sodium is in the manufacture of tetraethyllead, an anti-knock ingredient in gasoline (first introduced by the Ethyl Corporation). About 60% of the total production of sodium is used to manufacture the anti-knock gasoline by combining sodium lead alloy with ethyl chloride which created tetraethyllead. The second major use of sodium is in the reduction of animal and vegetable oils into long-chain fatty alcohols. These long-chain fatty alcohols are used to manufacture soaps and detergents. This use has been decreasing in favor of such fatty alcohols by high-pressure catalytic hydrogenation. Sodium is also used to make sodium hydride, sodium amide, and in the synthesis of isosebacic acid. Sodium chloride (salt) is used in the manufacture of sodium hydroxide, sodium carbonate, sodium sulfate, and sodium metal. In the manufacture of sodium sulfate, the co-product is hydrogen chloride. In metallic sodium manufacture, the co-product is chlorine gas. Rock salt (sodium chloride) is used in curing fish, packing meat, and curing hides; table salt, however, accounts for only a small percentage of sodium chloride use, as most of the use is industrial.

Sodium hydroxide is the most important industrial alkali as it is used to manufacture many chemicals, but many other sodium chemicals are important to industry. About 30% of the sodium hydroxide made is used to manufacture other chemicals; the next major use is for cellulose film and rayon (25%). Soap manufacture, petroleum refining, and pulp and paper manufacturing account for about 10% of the total sodium hydroxide uses. Another sodium compound, sodium sulfate, is used mostly in the kraft paper pulp industry. Sodium carbonate finds its major use in the glass industry (one-third); another third is used in the manufacture of textiles, paper, metals, and petroleum products. One chemical reaction involving sodium is useful on icy wintertime sidewalks and roads: when sodium is combined with water (snow or ice), the reaction liberates sufficient heat to melt the ice.

Some important sodium chemicals occur in nature: sodium chloride (salt), sodium carbonate (soda and trona), sodium borate (borate), sodium nitrate, and sodium sulfate. Sodium salts are found in sea water, salt lakes, alkaline lakes, and mineral springs. Rock salt deposits occur where salt lakes and ancient seas have existed.

Sodium can irritate the skin and burn the eyes. Probably just as too much sodium in the diet can be a problem, too much sodium is cosmetics may also not be beneficial. Since sodium is used in the manufacture of soaps and shampoos, a proper formula should be determined so that the sodium content of the shampoo is not too drying to the hair or irritating to the skin.

SODIUM ACETATE - Acetate is derived from acetic acid. This is combined with sodium and used as a preservative. It is an allergen.

SODIUM ALGINATE - Algin is a term for the hydrophilic substance isolated from brown algae: *Macrocystis, laminaria*, and *Ascophyllum*. Sodium alginate (also known as the salts of alginic acid) is made by prewashing seaweed whereby the undesirable salts are leached out. This is followed by the extraction process with a dilute alkaline solution which solubilizes the alginic acid present in the seaweed. Sodium alginate is not known to be toxic. It is used in foods, pharmaceuticals, and cosmetics. In cosmetics, it is used mostly as a thickening agent and emulsifier.

SODIUM ALUM - In ancient times, alum was obtained by burning herbs to obtain the ash, which was used as an astringent. Today we know alum as a naturally occurring mineral known as kalunite and the constituent of the mineral alunite. Alum as used in sodium alum is produced as aluminum sulfate by treating bauxite with sulfuric acid to yield alum cake. The industrial alums are potash alum, ammonium alum, sodium alum, and chrom alum (potassium chromium sulfate). These chemicals are used as astringents, styptics, and emetics. They are irritating to mucous membranes and may cause allergic reactions.

SODIUM ASCORBATE - A form of vitamin C that is believed to be a buffered version of ascorbic acid (kinder to the stomach). It is used as an antioxidant and preservative in cosmetics. It can also block the formation of nitrosamides just as other ascorbates do.

SODIUM BENZOATE - Benzoic acid is used as a preservative in some cosmetics, but it is only effective at a low pH. It is, for example, 99% effective at a pH of 2, 94% effective at a pH of 3, 60% at a pH of 4, 13% effective at a pH of 5, and hardly effective at all at a pH above 5. It is not, for example, effective in most shampoo formulas. Sodium benzoate is often used in soft drinks as a preservative. A natural source of benzoic acid is benzoin gum from the benzoin-producing *Styrax* tree growing in Asia. Sumatra benzoin gum contains 12% benzoic acid. Benzoin as an herbal extract is used as an antiseptic, astringent, and skin protector. The Siam benzoin is the highest in antioxidative and preservative properties. There have been allergic reactions to sodium benzoate when used in foods. It has been listed as moderately toxic due to the dermatitis that develops in some people.

SODIUM BICARBONATE - See **BICARBONATE OF SODA**.

SODIUM BISULPHITE - Corrosive synthetic chemical used as a hair relaxer and preservative.

SODIUM BORATE - Sodium salt of boric acid. Used as a detergent builder, emulsifier, and preservative in cosmetics. See **BORIC ACID**.

SODIUM CARBONATE - Sodium salt of carbonic acid; used as an alkali and humectant in cosmetics.

SODIUM CITRATE - Crystalline salt used in foods as a buffering agent; in cosmetics it is used as a sequestrant and alkali.

SODIUM FLUORIDE - Sodium salt of fluoride added to water in trace amounts to prevent dental caries (cavities). Sodium fluoride can cause mottling of teeth and, if taken orally, death.

SODIUM HYDROXIDE - Also called caustic soda or lye, this extremely alkali chemical (pH of a 0.5% by weight in water solution is around 12) is corrosive. It is used as an alkalizer and in hair-straightening products. Combined with fats, lye produces soaps.

SODIUM IODATE - See **CHAPTER 14 ON PRESERVATIVES**.

SODIUM LACTATE - Hygroscopic viscous sodium salt of lactic acid, used as an antiacid and as a substitute for glycerol.

SODIUM LAURYL SULFATE - White powder used as a detergent, emulsifier, and surfactant in over a thousand cosmetic products, including shampoos, toothpastes, lotions, and creams. SLS is a strong degreaser that dries skin and hair. It is a primary irritant in high concentrations. SLS is used in many so-called "natural" cosmetics, but it is not natural. It is produced synthetically via the Ziegler process and not with coconut oil (i. e., sulfur trioxide or chlorosulfuric acid). SLS has produced skin and hair damage, including cracking of the horny layer of the skin and a severe inflammation of the dermaepidermal tissue ("Denaturation of epidermal keratin by surface active agents, *Journal Invest. Dermatology*, 32:581, 1959). The presence of natural ingredients make little difference in the irritating action of these synthetic detergents. Any cosmetic that contains sodium lauryl sulfate can't be termed as natural, although many shampoos labeled as natural contain large amounts. Also SLS is frequently combined with triethanolamine (TEA) which may be contaminated with nitrosamines, a potent carcinogen. See **ALKYL SULFATE, DETERGENT, NITROSAMINES,** and **SURFACTANT**.

SODIUM LAURETH SULFATE - Synthetic detergent similar to **SODIUM LAURYL SULFATE**, except it is a yellow liquid and somewhat milder.

SODIUM METAPHOSPHATE - Any of several crystalline sodium salts of metaphosphoric acid. Used in cosmetics as an emulsifier or texturizer.

SODIUM PALMITATE - Sodium salt of palmitic acid, used as a texturizer in cosmetics.

SODIUM PCA - Another name for this chemical is NaPCA, or the sodium salt of pyroglutamic acid. This was a popular "buzz" word in cosmetics a few years old. The advertising copy said NaPCA is a substance in our own skin that can re-moisturize it from the outside in; however, when it is synthesized, it can cause strong allergic reactions and severely dry the skin by absorbing moisture from the skin.

SODIUM PYRITHIONE - See **CHAPTER 14.**

SODIUM SALICYLATE - Sodium salt of salicylic acid used as a sun filter, antiseptic and preservative. May cause allergic reactions, especially in people allergic to aspirin.

SODIUM THIOGLYCOLATE - One of the thioglycolate compounds used in permanents as hair relaxers. These chemicals are primary irritants.

SOFT EXTRACTS - British term equivalent to our "native" or "solid" extracts.

SOLID EXTRACTS - Also known as pilular extracts, solid extracts are thin to thick liquids or semisolids prepared from native extracts and diluted to the appropriate strength. Usually the same strength as powdered extracts.

SORBIC ACID - See **CHAPTER 14** on **PRESERVATIVES.**

SORBITAN LAURATE, PALMITATE, OLEATE, PALMITATE, STEARATE, ETC. - Synthetic cosmetic ingredients made from lauric acid and sorbitol compounds; used as surfactants (non-anionic), humectants, binders, and emulsifiers.

SORBITOL - Crystalline, slightly sweet alcohol, occurring naturally in mountain ash but usually produced industrially by a reduction reaction of D-glucose; used as an humectant, binder, plasticizer, and softener in cosmetics. See **MANNITOL.**

SOYBEAN OIL - Pale yellow oil consisting mostly of glycerides of linoleic, oleic, linolenic, and palmitic acids; used as emollient in cosmetics.

SPERMACETI - Whale oil, illegal for use in any products in the United States since 1971, when the Marine Mammal Protection Act was passed. Spermaceti may include all kinds of whale oil but refers specifically to the oil of the sperm whale. The oil is thought to protect the whale from the bends when it surfaces from its half-mile dives for giant squid because of its ability to absorb nitrogen. All species of whales are endangered from the hunting ravages of man, and many are extinct. Only Norway and Russia still kill whales (Japan has announced they will quit by 1988), and they kill a lot of them.

SQUALENE - A saturated hydrocarbon known as perhydrosqualene obtained by hydrogenation of squalene, an aliphatic triterpene from shark liver oil. This oil was isolated by Marcelet, Tsujimoto and Chapman at the beginning of the twentieth century and is used in cosmetics for its moisturizing effect on the skin. It is used in cleansing creams, make-up, moisturizing creams, antiwrinkle creams, lotions, hair products, lipsticks, massage and bath oils, and as a vehicle of pharmaceutical active principles. Nontoxic.

Discussion - When squalene was found in human sebum in quantities of around 10%, it became a point of interest to cosmetic chemists. Its high unsaturation, however, proved a major drawback because this made it vulnerable to oxidation. Using the hydrogenation process developed by Marcelet, et al, squalene became sufficiently stable to be used in food. Squalene is also emerging in Japan as a health food, but earlier it had definite medical applications. In Japan during the late 1940's and early 1950's, physicians administered squalene subcutaneously, intramuscularly, and intravenously to treat tuberculosis and diabetes. There are more recent claims that squalene is a bolster to the immune system, increasing oxygenation, improving the metabolism, and strengthening the liver. Unfortunately, the Japanese stress the value of the shark-derived squalene, and they are busy raiding the deep for a rare species of shark - Aizame - which they claim is the best. One wonders about the ethics of killing a rare species of life in order to obtain an oil which has been known to exist since ancient times in wheat germ oil, rice bran, and olive oil in quantities between 0.1% and 0.7%. The squalene from olives is exactly like the squalene from the Aizame shark, but the big difference is that there is no need to kill the sharks to get it. Olive oil squalene is also superior because it is more commercially feasible, more stable against oxidation, of a higher food grade due to its vegetarian source, and with a greater purity and compatibility with the skin than either lanolin or shark-derived squalene. Further, with olive oil squalene there is less danger of contamination with heavy metal than with the fish product. Olive oil squalene leaves the skin smooth and velvety soft. In comparing the shark oil squalene and the olive oil squalene, it is obvious that the vegetarian source is better.

STAPHYLOCOCCUS - Gram-positive bacteria that may contaminate cosmetics.

STEARALKONIUM CHLORIDE - Quaternary ammonium compound used almost universally in hair conditioners, both mass-merchandised and so-called "natural." Stearalkonium chloride was originally developed by the textile industry for use as a fabric softener, and it also has anti-static properties. These characteristics are important in a hair conditioner only if you think of your hair as a ball of yarn. If you think of your hair as protein that grows out of living tissue, then you will avoid this quat. Quats are poisonous and corrosive, and they are used in hair conditioners in large

STEARALKONIUM CHLORIDE Continued
amounts, typically in the top five ingredients. They are used in cosmetic formulas because they are readily available, cheap, and easy to use in formulas. Chemists will typically use a lot of quats in a conditioner and much less protein (which really does contribute to hair health) and herbal oils (which lubricate and rejuvenate hair). Quats do perform well in products on a short-term basis, giving an instantly soft feeling to the hair, which reassures consumers that the product "works." Stearalkonium chloride does not, however, work well with your hair over time: the hair becomes dry, brittle, and breaks. It also contributes to allergic reactions.

Not all quats are synthetically produced: one complex quaternary ammonium salt known as d-tubocurarine chloride has been isolated from a tropical plant and used as a muscle relaxant. Choline, a B vitamin, is a mixture of complex lipids such as lecithin and acetylcholine and can be accepted as a natural quaternary. Lecithin is a good replacement in hair rinses and conditioners for the classic ammonium salts. See **QUATERNARY AMMONIUM COMPOUNDS**.

STEARATE - Ester of **STEARIC ACID**.

STEARETH-2, 4, 7, 10, 20, 30 - Polyethylene glycol ethers of stearyl alcohol, used as emollients and emulsifiers. Synthetic chemicals.

STEARIC ACID - Waxy, crystalline, fatty acid derived from tallow and other animal fats; also in cocoa butter and other hard vegetable fats. Used as emollient and base in cosmetics. Some allergic reactions.

STEARYL ALCOHOL - Fatty alcohol found in whale, porpoise, and dolphin oils but usually produced by hydrogenating stearic acid; used similarly to cetyl alcohol. See **CETYL ALCOHOL**.

STEROIDS - Group name for compounds similar to cholesterol, including sex hormones, bile acids, sterols, and some cancer-stimulating hydrocarbons.

STEROLS - Class of compounds widely distributed in the unsaponifiable portion of lipids in animals and plants.

STILBENE - Aromatic hydrocarbon obtained from benzaldehyde.

STILBENE DYES - Class of usually yellow to orange direct cotton azo dyes or fluorescent brighteners derived from stilbene. See **COLORS IN COSMETICS**.

STRATUM CORNEUM - Outer horny layer of the epidermis.

STRENGTH OF EXTRACTS - The potency or strength of botanical drug extracts are generally expressed in two ways. If they contain known active principles, they are expressed in terms of the content of the active compounds. Otherwise, they are expressed in terms of their total extract in relation to the crude drug. Thus, a strength of 1:4 means one part of extract is equivalent to or derived from four parts of crude drug.

STILLINGIA OIL- Pale yellow drying oil obtained from the seeds of the Chinese tallow tree *(Sapium sebiferum* or *Stillingia sebifera).*

STRAMONIUM - Dried leaf of the thorn apple (Genus *Datura*) used in medicine for asthma; contains the alkaloids atropine, lyoscyamine, and scopolamine; similar to belladonna. Used in cosmetics for its antiperspirant properties, but is lethal if ingested.

STRONTIUM HYDROXIDE - Alkaline solid used to make soaps and greases and in refining beet sugar. Irritant synthetic chemical.

STYPTIC - Having an astringent or hemostatic effect, as alum or tannin.

SUCCINIC ACID - Formed as part of the Krebs cycle, this acid occurs naturally (e. g., in amber, lignite, turpentine, and animal fluids); used as an antiseptic, buffer, and neutralizer in cosmetics.

SUGAR - Alias sucrose; used in cosmetics as a demulcent and preservative.

SULFATED CASTOR OIL - See **TURKEY RED OIL**.

SULFATED OILS - Oils or fatty acids treated with sulfuric acid or oleum rendering them water-soluble; used as wetting and emulsifying agents.

SULFUR - A chemical element with the symbol S, atomic number 16, and atomic weight 32.064. Sulfur was discovered prior to recorded history. Its elemental character was first recorded by the pioneering French chemist A. L. Lavoisier in 1777. Sulfur is found in the Earth's crust, about 0.1%. Texas and Louisiana have the largest sulfur deposits in the world. Other large deposits are in California, Colorado, Wyoming, Nevada, Utah, Mexico, and South America. There are impure deposits of sulfur in Japan, Sicily, and Mexico in volcanic regions. Smaller deposits are found in New Zealand, Chile, Russia, Iceland, and Spain. Sulfur is removed from the ground by drilling a hole and inserting three pipes in the ore bed. Hot water is forced down one of the pipes, and the sulfur is melted (sulfur melts at 112.8° C.). Compressed hot air is pumped down another pipe, and the molten sulfur is forced up through the third pipe. This process renders 99.5% pure sulfer that contains no arsenic, selenium, or tellurium. There are various sulfur compounds used in the manufacture of chemicals, textiles, soaps, fertilizers, leather, plastics, refrigerants, bleaching agents, drugs, dyes, paints, paper, and other products. Two main compounds made with sulfur are sulfides and oxides. When hydrogen and sulfur are combined you have hydrogen sulfide (H_2S). The oxides of sulfur such as sulfur dioxide are prepared by roasting metallic sulfides in air or oxygen by the reaction of copper with sulfuric acid at high temperatures.

SULFUR Continued

The hair contains about 3.8% sulfur, and the structure of hair is linked with a disulphide bond. The sulfur-containing amino acids, including cysteine, cystine, and methionine, are important to the hair and skin. They are also essential to protein metabolism. During metabolism they give up their sulfur and thereby enable the body to synthesize its own amino acids. The natural sulfur in herbs (and amino acids) has a positive effect on the hair and skin. The herb coltsfoot, for example, is high in sulfur (26%) and is an important ingredient for hair and skin care products. Hair conditioners and shampoos that contain herbal sulfur or the sulfur-containing amino acids can correct damaged hair and aid in reducing scalp problems. The sulfur-containing amino acids can be used to treat acne and other skin problems.

SULFUR COLORS - Class of sulfur containing colors used in dying cotton and other cellulose fibers. See **COLORS IN COSMETICS**.

SUNSCREENS - Substances that are effective in reducing the power of the sun's rays to burn the skin; that act as UV light filters. The best sunscreen is to stay out of the sun; after that comes PABA, or para-amino-benzoic acid; other natural sunscreens include willow bark and shea butter.

SUPERFATTING - Containing unsaponified fat, e.g., superfatted soaps.

SURFACTANTS - Surface-active-agents; substances capable of emulsifying oils and holding dirt in suspension so that it can be rinsed away with water. Soap is a surfactant; so are synthetic detergents.

SYNERGISM - In chemistry this is the word used to describe how two elements or substances (or even parts of the body) can work together to bring about a positive result. The sum of two or more substances working together is greater than the sum of each individual substance on its own. For example, we can use vitamin C in the form of ascorbic acid as an antioxidant to protect the water phase of a cosmetic product, but if we combine ascorbic acid with ascorbyl palmitate (the lipid-soluble vitamin C) in a cosmetic, we will have protection of the water phase AND the oil phase of the cosmetic. If we combine ascorbic acid, ascorbyl palmitate, vitamin E, and vitamin A as antioxidants, they work together better than each one does alone. Herbal cosmetics and herbal medicines are often combined based on the synergistic action to be obtained from the combinations working together. The word comes from the Greek *synergos*, working together.

SYNTHETIC APOLOGISTS - Those who are taken in by the supposedly great advancements of the Chemical Industrial Complex and Medicine. The SAPS also usually think testing on animals

prove that a chemical is safe for human use and that no advancements can be made in medicine without vivisection. (See **CHAPTER 13** in this book). The SAP does not believe in organic foods and defines "organic" as any substance that contains carbon. What the SAP does not know is that our body may not see things exactly as the synthesizer charts it on his formula pad. Once in a while the SAP will back down on something but only after humans drop dead from a chemical in sufficient numbers to warrant taking it off the FDA's GRAS (Generally Regarded As Safe) list. The SAP always checks the GRAS list, and if the chemical is on there, then it must be okay. It is, in fact, okay until some bureaucrat takes it off the GRAS list. Some SAPS have a sense of humor and will point out that fluoride should be in the water if for no other reason than to prove it is not a communist plot as some health food faddists may claim. Here are some of the SAP comments on foods, cosmetics, and supplements: "A cosmetic must contain a synthetic preservative to protect consumers. Organic fruits and vegetables are no different in taste or nutritional value from those grown on chemically treated soil. Processed foods are just as nutritious as 'health foods,' which are a rip-off. There is no difference between natural cosmetics and mass-merchandised cosmetics." There are many other statements made by SAPS, but more and more they are finding that they have to apologize for more and more problems in our polluted, chemicalized, increasingly toxic environment.

SYNTHETIC SKIN - See **POLYMERS**.

T

TALC - Powdered soapstone used as a base in baby powder, make-ups, and as a filler in creams. Some sources of talc are contaminated with asbestos. Repeated inhalation of talc can lead to talcosis. Cornstarch, powdered silk, and rice starch are all good alternatives to talc; however, avoid inhalation due to possible allergic reactions.

TALL OIL - Recovered from pine wood liquor during paper-making process, tall oil contains rosin acids, oleic and linoleic acids, and long chain alcohols. Used in cosmetics as an aromatic and fungicide.

TALLOW - Derived from the fatty tissue of animals, as cows, horses, sheep, etc., tallow is mostly fatty acid glycerides. Used to make soap, glycerol, margarine, candles, and lubricants.

TANNIC ACID - Complex phenolic acid found in plants (powdered gallnuts, shredded tara, quebracho wood, chestnut wood, wattle, sumac, valonia); used in tanning, dyeing, making ink; in medicine as an astringent and formerly to treat burns.

TAR OIL - Volatile oil distilled from wood tar (usually pine). Used as an antiseptic and deodorant in cosmetics.

TARTARIC ACID - Found in fresh fruit, this acid is sometimes used to neutralize permanent wave solutions and as a buffer in cosmetics. May irritate the skin in strong concentrations.

TEA - See **TRIETHANOLAMINE**.

TEA-LAURYL SULFATE - Synthetic detergent, emulsifier, surfactant that is a combination of triethanolamine and the salt of lauryl sulfuric acid. This is a very popular shampoo ingredient, but it is not recommended because it may be contaminated with nitrosamines (because of the TEA) and because it is drying to the skin and hair. (Formulas containing the amines should also contain vitamins C and E as carcinogen blockers.)

TEA TREE OIL - Distilled from the leaves of the Australian tree *Melaleuca alternifolia*, this oil is used as an antiseptic and germicide.

TERPINEOL - Usually obtained from pine oil, (although it occurs in many herbal essential oils), this monoterpene alcohol is used in soaps and perfumes for its fragrance. One variety of terpineol smells like hyacinths, another like lilacs.

TETRACHLOROETHYLENE - Synthetic chlorinated hydrocarbon used in dry cleaning solutions, degreasing metals, and as a solvent.

TETRASODIUM EDTA - Sequestering agent in cosmetics. Eye and skin irritant. See **SEQUESTRANTS**.

THEOBROMA OIL - Synonym for cocoa oil or butter. Used in cosmetics as an emollient. See **HERB CHART**.

THIOINDIGOID - Class of dyes similar to indigo.

THIOGLYCOLATES - Ill-smelling chemical compounds that are the result of a reaction between chloroacetic acid and hydrogen sulfide; used mainly in its ammonium salt form for permanent waves and in its calcium or other salt form as a depilatory agent. These chemicals work by breaking the chemical bonds of the hair; in the case of depilatories, thioglycolates turn the hair into a gummy mass that can be washed away. Hopefully when used on the hair in the form of a permanent wave, they do not have the same effect, although the same chemicals are used. Thioglycolate compounds are toxic in small doses if ingested. They damage the hair and skin, as well as any metal and fabric with which they come into contact. The surfactants usually included in permanent wave solutions only increase the danger, as they remove any

oils from the skin and hair so as to optimize penetration of the corrosive and irritating thioglycolate compounds. A further complication is that many surfactants anesthesize the eyeball so that if any thioglycolate or other potent chemical compound gets into the eye, the injured individual would not be able to feel the burn until substantial damage had occurred. We recommend that you not permanent wave your hair.

THREONINE - Essential amino acid.

THYMOL - Crystalline phenol, occurring naturally in thyme and many other essential oils, but also manufactured synthetically. Used as a fungicide, antispasmodic, anthelmintic, diaphoretic, sedative, expectorant, carminative, counterirritant, rubefacient, antifungal, preservative, fragrance, and flavor.

TINCTURES - Alcoholic or hydroalcoholic solutions usually containing the active principles of botanicals in comparatively low concentrations. They are generally prepared either by maceration or percolation or by dilution of their corresponding fluid or native extracts.

TITANIUM DIOXIDE - Inorganic salt that is produced as a white powder; used as a pigment or opacifier in cosmetics for its covering power, brilliance, and reflectivity. Used in eye make-up, powdered and liquid foundation make-up, sunscreens; also in house paint, enamels, plastics, paper products, and shoe whiteners. Avoid inhalation of titanium dioxide.

TOCOPHEROL - Vitamin E; may be natural or synthetic depending on the isomer and the manufacturer. The D isomer only occurs naturally (but can be isolated from a synthetic vitamin E); the DL prefix indicates the vitamin E product is synthetic. If natural, vitamin E is made from vegetable sources. Look for the NSVEA label (Natural Source Vitamin E Association) on vitamin E supplements. Vitamin E is a fat-soluble antioxidant; it works well as a preservative in the oil phase of cosmetics, particularly when combined with vitamins C and A. See **SYNERGISM** and **VITAMINS IN COSMETICS**.

TOILET WATER - Also known as "Eau de Toilette," this contains less fragrance concentrate than perfume (4-8%) and an alcohol that is lower in grade (80%). See chart below:

TYPES OF PERFUME

Type of Fragrance	%Fragrance Concentrate	Grade of Alcohol
Perfume (Parfum)	15-30%	90-95%
Parfum de Toilette	8-15%	80-90%
Eau de Toilette	4-8%	80%
Eau de Cologne	3-5%	70%
Splash Cologne	1-3%	
Eau Fraiche	about 3%	about 80%

TOLUENE - Liquid aromatic hydrocarbon resembling benzene, produced commercially from petrochemicals; used as a solvent, especially for nail polishes, in cosmetics; also in dyes, pharmaceuticals, and as a blending agent for gasoline. Toxic and narcotic in high concentrations.

TRAGACANTH - See **HERB CHART**.

TRICHLOROETHANE - Hydrocarbon used in cosmetics as a solvent. Irritating. narcotic vapors. May be fatal if inhaled, ingested or absorbed through the skin.

TRICHLOROETHYLENE - Hydrocarbon used in astringent formulations; a known carcinogen and irritant.

TRICHOLOGY - Scientific study of the hair.

TRICLOCARBAN - Mostly commonly used antibacterial agent (bacteriocide) in deodorant soaps; used in concentrations of 1 to 2%. Allergic reactions and photosensitization reactions are possible with this chemical. Another problem is that triclocarban kills some bacteria but not all, causing an imbalance in the bacterial flora that surrounds the body. Triclocarban is absorbed by the body (one study lists absorption at around 14%), and long-term consequences of this absorption are unknown.

TRICLOSAN - Commonly used deodorant ingredient; bacteriocide. Although this chemical has shown low oral toxicity, and has been approved for use by the FDA in deodorant soaps, percutaneous absorption (which definitely occurs when the substance is used over the entire body) may cause liver damage.

TRIDECETH-3, -6, -10, ETC. - Polyethylene glycol ethers of tridecyl alcohol (made from paraffin, a mineral oil product). Used as emulsifiers and binders in cosmetics.

TRIETHANOLAMINE - Amino alcohol made from ammonia and ethylene oxide and used ubiquitously throughout the cosmetic industry (mass-merchandised and so-called "natural" products alike) in making fatty acid soaps, as a pH adjuster, as an emulsifier, and a preservative. This synthetic chemical may be contaminated with nitrosamines, a known and potent carcinogen. See **NITROSAMINES**.

TRYPTOPHAN - Amino acid formed by the body. L-tryptophan is said to help you relax and sleep by stimulating the production of serotonin, a neurotransmitter that biochemically predisposes your brain to sleep.

TURKEY-RED OIL - Sulfated castor oil used in shampoos since 1880: the first synthetic detergent. Turkey red oil shampoo is effective in hard or soft water but does not foam much and tends to strip color from the hair.

TURPENTINE - Natural hydrocarbon isolated from pine trees and used in cosmetics as a solvent. Irritates skin and mucous membranes and may cause allergic reactions.

TURTLE OIL - Oil obtained from the giant sea turtle *Chelonium*. This oil is no better emollient than a good vegetable oil and destroys an endangered species. This is another example of how advertising copy creates a damand for an unethical product.

TWEENS - Trade name for the **POLYSORBATES**.

TYROSINE - Amino acid that participates in the production of melanin.

U

ULTRA-VIOLET RAY - Having a wave-length shorter than visible light (beyond violet which is at the end of the color spectrum) and longer than x-rays. Over-exposure to ultra-violet radiation will damage the skin over time. See **SUNSCREENS** and **PABA**.

UMBELLIFERONE - Natural phenol found in many plants (e. g., galbanum or asafetida) and many synthetically. See **COUMARIN**.

UREA - A white, crystalline water-soluble compound. This is the end product of normal animal and human protein metabolism. It is made commercially from the partial hydrolysis of cyanamide, and by heating carbon dioxide and ammonia under pressure. In 1828 F. Wholer prepared urea from phosgene and ammonia by rearrangement of ammonium cyanate. Urea is used medically as a diuretic. It has a high nitrogen content so is used to manufacture fertilizer. Urea is also used in combination with formaldehyde to create a syrup which is mixed with cellulose and coloring matter to be used in textile treatment or in laminating operations. Many people are allergic to fabrics that contain urea-formaldehyde. Urea is also used in cosmetics. It causes allergic reactions and those who are allergic to ammonia will probably be allergic to urea. There is danger in using products containing urea around the eyes.

URIC ACID - Nitrogenous compound present in the urine of most mammals. Elevated uric acid is believed to be a symptom of gout. Uric acid is used in some cosmetics instead of allantoin or comfrey extracts, but allantoin (from comfrey) is a superior cosmetic ingredient.

V

VEGETABLE GUMS - See **GUMS**.

VEGETABLE HAIR DYES - See **HENNA** in the **HERB CHART**.

VEGETABLE OILS - See **OILS**.

VEGETARIAN - A person or product that avoids animal products. There are different types of vegetarian products, and there are different types of vegetarian people. Some people eat eggs, milk, and cheese: they are lacto-ovo-vegetarians. Some people eat no animal products at all: they are vegans. Some cosmetic products use no animal by-products in their formulas and call themselves vegetarian. However, they will test on animals, or they will use synthetic colors, detergents, and preservatives that have been animal-tested over and over again. It's difficult for a cosmetic manufacturer to tell a raw materials manufacturer what to do: sometimes ingredients will be animal-tested, and if you want to use that ingredient and if that manufacturer is the only source, then you will have to use it or re-formulate. BUT, if a cosmetic manufacturer avoids synthetic chemicals and uses only natural ingredients, then that manufacturer is MORE vegetarian and animal-conscious than one who uses no animal by-products but uses synthetic ingredients. A few ounces of collagen (a dermal protein) taken from a cow that has already been slaughtered for its meat does less damage to our animal friends than using a chemical that has blinded, tortured and murdered thousands and thousands of creatures so that it can be considered "safe to sell." As our earth becomes more crowded and more polluted, our species will be forced to become more conscious of the connections between our actions and other species: this issue will become increasingly important.

VERMILLION - From the Latin for little worm *vermis*, from whose scales the red dye was originally made. Vermillion, or mercuric sulfide, was also derived from the mineral cinnabar but now is synthesized from a reaction involving mercury, sulfur, and sodium hydroxide. The color varies from crimson to nearly orange; used primarily as an artist's color and in rubber.

VETIVER OIL - Obtained from khuskhus, Hindi aromatic grass *(Andropogon zizamoides)*, vetiver oil is used in perfumery, cosmetics, and soaps.

VINEGAR - Sour liquid containing around 4% or 5% acetic acid; used as a solvent or a pH adjuster in cosmetics. Vinegar may irritate the skin if used in concentrations that are too strong.

VITILIGO - Skin abnormality characterized by areas with loss of pigment surrounded by deeply pigmented borders.

VOLATILE OILS - See **ESSENTIAL OILS**.

W

WALNUT EXTRACT - Extract from the husk of the nut of *(Juglans regia)*; used as a natural deep brown color.

WAXES - Waxes have existed for several million years, but men and women only learned how to use them a few thousand years ago. Their cosmetic use can be traced back to ancient Egypt. Egyptian women would mix waxes and essential oils and melt the wax and coat their bodies with the melted wax. They would then attend a festive occasion (perhaps of a religious nature), and as they danced the wax would slowly melt, releasing the fragrance. Waxes were used to create emulsions for cosmetic creams, and it is known that Galen used beeswax in the first cold cream for this purpose. Waxes are still used by some cosmetic manufacturers for this purpose though synthetic waxes and petroleum waxes are more frequently used instead of vegetable or animal waxes.

One of the major wax manufacturers, the Frank B. Ross Co., Inc., Jersey City, New Jersey, has listed the following sources of wax from their company: Animal and Insect Waxes, including Beeswax and Shellac; Vegetable Waxes, including Bayberry, Candelilla, Carnauba, Japan, Ouricury, Rice Bran, and Jojoba; Mineral and Petroleum Waxes, including Montan, Ozokerite, Petro-Wax, Microcrystalline, Oxidized, and Paraffin; Synthetic Waxes, including Ross Wax 100, Ross Wax 140, and Ross Wax 160.

Waxes have certain constants; that is, little change from one batch of wax to the next. These constants are melting point, acid number, iodine number, flash point, ester number, refractive index, specific gravity, saponification number, and unsaponifiable matter. Other than these factors, wax can vary between batches. There can be a great color variance, so quite often waxes are bleached. Wax can be obtained in many forms: lumps, bricks, slabs, flakes, chips, ground, powdered, and atomized. For the most part, however, the structure of wax is crystalline, amorphoid, fibrous, and microcrystalline. The colors of wax can be white, brown, green, yellow, amber, or black.

WAXES Continued

Wax has many industrial uses, food uses, and cosmetic uses. For example, an aesthetician can use wax as a skin care mask and a means of "hydro-occlusion" or increasing absorption of skin care products into the skin. There is also a treatment for arthritis of the hand in which medication is combined with wax and the hot wax is spread over the hand where it is allowed to cool for therapeutic results.

Beeswax is an insect product excreted by the honeybee, *Apis Mellifera Linne* (Family *Apidae*), to construct the honeycomb. The beeswax is extracted by boiling the honeycomb in water and skimming the wax off the top. The color of the wax depends upon the type of flower from which the bee extracted the pollen: it varies from deep brown to a light amber shade. Melting point: 143.6-149° F. It is compatible with most other waxes, fatty acids, fatty alcohols, and plant glycerides. Some people are allergic to beeswax.

Bayberry Wax is obtained from the berries of the bayberry shrub. The wax is a coating on the berries and is removed by boiling water. The wax floats to the surface and is skimmed off. The bayberry shrub grows in the coastal states of North, Central, and South America. Most of this wax comes from Columbia. It is a gray-green color with a very aromatic odor. Melting point: 100-120° F. It is compatible with most other waxes, fatty acids, hydrocarbons, and plant glycerides.

Candelilla is a vegetable wax found in the form of scales covering a reed-like plant *(Euphorbiea Antisiphilitica, Euphorbiea Cerifera,* and *Pedilanthus Pavonis)* which grows wild on the rocky slopes and plains of northwest Mexico and southern Texas. The wax is obtained by boiling the plant in water (which must contain a small amount of sulfuric acid) and skimming the wax off the top. After it is skimmed from the water, it is strained and gently cooked to remove excess moisture. It is shipped in lump form. It is a light brown to yellow. This wax is not as hard as Carnauba and does not reach its maximum hardness for several days. Melting point: 155-162° F. It is compatible with all vegetable and animal waxes and some hydrocarbons.

Carnauba Wax is exuded by the leaves of the Brazilian tree *(Copernica Cerifera)* to conserve the moisture within the tree and leaves. The natives of Brazil use various products from this tree for many necessities which is why it has been named "Arbol del Vida," or "Tree of Life." There are many Carnauba Palms in parts of South America, Ceylon, and Equatorial Africa, but due to irregular rainy seasons only the Brazilian trees have the wax. From September to March, the leaves which contain the wax are cut from the trees. The wax is graded by area of origin: Parnahyba, Piaui, Ceara, and Bahia. The wax is yellow to medium yellow. Melting point: 181.4° F and higher. It is compatible with all vegetable, animal, and mineral waxes as well as many plant glycerides, fatty acids, and hydrocarbons.

Ceresin Wax is derived from Ozokerite (see below) by refining and bleaching. It is a petroleum product and is considered a higher grade paraffin. The color is white to tan. Melting point: 128-150° F. It is compatible with vegetable, animal, and mineral waxes, many synthetic chemical resins, fatty acids, plant glycerides, and hydrocarbons. Because it is a petrochemical, it is an allergen to some people.

Japan Wax is a vegetable wax obtained from the coating on the berry kernels of several Japanese Sumac (Hazel) trees. The berries are aged then crushed. The wax is extracted by pressure or by a solvent. The wax is refined by melting, filtering, and bleached by chemicals or by sunlight. It is a pale cream color with a gummy feel. Melting point: 115-120° F. It is compatible with beeswax, cocoa butter, and plant glycerides.

Jojoba Wax is made by hydrogenating the liquid wax of the jojoba shrub *(Simmondsia Chinensis)* to a hard white wax with nickel-copper catalyst at mild temperatures and pressures. Melting point: 65-68° C. It is compatible with most other waxes and plant glycerides.

Microcrystalline Wax is a matrix of small crystals known as amorphous wax. It is a mixture of hydrocarbons and paraffins. The colors are white, yellow, and black. Melting point: 140-205° F. Compatible with most other waxes. This is a petroleum product and should be considered to have the same allergic causing properties as other petrochemicals.

Montan Wax is derived from lignite which is a vegetable matter partly mineralized to a product related to bituminous coal. The lignites from Central Europe and California are used to make this wax. The lignites are crushed to a powder, and the waxy material extracted by solvents. The color is dark brown, brown, and tan. Melting point: 181-190° F. Compatible with vegetable waxes, hydrocarbons, and resins.

Ouricury Wax is exuded from the leaves of the Ouricury Palm *(Syagrus Coronata)* which grows in Brazil. The wax can only be removed from the leaves by scraping the leaves with a sharp instrument. The color is a greenish-brown but varies with the care taken during processing. Melting point: 180-184° F. Compatible with all vegetable, animal, and mineral waxes, resins, fatty acids, plant glycerides, and hydrocarbons.

Ozokerite Wax is a bituminous product occurring in minocene formations near petroleum deposits in Poland, Austria, Russia, Ukraine, Utah, and Texas. The ozokerites have long fibers which are unlike the paraffins and microcrystalline waxes. The hydrocarbon nature of this wax makes it less desirable in cosmetics, and it is regulated by the FDA (Reg. 21 CFR 175.105). It comes in white and yellow. Melting point varies according to grade. Most flakes melt at 152-165° F. Compatible with all vegetable waxes, resins, animal waxes, plant glycerides, and fatty acids.

Paraffin Waxes are hard white crystalline materials derived from petroleum. They are refined with various solvents. Paraffins can become ran-

WAXES Continued

cid, at which time they take on a dark color and strong rancid smell. They are white in color. Melting point: 112-165° F. Compatible with some waxes, vegetable, mineral, and animal. This wax is one of the most used. You can't escape it: cereal wrap, food wrap, corrugated containers, cheese and vegetable coatings, candles, and textiles. If you want to avoid petrochemicals, paraffin makes it difficult.

Rice Bran Wax comes from the bran that has been removed from rice during processing. Rice bran is a commericially important source of edible oil. The oil contains a wax which is removed through purification and crystallization. The color varies from tan to light brown. Melting point: 169-181° F. Compatible with all other waxes, fatty acids, plant glycerides, and hydrocarbons. This wax is better as a coating for fruits, vegetables, confectionary, and chewing gum than paraffins or petrochemical waxes. It is also suitable for cosmetics.

Spermaceti Wax comes from the sperm whale, and the murdering of this whale is forbidden by government regulation in the United States. Jojoba wax is an excellent replacement for this wax.

WETTING AGENTS - Substances that promote the penetration or spreading of a liquid; they are used in mixing solids with liquids. See **HUMECTANT**.

WHEAT GERM OIL - See **CHAPTER 6**.

WHITEHEAD - Small whitish mass beneath the surface of the skin caused by the retention of sebum.

WHITE LEAD - Also called ceruse, this highly toxic substance was used by women on their faces to give them a smooth porcelain finish from Elizabethean times to around 1900, when it was finally replaced by rice powder, an innocuous herbal substance. White lead is a good example of how women have distorted and poisoned their bodies in the pathological pursuit of beauty.

WOOL WAX - Also known as **LANOLIN**.

XANTHAN GUM - See **GUMS**.

XANTHENE DYES - Any of a group of bright yellow to pink to blue-red dyes distinguished by a xanthene nucleus; they include organic pigments and are used to dye textiles and paper, and for fluorescent effects.

XYLENOL - Phenol compound, a petroleum distillate, used as disinfectants and to make phenolic resins.

XYLITOL - Sugar (from the pentose class) from the cell walls of plants, especially straw, corncobs, oat hulls, cottonseed hulls, and wood.

YEAST - See **BREWERS YEAST**.

ZEIN - Alcohol-soluble protein obtained from corn *Zea mays*, used as a coating, protective film, and plasticizer.

ZINC - A chemical element, Zn, atomic number 30, and atomic weight 65.38. Zinc is in fourth place among all the metals produced (iron, copper, and aluminum exceed it). The largest use for zinc is as a protective coating to other metals.

Zinc was known to be present in ancient brass long before it was recognized as a separate element. An alloy found in prehistoric ruins in Transylvania contained 87% zinc. The Chinese use of zinc dates back to the 15th century. Indian metallurgists produced zinc in the 13th century by reducing calamine ore with such organic materials as wool. Paracelsus (16th century) is believed to be the first European to recognize zinc as a metallic element. He called it "zinckum." In 1743 William Champion produced zinc in England by reducing zinc carbonate with coke.

Zinc is an essential element in the growth of many kinds of organisms, both plant and animal. A deficiency of zinc in humans has been found to retard growth and produce anemia. Insulin is a zinc-containing protein. Children who have the skin disease known as *acrodermatitis enteropathica* (a disease which causes lesions on the skin, poor nutrient, absorption, bowel problems, stunted growth, and poor nutrient absorption) find relief with zinc supplements. A daily intake of 35 mg of zinc cleared up the skin and corrected the bowel problems. Zinc oxide clears up diaper rash (as do ointments containing vitamins A and D). A supplement of zinc of 20 mg per day

ZINC Continued

is said to help some cases of acne. Nutritional researchers say that zinc, protein, and vitamin C supplements are important nutrients for healing the body. *The Medical Journal of Australia* (November 22, 1975) reported that ten ulcer patients were given 90 mg of zinc three times per day, and eight patients with ulcers were given a placebo. The patients taking zinc had a healing rate three times that of the patients on the placebo. Zinc in an ointment form is said to clear up dandruff, though it isn't the best form of therapy since it leaves a white gummy residue in the hair. The hair contains 116 mg of zinc per kilogram of hair in women and 212 mg in men.

ZINC OXIDE - Water insoluble white solid, occurring in nature as zincite; used as a pigment in making rubber and in pharmaceutical and cosmetic products. Zinc oxide has astringent properties. In an ointment base it can be used to protect the skin from the sun's burning rays.

ZINC STEARATE - Salt of stearic acid and zinc (usually zinc oxide); used as pigment and to help cosmetics adhere to skin. May be harmful if inhaled.

Part III
Natural Organic Hair Care
And
Natural Organic Skin Care

or

The Natural Method

or

Mother Nature
As Cosmetologist

organitoons

THE NEW HUCKSTERS HAVE MD DEGREES AND FDA APPROVAL!

"Even a man who's pure of heart, and says his prayers at night; can become a werewolf when the wolfbane blooms and the moon is full and bright...Well, er, you can also try Minoxidil Cream."

CHAPTER XVI

How to
Save
Your Hair

As the cartoon at your left illustrates, our new "medicine show" hucksters come with degrees from prestigious universities, or they are established pharmaceutical manufacturers. Plus, they often have FDA approval. The case in point here is a drug called minoxidil. Originally developed as a drug to lower blood pressure, minoxidil works by relaxing and enlarging certain small blood vessels so that the blood flows more easily. Because side effects are common with this drug, it is only used with serious cases of high blood pressure. There are enough side effects, in fact, to scare most prudent people away from minoxidil: an increase in the heart rate by 20 beats or more, severe chest pains, rapid weight gain, difficulty in breathing, dizziness, and fainting. One side effect which seems to occur in about eight out of every 10 people is what I call the "wolfman syndrome." About three to six weeks after beginning the drug, hair grows on the forehead and temples, between the eyebrows, and on the upper part of the cheeks (regardless of whether there is a full moon, of course). This "wolfman" growth is not noticed by some patients. And, the brochure packaged with the drug says *this growth is not permanent and will disappear about one to six months after stopping the drug.* Just think: if Lon Chaney, Jr., could have traced his "wolfman syndrome" to minoxidil, his 1941 movie "The Wolfman" would have had a happy ending.

Originally the pharmaceutical manufacturer Upjohn sold 2.5 mg and 10 mg tablets of minoxidil under the trade name Loniten™. Then they began mixing the drug with a liquid and rubbing into the scalp to grow hair. They reasoned that if one bad side effect was hair growth, maybe this bad effect could be turned into a good effect. As far as sales were concerned, their reasoning was sound: marketing studies suggested that there was $200 million per year in a hair growing drug that was approved by the FDA and distributed by doctors on a prescription basis. FDA approval and M. D cooperation was essential, however, because the drug was imported from another country, and Upjohn didn't want an OTC drug which would eventually be copied by other manufacturers.

New York University research (underwritten by Upjohn) found that minoxidil in a 3% solution grew hair in 30% of those who applied it to the scalp. It was carefully arranged that this study would be released to TV shows such as "60 Minutes" and "20/20" for advance publicity.

What a product! It grows hair! You've got the market cornered! AND the person who starts using it has to use it for life! This is a merchandiser's dream come true!

Upjohn began building a plant to manufacture the hair grower even before they had FDA approval. (Did they know something the rest of us didn't?) They called their new hair growing drug Regain. Now there's one thing we can say for the FDA: they never give their total approval: manufacturers always have to change something. The FDA balked at the name Regain. (Was it that they knew hair wasn't "regained"?) Upjohn then changed the name to Rogaine, which the FDA approved. But what does Rogaine stand for? Does it sound enough like "regain" to get the consumer's hopes up or does it stand for the large quantities of lettuce (romaine) you're going to have to cough up to keep your new-found fuzz? Don't forget, too, that if you stop using Rogaine, all your new-grown hair will fall out, just as the wolfman's appearance returned to normal with the passing of the full moon. However, the FDA has approved the manufacture and marketing of Rogaine, and perhaps by the time you read this, you will have some to rub onto your head for the rest of your life.

While the FDA was considering the approval of minoxidil, I noticed they came down hard on any other product that made claims to grow hair or even prevent hair loss. Before the approval of minoxidil they were very lax with these products, but all that changed when Rogaine came onto the horizon. What's curious about this is that all the other hair growers work just as well as minoxidil, and most are far less dangerous.

I make it a priority to look at anything in the lab that rumor or research has suggested as a hair grower. But where to get sufficient quantities of minoxidil for testing? One day, a dermatologist asked me to make a stronger solution and to make minoxidil more pleasant for patients to use. He had found that commercially formulated 3% solutions left a white, gummy residue on the hair, and he wanted a 5% solution. I agreed to his request, but I had a different purpose. Does it really work?

I was able to make a fast-absorbing 5% solution that was totally invisible on the hair. My formula, made with all-natural ingredients, was far better than any being made by pharmacists across the country and left the hair feeling better than other commercial minoxidil solutions. Nevertheless, I discovered for myself that minoxidil does not grow hair and is no better than any other chemical that claims to do so.

Since minoxidil's approval for hair growth, American Cyanamid has begun to test their hair growing drug called Viprostol on 1000 volunteers. Foltene, a hair growth chemical from Europe, has also entered the scene. They join other treatments already being sold, like the Helsinki treatment (made with polysorbate, a fatty acid ester used as a food additive), and biotin, a B vitamin.

One of the first articles written about polysorbates was published in a book called *Life Extension*, by Durk Pearson and Sandy Shaw (New York: Warner Books, 1982). This one allusion brought about all kinds of hair growth products based on the polysorbates. Actually the fatty acids and their esters do have a positive effect on the hair, and I have been using them in hair formulas since 1967. They help the hair, *but they do not grow hair where the hair has come out completely.*

Does Anything Grow Hair?

Like most of the males in my family, my father was bald from a very young age. He spent much of his life creating "hair growing elixirs." He also tried hair growers sold in mail order catalogs and or drug stores in the 40's and 50's. Every day he massaged the various treatments faithfully onto his head. He'd see some fuzz and say "This one is doing the job!" but he never grew any hair that covered his head and looked like hair. He got the same results then as you would get from the various treatments around today, including minoxidil.

When I worked with minoxidil I asked the dermatologist to give me before and after pictures of anybody who grew hair. He had none to give. He said, however, that since patients began using my 5% minoxidil cream their hair was in much better condition and that hair was no longer falling out. It is not the minoxidil, though, that makes the difference: I have found this to be true with all the products and ingredients I suggest using in the **Natural Method of Hair Care**. What your hair care products contain and how you use them can help or damage your hair. Because my minoxidil formula contained various natural substances, like amino acids, it is far superior to any commercially made, but even the best minoxidil formula around is still not worth the money or the risk of side effects this treatment requires.

There is nothing on the market, either for four dollars or four hundred dollars, that will grow hair where hair is missing. However, and this is a big HOWEVER, you can prevent hair from coming out, and in some cases grow hair back if there is any possibility of reviving the root of the follicle.

You CAN prevent hair loss and in some cases grow hair. You will not do this with a magic shampoo or cream, so don't send in that coupon or call for that product advertised on TV. You can only get this with a system of hair care that relies on natural ingredients. Before I outline the **Natural Method of Hair Care** and the various substances that can give you a full, thick, healthy head of hair, let me tell you more about your hair.

The Hair Growth Cycle and Hair Loss

"The very hairs of your head are all numbered," says the Bible. While this refers to the number of years we are alive, we can take it literally: our hairs ARE numbered. Many cosmetic chemists say that hair is dead, but nothing could be further from the truth. each hair has its own life cycle that is completely independent of every other hair. Our scalp is made up of hairs which are actively growing, hairs which are at rest, and hairs which are dead and will either fall out and be replaced or will fall out and not be replaced.

One researcher studied the growth cycle on an area that contained 230 hairs over a period of two weeks. She found that 45% of all hairs grew in this two week period. She also measured the size of hair follicles and found that the small hairs had short periods of growth and longer resting periods (no growth) and that larger hairs had longer periods of growth and shorter periods of rest. (M. Trotter, "The life cycles of hair in selected regions of the body," *Am. J. Phys. Anthropol.,* 7:427, 1924).

The growth of hair depends on the production of cells by mitosis at the sides of the papilla. The cells are, at first, very soft and are funneled upward above the region where the follicle ceases to be narrow. At this point the cells are keratinized and become hard and horny so they retain their shapes for the life of the hair. The stage at which hair is actively growing is called anagen, which usually lasts from 18 months to several years. This anagen period dictates the life of the hair and how long the hair will be. Most hair never gets longer than 36 inches. Some people, though, can grow hair long enough to sit on, while others never grow hair longer than shoulder-length.

The period when the hair stops growing is called catagen. At this point the hair forms a brush-like mass when it is keratinized. The final stage of the hair growth cycle is known as telogen, which means no further growth occurs. The hair follicle begins to shrink upwards, the lower half folding or wrinkling, and it atrophies into this position, held by the brush-like mass formed during the catagen phase.

By understanding this growth cycle, we can also understand that proper hair care seeks to complement the natural process of hair growth. Massaging the scalp during the catagen phase may stimulate hair to grow again. Even when the hair is between the catagen and telogen phases, massaging or plucking out the brush-like mass may cause the hair to grow again.

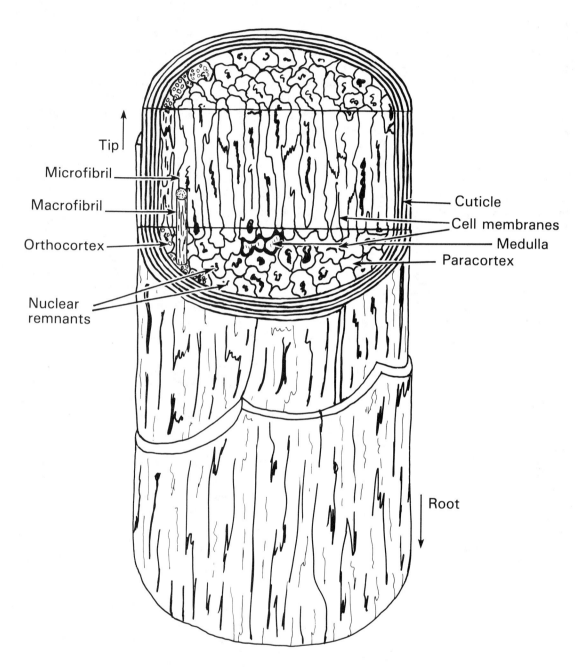

Tip

Microfibril

Macrofibril

Orthocortex

Nuclear
remnants

Cuticle

Cell membranes

Medulla

Paracortex

Root

Diagrammatic Sketch of a
Section of a Hair Fiber

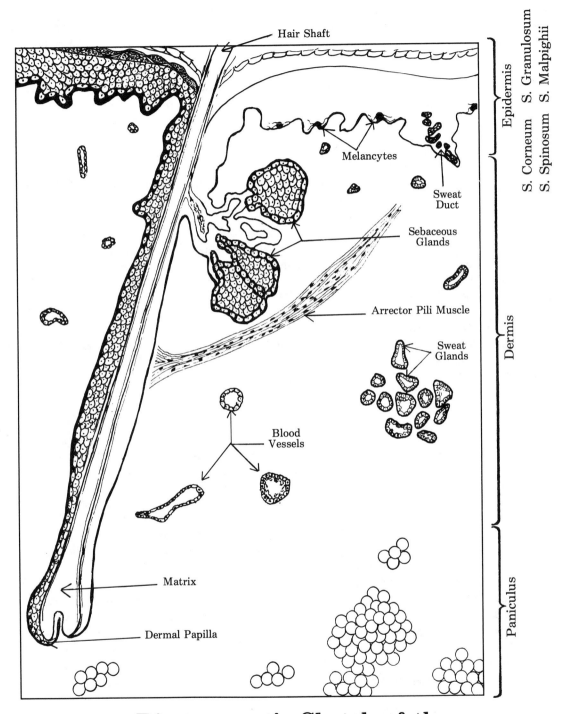

Diagrammatic Sketch of the Hair Root to Paniculus

You can't know exactly when each cycle is taking place because it happens on a hair-by-hair basis, depending on cell mitosis. This is the importance of daily natural hair care: to choose substances which encourage mitosis and a clean, clear scalp, and which encourage longer anagenic and catagenic stages of hair growth so that hair continues to grow and replenish.

The Structure and Chemistry of Your Hair

The hair is a far more complicated structure than most cosmetic manufacturers would have us believe: but don't take my word for this. Read the labels of hair care products, and you'll see for yourself. Practically all shampoos consist of synthetic detergents; hair conditioners contain a mixture of water, synthetic emollients, and quaternary ammonium compounds (predominantly stearylkonium chloride). Both the syndets and the quats originated in the fabric care industry, but your hair is a living fabric that needs a far more life-sustaining treatment than that afforded by these harsh chemicals. Only with a thorough knowledge of the hair's structure and biochemistry can you make an informed choice of the best ingredients to care for your hair.

Let's begin with the hair structure diagram on page 324. The hair shaft consists of an external layer of imbricated horny cells known as the cuticle, which is quite similar to that of the skin: an epidermis consisting of an outer and an inner coat. The hair cuticle surrounds a mass of spindle-shaped cells identified in our diagram as the paracortex and the orthocortex. Now, let's go deeper into the hair fiber. We find there a column of superimposed cells called the medulla. This is the central canal or the innermost section of the hair shaft. It has polygonal cells which contain keratohyalin, fat granules, air space, and pigment matter.

The diagram on page 324 shows the hair in relation to its support mechanisms in the body. The root of the hair contains a bulb which rests on the papilla through which run the blood vessels which supply hair nourishment. Along the hair follicles a fatty substance known as sebum is secreted, which gives the hair luster and pliability and keeps the skin surface soft and supple.

Sebum is a complex mixture of lipid substances secreted by the sebaceous glands. The exact composition of sebum is not known, but it does contain various fatty acids both saturated and unsaturated as well as straight-chained and branch-chained molecules, most of which are converted into triglycerides. Within the sebaceous ducts, the esters are acted on by enzymes and are broken down to diglycerides, monoglycerides and free fatty acids. Sebum may be analyzed as containing the following: free fatty acids 10-30%, triglycerides 20-40%, waxes 14%, cholesterol 2%, cholesterol esters 2%, sterols 0.4%, squalene 5-10%, paraffins 2-10%, diols 2%; other materials 2-5% (F. J. Ebling, *A Handbook of Cosmetic Science*, H. W. Hibbott, ed., Oxford: Pergamon Press, 1963). In cosmetic products, fatty acids or essential fatty acids is similar to sebum in their ability to lubricate the hair and skin.

A human hair is stronger than a similarly-sized fiber of aluminum, copper, or nylon. Its strength comes from its chemical constituents, amino acids, and their unique chemical arrangements. Hair is made of keratin, a protein containing eighteen amino acids. Keratin is also present in feathers, wool, horns, hooves, nails, and skin, although the ratio of amino acids with other forms of keratin varies (See **CHAPTER VIII** for a complete analysis of keratin). Keratin is held together by several different kinds of polypeptide bonds, but the one that gives it its extreme strength and insolubility is the disulfide bond, a chemical link between two sulfur atoms.

Human hair keratin contains two sulfur-containing amino acids, methionine (0.6%) and cystine (18%). In fact, keratin contains more cystine than any other amino acid. Due to its structure of two amine groups and two carboxyl groups, cystine enters into two polypeptide (amino acid) chains, which are then linked together by a disulfide bond.

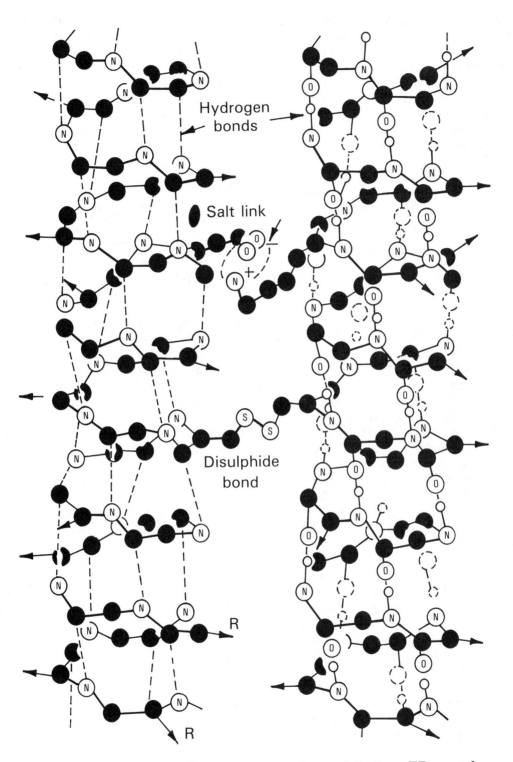

Pauling-Corey Structure for Alpha-Keratin

The complex arrangement of keratin fibers within a single strand of hair also contributes to the strength of the hair. Linus Pauling and his co-workers proposed a structure in which the polypeptide chains assume a double helix with 3.7 amino acids per turn. (See page 327.) Each turn of the helix is located relative to the next turn by hydrogen bond formation between the carbonyl and amine groups of amino acids (L. Pauling and R. B. Corey, *Proc. Nat. Acad. Sci. Wash.*, 37 [1951]; *Nature*, 171 [1953]; J. Am. Chem. Soc. 72 [1950]).

Pauling and Corey have suggested that the alpha-keratin helix may be a double helix coiled around an axis so that a compound helix is formed, resembling a seven-strand cable. The axis of this compound helix could be made up on the crystalline region of keratin.

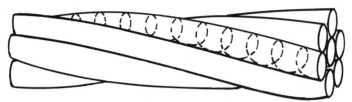

Structure of "crystalline regions" of keratin

This helix structure of the hair is not always well-organized due to the irregularities in the materials from which the keratin is formed. The difficulty of packing the side chains of 18 widely differing amino acids into a long polypeptide chain may lead to an unstable helix structure and a variable ratio between crystalline and amorphous material in the hair.

The correct balance of crystalline and amorphous material in the hair is unknown, but the structure of the crystalline regions of keratin seem to be important to the alpha-keratin helix as described by Pauling and Corey. Obviously if this region lacks a closely packed or a slightly imperfect crystalline, then the structure is weak and easily damaged. It can, of course, be damaged by chemicals based on the rendering of the insoluble keratin into soluble or dissolvable strands. (See diagram on page 327).

The hair structure is based on hydrogen bonds, salt links, and disulfide bonds. The disulfide bonds are formed from the amino acid cystine. Linkages involving other amino acids such as serine, threonine, and tyrosine, have been suggested, but there is no supporting evidence. Further, the chemical behavior of the hair can be explained in terms of hydrogen bonds, salt linkages, and disulfide bonds.

Hair keratin is insoluble in aqueous salt solutions, weak acids, weak alkalis, and neutral urea solutions. Water can alter its appearance, i.e., if you set your hair wet it will hold the set when it dries, but this change is temporary and will disappear when hair becomes wet again (as anybody caught in the rain with a fresh hair style will corroborate). In acid solutions between a pH of 1 and 2, swelling of the hair fibers occurs, and both hydrogen bonds and salt links are broken. Only the disulfide bond keeps the structure sound, but some hair damage occurs. In an alkaline solution at pH 10, the swelling occurs with the same results as the acid solutions of pH 1 and 2. At a pH of 12, the disulfide bonds begin to break down, and the hair is dissolved.

Both permanent wave solutions and depilatories use the same chemicals: the difference between the two is that depilatories are stronger solutions that completely dissolve the chemical bonds that hold hair together, while permanent waves seek to alter the chemical bonds while maintaining the integrity of the hair. This balance is difficult to judge, which is why permanent waving of the hair will cause severe hair damage. Even though the thioglycolate wave solution has only a pH of 9.5 and is considered mild, the chemical reaction on the alpha-keratin helix can be disastrous over an extended period of time. The continual waving of the hair in this manner leads to over-processed hair that is frizzy, dull, and brittle. Other chemicals that have been found to affect all three types of bonds are sodium sulfide, sodium thioglycolate, thioglycolic acid, ureabisulfite, potassium cyanide, chlorine dioxide, peracetic acid, phenol, and mercaptoethanol.

The chemistry behind hair color is very interesting. The color of our hair is inherited. The two main hair pigments are melanin and pheomelanin. These two coloring agents are formed in the melanocyte cells located on the upper part of the dermal papilla. These cells have long tentacles (called dendrites) which introduce the pigment particles into the cortical cells which are soft and unkeratinized. The melanin actually starts out as colorless granules, but contain the amino acid tyrosine. This is acted on by the enzyme tyrosinase and the melanin granules become black in color. If the granules are small, the color is lighter, but if they are large, the color is darker (the large granules are fewer but give a jet black hair color). The other pigment chemical, pheomelanin, is the result of the interference of tryptophan in the tyrosine-tyrosinase reaction. Tryptophan when combined with pheomelanin granules (which are brownish-yellow) yields colors ranging from brown to yellow. Minerals enter the picture as iron pigments combine with ash to create red hair. Red hair, according to Boldt, is made up of trichosiderins (iron complexes) combined with three distinct pigments whose color is not due to iron (P. Boldt and E. Z. Hermestedt, *Naturforsch*, B22, 7, 718, 1967).

One of the reasons hair turns gray is a copper deficiency which prohibits the formation of tyrosinase there by interrupting the pigmentation process. Perhaps the reason pantothenic acid has been reported to reverse graying is that this nutrient has some function in bonding copper to tyrosinase. Zinc deficiency can also cause a loss of pigment because this mineral plays a role in the decarboxylation process of dopachrome (the activation of tyrosinase requires the amino acid DOPA and ascorbic acid to produce dopachrome). As a person ages there is a loss of tyrosinase activity and in some instances this has been reversed with an intake of large amounts of para-aminobenzoic acid (PABA). The actor Robert Cummings is an example of someone who has successfully taken vitamins to prevent gray hair. In his seventies, he still has dark hair with no gray; in order to play the part of an old man his hair had to be artificially colored gray.

Synthetic hair dyes, bleaches, and permanent wave solutions chemically and drastically change the hair. Bleaching is damaging to the hair because it destroys the hair's melanin. Permanent dyes are harmful because they contain irritating chemicals, many of which are commonly known to be carcinogenic. Permanent waves weaken the hair's cystine bridge which gives it strength and elasticity.

Because the chemical structure of the hair can be altered or destroyed by some chemicals, we can't simply view it as fabric and work on the assumption that a detergent that washes pants and skirts will be fine for the hair. Nor will the chemicals that soften clothes restore hair after it has been damaged. And we certainly can't hope to maintain the structural integrity of the hair if we are constantly bombarding it with depilatory-type chemicals. Ingredients are of the utmost importance in hair care, but manufacturers of hair care products seem intent on ignoring the unique complex chemistry, physiology and structure of the hair.

One advertising strategy some cosmetic manufacturers use to put consumers off the scent of inherently harmful ingredients used in hair care products is the pH-balanced myth. Although I discuss this at length in **CHAPTER IV**, let me reiterate that there is no evidence that the pH range between 4.5 to 6 is best for the hair and skin. Soaps and shampoos are more effective at a pH of 8.0 to 10.0, and synthetic shampoos are effective at a pH of 6.0 to 9.0 (J. C. Harris, "Detergency evaluation testing," New York: Interscience Pub., 1954). It has been my observation that a natural shampoo with a pH of about 6.0 to 7.5 and a natural shampoo with a pH of 8.0 to 9.0 work about the same and leave the hair clean and healthy. I did find that the condition of the hair differed depending on whether it was shampooed with a natural coconut or palm kernel type soap or a synthetic detergent such as sodium lauryl sulfate. The synthetic detergent left the hair feeling brittle and straw-like, while the natural soap left the hair feeling clean but not stripped of all natural oils. When I added acid to the syndet, there was no change. The hair responded to the chemical formula itself and not to the pH. A shampoo and soap in the range of 5.5 to 10 has no influence on the irritancy of the product. Shampoos, soaps, and cleansers with this wide range of pH readings irritated the skin or damaged the hair when the product contained alkyl sulfates (like sodium lauryl sulfate). The hair reacts to the formula and not the altered pH of the formula. The pH is only an indicator. The pH of the aqueous solutions of the surface active agent is not characteristic of the compound but is influenced by the manufacturing process and does not in any way reflect the ingredients.

In hair care products (as in all cosmetics) the ingredients are what make the products succeed or fail in maintaining your health and beauty. The ingredients that I have found best support hair health: natural ingredients which nourish the hair at a very essential level. Of paramount importance among these ingredients are the sulfur-containing amino acids. These amino acids are essential to protein metabolism, which is to say, essential to life itself. During metabolism they give up their sulfur and thereby enable the body to synthesize its own amino acids (endogenous amino acids). Metabolism of the sulfur-containing amino acids proceeds via a complicated redox reaction and transmethylation, which are responsible for a satisfactory condition of the hair and skin.

Sulfur-containing amino acids are important in hair and skin care products because the majority of the body's sulfur (around 100 g) is located in the hair, skin, and nails. The hair protein keratin accounts for most of the sulfur in the body: human hair contains 3.92% to 5.47% sulfur. The cystine content of the hair varies, depending on the person's age and hair color, but hair which is falling out has a lower cystine and silica content.   The amino acid cystine (which makes up 18% of human hair keratin) provides for the regular intramolecular structure of keratin on which the elasticity and strength of the hair depend. Seborrhea (over-oiliness) of the scalp is also helped by cystine, as well as by methionine. Methionine, particularly, is indispensable for growth and renewal of bodily substances.

Shampoos and conditioners which contain the amino acid cystine, proteins combined with cystine, and the other sulfur-containing amino acids have been found to be excellent hair care products. Herbals high in cystine and organic silica are important hair care ingredients: horsetail *(Equisetum aruense)* has up to 7% silica and cystine; coltsfoot *(Tussilago farfara)* also contains both silica and cystine. These two herbs have been termed the hair care complex because of the positive effect they have on hair. A milk protein called lactalbumin has a positive effect on the hair and helps damaged hair, especially when combined with the sulfur-containing amino acids. I have found fatty acids when used in the shampoos and conditioners containing the amino acids and proteins discussed above have a positive effect on the dry hair that results from over-processing, chemicalizing, and mechanically traumatizing the hair.

The first hair conditioner I developed for damaged hair contained a mixture of protein and the sulfur-containing amino acids (as well as glycogen). The results on seriously salon-damaged hair were easy to observe within hours of the application. People who had hair damaged from hair straighteners (usually blacks who wished to straighten their hair) had excellent results when the conditioner was applied to the hair.

The conditioner contained the elements that could be used by the alpha-keratin structure: an essential fatty acid-amino acid base (which included the amino acids cystine, cysteine, and methionine), lactalbumin (a milk protein high in the eight essential amino acids); rosemary, sage, horsetail and coltsfoot (both high in silicic acid and cystine), nettle, glycogen, balsam tolu, vitamins A, B, C, and E. At the time I formulated the conditioner (1967-68) I thought the glycogen was correcting the damaged hair or perhaps the lactalbumin, but now I think the combined essential fatty acids and the sulfur-containing amino acids (including that in the herbals) were what made the difference. I can't discount the good effects of the other ingredients, but since then I have utilized herbals with cystine as well as a mixture of the sulfur-containing amino acids directly in products and have been able to observe the results over a 15 year period.

I have also tried other amino acids, such as the ones mentioned above, in hair care products for the purpose of restoring the "cystine bridge" and repairing hair damage, but only cystine gives good results. I have utilized all 25 amino acids to observe the results on the hair, and only the sulfur-containing amino acids give observable results, (i. e., hair repair, fuller hair, and overall healthier hair).

Dandruff and Other Scalp Problems

The disease known as dandruff can occur at any age in men and women. Several scalp conditions can cause a scaly condition of the scalp (skin) and the cause may differ widely. What happens in most dandruff cases is that the outer layer of the epidermis of the scalp does not disappear or powder off but forms large scales which are easily visible. When it is functioning properly, the scalp follows the usual growth cycle of the skin. The cells develop in the inner portion of the epidermis (stratum mucosum), and force the old cell layers outwards. When the old cells are forced away from the *stratum mucosum,* they lose their pigment (melanin) and become flatter, forming a cross-link structure void of water. They also lose all contact with the lymph which flows among the cells of the stratum mucosum. When this occurs the dead cells become a keratinous powder which usually is washed or groomed away unnoticed. The problem is when they form large visible scales. Obviously, though, the cause is not really known. Anything that upsets the keratinization or cell growth processes can contribute to the development of dandruff. Some of the chemical causes are hairsprays, strong synthetic shampoos that degrease the hair, alcohol lotions or grooming agents, and highly alkaline or acid products which can break down the *stratum corneum* into scales before the normal cellular cycle desquamates the old cells. Scales can also be caused by mechanical means such as excessive combing, brushing, scratching, or using a hairdryer on the hair.

One type of dandruff has been given a name: "pityriasis simplex capitis." This disease does not usually occur until after the age of 12. While there is no inflammation of the scalp, and at times no itching, it is the process of scratching that forms the scales: the more scratching, the more scales. Keeping the hair clean helps, but the scales return within 48 hours. It is believed that this form of dandruff is a malfunction of the scalp or other organs, but microbial attack of the scalp has also been suspected as a cause (perhaps it is both).

The factors within the body that can cause this type of dandruff are hormonal imbalance, impaired metabolic nutrition, dietary factors, and tension. The external factors are biochemical changes of the scalp, increased activity of bacteria and fungi, the use of topical medications, and cosmetics that irritate the scalp.

In 1874, a physician named Malassez discovered a yeast-like organism known as *Pityrosporum ovule* in dandruff scales. He believed it was the sole cause of dandruff. He also pointed out that this organism does not exist in nature away from humans (L. Malassez, *Arch. Physiol. Norm. Path.*, 1, 485, 1874).

It is doubtful if this particular organism causes all cases of dandruff, but perhaps a combination of the condition of the body, care of the hair, and bacteria could be a cause. Certainly a dry scalp and dry skin can cause dandruff whether the yeast-like organism is present or not.

A greasy scalp that is not kept clean will definitely cause a dandruff condition.

Can shampoos treat dandruff? The shampoos usually manufactured for dandruff contain a shampoo base plus a tar chemical, or a tar solution combined with the sodium salt of the sulphosuccinate of an undecylene alkanolamide. These chemicals can give a temporary control, but in order for a shampoo to prevent the recurrence of dandruff, it must work for a period of at least seven days, and then you would have to use it all the time to alleviate the dandruff completely. It doesn't work. Some of the chemicals that have been used are hexachlorophene, tar, salicylic acids, sulfur, resorcinol, cationic compounds, zinc pyridinium-thiol-N-oxide, zinc undecylenate. I will also add to this list some I have found very effective: selenium, sulfur amino acid complex (cysteine, cystine, methionine), and herbs predominantly rich in sulfur and silicic acid (i.e., stinging nettle, coltsfoot and horsetails). Other herbs such as rosemary, sage, and American bearsfoot are known as herbal-dandruff treatments.

Substances to Look for in Anti-Dandruff Products

Ingredient (Arranged according to natural quality, preference, and safety)	Comments and Use
Selenium	This is effective in a shampoo, but for best results should be combined in a formula that also contains amino acids (especially the sulfur-containing amino acids cysteine, cystine, and methionine) and the herbs coltsfoot, horsetail, allantoin, rosemary, and sage.
Sulfur-Containing Amino Acids (Cysteine, Cystine, Methionine)	The sulfur-containing amino acids are beneficial in a shampoo or conditioner. The use of both the shampoo and the conditioner daily may be required.
Sulfur	This ingredient should appear on a product label as sulfur, biosulfur, or organic sulfur. It can be used in shampoos, conditioners, or scalp ointments. The importance of sulfur for the skin and hair is apparent as it is found in protein (in the sulfur-containing amino acids) and in the tissue substances chondroitin sulfuric acid and hyaluronic acid. Homeopathy has long recommended the internal (oral) use of sulfur for functional disorders of the body. As early as the 16th century, Paracelsus employed sulfur-type preparations. Sulfur has a keratoplastic, keratolytic, vasconstrictive, and anti-parasitic action which would act against the dandruff organism *pityriasis simplex capitis*. A deficiency of sulfur or a disorder of the sulfur metabolism is characterized by atrophied mucous membranes, including the sebaceous glands. It is these problems that lead to dandruff, seborrhea, hair loss, and systemic susceptibility to infections. Sulfur can be absorbed into the skin and scalp and incorporated into the keratin of the hair.

Horsetails, Coltsfoot, Nettles

Rich in sulfur and silicic acid, these three herbals promote blood flow in the scalp which contributes to their anti-seborrheic and general positive effects on the hair. Coltsfoot is rich in sulfur, containing about 26%. Horsetails contain both cystine and up to 7% silicic acid as well as sulfur. Nettles contain a small amount of these elements. Look for horsetails and coltsfoot on the labels of shampoos or conditioners. It would be best to use both a shampoo and a conditioner containing these substances.

B Vitamins (D-Panthenol, Inositol)

The B vitamins are important to the hair and skin (scalp) as regulators of the metabolic function and components of an active group of enzymes essential for skin cell respiration. The two most important are d-panthenol and inositol. Regular treatment with d-panthenol mitigates various hair defects such as seborrhea and hair loss. Inositol exerts a generally favorable influence on the metabolism of the scalp, and prevents damage to the hair. These nutrients can be absorbed through the scalp and into hair keratin. They can be used in shampoos and conditioners.

Zinc

I have used the mineral "calamine" for zinc, but zinc can be obtained in several forms. The main problem with using zinc in products for the hair (though it is a dandruff treatment) is that it leaves a white or pinkish residue on the hair and skin. It can be used in a shampoo formula where the residue would be rinsed away, but as an ointment the formula would have to be prepared to compensate for the residue.

Salicylic Acid

This is also known as ortho-hydroxybenzoic acid. This is usually a synthesized chemical, but salicylates occur naturally in the following plants: cloves *(Syzygium aromatica)*, coca *(Erythroxylum coca)*, and yarrow *(Achillea millefolium)*. It also occurs naturally in the form of salicin (a glucoside of salicyl alcohol) in the buds of Balm of Gilead *(Populus tacamahacca)*. In birch oil *(betula lenta)*, salicylic acid is found in the form of methyl salicylate (98%), but methyl salicylate also occurs in cananga oil *(Cananga odorant)*, cassie absolute *(Acacia farnesiana)*, pipsissewa *(Chimaphila umbellata)*, tamarind *(Tamarindus indica)*, and of course, wintergreen oil *(Gaultheria procumbens)*. Like salicylates in general, methyl saliyclate has antipyretic, antiinflammatory and analgesic properties. However, as little as 4.7 grams of the pure chemical can be fatal to children. The highest use level in food should be 0.1%. It is a counterirritant and an antiarthritic in ointments and liniments. It probably does quite a job on dandruff, but has a very strong odor even in small amounts.

Salicylic Acid con't

Acetylsalicylic acid, a synthesized form of salicylic acid, is today the common drug known as aspirin, used as a pain reliever and analgesic. In traditional medicine Balm of Gilead buds were used for this same purpose with sores, cuts, bruises, pimples, and as a dandruff treatment as well.

Rosemary and Sage

Has offered some relief from dandruff in a hair rinse, shampoo and conditioner. Use all three forms.

Saponins

Saponins are glycosides (sugar-containing compounds which on hydrolysis yield one or more sugars) with sterols or triterpenes as part of their aglycone portions. Saponins are found in many plant extracts, such as yucca root, quillaya bark, sarsaparilla, ginseng, alfalfa, fenugreek seeds, and licorice. We are interested here in the saponins that have been beneficial in the treatment of dandruff. The most successful of these is quillaya bark *(Quillaja saponaria)*. This South American herbal is very effective in a shampoo for treating dandruff and was used for this purpose in folk medicine (see **HERB CHART**). I have created a shampoo using quillaya bark combined with coconut and castile soap for this purpose. Yucca root and ginseng root also seem to be an aid in the treatment of dandruff, itching, and as a tonic to the hair.

Tar

Though coal tar solutions are used to prepare antidandruff shampoos, they are not safe ingredients. Juniper tar oil, however, is a nontoxic replacement for coal tar. Juniper tar is the cade oil extract of *Juniperus oxycedrus*. Cade oil is obtained from the distillation of the branches and wood of this small tree native to the Mediterranean. Cade oil has been used for eczema, and to make a natural juniper tar antioxidant shampoo (see **HERB CHART**).

**Other Antidandruff Herbs:
Sweet Bay, Red Squill,
Valerian, Goldenseal,
Garlic**

Sweet bay *(Laurus nobilis)* has bactericidal and fungicidal properties. It has antidandruff activities and can be used in hair tonics and shampoos. **Red squill** *(Urginea maritima)* has a methanol extract with an active principle known as *scilliroside* that has been found to be effective in the treatment of dandruff and seborrhea. **Valerian** *(Valeriana officinalis)* has an ethanol extract that has antidandruff properties. **Garlic** *(Allium sativum)* has sulfur compounds that give it antimicrobial and antidandruff activity. If it doesn't work to clear up your dandruff, at least it will keep people far enough way they won't see the problem!

CHAPTER XVII

The Natural Method
of
Hair Care

In the last chapter we learned about the hair and some of the natural substances that will keep the hair healthy. We were also able to set aside the myth that there's a magic elixir that will grow hair. We had a chance to become familiar with the various ingredients that can help dandruff, scurf, and dead cells that can pile up on the hair. We will be talking about some of these same ingredients when we discuss **The Natural Method of Hair Care** because the substances that are beneficial to the hair as possible antidandruff treatments are also good for a full healthy head of hair. Now we will get down to the basics of taking care of your hair.

Exactly how do you take care of your hair (and scalp) in a way that assures you of a full, lustrous, healthy head of hair? There is so much information and so many products on the market, what do you do? In this book I try not to suggest products because taking care of your hair, just like taking care of your skin, is quite individual. My **Natural Method**, which has been so successful for thousands of men and women, is based on certain products and certain mixtures of ingredients, but at the same time it is possible to use it with various brands of products, although finding good natural products or the right combinations of natural ingredients is difficult. It's vitally important to ask yourself, the following questions though, before buying any product. What does the product have in it? Does it contain chemicals you should avoid? Does it have certain ingredients that have benefits for your hair and scalp? How natural is the product? Even if it is natural, what has the manufacturer added for your hair and not simply to sell you a product based on a specific advertised ingredient? Always read the label and base your purchase on these factors.

What is The Natural Method of Hair Care?

The Natural Method of Hair Care is so simple it can be stated in three steps: 1. Shampoo. 2. Herbal Rinse. 3. Condition. That's all there is to it. There is one catch to these three simple steps, though, and that is to use the correct ingredients in good natural formulas that are appropriate to your hair and scalp needs. I have already pointed out in **CHAPTER XVI** some of the important ingredients to look for in a product especially for scalp problems such as dandruff, and I pointed out that the structure and chemical composition of the hair tells you what to use on your hair and how to care for it. This is exactly how I developed **The Natural Method of Hair Care** and how I arrived at what ingredients to use.

What you don't put on your hair and into your scalp can be just as important as what you do, and it's also as important in **The Natural Method**. I can assure you of one thing: your hair will be full and healthy-looking if you put **The Natural Method** to work, and if you are a man worried about losing your hair it is very likely that you will not lose your hair. One thing is certain: you stand a better chance of keeping your hair than using any hair growing chemical.

I am going to discuss using **The Natural Method of Hair Care** according to hair type and special needs, but even if you aren't sure of what exactly your hair type is, **The Natural Method** still works the same. Since the three types of products you use on your hair are shampoo, herbal rinse, and conditioner, let's learn something about these three products.

Shampoo

Regardless of what ads tell you, **The Natural Method** works best if you change shampoos from time to time. Yes, you can have one you like most and use it most of the time, but my research has taught me that you can't have a perfect shampoo with every important ingredient in it. Also, hair goes through changes as does your environment. Hair responds in different ways to heat, cold, smoke, diet, and chemicals. Choose about three or four shampoos that work best for your, based on the ingredients in them. Alternate among them every few days. It will cost you no more and the benefits will be ample compensation for your hair.

Never use shampoos that contain alkyl sulfates. Never use a shampoo with amphoteric or anionic surfactants. Never use shampoos that contain propylene glycol or any other petrochemical. The trick is to read the label on the shampoo and simply NOT to buy it if it doesn't have a natural-type soap made with either coconut oil, palm kernel oil, or olive oil (such as a mild castile soap). Don't worry about hard or soft water or a film being left on your hair from these natural soaps because a good formula will not have this effect. Also, bear in mind that you are using **The Natural Method of Hair Care**, and the problem labeled "soap buildup" is not a problem for you: your insistence on a natural soap-based shampoo is a problem for cosmetic chemists and merchandisers. They will try to sell you synthetic detergents with the argument that they rinse out of the hair better or work better in all sorts of water. Synthetic detergents do suds better than natural soaps, but it's not the sudsing action that cleans your hair. This is not to say that natural shampoos don't suds at all: it's a question of degree, and once your hair is in good condition and is not too greasy or dirty, when you shampoo, you will get a little better sudsing action from even the natural shampoos. What's important is not the sudsing of the shampoo, not the fragrance of the shampoo, but if it is truly beneficial to your hair.

The shampoos you buy should be natural with natural ingredients to benefit the health of your hair. By the time you're through with this chapter you will know what those benefits are for your hair's health.

I know I've discussed exhaustively the pH question, but, again, let me emphasize that the pH of a shampoo has nothing to do with whether it will be good for your hair. I know you have heard so much advertising hype about this, but disregard these claims and this hype. What does it matter if the pH of a shampoo is 4.5 or 5.4 if it contains chemicals like sodium lauryl sulfate, TEA laureth sulfate, ammonium laureth sulfate, or triethanolamine? The perfect shampoo is not the pH balanced shampoo: it's the shampoo with the best ingredients.

Remember I said not to use amphoteric surfactants or detergents. The main reason for these chemicals is to improve the conditioning properties of a shampoo. It has been suggested that the amin oxides are excellent detergent additives for this purpose. They aren't, and you don't need them. The best conditioning additives for shampoos are natural fatty acids and herbal essential oils. They are so far superior to any synthetic chemical mixture that it is almost an insult to your hair to pour on it the various synthetic detergents and related chemicals. Also bear in mind that in **The Natural Method of Hair Care** you are not depending on a shampoo to do everything for your hair: you are using a *system* of hair care. All the books on shampoo chemicals are written without a solid hair care method in mind. They are written by chemists and self-styled beauty experts who got their knowledge from one of three sources (probably a mixture): from cosmetic manufacturers, from beauty "schools," or from the incidental and anecdotal "what works for them" approach. None of these methods affords a broad perspective and the first two are completely slanted towards synthetic chemicals and away from natural ones. The third approach, recommending products because the author has had good results on his or her own hair and skin, is unreliable, inconclusive, and untrustworthy.

When you choose a shampoo you are also not interested in the following additives (which do nothing for your hair): conditioning agents (except natural extracts for a specific purpose such as aloe vera, panthenol, jojoba, etc.); 2. pearlescent agents (that give shampoos a pearly look but are drying to the hair); 3. sequestrants (added to keep mineral ions from clouding solutions - i.e., added for merchandising concerns not for the improved health of your hair); colors (merchandising concern - plus, artificial or coal tar colors have carcinogenic potential); perfumes (most allergenic type of additive, although natural essential oils can be beneficial to the hair and at the same time add a pleasant aroma to the shampoo); synthetic preservatives (look instead for preservatives made with vitamins C and E which can also act as a blocking agent against the formation of the nitrosamine NDELA often found in shampoos). See **DICTIONARY**.

Herbal Rinse

The second step (or sometimes the third) in your **Natural Method of Hair Care** is using an herbal rinse. An herbal rinse for the hair is like a facial astringent and toner for the skin; it removes soap films, oils, and accomplishes other positive hair care chores. You can make your own herbal rinse or purchase in a health food store. Again, you want to read the ingredients. Don't use one that has isopropyl alcohol or acetone. Some of the best ingredients to look for are rosemary, sage, lemon balm, horsetail, coltsfoot, camomile, peppermint, and neutral henna (which is especially good for oily hair). If your hair tends to be dry, use the herbal rinse between the shampoo and conditioning steps. If your hair tends to be oily, use the herbal rinse as your last step (after conditioning the hair).

Conditioner

A good natural conditioner is important to you no matter what type of hair you have. If your hair has been colored, bleached, or otherwise chemicalized, a conditioner is utterly vital to your hair. A good conditioner can repair hair damage; it can rebuild the cystine bridge damaged by chemicals or heat or rough treatment. Here is a list of ingredients for the best hair conditioner you can use for all types of hair, including seriously damaged hair. It can even help reverse hair loss. This is a glycogen protein balanced conditioner. This means the conditioner can help repair damaged hair (with protein) and encourage mitosis (cell growth). Here are the ingredients to look for in this type of conditioner: essential fatty acids, amino acids (cysteine, cystine, and methionine), lactalbumin (this is a milk protein far superior to hydrolyzed animal protein), rosemary, sage, horsetail, coltsfoot (these herbs contain silicic acid and amino acids), nettle, and glycogen polysaccharide. I first used this combination of hair conditioning ingredients over 20 years ago in beauty salons in New York, in the kind of shops that perm, bleach, tone, color, straighten, and frost hair all day long. Sometimes the conditioner was used to save an over-processed head of hair that would have otherwise resulted in a lawsuit to the beautician. This combination of ingredients seems to work magic on all types of hair, and it does the very practical job of keeping a healthy head of hair full, lustrous, and beautiful. You can also use a very simple conditioner that gives good results with the following mixture of ingredients: jojoba oil, aloe vera, and coconut fatty acids.

You can find these conditioners in most good health food stores, but be sure to check the ingredients label to be sure chemicals such as hydrolyzed animal protein, stearalkonium chloride, or mineral oil derivatives such as propylene glycol aren't used in the hair conditioner. Natural herbal oils, fatty acids, amino acids, and milk protein are the best ingredients. A pH of about 4 or 5 is best for a hair conditioner.

What Type of Hair Do You Have?

Now that you know the three important steps in **The Natural Method of Hair Care**, let's find out how to use the **Method** depending on the hair type you have, but bear in mind that no matter what hair type you have, the three steps of shampoo, rinse, and condition will work just the same.

Oily hair feels and looks greasy at the roots of the hair, often just a few hours after shampooing. Yet the ends of the hair can be dry, particularly if hair has been permed or colored. Dandruff may be a problem; lack of body is very probably a problem if your hair is dry.

Dry hair feels brittle and strawlike at the ends. It is dull, and may be flyaway with many split ends. It may look bushy and frizzy, but it lacks true body that can be styled attractively.

Normal hair is glossy and manageable. It looks full, has plenty of body and can be styled effectively.

Test Your Hair For Body

Loss of body can be brought about by many things. UV rays, hair sprays (which seem to support hair body but actually makes the hair dry and limp in the long run), and a whole variety of chemicals reduce body. Remember, too, some people genetically have more body in their hair than other people. The problem with lack of body in your hair is that it leads to three other problems: less elasticity, less flexibility, and less strength.

Look carefully at your hair. Does it look limp and flat shortly after you've washed and groomed it? Hairspray can weigh it down and make it look flat and limp. If you use a commercial conditioner that contains a fabric softener such as stearalkonium chloride or some other quaternary ammonium compound, it will make the hair look flat and limp. It will destroy the body your hair naturally has.

Solution: If you already have fine or thin hair, you need a hair treatment that will build up the body in the hair. First, discontinue all commercial hair conditioners (especially those with chemicals such as the "quats" suggested above). Choose a conditioner with some of the ingredients discussed above. The conditioner should have a pH of of 4.5 to 5.5, but be sure it doesn't use a chemical to reach this pH, but rather that it is the result of the natural combination of ingredients. A blend of the various ingredients I've described would not need chemicals added to acidify the formula. If your hair tends to be oily, you may want to use the conditioner between shampoo steps, i.e., shampoo then condition and shampoo again. The best idea is to use an herbal rinse after you condition the hair. Thus your method would be to first shampoo your hair and rinse in warm water. Condition your hair; apply an herbal rinse, and finish with a rinse in plain water.

If your hair looks flat, then your hair may be oily. Choose a shampoo that cleans the hair thoroughly, and I suggest a shampoo with neutral, non-coloring henna. Look for henna in the ingredients list at no lower than the fourth or fifth position so there's enough to aid in building body and reducing oiliness. A henna rinse should have even more henna than the shampoo: in the second or third position. Follow this procedure: shampoo with the henna shampoo; condition hair, and rinse in plain water; rinse hair with henna rinse, and finish by rinsing in warm water. There are other shampoos and conditioners you can choose but look for good hair care ingredients as we've suggested in the preceding chapter and in this chapter (See **CHAPTER XVI**).

What else can give your hair body, since it is obvious that a shampoo alone can hardly do this job? Actually, if you put **The Natural Method of Hair Care** to work you will find out your hair will improve almost on its own. However, don't resort to hairspray and the so-called "body-building" hair care products advertised for mass consumption. The ingredients needed in a good hair care product could not be produced for the mass market. The best way to get natural body in your hair is to use a product with these two natural substances: panthenol (vitamin B_5) and cystine (a sulfur-containing amino acid). Let's take time out now to talk about these two ingredients.

Panthenol (also known as pantothenic acid, calcium pantothenate, and vitamin B_5) is an important vitamin to our body because it aids in the conversion of acetylcholine (a neurotransmitter in the brain) and is very important to our memory process. Panthenol is also important to the citric acid cycle, has a laxative action, reduces peroxidized fats, and perhaps even slows down cross-linking of our bodies' collagen. If panthenol is combined with PABA, beta carotene, vitamin C, and vitamin E, it helps reduce the toxic effects of UV rays and is also an excellent skin moisturizer.

As far as the hair is concerned, panthenol adds body and thickness to the hair without leaving it gummy, unlike so many hairsprays that contain synthetic gums and resins like PVP. If panthenol is combined with just a pinch of herbal gum, it will hold the hair, give it body, add luster, and reduce the dryness and the brittleness caused by the film-forming synthetic agents in hairspray.

Look for a hairspray or conditioner that contains panthenol. Here's a good ingredient list: natural grain alcohol (this acts as a carrying agent - don't settle for isopropyl or SD alcohols), panthenol, an herbal gum such as gum arabic, and aloe vera. Be sure the product has panthenol in at least the second or third position on the ingredients label so there's enough to do a good job.

As I discussed in the last chapter, cystine is one of the important sulfur-containing amino acids (along with cysteine, the non-oxidized form of cystine). This important amino acid can be used topically and is not only important to the hair but also to the skin. Cystine rebuilds hair that has been damaged by chemicals in hairsprays, perm solutions, colors, toners, bleach, hair straighteners, and even hair driers. See the previous chapter for more about the importance of cystine in hair care.

Read the labels of your hair care products see if they contain cystine, cysteine, and methionine, or the herbals that contain these elements (coltsfoot and horsetail) or all of these. When you check the ingredients of your hair care products, these sulfur-containing substances should be in at least sixth or seventh place on the labels of ingredients. If all these substances are in a hair conditioner, they can be in almost any position on the ingredient label since the product has been well-formulated to take advantage of the amino acids and herbals (see above suggestions under "conditioners").

Oily Type Hair

If you wash your hair in the morning and by afternoon it's oily, flat, and limp, then you probably have oily hair. The use of film-forming agents (hairsprays, body waves, gel sets, etc.) on the hair only adds to this problem. Oily hair also attracts more dirt - another reason to shampoo frequently. When it's time to shampoo your hair, the oily condition of your hair reduces the sudsing, and you should lather the hair two or three times. Alcohol solutions and grease-cutting detergents aren't the answer either: they actually make the problem worse. The scalp gets dry and the sebaceous gland pumps more oil along the hair shaft, and you have more grease and dirt on your hair. Sebum also builds up on the scalp, and this can cause a pile up of dead skin cells which comes out of the scalp like dandruff or psoriasis. Oily hair also makes your hair look thinner, so if you're a man with thinning hair which is also oily, your hair looks thinner than it is. What you want is *FAT* hair, and **The Natural Method of Hair Care** can do this for you!

How to Care for Oily Type Hair and Go from Flat Hair to Fat Hair

Use **The Natural Method** on your hair every day. Select about two or three shampoos. Look for some of the following ingredients in these shampoos: quillaya barka (excellent for oily hair and also for dandruff and sebum build-up on the hair); amino acid complex (a blend of amino acids is very helpful to excessive sebum flow in the hair); saponin extracts (like quillaya bark, these extracts which come from sarsaparilla root and yucca root are very helpful); henna (neutral, non-coloring).

Select an herbal hair rinse that contains some of the following ingredients: witch hazel, henna (non-coloring type), horsetail, coltsfoot, peppermint, rosemary, and sage.

1. **Shampoo.** Alternate from one shampoo to the other every few days. First, dampen hair with warm water, and apply shampoo. Massage shampoo through hair and well into scalp. Clean with a firm strong massage motion of the fingers, and then rinse with warm water. Apply shampoo again for a second sudsing, and rinse well with warm water.

2. **Condition.** Apply a conditioner to the ends of your hair only. If your hair is damaged or becomes dry, then apply conditioner all over your hair. Condition oily hair only as you feel it is necessary. Allow conditioner to stay in your hair for about two or three minutes, then rinse conditioner out of hair with warm water for one full minute. Be sure to rinse all the conditioner out of your hair.

3. **Rinse.** Pour the herbal rinse through the hair and massage well through your hair. Do this for about one full minute. Then rinse hair with warm water for one full minute.

Once per week, give your hair a treatment with *Rosa Mosqueta* rose hip seed oil. Pour a small amount in the palm of your hand. Rub the palms together and massage through the hair. Groom hair as usual. If your hair lacks luster you can do this more often. If your hair is salon-damaged or chemicalized, do this every day.

Another effective treatment for oily hair is apple cider vinegar. Before you shampoo (about 20 minutes if possible), part your hair and use a cotton ball soaked in apple cider vinegar and apply it to the scalp. I know it smells quite strong, but when you shampoo, the smell will disappear.

This may seem like quite a bit to do, but it will work magic on your hair and scalp. Within one week people will start saying, "What are you doing? Your hair looks beautiful!" If your hair has been flat and thin, your hair will now be full, thick, and lustrous. Even though you use two different shampoos when you lather, you still want to alternate with other shampoos from time to time.

Dry Type Hair

If you wash your hair in the morning and by the afternoon it is dry and like a head full of straw, then your hair is dry. Pouring oils on it won't work. Using shampoos that contain strong synthetic detergents, mineral oil, or propylene glycol, or some other petrochemical or oil won't work, either. One thing is a must. If your shampoo contains the synthetic detergents that we've already discussed, your hair will continue to become drier. Quite often dry hair has split ends and breakage, and this conditions worsens when hair is permed, colored, bleached, or processed. Hairspray, too, makes dry hair worse, and a blow dryer will eventually cause damage.

Look for a few good conditioning shampoos that use natural herbal oils found to benefit the hair. Check the shampoo labels for some of these ingredients: jojoba oil, jojoba butter, aloe vera, shea butter, evening primrose oil, panthenol (pantothenic acid or vitamin B_5), camomile (both golden and blue), *Rosa Mosqueta* rose hip seed oil, lanolin, and protein (soya or milk are best). Shampoo your hair only as often as needed, and you may wish to lather only once, unless your hair is particularly dirty (after strenuous exercise, for example).

Find a good natural hair conditioner with the ingredients listed above under "conditioners" and select some good quality herbal oils for a "hot oil" treatment.

1. **SHAMPOO.** Dampen hair with warm water. Apply shampoo and massage well through hair and into scalp. Rinse in warm water. If hair is particularly dirty, apply second application of shampoo and massage through hair. Rinse in warm water.

2. **RINSE.** Pour an herbal rinse through hair to remove any soap films. Rinse in warm water.

3. **CONDITION.** Apply hair conditioner and massage well through hair and into scalp. Allow this to stay in your hair as long as possible, at least five minutes if possible. Rinse hair in warm water.

Towel dry your hair: do not use hair dryer on hair.

Once a week, give your hair a hot oil treatment. Purchase some pure jojoba oil and *Rosa Mosqueta* oil. Alternate between these two oils. One week heat the jojoba oil and massage it through hair and into scalp. Allow it to stay on your hair for about 15 to 20 minutes before you shampoo hair. Another week pour some *Rosa Mosqueta* oil into your palms and work this through your hair and into your scalp. Do not shampoo it out.

For more luster, or if you must use a blow dryer, you can use a lusterizing spray. Look for these ingredients in a hair conditioning spray (and do NOT get an aerosol type): witch hazel, primrose oil, essential fatty acids, lanolin, pantothenate (B_5), and PABA (which help reduces drying and damage due to UV rays).

Using these ingredients and this method will completely change your hair from dry, drab, damaged hair to full, lustrous, healthy hair. Dry hair also lacks strength and elasticity. If just washing your hair leaves frizzies and split ends your hair lacks the elasticity essential to healthy hair. This is also a sign of chemical damage and over-processed hair. Follow the same procedure you would for dry hair.

Problem Hair

Problem	Try This:
If your hair is limp... OR fine-textured, lacks body, droops, doesn't hold a set, or has a flat look.	Follow the directions for "oily type hair." If you know your hair is dry, follow the method for dry hair. Choose products with panthenol and cystine.

If your hair is over-processed...
OR chemicalized by beauty salons who use petrochemicals and harsh permanent wave solutions and synthetic detergents which damage your hair. Damaged hair is more porous, and when it absorbs water, swelling results. Over-processed hair has breakage, split ends. Hair loss is possible.

Try this:
Follow the procedure for "dry type hair" above. Do not use commercial shampoos and conditioners which contain more of the chemicals you must avoid. A jojoba hot oil treatment once a week is very helpful. Daily use of *Rosa Mosqueta* oil on the hair to repair damage is vitally important.

If your hair has been damaged by chlorine...
The hair sustains damage when overexposed to chlorine just as if you had used cold wave solutions on it. It's dry, brittle, and lacks luster. Chlorine can also discolor the hair.

Try this:
There are swimmers' shampoos and conditioners in health food stores. The shampoo should contain protein, aloe vera, corn syrup (to help remove chlorine), vegetable glycerine (instead of propylene glycol) to re-moisturize hair, citric acid (to lower pH). African butter, pantothenic acid, almond oil, and allantoin (comfrey extract) are good ingredients to re-moisturize hair to keep it strong. Follow the method for dry hair.

If you have dandruff and scalp problems...
This can occur in oily or dry hair. It can be caused by many things: psoriasis, seborrhea, or dead skin cells that build up on the scalp and flake off like dandruff or psoriasis.

Try this:
Use the method for oily or dry hair, depending on your hair type. A good conditioner is important. Give your hair a hot jojoba oil treatment every week. Jojoba oil is good for controlling dandruff build-up on scalp. See **CHAPTER XVI**.

If you have hair loss...
When you shampoo do you find hair on the sink or in the tub afterwards? When your hair is wet does your scalp show through? Do you also have members on both sides of your family who are bald? Hair loss can be genetically or chemically caused.

If you start following **The Natural Method of Hair Care** and stay on the plan, you will probably notice a change: less or no hair loss and a thicker, healthier head of hair. Follow any of the programs for hair care here. Read all of **CHAPTER XVI** and **CHAPTER XVII**. Don't waste money on minoxidil or any of the "hair growers." You can consider a hair transplant, but even if you get one your hair will greatly benefit from **The Natural Method**. Nothing beats good natural products and our three simple steps: shampoo, herbal rinse, and condition.

organitoons

THE SECRET INGREDIENT FROM AN OLD MEDICINE
MAN STILL MUST MEET FDA LABELING LAWS

Diagram of the Skin

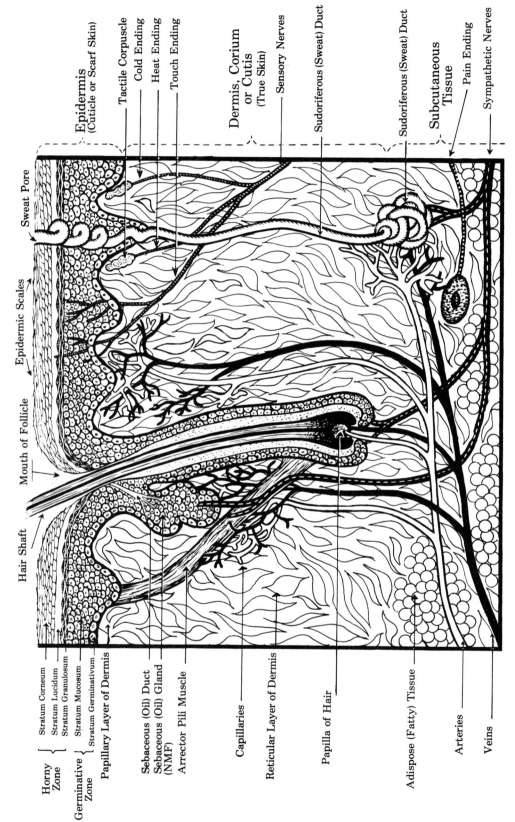

Epidermis
(Cuticle or Scarf Skin)

Tactile Corpuscle
Cold Ending
Heat Ending
Touch Ending

Dermis, Corium
or Cutis
(True Skin)

Sensory Nerves

Sudoriferous (Sweat) Duct

Sudoriferous (Sweat) Duct

Subcutaneous
Tissue

Pain Ending
Sympathetic Nerves

Sweat Pore
Epidermic Scales
Mouth of Follicle
Hair Shaft

Horny
Zone
{ Stratum Corneum
Stratum Lucidum
Stratum Granulosum

Germinative
Zone
{ Stratum Mucosum
Stratum Germinativum
Papillary Layer of Dermis

Sebaceous (Oil) Duct
Sebaceous (Oil) Gland
(NMF)
Arrector Pili Muscle

Capillaries

Reticular Layer of Dermis

Papilla of Hair

Adispose (Fatty) Tissue

Arteries
Veins

-344-

CHAPTER XVIII

What Your Skin Needs
Is Based On
How Your Skin Works

What your skin needs is based on how it works. While the diagram on the preceding page doesn't show exactly how complicated the largest organ of your body is, it can show you the basic structure and function of the skin. The three layers of the skin are epidermis, dermis (cutis), and subdermis (subcutaneous).

The *epidermis* is the outermost layer of the skin. It is often called the *cuticle* or *scarf skin*. The epidermis has no blood vessels, but it has many small nerve endings and consists of the following layers:

The *stratum corneum* consists of tightly packed, scale-like cells. These cells are continually being shed and replaced. Sometimes many of these "dead cells' will collect on the skin, and the skin will look dull and drab. A program of cleaning, steaming, masking, and moisturizing the skin will encourage proper shedding of these dead cells.

The *stratum lucidum* is a clear layer of transparent cells through which light can pass. Wouldn't it have been wonderful if nature had thought to make this transparent layer a UV protective coating, and thereby eliminate cancer due to overexposure? On the other hand, vitamin D (from light) must pass through this layer into the skin, and perhaps nature means for us to take proper care of our skin and not mess up our environment. If we do, we pay!

The *stratum spinosum* (prickle cells) is a layer of cells joined by prickle-like threads which works with the *germinative layer* or basal layer.

The *stratum germinativum* (also known as the *stratum mucosum*) is composed of various shaped cells. Some of these cells are responsible for the growth of the epidermis, and some of the cells contain a dark pigment called *melanin* which protects the cells deeper in the skin from the destructive effects of UV rays.

The *dermis* of the skin (also known as the *cutis*) is the underlying, or inner layer, of the skin. It is called "the true skin" because, unlike the epidermis, it is a highly sensitive and vascular layer of connective tissue which contains blood vessels, lymph vessels, nerves, sweat glands, oil glands, hair follicles, *arrector pili* muscles, and *papillae*. There are two layers in the dermis: the *papillary* layer and the *reticular* layer. The papillary layer is directly under the epidermis. This layer is made up of cone-shaped projections of elastic tissue that point upward into the epidermis (these pointed cone-like projections are called *papillae*). These projections contain looped capillaries and nerve endings. The *reticular* layer contains a complex network of fat cells, blood vessels, lymph vessels, oil glands, sweat glands, hair follicles, and *arrector pili* muscles.

One square inch of skin contains 65 hairs, 100 sebaceous glands, 650 sweat glands, 78 heat sensors, 13 cold sensors, 1,300 nerve endings that can record pain, 9,500 cells, 19 yards of blood vessels, 78 yards of nerves, 19,500 sensory cells at the ends of the nerve fibers, and 165 pressure apparatuses for the perception of tactile stimuli (touch).

The last layer which is below the dermis is the *subcutaneous* tissue. This is a layer of fatty tissue also known as *adispose* tissue or *subcutis*. According to your age, sex, and general health, the thickness of this fatty tissue varies. It gives smoothness and contour to your body, contains the fat we need for energy, and acts as a protective cushion for the outer skin, hair, and nails. Circulation is maintained by a network of arteries and lymph ducts. The subcutaneous tissue is usually considered as a continuation of the dermis. The skin gets its nourishment from the blood and the lymph as they circulate through the body. The blood circulates due to the pumping of the heart, but the lymph must circulate without the aid of the heart.

The lymph is a colorless watery fluid that is derived from plasma through a complex filtering system, and it circulates through the lymphatic system. It is the drainage system for the body tissues, to manufacture lymphocytes which are made up of white blood cells that produce antibodies to combat infection.

There's a close association of the skin to the nervous system which makes your skin "emotional." If you are nervous or anxious your skin can express this type of tension in hives or an outbreak of acne. Emotional stress or anxiety can cause psoriasis to flare up in those with this chronic condition. Massaging the skin can actually relax and reduce anxiety. One of the most important benefits of **The Natural Method of Skin Care** (discussed in **CHAPTER XIX**) is the relaxing effect it has on the body, the energizing effect on the lymphatic system, and the overall encouragement of the normal function of the skin. You can massage your skin according to the diagrams shown in this chapter, and you can have somebody else do it for you (and you to them) which is, of course, the best method. Skin problems are quite often your skin crying out for attention: emotional and physical. Infants who have not been given love and caring often develop eczema. It is believed that 56% of certain eczema and dermatitis (interchangeable names for the same group of conditions) are triggered by emotional upsets, 62% of psoriasis flare-ups, and emotional stress also accounts for severe scratching, hyperhidrosis (excessive sweating), alopecia areata (hair loss), and acne rosacea. Michael Scott describes in his book *Hypnosis in Skin Allergic Diseases* (an out-of-print book) the story of an airline pilot who developed herpes-type blisters on his forehead each time he flew over a particular canyon. Through hypnotherapy he recalled that the canyon had special significance to him because a friend and fellow pilot had been killed in a crash in that exact spot. He would have been with his friend during that fatal flight if he hadn't been ill. The skin problem gradually went away as he learned to deal with the guilt he felt over his friend's death (from *Skin Deep: A Mind/Body Program for Healthy Skin.* Ted A. Grossbart, Ph.D. and Carl Sherman, Ph.D. New York: William Morrow and Company, Inc., 1986).

Among all the senses, touch is the most important. Obviously, the 1,300 nerve endings that record pain through the skin are vital to our body. A condition known as *cutaneous alagia*, in which the individual can feel no pain in his skin, is a serious disorder which could result in serious burns and other injuries before becoming aware that one is in jeopardy.

The brain must receive sensory feedback from the skin in order to make adjustments in response to the information received. This continual feedback from the skin to the brain even goes on while we sleep. It is continuous.

In 60 B. C. Lucretius wrote in *De Rerum Natura* that "the paved highway of belief through touch and sight leads straightest into the human heart and the precincts of the mind." It is both the skin care massage and the substances used on the skin that will promote a healthy, youthful, clear skin (and complexion).

"The wiser mind mourns less for what age takes away than what it leaves behind," said Wordsworth. It is true, but today everybody wants to live a long time without growing old. The cult of youth is a multibillion-dollar industry, and most of the money is made by selling cosmetics to either hide signs of aging (by covering it up with makeup), or to rub supposedly "life-giving" and "wrinkle-removing" creams on the skin. Neither works. The make-up may cover slight discolorations of the skin, but as it lays on the face it actually increases the lines of the aged skin. It is, in a way ironic. You buy make-up and apply it to the skin, and for a little while perhaps you look younger (at a distance), but close-up the makeup dries and makes the lines even more noticable. In time this mixture of petrochemicals and coal tar dyes increases the lines. They become deeper, and the skin becomes older. You need to apply (and buy) more and more make-up. The answer is simple, but few people will accept a simple answer. The solution on a day-to-day basis is proper skin care using only natural substances, but, again, this solution requires that a few minutes be spent caring for the skin, which is often not given. This is due either to plain laziness or because we are a "quick-fix" society which believes not only in fast food but also in fast cosmetics. Women buy "Swiss collagen" creams for their face because they fall for the European hype and the pseudo-scientific claims that this one product will re-build their collagen and hold back the years. It doesn't work. Aging of the skin is a process that takes place. Everybody ages. Some, however, seem to look 40 in their late 50's, only 50 when they're in their late 60's, and so forth. This is often genetic. Nonetheless, by taking care of your skin with **The Natural Method** I suggest in this book, and following the step-by-step method and massage diagrams, you will look more youthful, regardless of your genes.

The Protective Action of Sebum AND the Importance of Moisture To Your Skin

Sebum is a complex oil. It is released onto the skin for the purpose of slowing down the evaporation of water on the skin. At the same time it prevents excess moisture from penetrating into the skin. The soft, moist, smooth skin can become dry and chafed due to our environment and cosmetics. For example, if you're out in a cold dry wind, your skin's oil barrier may lose its effectiveness and become dry and scaly. If you attempt to compensate for this loss with a mineral-oil based cream or lotion (which may make the skin feel better for a while but eventually inhibits the skin's natural moisturizing factor), you will only make the dry skin worse. This can happen in the summer heat, but it happens more frequently in the winter because the blood flow to the dermis is restricted by the cold and the lymph system may be slowed down as well. Sometimes the sebum which flows through oil ducts may become blocked and a blackhead forms. This block can be caused by many things: cold weather, make-up, powder, or some chemical in a cosmetic you apply to the skin. This is why deep cleaning with a facial cleanser, toner, mask, and so forth is important to the skin. Exfoliation is important as well because it encourages the turnover of dead skin cells.

Quite a bit has been written about the Natural Moisturizing Factor (NMF) of your skin. The NMF is part of the natural function of your skin, a biochemical mixture of oil and water, but it can be removed and altered by polar solvents and detergent systems. Make-up also upsets the NMF. During the past couple of decades several scientists have attempted to duplicate the NMF, and they have found some of the major components are sodium lactate, sodium pyrrolidone carboxylic acid (NaCPA), collagen amino acids. According to one researcher, it's a nucoprotein complex or a lipomucopolysaccharide complex (Curri, S. D., *Soap, Perfume, Cosmetic Magazine.* 40: 109, 1967).

One chemical mixture known as NaPCA was developed to supply the Natural Moisturizing Factor to the skin. It didn't work. These chemical glucosides upset the natural function of the skin, and the skin responded with allergic reactions and increased dryness. The low molecular weight of these glycols seems to draw moisture from the skin which results in a momentary feeling of smooth, moist skin, but in the long run the skin is actually made dry.

Another NMF called furyl glycine was synthesized in 1959, but this NMF didn't work either. Another chemical called adenine, an alkaloid obtained by purine (a component of nucleic acid), was patented in France in 1965. It was claimed that if the chemical was added to face creams it would act as an NMF. It wasn't successful: like NaPCA and the other so-called "NMF" chemicals, the results were not positive.

The problem with synthesizing the NMF is that these chemicals attempt to usurp the natural function of the skin. The best method of keeping the skin soft, moist, and smooth is to care for it naturally which encourages the proper functioning of the NMF. Many substances in plants and flowers have a more positive result on the skin. Used in synergistic formulations, without any synthetic chemicals, these substances reinforce the natural moisturizing function of the skin.

Some of the materials that have been used to penetrate the outer layers of the skin and increasing the NMF are collagen, placenta, elastin, reticulin, mucopolysaccharide, amino acid complex (as it occurs in skin keratin - 20 amino acids), gelatin, and hydrolyzed animal protein. In the area of fruit and vegetable extracts polyuronic acids, sugars, amines, and amino acids have been used to support the NMF. The fatty acids and fatty acid esters have a postive action, and when combined with amino acids have been found to encourage the NMF greatly.

Hormones have even been used though they are of little or no value, and they are carcinogenic. (A maximum use of 10,000 IU of hormone substance per ounce of product has been suggested as safe.) The hormones estrogen, progestin, pregnenolone, and androgens have very limited restorative effects on aging skin.

Oil and water soluble vitamins are taken in through the skin, and vitamin deficiencies can even be alleviated by topical application of vitamins. Vitamins in a skin care product work best in water soluble creams and lotions. In fact, the success of royal jelly and bee pollen in cosmetics is probably due to its content of B vitamins: pantothenic acid and its precursor and related materials panthenol, pantetheine, and pangamic acid. The B vitamins have a beneficial effect on the skin and hair. The panthenols actually make the skin moist and soft and increase the thickness of the hair. In a hair spray panthenol grooms the hair without leaving it feeling sticky and makes it appear thicker. Vitamins A, C, and E all are beneficial to the skin, and I have used them in skin care products. Vitamin E enhances percutaneous resorption as does vitamin F (essential fatty acids).

Very few natural ingredients are ever used in mass-produced cosmetics, and when they are, the formula is so compromised with chemicals that not only prevent the proper use of the important natural ingredients but have undesirable long-range effects. Mass-produced cosmetics also are not compounded with a skin care system in mind, and a natural system has never been tested and developed by any mass-produced cosmetic manufacturer or dermatologist clinic. Chemical manufacturers know very little about topical use though they lead you to believe in their technical bulletins that they do, and their aim is always to replace natural substances with cheaper synthetic substances which they claim are just as good. I have found otherwise. In fact, the whole concept of **The Natural Method of Skin Care** is to use ONLY natural substances and avoid synthetics or petrochemicals which have an adverse and aging effect on the skin.

What Causes The Skin To Age?

Gerontologists pretty much agree that it is within the connective tissues of the dermis that aging of the skin takes place. Since collagen makes up 70% of our connective tissue it has been studied carefully. On page 277 you can see a skin diagram showing an example of non-cross-linked and cross-linked collagen. If you lace your fingers together you can move them up and down like a gate hinge, but if somebody places their hand in the way this movement is prevented. This is a visual example of cross-linked collagen. The skin becomes tight, dry, and wrinkled. It is not flexible.

The aging that takes place seems to be due to not only genetic factors but to several other reasons: topical chemicals, UV light (the sun's effect on the skin), and the diet. I have found that combining the **Natural Method of Skin Care** with various natural substances will reduce the signs of aging. In the next two chapters I will discuss the various natural substances and the methods of application and skin care.

organitoons

"BAA... BAA, BLACK SHEEP, HAVE YOU ANY YOUTH REVIVING SECRET CELLULAR EXTRACTS THAT CAN BE USED IN A MOISTURIZING CREAM SO GULLIBLE WOMEN WILL PLUCK DOWN OVER A HUNDRED BUCKS TO RUB ON THEIR MUG AND DREAM OF YOUTH?"

CHAPTER XIX

Substances Found In Nature That Promote A Healthy, Youthful Skin

As the cartoons on page 350 demonstrate, the cosmetic industry is interested in making money with pseudo-scientific slogans and "vital juices" from slaughtered animals which, they tell us, will encourage the growth of healthy and youthful-looking skin. Our normal intelligence is compromised every time it is suggested that by killing animals and rubbing their tissue extracts on our faces we will look younger. Though collagen implants and topical applications of collagen do temporarily improve the skin, they are at best temporary treatments with no long range implication in creating a healthy, youthful skin.

In this chapter I will discuss vegetal alternatives to animal extracts including "vegetarian collagen" and some excellent herbal extracts far superior to all the "animal cell" substances touted by the cosmetic industry. You will soon see how far behind those cosmetic chemists are who still grub in the entrails of animals for the secrets of youth. Ironically, when they walk to and from their animal testing labs, they are treading on the herbs that contain the very elixirs they're looking for. I suppose their ignorance is understandable since they still base their work on animal torture and synthetic chemicals in the ancient belief that man is better than nature, the lord of the universe. Whether or not man is the most evolved and learned species is a philosophical question, but obviously superstition and ignorance abounds in the scientific community. On the one hand, they've created anti-aging creams (which don't work) from cellular extracts using black sheep raised especially for that purpose; on the other, animals are used to test the toxicity of products to be used on humans, who are an entirely different species.

Future anthropologists will undoubtedly study our modern anti-aging ritual of rubbing purified animal cells on our skin and find parallels with ancient myths in which warriors ate the hearts of the lions they killed to absorb their courage. It amazes me how any self-respecting scientist could actually believe such tommyrot and even spend years writing monographs about various combinations of cellular fluids that will make an aging face young again. However, I think very few actually believe the stuff they are writing; I prefer to think they are enamored of the money that can be made by distorting nature instead of the true discoveries that lie within nature.

Obviously, if animal slaughter and animal testing (and the money to buy their wares) could be translated into a youthful, healthy complexion we would already have some extraordinarily young-looking people, and we don't. Of course, genetic predisposition, a natural lifestyle, and minimal UV exposure play a big part in keeping the skin looking young. But, without a doubt, mass-produced cellular creams are not what the young-looking people I know use for their youthful appearance. They use natural products and **The Natural Method of Skin Care.**

Reverence for life and the quality of life must extend beyond mere slogans and be translated into a respect for all species and our entire eco-system. No matter what you may do to look younger or prevent lines and wrinkles it seems to me that if part of your method includes rubbing dead extracts of another species on your skin (or even having their glandulars shot into your body), you will be destroying the very principal of youth and life. The people who strut around in fur coats exhibit themselves as rich, but they also exhibit themselves as callous and ignorant about the importance of the animals who originally owned the coat and their importance to the survival of all species. In the same context, the woman or man who rubs dead animal cells on their skin because he or she can afford to do so is displaying the same callous disregard or ignorance.

If for the sake of argument, however, I suggested human cellular extracts instead of animal products, people would be aghast. "What," they would gasp, "you're making that product from human cells?" Yet if we are to buy the cosmetic hype for using the cells from a special breed of black sheep, wouldn't it seem far more logical to use cellular extracts from our own species?

Within the vegetal world there are more natural substances for skin (and hair) care treatments than in the entire animal kingdom. These herbal extracts also work far better to improve the skin and are better tolerated than any animal extract. Even collagen and hydrolyzed animal protein, two animal substances that work very well on the skin and hair, can be replaced with vegetal substances (and milk protein) that work better and are safer. (Recent research has suggested, for example, that hydrolyzed animal protein may be contaminated with the carcinogen NDELA.)

Take just one example: the substance known as squalane. This unique natural substance makes up about 10% of our sebum so it is obviously something the cosmetic "bandwagon" wants to advertise. One place it is found is in the liver of the rare species of shark known as the Aizame which the Japanese hunt and murder. They then sell the squalane to manufacturers who bottle it and sell it as a cosmetic and a medicinal. Squalane has always existed in wheat germ, rice bran, and olive oil. In fact, I've worked with olive oil squalane, and there are far fewer allergic reactions than with that ripped out of the Aizame shark's liver. But olives are not as exotic-sounding as Aizame sharks, and cosmetic and chemical manufacturers like to have exotic, hard-to-find chemicals, so they can corner the market and have no competition.

Why wouldn't an intelligent scientist engaged in the study of dermatologicals and the formulation of skin care products give up murdering animals if he or she knew herbals could do far more for signs of aging?

The animal exploiting scientists would do well to learn Gertrude Stein's statement: a rose is a rose is a rose, and then question the premise. What if a rose is not just a rose? What if a rose by any other name would not smell as sweet (some roses have no odor)? What if among the 3,000 species of *Rosaceae* there were tiny but important biochemical changes? And what if and if and if . . . That is the mind of the true researcher at work. The asking of questions and seeking for answers, and there are so many questions to be asked about the vegetation that springs up from the soil, so many discoveries yet to be made. In any case, I start off by giving you a bouquet of roses because one rose has proven its worth in restoring skin to petal-like softness - and so much more!

Rosa Mosqueta Rose Hip Seed Oil Actually Reduces Wrinkles, Lines, Scars, Heals UV Damaged Skin, and Improves the Skin and Hair

One rose that grows in the southern Andes of South America is called *Rosa aff. Rubiginosa*, but the natives call it *Rosa Mosqueta*. The flowers are pink and only live for about 24 hours. Then the petals drop away and are replaced by a fruit: the rose hips. (*See Color Plate 1, Fig.. 2, Rose Hip Seeds)*. This fruit is used to make a delicious tart jam and tea high in vitamin C. Inside the hips there are some tiny amber seeds which contain an oil high in essential fatty acids (especially linoleic and linolenic acids) and other unique phyto-substances (See chart below).

ROSE HIP SEED OIL TECHNICAL SPECIFICATIONS

	Average
Viscosity	42.30
Iodine Index	181.20
Saponification Index	190.00
Saponification Equivalent	893.37
% Unsponifiable Residue	0.76
Acidity Index	0.82
pH (20° C.)	5.10
Ester Index	189.18
% Neutral Fat	99.57
% Acid Fat	0.43
% Linoleic Acid	41.00
% Linolenic Acid	39.00
% Oleic Acid	16.0
% Palmitic Acid	3.00
% Stearic Acid	0.80
% Other Fatty Acids	0.20
% Ascorbic Acid (Vitamin C)	1.25
% Carotenoids	0.05
% Flavonoids	0.35
% Pectin	4.60
% Polyphenols	2.64
% Leucoanthocyanins	1.75
% Catechins	0.91
% Glycosides	17.00

In 1978 Carlos Amin Vasquez, M. D. discovered that the unique oil from the seeds of this species of rose hips was excellent in treating seriously burned patients. Healing was faster, and the rejuvenation of skin tissue was superior to other treatments.

Radiologist and oncologist Dr. Hans Harbst found that *Rosa Mosqueta* oil was excellent as a treatment for the "tracking" and other dermatological problems following radiation therapy. "As a radiotherapist, I work with many patients who have undergone surgery and therefore have scars," explains Dr. Harbst. "In addition, subsequent radiation causes secondary reactions to the skin such as inflammation, darkening, and dermatitis. These effects are inevitable following radiation treatments. This presents an aesthetic problem for patients, but the application of *Rosa Mosqueta* oil has produced faster healing of these lesions. Also, treatment of scars that cause tightening of the skin and difficulty in moving the arms and legs has been greatly improved with *Rosa Mosqueta* oil. We have achieved a loosening of the tension in the skin with *Rosa Mosqueta* oil. Results have been very good with some patients and spectacular with others."

"A man who had his whole head radiated due to a brain tumor had no signs of radiation after four weeks of treatment with *Rosa Mosqueta* oil. Another patient who showed an acute dermatitis after radiation had an excellent recovery 24 hours after treatment with the oil. The skin had actually regenerated."

I have found that *Rosa Mosqueta* rose hip seed oil will heal skin damaged with UV rays and reverses the aging effect due to this type of damage, but I was not the first to make this discovery. In 1978 Dr. Fabiola Carvajal, M. D., was working in the microbiology department at Concepción University in Santiago, Chile (*See Color Plate No. 1, Fig.. 1*). One of her colleagues, a pharmaceutical chemist, brought her a reddish-amber colored oil and told her it was *Rosa Mosqueta* oil and that it had a high percent of essential fatty acids which seemed to improve the skin.

"I was already familiar with the flower," she said, "which is found in Chile's 8th region. I had eaten *Rosa Mosqueta* jam and it was delicious."

Dr. Carvajal decided to test this unusual natural oil in clinical dermatological tests. Below, in her own words, are the results of her clinical studies.

"The results were superb using Rosa Mosqueta oil and cream in all our clinical studies, even with scars over 20 years old and with patients who had not improved using other therapies. Burns (including UV damaged skin and radiation burns) chronic ulcerations of the skin (such as that with paraplegics and bedridden invalids) skin grafts, brown spots, prematurely aging skin, dry skin: all benefited with *Rosa Mosqueta.*

"I have also found that the oil is beneficial in hair care as well: particularly with colored hair, permed hair, tinted hair, or hair that has been damaged by too much sun or cold weather." (*See Color Plate No. 4, Hair Repair with Rosa Mosqueta*).

Dr. Carvajal's photographs of some patients who have improved by treatment with *Rosa Mosqueta* demonstrate the good results of which she speaks.

One of the most dramatic examples of improvement was a young woman, 33 years old, whose face sustained extensive damage in a car wreck which caused extensive hypertropic scars (*Color Plate No. 1, Fig. 3*). Her traumatism was both physiological and psychological. She couldn't stand to look at her face in a mirror, and even had all the mirrors removed from her house. Dr. Carvajal treated her for four months with *Rosa Mosqueta* oil and cream. The improvement was amazing with excellent regeneration of the skin. The patient was very pleased with the results and was able to feel good about her appearance again (*Color Plate No. 1, Fig. 4.*)

Extensive aging of the skin, especially where UV damage is apparent, often takes on the appearance of deep lines in the skin which even resemble the cross-linked appearance of collagen. A 62-year old woman had the deep lines associated with premature aging due to UV rays and other external causes. In *Color Plate No. 2, Fig. 5*, we see signs of aging and in *Color Plate No. 2, Fig. 7*, a close-up shows how deep the cross-linked lines go into the skin. After two months of daily use of *Rosa Mosqueta* her skin is visibly improved. (*Color Plate No. 2, Figs. 6 and 8*).

The close-up of another woman with premature aging of the skin and the improvement after three months of using *Rosa Mosqueta* cream demonstrates that herbals high in fatty acids can smooth the topical appearance of the skin, thereby preventing the aging we saw in *Color Plate No. 3*. Daily care of the skin is a preventive measure (*Color Plate No. 3, Figs. 9 and 10*).

Though Dr. Carvajal doesn't recommend *Rosa Mosqueta* for the treatment of acne (due to the high amount of essential fatty acids and oils) she did find the treatment successful in the removal of acne scars. A dermatology treatment was used to electrically remove acne from a young woman's face but left acne scars. We see the scars four months after treatment (*Color Plate No. 3, Fig 11*). The scars were treated with *Rosa Mosqueta* cream for six months with excellent results (*Color Plate No. 3, Fig. 12*).

The examples of skin improvements using *Rosa Mosqueta* oil and cream seem almost miraculous, but when combined with other anti-aging herbs that I've discovered in two decades of formulating natural cosmetics, the results are even better. After introducing pure Rosa Mosqueta oil for skin care in the United States in 1986, I compounded a cream made with *Rosa Mosqueta* which also contained the following herbals: aloe vera, horsetail, coltsfoot, nettles, coneflower, St. John's wort oil, calendula, almond oil, vitamins A, C, and E. I compounded these in an essential fatty acid base. I found that other rose hip creams didn't work when compared with this one, and even creams containing *Rosa Mosqueta* didn't work as well as the one containing the mixture of herbs I've suggested here.

Because of the excellent results Dr. Harbst obtained with his treatments of patients after radiation exposure, another obvious use for *Rosa Mosqueta* is in sun care products. A sun care product could combine *Rosa Mosqueta* with aloe vera and other herbals for an excellent "after sun" cream as well as a sunscreen. An excellent sunblock could contain *Rosa Mosqueta*.

I tested my *Rosa Mosqueta* herbal mixture against animal cellular products found in the marketplace: the herbals were far superior. None of the animal-containing cosmetics gave the skin-smoothing and regenerating effects obtained by the *Rosa Mosqueta* cream combined with the herbals. One may ask "why don't the huge cosmetic manufacturers jump on the herbal bandwagon, especially with herbals such as *Rosa Mosqueta*, St. John's wort, calendula, horsetail, coltsfoot, etc.?"

If you've read this far, then you know the answer: the mass-produced cosmetic is NEVER formulated from the natural viewpoint because cosmetic chemists aren't trained in an understanding of herbals. They also simply don't believe in them. For example, when Dr. Amin and his associates tried to interest the largest cosmetic manufacturers in the U. S. as well as in Europe in their *Rosa Mosqueta* research, they got plenty of nods, smiles, skeptical glances, but no true interest. Within a few weeks after I reviewed their excellent medical studies I was using *Rosa Mosqueta* for cosmetic tests, and within one month I had gone to market with a line of cosmetic hair and skin products utilizing *Rosa Mosqueta* (including sun care products).

Of course, I have three advantages over larger and more prestigious cosmetic manufacturers: I recognized the results obtained from *Rosa Mosqueta* because of my firsthand knowledge of the good results with other herbals high in essential fatty acids; 2. I am curious and therefore test everything; 3. I like the adventure and the satisfaction of creating products that work.

After I established *Rosa Mosqueta* in hair and skin care products, other larger cosmetic manufacturers became interested, but this is the result of their desire to simply copy something somebody else has. Plus, they are more interested in hyping a product than in creating one that really works. In fairness to them, however, the FDA tries to limit creative thinking in compounding of quality cosmetics by always crying the prohibitive word "drug" when a manufacturer makes a cosmetic that really helps the hair and skin and wants to tell the public what it does. Herbal remedies have been with us far, far longer than the FDA, but nonetheless the FDA looks with contempt on anything they think smacks of "snake oil" unless they are the ones who okayed it. Few cosmetic chemists have the "ancient magic" that alchemists and herbalists had, and the cosmetic chemist of today is just an extension of the chemical manufacturer just as the M. D. is an extension of the pharmaceutical manufacturers. They are not only limited by their training and belief in animal testing, but by the limits of their imagination imposed by government ideology.

Collagen and Celltherapy for Vegans

The whole idea behind applying collagen creams to the skin is to accomplish the following: to increase elasticity of the skin, to arrest or compensate for collagen loss by topical application, and to stimulate the formation of new collagen fibrils that would consequently lead to regeneration of the skin. Dr. Kurt Richter conducted tests on humans with topically applied collagen in his lab in West Berlin and claims that it does give these three results.

The same results can obviously be obtained, as we have seen, from *Rosa Mosqueta* seed oil. The same results can also be obtained by using any herbal that encourages the formulation of collagen fibrils. Two such herbs are horsetail (*Equisetum*) and coltsfoot (*Tussilago farfara*). When they are compounded in a cream or lotion they have the same good effects on the skin that regular soluble collagen has. This is probably due to the high amount of organica silica in the herbs (silica is identified by the body as collagen). Vegetarian collagen can be created by combining horsetails and coltsfoot with aloe vera, St. John's wort, coneflower, calendula, aristolochia, and echinacea root.

Two of the herbs used in the vegetarian collagen have unique skin-regenerating properties: aristolochia and echinacea. The green parts of the aristolochia clematis provide an old and well-tried medicinal, still used in modern pharmacy as a wound-healing agent. Skin afflictions, like burns and inflammations, are treated with tinctures or ointments containing this herb. Aristolochia has active substances that increase the body's own defensive powers and promotes granulation in the connective tissue. It also stimulates the formation of new cells in the outer layers of the skin. Echinacea root was used by the American Indians as a remedy for snakebites and infected wounds. In skin injuries and infections, extracts from the root support the natural defensive powers of the body and help regenerate cellular tissue.

How herbs are combined is important when making skin care products. Often an herbal cosmetic is made in three or four steps and then combined; This means using one herb in various complexes that emphasize certain characteristics then combining the complexes; i. e., taking advantage of natural synergism. This method produces specified results, a targeted effect on the skin, whereas the overall organism is only minimally and non-specifically influenced. One example is vegetarian celltherapy lotion that combines several herbs for specific purposes.

Combing herbs with similar properties strengthens the ability of the entire mixture. To make a vegetarian celltherapy, combine hydroglycolic extracts of the following herbs as indicated: lotion base: aloe vera gel, sea ware, chlorella, laminaria, and bladderwrack (these are all seaweeds); hydroglycolic extracts for desensitizing, anti-inflammatory, and healing: Roman camomile, St. John's wort, blue bottle, feverfew, calendula, comfrey, limetree; Hydroglycolic extracts for hydrating, anti-wrinkle, cellular growth: hops, rosemary, horsetail, pine-tree, lemon, arnica, cucumber, elder, mallow, pellitory of the wall, pantothenate (vitamin B_5), vitamin F, allantoin (comfrey extract): Hydroglycolic extracts for anti-blotchiness and anti-varicose: red vine, arnica, St. John's wort, chestnut, ivy, and witch hazel.

Tea Tree Oil

The essential oil distilled from the leaves of the *Melaleuca alternifolia* is quite unique. The tree grows on the north coast of New South Wales, Australia, and the oil from that tree has been used "down under" for over 50 years for a variety of topical skin problems.

The name "tea tree" came about when Captain Cook and Joseph Banks, the famous botanist, first discovered the aboriginal people of the great southland known as *Terra Australia*. The natives there used the leaves of the species of *Melaeuca* trees to make a tea. Joseph Banks called the trees: tea trees. Hence, we get the name "tea tree oil."

There are over 180 species of *Melaleuca* or "tea trees," but the oil taken from one specific species (*Melaleuca alternifolia*) has a broad spectrum of antiseptic and fungicidal action. The action of this oil, in a way, is similar to the oil taken from the leaves of the eucalyptus tree. When tea tree oil is put in steam and inhaled it soothes a throat infection and is a treatment for sinus problems (as is eucalyptus oil). It is risky to compare essential oils from one plant to another so obviously tea tree oil is not like eucalyptus oil. To my nose the odor of tea tree oil is not as pleasant as eucalyptus oil, but this is a matter of personal choice.

In Australia tea tree oil is used for the treatment of vaginal infections such as *moniliasis* (caused by *candida albicans*, trichomonal vaginitis, cervicitis, and endocervicitis), it is used for the treatment of athlete's foot, and other fungal infections, for burns, sunburns, pimples, boils, stings, toothache, gum infections, cuts, abrasions, and sore throat.

If used on the skin, tea tree oil should not be used full strength but mixed with one part of tea tree oil to 10 parts olive oil, coconut oil, almond oil, or any natural vegetable oil.

On a burn tea tree oil is used pure without dilution swabbing it onto the burn and then using ice packs to lower the heat in the burned area. On a pimple or boil the oil is applied with a cotton ball to the affected area. Tea tree oil is applied directly to the site of a toothache, gum infection, or mouth ulcer. Vaginal infections are treated by adding about one teaspoonful of tea tree oil to a quart of douche, and a sitz bath can be prepared for the same types of infection by adding 10 ml to a tub of warm water.

Keep tea tree oil away from the eyes, and if you get a rash from using it, discontinue use. The oil will cause a temporary warm sensation when it comes in contact with the skin.

I have found that tea tree oil is not a good skin care ingredient in the sense that aloe vera is (as a moisturizer), though tea tree oil is beneficial in very tiny amounts in a facial cleanser or as a first aid type-antiseptic. The taste is not pleasant.

Neem Oil

The neem or *nimba* tree (*Melia azadirachta*) is found in southeast Asia, India, Andamans, Pakistan, Ceylon, Burma, Malaya, Indonesia, Japan, and tropical regions of Australia and Africa. It is a hardy evergreen glaborous tree that grows 40 to 60 feet high. From February to March it sheds its old leaves, and in the first week of April it produces glossy young leaves and fragrant white flowers. After a rain the flowers and fruits of the tree give off an awful stench, yet because of the large number of leaves the photosynthesis of the Neem tree is high. Consequently it gives off more oxygen during the daytime as compared to other trees, and its reputation as a purifier of air is not unjustified. The Neem trees grow in all parts of India from Cape Comorin to the Himalayas.

The Neem tree is held sacred by the Hindus and various parts of the tree are used in many of their rituals and ceremonies. It is believed that Sri Chaitanya, the father of the *Vaishnava* cult, was born under a Neem tree and therefore he has been given the nickname *Nimai*. A festival called *Ghastahapana* (installation of the sacred pot) is well-known in many parts of India. On certain occasions, the villagers collect together and install at a public place a pot filled with water on which they put five branches of Neem and a coconut. This is covered with flowers and worshipped. Sacrifices *(bali)* are made before it. The purpose of this festival is to avert ill luck and disease.

The bark, leaves, and fruits of the Neem have been used in ayurvedic medicines from a very remote period and are mentioned in the ancient Sanskrit writings of *Shushruta*. The very name of the tree, *nimba*, is synonymous with *Arishta*, meaning the relief of sickness. The bark is a bitter tonic and astringent, used to lower fevers, help thirst, and in the treatment of diseases of the skin. As a topical for the skin, the leaves of the tree are used as a wash, ointment, and liniment for skin problems and ulcers.

In India various medical practitioners agree that the efficacy of neem in cases of skin afflictions of an obstinate nature is excellent. Here neem oil is combined with chaulmoogra oil (*Hydnocarpus kurzii*) to treat leprosy. Since neem oil readily saponifies, a neem soap for washing problem skin (or used as a carbolic soap) is possible. When applied as an oil or cream, neem seems to make fingernails stronger and less liable to split or break.

Neem is an excellent problem hair treatment used as a rinse or shampoo, particularly for stubborn cases of dandruff. Because of its antiseptic qualities, neem is an ideal ingredient to combine with other herbals such as rosemary oil and sage oil for a scalp treatment rinse and shampoo.

Borage Oil

Evening primrose seed oil (*Oenothera biennis*) became one of the hot-selling items in the health food industry in the late seventies and early eighties, mainly based on its content of gamma-linolenic acid (GLA). GLA is a unique fatty acid which, as researchers such as David Horrobin, C. R. Lovell, and T. F. Burton told us, is only available through evening primrose oil and mother's milk (See **CHAPTER VI**, pp. 67-72). GLA is alleged to help a long list of ailments: heart disease, hyperactivity in children, premenstrual syndrome, eczema, arthritis, and hangovers. Evening primrose seed oil contains up to 10% GLA, and some manufacturers boasted that this oil was the only [practical] source of this fatty acid. For many years I have used evening primrose oil in hair and skin care cosmetics and have also found that the pure oil could soften and dissolve psoriasis lesions. However, when researchers make outlandish blanket statements they sometimes find they're wrong. Black currant seed oil and borage oil both have been discovered to contain GLA as well, which meant that mom's milk and the evening primrose flower didn't have the market cornered on GLA. Actually, of all three oils, borage oil (*Borango officinalis*) contains the highest amount of GLA (between 19% and 24%) which makes the researchers' mistake a big one.

Borage originally came from Syria where it was used in the Middle Ages to improve the quality of the blood. Later, during the Renaissance, it was recommended for depression and certain heart ailments. Pliny called it *euphrosinum* because it "maketh many merry and joyful." According to Dioscorides and Pliny, borage was the famous *nepenthe* of Homer which, when drunk steeped in wine, brought about forgetfulness.

I have found that for both internal and topical use borage is better than evening primrose oil (EPO) in several significant ways. Borage oil tastes bland, but EPO tastes terrible and can burn the throat. If you wish to supplement your diet with GLA, your choice would probably then be borage oil, which supplies more GLA than EPO and tastes better. The odor of borage is pleasant, while EPO has a strong unpleasant odor. Third, EPO is harsh to the skin, while borage is soothing. In fact, borage oil (like *Rosa Mosqueta*) reduces the aging process and the damage caused by UV rays.

Borage has some extra good constituents, besides the high amount of GLA: calcium, potassium, and mineral acids. Old herbalists used it externally as a poultice for inflammatory swellings.

Herbs for the Skin

The following chart is useful for recognizing herbs used to care for the skin and for internal use as well. It is a supplement to the **HERB CHART** in Part I, Chapter 7, pp. 80-126. This quick reference chart will allow you to visualize how several herbs can be combined for a specific purpose. If you have trouble obtaining one herb you may be able to find another to replace it in your skin care formula. For example, several herbs have a positive effect on the veins and capillaries: calendula, comfrey, orange blossom oil, rose oil, rhatany, rosemary, St. John's wort, witch hazel, and yellow dead nettle. To improve the condition of the veins and capillaries, combine these herbs together or use any one or two of them.

There are several ways of extracting the "magic elixirs" from these herbs. Here are some of the best methods:

Herbal Tea

Prepared as an INFUSION: usually equal amounts of the herbs are placed in a teapot (non-metal) and boiling water is poured over the herbs. Steep about one minute. If the herbs are fresh (not dry), steep for only half a minute. Roots and bark should be boiled in the water and steeped for three minutes. Use one heaping teaspoon of herb for every quart of water. The color should be a light yellow or green depending on the herb.

A cold infusion can be used, and some herbs should be be prepared in hot water. If in doubt use cold water as follows: steep the herb in cold water overnight (about eight to 12 hours). If you are going to drink the tea, heat it until it is warm but not hot. It also can be taken as a cold tea. When used topically on the skin (or in the hair) it should be used cool or at room temperature.

A combination of cold and hot infusions can be prepared, and I've prepared many herbs in this way. I go to this extra trouble because some active substances are obtained from a hot water infusion and some from a cold water infusion. Herbs from the minty family and eucalyptus, curiously enough, respond to both hot and cold extractions, each type giving an active substance. When using both a hot infusion and cold infusion method, combine them at room temperature. Keep fresh water infusions in the refrigerator when not in use. Store in a tightly capped glass container.

Ointments and Oils

Two oils are excellent for extractions: olive oil and sweet olive oil. On previous pages I discussed jojoba oil which is also an excellent extraction base (*see pages 59; 70-74*). The more unsaponifiable substances the oil contains, the better herbal oil or ointment you will obtain. Avocado (2 to 6% unsaponifiables) and African or karite butter (3.5% to 11% unsaponifiables) also make excellent base oils.

Weigh 500 grams of the oil of your choice or about 19 liquid ounces. Weigh four heaping handfuls of herbs (I base my recipe on my hand, or a little over 80 grams, around three ounces) and chop herbs to a fine consistency. Place the herbs in a non-metal container and pour the oil over the herbs. Remember, if you use several herbs you will want to make the total amount of combined herbs come to three ounces. After you've poured the oil over the herbs, allow this mixture to stand for two weeks in the sun for a natural extraction process. Do not use chemicals. Use only pure oil (cold-pressed) that contain no chemicals. Filter this mixture through linen or cheese cloth as often as needed to remove herbal flakes. Bottle and keep in refrigerator.

Most books recommend preparing ointment with either petrolatum or lard. I don't like either and feel they make very poor herbal ointments. I don't like lanolin either. Remember, these are herbal extracts you're preparing so keep the animal extracts out of the mix! The finest ointments are made with herbal butters. You can use jojoba butter or African butter. Use finely chopped herbs, the same amount as when you prepared the oil. My tiny handfuls (four of them), or around three ounces, are placed in a non-metal container. Heat 500 grams or 19 liquid ounces of herbal butter until it comes to a boil. Slowly add the herbs to the hot melted butter. Allow this mixture to stand for about eight hours until it is of an ointment consistency, then heat it until it is a warm ointment (don't boil). Filter this through a linen cloth into ointment jars. Keep tightly capped and in refrigerator when not in use.

Tinctures

These herbal extracts are also known as essence and are prepared with corn spirits. A bottle is filled with herbs, and the grain alcohol poured over them. Let this stand for 14 days in a warm area, not cooler than 68°. Every few days shake this mixture well. Strain and squeeze out residue. Tinctures are strong and therefore used by drops (*see pp. 234-235 on how to make an herbal astringent*).

Herb Pulp

Maria Treben in her excellent book *Health Through God's Pharmacy* suggests using a wooden board and a heavy wooden rolling pin to crush stems and leaves. The herbs should be fresh. They are used as a poultice. Place the herbal pulp on a linen cloth, and affix it to the part of the body to be treated with a plastic wrap or piece of cloth. Aloe vera pulp is removed from the inside of the leaf and applied directly to the skin as a moisturizer.

Herbal Packs

These poultices are steamed. Fresh or dried herbs can be used. Use a double boiler or a sieve which can be hung over boiling water. Place a cover on the pot with the herbs hanging over the boiling water so the steam rises to the herbs. Remove the warm damp herbs after they have been steamed like this for a while and place them on a piece of cheese cloth. Place this on the affected area and bind with a cloth. Warm poultices of this type are left on from one hour to overnight. Facial use is usually left on for about 30 to 45 minutes.

Herbal Bath Emulsions

There are several ways of using herbs in the bath for the skin and for body care. The first product I ever manufactured was an herbal bath emulsion called **Relax-R-Bath**. This was made by grinding the herbs into a powder and blending them into a coconut oil that gave a slight sudsing action. I used dried herbs, fresh herbs, tinctures and extracts from herbs. I also prepared "spa herbal solutions" which are used in regular hot tubs or in whirlpool baths. Here's how to prepared the suggested herbs used on our charts:

Fill a bucket with hot or warm water (8 liters) and place 250 grams of herbs in the water (around 9 ounces). Allow the herbs to steep in this water overnight. The next day reheat the bucket of water and herbs. Strain this into a tub of hot water (you can strain it through a towel that you don't mind staining). Get in the tub, relax, and allow the steam to rise off the water as you breathe and relax. Most herbalists suggest that your heart be above the water. The heat of the water depends on what is comfortable for you. Soak for about 20 minutes. When you are through, wrap yourself in a huge towel; put on a robe, and lay back to allow a natural perspiration and drying take place. Stay out of drafts.

For a quick reference guide to learn which herbs have healing, soothing, or astringent qualities, etc., turn to the chart on the next page.

Topical Applications of Herbs

	Astringent	Calmative	Cleansing	Circulation of (internal-external)	Cuts, bruises skin, massage	Eczema, acne, skin disorders	Inflammation	Moisturizing, softening	Muscle tension	Pain relief	Rejuvenation	Soothing qualities	Stimulant	Veins, capillaries
AGRIMONY	•				•	•	•							
ALOE					•	•	•	•		•	•	•		
ALMONDS								•				•		
ALTHEA ROOT	•							•				•		
ANGELICA		•												
APRICOT								•						
ARAROBA (GOA)	•					•								
ARISTOLOCHIA					•		•				•	•		
ARNICA				•	•			•					•	
AVOCADO				•		•		•						
BALM OF GILEAD					•								•	
BALSAM OF PERU	•		•					•						
BALSAM TOLU	•		•					•						
BEARSFOOT													•	
BEDSTRAW	•		•			•							•	

-361-

	Astringent	Calmative	Cleansing	Circulation of (internal-external)	Cuts, bruises skin, massage	Eczema, acne, skin disorders	Inflammation	Moisturizing, softening	Muscle tension	Pain relief	Rejuvenation	Soothing qualities	Stimulant	Veins, capillaries
BENZOIN	•					•								
BERGAMOT OIL	•					•								
BETULLA	•		•	•										
BISTORT	•													
BLADDERWRACK				•		•		•				•		
BONESET				•		•							•	
BORAGE					•		•	•			•	•		
BUTCHERS BROOM	•													
CADE OIL					•	•								
CAJEPUT OIL	•												•	
CALAMUS, SWEET FLAG			•											
CALENDULA (Marigold)	•		•	•	•	•	•	•	•	•			•	•
CAMOMILE	•	•	•		•	•	•	•		•		•		
CAMPHOR	•						•					•	•	
CATHECHU (Black/Pale)	•													
CENTAURY	•	•										•		
CHAULMOOGRA	•	•			•	•	•							
CINNAMON	•													

	Astringent	Calmative	Cleansing	Circulation of (internal-external)	Cuts, bruises, skin, massage	Eczema, acne, skin disorders	Inflammation	Moisturizing, softening	Muscle tension	Pain relief	Rejuvenation	Soothing qualities	Stimulant	Veins, capillaries
COCOA								•						
COLTSFOOT	•		•		•									
COMFREY			•	•	•	•	•	•		•	•	•		•
COWSLIP		•	•											
CUCUMBER	•							•				•		
DANDELION			•			•							•	
ECHINACEA					•						•			
ELDER FLOWERS	•												•	
ELECAMPANE	•		•			•		•	•					
EUCALYPTUS	•		•	•		•								
EVENING PRIMROSE	•	•	•			•		•						
EYEBRIGHT	•		•											
FENNEL			•			•								
FRANKINCENSE				•				•					•	
GERANIUM	•		•											
GINGER								•					•	
GINSENG	•	•											•	
GOLDEN ROD		•	•											

-363-

	Veins, capillaries	Stimulant	Soothing qualities	Rejuvenation	Pain relief	Muscle tension	Moisturizing, softening	Inflammation	Eczema, acne, skin disorders	Cuts, bruises, skin, massage	Circulation of (internal-external)	Cleansing	Calmative	Astringent
GOLDENSEAL									•					•
GRAPEFRUIT OIL									•			•	•	
GREATER CELANDINE									•		•	•		
HAWTHORN														•
HEARTSEASE									•					
HENNA														
HOPS							•							
HORSE CHESTNUT											•		•	•
HORSETAIL					•				•	•		•	•	•
HYSSOP									•	•				
IMMORTELLE			•				•		•	•				
IVY							•				•		•	
JASMINE													•	
JUNIPER BERRIES									•		•	•		•
KELP											•			
LADY'S MANTLE										•		•		•
LAVENDER			•	•		•	•	•	•	•	•	•	•	•
LICORICE ROOT								•						

	Astringent	Calmative	Cleansing	Circulation of (internal-external)	Cuts, bruises skin, massage	Eczema, acne, skin disorders	Inflammation	Moisturizing, softening	Muscle tension	Pain relief	Rejuvenation	Soothing qualities	Stimulant	Veins, capillaries
LINDEN TREE		•	•					•			•	•		
MALLOW, BLUE			•		•	•		•		•				
MISTLETOE		•	•	•						•				
MUSK SEED		•	•			•								
MYRRH	•													
NETTLE	•							•					•	
OATS		•	•										•	
OLIVE OIL	•		•			•		•						
ORANGE OIL (BLOSSOM)	•			•			•	•			•			•
PAPAIN			•		•	•	•	•			•			
PARIS HERB						•						•		
PIPSISSEWA	•		•			•								
PLANTAIN, RIBWORT			•		•	•	•							
QUILLAIA			•			•	•							
RAMSONS			•			•								
ROSA MOSQUETA					•		•	•		•	•	•		•
RHATONY	•							•			•			
ROSEMARY			•	•		•			•		•			•

-365-

	Astringent	Calmative	Cleansing	Circulation of (internal-external)	Cuts, bruises, skin, massage	Eczema, acne, skin disorders	Inflammation	Moisturizing, softening	Muscle tension	Pain relief	Rejuvenation	Soothing qualities	Stimulant	Veins, capillaries
RUTIN							•							•
SAGE		•	•			•		•						
SHEPHERD'S PURSE			•		•				•	•				
SPEEDWELL		•	•		•	•	•			•			•	
STINGING NETTLE			•	•	•	•				•			•	
ST. JOHN'S WORT	•			•		•	•	•				•		•
STORAX	•					•								
STRAWBERRY	•													
SUNFLOWER OIL			•	•										
THYME		•	•		•									
WALNUT			•		•	•								
WILLOW (Small Flowered)			•											
WINTERGREEN OIL	•		•	•					•			•	•	
WITCH HAZEL	•		•	•	•	•	•	•						•
WOOD SORREL			•			•								
YARROW			•	•		•	•	•				•		
YELLOW DEAD NETTLE			•									•		•

-366-

organitoons

COLOR PLATE NO. 1

Fig. 1. In 1978 Dr. Fabiola Carvajal conducted clinical dermatological tests using *Rosa Mosqueta* Rose Hip Seed Oil and *Rosa Mosqueta* Rose Hip Seed Oil Cream. She had success in treating patients with conditions that had not improved with other therapies, including UV-damaged skin, radiation burns, chronic ulceration of the skin that occurs with paraplegics and bedridden invalids, skin grafts, dry skin, and serious scars over 20 years old.

Fig. 2. *Rosa Mosqueta* grows wild in the southern Andes. Because the land has not been chemicalized, the natural properties of the flowers are intact. The bright red hips are used to make a delicious tart jam and rose hip tea. The amber seeds inside the hips contain an oil high in essential fatty acids and vitamin C. Dr. Carvajal and her associates have found that the oil and cream made with the oil are excellent for the hair and skin.

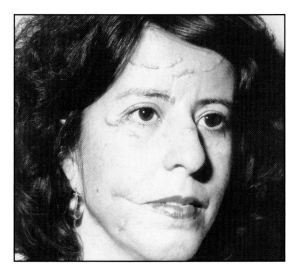

Fig. 3. A 33-year old patient of Dr. Carvajal sustained serious damage due to an automobile accident. Hypertropic scars were left after the accident.

Fig. 4. Dr. Carvajal treated the patient for four months with *Rosa Mosqueta* Rose Hip Seed Oil. The results were excellent.

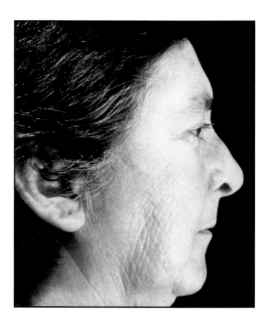

Fig. 5. A 62-year old woman with signs of aging due to UV exposure and loss of collagen.

Fig. 6. After two months of treatment with *Rosa Mosqueta* Rose Hip Seed Oil and *Rosa Mosqueta* cream, her skin is improved.

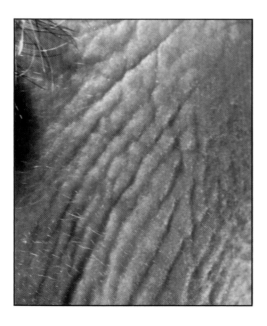

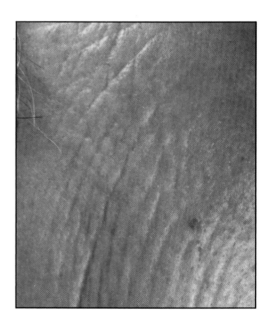

Fig. 7. A close-up of the woman's skin shows the depth of the wrinkles. They resemble the cross-linking that takes place when collagen becomes insoluble.

Fig. 8. A close-up after three months of treatment with *Rosa Mosqueta* shows reduction of lines and a smoother skin.

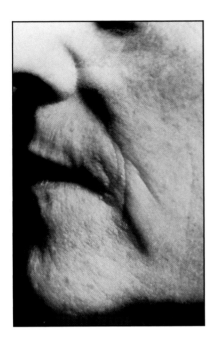

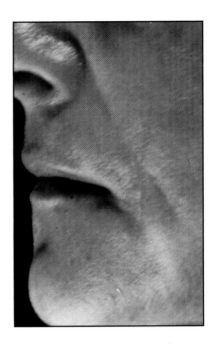

Fig. 9. A woman with premature signs of aging and a pronounced buccal crease (running from the sides of the nose to the corners of the mouth).

Fig. 10. After three months of treatment with *Rosa Mosqueta* Rose Hip Seed Oil, the buccal crease is less noticable, and the skin is smoother.

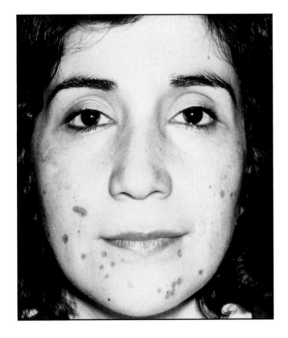

Fig. 11. Thirty-old woman with scars after treatment for acne.

Fig. 12. After four months of treatment with *Rosa Mosqueta* cream.

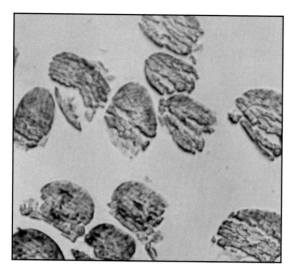

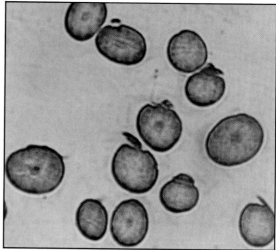

Fig. 13. Damaged hair before treatment with *Rosa Mosqueta*. Notice the damage to the cuticle of the hair as well as the medulla.

Fig. 14. Twenty-four hours after applying *Rosa Mosqueta* to the hair, the cuticle is repaired, and even the medulla of the hair shaft can be recognized.

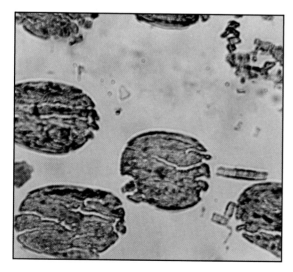

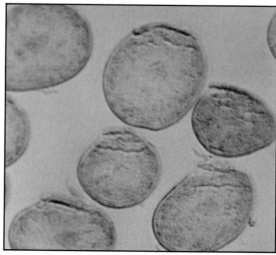

Fig. 15. Dry hair before treatment with *Rosa Mosqueta*.

Fig. 16. Twenty-four hours after treatment with *Rosa Mosqueta* Rose Hip Seed Oil.

Fig. 1. Diane is applying a hot towel to her face. This step relaxes the tissues and allows for a deeper cleansing of the skin.

Fig. 2. Spoon natural cleansers out of jar to avoid contamination.

Fig. 3. A cleansing pad or washcloth is preferable for cleaning the skin. Loofahs tend to be too rough for sensitive facial skin.

Fig. 4. Herbal steam penetrates deep into your skin's pores.

Fig. 5. Pour very hot water over the facial steaming mixture into a ceramic or glass bowl (be sure bowl is heat-proof).

Fig. 6. Make a tent over your head with a large towel. Hold your face over the herbal steam for two to three minutes.

Fig. 7. Use a natural herbal oil for your **Natural Method Massage.**

Fig. 8. Massaging your skin over herbal steam is extemely beneficial.

Fig. 9. Spoon herbal mask out of jar and apply to face and neck.

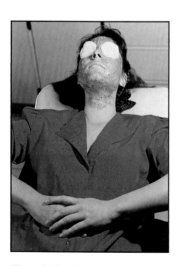

Fig. 10. Soak two cotton balls with natural herbal astringent or natural witch hazel. Place them over your eyes, and relax. Very important!

Fig. 11. Here Diane is applying a natural clay-based mask. This mask is very good for oily skin.

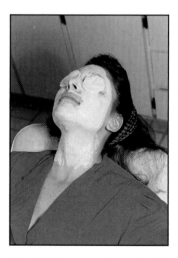

Fig. 12. Leave mask on for 10 minutes or so. Don't fall asleep!

Fig. 13. Toning the skin with a natural herbal astringent removes soap films and cellular debris, and tightens tissues. Plus, it leaves your skin feeling fresh and clean.

Fig. 14. Saturate a cotton ball with a natural herbal astringent, and wipe upwards. Change cotton balls as they become soiled.

Fig. 15. Apply just a dot of natural moisturizer to your fingertips. You don't need too much!

Fig. 16. Diane is distributing the moisturizer evenly on her fingers before applying it to her face.

Fig. 17. Apply moisturizer to face in light, upward strokes. A natural moisturizer will be absorbed into the face almost instantly.

Fig. 18. Natural celltherapy treatments can rejuvenate your skin. They can be either vegetarian or of animal origin.

Fig. 19. *Rosa Mosqueta.* rose hip seed oil is high in essential fatty acids and has a mild pH. Apply it to dry, prematurely aging, or UV-damaged areas of your skin.

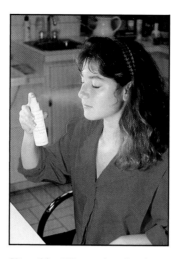

Fig. 20. Water is the best moisturizer, but look for a natural mineral water spray enriched with vitamins and herbal extracts.

Fig. 21. A natural powdered make-up base needs no preservatives and can be colored naturally. It protects your skin from the elements and keeps oily skin from looking shiny.

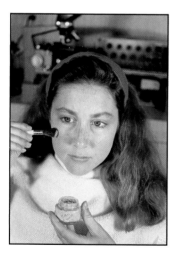

Fig. 22. Look for powdered blush that uses hematite or another natural color.

Fig. 23. Various shades of powdered make-up can be used on your eyelids, in the crease of your eyelids, just below the browbone, or on your lips.

Fig. 24. Diane has applied some eye pencil for a dramatic evening look. The rest of her make-up is 100% natural. After applying make-up, set it with a spritz of mineral water spray.

CHAPTER XX

The Natural Method of Skin Care

Step-By-Step
In Descriptions, Photos, and Diagrams

I introduced **The Natural Method of Skin Care** almost two decades ago, and have over the years refined it to meet the changing requirements caused by both environmental changes (which affect our skin) and various herbal discoveries (most of which are discussed in this book). If you study the herb charts and the many chapters devoted to natural substances for hair and skin care you will discover that cosmetic applications of these substances have been known for hundreds of years (sometimes thousands of years); thus, there are few really new discoveries. In fact, new discoveries are usually rediscoveries or mere updates.

It's important you use natural products with **The Natural Method of Skin Care**, but they should be more than just natural. They should contain substances that complement how your skin works, and they should be formulated with a *relative specificity*. This means that ingredients are combined to enhance their respective characteristics so that they have a targeted effect on particular functions of the skin, but a minimal effect on the skin in general. Most skin (and hair care) cosmetics aren't formulated with this special synergetic action in mind, but **The Natural Method of Skin Care** was designed to work in this manner.

This means that whether you have dry skin, oily skin, combination skin, or normal skin The Natural Method of Skin Care will work for you due to the law of relative specificity.

Over the years I have received many, many letters from people who have used **The Natural Method of Skin Care**. Although they had visited many skin care experts, American and European, and tried many systems and products from all over the world, they found to their amazement **The Natural Method** gave them the best results. **The Natural Method** works because it uses natural products free of petrochemicals, coloring agents, synthetic preservatives, and synthetic fragrance chemicals. Here are some criteria to use in choosing products.

Don't worry about claims that aren't relevant to natural products: e. g., "is the product pH balanced? Does it contain oils? Is this herb or that one dangerous?" These are marketing red herrings created by the cosmetic industry to sell products. They are utterly unimportant to the care of your skin. The whole purpose of **The Natural Method** is to protect your skin and support its normal function. Because your skin is designed to work within a fairly wide

-377-

range of pH values, a product's pH is not what adds or subtracts from your skin's health, but rather whether or not it contains good ingredients. Oils are not always bad for your skin even if you have oily skin. Essential oils are of all types and with **The Natural Method** can be used on what is termed oily skin as well as dry skin. Remember, very oily or dry skin is abnormal: the purpose of **The Natural Method of Skin Care** is to normalize the skin.

Don't worry about so-called "dangerous herbs." Unless the cosmetic manufacturer is a rank amateur, he or she will know which herbs are dangerous: this has been well documented. Also, most herbs said to be "toxic" and "carcinogenic" are not a risk and often are very beneficial to the skin. Take, for example, eucalyptus oil. The leaf of the eucalyptus tree is poisonous to humans, but when used in tiny amounts has excellent properties in a skin care cream. The same is true of menthol and camphor. Used properly they are safe and beneficial. Another herb that has been unjustly maligned is St. John's wort oil, which is said to increase sensitivity to the sun. I tested this herbal extensively on humans and used it for years in sun care lotions. A Chilean dermatologist, Dr. Carvajal, is researching the benefits of St. John's wort to the hair and skin, but I have found this herbal oil safe and a protection for sensitive skin.

There are ten steps to **The Natural Method of Skin Care**: 1) *Towel* steam to soften and relax tissues); 2. *Cleanse;* 3) *Herbal steam;* 4) *Massage* with **The Natural Method Massage** over the herbal steam; 5) *Apply an herbal or clay mask* (a weekly or monthly step depending on need); 6) *Tone* with an herbal astringent or pure aloe; 7) *Moisturize*; 8) *Rejuvenate* with a cellular treatment; 9) *Hydrate* with an herbal mineral water spray; 10) *Apply natural make-up* (this is optional and depends on the time of day of the facial).

If you went to a natural aesthetician who used **The Natural Method of Skin Care** he or she would go through all these steps (and more) except he or she would use equipment like a towel steamer, or a facial vaporizer, or an electric pulverizer. This last device is a unique atomizer spray that originated in France and is used by most European aestheticians. It carries plant extracts, herbal teas, and skin fresheners in a fine mist spray to the skin, but a fine mist pump bottle containing mineral water and herbs does just as well. Most natural aestheticians will use a pump spray (though the other looks quite impressive). One of the most important steps is number four, the **The Natural Method Massage** with herbal oil over herbal steam. Of course an aesthetician can do this to you better than you can do it to yourself. Nonetheless, practice **The Natural Method Massage** on your skin, and you will see results. There are 11 steps to **The Natural Method Massage**, but it's extensively diagrammed on pages 382 to 387. The best way to take care of massaging your skin is a shared facial: someone does it for you and you do it for him or her. Men as well as women can benefit from **The Natural Method of Skin Care** and the **The Natural Method Massage**. Why shouldn't a man's skin be just as youthful and healthy as a woman's skin?

Over the years I have worked with many aestheticians, bringing **The Natural Method** to them and raising their awareness of natural substances in cosmetics. One natural aesthetician has been with me well over a decade: Marianne Blakeslee. She helped me develop **The Natural Method** by using it on thousands of clients whose skin attests to its superb life-giving effects. Ms. Blakeslee gives **Natural Method** facials at her skin care clinic in Belmont, California. Further, she makes it her business to study and know about products and methods worldwide and has been very helpful over the years.

Luc Bodin is another natural aesthetician who gives seminars in how to use natural substances for the care of the skin. He has also made it his business to study methods and investigate products in his native France and all over the world. We constantly trade information.

Color plates 5 through 8 show Diane D'Ambrosio demonstrating **The Natural Method Facial**. Notice how great her skin looks. She is doing the complete **Natural Method**, but I have included a chart showing the "easy version" of **The Natural Method Facial** at the end of this chapter.

STEP ONE - Soften and Relax Tissues

If you wear make-up, remove it before you begin **The Natural Method Facial**. I suggest that to get the best benefit from your facial that you do it in the evening when you aren't going to put make-up back on the skin. I have some suggestions about wearing make-up, but they come later.

There are several different herbal oils you can use to remove make-up, but don't use mineral oil or mineral-oil based products. Pure jojoba oil works very well, and will remove eye make-up gently from the eyes. If your eyes burn, this is the eye make-up being liquified by the oil and getting into the eyes. Be sure ALL MAKE-UP is off the skin.

In the days of the old-fashioned barber shop, one of the things most beneficial to the skin was the hot towel the barber put on the man's face before he began the shave. This was soothing and relaxing, but it also made it easy to whisk the man's beard away. I have a towel warmer in my skin care clinic, but you don't need anything that fancy: just a hot towel.

Towel steaming your face opens follicles and allows a deeper cleansing of dirt, grease, blackheads, and other cellular debris. The hot towel also softens dead surface cells which aids in their removal during the facial. There are other important reasons for the hot towel: it stimulates the sebaceous glands; it increases blood circulation to the face which naturally nourishes tissues. Remember that after applying a hot towel your skin is very vulnerable to contamination: don't put synthetic chemicals or petrochemicals on your skin. Even mineral oil, which generally is not absorbed by the skin, will be absorbed after a hot towel treatment.

You will want to prepare two towels and go from one to another, which will take about two minutes per hot towel.

Color Plate 5, Fig. 1 shows Diane applying a hot towel to her face. The nose and mouth are kept uncovered.

STEP TWO - Cleanse

After you have applied the hot towel, you are ready to clean your skin. You can use plain cotton cleansing pads. I don't recommend loofahs for several reasons. They are entirely too rough for the skin, and you don't need that kind of "scrub action" in **The Natural Method of Skin Care**. Loofahs are also a breeding ground for bacteria. I have looked at freshly-cleaned loofahs under a microscope and have found plenty of bacteria and debris there. It's best to use cleansing pads that can be thrown away after use.

The cleanser you use is important, so let me give you a guide for reading facial cleanser labels. Here are three sets of ingredients (only natural substances) that have worked well with **The Natural Method**.

1. For skin that tends to be oily. Coconut fatty acid base, castile soap (olive oil type), aloe vera gel, witch hazel, eucalyptus oil, menthol oil, camphor oil, avocado oil, elder, nettle, rosemary, sage, camomile, myrrh, peppermint, lemon grass, vitamins A, B, C, and E.

2. For skin that tends to be dry. Mineral water, protein (soya if possible), coconut oil (acts as a soap), sea ware, chlorella, kelp (these three are seaweeds), a combination of vitamin and plant extracts, a natural preservative.

3. For skin that is aging (featuring Rosa Mosqueta). Olive oil castile soap, water, vegetable glycerine, *Rosa Mosqueta* (rose hip seed oil), laminaria, fucus, bladderwrack (these are seaweed extracts), St. John's wort, alfalfa extract, borage oil, comfrey, shea butter (also known as karite or African butter), peppermint oil, almond oil, vitamins A, C, and E. (A natural preservative should be used.)

The first cleanser contains no water except the amount that is in the various extracts so it will usually be a thick white cream. It has been used on dry and oily skin, but seems to work best on oily-type skin. The second cleanser is a mixture of seaweed extracts that is soothing and very good for dry type skin. It contains more water (mineral water) so it will be slightly thinner than the first cleansing cream. The third cleansing cream is closer to a liquid soap since it contains quite a bit of castile and more water. The ingredients are excellent for dry skin and aging skin because of its soothing qualities and the herbals *Rosa Mosqueta*, St. John's wort, alfalfa extract, and borage oil. It is an expensive list of ingredients, but an excellent cleanser. Any of these selections of ingredients will do quite well.

Cleansing the Skin

Wet the cotton pad. Squeeze the excess water out and apply a small amount of cleanser to the pad. Avoid using too much cleanser. If the cleanser is in a jar, scoop a small amount onto the pad with a spatula or spoon. If the cleanser is in an applicator bottle, simply squeeze a small amount onto the pad.

Starting at the base of the neck, cleanse the neck using upward strokes. Go on to the chin and slide the pad along the jawline to the left ear, and then repeat this movement along the jawline to the right ear. Alternate back and forth a couple of times from one side to the other, ear-to-ear. Usually aestheticians will not clean inside the ears, but you should do so. Rub the pad behind the ears, around, and then inside the configurations of the ears.

Starting at the jawline again, use upward movements to cleanse each cheek. Go from one cheek to the other for about seven strokes for each cheek.

Cleanse the area directly under the nose starting at the center and working outward toward the corners of the mouth alternating the movements back and forth several times.

Starting on the bridge of the nose, cleanse the right side of the nose and the area next to it, then slide back along the same area to the bridge of the nose, and then to the left side of the nose and the area next to it. Alternate the movements and clean the nose area in this manner three times on each side.

Place the pad flat on the center of the forehead and slide to the right temple. Massage this area with the pad in a tiny circular movement, then slide back to the center of the forehead and on to the left temple. At this point again apply a slight pressure and tiny circular movements. Follow this procedure from the left temple to the right temple and back again about three times or so.

With the eyes closed, lift the eyebrow, and using the pad, clean the eyelids and lashes. Repeat this step for each eye. Be very gentle and do not press on the eye or force cleanser into the eye. When cleaning the eye (especially if there's still some make-up on the eye), rotate the pad to be sure you have a clean area on the pad. If needed, prepare a new pad with cleanser.

Place the pad under the lower lashes at the outside corner of the eye and move across to the inner corner of the eye. Follow this same procedure for both eyes. Remember, be gentle when cleaning the skin around the eyes because it is very sensitive and can become irritated.

Color Plate 5, Figs. 2 and 3 - Diane is applying facial cleanser to a pad and cleaning face.

STEP THREE - Applying herbal steam to your face

The aesthetician will use a facial vaporizer to steam your skin, but you can do the same thing without a vaporizer. In fact, unless the aesthetician goes to quite a bit of trouble the steam he or she uses will be just plain steam whereas you can prepare herbal steam. Look for a mixture of herbs for the skin in your health food store or put together your own blend. Here is a list of the herbs that should be used. Use this list to check out any mixture you buy in a store. **Herbs for making facial steam:** Calendula blossoms, camomile flowers, coltsfoot, horsetail, comfrey root, rosemary, sage, peppermint, elder berries, lavender flowers, marshmallow root, nettle leaves, blueberry leaves, eucalyptus leaves, St. John's wort, coneflower, and benzoin bark.

Herbal steam is better than plain steam on the face. Either type, though, is excellent for the skin: 1) it softens surface cells so they be can sloughed off during **The Natural Method Massage**; 2) steams opens follicles so they can be easily cleaned; 3) the vapor penetrates into the skin thereby helps pores to eliminate toxins (here's where the herbal steam is far better than plain steam because herbal essences are carried into the skin and improves cellular metabolism); 4) lines are softened and the skin responds well to the toner and moisturizer; 5) the vapor mist increases blood circulation.

Place a handful of herbs into a bowl and pour about a quart of boiling water over the herbs. Create a tent with a towel and allow the steam to rise onto your face. Skin that has large couperose areas should be held about 24 inches away from the vapor. Thick or oily skin can be closer to the vapor (about 15 or 16 inches).

Colors Plate 5, Figs. 4, 5, and 6: Diane pours a handful of herbs in a bowl, pours in hot water, and steams face under towel made into tent.

STEP FOUR - Natural Method Massage

After steaming your face for a couple of minutes under the towel, remove it and give your skin a **The Natural Method Massage** with herbal oils. **Color Plate 6, Figs. 7 and 8** show Diane applying an herbal oil to her fingers and beginning massage. A single oil can also be used as a facial massage oil, make-up remover, and beauty oil such as jojoba oil, borage or *Rosa Mosqueta* rose hip seed oil. Our recommendations for a beauty massage oil follow:

Herbal Complexion Oil - Jojoba oil, wheat germ oil, *Rosa Mosqueta* oil, vitamin F complex, vitamin E, panthenol (B₅), avocado oil, St. John's wort oil, borage oil, carrot oil, arnica blossom oil, aloe vera juice, evening primrose oil, and alfalfa extract. (Check ingredients list or mix your own.)

A single oil can also be used as a facial massage oil, make-up remover, and beauty oil such as jojoba oil, borage or *Rosa Mosqueta* rose hip seed oil.

Apply a small amount of oil in the palm of your hand; rub hands together, and begin massage on the forehead. Follow the 11 steps of **The Natural Method Massage**, as pictured in the following diagrams and photos showing each step. Use a gentle but firm touch and never lift your fingers from the skin. The movements are fluid and move from one step to the other. If possible, get somebody do to the massage on you, but if not do the massage on yourself. Enjoy!

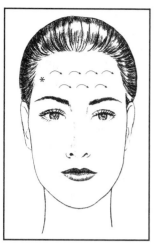

STEP ONE
Circular Massage of Forehead.

Use the middle and index fingers of both hands in a semi-circular movement. Apply light strokes *(effleurage)* toward the left temple. Begin at the * on the right temple, moving left and finishing in the center of the forehead. Do this across the forehead five times. Do not lift your fingers: movement must be smooth and even.

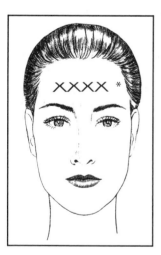

STEP TWO
Criss-Cross Massage of Forehead.

Use the index and middle fingers of both hands. Begin at the left temple, and work from left to right using criss-cross motions. Finish this step in the center of your forehead by pressing lightly. Do this five times.

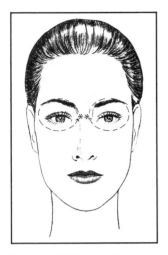

STEP THREE Eye Area Massage.

Use a very gentle touch on the thin and delicate skin around the eyes. Place the middle fingers at the inner corners of the eyes and the index fingers over the brows. Slide to the outer corner of the eyes and back again. Do this five times.

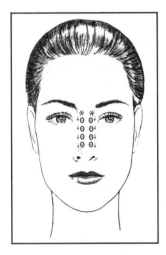

STEP FOUR Massage of the Nose Area.

Slide your fingers from the eye area to each side of the bridge of the nose. Press firmly and rotate one time, then slide down the nose in a circular movement *(effleurage)*. Press and rotate; press and rotate. End by pressing and rotating on the tip of your nose, then return to the beginning position, and repeat three times.

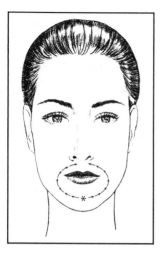

STEP FIVE
Massage
Around the
Mouth.

Slide your right hand under the chin, and bring thumb and middle fingers up to the corners of the mouth. Do a circular *effleurage* five times. Continue around the mouth; press and rotate until you reach the cleft in the upper lip. Repeat this massage three times.

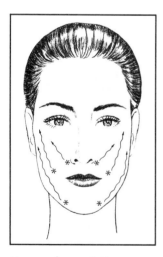

STEP SIX
Massage
The Cheeks.

Using the middle and index fingers of both hands, massage from the chin across the cheeks to the earlobes, from the corners of the mouth to the earlobes, and from the corners of the nose to the tips of the ears. Repeat this massage five times.

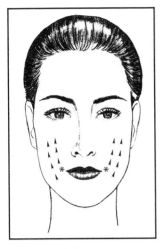

STEP SEVEN Pressing Massage of the Cheeks.

Beginning at the corners of the mouth, gently but firmly tap the face with a lifting and dropping motion of both hands on both sides of the face at the same time. Repeat this five times.

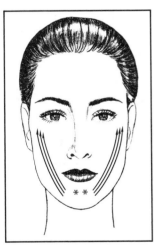

STEP EIGHT Massage The Sides Of The Face.

Grasp the flesh at the chin with the thumb and knuckle of the first finger of both hands. Work up the face with a "plucking" movement. Go up both sides of the face in this manner, and come down repeating the movement five times.

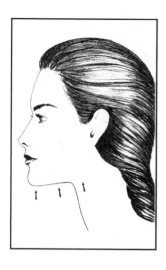

STEP NINE
Massage Under The Jaw Line.

Gently lift the jaw line with the tips of the fingers and slide back toward the ears.

STEP TEN
Massage Under Jaw.

Place both hands (palms down) with the fingertips en-twined under the neck. Begin a scissor-like move-ment back and forth keeping the fingertips together. Repeat this movement five times *(See diagram 10).*

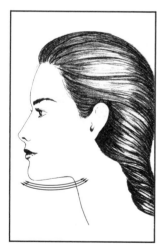

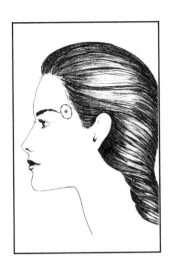

STEP ELEVEN
Completing The Facial Massage.

Complete the facial massage by gently rotating temples, then pressing for three seconds. Repeat five times and gradually taper off pressure.

STEP FIVE - Herbal or Clay Mask

Why are masks put on the skin, and what do they do? Masking the skin goes back to antiquity. It is believed that clay masks, herbal masks, and occlusive "leaf" masks were used in ancient Egypt as far back as 30 B. C. The American Indians used occlusive "leaf" masks for their healing properties, knowing that the drawing effect would cleanse a wound and increase healing. Professional aestheticians use clay masks, jelly masks, and wax masks. The jelly mask, which is called an Herbal Jelly Mask by aestheticians, is made by blending an herbal tea into glycerine and adding dry pectin to create a gel. You can create your own Herbal Jelly Mask every bit as good as any you could get from an aesthetician or buy in a store. Here is how you make it.

Herbal Jelly Mask

For Most Skin Types
3 oz. (85 grams) herbal tea
3 oz. (85 grams) glycerine
½ oz. (14 grams) pectin

For Dry Skin Types
3 oz. (85 grams) herbal tea
3 oz. (85 grams) glycerine
1 oz. (28 grams) jojoba oil
½ oz. (14 grams) pectin

Procedure: put glycerine into bowl and stir as you gradually add pectin powder. Be sure the pectin powder is blended into glycerine (no lumps). You can use an electric mixer if you wish. When the glycerine and pectin blend is uniform, add the herbal tea, stirring as you do to get the tea into blend. (If you are adding the jojoba oil, add it before the herbal tea.) This mixture should be left overnight as it takes about 8 to 12 hours to thicken into a gel. When you choose an herb, choose one for the desired effect (see **CHARTING THE HERBS** in **CHAPTER 6**) or mix several together for a desired effect (see **CHAPTER 19**). Choose herbs with a hydrating or moisturizing effect for the dry skin gel mask. If you wish, you can add one ounce of honey to the mask mixture (especially the dry skin type), but be sure you aren't allergic to honey (or for that matter to any of the herbs used). Be sure to brew your tea in distilled water.

These are some of the ingredients used for masking the skin:

Glycerine - For moisturizing benefits.
Calamine - Zinc powder that soothes and heals.
Fuller's earth - Or kaolin or other clays that stimulate and draw. Because they absorb oils, clays can be very drying to the skin. Avoid so-called "magic clays"; they may contain impurities.
Magnesium - Astringent.
Sulfur - Drying action, indicated for skin problems.
Jojoba oil - Moisturizing, indicated for some skin problems.
Honey - Moisturizing and drawing effect.
Sweet almond oil - Reduces the drying effect in clay type masks; desirable for dehydrated skin.
Rose water - Mild toning effect on the skin; refreshingly fragrant.
Orange water - Mild toning effect; refreshingly fragrant.
Witch hazel - Mild astringent with soothing qualities for irritated skin.

Many masks found on the market are loaded with synthetic chemicals. Always get only natural ingredients in a mask (read the label); if you can't find one you like in a store, you are better off making your own. Choose a mask for your skin type. If you have combination skin, apply a mask with moisturizing properties on the dry areas and a more astringent mask on the oily areas.

The desired effect is for the mask to dry and then be rinsed away or peeled away, but a mask can remain "damp" on the skin and remain on the skin a certain period. This type of mask is desirable for dry type skin or combination skin and is often sold as a "sea type mask." It will usually contain sea herbs (seaweeds, etc.), with clay (kaolin), honey, and herbal oils. The mask does not have to become dry and brittle to have a drawing effect or occlusive effect on the skin.

You can create an herbal and meal type mask by blending dry materials with water, honey, egg, etc. You can also purchase combinations of herbs and meals for mixing a mask or get a ready-mixed meal mask. They can act as a skin scrub as well as a mask.

The herbal and meal mixtures you can purchase are blended with fruits, vegetables, milk, etc. Here are some kitchen cosmetic suggestions:

Strawberries - Crushed and added to a herbal or gel mask, they have an astringent effect on the skin. This mask is stimulating.

Bananas - Crushed and added to an herbal or gel mask, they leave the skin soft and smooth.

Avocados - Crushed and added to a mask (or used directly on the skin), these are beneficial for dry type skin. They don't work as well in a clay mask as they do in herbal and meal mixtures.

Papaya - Due to certain enzymes in this fruit (e. g., *papain*, which is also used as a meat tenderizer), it has a softening effect on tissues.

Honey - When added to any mask mixture, it has a toning, tightening, and hydrating effect.

Vitamin B Complex - Though it has an unpleasant odor, the B complex is beneficial to the skin. It hydrates the skin and leaves it smooth and moist.

Vitamin C - Adding ascorbic acid powder to a mask gives it an exceptional astringent effect. This is probably kinder to the skin than lemon juice which may be too acidic and harsh (though lemon juice has a slight bleaching effect that may be desirable).

Oatmeal - Very soothing to the skin, it gently exfoliates (also a slight bleaching effect).

Vitamin D - Has healing properties and is soothing to irritated skin.

Vitamin E - Is known for its healing effects. When applied to an open wound, it can eliminate scarring and speed healing. It is superb mixed with aloe vera. In a mask it lubricates and softens dry skin.

Camomile tea - Good for steaming the skin. In a mask it has a calming, soothing effect, and is a skin softener.

Comfrey tea - Will heal wounds, skin ulcers, and soothe the skin. Comfrey contains a substance known as allantoin which reportedly has excellent healing and cell-proliferating properties.

Menthol - Derived from peppermint and is somewhat stronger. It is cooling, healing, and mildly antiseptic.

Peppermint tea - It has a cooling, soothing, and antiseptic action. This tea is rich in vitamins A and C and (like menthol) is good for the skin.

The herb charts in this book will give you their various benefits for the hair and skin. This can help you create other masks for your specific needs. There are many masks for various types of skin, but here are two mixtures that work very well.

Herbal Mask with Oatmeal and Jojoba Meal - Coconut fatty acid base, jojoba meal, oatmeal flakes, aloe vera gel, eucalyptus, menthol, wheat germ oil, carrot oil, avocado oil, lemon oil, citrus seed extract, vitamins C and E.

Clay Mask With Seaweed Extracts - Seaweed mixture of fucus, laminaria, sea ware, and bladderwrack blended into kaolin, honey, jojoba oil, almond oil, peppermint oil, papaya, and citrus seed oil.

The first mask is a "grainy" thick herbal mask, brown in color due to the jojoba meal and other herbs. See **Color Plate No. 6, Figs. 9 and 10** where Diane is applying the mask. Remove mask with damp wet cotton or a wet towel. You can also massage your skin and use the mask as a "scrub" on the skin.

Natural aesthetician Marianne Blakeslee uses this mask in a unique way. She stirs in a few drops of *Rosa Mosqueta* oil and a tablespoon of honey and allows steam to go into the mask and honey blend. She then applies the mask to the face, neck, and shoulders of her client.

During the masking step, Marianne massages the skin: she pushes her fingers into the mask and lifts, performing this movement over and over on the face, neck, and shoulders. It has a wonderful "pulling" effect, almost like an acupressure massage. She does the same massage with the clay mask, mixing it with *Rosa Mosqueta* oil and honey, heating it, and doing the same beneficial massage. It's worth a trip to her skin care clinic in Belmont, California, just to get this unique "mask massage."

Leave the mask on for 15 to 20 minutes. The two masks discussed here do not dry hard but remain slightly moist. To remove them, rinse them away or use a wet towel to get all the herbs or clay off the skin. Take care not to get any in the eyes. Keep your eyes closed while you rinse and wipe the mask away. Give yourself a mask treatment every couple of weeks or so. Sometimes you will skip Step 5 and go right to Step 6.

STEP 6 - Toning Your Skin

Applying a toner or astringent to your freshly cleaned skin is an important step in the facial. The toner or astringent acts to clear the skin of soap films, cellular debris, and any trace of oil. It also softens and emulsifies deposits and blackheads in the follicles. One feat an astringent cannot perform is to make large pores smaller: this is genetic. It can, however, make them appear smaller.

Don't use an astringent or toner that contains alcohol or acetone or synthetic chemicals of any kind. Please, PLEASE read labels. Use an herbal astringent with a witch hazel base. Look for a formula high in aloe vera which is, on its own, a good skin toner. Here is the perfect list of ingredients for an astringent: witch hazel base, nettle, myrrh, camomile, benzoin gum, elder blossom, marshmallow, aloe, rosemary, fennel, balm-mint, menthol, kelp, vitamins B, C, E, F, and citrus seed extact.

Dampen cotton pads with the herbal astringent.Start at the base of the neck and wipe the face in an upward and outward direction. Use the same general movements as described in cleaning the skin. Turn to a clean side of the cotton from time to time or use a new cotton pad dampened with herbal astringent. **Color Plate No. 7, Figs. 13 and 14,** show Diane applying astringent to a cotton pad and toning her skin.

STEP SEVEN - Moisturizing Your Skin

Choose a natural moisturizer for your skin. If you've read this far you will know what ingredients to look for and what to avoid. One type of moisturizer you may not be familiar with is vegetarian collagen. Here's what to look for in a product of this type:
Vegetarian collagen moisturizer - Essential fatty acid base, horsetail herb, coltsfoot herb, St. John's wort herb, coneflower herb, calendula herb, aristolechia herb, echinacea root, vitamins A, C, and E.

Moisturizers are used on oily as well as dry skin, but look for different ingredients in moisturizers for different skin types.
Collagen Moisturizer (15% Soluble Collagen [bovine]) - essential fatty acid base, vitamin F, aloe vera, soluble collagen, elastin, reticulin (these three are dermal proteins), vitamins A, C,

E, and citrus seed extract. Moisturizers with dermal proteins should not contain methyl and propyl paraben which are not compatible. Label should specify "soluble collagen."

Elastin Moisturizer - Essential fatty acid base, aloe vera, elastin, reticulin, natural moisturizing factor (this is calcium, lactic acid, vitamin F), Echinacea root, aristolochia herb, wheat germ oil, avocado oil, carrot oil, vitamin E oil, provitamin A, vitamins B, C, E, and elastase (this is the elastin enzyme).

Some people alternate between collagen and elastin moisturizers, but another type of moisturizer is a placenta type: **Placenta/herbal moisturizer with vitamins** - Essential fatty acid base, aloe, balm-mint, fennel, yarrow, lavender, vitamins B, C, E, placenta, and soluble collagen. **Herbal moisturizer for oily-type complexions** - coconut fatty acid base, balsam, coltsfoot, nettle, balm-mint, allantoin (comfrey extract), goa herb (tonic herb for oily or acne-prone skin), vitamins A, B, C, and E.

The placenta-type moisturizer is for very dry skin, but **The Natural Method Facial** as outlined does not necessarily call for a special moisturizer for dry-type skin, since the entire facial improves all skin types.

The moisturizer for oily skin does leave the skin soft and smooth. It is not oily in consistency. You will notice that in the facial I include the use of oils and the skin therefore gets its share of herbal oils. In the "celltherapy" step of the facial I suggest using *Rosa Mosqueta* oil if your skin is dry or has premature aging or UV damage.

Apply the moisturizer to the finger tips as Diane is doing in **Color Plate 7, Fig. 15**, and then spread it on the fingers as she is doing in **Fig. 16**. Don't use too much moisturizer, and if any remains after application, blot it off your face with a tissue. Apply the moisturizer using the same general movements you would use for the facial massage and be sure you use the moisturizer on the neck area as well as the face. **Color Plate No. 7, Fig. 17** shows Diane applying moisturizer.

STEP EIGHT - Rejuvenate With A Cellular Treatment

This step appears to be just using another moisturizer, but it is a very specific step. You must choose skin care treatments that are specifically formulated for the improvement of skin cells. Again, this doesn't mean you're leading black sheep to slaughter, and it doesn't mean that you need a tiny glass ampoule that you break and pour on your skin. A celltherapy treatment can contain animal tissue extracts, but it can also be vegetal. In the past few years I've found that a vegetarian celltherapy is every bit as good (and better for our animal friends) as any animal cellular mixtures, and this holds true for the use of collagen and elastin too. Research has proven better results with botanicals for the skin. (See **CHAPTER 19**.)

Use a spatula to put the celltherapy treatment on the forehead, cheeks, and chin (just a spot in each area), and then massage the treatment into the skin (See **Color Plate No. 7, Fig. 18**).

If your skin is very dry, developing signs of premature aging, or has UV damage, I suggest you apply *Rosa Mosqueta* oil and *Rosa Mosqueta* cream during the cellular treatment just as Diane is doing in **Color Plate No. 8, Fig. 19**).

STEP NINE - Hydrate Your Skin

The last step in **The Natural Method of Skin Care** is primal: we return to water. Use a good quality mineral water in a fine mist pump spray bottle. If you purchase a mineral water spray from your health food store, look for more than just water and glycerine in a bottle for your money. Here's the best list of ingredients for a good mineral water spray with herbs and vitamins: Natural mineral water base, aloe vera gel, vitamin A, vitamin E, vitamin F, PABA, inositol, pantothenate, horse chestnut, fennel, hops, camomile, balm-mint, and yarrow.

Close your eyes and spray the mineral water spray on the skin as Diane is doing in **Color Plate No. 8, Fig. 20.**

STEP TEN - Natural Make-Up

This step is optional. In fact, I recommend NOT using make-up just after a facial. Let your face go bare for a few hours and relish its healthy, natural beauty. If you are going to use make-up, get natural make-up, which uses no talc or petrochemicals but powdered silk and natural colors.

First apply a base powder to protect your skin, but not talc or a pressed powder that uses synthetic colors and other petrochemicals.

In **Color Plate No. 8, Fig. 21,** Diane is applying a translucent base powder. Notice it doesn't color the skin but it does even skin tones slightly. It won't make your skin look dry or oily, but an added benefit is that if your skin tends to be oily and look shiny, it will reduce the shiny look. Here is a blend of ingredients to look for in a good base powder:

Translucent Base Powder - silk powder, cinnamon powder, aloe vera powder, henna (neutral), and allantoin (comfrey root).

If you wish to add color, look for coloring powders that you can use as a blush, eye shadow, on the lips, etc. In **Fig. 22,** Diane is applying a rose tone to her cheeks. **Fig. 23** shows Diane apply medium tone to her eye lids and a deep tone in the creases below the browbone. In **Fig. 24,** she is using a natural red lip gloss. Except for eyeliner around her eyes, Diane has used absolutely no mass-produced chemicalized make-up.

If you don't wish to go through the entire procedure of **The Natural Method,** you can scale it down to your needs, but you should follow the full nine-step procedure once a week. On page 394 is a diagram of an abbreviated version of **The Natural Method of Skin Care.**

Hydro-Occlusive Mask Treatment

Some aestheticians and skin care clinics give a collagen mask treatment to the skin for the purpose of getting more collagen into the skin. I call this a "hydro-occlusive mask treatment," and my method of doing it at home is much better (and costs far less) than the ones you'll get in skin care clinics.

To create your own mask, use a section of plastic wrap. Create a mask pattern, and lay the plastic wrap on the pattern. Cut out eye sections, a nose section, and mouth section. This is easily done with a single-edged razor blade. Put this aside. Then follow the easy version of **The Natural Method** as shown on page 394. Hydrate your face more than usual so that the plastic wrap will adhere. Apply the plastic wrap to the skin, and press it on. Spray on more mineral water if needed. Use a hand dryer to dry the film mask on the skin for two to three minutes. Turn the dryer to "hot" so the mask will shrink onto the skin. Peel the mask away. Your skin will be smooth and soft. The occlusive action of the plastic wrap against the skin will increase absorption of the moisturizing and/or rejuvenating treatments you have used.

The "hydro-occlusive mask treatment" can be done as needed, and you may want to use other products under the mask, such as *Rosa Mosqueta* oil and cream. At first you will find it difficult to work with plastic wrap because they tend to cling, but this is the best mask you can use.

The secret to **The Natural Method of Skin Care** is using good quality products and ingredients and following the many steps. As you do it more and more, you will become an expert. The difference it will make in the health and appearance of your skin will surprise you. It works, and it really is worth the effort.

Hydro-Occlusive Mask Step-By-Step

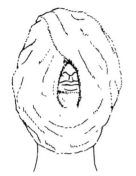

1. Towel steam skin.

2. Clean skin with natural cleanser.

3. Tone skin with natural astringent.

4. Apply natural moisturizer or celltherapy.

5. Hydrate skin with mineral water spray.

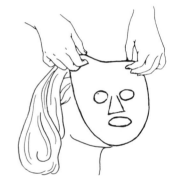

6. Apply "film" mask to wet skin and press on.

7. Dry "film" mask with hair dryer.

8. Peel away film mask.

Easy Version of Natural Method Facial

Hot Towel   *Cleanse*

Herbal Steam

Massage   *Tone*

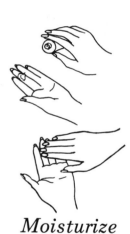

Moisturize

Hydrate

Part IV

Resources

or

Mother Nature's Buying Guide

organitoons

RESOURCES

Natural Cosmetics Manufacturers and Herbal Suppliers

"Resource" is the name we apply to what we acquire that complements our lives, that gives substance to our beliefs, and that even sends a message about who we are to those we meet.

Of course, some resources are purchased or obtained without thought. Somebody tells us to get this or that because it's great, and because we value their judgement we do.

Quite often little thought is given to the choice of cosmetics, yet, it should be analyzed. Hopefully, this book can be of value in that respect because this choice isn't really as casual and unimportant as we suppose. It holds "brand name" elitist overtones and many psychological factors, including how we want others to see us and how we feel about ourselves and the surrounding world. It is both simple and complex. During many centuries of recorded history, cosmetics have been part of religion and the morality, and during some periods a woman who wore make-up was thought a prostitute. Even today the use of make-up still has moral connotations for some segments of society.

Some men and women are more comfortable with certain brands of cosmetics (even brands of shampoo) for reasons that have nothing to do with what they contain. One name brand skin toner, for example, sells for ten dollars yet is made of the worst possible chemical mix, while a natural brand made of the finest natural substances for the skin (as well as our environment) sells for half that amount. But many supposedly intelligent people will purchase the more expensive, highly-chemicalized name brand, just because of the elitist image the brand name conveys. (These same consumers could make a far superior product in their own homes for less money.) By the same token, there are cheap mass-produced toners with the same chemicals as the overpriced varieties, available in discount and chain stores for less money.

Buying cosmetics is like buying art. Most art and certain cosmetics are elitist. Some rich people go to an exclusive department store and purchase a "famous national brand" celltherapy cream at an outrageous price and shun a cheap chain store brand and a more effective natural brand. These people, who obviously don't read labels, have adopted an elitist attitude. They can afford the famous brand celltherapy; they believe the hype about rubbing dead animal extracts on their skin, and they are attracted to the name of the manufacturer on the label.

There are exceptions. Some informed consumers, in every social and economic class, read ingredients labels and buy with intelligence. They know more than department store buyers.

I have found that more and more people are learning about cosmetics and the value of natural ingredients. They are also learning that the chemicalization of cosmetics via animal testing and animal extracts is a danger to all species and our environment. Mass-merchandised cosmetics try to zero in on this by creating products that have existed for some years in the health food industry - such as Jojoba Shampoo, Aloe Vera Cosmetics, etc. However, mass producers always compromise their so-called "natural" formulas with chemical additives which most concerned and informed consumers don't want. So the famous brands go on selling to people who don't know or care about ingredients and the implications chemicals have to man and his environment.

Creating Natural Cosmetics Is An Art

The creation of a natural cosmetic is an art, very much like composing a piece of music or writing a beautiful drama. The perfumer Fred Peronne says, "Cosmetic chemists are magicians." It is true that the best of them are, but the worst of them are merely chemical merchants: the producers of formulations for a dollar-and-dime mass consumption ideology based strictly on cost and profit with no regard for quality and content. The corporate structure of private enterprise turns the cosmetic sleight-of-hand artist into a mere illusionist: the cosmetic maven becomes a peddler of chemicals for the industrial chemical complex. He or she creates cosmetic illusions instead of real products that actually do something for the hair and skin.

The natural cosmetic compounder dips his hands into the essence of nature to create. The synthetic cosmetic chemist dips his hands into the chemical beaker.

Even when the synthetic cosmetic chemist does create a supposedly "natural" product he or she always takes the synthetic compounding path (based on cheap, synthesized ingredients and combining a drop from nature for every cup taken from the chemical brewmasters). Because they deal in mere illusions, with neither their hands (nor their hearts and minds) involved with nature, they can't make natural products.

Even though natural hair and skin care products may not be perfect, because nature herself is imperfect, they are far safer and more valuable than the chemical brews. The biggest fear which has been suggested to consumers by the synthetic name-brand manufacturers and the FDA is that a natural cosmetic could contain dangerous microogranisms if it doesn't contain preservatives such as methylparaben, propylparaben, etc. This is totally untrue. Synthetic chemical mixtures (based mostly on inaccurate animal tests) are far more dangerous than almost any microorganism that would develop in a natural cosmetic. Plus, there are natural preservatives that are far less toxic to us and our environment than the usual synthetic preservatives (which are put in products not to protect humans but to protect mass-produced, warehoused products). There is no perfect preservative, synthetic or natural. Furthermore, all allergic reactions can be traced to specific substances or mixtures of substances, rather than to microorganisms. The allergen can be synthetic or natural.

At first I didn't know whether to put this section in the book. A resources section is almost out of date as soon as you print it. This is especially true with manufacturers who sell aloe (in particular) and those who make natural cosmetics (in general).

Aloe manufacturers and packagers spring up like weeds in a garden. Most of them seem to be located in Texas. They want you to use aloe for everything: they want you to drink it (whether it gives you diarrhea or not). They want you to rub it on your face (and other parts of the body). They want you to brush your teeth with it (the Russians say it cures gum disease). As they say all this, they also warn you that some manufacturers "water down" their aloe.

"Buy our aloe," they proselytize, "because it's the real thing." This amuses me because when I look at many aloe cosmetics, guess what I find besides aloe? I find the same old synthetic chemicals and petrochemicals used in most cosmetics. Because there are so many aloe products, how do you know which ones to buy? You can't trust a certain type of outlet because aloe manufacturers sell anywhere they can: in drug stores, discount stores, supermarkets, health food stores, flea markets, multilevel pyramid sales, out of the trunks of their cars, or at prayer meetings (yes, there is a "born again" aloe). My only advice for buying aloe products is the advice I give for everything else: **READ THE LABEL.**

There are also quite a few jojoba cosmetic manufacturers (almost as many as aloe pushers). Their main slogan is "Save the Whales" (even though it became a crime to murder sperm whales for their oil some years ago). I suppose it's still a good one, but slogans can be misleading because the same old synthetic chemicals we see in many aloe products crop up in many jojoba products as well, so the above advice holds true here as well.

"We don't test on animals" is another slogan that can be misleading because many of the chemicals used by the sloganizers are tested on animals by the chemical manufacturers who supply the cosmetics companies. If cosmetic companies insist on using slogans, here's one I invented that covers most of the bases: Save The Whales, Protect The Environment From Petrochemicals, Don't Test On Animals, and Don't Use Animal Tested Chemicals Which Are Assumed Safe or Make Claims Based On Animal Testing. It's long. but it has to be to say it all.

When you check out the cosmetic companies in this section, **READ THE LABELS.** It doesn't matter whether or not they say they don't test on animals. It doesn't matter whether they say they don't use animal extracts. It does matter if they use chemicals that pollute our environment, chemicals which are used as safe and effective based on animal testing. This is what you find out by reading the product label. A label may say: This Cosmetic Is Not Tested On Animals, but may still have ingredients such as sodium lauryl sulfate, methyl paraben, propyl paraben, benzalkonium chloride, etc. These chemicals have only been proven safe with animal testing. If you put them in your product you rely on or accept those tests (unless you've proven their safety with human or *in vitro* testing). Also, many of these chemicals pollute our environment because they aren't biodegradable. This affects all species. You won't know any of this if you don't read the label.

I decided to include this resources section as a service to readers, but I don't say that all the products are natural or that they work as claimed. There are a few manufacturers listed here whose products I've used quite successfully with **The Natural Method of Hair And Skin Care.** However, I'm not suggesting any products, even the ones I've found to be superior and natural, because I'm not in control of their formulation. Control and concern is the whole name of the natural cosmetics game, and these are things which aren't printed on the labels. And if I'm not in control and my concern isn't there, then I can't approve or disapprove of any brand.

If aloe manufacturers spring up like weeds in a garden then cosmetic manufacturers grow like kudzu in Georgia. The *Pueraria thumbegiana* has been known to grow so dense that it takes over abandoned houses, cars on cinder blocks, and whole areas within months. Natural cosmetic manufacturers have come on the scene like kudzu, but they don't often last that long. Hence, some listed in this section may not be around long after this book's publication, and new companies will also doubtless spring up after the book's appearance. Look for most of the brands listed here in health food stores, and check them out against the list of synthetic and natural substances I've discussed in this book.

If you continue your research by writing (or calling) cosmetic manufacturers, don't ask them for samples. Let's be logical. A manufacturer who has to give away samples is pretty desperate to sell you his or her products. If they were in demand and worth buying there'd be no need to give them away.

Another rule of being a good consumer is not to ask cosmetic manufacturers about other brands. What can manufacturers say to you? If they say, "that brand is great," then why should you buy their brand? If the manufacturer says, "that brand stinks," how would you know if they were being honest? All you should ask about is the products made by the manufacturer you are querying. Also, be considerate. Don't think you have the right to tie up the phone with a long chat with a manufacturer. They're busy. Give them the same courtesy you'd want from somebody who called you on the job or at home.

Don't call a cosmetic manufacturer and ask dumb questions or something you could find out on your own. "Hello, I called to ask you what collagen is ... " That's a dumb question because if you want to know what collagen or any other ingredient is you can find the information in a dictionary, or this book. Just because a manufacturer has an ingredient in their product doesn't mean they have to give you unending data about it. If you must know and can't find out about an ingredient on your own, then write to the manufacturer and inquire in writing. Above all, don't call them collect. Why should a manufacturer take your collect call to answer something they could send you with a postage stamp?

Don't be a "can I get it wholesale" type. Cosmetic manufacturers have price schedules and discounts based on volume buying from established wholesalers or retailers. When you try to get a product wholesale you are making it difficult for the manufacturer in many ways. If their wholesalers and/or retailers find out they sold to a consumer for a wholesale price (or at cost) it could cause a real business problem. It's inconsiderate and selfish to think that you are so special you should get the same price a retailer gets. You have none of the overhead a retailer has, and you aren't running a business. If a product is good, if it helps your hair and skin, if it's a superior natural formula, and if you like it, then it's worth the price you pay. I firmly believe that a cheap price usually means cheap merchandise, in most cases. I know from selecting natural ingredients from all over the world that a good natural quality hair and skin care product can't be compounded cheaply. Oh, it is possible to make a "natural" product that isn't really natural, and to make it with synthetics that claim to be natural (such as synthetic jojoba). But if you read the label you will know if it contains enough good quality natural substances to warrant the price. This book is also a service in that regard since I've written about all the various natural substances.

Don't suffer from the "If it's from Europe it must be good" syndrome. Just as you may be enamored by cosmetics that use European hype (i.e. Swiss Skin Care, German Cosmetics, French Extracts), in other countries they often want to buy products sold to them with American hype. There's only one rule: **READ THE LABEL.** Not the "hype" label, but the ingredients label. But be aware that products from Europe may not have all the ingredients listed or they may not be listed accurately. The FDA is not staffed well enough to keep up with the labeling of cosmetic imports. And what can they really do against a foreign cosmetic firm if they fail to label properly? I once read a cosmetic label written in several languages (including English) and the ingredients were slightly different in each language. Quite the opposite of what you may think, products in Europe are not all natural. They use the same synthetic chemicals that are often used in American mass-produced cosmetics, and they test on animals and pollute the environment with chemicals in cosmetics just as do many American manufacturers. In fact, there are more natural cosmetic manufacturers in the United States than there are in Europe, and they are far superior. So you see, the European Brand Cosmetic is largely hype. There are some good natural brands in other countries just as there are in the United States, but the only true measure is to read the ingredients label and make your judgement based on that.

You can be allergic to any ingredient, natural or synthetic. My suggestion is to do a patch test. Here is a quick patch test method:

Patch Test

1. Clean a small area on the inside of your arm by wiping it with alcohol.
2. Use a spatula or a butter knife and apply a small amount of the cosmetic you plan to use.
3. Cover this area with a bandage strip.
4. Allow 24 hours and then look at the area. If it is red, if it itches, or if a rash has formed, then you may be allergic to something in the cosmetic.
5. If you wish, wash the area and apply the same product to the same area once again.
6. Cover it with the bandage strip.
7. Allow 24 hours and then look at it again. If you got the redness and/or rash a second time, do not use the product.

The patch test isn't a perfect method of finding out if you're allergic to something, but it's helpful. You may also be temporarily allergic to a new product, and by using it often the allergic reaction will go away. The best method to know if this will occur is to do the patch test about seven times (daily for a week) and see if the rash or redness clears up. However, I only recommend this if you want to use the product and it's important to you to use it. However, ideally, I feel if the patch test tells you you're allergic to something it is best not to use the product.

Reading Labels

When you walk into a cosmetic section of a health food store, department store, or drug and/or discount store, you are hit with a rainbow of colored labels and boxes. Sometimes even the product inside the bottle is colored to match the packaging. The first thing most people do (and I've watched them) is pick the product up, glance at the product name and the slogans on the bottle or box, and then open the bottle and smell the contents. Since these three factors - packaging, color, and odor - probably influence buyers most, the cosmetic industry spends millions of dollars trying to come up with a winning slogan/product name, color, and odor.

Not very many people read the labels of what they buy. Oh yes, people do read food labels for diet and health purposes (to avoid sugar, etc.). But choosing cosmetics is a whole different ball game - and the stakes are equally high!

A study by Product Marketing's Consumer Expenditure reported that in 1985 (this book went to press in early 1987) sales for skin care products were $2.6 billion. The top area of sales was in products designed for those concerned about aging skin: 1. face creams and cleansers ($57 million); 2. face lotions and moisturizers ($51 million); body lotions and emollients ($41 million); suntan products ($25 million).

In 1987, *People Magazine* commissioned a study of 900 women to find out what treatments were most important to them in the use of facial cleansers (not soap), moisturizing and skin care treatments. The consumers reported that the most important ingredients in a skin care product are those that are hypo-allergenic, provide a sunscreen, and prevent wrinkles. Moisturizing the skin was considered the most important skin care product function, followed by deep-cleansing, sunscreening, and minimizing wrinkles. Concern that the products not cause allergic reactions was the most important consideration.

We are obsessed with aging, and we are worried about product safety. Even though the term hypo-allergenic is a misnomer (products marked as hypo-allergenic may contain synthetic chemicals that cause short and long-range problems) the concern is still there.

Most of the people surveyed bought their products from drug and chain stores, and the rest bought from department stores, discount outlets, and supermarkets. Cosmetic buyers for these various outlets were also interviewed. Most felt that what they wanted for skin care were single-purpose products and sun protection products. A Marshall Fields spokesperson said the trend for the future was simple products that work in a simple regimen and that complicated products are not going to work. The 'hype word' today is hypo-allergenic, said one buyer. He added that consumers don't know the difference between the phrases dermatology-approved and dermatology-tested. Most people look for unscented and lanolin-free products.

What all this tells me is that the buyers in department, drug, discount, and supermarkets don't know anything about the chemicals that go into cosmetics, and they assume their customers don't know much either. They are neophytes of the first order if all they are concerned with is the slogans "hypo-allergenic," "fragrance-free," and whether or not a cosmetic has lanolin. Let's face it, if you don't read the label you don't know what you're getting.

When a "hypo-allergenic" product contains mineral oil, is it really hypo-allergenic or, for that matter, when it contains any of the FD&C or D&C colors is it still hypo-allergenic? If you use a hypo-allergenic shampoo and you're not allergic to it but it contains the chemicals that may be contaminated with the cancer causing chemical NDELA (see pp. 271-272), is this hypo-allergenic? Well, you don't break out in a rash. Maybe you just get cancer!

I have renamed "Hypo-allergenic" as "Hype-allergenic" because that's exactly what it is: hype. There is only one way to get a hypo-allergenic product and that is to buy based on the ingredients label and how well the product works for you. For example, it doesn't make sense to me for somebody to avoid lanolin and buy a product that has mineral oil, DEA-oleth-10 phosphate, imidazolidinyl urea, disodium EDTA, etc., etc. These chemicals are far more dangerous than lanolin, and there's a long list of chemicals that are wolves in sheep's clothing. At least lanolin is the real thing, and you know what you're getting (whether you like lanolin or not). In any case lanolin is chemicalized and processed in many different ways.

I can understand avoiding lanolin if you want no animal extracts of any kind in your cosmetic product; you're a purist vegetarian, but to avoid lanolin for any health reason and use all the other chemicals they throw into cosmetics is absurd.

In all the cosmetic articles and books written each year, very few suggest that you learn what the various chemicals in cosmetics are, what they do, if they're safe, and that you put this information to work by reading labels.

Only you can read the label and trust your own eyes and judgement. I have never met one cosmetic counter person who knows what all the chemicals are, what they do and if they're safe. Here's a conversation I had recently at a cosmetic counter.

AUBREY: What's in this Eye Zone Gel? There's no label on the bottle?

COSMETIC CLERK: Oh, it isn't on the bottle.

AUBREY: I was looking on these brochures. It isn't on any of the brochures.

CLERK: No, it isn't on the brochures.

AUBREY: Since this product is used around the eyes, isn't it a good idea to know what's in it? I mean, maybe it has something that could be harmful.

CLERK: Oh, no. That's not possible. It's been tested.

AUBREY: I'd still like to see the ingredients.

CLERK: Wait. It's here on the box.

AUBREY: I see. No way of being able to read this without buying the product, I suppose? I mean, the person I'm getting it for needs to check it out.

CLERK: Oh, we have to account for every box.

AUBREY: The cost is thirty-five dollars?

CLERK: Yes. But all the ingredients are safe.

I spent the thirty-five dollars so you can read the ingredients for this Eye Zone Gel (which goes by a different spelling and name, because I have withheld the brand name): purified water, polyglyceryl-methacrylate, tissue matrix extract, glycerine, butylene glycol, TEA-carbomer

940, propylene glycol, TEA-acrylamide copolymer, trisodium EDTA, imidazolidinyl urea, methylchloroisothiazolinone, methylisothiazolinone and other ingredients

Now here we have an example of labeling that makes me mad. I paid $35.00 to read the label on the box, and what do I get? I get an abundance of synthetic and petrochemicals and the statement at the end of the label that says: "And other ingredients." As if the ingredients I see aren't bad enough: they also throw in some more stuff and don't tell me what it is.

Now you are apt to say, "But don't FDA regulations say you have to list ALL ingredients?" The truth is, the FDA doesn't say that. You have to list the main ingredients, but you are not responsible for ingredients that you did not put in and ingredients that are added in such tiny amounts that they feel listing them would be ludicrous. To return to the ingredients in the eye cream: what is "tissue matrix extract"? The manufacturer claims this is a "trade secret." However, it is simply an animal cellular extract which do not make you look younger, don't take away wrinkles, are rendered useless (even if they did work which they don't) by the synthetic chemical formula. Let's examine some of the chemicals in this Eye Zone Gel.

TEA-Carbomer 940 - This is how they create the "gel" look of the Eye Zone Gel. They call it a "cool clear gel." Carbomer 940 is a synthetic emulsifier and thickener. Guess what? It can cause eye irritation! (See page 272, Carbomer 934, etc.)

This gel agent also contains TEA. That's triethanolamine, which has been found to be contaminated with the nitrosating agent NDELA. (See pages 271-272 Carcinogenecy In Cosmetics.)

Butylene Glycol & Propylene Glycol - Butylene Glycol is used in the manufacture of polyester and cellophane. Propylene Glycol is a petrochemical and is used as an antifreeze and hydraulic brake fluid. On the skin it causes allergic reactions, and though, like mineral oil, it gives a temporary moisturizing effect, it will in the long run make the skin dry (see pp. 270, 301).

TEA-Acrylamide Copolymer - They weren't happy enough chemicalizing us with one dose of TEA (triethanolamine) - they had to give us another dose, along with more synthetic copolymers. Acrylamide or acrylates causes various skin problems whether used in cosmetics or in fabrics (see pp. 272 and 261).

Trisodium EDTA - EDTA is an acronym for ethylene diamine tetra acetic acid. It binds metallic ions and acts as an antioxidant. It causes many allergic reactions.

There's no need to go on and list all the various chemicals and discuss them. It is obvious that the products aren't prepared with sufficient regard for formula and the skin or hair of the person who is buying the product.

The only way to know what you're using and what you're paying for is to read the label. There is absolutely no other way to know. If the manufacturer admits that they are leaving some chemicals off the label my advice is NOT to buy the product.

This book gives enough information so you can learn quite a bit about almost any ingredient listed on a cosmetic, but the chemical industry is always coming out with chemicals so it's impossible to list them all in any book and be up to date. If the chemical on the label is long and complex sounding and you can't find it in this book, my advice is: don't buy that product.

Most cosmetic chemists are so unimaginative that they toss chemicals together without any sense of quality or aesthetics or consideration for the hair and skin. All you have to do is read a label and see the variety of chemicals to know that the product is a conglomeration of chemicals without any relationship to the real world or to our hair and skin. The product lacks harmony or purpose, which is what sets a good cosmetic product apart from an inferior one.

Again, I think compounding a good quality natural cosmetic is an art - like composing music or writing a play. The cosmetic must be thought out and planned just like a composition or a drama. The cosmetic must have harmony. The formula should fit together and every ingredient be related in some way to the others so that whole will benefit your hair or skin.

The natural cosmetic compounder wants a hair or skin care product with that kind of harmony. This means it's part of nature as much as possible. It means that the safety and quality of the product is not based on animal tests but on the test of time. If at the very beginning the cosmetic chemist sets out to make a product to sell for a high price based simply on a designer's name or on a rare ingredient, or based on advertising hype, there is absolutely no way a good, natural cosmetic will be the outcome.

The following cosmetic ingredients labels are based on products that can be purchased in various outlets. My purpose in including them here is to demonstrate that by reading a label you can know the following: 1. The quality of the ingredients, 2. If the cosmetic is natural, 3. If the price is reasonable for the ingredients listed.

I hope that by showing a variety of cosmetics and brands you will become adept at reading a cosmetic label and that this book will help you become a "natural cosmetics maven."

Sample Label of Hair Care Product
Found in Health Food Stores,
Department Stores, and Drug/Discount Stores

Swiss Shampoo
This exclusive formula contains: Purified Water, Sodium C14-16 Olefin Sulfonate, Propylene Glycol, Cocoamphocarboxypropionate, Lauramide DEA, Sodium Laureth Sulfate, Cocamidopropylamine Oxide, Citric Acid, Fragrance, Steartrimonium Hydrolyzed Animal Protein, Arnica Extract, Polyquaternium 10, Hayflower Extract, PEG-150 Distearate, Calendula Extract, Imiazolidinyl Urea, Disodium EDTA, Methylparaben, Propylparaben, FD & C Green No. 3, D & C Yellow No. 10.

This is a national brand shampoo sold in exclusive department stores.

RETAIL PRICE FOR 6 oz. - $7.50

COMMENTS: You could buy a good quality natural shampoo for this price or if you want a petrochemical brew you could buy a cheaper shampoo with the same chemicals in it. These herbal extracts are expensive but wasted in this formula. A simple coconut oil soap would clean the hair as well as the petrochemical mixture.

You pay for the name on the label, but not the juice in the bottle. Forget the famous name and read the label!

These are all petrochemicals. (See p. 263 on Alkyloamides).

Added to the product to lower the pH.

Synthetic fragrance!

The animal protein is supposed to repair damaged hair, but it is wasted in this formula (see p. 289 on Hydrolyzed Protein).

Instead of propylene glycol they could use vegetable glycerine.

Maybe these herbals are why the manufacturer called this a "Swiss Shampoo." These have little effect on the hair in such a synthetic formula.

Sequestering agent (p. 283).

Shampoo has paraben preservatives. They are not compatible with protein nor with synthetic detergents. Also, the parabens will not prevent the formation of nitrosamines. Vitamins C and E act as blocking agents against the formation of NDELA (see p. 294 on Nitrosamines).

Shampoo has artificial colors which are possible carcinogens.

Sample Label of Hair Care Product Found in Health Food Stores, Department Stores, and Drug/Discount Stores

Shampoo With Elastin
For Permed, Dry
Or Damaged Hair

Ingredients: Water, Ammonium Lauryl Sulfate, Cocamidopropyl Betaine, Cocamide DEA, Hydrolyzed Animal Elastin, Soluble Animal Collagen, Silk Amino Acids (Hydrolyzed Silk Protein), Hydrolyzed Animal Protein Sorbitol, Panthenol, Extracts of Camomile, Sage, Rosemary, Balsam Tolu, Yarrow, Comfrey, Witch Hazel, Lavender, Licorice, and Lemon Grass, PABA, Polyquaternium-10, Citric Acid, Quaternium-22, PEG-75 Lanolin, Stearamidopropyl Dimethylamine Lactate Ammonium Chloride, Sodium Styrene (and) Acrylates (and) Divinylbenzene Copolymer (and) Ammonium Monoxynol-4 Sulfate, Fragrance, Methylchloroisothiazolinone (and) Methylisothiazolinone, Diazolidinyl Urea.

National Health Food Chain Brand.

RETAIL PRICE FOR 6 oz. - $2.49

COMMENTS: If you compare this brand to the mass-produced name brand shampoo, you will find many of the same chemicals. This one, which is cheaper, actually has MORE HERBS and is more shampoo. Notice that this health food store brand has more synthetic chemicals than the non-"natural" brand.

This is a petrochemical combined with an ammonium compound (one of the least desirable synthetic detergents (see p. 265).

Synthetic detergents, including one with DEA (see p. 263).

The hydrolyzed animal extracts are included for hair repair, but this formula contains too many syndets and other synthetic chemicals for the protein to be of any value.

All these herbs are valuable, but why did they put them in such a synthetic formula?

This B vitamin is of no value in this shampoo. The sun dries out the hair, but so do ammonium sulfate and the quaterniums!

Don't buy shampoos (or conditioners) with quats in them! (See p. 303.)

Synthetic fragrance!

Causes allergic reactions and contains ammonia (p. 312, Urea).

Lactate is okay, but why the chemical junk with it?

Acrylates and other polymers cause allergic reactions (p. 261).

Sample Label of Hair Care Product
Found in Health Food Stores,
Department Stores, and Drug/Discount Stores

Jojoba/Aloe/Yucca Shampoo
Ingredients: Coconut Oil, Olive Oil Castile, Desert Herb Complex (Jojoba Oil, Aloe Vera, Yucca Root), Water, Citrus Seed Extracts with Vitamins A, C, and E.

Natural shampoo found only in health food stores.

RETAIL PRICE FOR 8 oz. - $7.50

COMMENTS: This looks like a simple shampoo, and in many ways it is. On the other hand, it's a good formula with no synthetic detergents or other chemicals. The high amounts of jojoba, aloe, and yucca make it a good quality buy. If you compare it to the other shampoos you will notice you're paying for lots of synthetic additives, which you don't need on your hair. This shampoo is somewhat expensive but compounded exclusively with good, natural ingredients.

The coconut oil and olive oil castile soap are natural hair cleansers (no sodium lauryl sulfate or other alkylamides).

Jojoba, aloe, and yucca root are excellent for the hair and scalp. Jojoba is an excellent hair and scalp conditioner. Aloe vera not only helps thicken shampoo formulas but is a good moisturizing agent. Yucca root is a mild cleanser.

Water is lower on the list of ingredients which means a higher amount of cleansers and herbals are used. The shampoo relies mostly on "wet hair" as the solvent.

The preservative is natural and includes Vitamins A, C, and E as "blocking agents" against the formation of nitrosamines (see pp. 271, 282-283, 294-295).

Sample Label of Hair Care Product
Found in Health Food Stores,
Department Stores, and Drug/Discount Stores

Ginseng Shampoo
Ingredients: Water, Coconut and Soya
Protein Soap, Aloe Vera, Hair Complex
Herbs (Nettle, Coltsfoot, Horsetail,
Cystine, d-Panthenol, Inositol), Ginseng
Root, Siberian Pine Extract with Vitamins
A, C, and E.

This natural shampoo is sold only in health
food stores.

RETAIL PRICE FOR 8 oz. - $6.50

COMMENTS: This is a natural shampoo
and no synthetic chemicals are used. It is
well-conceived and contains natural ingredients known to be hair care aids.

Natural cleansers for the hair; made
with coconut oil and soy protein.

High amount of aloe vera.

This shampoo includes the herbs
found to be excellent for hair repair, dandruff problems, and hair loss (see pp. 332-,
333, 333, 341).

Extra cystine in this formula, even
though horsetail herb has some cystine.
Important for repair of damaged hair and
the disulfide bond.

Ginseng root is a tonic but may not
be an important hair care ingredient.

Siberian pine extract has preservative qualities and gives a pleasant
natural fragrance. A clean and fresh-type
odor.

Vitamins A, C, and E are used as
natural preservatives, and they also act as
natural blocking agents to the formation
of nitrosamines.

Sample Label of Hair Care Product
Found in Health Food Stores,
Department Stores, and Drug/Discount Stores

Hot Oil Treatment
Ingredients: Water, Propylene Glycol, PEG-150 Distearate, Soyatrimonium Chloride, Isopropyl Alcohol, PPG-12-PEG-65 Lanolin Oil, Hydrolyzed Animal Keratin, Laureth-23, Disodium Phosphate, Citric Acid, Propylparaben, Methylparaben, Fragrance, Phenoxyethanol, D & C Yellow No. 10, D & C Green No. 5, and FD & C Red No. 40.

The usual petrochemical that is used instead of natural vegetable glycerine!

The usual polyethylene glycol and polypropylene glycol chemicals (more petrochemicals)

Lanolin oil is the ONLY natural oil in this formula.

Isopropyl alcohol isn't needed as a solvent, but it's there to make the product cheaper and as a carrying agent for all the synthetic oils and the lanolin.

The usual "paraben twins" are in the formulas as preservative, but they aren't compatible with the proteins which makes one wonder why they're there.

Who needs a synthetic fragrance in a hair treatment?

Why are the artificial colors there? They may be carcinogens.

National Brand Hair Conditioning Oil for Hot Oil Treatment of Hair. Sold in department, drug, and discount stores.

RETAIL PRICE FOR TWO BOTTLES OF 5/8 oz. EACH - $3.35

COMMENTS: This product is a good example of what mass-marketing cosmetic manufacturers do to a good idea. They give you a few drops of a substance currently popular in hair treatments - keratin -and throw it in to the usual mixture of synthetic chemicals and petrochemicals. You don't need artificial coloring, and you don't need synthetic preservatives (vitamin E would be a good natural preservative).

Note: you can locate many good natural oils for hot oil treatments in health food stores. Try pure jojoba oil or *Rosa Mosqueta* oil. Both are superior to this synthetic brew.

Sample Label of Hair Care Product
Found in Health Food Stores,
Department Stores, and Drug/Discount Stores

Swiss Instant Hair Conditioner
Ingredients: Purified Water, Cetearyl
Alcohol, Distearyldimonium Chloride,
Cetrimonium Chloride, Steartrimonium
Hydrolyzed Animal Protein, Quaternium
22, Quaternium 26, Dimethyl Stearamine,
Arnica Extract, Panthenol, Amidomethi-
cone, Calendula Extract, Tallowtrimonium
Chloride, Cetyl Alcohol, Hayflower Ex-
tract, Nonoxynol-10, Propylene Glycol,
Fragrance, Hydroxypropyl Methylcellu-
lose, PEG-40 Stearate, Citric Acid, Im-
idazolidinyl Urea, Methylparaben, Propyl-
paraben, D & C Green No. 5, D & C Yellow
No. 10.

National Brand Hair Conditioner
sold in exclusive department stores.

RETAIL PRICE FOR 6 oz. - $7.50

COMMENTS: This is the usual blend of
ammonium compounds and animal protein
found in many hair conditioners. Instead
of the usual stearalkoniunm chloride this
hair conditioner uses several ammonium-
type chemicals.

Fatty alcohols which can be natural
or synthetic (mixture of cetyl and stearyl
alcohols) used as emulsifiers and
emollients.

A quaternary ammonium salt. Synthetic. Irritating (p. 274).

Animal protein is an aid in repairing
damaged hair; however, this animal protein is not the best choice for that job (see
p. 289).

Quats are caustic ammonium
chemicals (p. 303).

Synthetic fragrance!

Arnica, calendula, hayflower, and
panthenol are good natural ingredients,
but they are ruined in this synthetic
chemical mismatch.

The usual synthetic preservatives
that are not compatible with protein and
should not be used in a protein hair or skin
product.

Synthetic colors that may be carcinogens. This particular mix is in the product to match the packaging. What do
they have to do with hair care?

Once again, the petrochemical propylene glycol because it's cheap. Vegetable
glycerine is far superior in hair and skin
care!

Sample Label of Hair Care Product
Found in Health Food Stores,
Department Stores, and Drug/Discount Stores

Glycogen Hair Conditioner

Ingredients: Essential Fatty Acid Base (with Amino Acids: Cysteine, Cystine, and Methionine), Lactalbumin (Milk Protein), Rosemary, Sage, Horsetail, Coltsfoot, Nettle, Glyco-Protein (Glycogen Polysaccharides), Balsam Tolu, Vitamins A, B, C, and E in Citrus Seed Extract. pH 4.5 to 5.5

Natural brand hair conditioner sold only in health food stores.

RETAIL PRICE FOR 8 oz. - $6.00

COMMENTS: This hair conditioner is a rich natural formula without the ammonium compounds and the industrial fabric softeners like stearalkonium chloride usually found in hair conditioners.

This formula also contains balsam tolu for those who like a "balsam instant conditioner." Balsam canada (*(Abies balsamea)* is the type used in most balsam conditioners because of the body it gives hair, but balsam tolu *(Myroxylon balsamum)* is far better and also has a mild antiseptic action. Balsam tolu and balsam peru are the only true balsams.

This is a good base for hair care as it contains the essential topicals for hair problems: essential fatty acids and the sulfur-containing amino acids.

Lactalbumin (milk protein) is the best type of protein for hair care.

Rosemary, sage, horsetail, coltsfoot, and nettle are excellent herbals for hair care.

Glycogen blended with protein is helpful to the scalp.

Balsam tolu leaves hair soft and smooth and also has a pleasant natural fragrance.

The natural preservative system of vitamins A, B, C, and E, and citrus seed extract also acts as a blocking agent against nitrosamines.

Sample Label of Skin Care Product
Found in Health Food Stores,
Department Stores, and Drug/Discount Stores

Tender Facial Cleanser
Ingredients: Purified Water, Mineral Oil, Glycerine, Squalane, Glyceryl Stearate, Cetearyl Stearate, Cetearyl Alcohol, Isocetyl Stearate, Tocopherol, Retinyl Palmitate, Allantoin Acetyl Methionine, DEA-Oleth-10 Phosphate, Ceteareth-20, Butylene Glycol, Stearyl Alcohol, Disodium EDTA, TEA-Carbonmer 934, Imidazolidinyl Urea, Phenoxyethanol, Benzyl Alchohol, Fragrance.

National Brand Facial Cleanser sold in exclusive department stores.

RETAIL PRICE FOR 4 oz. - $11.00

COMMENTS: This facial cleanser supposedly for normal skin, is loaded with petrochemicals which dry out the skin. It also contains chemicals that can be contaminated with the nitrosamine NDELA (N-nitrosodiethanolamine), but doesn't have nitrosamine-blocking agents: vitamins C, and E (even though it does have vitamin E in formula). I'm not so sure that if you actually had tender skin you would want to use this this "tender facial cleanser" on your skin!

Mineral oil!

At least it doesn't have propylene glycol.

Has squalane from murdered Aizame sharks (becoming an endangered species). Why not olive oil squalane? (See p. 308.)

Synthetic vitamin E?

Diethanolamine (DEA) - may be contaminated with nitrosamines.

Ceteareth-20 is a petrochemical (contains polyethylene glycol).

Synthetic emulsifier that can cause eye irritation and allergic reactions. This one is doubly bad as it also contains triethanolamine (TEA), which can be contaminated with the nitrosamine NDELA. (See pp. 271-272.)

Contains Urea! (see p. 312).

Benzyl alcohol is synthesized. It can be irritating to skin (p. 269).

Synthetic fragrance!

Sample Label of Skin Care Product Found in Health Food Stores, Department Stores, and Drug/Discount Stores

Natural Organic Facial Cleanser
Ingredients: Coconut Fatty Acid Base, Castile soap (Olive Oil Type), Aloe Vera Gel, Witch Hazel, Eucalyptus Oil, Menthol Oil, Camphor Oil, Avocado Oil, Elder, Nettle, Rosemary, Sage, Camomile, Myrrh, Mint, Lemon Grass, Vitamins A, B Complex, C, and E.

Coconut fatty acid base and olive oil castile are far better cleansing agents than detergents and mineral oil (petrochemicals).

Lots of aloe vera gel which is useful in facial cleansers for a soft, clean feel.

Witch hazel has tonic effect on skin.

Eucalyptus, menthol, and camphor are medicinal herbs for skin problems. The other oils are specific for all skin types.

Natural preservative created with vitamins. Also vitamins C and E act as blocking agents against nitrosamines.

Natural brand facial cleanser sold only in health food stores.

RETAIL PRICE FOR 8 oz. - $7.00

COMMENTS: This cleanser contains none of the petrochemicals usually found in cleansers and creams. It uses many herbal oils and extracts which make it a good natural formula. It is usually used on normal or oily-type complexions, but can be used on all skin types.

Sample Label of Skin Care Product Found in Health Food Stores, Department Stores, and Drug/Discount Stores

THREE TONERS FOR VARIOUS SKIN TYPES

Gentle Toner
Ingredients: Purified Water, Sodium Phenylbenzimidazole-5 Sulfonate, Isoceteth-20, Ammonium Glycerrhizinate, Horse Chestnut Extract, Allantoin, Menthol, Polyacrylamide, Diazolidinyl Urea, Phenoxyethanol, Methylparaben, Propylparaben, D & C Red No. 33, Ext. D & C Violet No. 2.

Mild Action Toner (Tonic)
Ingredients: Purified Water, SD Alcohol 50, Sodium Phenylbenzimidazole-5 Sulfonate, Isoceteth-20, Ammonium Glycerrhizinate, Horse Chestnut Extract, Allantoin, Menthol, Polyacrylamide, Imidazolidinyl Urea, Phenoxyethanol, Methylparaben, Propylparaben, FD & C Blue No. 1, Fragrance.

Full Strength Toner (Tonic)
Ingredients: Purified Water, Witch Hazel, Acetone, Ammonium Glycerrhizinate, Horse Chestnut Extract, Cortisol, Glutathione, Allantoin, Polyoxyethylene 20 Isohexadecyl Ether, Polyacrylamide, Benzophenone-1, Menthol, FD & C Yellow No. 5, D & C Red No. 33.

National brands of toners for normal to dry skin sold in exclusive department stores.

RETAIL PRICE FOR 6 oz. - $10.00

These three toners are national brands sold in exclusive department stores. The formula No. 1 is a "gentle tonic" for normal to dry skin that is sensitive skin. Formula No. 2 tonic is for normal to dry skin called a "mild astringent." Formula No. 3 is said to be a neutral lotion that protects against environmental pollution, irritants, and sun damage.

All three contain environmental pollutants so it's hard to see how they could protect against pollution. None can aid sun damaged skin, since they contain petrochemicals (pollutants); none contain PABA (the sunscreen agent), and all contain artificial carcinogens and are phototoxic.

The solvent acetone, in the No. 3 formula, is disastrous to the skin. Formula No. 2 is specified for normal skin and has SD Alcohol 40 as the second ingredient (a disaster to dry skin).

Sample Label of Skin Care Product
Found in Health Food Stores,
Department Stores, and Drug/Discount Stores

Herbal Astringent (For All Skin Types)
Ingredients: Witch Hazel Base, Nettle, Myrrh, Camomile, Benzoin Gum, Elder Blossom, Marshmallow, Aloe, Rosemary, Fennel, Balm-Mint, Menthol, Kelp, Vitamin B Complex, Vitamins C, E, F, and Citrus Seed Extract.

Witch hazel is the best astringent base as it usually contains no more than 15% alcohol content (unless alcohol is added). It is mild yet has a soothing and cleansing effect on the skin.

Benzoin gum acts as a natural preservative and has a fairly good antiseptic action.

Natural brand herbal astringent sold only in health food stores.

RETAIL PRICE FOR 8 oz. - $5.75

Myrrh was used by the ancient Egyptians as a healing agent, and by the ancient Greeks to care for the skin.

COMMENTS: This astringent or toner is far superior to all the formulas that contained the petrochemicals, acetone, and alcohol. There should be no need for a variety of formulas for toning the skin unless they are very different from each other. The three formulas on the preceding page are chemical brews. The only differences seem to be in the alcohol or acetone content.

Vitamins C, E, F and citrus seed extracts are refreshing to the skin and are also natural preservatives.

Menthol is an antiseptic and cooling agent. There is only a small amount, but this is a very active extract. Little is needed.

Carcinogens and Suspected Carcinogens

In addition to the chemicals discussed in the chapters, there are several commonly used chemicals (natural and synthetic) which are suspected carcinogens, teratogens, or toxic as so defined by the GAO, NIOSH, FDA, EPA, and the WHO. Here is the list as of 1978. Bear in mind, however, that this list does not mean that there aren't other substances not on this list that could be carcinogens or co-carcinogens.

1. Acacia
2. Acid Blue 9
3. Acid Blue 9 ammonium salt
4. Acid Blue 74
5. Acid Green 5
6. Acid Red 18
7. Acid Red 27
8. Acid Red 87
9. Acid Violet 49
10. Acid Yellow 73 sodium salt
11. Alcohol
12. 4-amino-2-nitrophenol
13. o-Anisidine
14. Asbestos
15. Basic Orange 2
16. Basic Violet 1
17. Basic Violet 3
18. Basic Violet 10
19. Boric acid
20. Butyrolactone
21. Calcium carrageenan
22. Calcium saccharin
23. Captan
24. Carrageenan
25. Chloroamine-T
26. Chloroacetic acid
27. Cholesterol
28. Chromium oxide greens
29. Coal tar
30. Coumarin
31. Creosote
32. D&C Blue No. 1
   Aluminum Lake
33. D&C Blue No. 2
   Aluminum Lake
34. D&C Blue No. 4
35. D&C Green No. 3
   Aluminum Lake
36. D&C Red No. 4
   Aluminum Lake
37. D&C Red No. 9
38. D&C Red No. 9
   Barium Lake
39. D&C Red No. 9
   Barium/Strontium Lake
40. D&C Red No. 9
   Zirconium Lake
41. D&C Red No. 17
42. D&C Red No. 19
43. D&C Red No. 19
   Aluminum Lake
44. D&C Red No. 19
   Barium Lake
45. D&C Red No. 19
   Zirconinum Lake
46. D&C REd No. 22
47. D&C Yellow No. 6
   Aluminum Lake
48. D&C Yellow No. 8
49. Dehydroacetic Acid
50. Dimethoxane
51. Dimethyl sulfate
52. Direct Black 38
53. Direct Black 131
54. Direct Blue 6
55. Direct Brown 1
56. Direct Brown 1:2
57. Direct Brown 2
58. Direct Brown 31
59. Direct Brown 154
60. Disperse Yellow 3
61. Estrone
62. Ethyl carbonate
63. Ethylene oxide
64. Ethylene urea
65. Ethynylestradiol
66. FD&C Blue No. 1
67. FD&C Blue No. 1
   Aluminum Lake
68. FD&C Blue No. 2
69. FD&C Blue No. 2
   Aluminum Lake
70. FD&C Green No. 3
71. FD&C Red No. 4
72. FD&C Red No. 40
73. FD&C Yellow No. 6
74. FD&C Yellow No. 6
   Aluminum Lake
75. Formaldehyde
76. JC Red No. 6
77. Hydroquinone
78. Hydroxystearic acid
79. Iron oxides
80. Karmeria extract
81. Lactose
82. Lead acetate
83. Maleic anhydride
84. Methenamine
85. 4-Methoxy-m-phenylene-
   diamine
86. 4-Methoxy-m-phenylene-
   diamine sulfate
87. Methyl hydroxystearate
88. Methyl methacrylate
89. Methyl oleate
90. Methyl stearate
91. 2-Nitro-p-phenylene-diamine
92. N-nitrosodiethanolamine
   (NDELA) (formed with
   TEA, DEA, or MEA and a
   nitrosating agent like sodium
   lauryl sulfate)
93. Nylon
94. Oleic acid
95. Oxyquinoline
96. Oxyquinoline sulfate
97. Paraffin
98. PEG-8
99. Phenol
100. Phenylalanine, D-
101. o-Phenylenediamine
102. Phenyl mercuric acetate
103. Pigment Red 53:1
104. Pigment Red 53
105. Polyethylene
106. Polysorbate 80
107. Polyvinyl alcohol
108. Propyl alcohol
109. Propylene oxide
110. PVP
111. Ricinoleic acid
112. Saccharin
113. Silver
114. Sodium saccharin
115. Solvent Red 23
116. Sorbic acid
117. Succinic anhydride
118. Thiourea
119. Toluene
120. Toluene-2,4-diamine
121. Trichloroethylene
122. Tristearin
123. Ultramarine green
124. Zinc chloride
125. Zinc sulfate

TERATOGENIC SUBSTANCES

1. Acid Red 27
2. 6-Aminocaproic acid
3. BHT
4. Butylmethacrylate
5. Captan
6. Carbon dioxide
7. Cetrimonium bromide
8. Dibutyl phthalate
9. Dimethyl phthalate
10. Dioctyl phthlate
11. EDTA
12. Estrone
13. Ethyl methacrylate
14. Ethyl phthalate
15. Hexachlorophene
16. Lead acetate
17. Lithium chloride
18. MEK
19. Nitrous oxide
20. Phenyl mercuric acetate
21. Retinol
22. Retinyl palmitate
23. Salicylamide
24. Sodium chloride
25. Sodium salicylate
26. Theophylline

ABUNDA LIFE OF AMERICA, P. O. Box 151, Avon by the Sea, NJ 07762; (201)-775-7575. Dr. Robert H. Sorge, general manager.
Product Categories - Bath salts, oils
Literature - Semi-annual catalog.
Brand Names - Same.

ACTIVE ORGANICS, 7715 Densmore Ave, Van Nuys, CA 91406; (818)-786-3310. Michael A. Bishop, president.
Product Categories - Hair, skin and body aids; men's and pet's grooming products.
Literature - Annual product lists.
Brand Names - Bishop's Formula (animal grooming).

AGRI-PRODUCTS MARKETING CORP., div. Agrifuture, Inc., 3651 Pegasus Dr., Ste. 101, Bakersfield, CA 93308; (805)-393-3732. Gordon L. Fisher, president.
Product Categories - Jojoba oil.
Literature - Yearly Agrifuture Report.
Brand Names - Puroba, Golden Jojoba Oil.

ALBA BOTANICA COSMETICS, (formerly Life Tree Inc.), P. O. Box 1858, Santa Monica, CA 90046; (213)-451-0936. K.J. Grand, president.
Product Categories - Herbal lotions and creams, bath oils/salts, men's grooming aids; skin and hair care products.
Brand Names - Alba Botanica Cosmetics.

ALL WAYS NATURAL, Brooklyn Navy Yard, Flushing & Cumberland Aves., Brooklyn, NY 11205; (718)-935-0222, outside NY (800)-233-5353. Peter Neuer, president.
Product Categories - Herbal hair care for black consumers and skin tone cream.
Literature - Price lists and catalogs every two months.
Brand Names - All Ways Natural Indian Hemp.

ALOE FARMS, Box 125 Los Fresnos, TX 78566; (512)-425-1289. M. Elliot Berry, president.
Product Categories - Aloe vera powder, comfrey/aloe capsules, gel and juice.
Literature - Yearly price lists, brochures.
Brand Names - Aloe Farms.

ALOEFIRST, P. O. Box 171 Westfield, NJ 07090; (201)-232-6365.
Product Categories - Body/face creams, lotions, sunscreens, lip balm.
Brand Names - Aloefirst.

ALOE FLEX PRODUCTS, INC., P. O. Box 1185, Dickinson, TX 78566; (713)-337-2240, (800)-231-0839. James S. Flex, president.
Product Categories - Orthopedic/tennis elbow cream and liniment, body/face lotion and cream, men's and pet grooming products, vitamins, and aloe juice.
Literature - Annual catalogs.
Brand Names - Flex Gard, Aloe Flex.

ALOE GOLD VERA PRODUCTS, P. O. Box 1323, Englewood, CO 80150; (303)-761-0174. Ron Harris, president.
Product Categories - Hair and skin care, make-up, deodorants, aloe vera products, first aid spray, and liniment.
Literature - Yes.
Brand Names - Aloe Gold.

ANANDA COUNTRY PRODUCTS, 14618 Tyler Foote Rd., Nevada City, CA 95959; (916)-292-3505. Suzanne Betts, manager.
Product Categories - Fragrance oils, incense.

AROMA VERA CO. (formerly Rhizotome Co.), P. O. Box 3609, Culver City, CA 90231; (213)-675-8219. Marcel Lavabre, president; Sylvain Michelet, U. S. manager.
Product Categories - All vegetal, non-animal bath, hair and skin aids, deodorants, massage products, essential oils, aromatherapy products, essential oils for perfume industry, and aromatic diffusors.
Literature - Annual catalogs, newsletter on aromatherapy, price lists several times a year, samples.
Brand Names - Quintessence, Kosmarom, Fleur De Brume.

ARYA LAYRA, M. E. G. Gottlieb, Diaderma-Haus GMBH & Co., 6900 Heidelberg, West Germany; Gabriella Moore, U. S. A. Distributor.
Product Categories - Body lotions, cleansers, toners, masks, moisturizers.
Literature - Brochure explains daily skin care program using products.
Brand Names - Arya Layra.

ATLANTIS NATURAL PRODUCTS, 686 S. Arroyo Pkwy., No. 117, Pasadena, CA 91105; (818)-440-1774, (213)-264-1231. Gary J. Ryan, president.
Product Categories - Hair products, soap, cleansers.
Literature - Brochures.
Brand Names - Aloe Apri, Aqua Azulene.

AUBREY ORGANICS, 4419 N. Manhattan Ave., Tampa, FL 33614. (813)-877-4186. Aubrey Hampton, chief executive officer.
Product Categories - More than 100 all-natural, non-animal-tested hair, skin and body care products; men's and pet's grooming; hair and skin products for people of color; chewable food supplement.
Literature - Catalogs and bulletins; *Organica* (quarterly international newspaper on animals, environment, science and the arts); book: Aubrey Hampton's *Natural Organic Hair and Skin Care with A-to-Z Natural/Synthetic Cosmetic Dictionary* and *Resources Section.*
Brand Names - Aubrey Organics, Men's Stock, Nyaanza Naturals, Organimals, Organowafers, Rosa Mosqueta.

AUROMERE AYURVEDIC IMPORTS, 1291 Weber St., Pomona, CA 91768; (714)-629-8255. Dakshina Vanzetti, president, general manager.
Product Categories - Skin-care products, herbal toothpaste, incense, bath powder, exercise equipment, herb teas, gifts, books, journals.
Literature - Catalogs, brochures, price lists, free and updated several times a year.
Brand Names - Vicco, Herbomineral, Chandrika, Ashram, Auromere Ayurvedic, Dr. Pati's.

AUTUMN EARTH, (div. Natural Thoughts, Inc.), 3536 Adams Ave., San Diego, CA 92116; (619)-281-4228. Jean Shea, president.
Product Categories - Hair and skin products, clay products, sun products, soaps/cleansers.
Literature - Catalogs, price lists, samples.
Brand Names - Autumn Earth.

AUTUMN HARP, 28 Rockydale Rd., Bristol, VT 05443; (802)-453-4807. Kevin Harper, president.
Product Categories - Skin and personal-care products, baby products, comfrey salve, first-aid ointment.
Literature - Annual catalogs, price lists, posters.
Brand Names - Earthchild, Autumn Harp.

BEAUTYMASTERS, INC., P. O. Box 2069, Michigan City, IN 46360; (219)-874-2260. Richard D. Waskow, president.
Product Categories - Hair, skin and body products, extensive makeup products.
Literature - Annual price lists, brochures, samples, Guide to Cosmetic Ingredients and Technical Terms available for consumers.
Brand Names - Beautymasters.

BODY LOVE NATURAL COSMETICS, P. O. Box 7542, Santa Cruz, CA 95061; (408)-425-8218. Elizabeth Van Buren, owner-manager.
Product Categories - Skin cosmetics/cleansers; herbal facial steams; bath mitts.
Literature - Biannual price lists, free brochures.
Brand Names - Amazing Grains, Body Love, Love Mitts, Herbal Facial Steams.

BORLIND OF GERMANY, P. O. Box 1487, New London, NH 03257; (603)-526-2076, (800)-447-7024. Polly Kulow, manager.
Product Categories - All-natural, herbal skin-care products, sun products, men's grooming, face creams/lotions, soaps, sponges, masks, ampoules.
Literature - Catalogs, price lists.
Brand Names - Annemarie Borlind, Sunless Bronze.

CARME, INC. 84 Galli Dr., Novato, CA 94947; (415)-883-8844, (800)-227-2628. James A. Egide, chief executive officer.
Product Categories - Hair, skin, body and baby products.
Literature - Catalogs, promo aids.
Brand Names - Carme, Jojoba Farms, Biotene H-24, Mild & Natural, Loanda, Revitacyl, Sleepy Hollow Botanicals, Country Roads, Mountain Herbery, Mill Creek, Golden California, Country Road, Bakuhaan, Golden Cal.

CHENTI PRODUCTS, INC., 21093 Forbes Ave., Hayward, CA 94545; (415)-785-2177. Don Gieseke, president.
Product Categories - Hair, skin, body, sun products.
Literature - Bulletins upon request.
Brand Names - Chenti.

COESAM, div. cosmetica, Josue Smith Solar 507, Providencia, Santiago, Chile.
Product Categories - Cosmetic products made with Rosa Mosqueta rose hip seed oil.
Literature - Full color brochures and information about Rosa Mosqueta rose hip seed oil.
Brand Names - Coesam, Rosa Mosqueta.
Comments - Products available in South America. Product do not contain an ingredients label as this is not a legal requirement in Chile. (In Chile, cosmetics are registered with the government and given a number by the state which appears on the product containers.) NOTE: The trade name *Rosa Mosqueta* is a U. S. trademark belonging to Aubrey Organics and supplied by that company in the United States.

COLORA, div. Milady Cosmetics, 217 Washington Ave., Carlstadt, NJ 07072; (201)-939-0969, (aff: Pareto, Inc.); Nisso Benattar, president.
Product Categories - Henna, hair removers, bath salts, ethnic products.
Literature - Annual catalogs.
Brand Names - Colora, Moriah, Caramelle.

COMFREY INTERNATIONAL CO., P. O. Box 540, Woodburn, OR 97071; (503)-982-8550. Joe A. Phillips, president.
Product Categories - Grows, harvests, processes and markets comfrey-based products, including hair and face products, mouthwashes, capsules/tablets, bulk and packaged herb teas.
Literature - Price lists and product information.
Brand Names - Mt. Angel Health & Beauty Aids, Comfrey Farms, Comfrey International, Inc.

COMMUNITY SOAP FACTORY, P. O. Box 32057, Washington, DC 20007; (202)-347-0186. Judith G. Oakley, president.
Product Categories - Natural soaps, shampoo, pure coconut oil (edible and massage).
Literature - Annual price lists, brochures.
Brand Names - Community Soap Factory.

COSMETICS BY JEANNE, c/o Thomas Health Foods, 8182 Beechmont Ave., Cincinnati, OH 45230; (513)-475-4995. Jeanne Thomas, Jay Davis, owners.
Product Categories - Cosmetics.
Literature - Catalogs every 3-6 months.

COUNTRY COMFORT, div. Traditional Medicinals, 215 Classic Ct., Rohnert Park, CA 94928; (707)-584-3057. Drake Sadler, president.
Product Categories - Baby products, salves, lip creams.
Literature - Catalogs, flyers.
Brand Names - Country Comfort, Herbal Savvy.

D & P PRODUCTS, 2810 E. Long Street, Tampa, FL 33605; (813)-248-6640. Paul Penders, president.
Product Categories - Hair, skin and body care products, men's grooming, lip care, make-up.
Literature - Price lists every six weeks.
Brand Names - Paul Penders.

DESERT ESSENCE, 1732 Arteique Dr., Topanga, CA 90290; (213)-455-1046. Steven Silberfein, president.
Product Categories - Hair, skin, sun products, also Dr. Xavier Gomez Shampoo (Mexican).
Literature - Brochures, price lists, literature, samples.
Brand Names - Desert Essence.

DESERT WHALE JOJOBA CO., P. O. Box 41594, Tucson, AZ 85717; (602)-882-4195. Jeff Kazansky, president.
Product Categories - Jojoba oil.
Literature - Price lists, specifications.

DESMO CHEMICAL CORP., 2601 South Hanley Rd., St. Louis, MO 63144; (314)-968-2376. Dr. Bill Scott, executive vice-president.
Product Categories - U.S. dist. Flachsmann (Swiss) natural plant extracts for health food/pharmaceutical industries. Available in fluid, solid or powder.
Brand Names - Flachsmann Ltd. Botanicals, Descote, Destab, Eflaplant.

DURHAM PRODUCTS CO., Div. Durham Pharmacal Corp., Route 145, Oak Hill, NY 12460; (518)-239-4195. Kevin M. Reeth, president.
Product Categories - Personal care soaps.
Brand Names - Ye Old Fashioned Soaps.

EARTH SCIENCE, INC. 620 N. Berry St., Brea, CA 92621; (714)-630-6270. (800)-222-6720. Kris M. Schoenaur, president.
Product Categories - Hair, skin, and body care products; vitamins.
Literature - Quarterly catalogs.
Brand Names - Earth Science.

ESSENCES FOR AROMATHERAPY, P. O. Box 606, San Rafael, CA 94915; (415)-459-3998. Dr. K. Schnaubelt, owner.
Product Categories - Essential oils.
Literature - Semiannual catalogs, in depth information.
Brand Names - Essences for Aromatherapy.

THE ESSENTIAL OIL CO. (formerly Rainbow Oils, Inc.), P. O. Box 88, Sandy, OR 97055; (503)-695-2400. Robert Seidel, owner.
Product Categories - Essential and perfume oils, incense; bath oils; insecticides/repellents, candles; flea/tick control products.
Literature - Quarterly price lists.
Brand Names - Rainbow Oils.

ESSQUE BODYCARE, P. O. Box 3434, Stamford, CT 06905; (203)-322-8778. Steve Evans, president.
Product Categories - Bodycare soaps/cleansers.
Literature - Customer handouts, displays.
Brand Names - Dermelle.

EVE COSMETICS, P. O. Box 131, Pebble Beach, CA 93953. Maxamillion Se Ale, president.
Product Categories - Baby products, natural shampoo and conditioner.

4-D HOBE MARKETING CORP., 201 S. McKemy, Chandler, AZ 95226; (602)-257-1950. Erne Terrazas, president.
Product Categories - Hair and skin care products; food supplements (including herbs, protein vitamins/minerals).
Literature - Catalogs and brochures.
Brand Names - NuHairtrition, 4-D, Super, Players' Choice.

GARI M. BEAUTY CARE PRODUCTS, P. O. Box 701, Woodland Hills, CA 91365; (714)-859-2218 sales office. John Matsukas, chief executive officer.
Product Categories - Hair, skin, and body care products; sun products.
Literature - Catalogs, bulletins, price lists published as necessary.

GIOVANNI COSMETICS, P. O. Box 205, Reseda, CA 91335; (213)-833-3236. Arthur C. Cuidotti, president.
Product Categories - Hair care products.

GISELLE'S PROFESSIONAL SKIN CARE LTD., 7-1742 Marine Drive, Vancouver, B.C. V7V 1J3, Canada; (604)-925-2711.
Product Categories - Hair, skin, and body care products, bath brushes, foot care products, sponges, toothpaste.
Literature - Catalogs.
Brand Names - Dr. Grandel, Marvin, Revita, Muko.

GOA LABORATORIES, 3270 Pineda Avenue, Melbourne, FL 32940; (305)-259-8607. James M. Terry, president.
Product Categories - Aloe vera burn care, skin, and sun protection products; aloe vera juice.
Literature - Catalogs, price lists.
Brand Names - Gel of Aloe.

GOEMAR INTERNATIONAL, div. Les Laboratoires Goemar S. A. (France), Thornridge Drive, Atlanta, GA 30340; (404)-493-7026. Harriet Hessam, vice-president.
Product Categories - Seaweed-based hair, skin, and body care products, magnesium, calcium supplements, and nutritional drinks.
Brand Names - Tonialg.

GOLDEN LOTUS, P. O. Box 1323, Englewood, CO 80150; (303)-761-0174. R. S. Hervey, vice-president of marketing.
Product Categories - Hair and bodycare products; home care products.
Literature - Annual price list, consumer brochures.
Brand Names - Golden Lotus.
Comments - Company states it does not test on animals and that its products are free of animal ingredients.

GOLDEN TEMPLE NATURAL PRODUCTS, P. O. Box 1095, Taos, NM 87571; (505)-758-3247. Sananda Ra, president.
Product Categories - Lip and balm-type products, herbs.
Literature - Catalog, and product literature.
Brand Names - Lip smoothies.

GOLDSCHMIDT COSMETICS, INC., 90 Plant Ave., Happauge, NY 11788; (516)-434-1880. Les Goldschmidt, vice-president.
Product Categories - Baby products; hair, skin, and body care products; ethnic products, eye and face make-up, food care products, men's products.
Literature - Catalogs as needed.

IDA GRAE COSMETICS (formerly Nature's Colors), 424 La Verne Avenue, Mill Valley, CA 94941; (415)-388-6101. Ida Grae, president.
Product Categories - Powder, rouge, eye-shading powders, eye-lip cream, moisturizer, creme rouge, solid fragrances.
Literature - *Nature's Colors - Dyes From Plants*, book by Ida Grae. Also yearly brochures, price lists, literature.
Brand Names - Ida Grae cosmetics.
Comments - Products claim to be 100% natural without preservatives, synthetics, or animal tests.

GREAT HEALTH, 2663 Saturn Street, P. O. Box 1749, Brea, CA 92622; (714)-996-8600. Graham Bell, president.
Product Categories - Hair, skin, and body care products; brushes, fragrances, sponges, tools, products and equipment, cards, insecticides, plants; flea/tick control, pet supplements; honey, full line of vitamins & minerals.
Literature - Product literature, quarterly catalog, monthly newsletters.
Comments - Most eclectic company we've seen!

GREEN MOUNTAIN HERBS, LTD., P. O. Box 2369, Boulder, CO 80306; (800)-525-2696. David Rainey, president.
Product Categories - Essential oils (over 50 varieties of true plant oils); herbal tea capsules (55 varieties) in 90 caps/bottle or bulk pack 500/bag; herbal beverage blends (12 varieties of bulk beverage teas). Imports bulk herbs from Europe, Africa, South America. Also sprouters; bodycare accessories, hair, skin, and body care products, massage tools, toothbrushes, toothpaste, pet flea/tick control, food supplements.
Brand Names - Green Mountain, Olive's East, Herbal Reign, Quintessense Aromatherapy.

DR. HAUSCHKA COSMETICS, INC., Wala-Heitmittel GMBH, D-7325 Eckwalder/Bad Boll, West Germany; U. S. Distributor - Meadowbrook Herb Garden, Rt. 138, Wyoming, RI 02898; (401)-539-7603.

Product Categories - Bath oils, massage oils, moisturizers, cleansers, lotions, make-up, etc.

Literature - Good literature about natural cosmetics and an excellent booklet *The Herb Book* by Dr. Hauschka, with beautiful color and line illustrations by Stella Aurora Ormai.

Brand Names - Dr. Hauschka.

Comments - Dr. Hauschka says "Certain irregularities in the intensity of color or aroma of plant oils are to be expected." This is one tip that tells us his products are natural and not perfumed or loaded with synthetic chemicals. All the products are natural as possible and every effort is made to keep them that way. Still, we encourage "label consciousness" and not "brand name consciousness": read the labels.

HAWAIIAN RESOURCES CO., LTD., 1123 Kapahulu Avenue, Honolulu, HI 96816; (808)-737-8726. Peter W. Cannon, president.

Product Categories - Coconut oil from Tahiti, scented and unscented.

Literature - Informational brochures about Monoi Taire Tahiti.

Brand Names - Monoi Tiare Tahiti, Monoi Pitate, Monoi Tipani, Monoi Ylang-Ylang.

Comments - Sole U. S. distributor of Monoi Tiare Tahiti Scented Coconut Oil.

HEAD SHAMPOO, INC. 20626 Belshaw Ave., Carson, CA 90746; (213)-979-3322. Michael Hsu, president.

Product Categories - Shampoo, conditioner, natural deodorants, soap, body scrub.

Literature - Displays.

Brand Names - Pure & Basic, Head.

HILLTOP GARDENS, Rt. 1, Box 161, Lyford, TX 78569; (512)-262-1912. R. C. Benson, president.

Product Categories - Aloe vera products, including complete hair, skin, and body care. Also, aloe vera plants.

Literature - Brochures and price lists.

Brand Names - Mrs. Ewald's R. Charles, Aloe-Labs, Benson's Aloe Capsules and Aloe Juice, Aloe Up.

THE HERITAGE STORE, P. O. Box 444-HB, Virginia Beach, VA 23458; (804)-428-0100. Tom Johnson, owner/president.

Product Categories - Edgar Cayce cosmetics, formulas, and oils; pure lanolin, herbs (teas, roots, herbal tonic and formulas); inhalant, cough syrup, massage liniment, other hair, skin, and body care products.

Literature - Yearly catalogs.

Brand Names - Heritage Products.

HIMALAYAN LABS, RD 1, Box 88, Honesdale, PA 18431; (717)-253-5551. Kevin Hoffman, president.

Product Categories - Hair, skin, and body care products.

Brand Names - Natural Grace.

HOLISTIC PRODUCTS CORP., 10 West Forest Ave., Englewood, NJ 07631; (201)-569-1188 in NJ; (800)-221-0308 in USA. Arnold H. Gans, president.

Product Categories - Holistic home remedies, moisturizers, mouthwashes, homeopathic formulas, hair products, sun products, propolis products; herb tablets, insecticides/repellents; snack bars.

Literature - Semiannual catalogs, bulletins, price lists, promo ads.

Brand Names - Holistic.

HOME HEALTH PRODUCTS, INC., P. O. Box 3130, Virginia Beach, VA 23454; (804)-491-2200 in VA; (800)-468-7313 in USA. Samuel H. Knoll, president.

Product Categories - Edgar Cayce healthcare products; hair, skin, and body care products; laxative, tooth powder, food and food supplements.

Literature - Quarterly catalogs and price lists on request.

Brand Names - Almond Glow, Myo Rub, Herbacol, Nature's Oil, New Seasons, Palma Christi, Peri-Dent, Salt 'N Soda.

HOMESTEADER SOAP CO., P. O. Box 66, Fiddler's Elbow Road, Middle Falls, NY 12848; (518)-692-9469. Virginia Trembray, president.

Product Categories - Soap, soft soap, pumice hand cleaner.

Literature - Brochures, etc.

Brand Names - Homesteader.

INNER TRADITIONS INTERNATIONAL, LTD., Park Street, Rochester, VT 05767; (802)-767-3174. Ehud Sperling, president.

Product Categories - Body care, complete line of essential oils and aromatherapy products.

Literature - Semiannual catalogs and order forms.

INNERCLEAN, (div., Alvin Last, Inc.), 145 Palisades St., Dobbs Ferry, NY 10522; (914)-693-2221. Alvin Last, president.
Product Categories - Herbal blends (internal use), henna-type hair color, hair and skin care products, make-up, baths, toothpowder, coconut oil.
Literature - Price lists.

INSTITUTE SWISS, div. Minnetonka, Inc., Jonathan Industrial Park, Chaska, MN 55318; (612)-448-4181.
Product Categories - Bath salts, oils, body lotions, moisturizers, shampoos/conditioners, soaps and cleansers.
Literature - Catalogs as needed.
Brand Names - Institute Swiss.

IVO OF CALIFORNIA, 8533 Seranata, Whittier, CA 90603; (213)-947-4100. George Macura, president.
Product Categories - Body lotions, deodorants/anti-perspirants, facial cleansing cremes, face make-up, lip care products, moisturizers, soap/cleansers, sun products, eyeblack for sports.
Literature - Quarterly flyers.
Brand Names - IVO.

JASON NATURAL COSMETICS, Div. Jason Natural Cosmetics, 8468 Warner Drive, Culver City, CA 90232; (213)-838-7543. Jeffrey B. Light, president.
Product Categories - Complete hair and skin care products (163 items).
Literature - Consumer brochures.
Brand Names - Apricot Scrubble, Satin Soap, Aussie Gold, Duck Oil, Sunbrellas of Jason.

JERICHO BATH SALTS, INC., 555 Fifth Avenue, New York, NY 10017; (212)-286-9290. Emmanuel Pepis, president.
Product Categories - The Living Dead Sea mineral bath salts, facial mask, mineral soap, clay soap, black mud, mineral shampoo, foot care, moisturizers, conditioners.
Literature - Yes.

JEUNESSE NATURAL SKIN CARE, 6150 Reseda Blvd., No. 311, Reseda, CA 92335; (818)-342-0750. Selma Myers, president.
Product Categories - Eye make-up, face make-up facial cleansing creams, lotions, lip care, moisturizers, soaps/cleansers, toners.
Literature - Demos, etc.
Brand Names - JEUNESSE.

JOJOBA SERVICES INTERNATIONAL, P. O. Box 891, Milpitas, CA 95035; (408)-263-2450. Barry Atsatt.
Product Categories - Jojoba oil.
Literature - Quarterly catalogs, price lists, product sheets, brochures.
Brand Names - Moby Jojoba Oil.

KISS MY FACE CORP., P. O. Box 804, New Paltz, NY 12561; (914)-255-0884. Robert MacLeod, president.
Product Categories - Olive oil soap, moisturizer, shampoo, and conditioner; Aegina virgin olive oil. Also accessories, body lotions, brushes, facial cleansing creams, men's grooming aids, sponges, toners, and scrub masques.
Literature - Brochures.
Brand Names - Kiss My Face, KMF, Aegina, Olive & Aloe.

LA CRISTA ALL NATURAL SKIN CARE, P. O. Box 240, Davidsonville, MD 21035; (301)-956-4447. Linda Collinson, president.
Product Categories - Moisturizers, baby products, bath salts, etc., sun products.

LAN LAY INTERNATIONAL, INC., P. O. Box 766, San Jose, CA 95106; (408)-971-8211. C. P. Lawrence, president/owner.
Product Categories - Lanolin and other natural oils, men's grooming aids, lotion.
Brand Names - Lan Lay, Cheryla.
Literature - Annual catalogs.

LEVLAD, INC., 9183-5 Kelvin Avenue, Chatsworth, CA 91311; (818)-882-2951, (800)-327-2010. Vlad Weinstein, president.
Product Categories - Shampoos, conditioners, lotion, facial care system, toothpaste and bath oils.
Literature - Catalogs, ad reprints, brochures.
Brand Names - Nature's Gate, Springbrook, Aloegen.

LP DISTRIBUTORS, 7422 Mountjoy, Huntington Beach, CA 92648; (714)-848-5551. Lou Paulsen, president.
Product Categories - Body lotions, moisturizers, shampoos and conditioners, vitamins and supplements.
Literature - Monthly newsletter.
Brand Names - Dr. Donsbach.

MAGICK MUD, 3412-K West MacArthur, Santa Ana, CA 92704; (714)-957-0674. Mary Lou Lang; Roger Derryberry, gen. partners.
Product Categories - Facial masks.
Literature - Yes.
Brand Names - Magick Mud.

MAISON NATURELLE USA, INC., P. O. Box 730, Pine Brook, NJ 07058; (201)-882-1305. Torben Friis Madsen, president.
Product Categories - Bodycare products; baby products, bath salts and oils, skin care products, foot care, fragrances, lip care, men's grooming aids, hair care products, sponges, sun products.
Literature - Annual catalogs, flyers.
Brand Names - Naturalia.

MARCAM CORPORATION, P. O. Box 355 Westwood, NJ 07675; (201)-933-6345. Irwin Sieger, president.
Product Categories - Hair care products, temporary dyes, soaps, musk perfume, suncare products, cosmetics and toiletries, nail and cuticle products, cosmetic brushes, vitamin E oil, jojoba oil, essential oils; PABA.
Literature - Price lists, literature.
Brand Names - Marcam, Born Again.

MARGARITE COSMETICS, div. Moon Products, Inc., 2138 Okeechobee Blvd., West Palm Beach, FL 33409; (305)-686-1466. Margarite Moon, vice-president.
Product Categories - A complete line of skin-care and make-up products including make-up remover pads.
Literature - Annual brochures.
Brand Names - Margarite.

MICHAEL'S HEALTH PRODUCTS, 4220 N. 22nd "E", McAllen, TX 78504; (512)-686-4433. Michael Schwartz, president.
Product Categories - Herbal creams, body lotions, facial cleansing creams and lotions, moisturizers, sun care products; herbs in capsules/tablets with vitamins/minerals, vitamins with others, nutritional "programs" in a bottle.
Literature - Monthly catalogs.
Brand Names - Michael's.

MIRACLE OF ALOE, (div. Jess Clark & Sons), 530 Westport Avenue, Norwalk, CT 06851; (203)-846-1813. Jess F. Clarke, III, president.
Product Categories - Bath oils, body lotions, facial cleansing creams, lotions, foot care products, lip care products, moisturizers, shampoos/conditioners, soaps/cleansers, toothpaste, aloe vera juice; 42% aloe rub, 70% aloe ointment; aloe plants.
Literature - Semiannual catalogs, price lists, free literature.
Brand Names - Miracle of Aloe.

MODDRELL'S HEART OF ALOE VERA, INC., Rt. 4, Box 1994, 612 Oakdale Road, Cleburne, TX 76031; (817)-641-7555 in TX; (800)-433-2222 in USA. W. Murel Moddrell, president.
Product Categories - Aloe vera juice, skin care items, shampoo, conditioner, mouthwash, sun products.
Literature - Brochures and price lists, store demos, samplings.
Brand Names - Heart of Aloe Vera.
Comments - "Heart of Aloe Vera" is a member of the National Aloe Science Council.

MONOI, INC. (formerly Dulac Corp./Monoi), 72-47 Ingram St., Forest Hills, NY 11375; (718)-544-3956, (718)-263-5554. Rana Rivelo, vice-president
Product Categories - Full line of natural hair, bath, and body beauty treatment products from France and Tahiti.
Literature - Full-color brochures.
Brand Names - Monoi Originale, Monoi Moisturizing Fluid, Monoi Moisture Milk, Monoi Bath and Shower Gel, Monoi Eau de Toilette, Monoi Outdoor Oil SPF 4.

NATIONAL ALOE VERA, 11260 Mt. View Road, Tracy, CA 95376; (209)-836-4944. Jean Tolle, owner/manager
Product Categories - Bottled aloe vera juice and aloe vera body lotions, facial cleansing creams, first aid gels.
Brand Names - Tolle Health Products.

NATURADE PRODUCTS, 7110 E. Jackson St., Paramount, CA 90273; (213)-531-8120. Allan Schulman, president.
Product Categories - Shampos and conditioners, plus full skin treatment line, nailcare products, make-up.
Literature - Research update bulletins on request. Catalogs as needed, semiannual price lists.
Brand Names - Aloe Vera 80 Collection, Nutricolor.

NATURE COSMETICS, INC., (div. Avanza Corp.), 881 Alma Real No. 101, Pacific Palisades, CA 90272; (213)-459-9816. John M. Van Zandt, president.
Product Categories - Body care accessories, bath salts, oils, body lotions, clay products, eye make-up, face make-up facial cleansing cremes, lotions, fragrances, lip care products, moisturizers, nail care products, shampoos/conditioners, toners, aloe vera juice.
Literature - Brochures.
Brand Names - Nature.

NATURE DE FRANCE, 145 Hudson St., New York, NY 10013; (212)-925-2670. Stewart F. Levy, president.
Product Categories - Skin and body care products made from imported French clay.
Literature - Biannual bulletins.
Brand Names - Nature De France.

NEW ENGLAND NATURAL SPONGE, 2495 Long Beach Rd., Oceanside, NY 11572; (516)-678-5600. Sanford H. Stevens, marketing director.
Product Categories - Baby products, men's grooming aids, massage tools, toothbrushes, face make-up, loofah products, straps, pads, wooden bath brush, discs, seawool bath sponges, and natural pumice. Brushes: make-up/body/sauna, nail and complexion; foot file. Also: bath pillows, nail and pedicule kits; travel essential kit; natural bath products kit.
Literature - Semiannual catalogs, floor and counter displays.
Brand Names - New England, Deep Facial, Nature's Scrub Brush.

NORIMOOR, INC., 23-26 Broadway, Long Island City, NY 11106; (718)-278-7171. Eleanor M. Krupa, president.
Product Categories - Mineral water, body lotions, clay products, face make-up, facial cleansing cremes, lotions, etc., foot care, shampoos/conditioners, soaps/cleansers, toothpaste, pet supplements.

O'NATUREL, INC., 535 Cordova Road, Suite 472, Santa Fe, NY 87501; (505)-982-6677. Aida Reed, president.
Product Categories - Herbal shampoos, conditioning pack, clay products, cleansing lotion, body lotion, facial scrub and moisturizing cremes.
Literature - Catalogs, price sheets.
Brand Names - O'Naturel, Les Provencales.

ORGANIC AID, (div. Buty Wave Products), 7323 Beverly Blvd., Los Angeles, CA 90036; (213)-936-2191. Joseph Simon, president.
Product Categories - Soaps, shampoos, conditioners, moisturizers, sun products, body lotions, men's and children's products.
Literature - Booklets, photos, price lists.
Brand Names - Organic Aid, Restor.

ORJENE NATURAL COSMETICS, 5-43 - 48th Ave., Long Island City, NY 11101; (718)-937-2666. Gene Gomory, president.
Product Categories - Complete line of hair and skin care products, including make-up.

Literature - Consumer catalog, retail price lists, monthly bulletins.
Brand Names - Orjene, Vit-A, Jog® R, Proforma-Complex.
Comments - Products manufactured in own laboratory.

PACIFICA RESEARCH LABORATORY/BON SANTE, 132 W. 132nd St., Los Angeles, CA 90061; (213)-323-8881. Maq Hussain, president.
Product Categories - Hair, skin, and body care products.
Literature - Catalogs as needed, brochures.
Brand Names - Bon Sante.

PALM BEACH BEAUTY PRODUCTS, 950 Xenia Ave., S. Minneapolis, MN 55416; (612)-546-0322; (800)-328-8205. Ben B. Kaitz, president.
Product Categories - Hair, skin, and body care products.
Literature - Annual catalogs, semiannual price lists, pamphlets, flyers.
Brand Names - Medical, Forever 29, Bee Pollen, Nucleic Plus.

PARA LABORATORIES, INC., 100 Rose Ave., Hempstead, NY 11550; (516)-538-4600. Alan Estrin, president.
Product Categories - Hair, skin, and body care products. Mint julep mask is most widely-distributed product.
Literature - Semiannual catalogs, quarterly bulletins, price lists, circulars.
Brand Names - Queen Helen, Batherapy, Foot Therapy.

PIBBS' INDUSTRIES, 36-25 Prince St., Flushing, NY 11354; (718)-445-8046; Biagio Petrucceli, president.
Product Categories - Shampoo and hair conditioners; hair waving lotions, skin care products, brushes.
Brand Names - Pibbs, Liv-Agen.

PRECISION LABORATORIES, LTD., 8585 123rd St. Surrey, BC Canada V3W 6E2; (604)-596-1581.
Product Categories - Baby products, hair and skin products.
Literature - Samples.
Brand Names - Vita Herb, Hairobics, Meadow-Brook, Prevale.

RA-BOB INTERNATIONAL, 320 Hillsdale Dr., Wichita, KS 67230; (316)-733-0904. B. R. Goodman, owner.
Product Categories - Essential oils; jojoba oil and jojoba-vitamin E combos; concentrated perfume oil bases, vitamin E oil.
Literature - Seminannual catalogs.
Brand Names - Ra-Bob International Perfumes, Essential Oils.

RACHEL PERRY, 9111 Mason Ave., Chatsworth, CA 91311; (818)-888-5881. Rachel Perry, president.
Product Categories - Cosmetics (make-up), skin and body care products
Literature - Product lists, brochures.
Brand Names - Rachel Perry.

RAINBOW RESEARCH CORP., 170 Wilbur Pl., Bohemia, NY 11716; (516)-589-5563. Tony Farish, president.
Product Categories - Thirteen henna colors, hair and skin products, sports protection cream and sports massage, sun products.
Literature - Catalogs, brochures.

THE REAL ALOE COMPANY, INC., Box 3428 Simi Valley, CA 93063; (805)-522-5310. Frank Mundell, president.
Product Categories - Aloe vera gel/juice, soap and cosmetics; hair and sun products.
Literature - Annual price lists.

REVIVA LABS, INC., 705 Hopkins Rd., Haddonfield, NJ 08033; 609-428-3885. Stephen Strassler, president.
Product Categories - 105 skin products, including make-up.
Literature - Annual catalogs, bimonthly bulletins.

RIO GRANDE ALOE VERA CO., 1318 39th St., NW, Fargo, ND 58100; (701)-282-5184, (800)-437-2733. Peggy Gillen, president.
Product Categories - Aloe vera: juice, caps, jelly; ecualyptus liniment, body face, sun products.
Literature - Brochures, price lists.
Brand Names - Rio Grande.

RNA COSMETICS, INC., 10 Daniel St., Farmingdale, NY 11735; (516)-293-0030; 2500 Grand Ave., Long Beach, CA 90815; (213)-494-2500. Gerald Kessler, president.
Product Categories - Hair, skin and sun products with ribonucleic acid (RNA) as base.

JEANNE ROSE HERBAL BODYWORKS, 219A Carl St., San Francisco, CA 94117; (415)-564-6785. Jeanne Rose, president.
Product Categories - Herbal hair, skin, bath products, bulk herbs, essential oils, salves, massage oil.
Literature - Yearly catalogs.
Brand Names - New Age Creations, Jeanne Rose.

ROYAL LABS COSMETICS, PO Box 900, Waterbury, CT 06708; (203)-753-2737. Paul M. Lieber, president.
Product Categories - Bodycare products, bath and sun products, makeup, men's grooming.
Literature - Semiannual catalogs, literature, price lists.
Brand Names - Royal Labs, Daniela.

SAN-MAR LABS., INC. 399 Executive Blvd., Elmsford, NY 10523; (914)-592-3130. Frank V. Penna, executive vice-president.
Product Categories - Body lotions, ethnic products, sun products, men's grooming.
Literature - New catalogs, as needed.

SHIKAI PRODUCTS (Div. of Trans-India Products), Box 2866, Santa Rosa, CA 95405; (707)-584-0298. Dr. Dennis T. Sepp, president.
Product Categories - Hair, skin and body products.
Literature - Annual catalog.
Brand Names - Shikai, Skin Moist, Henna Gold.

SOMBRA COSMETICS INC., 5600 McLeod, Suite G, Albuquerque, NM 87109; (505)-888-0288. Alfredo Cortazar, president.
Product Categories - Body, face, skin, hair and sun products.
Brand Names - Sombra.

STEARN'S INC., 14328 Victory Blvd., Ste. 205, Van Nuys, CA 91401; (818)-902-9867, (800)-521-3342. Sam Stearn, chief executive officer.
Product Categories - Skin and hair products.
Literature - Bulletins, bimonthly catalogs and price lists.
Brand Names - Stearn's, Derma E.

SUMERU GARDEN HERBALS, Box 2847, Santa Cruz, CA 95063; (408)-728-4525. Madhu Mascaro-Brodkey, Ken Brodkey, co-owners.
Product Categories - Hair, body and baby products; essential perfumed oils, fragrances, essential oils.
Literature - Price lists, brochures.
Brand Names - Sumeru Garden Herbals.

SUN-PRO OF CALIFORNIA, INC., 4238 Hilldale Rd., San Diego, CA 92116; (619)-282-8364. Rita Redlinger, president.
Product Categories - Sun protection and skin-care products.
Literature - Annual catalogs, brochures.
Brand Names - **Sun-Pro, Sun Block, Lip-Pro, Pure Gold, Tanning Body Lotion.**

SUNSHINE NATURAL PRODUCTS, LTD., Rt. 5W, Renick, WV 24966; (304)-497-3163. Barry Glick, president
Product Categories - Body, face, skin, hair products; pet products; deodorants.
Literature - Semiannual catalogs.
Brand Names - **Sunshine.**

TOM'S OF MAINE, INC., Railroad Ave., Kennebunk, ME 04043; (207)-985-2944. Thomas M. Chappell, president.
Product Categories - Natural toothpaste, deodorant, skin and hair care.
Literature - Catalogs.

TROPICAL SOAP CO., P. O. Box 31673, Dallas, TX 75231; (214)-243-1991. Clifford C. Sasfy, president.
Product Categories - Coconut oil soap, vitamin E products.
Literature - Bulletins when prices change.
Brand Names - **Sirena.**

UNCOMMON SCENTS, INC., 555 High St., Eugene, OR 97401; (503)-345-0952. Chuck Agol, president.
Product Categories - Body-care, bath, lip-care products, fragrances; essential oils.
Literature - Semiannual catalogs.

VERA PRODUCTS, INC., 601 W. Jackson, Harlingen, TX 78550; (512)-428-6712. Keith J. Seiler, president.
Product Categories - Aloe vera gel, juice and shampoo. Skin and sun-care prods, lip balm.
Literature - Yes.
Brand Names - **Lily of the Desert.**

VITA WAVE PRODUCTS, LTD., 7131 Owensmouth Ave., Ste. 94-D, Canoga Park, CA 91303; (818)-886-3808. Stephen Molchan, president.
Product Categories - Hair, sun and skin products.
Literature - Annual brochures, price lists.
Brand Names - **Vitawave, VeBourne Labs.**

VIVA VERA ALOE VERA, 915 Whitmore Dr., Rockwall, TX 75087; (214)-722-0011, (800)-772-0110 in TX, (800)-527-4835 in USA. Luci Flint, president.
Product Categories - Aloe vera body care products; baby products, eye make-up, face make-up, food care products, skin care products, nail care, sun products. Also food supplements.
Brand Names - **Viva Vera Aloe Vera.**

WEEDS OF WORTH, LTD., SR. 65, Box 140, Great Barrington, MA 01230; (412)-229-3348; Linda Burnham, owner.
Product Categories - Herbal healing salve, herbal body oils, herbal insect repellent, cough syrup, massage oil.
Literature - Annual catalogs.
Brand Names - **Weeds of Worth.**

WELEDA, INC., 841 S. Main St., P. O. Box 769-HFB, Spring Valley, NY 10977; (914)-356-4134. Finbarr Murphy, president.
Product Categories - Baby products, bath oils, facial cleansing lotions, moisturizers, mouthwash, shampoos/conditioners, soaps, toothpastes.
Literature - Annual catalogs, brochures, quarterly product information leaflets, periodical *Weleda News.*
Brand Names - **Weleda.**

WEST CABOT COSMETICS, 165 Oval Drive, Central Islip, NY 11722; (516)-582-4222; (800)-645-5048; Lawrence Kalur, president.
Product Categories - Soaps, moisturizers, cleansing cream and pore toning lotion.
Literature - Bulletins.
Brand Names - **Physicians and Surgeons.**

WINDFLOWER HERBALS, P. O. Box 987, Columbia, CA 95310; (209)-533-2238; Kim Blair, owner.
Product Categories - Lip balm and herbal salves, poison oak/ivy treatment, fragrant body oils.
Literature - Brochures, ingredient summaries.
Brand Names - **Windflower Herbals.**

ACTIVE ORGANICS, 7715 Densmore Ave., Van Nuys, CA 91406; (213)-786-3310.
Comments - Supplies herbal extracts under the trade name **Actiphyte**. Also is a manufacturer of cosmetics. Manufacturer/wholesaler.

ALBAN MULLER INTERNATIONAL, 19 Rue St. Just, 93100 Montreuil, France.
Comments - Supplies many plant extracts and essential oils. Has some specialty raw materials to use as ingredients in sun protection products (other than PABA) though these are not approved for an SPF rating by the FDA; also natural hair dye ingredients made from herbs. Has no U. S. office. Works through distributors in U. S. Manufacturer/distributor/wholesaler.

AMERCHOL, 136 Talmadge Road, Edison, NJ 08818; (201)-287-1600.
Comments - One of the largest and best known suppliers of lanolin and lanolin derivatives. Also has other cosmetic raw materials both natural and synthetic. Manufacturer/wholesaler.

AROMA VERA, P. O. Box 3609, Culver City, CA 90231; (213)-675-8219.
Comments - This company has a variety of completely natural essential oils for aromatherapy purposes and for use in cosmetics and natural perfumes. Very high quality blue camomile oil and lemon skin oil (for use in astringents, etc.); also, lavender, lavadin, neroli (orange blossom), peppermint (delicious), tea tree oil (see pp. 356-357), vetiver, etc. Manufacturer/wholesaler.

APPLEWOOD SEED COMPANY, 833 Parfet St., Lakewood, CO 80215.
Comments - This is a unique herb seed shop with herbal seeds from Shakespeare's era. Why not start an herbal cosmetic line called "Shakespeare's Herbal Cosmetics?" "Here's rosemary for remembrance." (Remember where you got the idea!) You can order by mail; send for the catalog. Retail/mail order.

BERJE, INC., 5 Lawrence St., Bloomfield, NJ 07003; (201)-748-8980.
Comments - Supplies natural essential oils and botanical extracts for use in aromatherapy, perfumes, or as cosmetic ingredients. They have blue camomile, rosewater (from France), good quality almond oil, pine needle oil, rosemary oil, avocado oil, and a large list of vegetable oils. Manufacturer/wholesaler.

BERTIN, 38 rue Jules-Ferry, 92400 Courbevoie, France.
Comments - Superb quality of essential oils and various plant extracts. Good quality alfalfa extract and borage oil (high GLA). Manufacturer/wholesaler.

BIO-BOTANICAL, Inc., 2 Willow Park Center, Farmingdale, NY 11735.
Comments - Supplies over 50 herbal extracts. They say they use a cold, not heat, process to prepare the extracts. Their extracts are concentrated. Line can be found in most health food stores. Manufacturer/wholesaler.

CENTERCHEM, 475 Park Dr. S., New York, NY 10016; (212)-725-5565.
Comments - Supplies various organic materials for use in cosmetics, including soluble collagen, elastin, also various herbal extracts. Manufacturer/distributor/wholesaler.

M. LUDO CHARDENON, Le Paradis des Plantes, Route d'Aubais, 30250 Sommieres, France.
Comments - M. Chardenon is one of the few herbal experts in the world, and his paradise of plants offers many herbs for sale. His book *In Praise of Wild Herbs* (with an introduction by Lawrence Durrell (Santa Barbara, CA: Capra Press, 1984) is a must for your collection with many unique medicinal uses of herbs. We've known M. Chardenon and have used his herbs. (He even makes a rosemary dandruff treatment that's really natural). When you buy herbs from him you know he actually went out himself, collected them from non-chemicalized soil (in the wilds of France), chopped them, packaged them, and sent them to you. You can write to him, but he will probably answer you in French (though he'll have somebody translate your letter to him). His cooking herbs are superb. All you have to do is feel them and smell their aroma and you know they're superior to the mass-produced and packaged herbs. In France they call these herb teas *tisanes*. M. Chardenon is 71 years old, and he is out every day collecting herbs and preparing them for sale as if he were a man of 40. Manufacturer/retail/mail order.

COESAM, (div. Cosmetica), Joseue Smith Solar 507, Providencia, Santiago, Chile.
Comments -Manufactures *Rosa Mosqueta* rose hip seed oil. This superior product is naturally extracted from a species of rose that grows high in the Andes mountains *(Rosa aff. Rubininosa)* and has been extensively researched as a healing and anti-aging agent. *Rosa Mosqueta* is an exclusive trademark for Coesam (in South America) and Aubrey Organics (in the United States). Manufacturer/wholesaler.

CRODA, 183 Madison Ave., New York, NY 10016; (212)-683-3089.
Comments - Supplies various proteins for use in cosmetics including thermal proteins such as collagen, elastin, and reticulin. Manufacturer/wholesaler.

CULPEPPER THE HERBALIST, 21 Burton St., Berkeley Square, London, WIX7DA, England.
Comments - England's Society of Herbalists organized this first of six herbal shops. They supply herbs, herbal products (e.g., almond milk lotion). Send for their catalog (you pay postage). Retail/mail order.

E. E. DICKENSON, 40-46 N. Main St., Essex, CT 06426; (283)-767-8261.
Comments - One of the oldest manufacturers of witch hazel (it has a 15% alcohol content). Their brand of witch hazel can be found in any store and is also sold in bulk. Manufacturer/wholesaler.

FRAGRANCES & DESIGNS, 516 Fifth Avenue, Suite 507, New York, NY 10036; (212)-840-8460. Daniel Akerib, president.
Comments - This is the New York office of the French vegetarian soap company, L'Occitane. These soaps are of a very high quality. Manufacturer/wholesaler.

GREEN MOUNTAIN HERB CO., P. O. Box 2369, Boulder, CO 80306; (800)-525-2696).
Comments - This herb company supplies many botanicals in various forms: cut and sifted, whole, ground, etc., to order. They sell essential oils and distribute many herbal products. Manufacturer/distributor/wholesaler/retail/mail order.

HAARMANN & REIMER, P. O. Box 175, Springfield, NJ 07081; (201)-686-3132.
Comments - Blends essentials oils for use in perfumes and also has herbal blends with the trade name Cremogens. H & R also published through Johnson Publications, Ltd., in London, an excellent four-volume set of perfume books, collectors' items containing herbals, essential oils, perfumes, etc., and beautiful color plates. Manufacturer/wholesaler.

HENKEL, 1301 Jefferson St., Hoboken, NJ 07030.
Comments - This company was begun by Dr. Kurt Richter in Berlin and manufactures various herbal extracts for cosmetic formulas. Has many active ingredients as well as collagen, elastin, and placenta extracts. Manufacturer/wholesaler.

INDIANA BOTANICAL GARDENS, Hammond, IN 46325.
Comments - Supplies herbs, gums, essential oils, resins, and herbal preparation. Write for catalog. Retail/mail order.

INTERNATIONAL SOURCING, INC., 555 Rt. 17 S., Ridgewood, NJ 07450.
Comments - Supplies many plant extracts for use in cosmetics including seaweed extracts and herbal mixtures. Manufacturer/wholesaler.

INVERNI DELLA BEFFA S. A., 1 Rue de Stockholm, 75008 Paris.
Comments - Inverni (also known as Indena) supplies extracts from many plants and specializes in medicinal plant derivatives. Manufacturer/wholesaler.

JANCA'S JOJOBA OIL & SEED COMPANY, 1407 S. Date, Mesa, AZ 85202; (602)-833-4940.
Comments - Tom Janca founded this company before jojoba oil was a household name for a good moisturizing shampoo and a method of "saving the whales." Janca has jojoba oil, jojoba meal, jojoba butter, jojoba wax, and even jojoba seeds. Manufacturer.

KIEHL PHARMACY, 109 Third Ave., New York, NY 10003.
Comments - They have dried herbs, fragrances, lanolin, neutral and colored henna. Retail/mail order.

LABORATORI VEVY, INC., 1 Dag Hammarskjould Plaza, New York, NY 10017.
Comments - Vevy is located in Genoa, but has an office in New York. They have a great variety of water-soluble fractions of herbal essential oils for use in cosmetics. Manufacturer/wholesaler.

LABORATOIRES GALENIQUES VERNIN, B. P. 28-1, Rue Dajot, 77002 Melun, France.
Comments - Vernin supplies vegetal extracts known as **Phytelenes** in liquid and powdered form for use in cosmetics. Manufacturer/wholesaler.

LIPO CHEMICALS, INC., 207 - 19th Ave., Patterson, NJ 07504; (201)-556-2568.
Comments - Lipo supplies natural emollient oils such as avocado oil, sesame, oil, wheat germ oil, and other natural herbal extracts. Manufacturer/wholesaler.

MAGUS, P. O. Box 254, Cedar Grove, NJ 07009.
Comments - This company supplies herbs they say are organic and wild that were picked along the Appalachian Trail. Retail/mail order.

MEADOWBROOK HERB FARM, Route 138, Wyoming, RI 02898.
Comments - This organic herb farm has a wide selection of herbs. Available in health food stores. They also distribute the natural West German cosmetic line known as Dr. Hauschka. Manufacturer/distributor/wholesaler.

MEER CORPORATION, 9500 Railroad Ave., N. Bergen, NJ 07047; (201)-861-9500.
Comments - Supplies many herbs in bulk and in many forms: cut and sifted, whole, powdered, or as essential oils. Manufacturer/wholesaler.

MIAMI CLAY CO., 18954 N. E. 4th St., Miami, FL 33179.
Comments - Supplies a great variety of clays in bulk for use in cosmetics and other uses. Manufacturer/distributor/wholesaler.

D. NAPIER & SONS, 17 Bristol Place, Edinburgh, EHI, Scotland.
Comments - Napier, the herbalist, created this herb pharmacy in 1860. It is still one of the most unique herb stores around. Retail/mail order.

ORGANIC EXTRACTS, INC. 9626 A Cozycroft Ave., Chatsworth, CA 91311.
Comments - Supplies botanical extracts under the trade name of Cytosolv. Manufacturer/wholesaler.

OTTO RICHTER & SONS, LTD., Box 26A, Goodwood, Ontario, Canada.
Comments - Has a selection of 300 different herb seeds, and a good catalog for 50 cents. Also has a wide variety and excellent selection of rare herbs. Retail/mail order.

S. B. PENICK & CO., LTD., 100 Church Street, New York, NY 10007.
Comments - Penick is a world famous importer of botanicals and has a variety of domestic herbs as well as some herbal extracts in bulk. They have a good quality neutral henna extract (non-coloring), quillaya bark extracts, and many herbal gums. Sells only in large quantities. Manufacturer/distributor/wholesaler.

PHILLIP ROCKLEY, LTD., 20505 Dag Hammarskjould Plaza C. C., New York, NY 10017; (212)-355-5770.
Comments - Supplies natural ingredients for cosmetics. Has excellent seaweed extracts. Manufacturer/wholesaler.

ROCKY HOLLOW HERB FARM, Lake Wallkill Road, Sussex, NJ 07461.
Comments - You can find this brand of herbs in many health food stores. Rocky Hollow has their own herb farm. Manufacturer/wholesaler.

FRANK B. ROSS COMPANY, INC., 6 Ash St., Jersey City, NJ 07304; (201)-433-4512.
Comments - Supplies waxes used in industry and for cosmetics. Natural and synthetic waxes of all types. Sells only in bulk. Manufacturer/wholesaler.

SEDERMA, 24 Bis, Bd Verd de St. Julien, 92190 Meudon, France.
Comments - Supplies many plant extracts for use in cosmetics as well as mucopolysaccharides and other organic extracts. Manufacturer/wholesaler.

TAYLOR'S HERB GARDENS, INC., 1535 Loan Oak Road, Vista, CA 92083.
Comments - They have over 200 medicinal, culinary, and aromatic herbal plants growing in their beautiful gardens since 1947. Their catalog is free, and they supply live plants as well as seeds. Retail/mail order.

TERRY CORPORATION, 3270 Pineda Ave., Melbourne, FL 32935; (305)-259-1630.
Comments - They supply aloe extracts for cosmetic manufacturers, including aloe oil, aloe extract, aloe powder. Manufacturer/wholesaler.

WHITE MOUNTAIN FARM, Litchfield, CT 06759.
Comments - Supplies herbs by mail. They have excellent English lavender *(Lavandula augustifolia)*. Retail/mail order.

WHOLE HERB CO., P. O. Box 1085, Mill Valley, CA 94942; (415)-383-6485.
Comments - Essential oils. Manufacturer/wholesaler.

YELLOW EMPEROR, INC., 4091 W. 11th Ave. E., Eugene, OR 97402.
Comments - The people at Yellow Emperor will prepare any herbal extract in any strength desired for commercial use. Manufacturer/wholesaler.

NOTICE: No health food stores appear on this list; however, many health food stores supply herbs, herbal extracts, essential oils, and herb products.

organitoons

Index

A

Abbott Labs, Inc., 143
ABC television network, 29
Absolutes, 55
Absorption base, 42, 43
Academic Press, 247
Academy of Athens, 24
Acetone, 168, 240, 391
Acetylsalicylic acid (see aspirin)
Acid mantle, 64, 75
Acidophilus, 8, 134-135
Acne, 73, 135
Aconite, 3
Acupressure (also see acupuncture), 177-185, 391
    face lift chart, 178-182
    points on body, 183-185
Acupuncture (also see acupressure), 57, 60
Acupuncture - The Chinese Art of Healing, 174
Adrien Arpel Bio-Cellular Cream, 250
Advertising Age, 154
Aesthetician (or esthetician), 378, 380, 389, 393
Aesthetics World, 63
African butter (see Karite Butter)
African Butter Shampoo, 246
Agar-agar, 63
Aizame shark, 321
Alanine, 141
Alcohol, 168, 391
Alcohol, isopropyl, 240, 339
Alcohol, SD, 220, 240, 250, 339
Alexander The Great, 1
Aldehydes, 42
Alfalfa, 77, 334, 379, 381
Alfin, Inc., 150
Algae, 64, 75, 144, 145
Algotherapy, 64
Alkanna root, 163
Alkyl sulfates, 330
Allantoin (also see Comfrey), 135-136, 170, 249, 332, 342, 356, 390, 392, 393
Allen, Margaret, 154
Allergies, 3
Almond oil, 58, 244, 251-253, 342, 354, 357, 379, 389, 390
    almond oil facial cleanser, 244
Aloe vera gel, 6, 47, 49-51, 58, 59, 131, 133, 136, 145, 150, 152, 170, 241, 249, 251-253, 337, 338, 339, 341, 342, 354-356, 360, 379, 381, 390-393
Alum, 58
Alpha-keratin helix, 328, 330; diagram of, 327
Aluminum, 48, 326

Aluminum lake colors, 160
Ambrette seeds, 131
American Anti-Vivisection Society, 218
American bearsfoot, 332
American Board of Plastic Surgery, 45
American Cyanamide, Inc., 322
American Journal of Physical Anthropology, 323
American Medical Association (AMA), 174
American Society of Pharmacognosy, 133
American Vegan Society, 218
American Vegetarians, 218
Amin oxides, 337
Amino acids, 43-44, 63, 65, 135, 140, 141, 224, 326, 328, 337-340
    amino acid complex, 144
Ammonia-N, 141
Ammonium laureth sulfate, 336
Amory, Cleveland, 213
Amphoteric, 336
Anagen, 323
Anchor Press, Inc. 168
Animal Liberation, Inc. 218
Animal Models in Dermatology, 221
Animal toxicity evaluation, 220, 236, 237
Anionic surfactants, 336
Annatto, 162, 166
Anthony, Susan B., 213
Anthraglycosides, 131
Antiaging treatments, 355-358
Antibiotics, 136
Anti-blotchiness, 139
Anti-inflammatory, 139
Antiseptics, 58, 76, 139
Antioxidants, 60, 73, 76, 143, 247, 251
Antioxidants and the Autooxidation of Fats, 144
Antioxidant shampoos, 334
Anti-varicose, 139
Apigenin-7-apioglycoside, 131
Apple oil, 59
Apple cider vinegar (in a rinse), 340
Apri Cosmetics, 11
Aquarian Gospel, 57
Arachidonic acid, 43
Arco Publishing Co, Inc., 135
Arginine, 141, 145
Argus Archives, 218
Aristotle, 1, 23
Aristolochia clematis, 356, 391, 392
Arizona, University of, 73
Arnica, 63, 139, 142, 145, 356, 381
Aromatherapy, 54, 55, 56-62, 77
    bath oils, 61-62
    body care, 59-61
    facial massage, 58-59
    massage oils, 61, 62

Aromatherapy, cont'd
  arthritis, 65, 146, 358
Art of Aromatherapy, The, 58
Aspartic acid, 141, 145
Aspirin, 171, 175
Astringent (toner), 58, 240-242
Aubrey's Homemade Herbal Astringent, 241
Aubrey Organics, 138
Avocado oil, 42, 48, 54, 59, 64-65, 247, 252,
  379, 381, 390, 392
Avon Rich Moisture Face Cream, 250
Ayurvedic medicine, 357
Azo (and Monoazo) dyes, 161-163
Azulene (from camomile), 166

B

B-amyrine (antioxidant), 247
Bach's Brandenburg Concertos, 15
Baer, R. L., 41
Baker & Cummins, 8
Balm, 58
Balm-mint, 391, 392, 393
Balm of Gilead, 333, 334
Balsam, v, 240, 392
  as a conditioner, 240
Bananas, 390
Banks, Joseph, 356
Barefoot doctors of China, 57, 173
Barnard, Christiaan, 150
Beauty Without Cruelty, 28, 218
Bee pollen, 175
Beeswax, 22, 243, 244, 245, 251-253
Bentham, Jeremy, 213
Benzanthracene, 224
Benzoic acid, 220
Benzoin gum, 241, 381, 391
Bergamot, 59
Bergh, Henry, 214
Bergman, Ingrid, 154
Berke, P. A. Z., 221
Berzelius, Jons Jacob, 4, 5
Beta carotene (see Carotene and Vitamin A)
BHA, BHT, 2, 3, 60, 149, 220, 221, 224
Bianco, Renato (Rene of Florence), 26
Biotin, 75, 322
Birch, 63, 145, 333
Bixin, 162
Bladderwrack, 63, 144, 145, 356, 379, 390
Blake, William, 213
Blakeslee, Marianne, 378, 391
Bleaches, 329
Bloomingdales, 150
Blue bottle, 139, 150, 356
Blue-green manna, 145-146
Blueberry leaves, 379
Bodin, Luc, 378
Boissier, J. R., 247
Boldt, P., 329
Bombast, Philippe Aureolus (Paracelsus), 24,
  25
Bonnardiere, Dr., 62

Borage oil, 358, 379, 380, 381
Borax, 22, 244, 251
Boron, 145
Bricklin, Mark, 8
British Biological Research Assoc., 3
British Food Standards Committee, 3
British Journal of Dermatology, 45
British Union for the Abolition of Vivisection
  (BUAV), 212, 218
Brunnschwick, Hieronymus, 26
Buckley, William F., 15
Bullocks (department store), 150
BUAV Newsletter, 212
Butler, Samuel, 213
Butylene glycol, 134
Butyrosperum parki kotschy (see Karite
Butter),

C

Cabbage, 59
Cade oil, 334
Calamine (also see zinc), 333, 389
Calcium, 48, 63, 145, 392
Calendula, 65, 150, 241, 249, 354-356, 358, 381,
  391
Camomile, 33, 55, 58, 59, 63, 131, 132, 139,
  150, 241, 249, 337, 341, 356, 379, 381, 390,
  391, 393
Camphor, 54, 136, 378, 379
Candellia wax, 74, 245
Candida albicans, 131, 134, 136, 356
Cananga oil, 333
Canthanaxin, 34, 168, 170
Carboxyl groups, 326
Carcinogenic substances, 75, 236, 378
Carcinogens in colors, 160-164
Cardinal Manning, 213
Cardinal Newman, 213
Carmel, 166
Carmine, 162, 166
Carnauba wax, 74, 245
Carotene, 339
Carrot oil (also see Vitamin A), 65-66, 247, 381,
  390, 392
Carson, Rachel, 213
Carter, Lynda, 154
Carvajal, Fabiola, M. D., 353-354, 378
Cassie absolute, 333
Castile soap (also olive oil soap), 75, 334, 379
Castor oil, 42, 54, 66-67, 149, 154
  leprosy ointment, 66
  lipsticks, 67
  soaps, 67
Catagen, 323
Cedarwood, 59
Celltherapy, 77, 142, 146, 150, 245, 247, 251,
  355, 392
Cellulite, 62, 63, 142, 146
Cellulose, 27
Ceratum refrigerans, 243
Cetyl alcohol, 154, 245, 249
Cetyl palmitate, 154

Chain, Ernst Boris, 216
Chamazulene (azulene), 131
Chanel, Coco, 250
Chanel Lotion Vivifiante, 240
Chaney, Jr., Lon, 321
Chaulmoogra oil, 357
Chemie Research and Manufacturing, Co.,
   Inc., 223
Chestnut, 356
Ch'i, 60, 176
Chiffon margarine, 5
Chinese medicinal herbs (chart), 186-209
Ching Ch'i Shin Longevity Tonic, 176
Chlorella, 356, 379
Chlorine, 220
Chlorine dioxide, 329, 342
Chlorocresol, 220
Cholesterol, 154, 245, 248, 326
Choline, 145
Chlorophyll, 64
Chondria, 63
Cinchona, 1
Cinnamon, 362
Citric acid, 75, 342
Citrus seed oil, 389
CIVITAS Publishing, 216
Clairol, 29
Clairol's Herbessence Shampoo, 12
Clay, 47, 48, 139, 163
Clay masks, 389, 390, 391
Cleopatra, 27, 47-51
Clinique Clarifying Lotion, No. 2, 240
Clove, 58, 333
Coal tar (also see Tar), 334, 337
Coal tar dyes, 162, 163, 215
Cobalt, 145
Coca, 333
Cocamide DEA, 6, 75
Cochineal (also see Carmine), 162
Coco Cream No. 1 Skin Equilibrium Supple-
   ment, 250
Cocoa butter, 244, 245
Coconut fatty acids, 170
Coconut oil, 6, 42, 247, 330, 334, 336, 357, 379
Cod liver oil, 42
Collagen, 41, 42, 44-46, 64, 139, 140, 167, 170,
   351, 352, 355, 392, 393
Colors (artificial), 154, 155, 159-164, 215
   Chart on FD & C Colors, 165
   Chart on Non-Certified Colors, 166
Coltsfoot, 59, 170, 241, 330, 332, 333, 337, 339,
   340, 354-356, 381, 391, 392
Comfrey, 58, 135, 146, 241, 249, 342, 356,
   358, 379, 381, 390, 392, 393
Compassion in World Farming, 218
Condillac de, E. B., 213
Coneflower, 150, 354, 356, 381, 391
Conry, Tom, 168
Consumer's Guide to Cosmetics, 168
Cook, Captain, 356
Copeland, Aaron, ii
Copper, 145, 326, 329
Corey, R. B., 327, 328
Corn flower, 249
Corn syrup, 342

Cosmetic Ingredients, Dictionary of, 133
Cosmetic and Drug Preservatives, 221
Cosmetic, Toiletry, and Fragrance Association
   (CTFA), 133, 161, 164, 215, 224, 246
Cosmos, 15
Coty Equation One Perfect Ounce Max.
   Cream, 250
Countess of Chinchon, 1
Country Road Cosmetics, 12
Crispus, 63
Crybroyage (microburst), 63
Crocus sativus (also see Saffron), 163
Cucumber, 139, 356
Cummings, Robert, 329
Cuticle, 64, 326
Cyanocobalamin, (B_{12}), 145
Cypress, 59
Cysteine, 144, 330, 332, 337, 339
Cystine, 141, 142, 143, 144, 330, 331, 332, 333,
   337, 339, 341
   "cystine bridge" of hair, 329, 331
Cytoxic testing, 136
Cytoplasm, 43

D

Daisy, 58,
Dandruff, 59, 143, 144, 145, 331-334, 340, 342
D'Ambrosio, Diane, 378
   and the Natural Method Facial, 373-376
   and the Natural Method Massage, 382-387
Darwin, Charles, 213
da Vinci, Leonardo, 213
Debussy, Claude, ii
Deneuve, Catherine, 153, 154,
Denniel, Raymond, 63
Dermagraphic skin, 247,
Dermatitis, 247,
Detergency evaluation testing, 329
Derma Labs, 8; X-5T shampoo, 8
DHS Tar Shampoo, 8
Dihomogammalinolenic acid, 69, 137
Diane von Furstenberg's Cream Cleanser
   Facial Spa, 243
Diethyltoluamide, 220
Diethanolamine (DEA), 75
Dihydroxyacetone, 166, 168, 170
Diols, 326
Disodium EDTA-copper, 166
Disulfide bond, 326, 328
DMSO, 41, 43
DNA, 43, 64
Dr. Graham's Temple of Health, 26
Donahue Show, Phil, 159
DOPA, 329
Dopachrome process, 329
Dorothy Gray 2-Minute Magic Moisturizer,
   243
Docosahexenoic acid, 137
Dow Chemical, Inc., 131, 132
Draize, J. H., 214
Draize test, 214, 216, 217, 220
Dry hair treatments, 338, 341

Duchesne-Dupart, Dr., 63
Duke, Mark, 174

E

Ebling, F. J., 326
Echinacea root, 356, 391, 392
Eczema, 65, 145, 249, 334, 358
Effleurage, 60
Egg, 48
Eicosapentaenoic acid (EPA), 136-137
Eilerman, Heinz, 23
Einstein, Albert, 213
Elastin, 42, 44, 139, 142, 392
Elder, v, 58, 139, 241, 356, 379, 381, 391
Elizabeth of Hungary, 26
Eller, J. J., 45
Elm, 58
Emperor Julian, 23
Emperor Justinian, 24
Emperor Trajam, 21
Encyclopedia of Common Natural Ingredients, 133
Encyclopedia of Medicinal Herbs, 135
Epidermal cells, 141
Enzymes, 55, 56, 74, 136, 138, 140, 326, 333 390, 392
Epidermis, 331
Escin, 63, 145
Estee Lauder Whipped Cleansing Cream, 243
Essential fatty acids (EFA's), 12, 43, 46, 67-71, 137, 140, 337, 341
Essential fatty acid base, 58
Essential oils, 54-55, 56, 57, 58, 63, 77, 141, 337, 378
Ether, 42
Essex Testing Clinic, Inc., 139
Ethoxidiglycol, 134
Ethoxylate phytosterols, 137
Ethylene glycol, 245, 249
Eucalyptus, iv, 58, 136, 241
Eucalyptus oil, 356, 378, 379, 381, 390
European Economic Community (EEC), 221
Evening primrose oil, 12, 137, 248, 252, 341, 358, 381
Exfoliation, 390
Exxon, 29
EZ-I-TOX, 216

F

Faberge, 11, 23, 34
Farm and Food Society, 218
Fatty acids (also Vitamin F, Essential Fatty Acids), 246, 248-249, 321, 322, 337, 341, 355

Fatty acid base (coconut), 354, 390, 392
Fatty alcohols, 245, 248-249
Fatty alcohol esters, 248
Fatty alcohol ethers, 245
Fawcett, Farrah, 33
FDA (Food and Drug Administration), 23, 29, 31, 34, 41, 53, 135, 159, 162-164, 167, 170, 215, 221, 240, 321, 322, 355
FDA Act (1938), 28
FD & C colors (see Artificial Colors)
FD & C dyes, 29
Fennel, 58, 241, 391, 392, 393
Fenugreek seeds, 334
Feverfew, 139, 356
Filatov, Vladimir, 150
Fitzpatrick, Thomas, 170
Flack, Roberta, 154
Flax oil, 247
Fleishner, Albert M., 151
Fleming and Florey, Profs., 216
Flori Robert's Anti-oil Lotion, 243
Flour, v
Foltene, 322
Formaldehyde, 45, 156, 220, 224, 236
Formalin, 45
Four D Marketing, Inc., 72
Fragrance (as specific types, see Essential oils and Aromatherapy)
Fragrances, artificial, 377
"Fragrance-free," 53
Frances Denney pHormula ABC, 240
Francois I, 25
Frangipani, Mutio, 26
Freberg, Stan, iii
Freud, Sigmund, 213
Friends of the Animals, Inc., 218
Frost, P., 39
Fucoxanthin, 64
Fucus, 63, 379, 390
Fuller's earth, 389
Fund for Animals, Inc., 218
Fund for the Replacement of Animals in Medical Exp., 218

G

Gale, Roger, 212
Galen, 21-24, 42, 217, 243
Galen's cold cream, 22
Gallic acid, 221
Gamma-linolenic acid (GLA), 12, 137, 249, 358
Gamophene, 221
Gandhi, Mahatma, 213
Garlic, 334
Gattenfosse, Rene-Maurice, 57, 58
Gaul, E. I., 42
Gazet Medicale de France, 247
GBS: A Full Length Portrait, 214
Gelatin, 139

General Motors, Inc. 159
General Nutrition Centers, 12
Geranium, 58
Germall 115 (see also Imidazolidinyl urea), 221-223
Gershwin, George, ii
Gettysburg Address, 15
Ghastahapana, 357
Gillette Corporation, 5, 11
Ginger, 58
Ginseng, 58, 175, 176, 196, 334
Glucomannan, 131, 137-138
Glutathione peroxidase, 143
Glutamic acid, 141, 145
Glutathione, 143-144
Glycine, 141, 145
Glycel, 150
Glycerine, iii, 17, 42, 75, 149, 240-241, 245, 249, 251-253, 342, 379, 389, 392
Glyceryl monostearate, 22
Glycogen, 330, 331, 337, 338
Glyoxylic acid, 249
Goa, 392
Godeau, G., 247
Goldenseal, 334
Goldman, C. L., 222
Goldschmidt and Kligman Technique, 139
Gomez, Javier, 75
GQ Magazine, 155
Grandmaw's lye soap, iii
Grape, 58, 59
Grapefruit, 58
Grapefruit seed extract, 224
Greeley, Horace, 213
Goethe, Johann Wolfgang von, 213
Guaicol, 221
Gum arabic, 339

H

Hair dyes, 329
Hair growth cycle, 323
Haldane, J. B., 214
Harbst, Hans, 353, 355
Harich, Jakob, 223-224
Harper & Bros., 214
Harris, J. C., 329
Harry, R. G., 45
Harvard Medical School, 170
Healing agents, 249, 389, 390
Health Through God's Pharmacy, 360
Heather, 58
Heckler, Margaret
Helsinki treatment, 322
Hematite, 392
Henna, iii, 6, 27, 47, 48-49, 51, 166
    neutral, 337, 339, 340,
    in non-color rinse, 340
Herbal masks, 389-391
Herbal packs, 360
Hermann, F., 41
Hermestedt, E. Z., 329
Hesse, Bernard C., 162

Hesse, Hermann, 211
Heterphenes, 47
Hexachlorophene, 41, 215, 221, 224, 332
Hexosan, 221
Hibbott, H. W., 326
Hippocrates, 21, 24, 28, 217
Histidine, 43, 141, 145
Hollyhock, 58
Honey, 139, 389, 390, 391
Hops, 139, 356
Horrobin, David, 12
Horowitz, S., 39
Horse chestnut, 58, 63, 135, 139, 145, 391
Horsetail, 59, 139, 170, 330, 332, 333, 337, 339, 340, 354-56, 381, 391
Hsu, Yu-Chih, 222
Huang Ti, 57
Hugo, Victor, 213
Humectants, 42
Hyaluronic acid, 138, 139, 142
Hyaluronidase, 138
Hydnocarpus kurzii (chaulmoogra), 357
Hydro-occlusive mask, 138-140, 393
Hydrocarbons, 43, 244, 245, 248, 250, 254
Hydrocortisone, 151, 152
Hydrogen bonds, 328
Hydroglycolic extracts, 151, 356
Hydrolyzed animal protein, 337, 338, 352
Hydrolyzed mucopolysaccharide (HMP), 142
Hydroxyproline, 44-45, 140-142
Hypericum (St. John's wort), 155
Hypo-allergenic cosmetics, 9,
Humboldt, A. Von, 15

I

I Ching, Book of Changes, 176
I. Magnin, 150
Ibn Sina, 24
Ibsen, Henrik, 213
Immune system, 136
Indian snakeroot, 133
In vitro testing, 216-217
Infusions, 359
Inositol, 391
Indigo *(Indigofera)*, 163
International Sourcing, Inc., 151
Interscience Publishing, 329
Iron, 48, 145, 329
Iron oxides, 166
Isoleucine, 141, 145
Isopropyl myristate, 243
Ivy, 63, 139, 142, 145, 356

J

Janca Oil and Seed Company, 73
Janca, Tom, 73
Jasmine, 55, 58, 59
Jelly mask, 388
Jergen's All-Purpose Face Cream, 243

Jesus, 57, 218
Johns Hopkins University Hospital, 216
Johnson, A. R., 3
Jojoba meal mask, 389
Jojoba oil (and butter), 5, 12, 16, 17, 33, 56, 58,
    59, 60, 61, 72-76, 154, 170, 244, 245,
    251-253, 337, 338, 341, 342, 359, 381, 389,
    390,
    in face cleanser, 245
    in hair conditioner, 148
    in hot oil treatment, 341-342
    in moisturizer, 251
Jojoba wax, 74-75
Journal de Pharmacologie, 247
Journal of American Chemical Society, 144,
    328
Journal of Investigative Dermatology, 42
Jovan Oil of Mink, 250
Jung, C. G., 213

K

Kabara and Dekker, Inc., 221
Kadans, Joseph, 135
Kaolin (clay) 48, 390; also Mt. Kaolin, 48
Karite butter (also shea and African
    butter), 245, 246-247, 254, 341, 342, 359,
    379
    as sunscreen, 247, 253-254
Kellogg's, 41
Kelp, 58, 145
Keratin, 141, 143, 144, 326, 328
    Alpha-keratin helix, 327, 328
    Shampoos, conditioners, 141
Keratinization, 323, 329
Keratohyalin, 326
Kipling, R., 2
Kimberly-Clark, Inc., 34
Kingsford, Anna, 218, 218
Kirlian photography, 174
Kohl, 47
Konjac root, 137
Kramer, Sylvia, 9
Krutch, Joseph Wood, 213

L

LD50/60 test, 212, 215, 217
Lactalbumin, 330, 331, 337
Laminaria, 144, 356, 379, 390
Lancome Galatee Milky Creme Cleanser, 243,
Lancome Tonique Fraicheur, 240
Lanolin, 42, 245, 248, 251, 341, 359
Lavender, iv, 55, 57, 58, 59, 61, 241, 252, 381,
    391
Lawsone, 48
Lawsonia inermis, 48
Lawsonia spinoza, 48
Lecithin, 9, 245, 248,
Leewenhoek, Anton van, 4
Lemon, 55, 58, 59, 139, 148, 356, 390

Lemon balm, 337
Lemongrass, 58, 59, 379
Lemon oil, 240, 241
    as antioxidant, 223-224
Le Fournier, Jean, 25
Let's Live, 136
Lettuce, 58
Leucine, 141, 145
Leung, Albert Y, 133
Li Ch'ing Yuen, 175-176
Licorice root, 334
Liebaut, Jean, 25
Life Extension, 322
Lime, 58, 59
Limetree, 139
Linden (Limetree), 150, 249, 356
Lincoln, Abraham, 15
Linee, Karl von, 1
Link, H. F., 72
Linoleic acid, 43, 65, 247, 248, 249
Linolenic acid, 43
Lipase, 74
Lipids, 142
Liquid Gold From the Desert, 73
Lithotamia, 63
Litmus paper, 37, 39
Livingston, Churchill, 221
Loniten, 321
Lorenzani, S. S., 136
Louis XIII, 26
Louis XIV, 1
Louisville, iv
Lovage, 58
Love and Mr. Lewisham, 214
Luce, Clare Booth, 213
Lusterizing spray, 341
Lwoof, J. M., 247
Lycium chinensis, 175
Lymphocytes, 140
Lysine, 141, 145

M

Macadamia nut oil, 252
Macalister, C.J., 135
Magnesium, 48, 63, 145, 389
Magnolia, 58
Ma Huang Tonic of Clear Thinking, 176
Mahmoudi, J., 48
Mailbach, H.I., 221
Malassez, L., 331
Marigold, 139
Marjoram, 58
Marshall Field's Dept. Store, 150
Marshmallow (Mallow), 58, 139, 241, 356, 381,
    391
Mattill, H.A., 144
Martinello, Giovanni, 25
Marx, Groucho, 47
Mary Kay, 154
Mary Queen of Scots, 25
Massachusetts General Hospital, 19
Materia Prima, 16

Maybelline, 154
Max-EPA, 137
Max Factor Skin Freshener, 240
Mecca, S. B., 135
Medical and Health Annual Encyclopedia, 136
Medici, Catherine de, 25, 26
Medulla, 326
Melaleuca alternifolia (tea tree oil), 356
Melanin, 170, 329
Melanocyte cells, 329
Mennen, 9
Menthol, 53, 54, 136, 378, 379, 389, 391
Meridians, 174
Methionine, 141, 144, 145, 326, 330, 332, 337, 339
Methoxysalen, 19, 170
Methylparaben, 6, 45
Methyl p-hydroxybenzoate, 160
Microorganisms, 4, 219, 220, 222
Millerpertuis (St. John's wort), 155
Mill Creek Cosmetics, 12
Mineral oil, 22, 43, 45, 154, 168, 170, 243, 244, 245, 250, 252, 338, 341, 379
Mineral water, 379, 391-392
Minoxidil, 151, 321-323, 342
Miskulik, M., 247
Mistletoe, 58
Molasses, v
Mondeville, Henri de, 24, 159, 160
Monilia abrican, 134
Moniliasis, 356
Montecorvino, Giovanni di, 25
Moss, Randolph, M. D., 3
Moxabustion, 175
Mucopolysaccharides, 6, 138, 142
Mustard plaster, 57
Mycologist, 134
Mycostatin, 136
Myristeryl alcohol, 154
Myristic acid, 248
Myrrh, 379, 390

N

Nader, Ralph, 29, 159, 160
NaPCA, 7
National Academy of Science, Washington, 328
National Anti-Vivisection Society, 218
National Cancer Institute, 236
Natural Method (Hair and Skin Care), The, iii, 8, 13, 14, 17, 18, 58, 140, 152, 161, 323, 336-342, 352, 377-394
Natural Organic Hair and Skin Care, 6
Natural Organics Plus, Inc., 11
Natural Source Vitamin E Association, 29
Natural Way to Super Beauty, The, 7, 8
Nature Magazine, 221, 328
Naturforsch, 329
NBC (television), 29
NDELA (N-nitrosodiethanolamine), 337, 352
Neem oil, 357-358; (for dandruff, 357)
Nei Gung (inner alchemy), 175

Neroli, 59
Nettle, 241
Nettle, stinging, 330, 332, 333, 338, 354, 379, 381, 391
   yellow dead nettle, 358
Neutral henna, 48
Neutrogena, 8
Newhall, Nancy, 213
New York State Medical Journal, 41
New York University, 151, 321
Neiman-Marcus Dept. Stores, 150
Niacin (B$_3$), 68, 69, 145
Nitrogen, 73
Nitrosamines, 337
Nixon, Richard, 171
Noxema Complexion Lotion, 243
Nutmeg, 58
Nyaanza Naturals, 246
Nylon, 326

O

Oatmeal, 389
Occlusive bonds, 135, 138, 139
Octacosanol, 142-143
Odorceptor, 55
Odorvector, 55
Ohsawa, George, 147, 148
Oil of Olay, 154, 239, 250
Oily hair treatments, 338, 340, 341
Olcott, H. S., 144
Oleanolic acid, 151
Oleic acid, 65, 245, 248, 249
Olfactory response, 53, 55-56
Olive oil, 22, 42, 247, 336, 352, 357, 359
Orange, 58
Orange blossoms, 58, 241
Orange blossom oil, 358
Orange water, 389
Orthocortex, 326
Organic (discussed), 4
Organica, 212
Oribasios of Pergamum, 23
OSHA, 236
Over-processed hair, 329, 338, 342
Oxtoxynol, 243
Ozokerite, 22, 43, 243, 244, 245
Ozonosphere, 168, 169

P

PABA (para-aminobenzoic acid), 167, 168, 247, 253, 254, 250, 329, 339, 341, 391
Palm kernel oil, 336
Palmitoleic acid, 65
Pansy, 58
Panthenol (also pantothenic acid), 13, 170, 329, 333, 337, 342, 356, 381, 391,
Pantothenate (Panthenol, d-panthenol, B$_5$), 138, 139, 145
Papaya (papain), 389

Papilla, 326, 329
Parabens, 131, 154, 221-224, 391
Paracelsus, 16, 332
Paracortex, 326
Paraffin, 43
Pauley, Gay, 154
Pauling, L., 327, 328
Pavlov, 214
Peach, 59
Peanut, 56, 58
Peanut oil, 247
Pearson, Durk, 322
Pearson, Hesketh, 214
Pectin, 389
Pellitory of the Wall, 139, 356
Penicillin, 216
Pennsylvania Radiology Dept., 133
People for the Ethical Treatment of Animals
    (PETA), 218
Peppermint, iv, v, 57, 58, 337, 340, 379, 381,
    389
Peracetic acid, 329
Pergamon Press, 326
Permanent waves, 328, 329
Peronne, F., 56
Peronne Perfumes and Flavors, Inc., 56
Person & Covey, 8
Peruvian bark, 2
Petrochemicals, 6, 240, 243, 245, 250, 336, 341,
    377, 392
Petrolatum, 22, 43, 243, 245, 359
Petrolatum PEG-15 cocoate, 168
pH, 32, 37-40, 45, 153, 328, 329, 330, 336, 338,
    377, 378
Pharaoh Cheops, 47
Pharaoh Teta, 27, 47
PHB esters (also see Parabens), 220
Phenol, 329
Phenylalanine, 141, 145
Pheomelanin, 329
Phenols, 42, 221-222
Phenonip, 221
Phenoxetol, 221
Phospholipids (also see Lecithin), 245, 248
Phosphorus, 145
Photosensitizing agents, 139
Phototoxins, 168
Pytotherapy, 54
Pilo-sebaceous apparatus, 41, 60, 139
Pine, 139
Pine-tree, 356
Pipsissewa, 333
Pityrosporum ovule, 331
Placenta, 46, 391
del Plan, Giovanni, 25
Plato, 23
Plus Natural Vitamins, Inc., 11
PMS, 358
Polo, Marco, 25
Polyethylene glycol (PEG), 240, 245
Polyethylene glycol ether, (Oleth-10), 240
Polyethylene sorbitol, 245
Polygonal cells, 326
Polypeptide bonds, 326, 328
Polysaccharides, 63, 139

Polysorbates, 322
Polyunsaturated fatty acid, 43
Polytar shampoo, 8
Pond's Lemon Cold Cream, 243
Porta, Giovanni-Battista, 25
Potassium, 48, 63, 136, 145
Potassium carbomer-934, 154
Potassium cyanide, 329
Potassium laurate, 154
Potassium myristate, 154
Potassium palmitate, 154
Potassium stearate, 154
Power-Cobbe, Frances, 214
Preservatives, 219-224, 225-234, 236, 237, 377
Preventive Diagnostics Corp., 216
Primrose, Evening, 58, 67-72
    arthritis and, 70
    alcoholism and, 71
    chart: "Prostaglandin Synthesis," 69
    gamma-linolenic acid, 67-72
    hair lusterizing spray, 71
    hyperactive children, 70
    PMS, 70
    prostaglandins, 68-71
    psoriasis, 71-72
    shampoo, 72
Proline, 141, 145
Propyl gallate, 221
Propyl p-hydroxybenzoate, 221
Propylene glycol, 17, 33, 42, 134, 160, 168,
    240, 243, 245, 249, 250, 336, 338, 341, 342
Propylparaben, 45
Prostaglandins, 137, 140
Proteins, 43, 65, 137, 141, 142, 146, 222, 337,
    338, 379
Protein metabolism, 330
Protozoa (discussed), 4
Proust, M., 55
Provitamin A (beta-carotene), 145
Psoriasis, 19, 63, 139, 145, 146, 170, 224,
    249, 340, 342, 358
Public Citizen Health Group, 29, 163, 215
PUVA (Psoriasis UV-A treatment), 170
Pyorrhea, 65
Pyramid of Giza, 47
Pyridoxine (B_6), 68-69, 145
Pythagoras, 15
Pugliese, Peter T., 139

Q

Quaternary ammonium compounds, 220,
    338
Quillaya bark, 153, 154, 334, 340
Queen Elizabeth I, 25
Queen Ses, 47, 48
Quillaya, 16
Quinine, 1

R

Randolph, T. G., 3
Red henna, 48, 49
Redken, Inc., 32
Redken pH Moisturizing Skin Balancer, 250
Red squill, 334
Red vine, 139, 356
Regan, Tom, 213
Relative specificity (in herbs), 356, 377
Relax-R-Bath, 360
Remembrance of Things Past, 55
Resorcinol, 332
Reticulin, 44, 45
Retinyl palmitate (see Vitamin A)
Revlon Eterna 27 Moisturizer, 250
Rhatany, 358
Rhubarb, 58
Riboflavin (B₂), 145, 168
Ribonucleic acid (RNA), 43
Ribosomes, 43, 141
Rice oil, 247
Rice polishings, 135
Richter, Kurt, 355
Robert, A. M., 247
Robert, L., 247
Rockwell, Norman, 54
Rodale Press, 8
Rogaine, 322
Rosa aff. rubiginosa, 353
Rosa Mosqueta, 170, 340, 341, 342, 353-355,
    379, 380, 381, 390, 391, 392
    for aging skin, 354, 391
    for hair repair, overprocessed hair, 340, 342,
    354
    color plates of hair and skin use, 369-372
Rose, 55, 58
Rose hips, 58, 353-355
Rosemary, iv, 58, 139, 148, 330, 332, 334, 337,
    340, 356-358, 379, 381
Rosen, W. E., 221
Rose petals, 58
Rosewater, iii, iv, 22, 42, 58, 244, 389
Rossellini, Isabella, 154
Rousseau, Jean-Jacques, 214
Royal College of Surgeons, 212
Royal jelly, 175, 205
Royal Society for the Prevention of Cruelty to
    Animals, 218
Ruesch, Hans, 213, 216
Ruscelli, Girolamo, 25
Rush, J. A., 213
Ruskin, John, 213
Russell, Dr., 63

S

Sagan, Carl, 15
Sage, 58, 330, 332, 334, 337, 340, 357-358, 379,
    381

Saks Fifth Avenue, 150
Salicyclic acid, 220, 332, 333, 334
Salt, Henry S., 214
Sampson technique, 139
San Carlos Apache Indians, 73
Sandalwood, 58
Saponins, iv, 334
Sarsaparilla, 334, 340
Sassafras, 58
Schiller, Ferdinand, 213
Schopenhauer, Arthur, 213
Schuykill Chemical Co., Inc., 135
Schweitzer, Albert, 213
Scleroderma, 65
Scottish Soc. for the Prevention of Vivisection,
    218
Sea pod liniment, 63
Sea ware, 144, 145, 356, 379, 389
Seaweed extracts, 139, 144, 145, 379, 380, 389
Sebaceous glands, 75, 326, 332
Seborrhea, 330, 332, 342
Sebum, 43, 64, 75, 144, 326, 340, 352
Sebutone shampoo, 8
Secol Corp., 139
Secundus, Gaius Plinius, 21
Sederma Corp., 246
Selenium, 143-144, 332
Selling Dreams: Inside the Beauty Business,
    154
Sequestrants, 337
Serine, 141, 145, 328
Serjeant, Richard, 213
Serra, Junipero, 72
Sesame oil, 247
Seven Seas Health Care, Ltd., 137
Shaftsbury, Lord, 213
Shaw, George Bernard, 136, 211, 213-215
Shaw, Sandy, 322
Shea butter (see Karite Butter)
Shelly, Mary, 213
Shelly, Percy, 213
Shepherd's purse, 58
Shiatsu, 60
Shin, 176
Silica (silicic acid), 48, 330, 333, 337, 355,
    356
Silicons, 245
Simon & Schuster, Inc., 154
Slaughter of the Innocent, 216
Slippery elm, iv
Society for Alternatives to Animal Testing, 32
Society of Animal Rights, 218
Society of Cosmetic Chemists, 217
Sodium, 48, 145
Sodium benzoate, 220
Sodium chloride, 75
Sodium hydroxide, 168
Sodium hypochlorite, 220
Sodium laureth sulfate, 222
Sodium lauryl sulfate, 75, 222, 243, 330, 336
Sodium myristate, 154
Sodium palmitate, 154
Sodium stearate, 154
Sodium sulfide, 329
Sodium thioglycolate, 329

Sorbic acid, 220
Sorbitol, 42, 249
Soy bean oil, 247
Soya, 137, 341
Soya oil, 65
Spearmint, 58
Sperm whale, 73
Spermaceti, 73, 245
Spring Brook Cosmetics, 12
Spirulina, 144-146
Squalene, 326, 352
Sri Chaitanya, 357
Stearic acid, 243, 245, 248, 249
Stage Ten Lemon E Toner, 240
Stanton, Elizabeth, 213
Staphylococcus aureus, 131
St. Francis of Assisi, 213
St. Jerome, 213
St. John's oil, 139, 249
St. John's Wort, v, 76, 154, 155, 170, 354-356,
    358, 378, 379, 380, 381, 390
Stein, Gertrude, 352
Steinberg, M., 221
Stiefel Inc., 8
Stigmasterol, 247
Stomata, 64
Stearalkonium chloride, 240, 326, 338
Stearyl alcohol, 154
Stearyl dimethyl benzyl ammonium chloride,
    240
Steroid alcohols, 245
Stratum corneum, 221, 223, 331
Stratum mucosum, 331
Strawberries, 58, 389
Sulfur, 42, 332, 333, 389
Sulfur-containing amino acids, 326, 330-333,
    339
Sulzberger, M. B., 41
Sumac, 58
Sun protection (sun screens), 249, 252, 253
    sun protection oil (SPF 15), 252-253
    sun protection lotion (SPF 15), 253
    sun protection butter (SPF 15), 253
    sun protection factor (SPF), 167, 252-254
Sunflower, 56, 58, 59, 61
Su wen, 173
Sweet bay, 334
Sycamore leaves, 135
Synergistic, 77
Synthetic chemicals, 58, 143, 246, 250, 254,
    389, 391
Synthetic detergents (syndets), 326, 330, 336,
    337, 341

T

T-Gel Shampoo, 8
Tai Ch'i Chuan, 175
Talbot, Robert, 1, 2
Talc, 176, 392
Tan accelerator, 168-170
    tyrosine and riboflavin as, 168
    chart of UV rays, 169

Tan Accelerator, con't
    psoriasis treatment with, 170
Tao te Ching, 173
Taoist longevity tonic, 176
Tamarind, 333
Tar solutions, 332, 334
TEA laureth sulfate, 336
TEA lauryl sulfate, 6
Tea tree oil, 356-357
Tennyson, Alfred, 213
Thalassotherapy, 54, 55, 62-64, 77
Thalidomide, 215-216
Thiers, H., 65
Thioglycolate, 54
Thioglycolic acid, 329
Thomson, Samuel, 10
3-dehydronoblin, 131
3-epinobilin, 131
Threonine, 328
Thyme, 58
Time Magazine, 5, 215
Tinctures, 360
Tisserand, Robert B., 58
Tocopherol, 76-77
Tolstoy, Leo, 213
Tommasi, 49
Topical Applications of Herbs (chart), 361-366
Tozian, Greg, 212
Transmethylation (also Redox reaction), 330
Treben, Maria, 360
Trentepohlia, 64
Triethanolamine (TEA), 22, 32, 75, 153, 168,
    220, 336
Triglycerides, 245, 246, 326
Trippett, Frank, 5, 6
Trotter, M., 323
Tryptophan, 329
Twain, Mark (S. Clements), 213
Tween 40, 22
(2)-5-tetradecen-14-olide, 131
Tyrosine, 168, 328, 329

U

Undecylene alkanolamide, 332
Underwood, G. B., 42
United Action for Animals, 218
University of Paris, 25
Unsaponifable substances, 65, 247, 359
Upjohn pharmaceuticals, 321, 322
Ureabisulfite, 329
UV damage of the skin, 358, 391
UV-400, 170
UV rays, 167-170, 247, 254, 338, 339, 341

V

Vangelis, 15
Vanseb-T Shampoo, 8
Valerian, 334
Valine, 141

Valium, 171
Vasquez, Carlos Amin, M. D., 353, 355
Vegetarian Activist Collection, 218
Vegetarian celltherapy, 355-356, 391
Vegetarian collagen, 351, 355-356, 390
Vegetarian Society, The, 218
Veith, Ilza, 57
Viprostol, 322
Vitamin A, 5, 65-66, 141, 224, 331, 379,
   390, 391
Vitamin B, 55, 145, 223, 224, 331, 389, 390,
   391
Vitamin C (also ascorbic acid), 68-69, 75, 145,
   223, 224, 329, 331, 337, 339, 379, 389-392
Vitamin D, 65, 389
Vitamin E, 9, 65, 75-77, 138, 139, 142-145, 223,
   224, 331, 337, 339, 379, 381, 389-392
   Vitamin E oil (in formulas), 244, 251-253
Vitamin F, 43
Vitamins and hormones, 247
Vivaldi's "The Four Seasons," 16
Vulneray (see healing agents), 135

W

Wagner, Richard, 213
Wagten-donk, W.J. Van, 247
Warner Bros., Inc., 322
Washington Post, 236
Wax esters, 245
Weleda Cosmetics, 23
Wellcome Research Laboratories, 68
Wells, H.G., 35, 214
Westwood, Inc., 8
Wheat germ, 59, 61, 62, 76, 77
Wheat germ oil, 5, 135, 142, 143, 381, 389, 391
Whirlpool bath, 57
White willow bark, 58
Wickhen Products, Inc., 16, 72
Witch hazel, 58, 139, 240-242, 340, 341, 356,
   358, 379, 389, 390
Wohler, F., 4
Wolff, S., 45
Wolfman syndrome, 321
Wolfman, The (Movie), 321
Wollstonecraft, Mary, 213
Wood's Lamp, 18
Wright, Sir Almroth, 214
Wulzen, R., 247

X

Xienta Institute for Skin Research, 139
Xseb-T shampoo, 8

Y

Yamamoto Skin Clinic, 217
Yamamoto, Shigeru, 217

Yarrow, 333, 391, 392
Yeh Ch'ing-Chiu, 174
Yellow Emperor's Classic of Internal Medicine,
   57
Yin and Yang, 170, 172-176
Young, Frank, 163
Yucca, 74, 334

Z

Zetar shampoo, 8
Zinc, 22, 68, 69, 145, 329, 332, 333
Zinc pyridinium-thiol-N-oxide, 332
Zinc undecylenate, 332
Zyderm, 45

NOTE: This index contains words as they are
used in text. Words used in charts, tables, etc.,
are not contained in this index. If you have a
question about a particular herb or synthetic
chemical, see the appropriate table.

NOTES

NOTES

NOTES

NOTES

NOTES